KAMI·KAZE™

Volume 1

By Shiki Satoshi

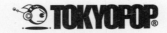

HAMBURG // LONDON // LOS ANGELES // TOKYO

Kami-Kaze Vol. 1
Created by Shiki Satoshi

Translation - Ray Yoshimoto
English Adaptation - Jerome Halligan
Copy Editors - Peter Ahlstrom and Eric Althoff
Retouch and Lettering - Jason Milligan
Production Artist - Erika "Scooter" Terriquez
Cover Design - Gary Shum

Editor - Luis Reyes
Digital Imaging Manager - Chris Buford
Production Managers - Jennifer Miller and Mutsumi Miyazaki
Managing Editor - Lindsey Johnston
VP of Production - Ron Klamert
Publisher and E.I.C. - Mike Kiley
President and C.O.O. - John Parker
C.E.O. - Stuart Levy

A 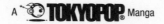 Manga

TOKYOPOP Inc.
5900 Wilshire Blvd. Suite 2000
Los Angeles, CA 90036

E-mail: info@TOKYOPOP.com
Come visit us online at www.TOKYOPOP.com

ISBN: 1-59532-924-2

First TOKYOPOP printing: February 2006
10 9 8 7 6 5 4 3 2 1
Printed in Canada

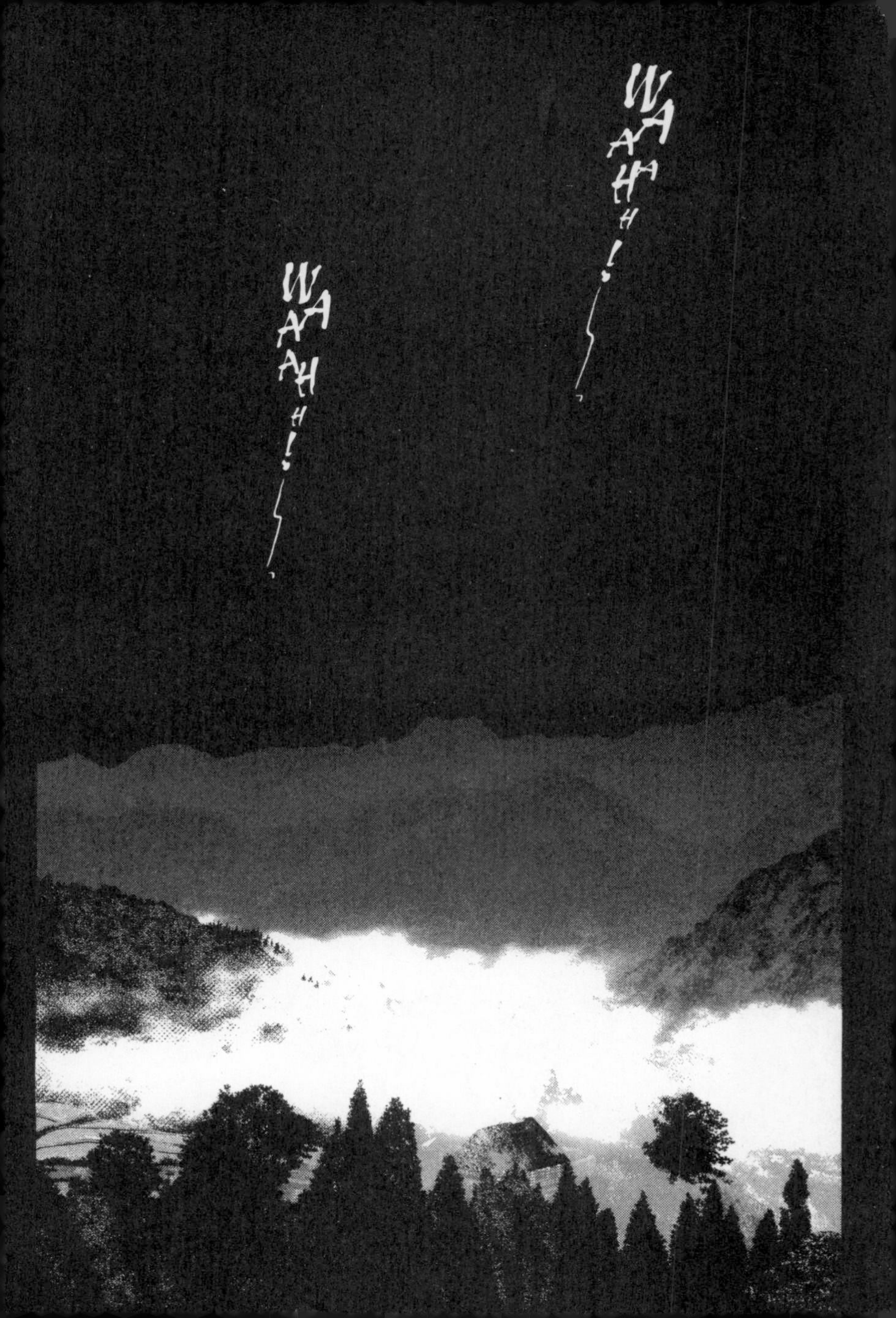
WAAAHHH!!
WAAAHHH!!

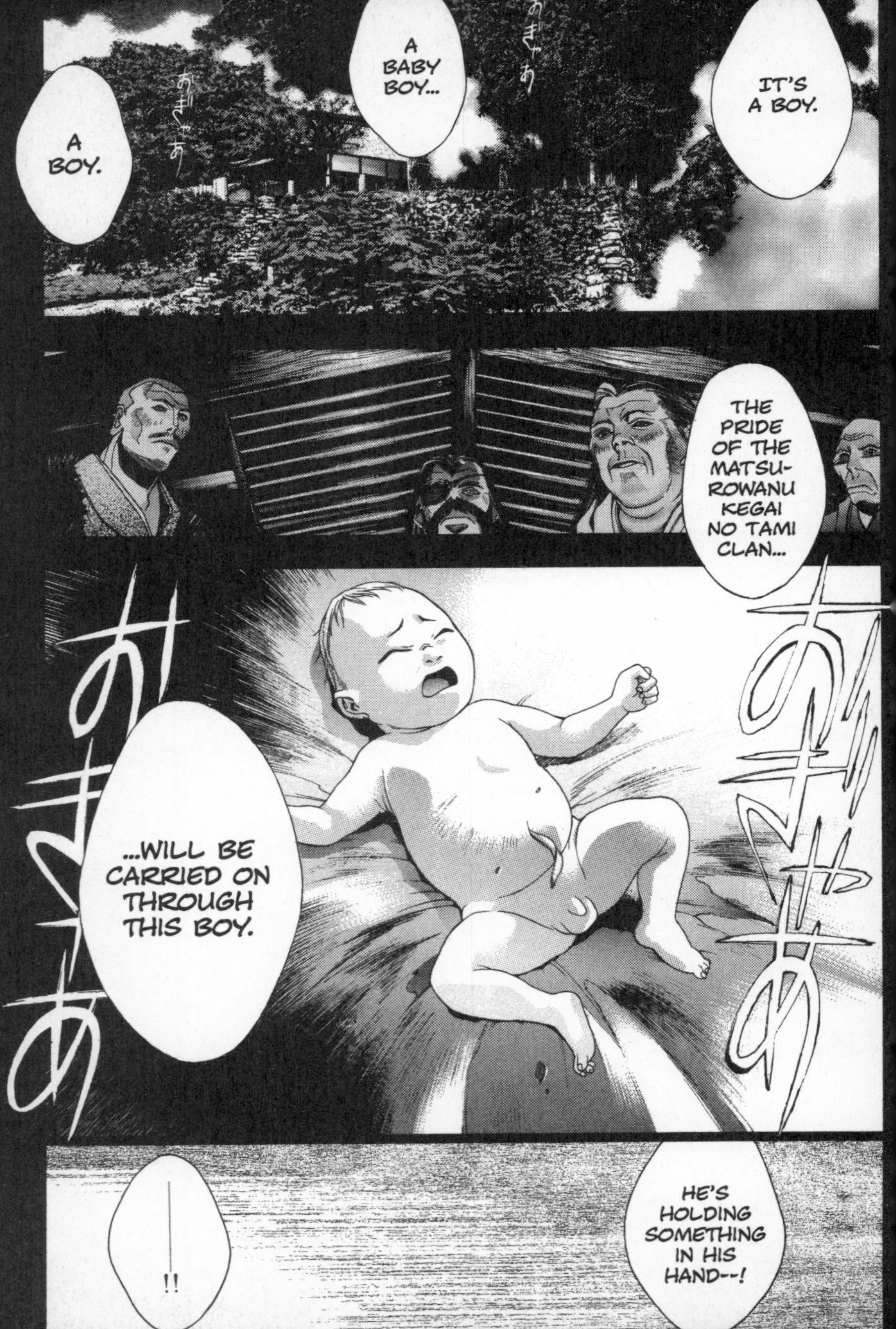
IT'S A BOY.
おぎゃあ
A BABY BOY...
おぎゃあ
A BOY.
THE PRIDE OF THE MATSU-ROWANU KEGAI NO TAMI CLAN...
おんぎゃあ
...WILL BE CARRIED ON THROUGH THIS BOY.
おぎゃあ
HE'S HOLDING SOMETHING IN HIS HAND--!
—!!

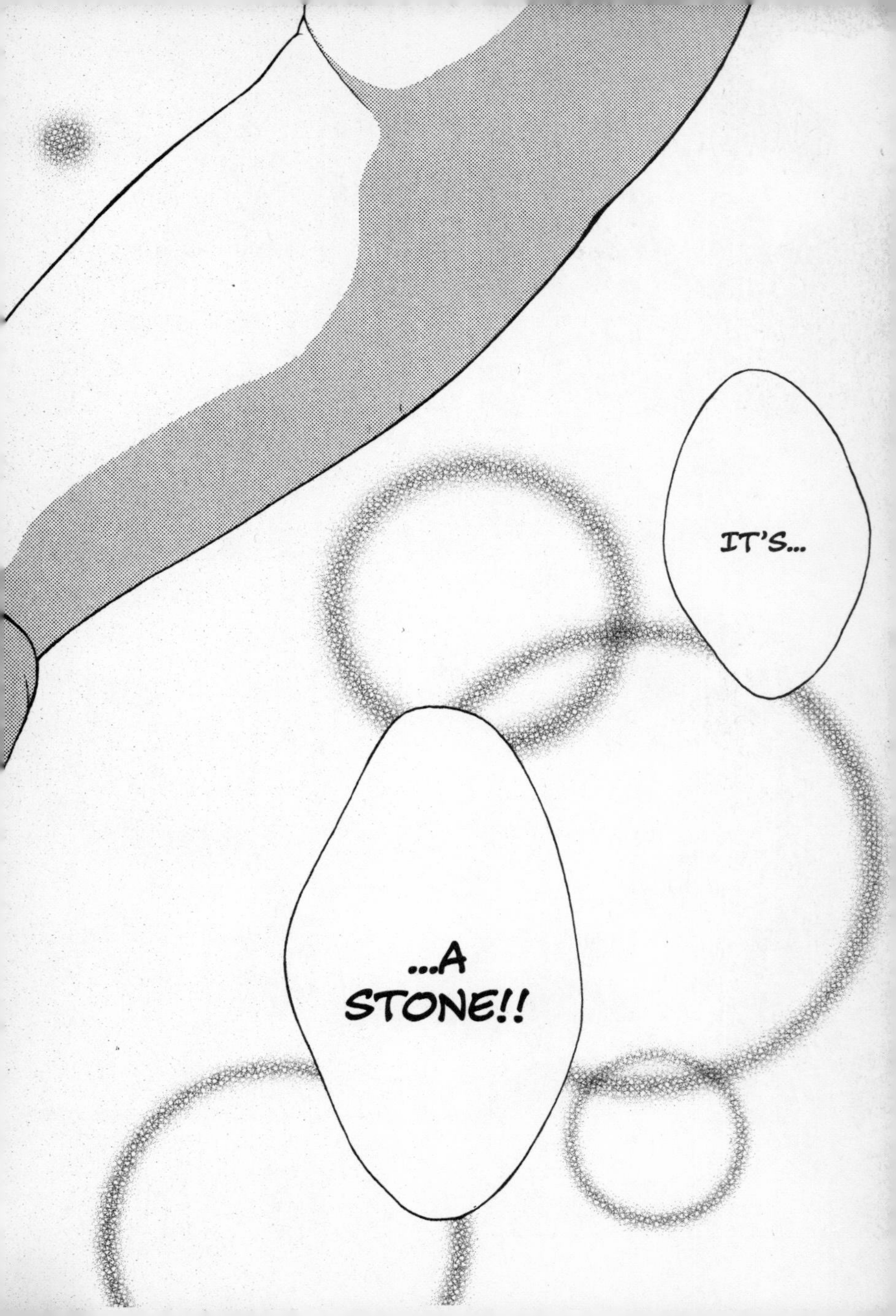
IT'S...
...A STONE!!

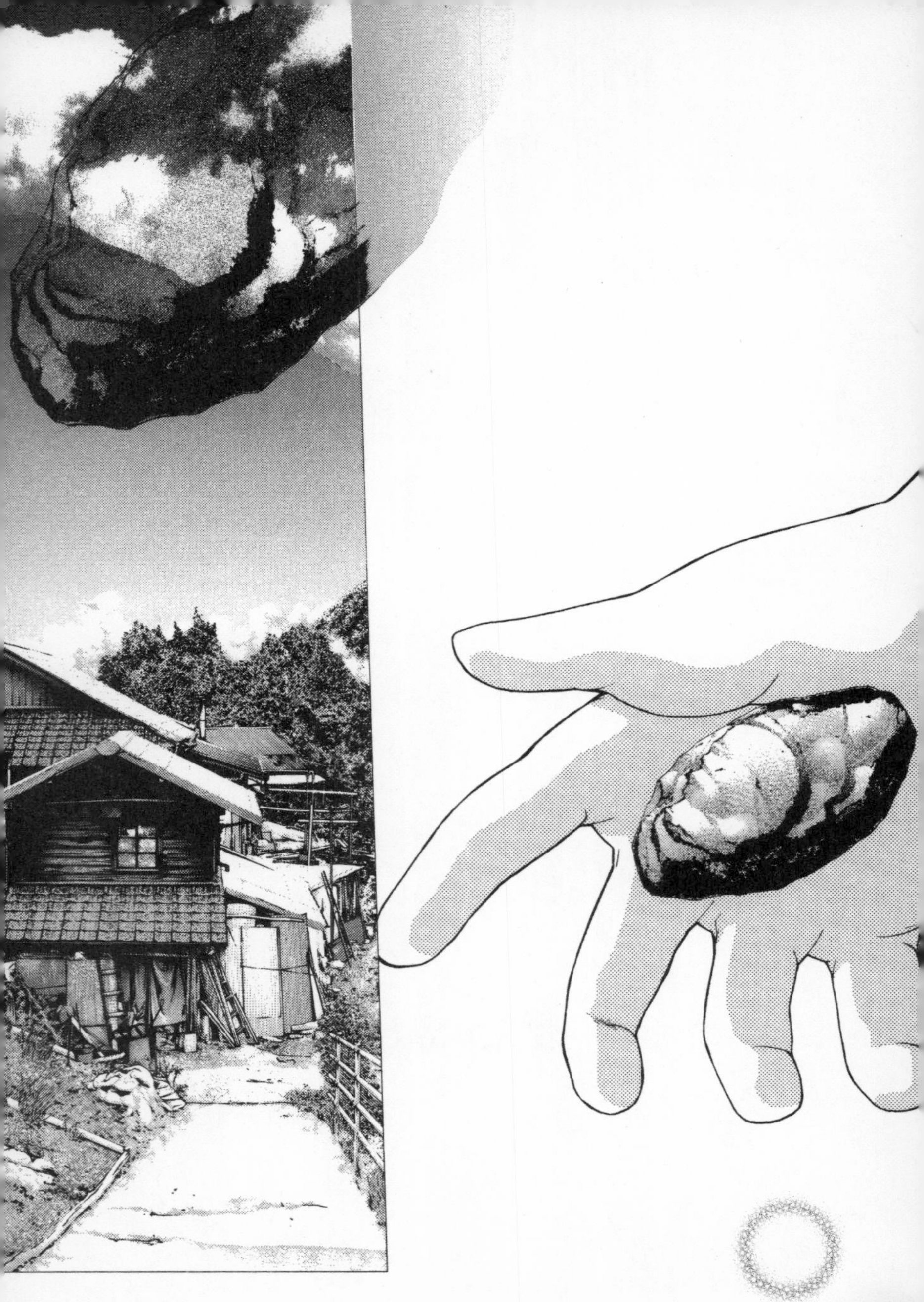

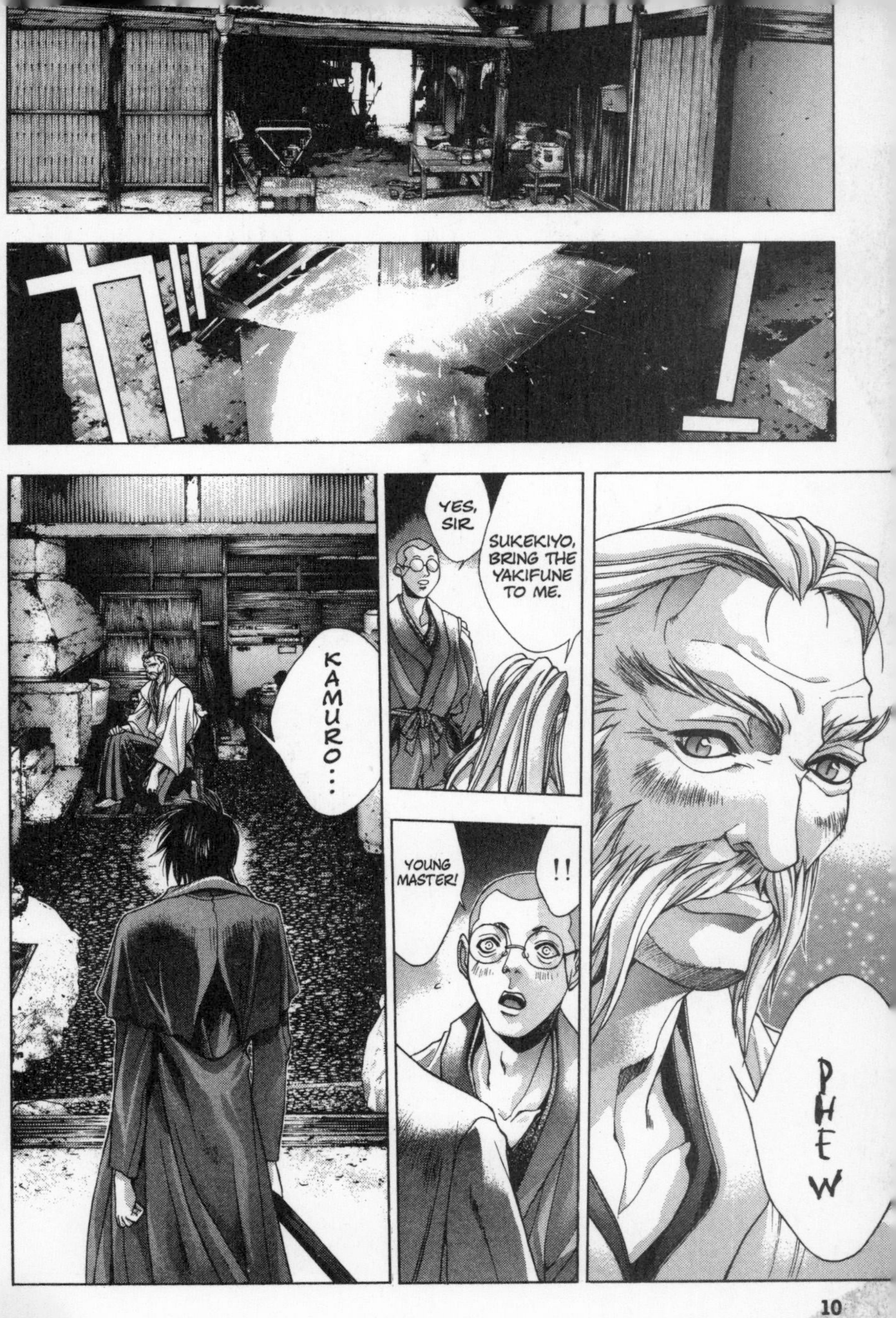
PHEW
SUKEKIYO, BRING THE YAKIFUNE TO ME.
YES, SIR
!!
YOUNG MASTER!
KAMURO...

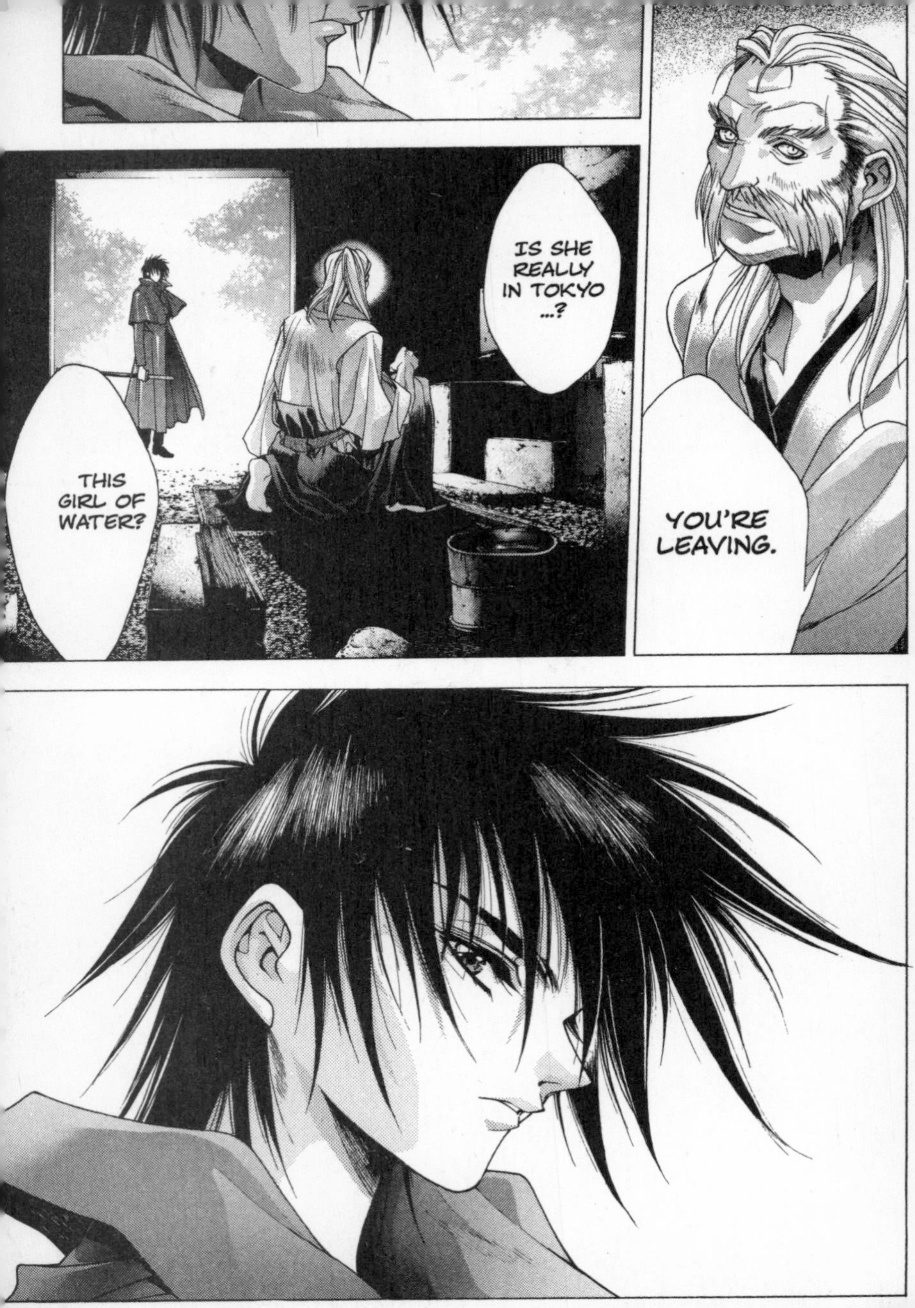
YOU'RE LEAVING.
IS SHE REALLY IN TOKYO ...?
THIS GIRL OF WATER?

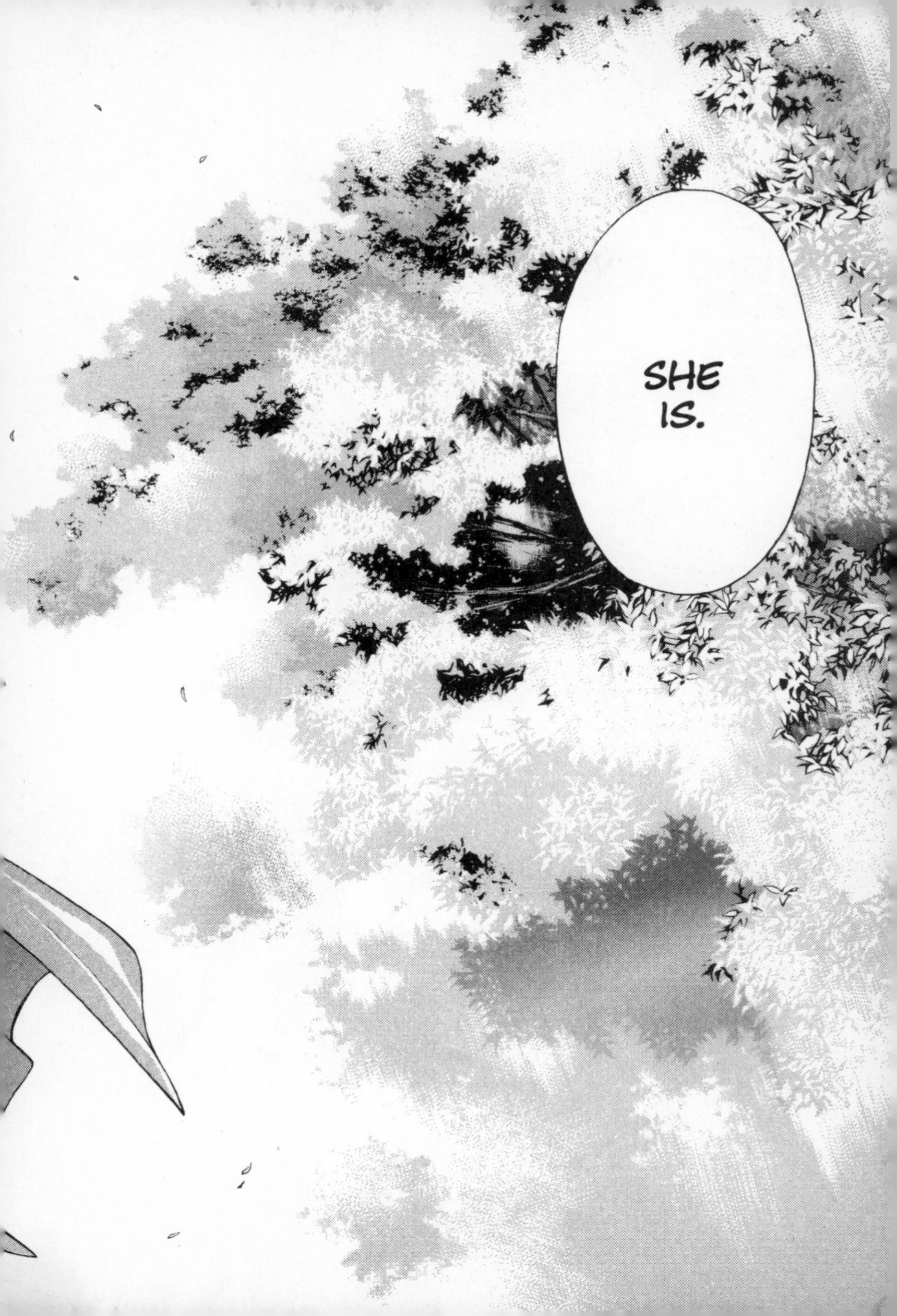
SHE IS.

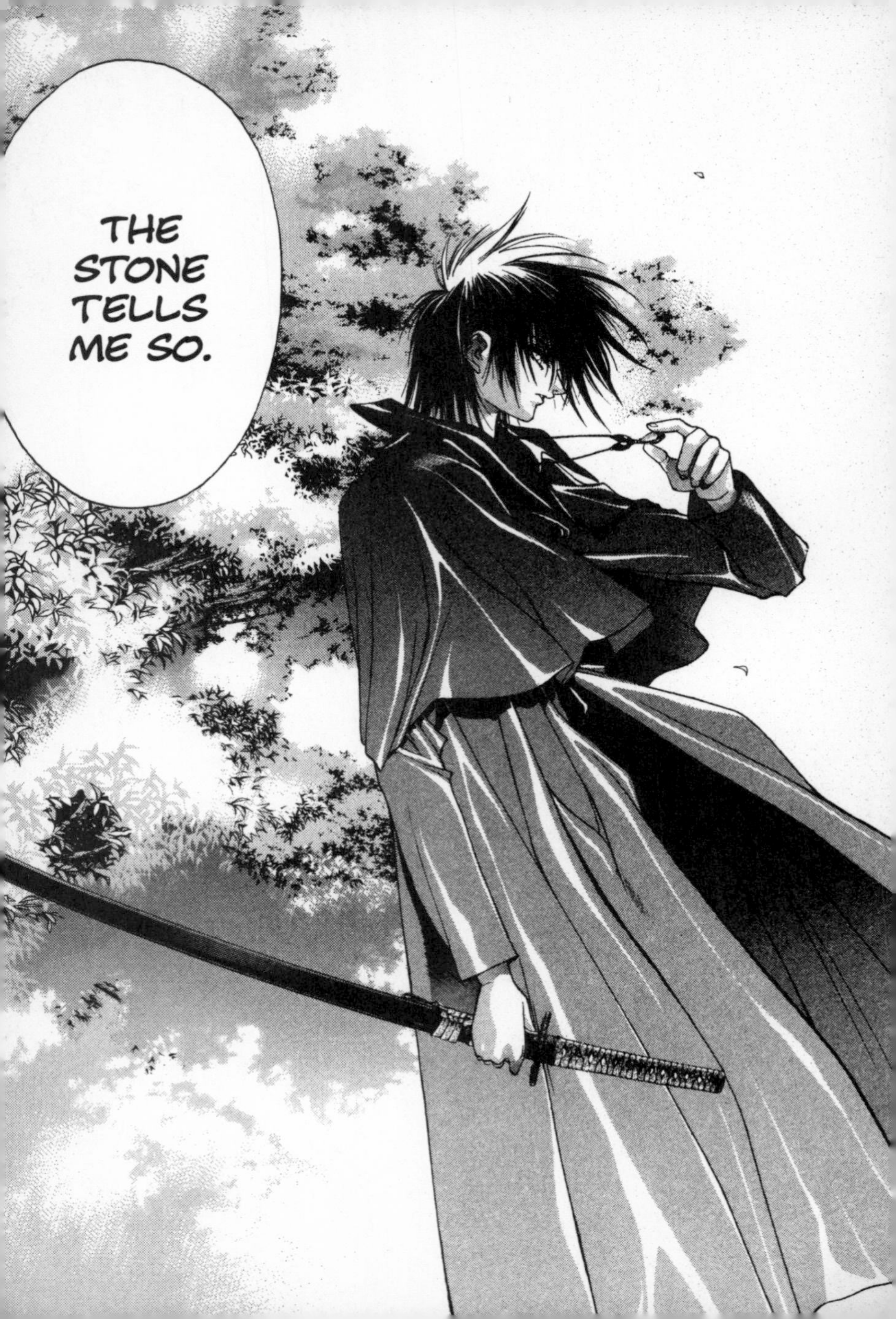
THE STONE TELLS ME SO.

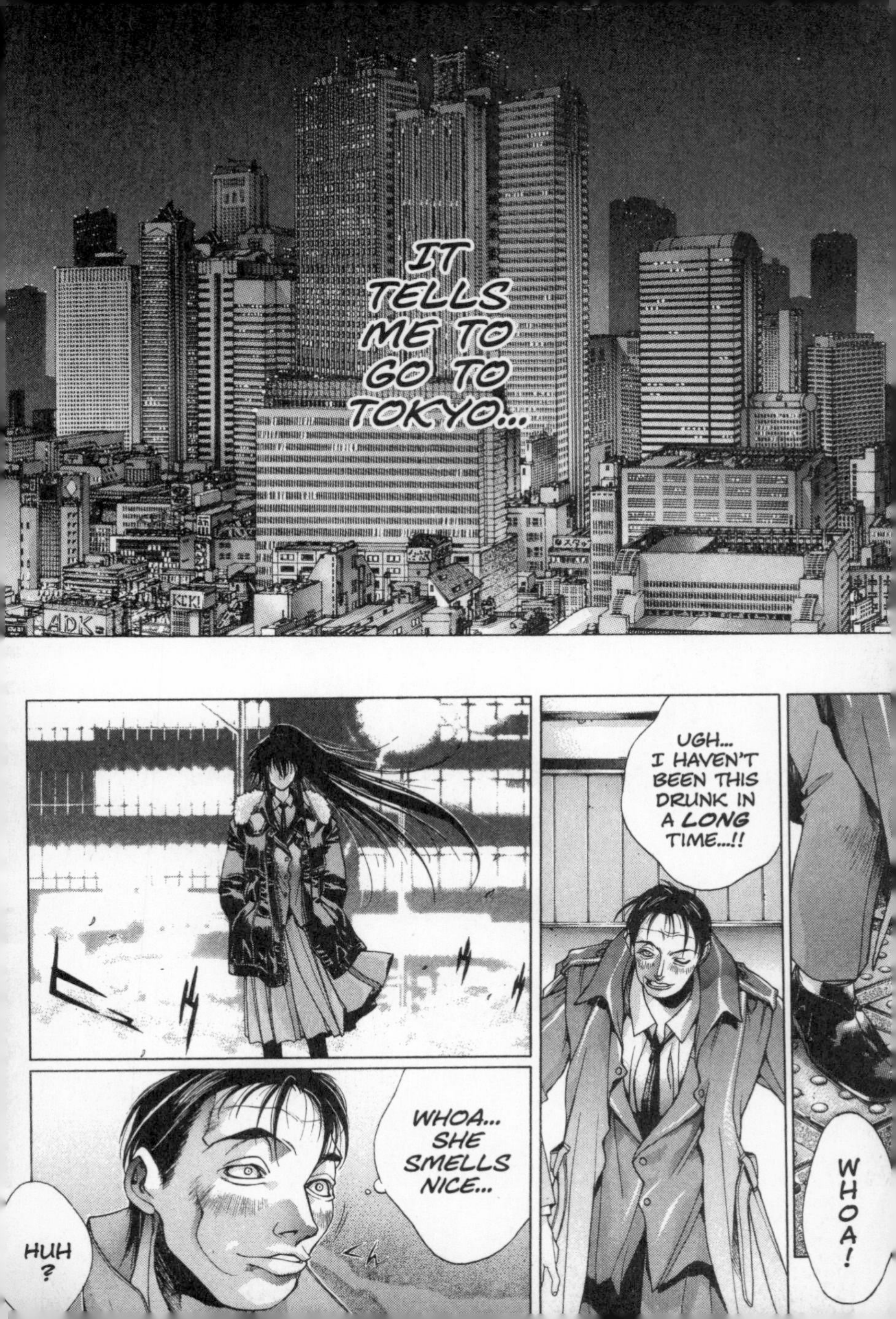
IT TELLS ME TO GO TO TOKYO...
WHOA!
UGH... I HAVEN'T BEEN THIS DRUNK IN A LONG TIME...!!
WHOA... SHE SMELLS NICE...
HUH?

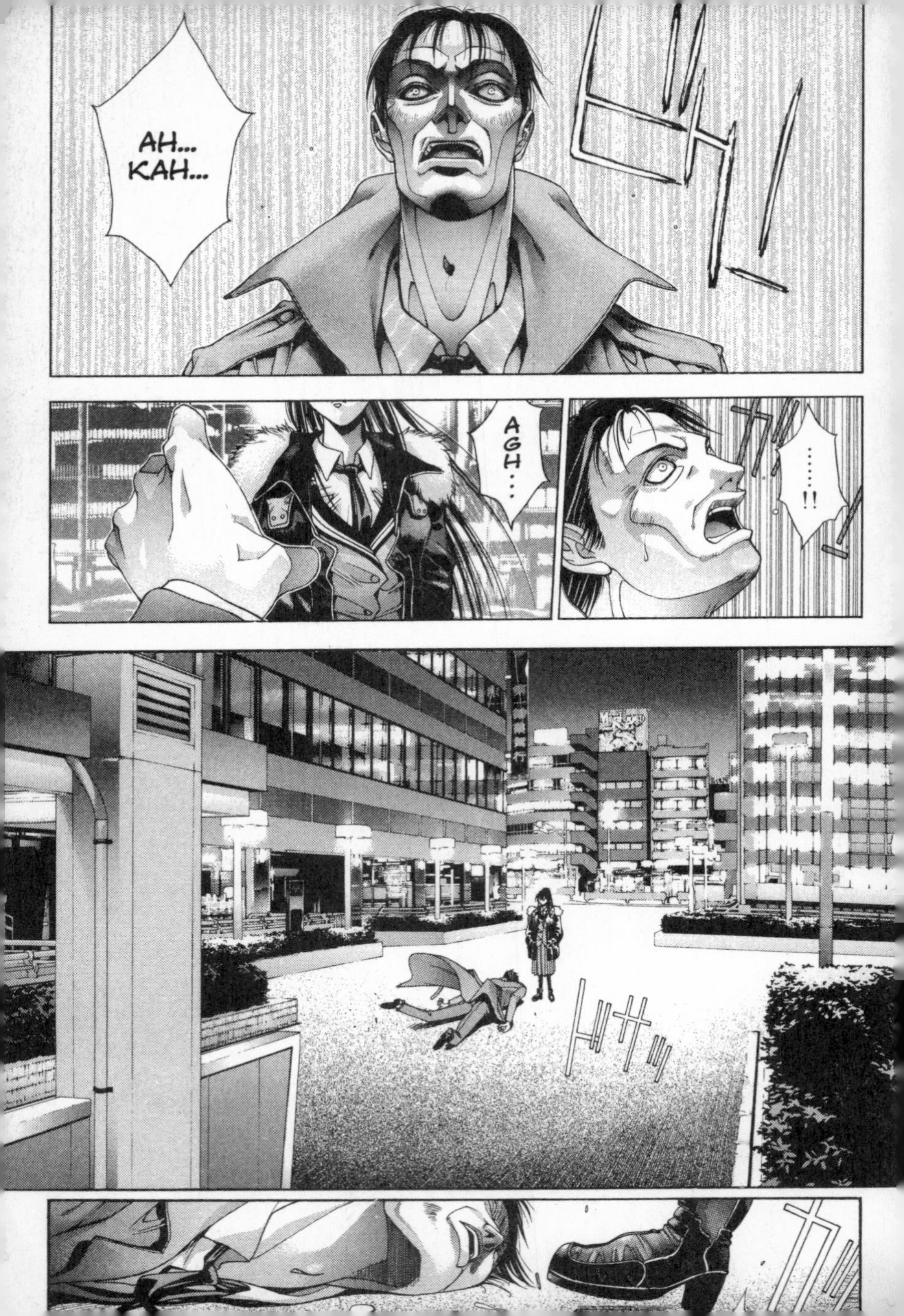
AH... KAH...
......!!
AGH...

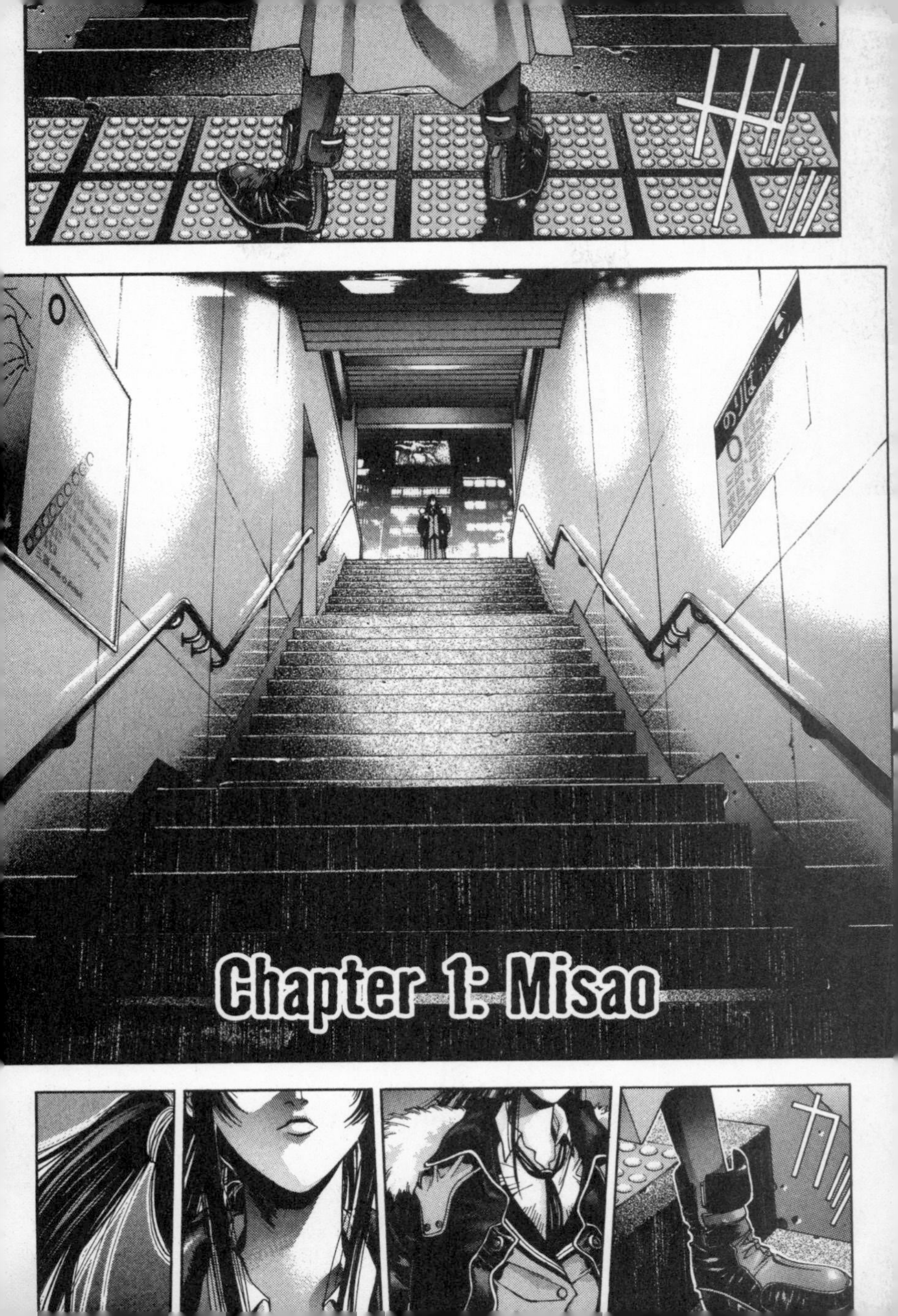
Chapter 1: Misao

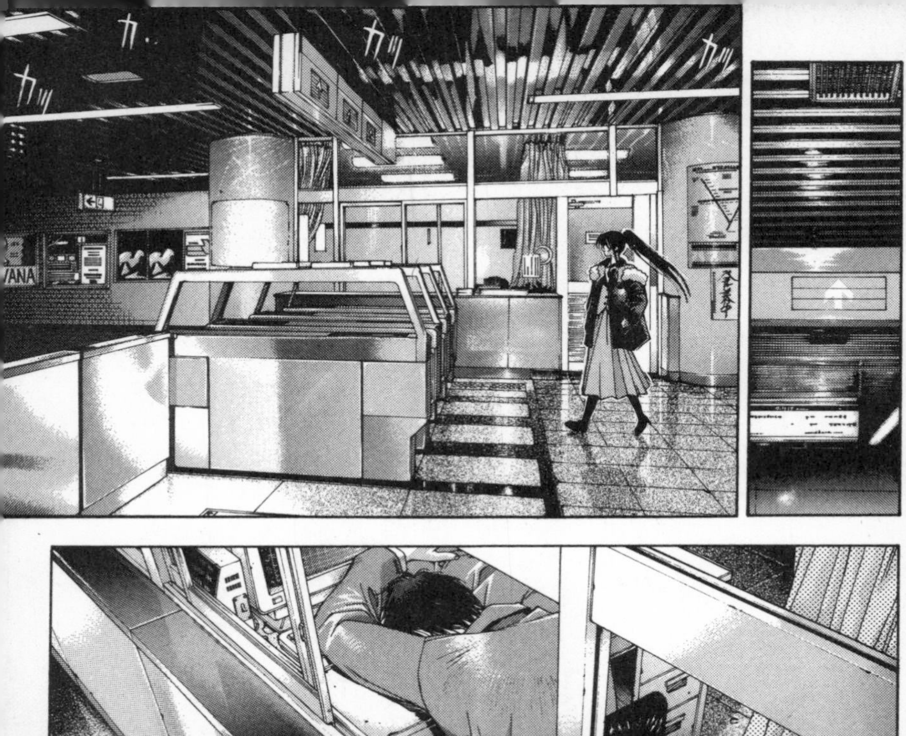
カッ
カッ
カッ
カチッ

Sign: Subway Map

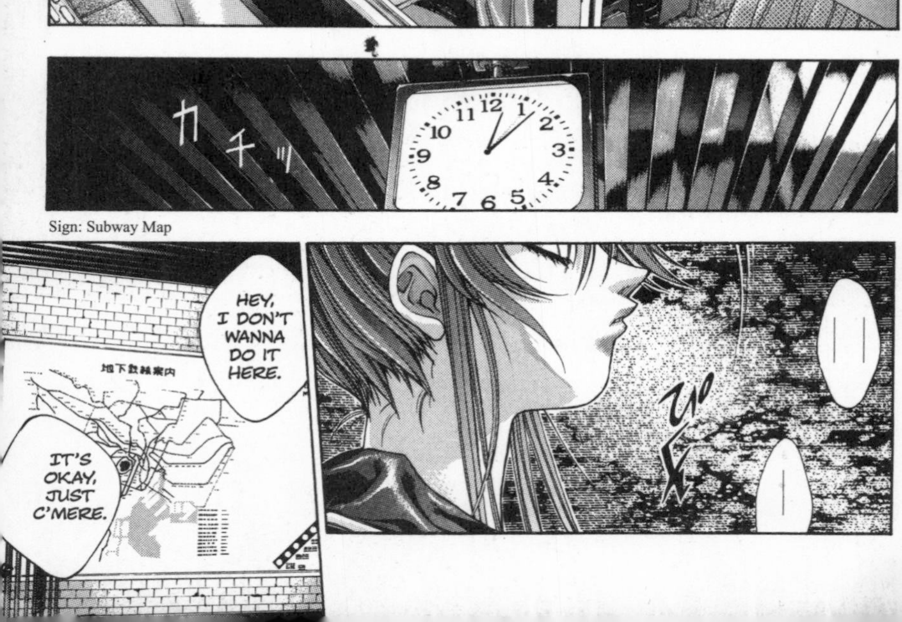
地下鉄線案内
HEY, I DON'T WANNA DO IT HERE.
IT'S OKAY, JUST C'MERE.

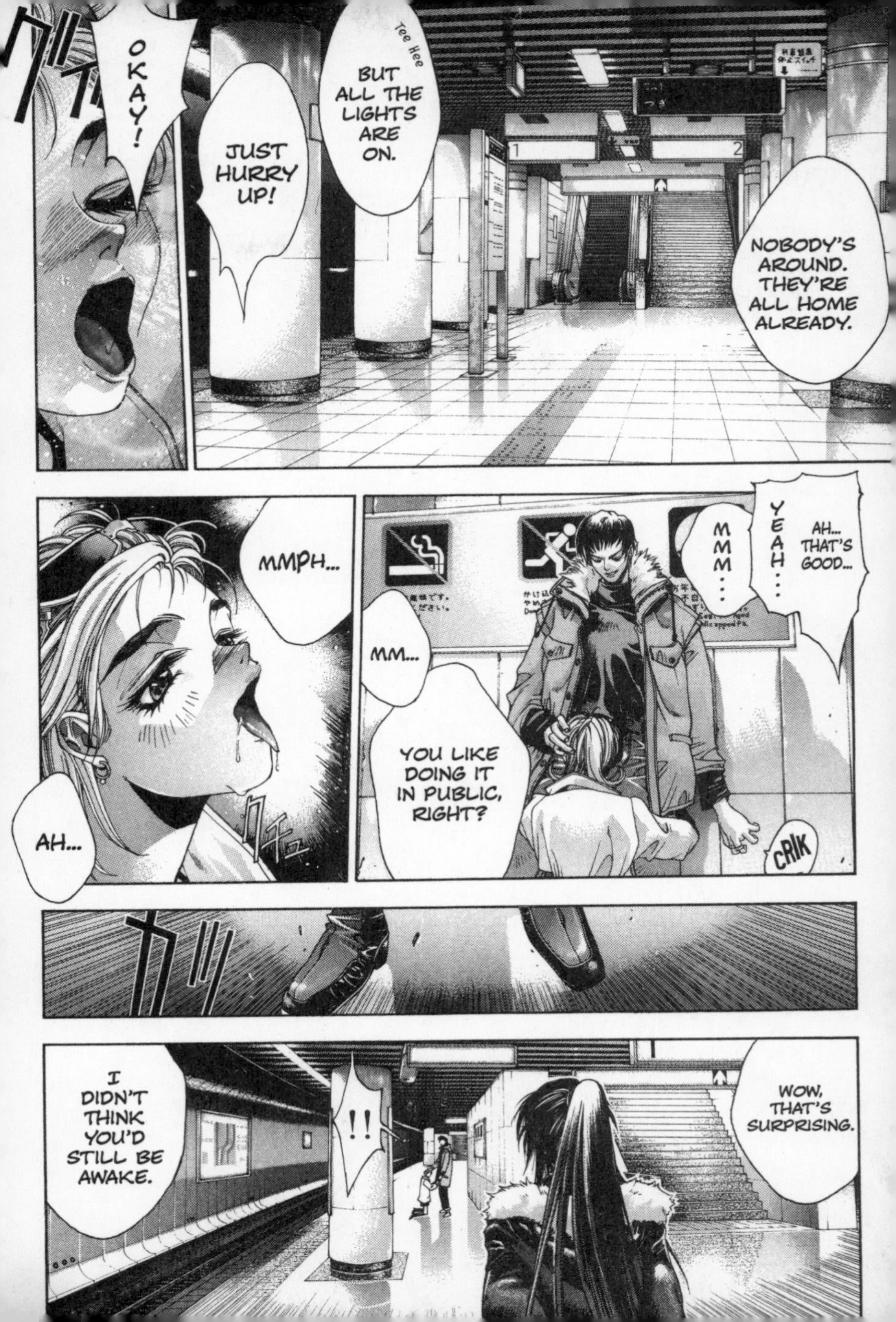
NOBODY'S AROUND. THEY'RE ALL HOME ALREADY.
Tee Hee
BUT ALL THE LIGHTS ARE ON.
JUST HURRY UP!
OKAY!
AH... THAT'S GOOD...
YEAH...
MMM...
MM...
YOU LIKE DOING IT IN PUBLIC, RIGHT?
CRIK
MMPH...
AH...
WOW, THAT'S SURPRISING.
!!
I DIDN'T THINK YOU'D STILL BE AWAKE.

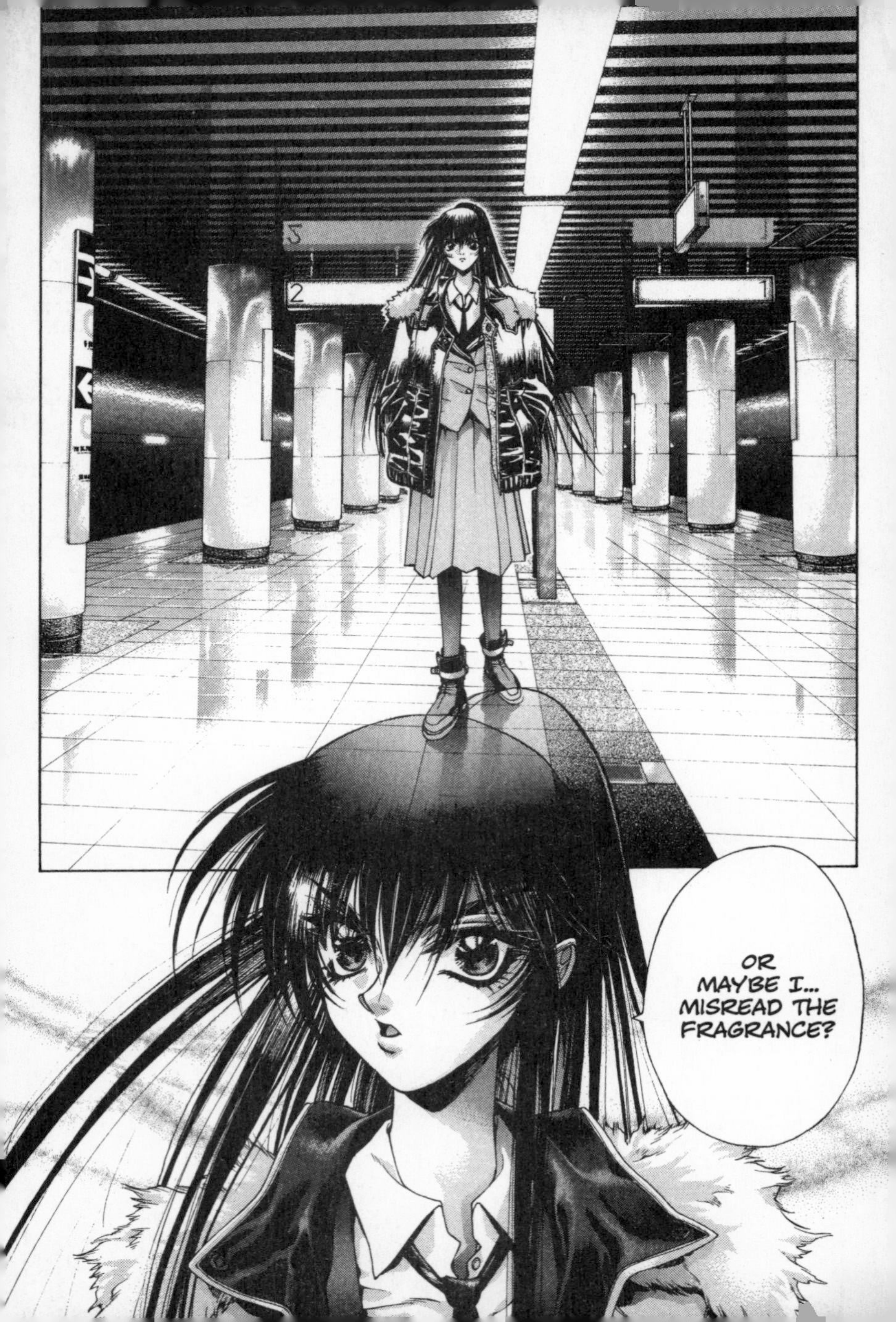
OR MAYBE I... MISREAD THE FRAGRANCE?

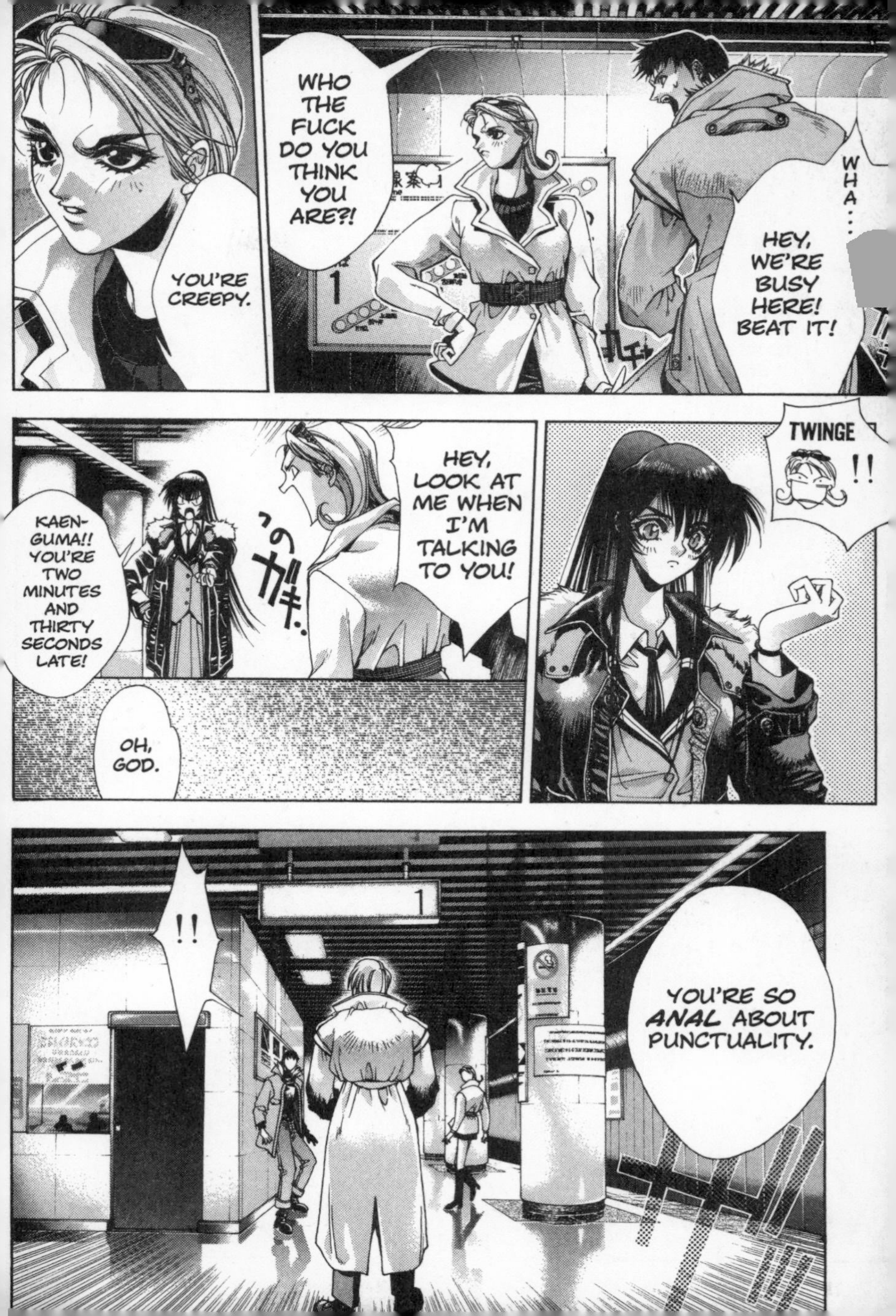
WHA...
HEY, WE'RE BUSY HERE! BEAT IT!
WHO THE FUCK DO YOU THINK YOU ARE?!
YOU'RE CREEPY.
TWINGE
!!
HEY, LOOK AT ME WHEN I'M TALKING TO YOU!
KAEN-GUMA!! YOU'RE TWO MINUTES AND THIRTY SECONDS LATE!
OH, GOD.
YOU'RE SO ANAL ABOUT PUNCTUALITY.
!!

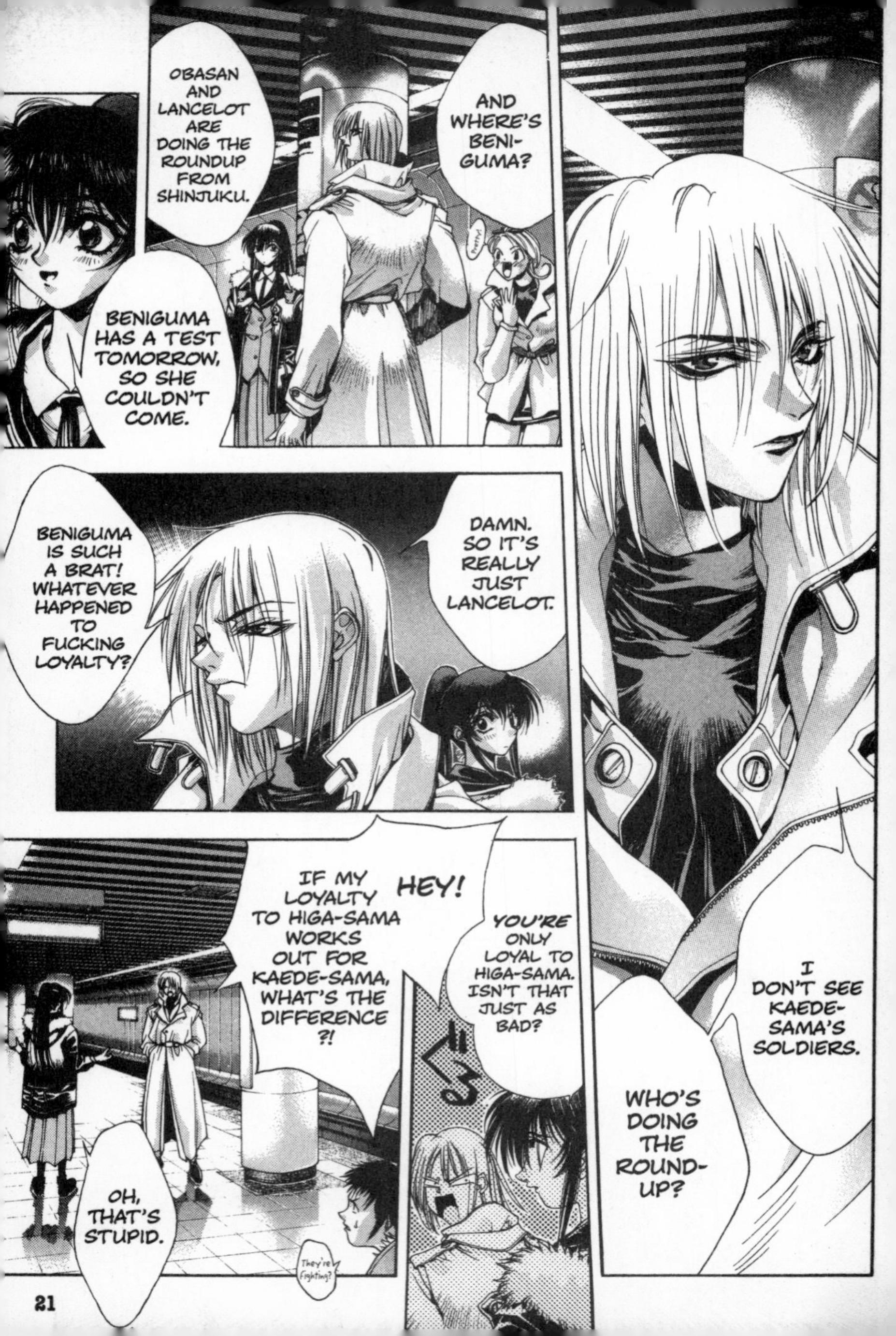
I DON'T SEE KAEDE-SAMA'S SOLDIERS.
WHO'S DOING THE ROUND-UP?
AND WHERE'S BENI-GUMA?
Pretty!
OBASAN AND LANCELOT ARE DOING THE ROUNDUP FROM SHINJUKU.
BENIGUMA HAS A TEST TOMORROW, SO SHE COULDN'T COME.
DAMN. SO IT'S REALLY JUST LANCELOT.
BENIGUMA IS SUCH A BRAT! WHATEVER HAPPENED TO FUCKING LOYALTY?
YOU'RE ONLY LOYAL TO HIGA-SAMA. ISN'T THAT JUST AS BAD?
HEY!
IF MY LOYALTY TO HIGA-SAMA WORKS OUT FOR KAEDE-SAMA, WHAT'S THE DIFFERENCE?!
OH, THAT'S STUPID.
They're fighting?

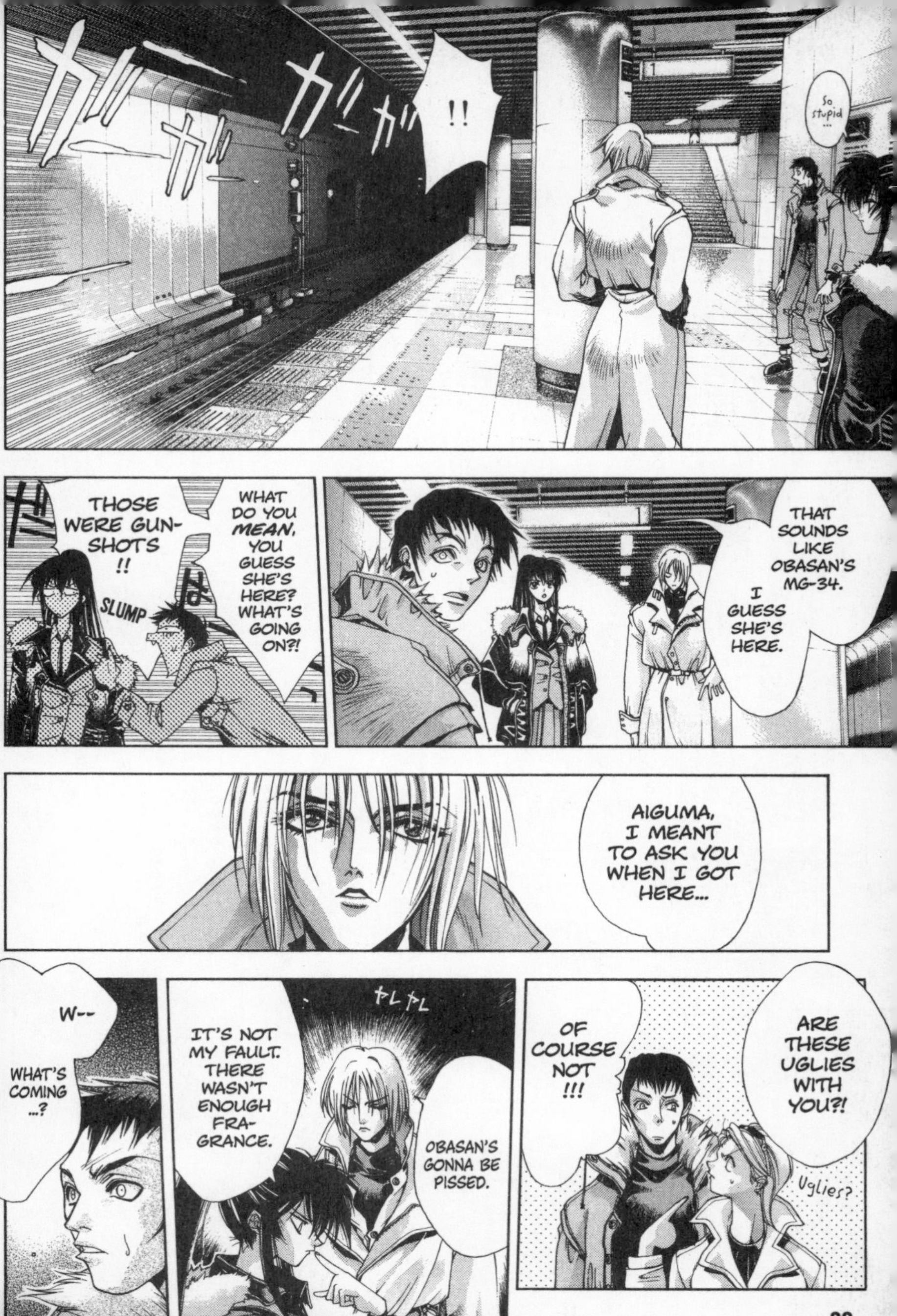
!!
So stupid...
THAT SOUNDS LIKE OBASAN'S MG-34.
I GUESS SHE'S HERE.
WHAT DO YOU *MEAN*, YOU GUESS SHE'S HERE? WHAT'S GOING ON?!
THOSE WERE GUN-SHOTS!!
SLUMP
AIGUMA, I MEANT TO ASK YOU WHEN I GOT HERE...
ARE THESE UGLIES WITH YOU?!
OF COURSE NOT!!!
Uglies?
IT'S NOT MY FAULT. THERE WASN'T ENOUGH FRA-GRANCE.
OBASAN'S GONNA BE PISSED.
W--
WHAT'S COMING...?

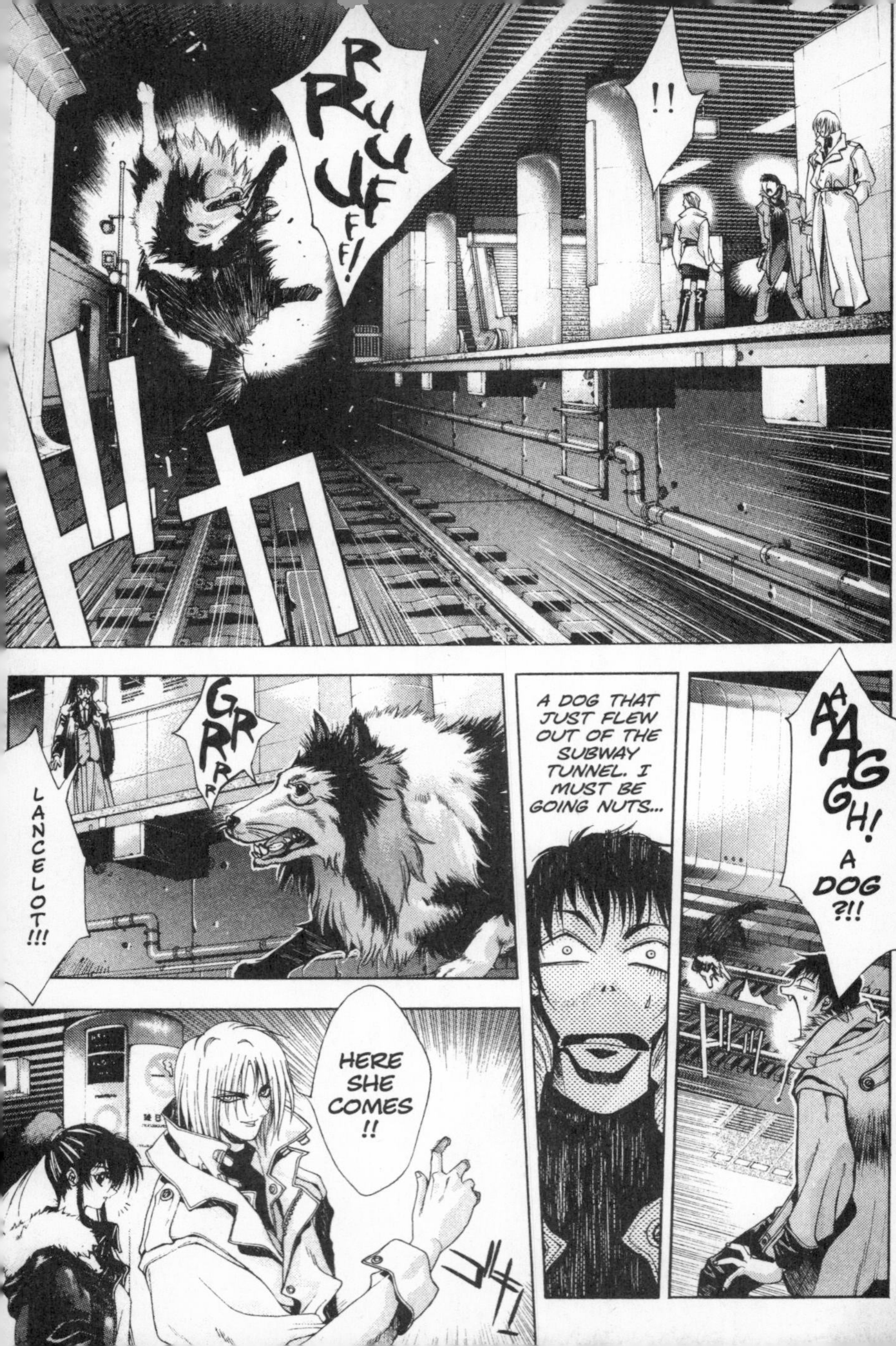
!!
RRUUUFFF!
AAAGH!
A DOG ?!!
A DOG THAT JUST FLEW OUT OF THE SUBWAY TUNNEL. I MUST BE GOING NUTS...
GRRRR
LANCELOT!!!
HERE SHE COMES !!

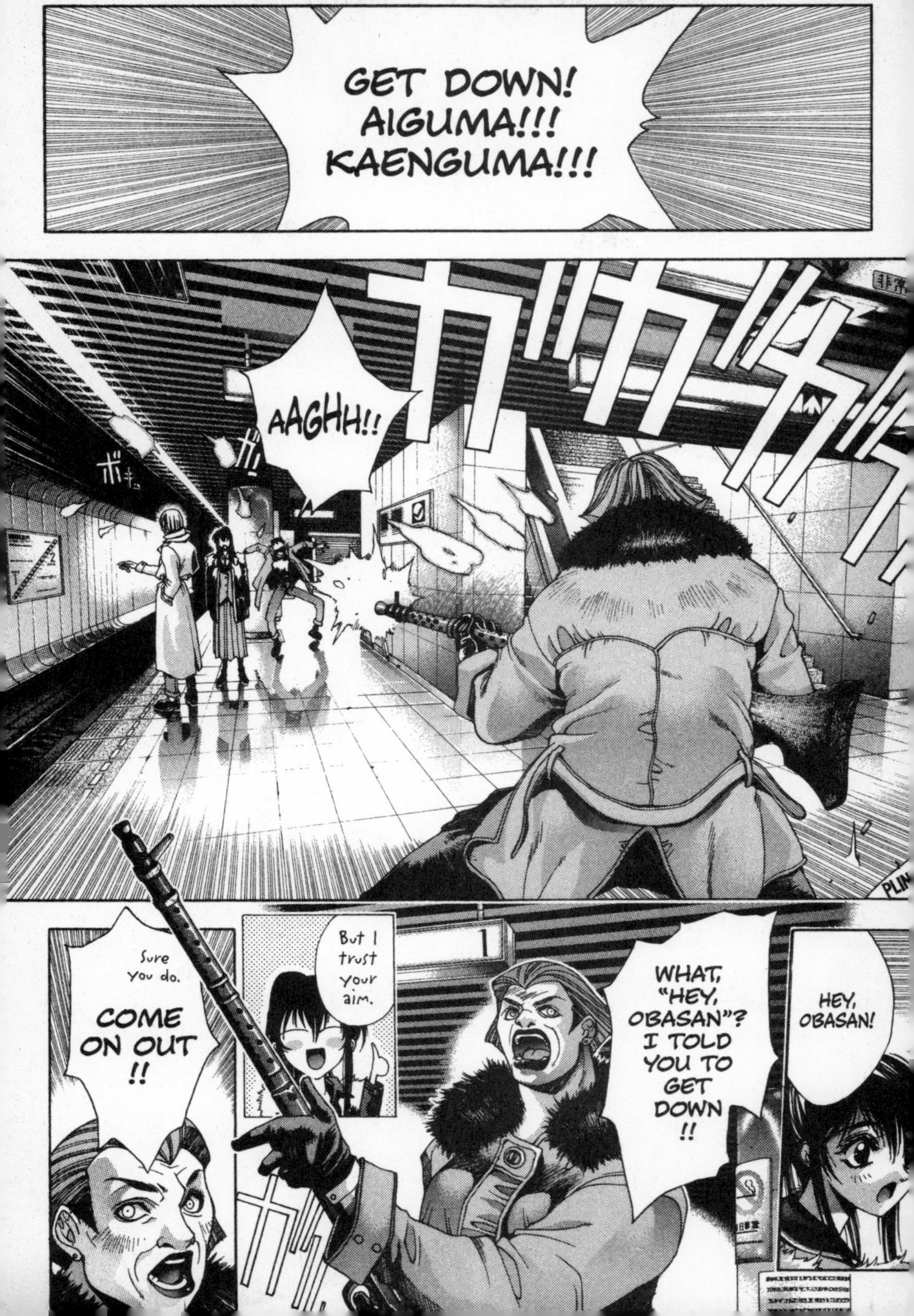
GET DOWN! AIGUMA!!! KAENGUMA!!!
AAGHH!!
HEY, OBASAN!
WHAT, "HEY, OBASAN"? I TOLD YOU TO GET DOWN !!
But I trust your aim.
Sure you do.
COME ON OUT !!

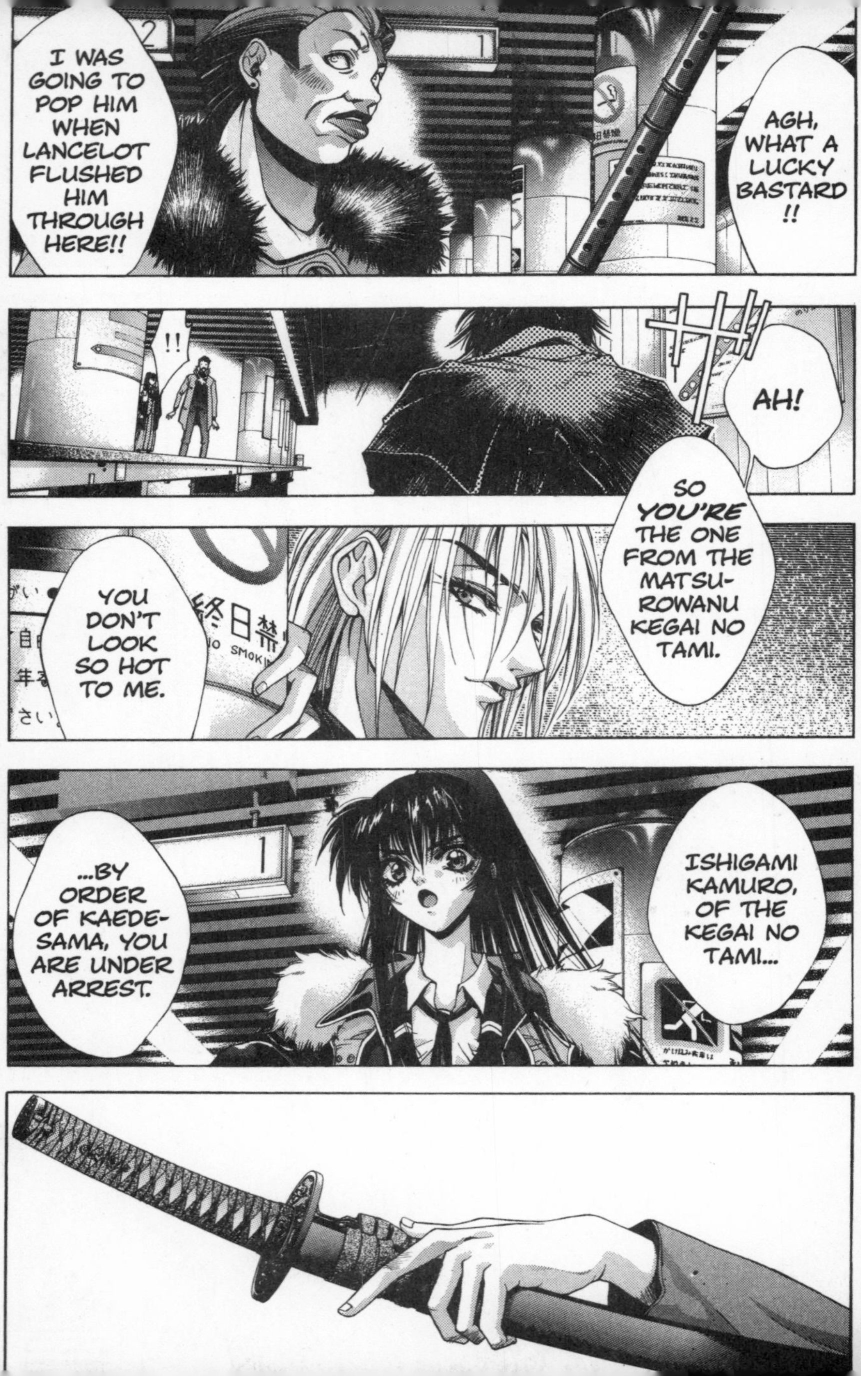
AGH, WHAT A LUCKY BASTARD!!
I WAS GOING TO POP HIM WHEN LANCELOT FLUSHED HIM THROUGH HERE!!
AH!
!!
SO *YOU'RE* THE ONE FROM THE MATSU-ROWANU KEGAI NO TAMI.
YOU DON'T LOOK SO HOT TO ME.
ISHIGAMI KAMURO, OF THE KEGAI NO TAMI...
...BY ORDER OF KAEDE-SAMA, YOU ARE UNDER ARREST.

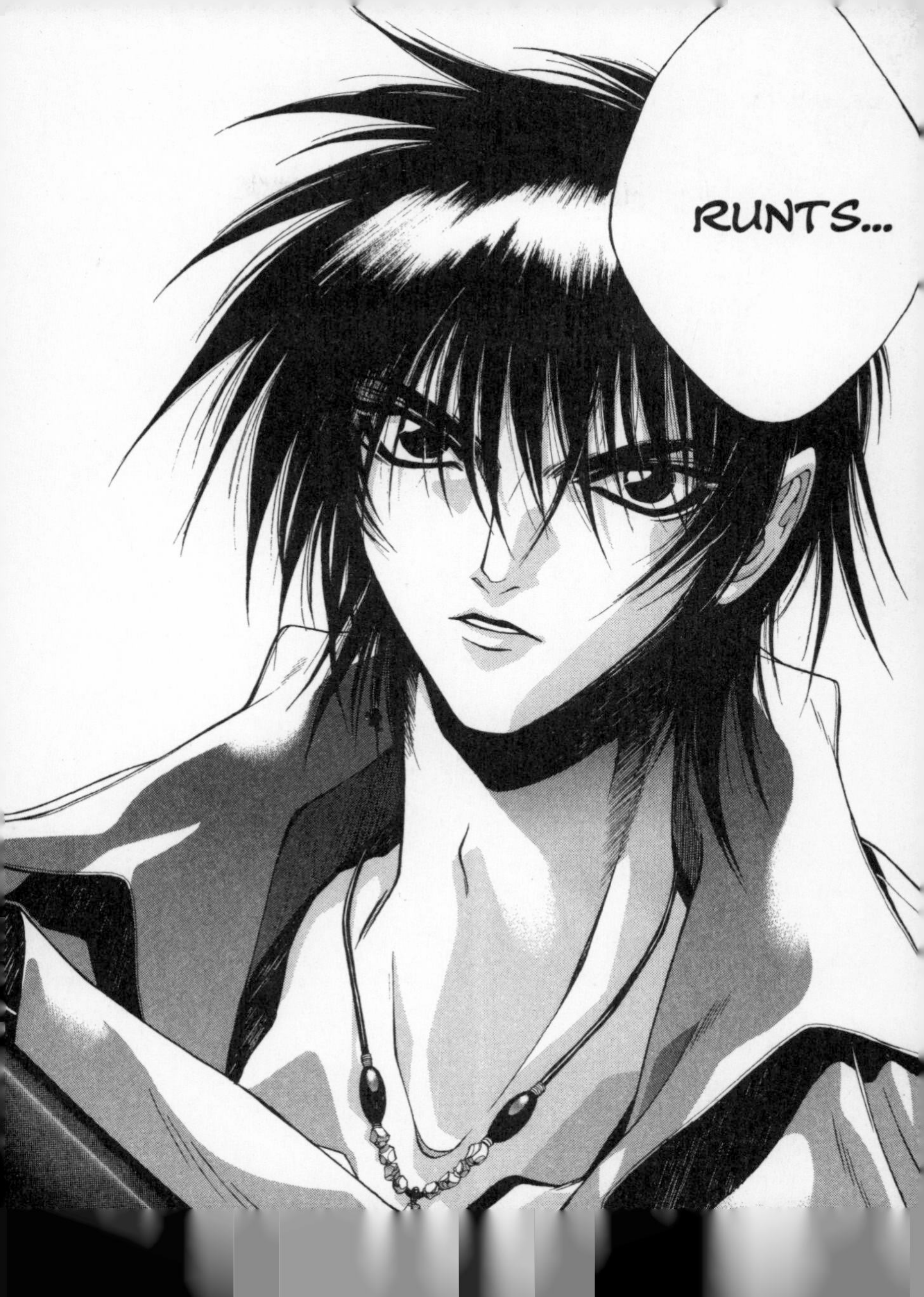
RUNTS...

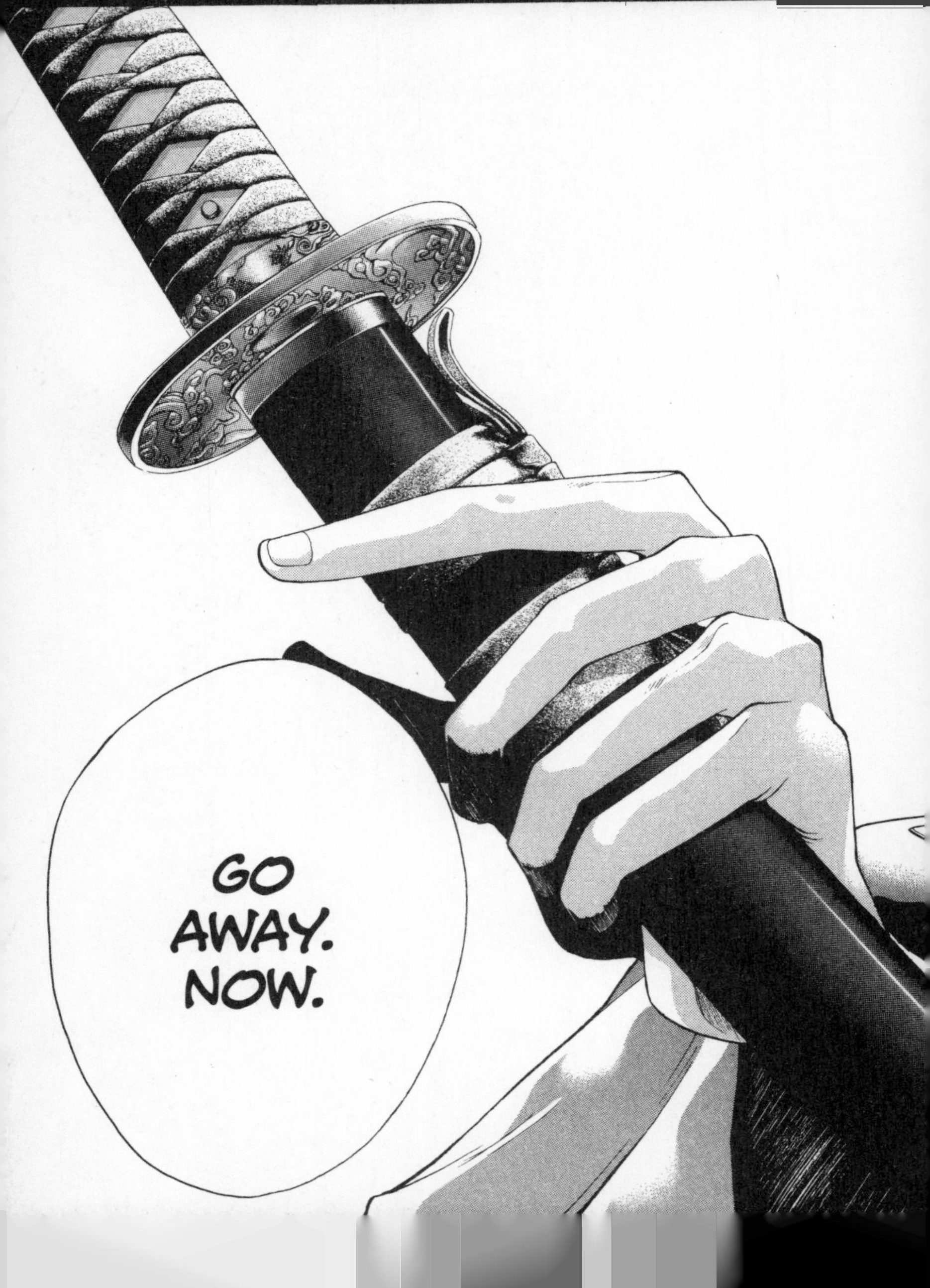
GO AWAY. NOW.

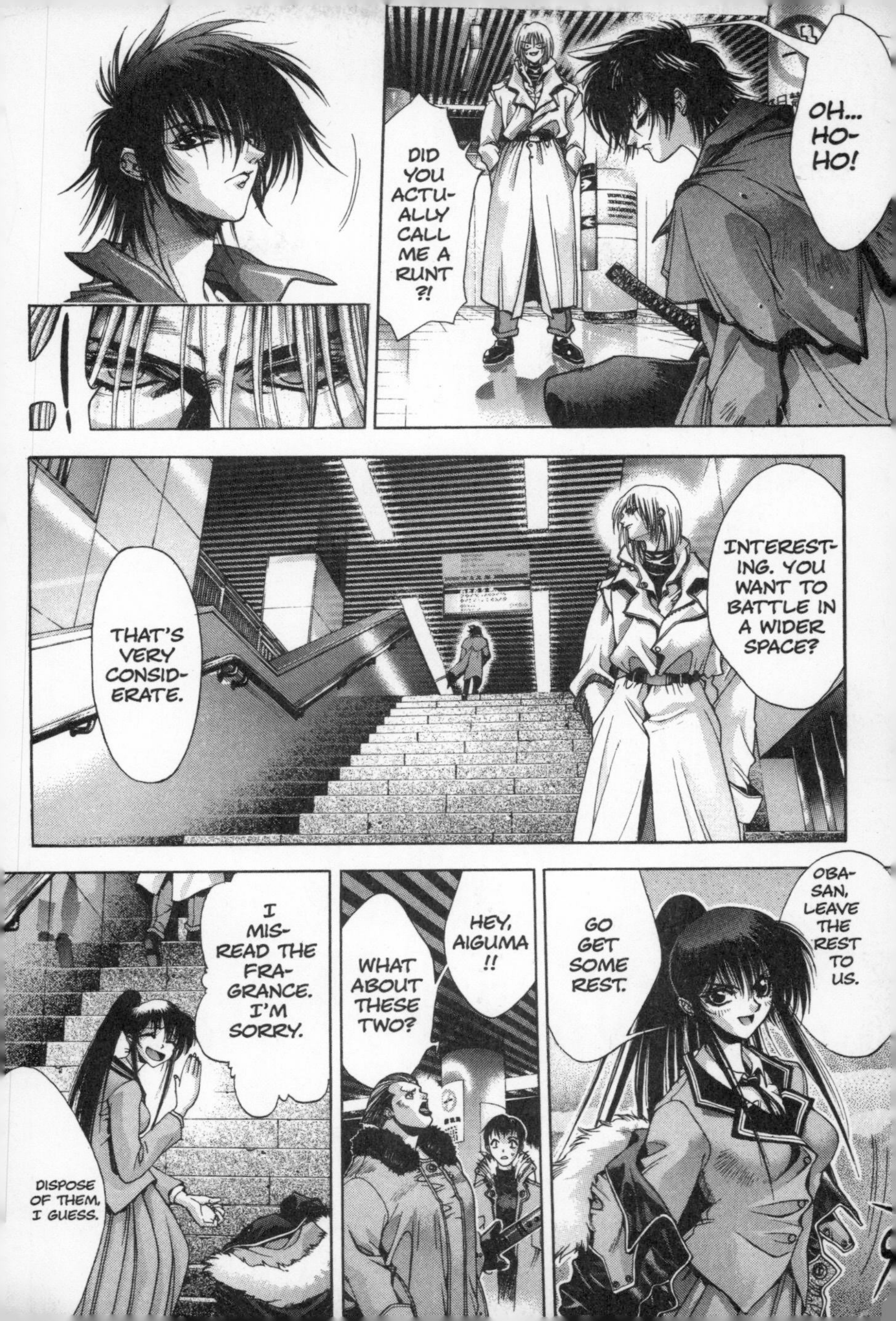
OH... HO-HO!
DID YOU ACTUALLY CALL ME A RUNT?!
INTERESTING. YOU WANT TO BATTLE IN A WIDER SPACE?
THAT'S VERY CONSIDERATE.
OBASAN, LEAVE THE REST TO US.
GO GET SOME REST.
HEY, AIGUMA!!
WHAT ABOUT THESE TWO?
I MISREAD THE FRAGRANCE. I'M SORRY.
DISPOSE OF THEM, I GUESS.

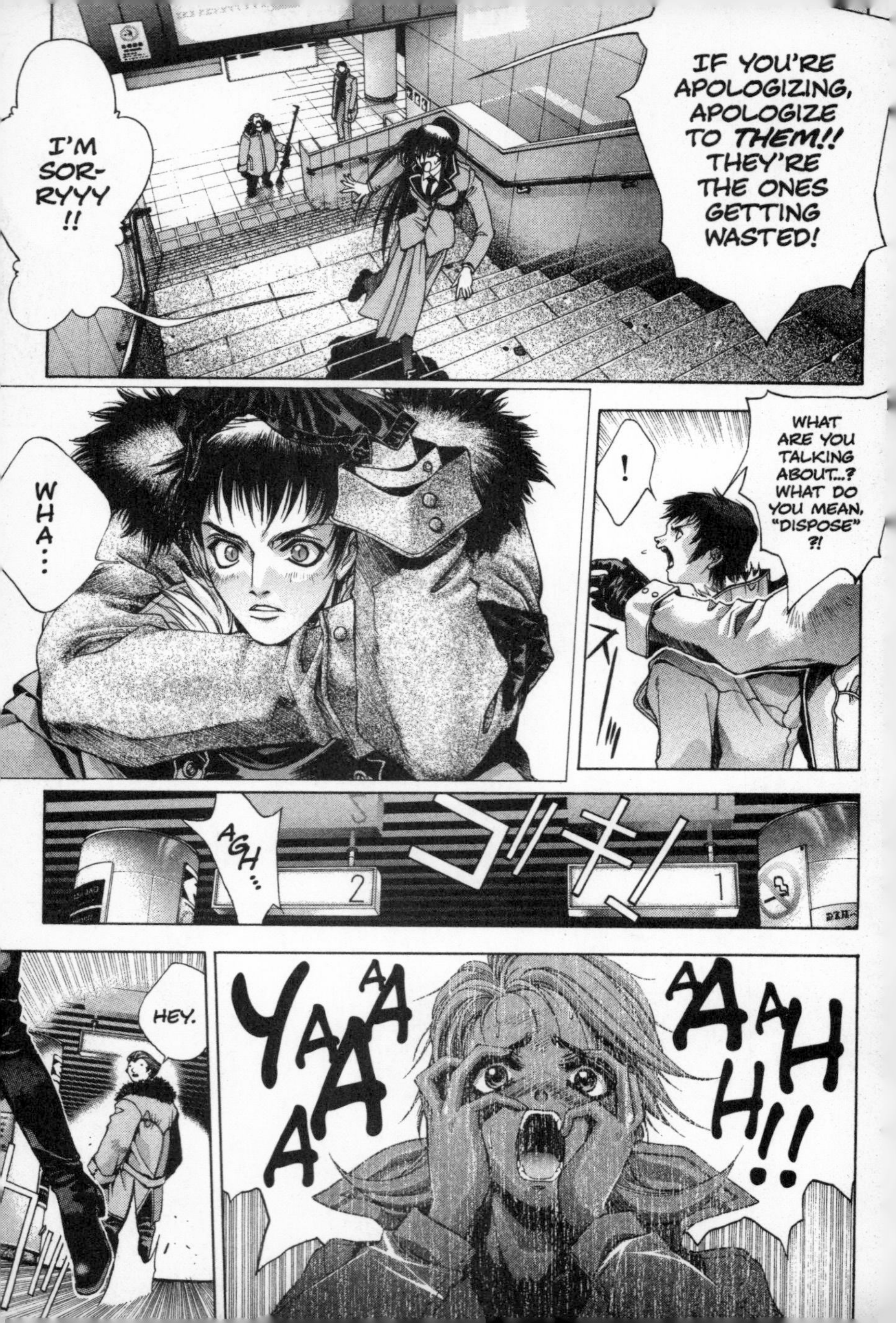
IF YOU'RE APOLOGIZING, APOLOGIZE TO *THEM!!* THEY'RE THE ONES GETTING WASTED!
I'M SORRYYY!!
!
WHAT ARE YOU TALKING ABOUT...? WHAT DO YOU MEAN, "DISPOSE"?!
WHA...
AGH...
YAAAAAAAAAAHH!!
HEY.

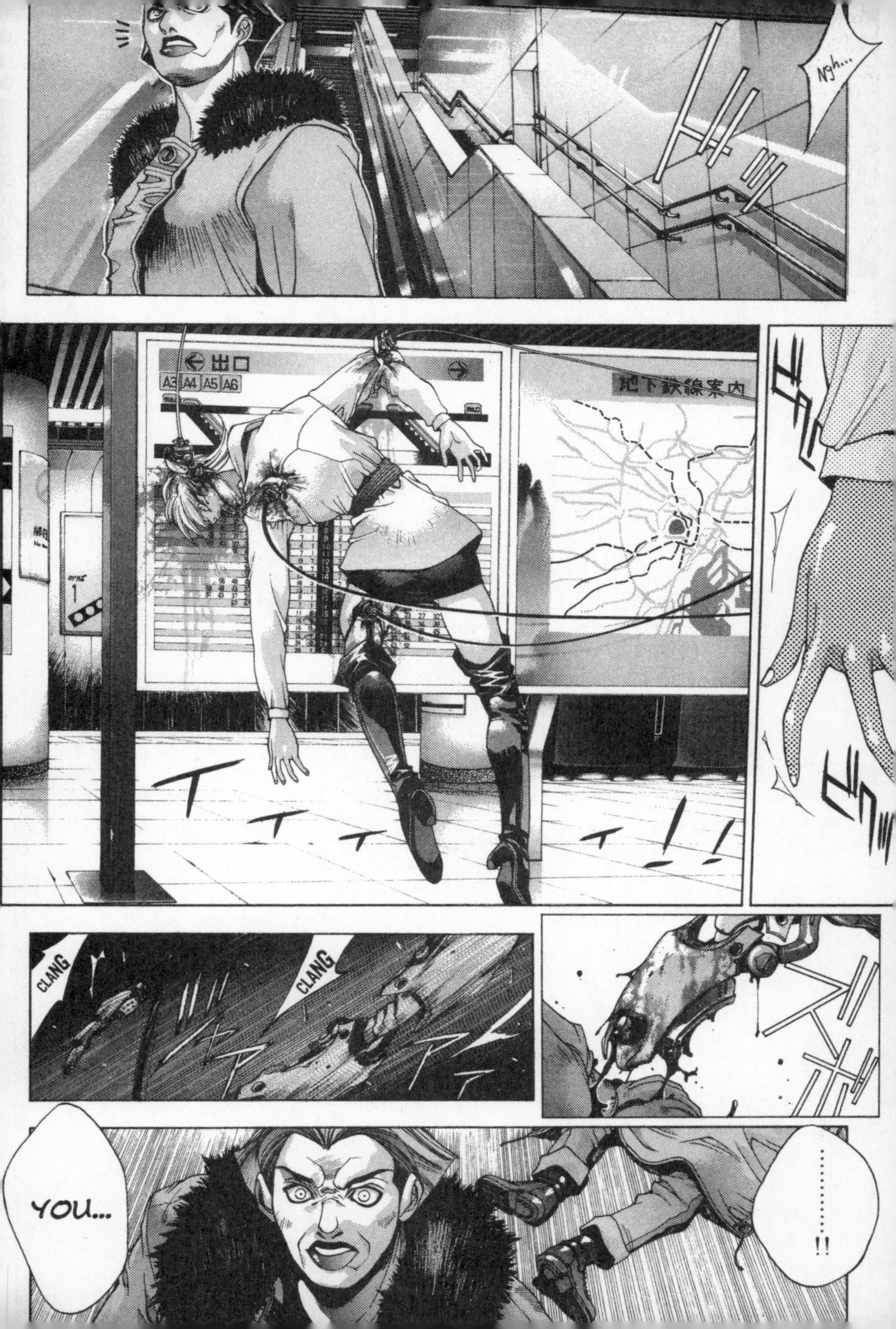
Ngh...
出口
A3 A4 A5 A6
地下鉄線案内
CLANG
CLANG
......!!
YOU...

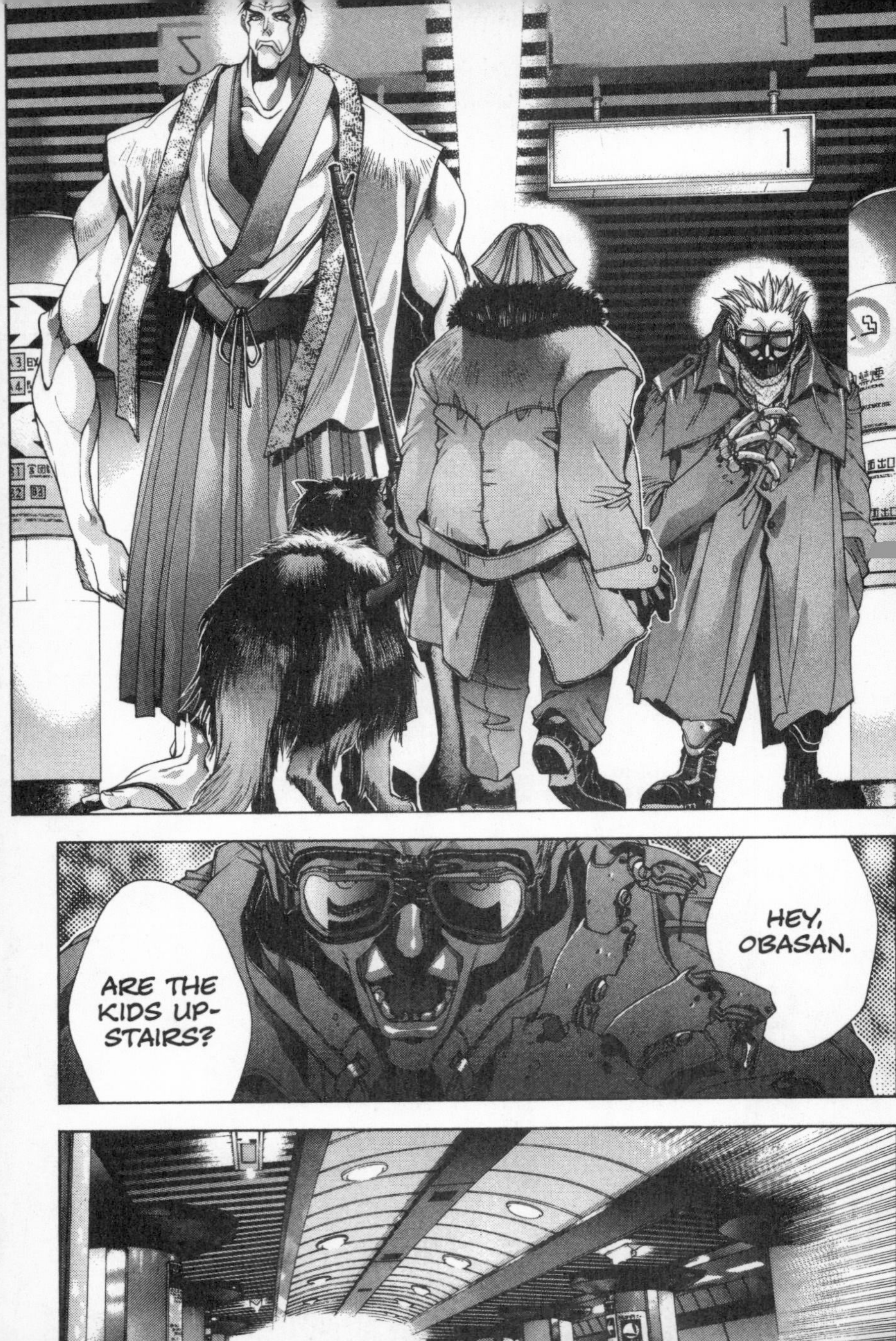
HEY, OBASAN.
ARE THE KIDS UP-STAIRS?

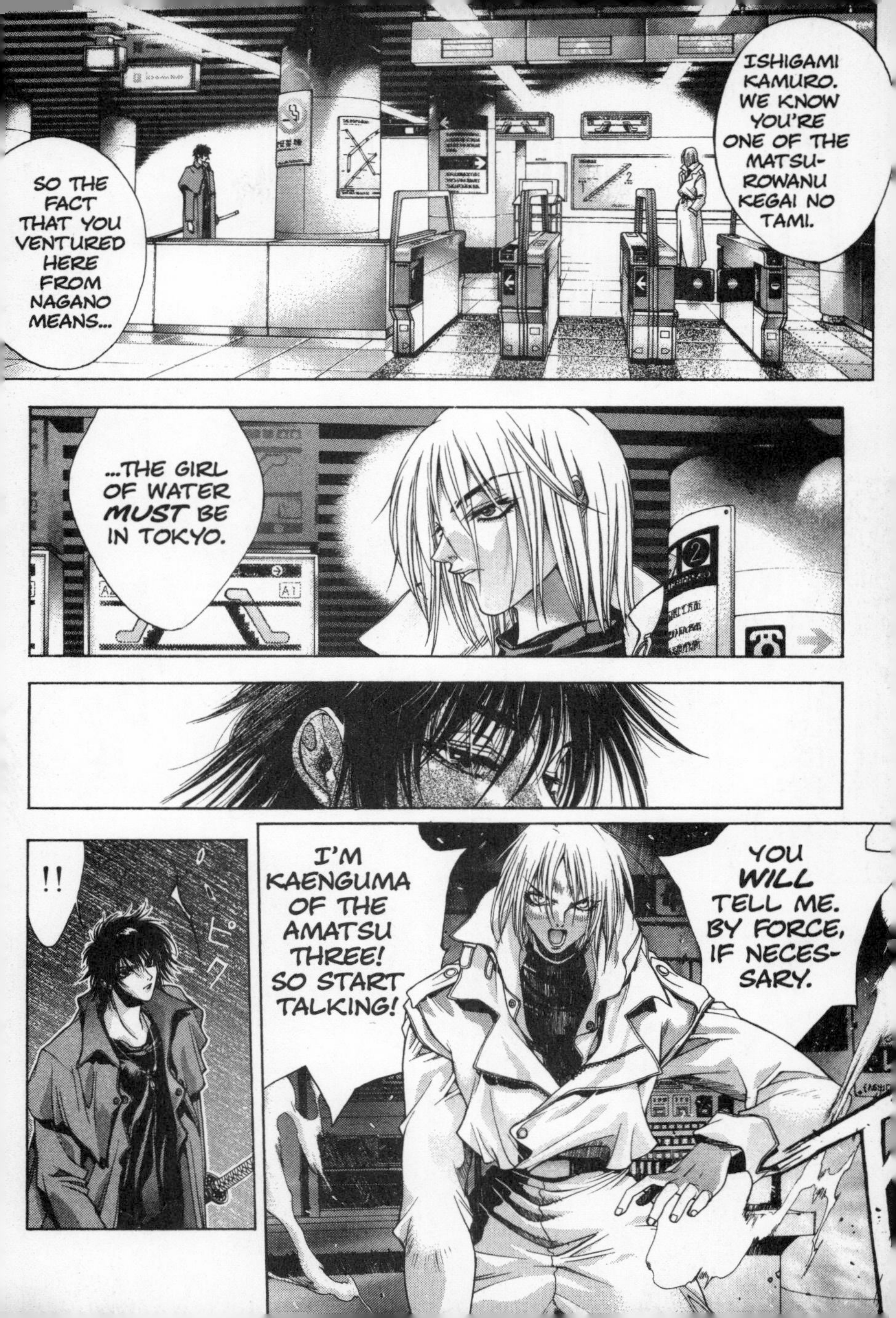
ISHIGAMI KAMURO. WE KNOW YOU'RE ONE OF THE MATSU-ROWANU KEGAI NO TAMI.
SO THE FACT THAT YOU VENTURED HERE FROM NAGANO MEANS...
...THE GIRL OF WATER *MUST* BE IN TOKYO.
YOU *WILL* TELL ME. BY FORCE, IF NECES-SARY.
I'M KAENGUMA OF THE AMATSU THREE! SO START TALKING!
!!

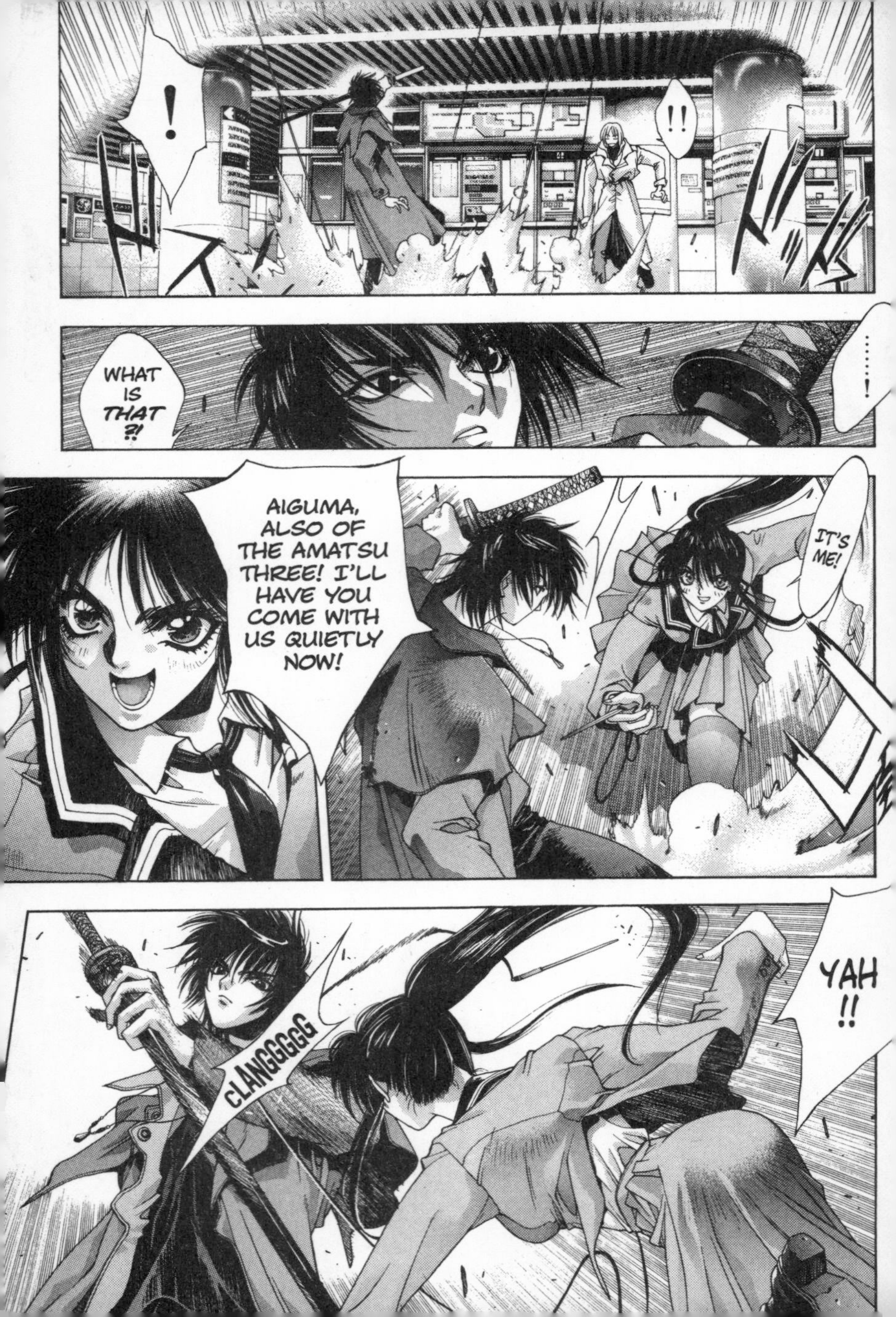
!!
!
......!
WHAT IS THAT ?!
IT'S ME!
AIGUMA, ALSO OF THE AMATSU THREE! I'LL HAVE YOU COME WITH US QUIETLY NOW!
YAH !!
CLANGGGGG

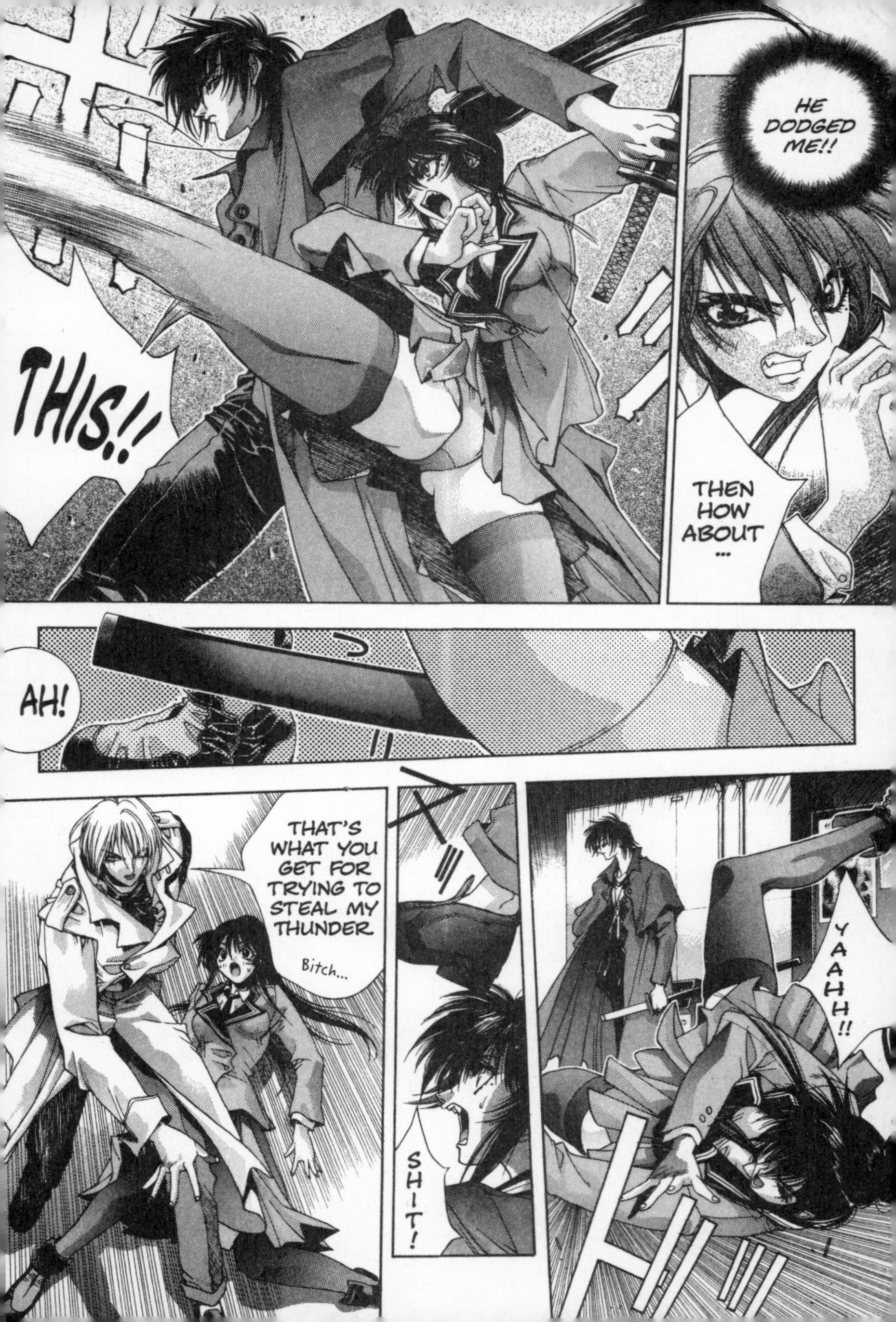
HE DODGED ME!!
THEN HOW ABOUT ...
THIS!!
AH!
YAAHH!!
SHIT!
THAT'S WHAT YOU GET FOR TRYING TO STEAL MY THUNDER
Bitch...

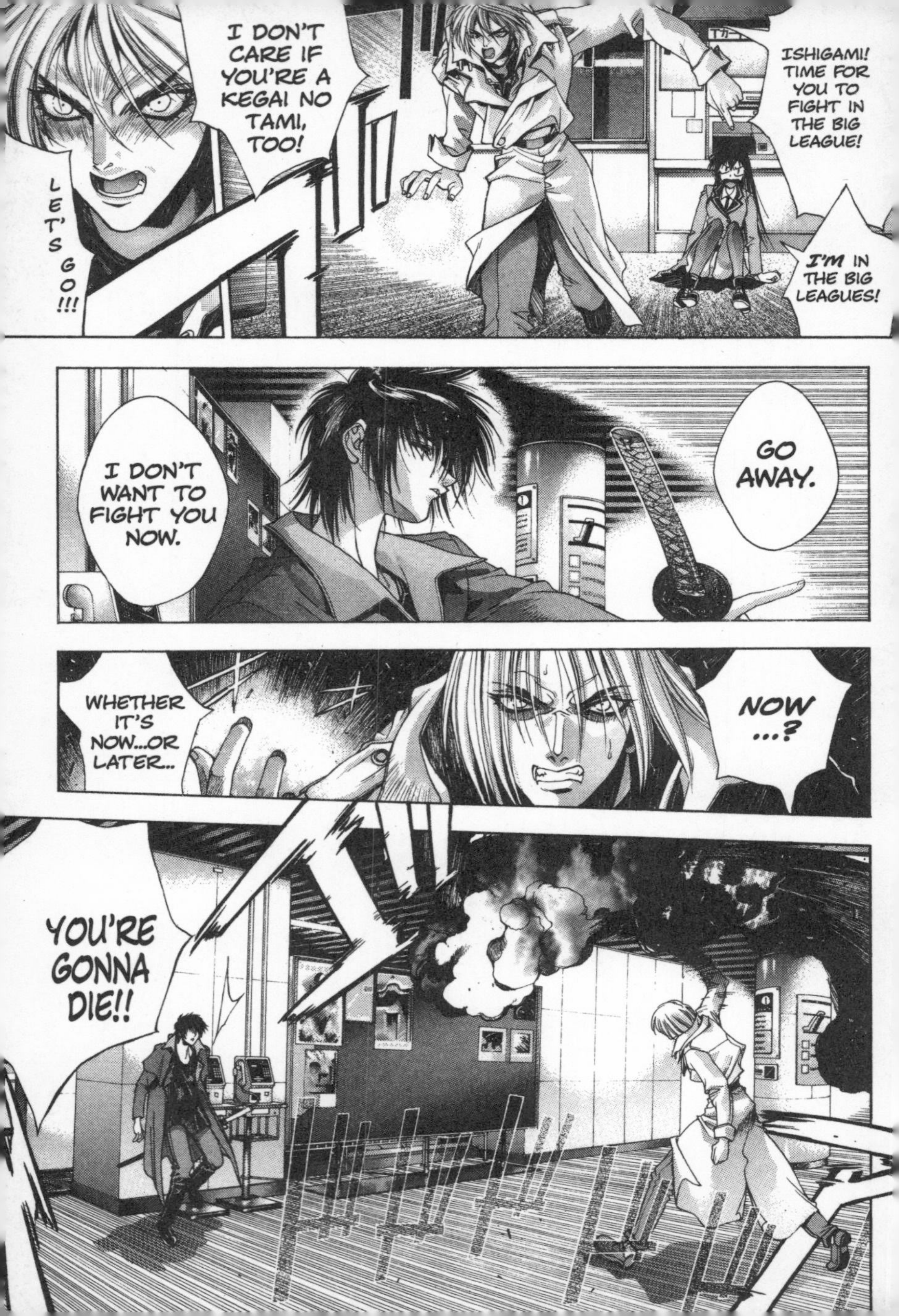
ISHIGAMI! TIME FOR YOU TO FIGHT IN THE BIG LEAGUE!
I'M IN THE BIG LEAGUES!
I DON'T CARE IF YOU'RE A KEGAI NO TAMI, TOO!
LET'S GO!!!
GO AWAY.
I DON'T WANT TO FIGHT YOU NOW.
NOW ...?
WHETHER IT'S NOW...OR LATER...
YOU'RE GONNA DIE!!

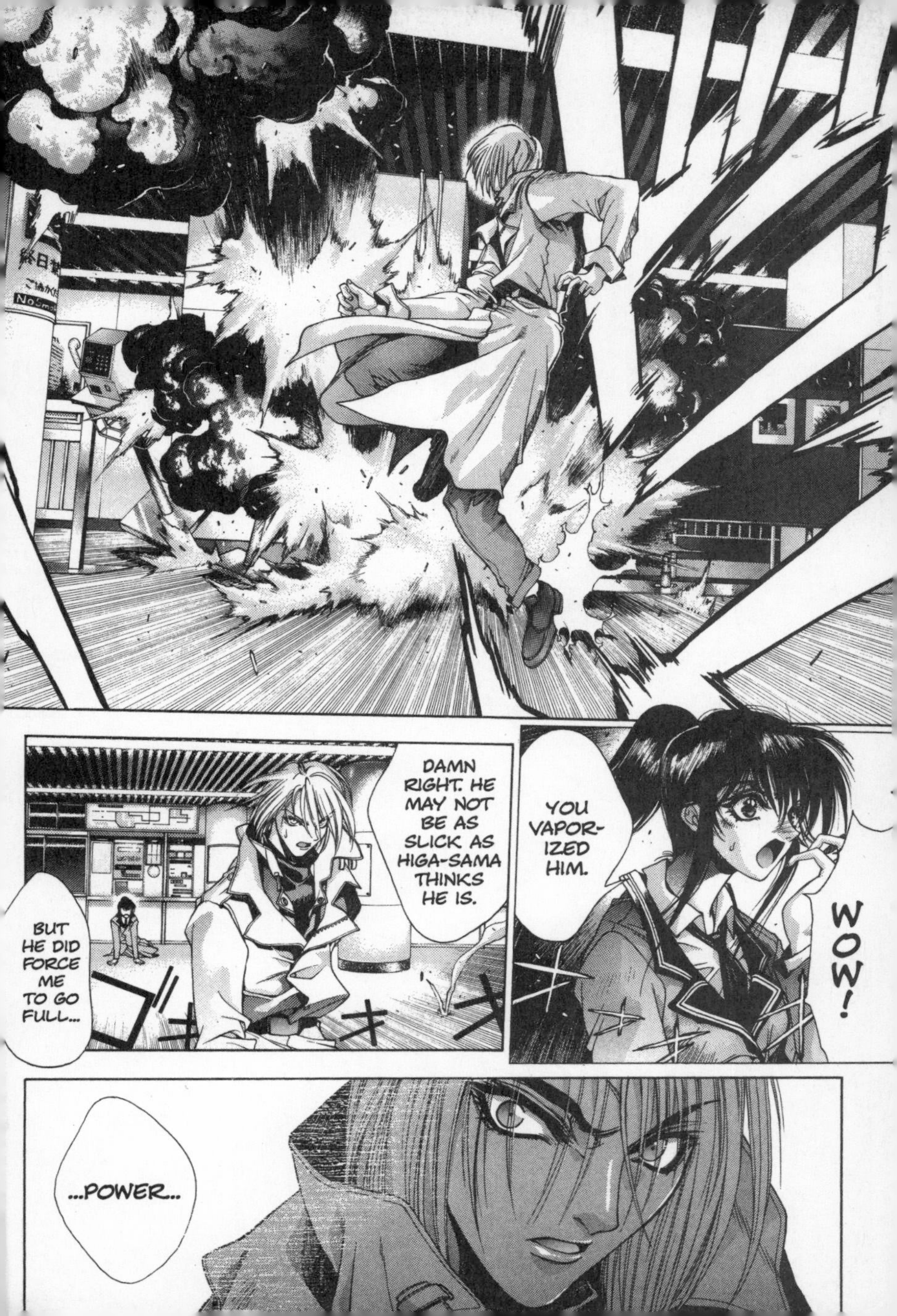
YOU VAPORIZED HIM.
WOW!
DAMN RIGHT. HE MAY NOT BE AS SLICK AS HIGA-SAMA THINKS HE IS.
BUT HE DID FORCE ME TO GO FULL...
...POWER...

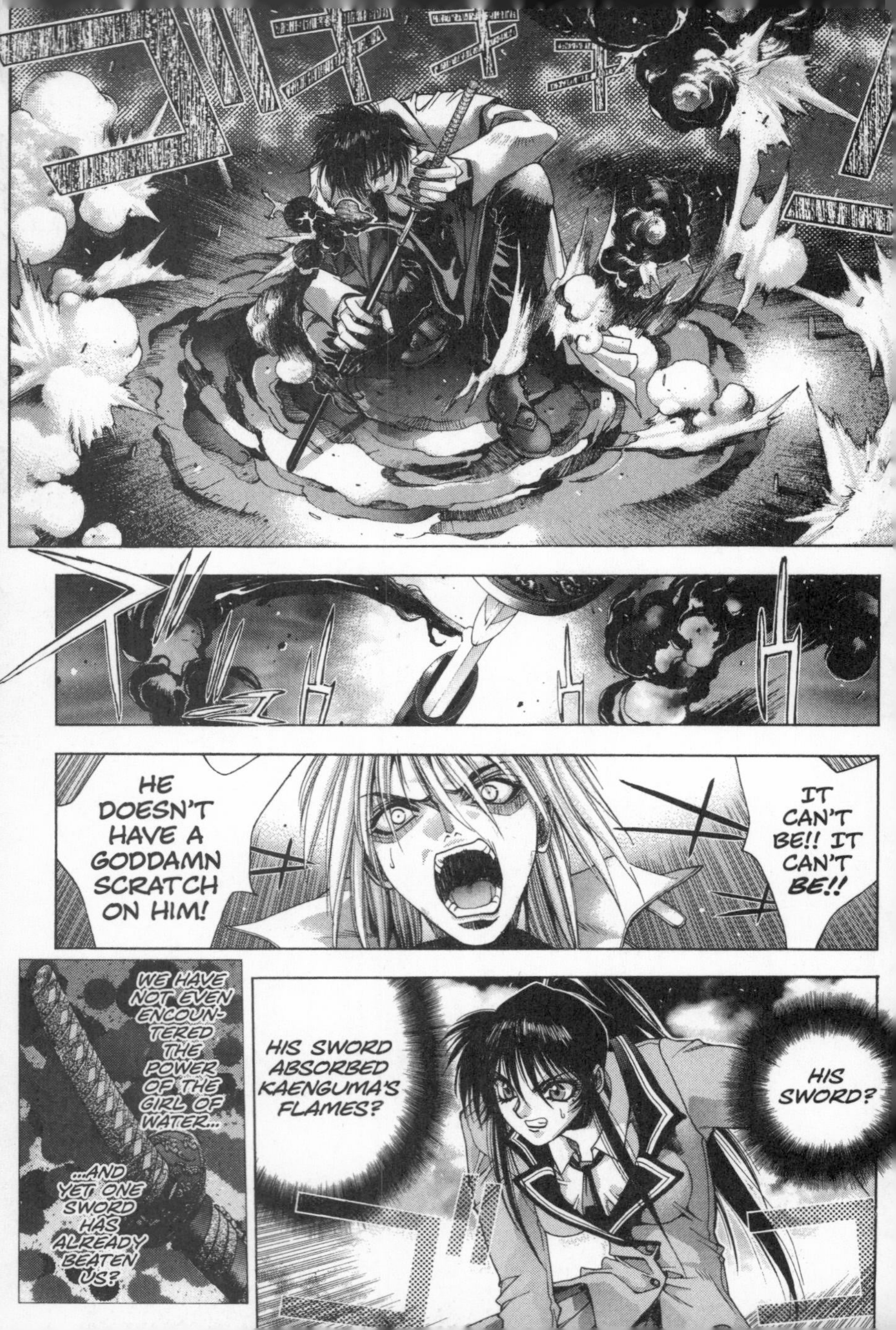
IT CAN'T BE!! IT CAN'T BE!!
HE DOESN'T HAVE A GODDAMN SCRATCH ON HIM!
HIS SWORD?
HIS SWORD ABSORBED KAENGUMA'S FLAMES?
WE HAVE NOT EVEN ENCOUNTERED THE POWER OF THE GIRL OF WATER...
...AND YET ONE SWORD HAS ALREADY BEATEN US?

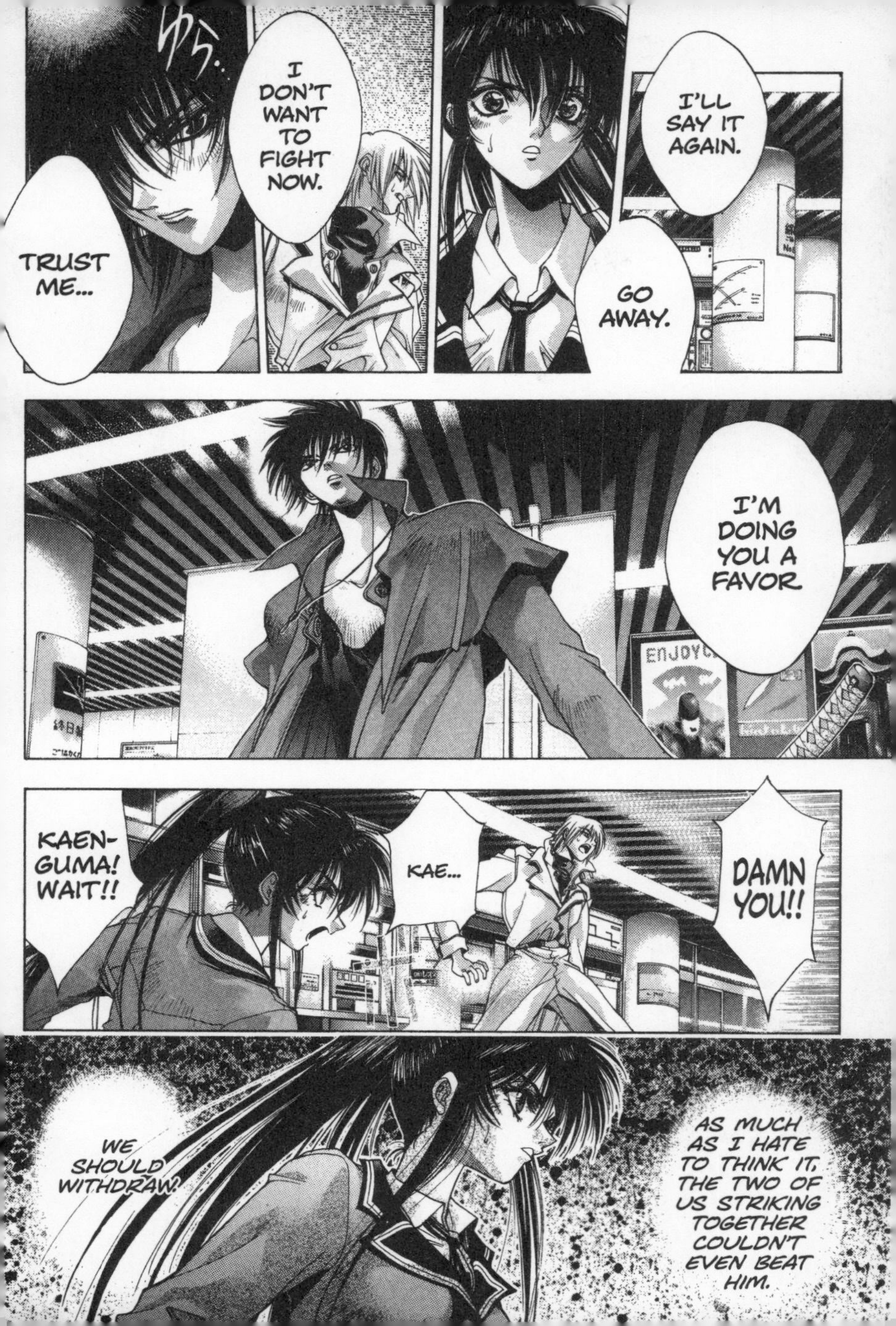
I'LL SAY IT AGAIN.
GO AWAY.
I DON'T WANT TO FIGHT NOW.
ゆら...
TRUST ME...
I'M DOING YOU A FAVOR
DAMN YOU!!
KAE...
KAEN-GUMA! WAIT!!
AS MUCH AS I HATE TO THINK IT, THE TWO OF US STRIKING TOGETHER COULDN'T EVEN BEAT HIM.
WE SHOULD WITHDRAW.

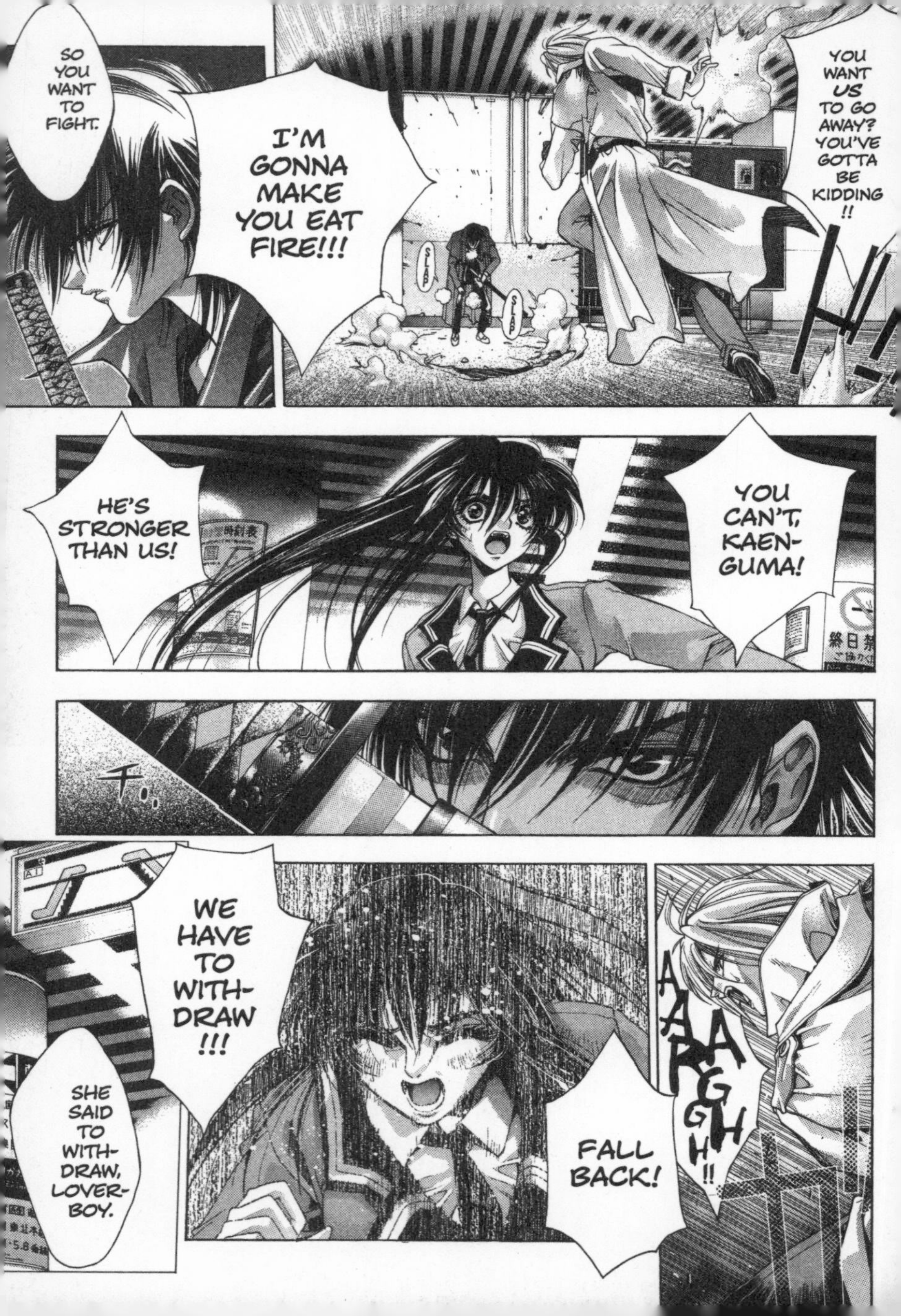

YOU WANT US TO GO AWAY? YOU'VE GOTTA BE KIDDING!!
I'M GONNA MAKE YOU EAT FIRE!!!
SLAP
SLAP
SO YOU WANT TO FIGHT.
YOU CAN'T, KAEN-GUMA!
HE'S STRONGER THAN US!
チ..
AARGGHH!!
FALL BACK!
WE HAVE TO WITH-DRAW!!!
SHE SAID TO WITH-DRAW, LOVER-BOY.

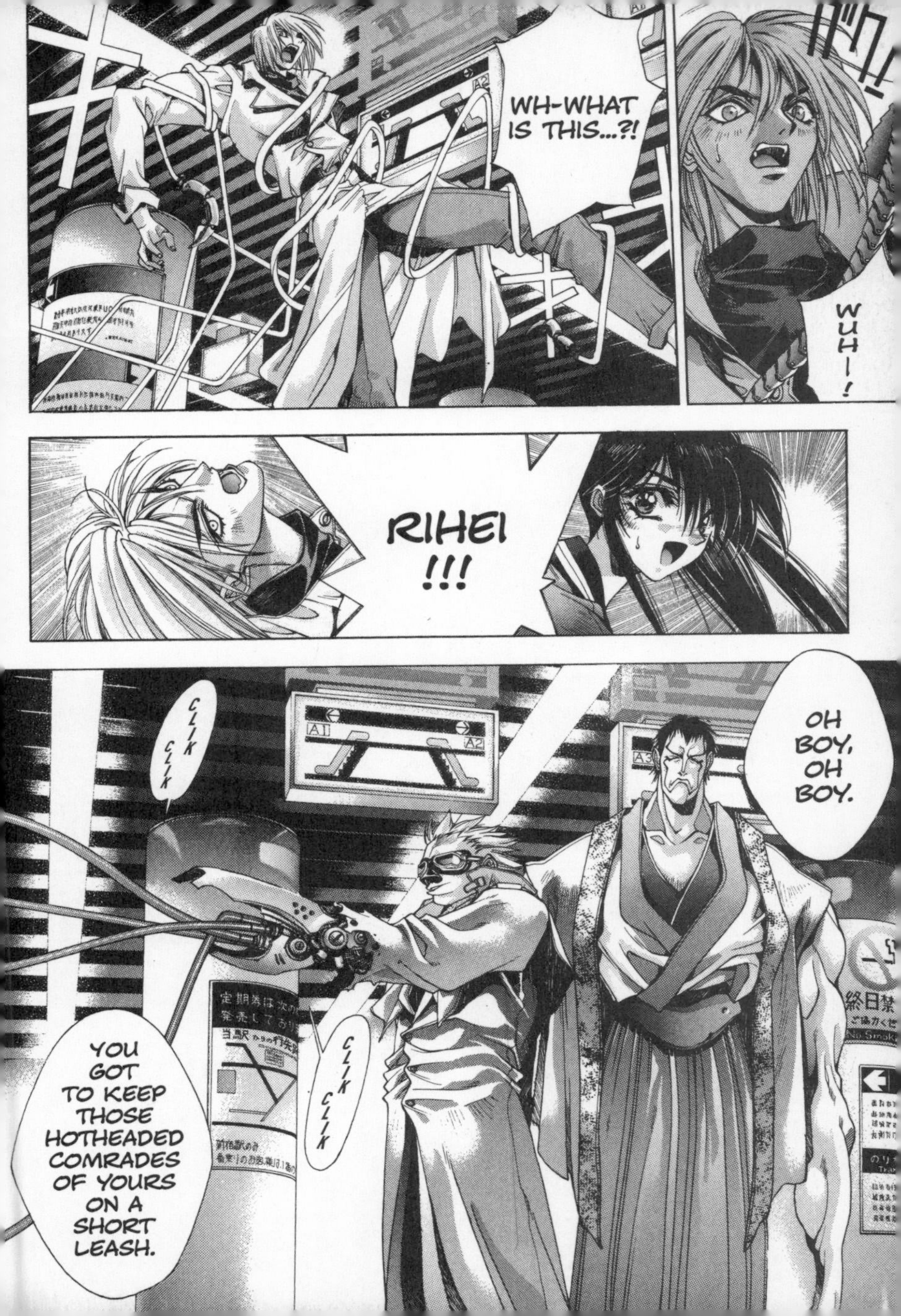
WH-WHAT IS THIS...?!
WUHI-!
RIHEI !!!
OH BOY, OH BOY.
CLIK CLIK CLIK
CLIK CLIK CLIK
YOU GOT TO KEEP THOSE HOTHEADED COMRADES OF YOURS ON A SHORT LEASH.

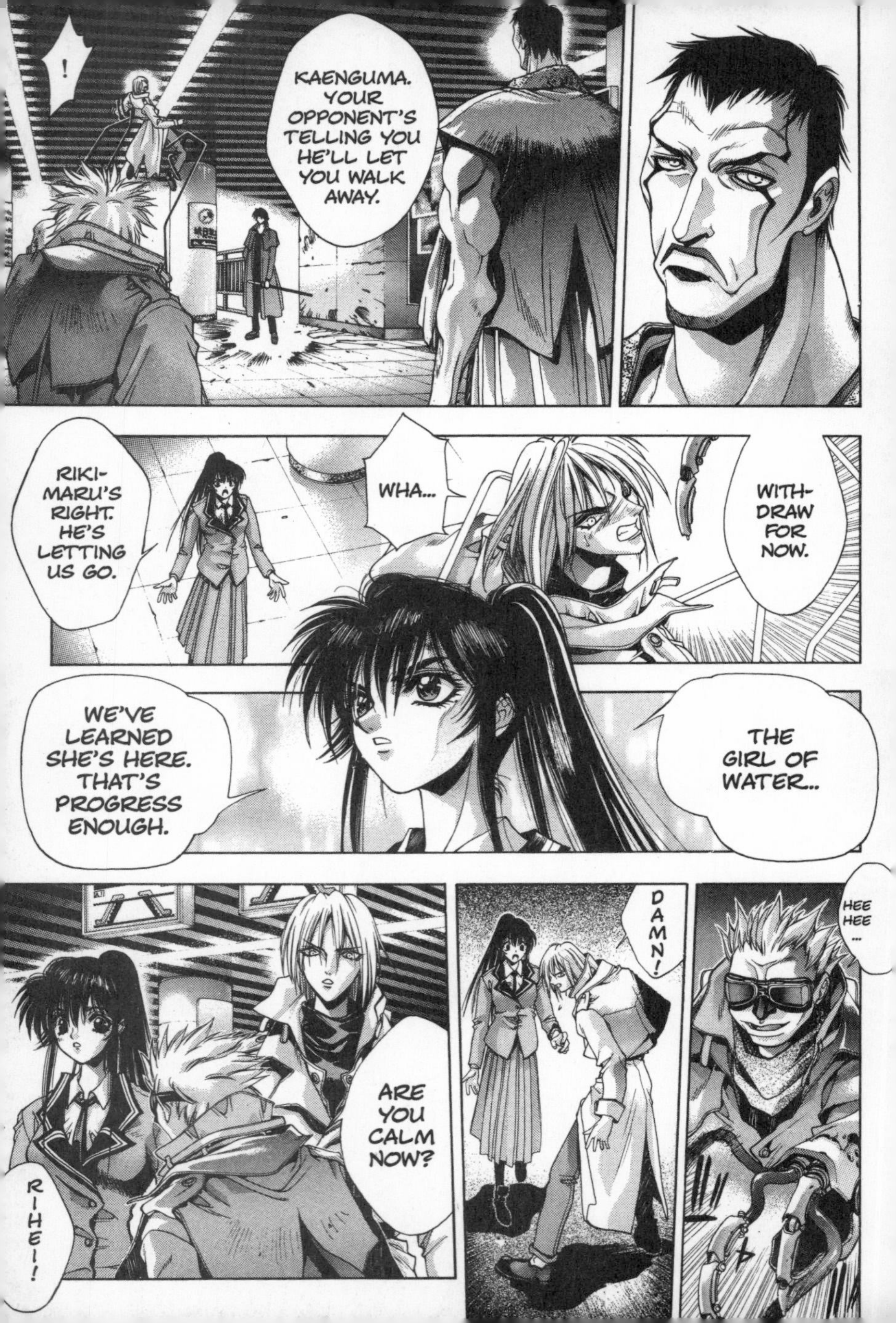
KAENGUMA. YOUR OPPONENT'S TELLING YOU HE'LL LET YOU WALK AWAY.
!
WITH-DRAW FOR NOW.
WHA...
RIKI-MARU'S RIGHT. HE'S LETTING US GO.
THE GIRL OF WATER..
WE'VE LEARNED SHE'S HERE. THAT'S PROGRESS ENOUGH.
HEE HEE ...
DAMN!
ARE YOU CALM NOW?
RIHEI!

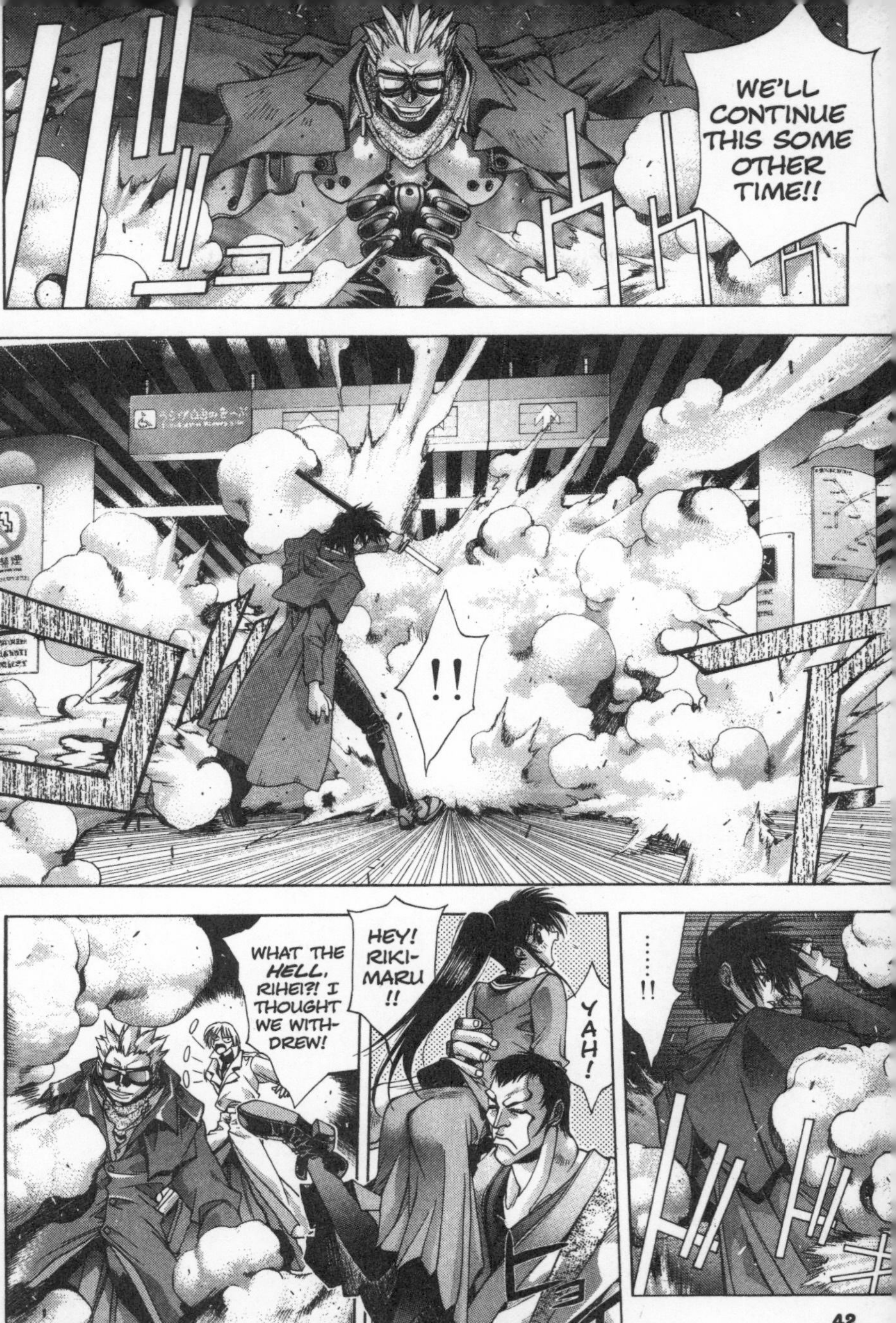
WE'LL CONTINUE THIS SOME OTHER TIME!!
!!
......!!
YAH!
HEY! RIKI-MARU!!
WHAT THE *HELL*, RIHEI?! I THOUGHT WE WITH-DREW!

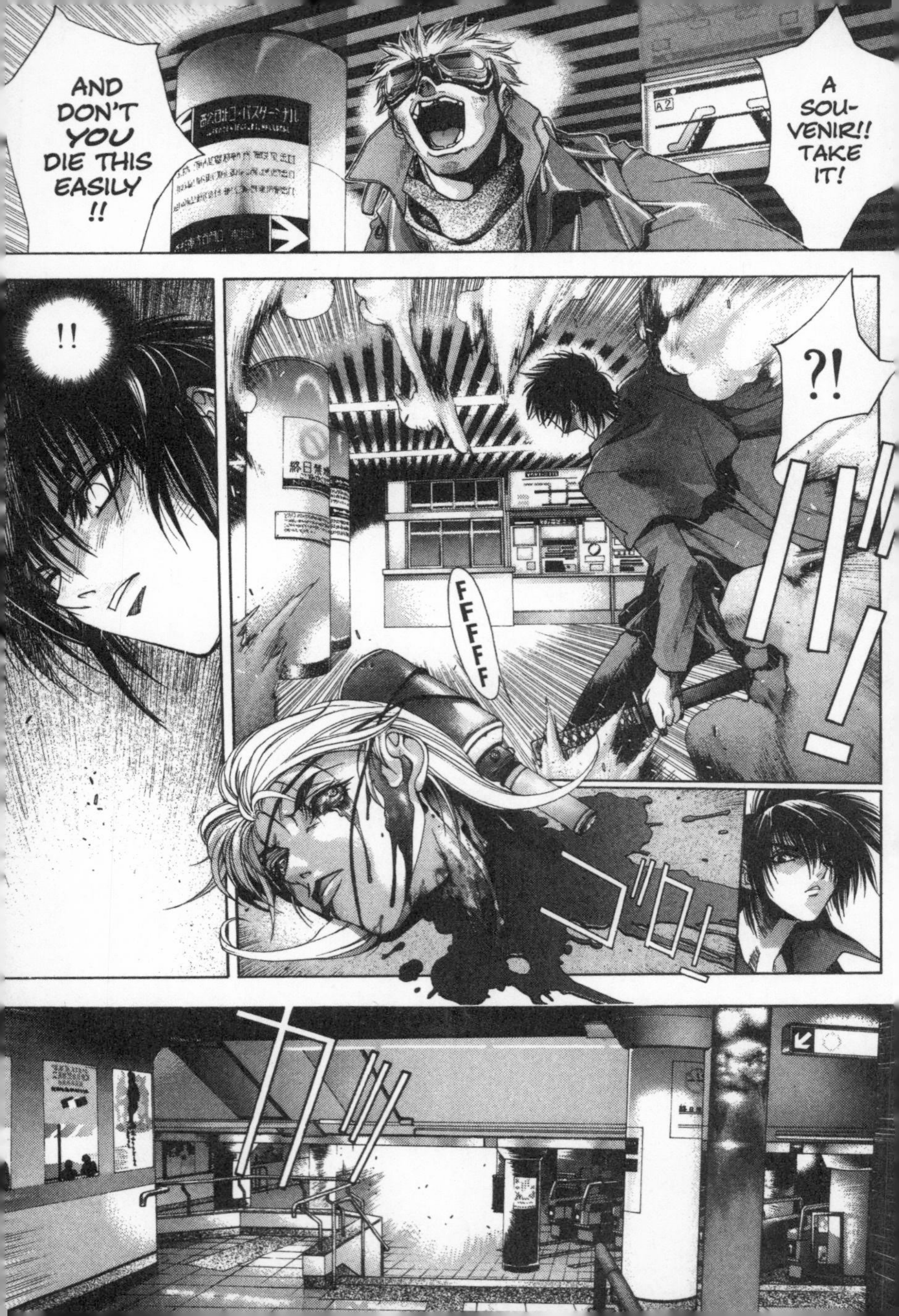
A SOUVENIR!! TAKE IT!
AND DON'T YOU DIE THIS EASILY!!
?!
FFFFF
!!

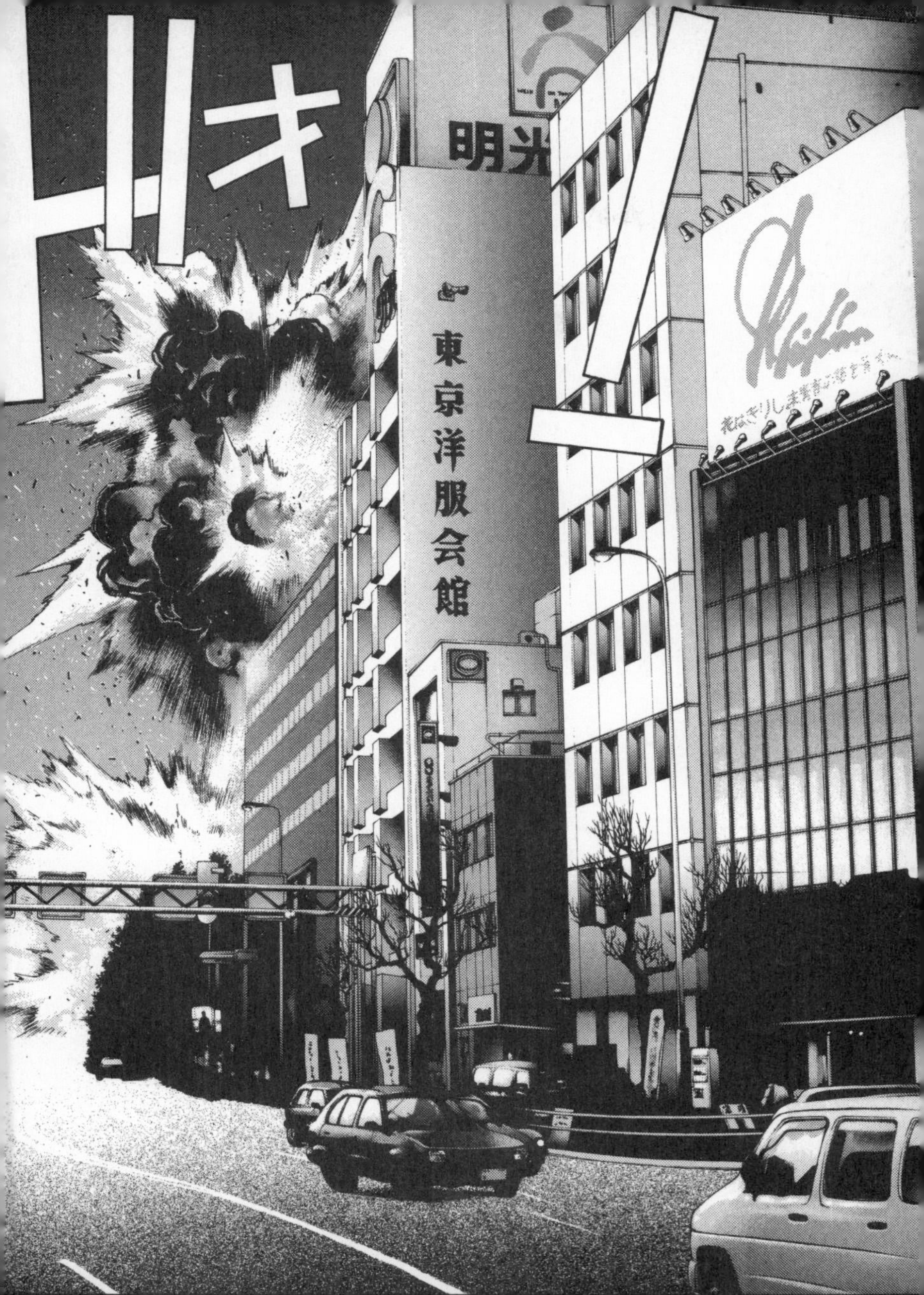
明光
東京洋服会館

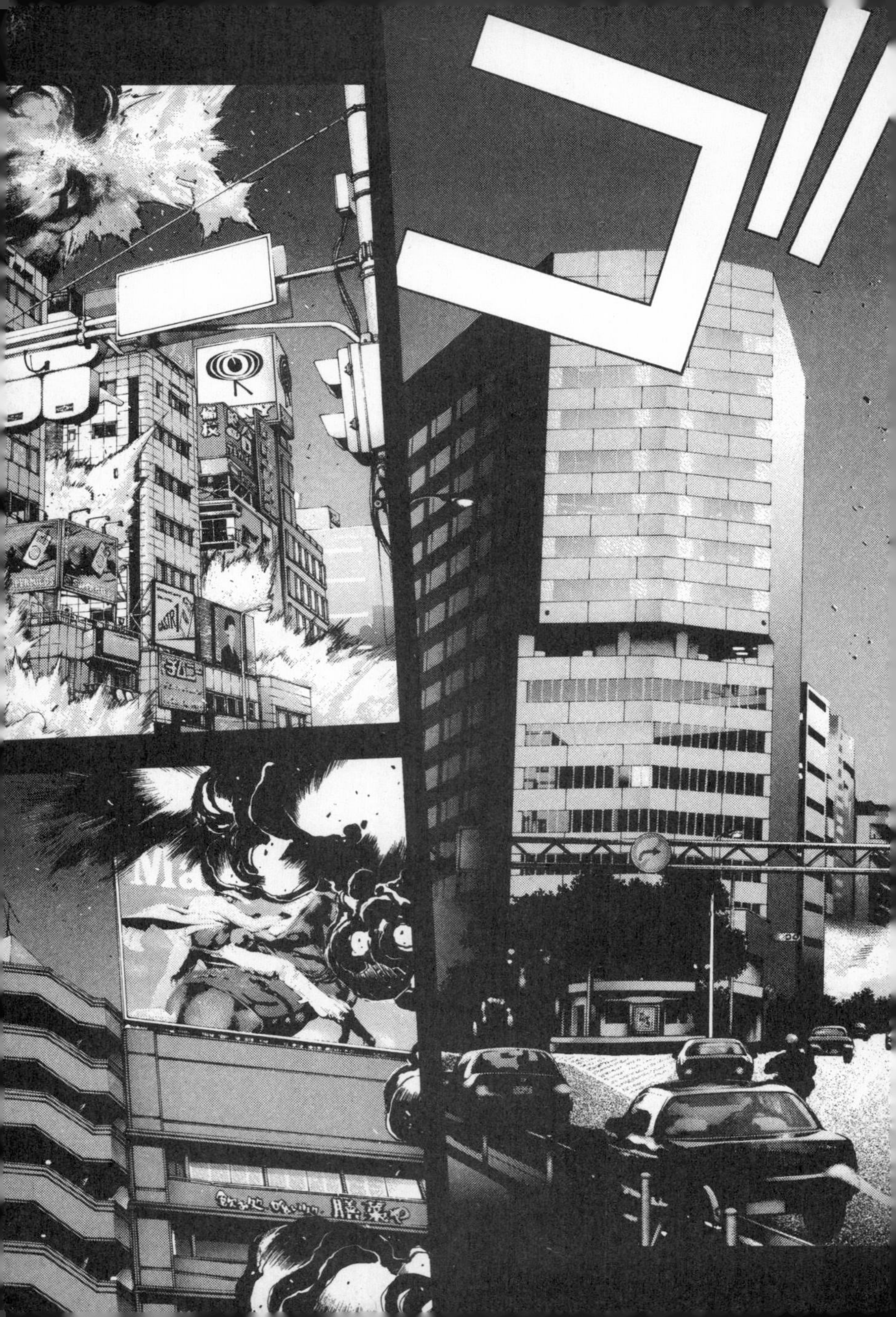
ゴ

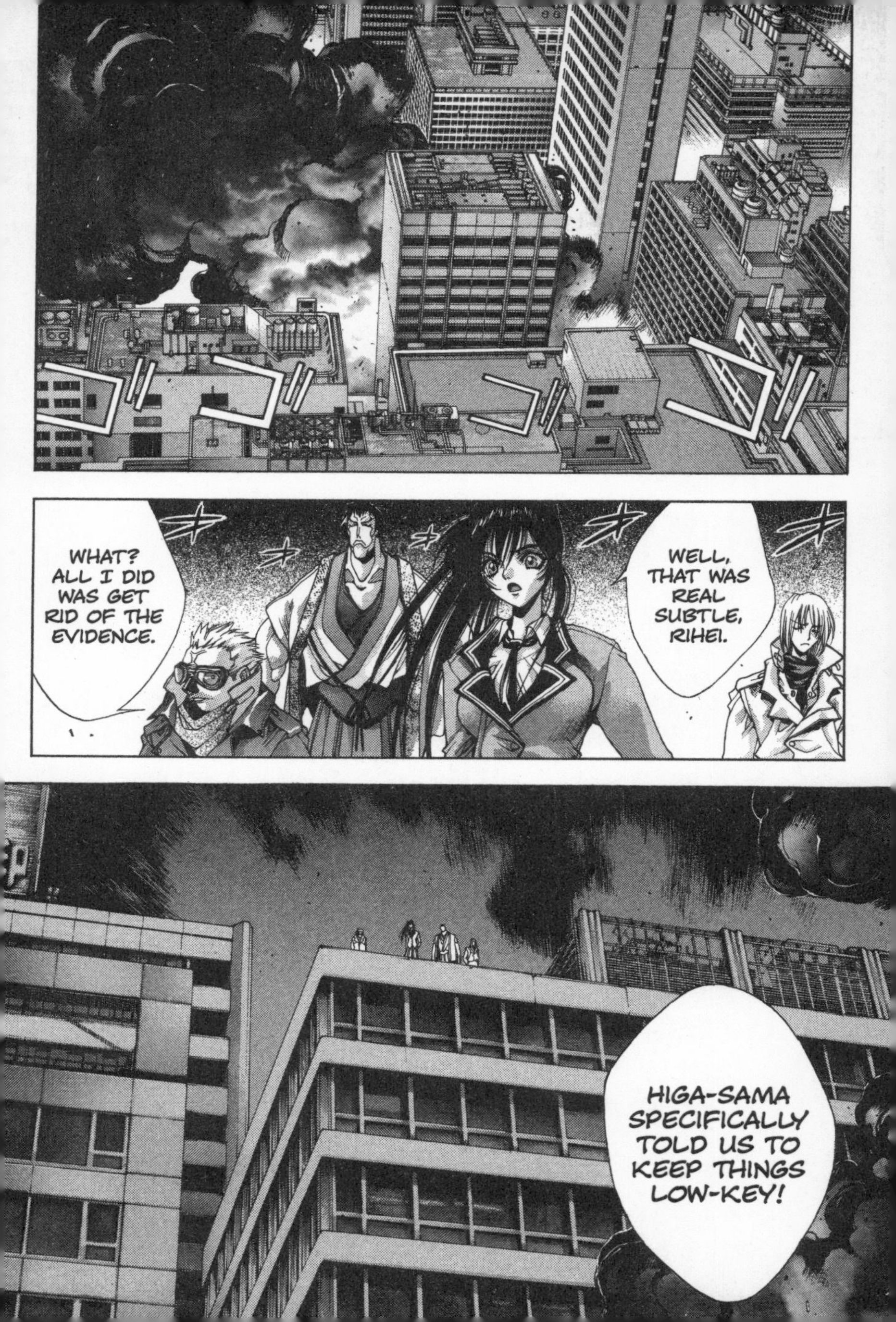
WELL, THAT WAS REAL SUBTLE, RIHEI.
WHAT? ALL I DID WAS GET RID OF THE EVIDENCE.
HIGA-SAMA SPECIFICALLY TOLD US TO KEEP THINGS LOW-KEY!

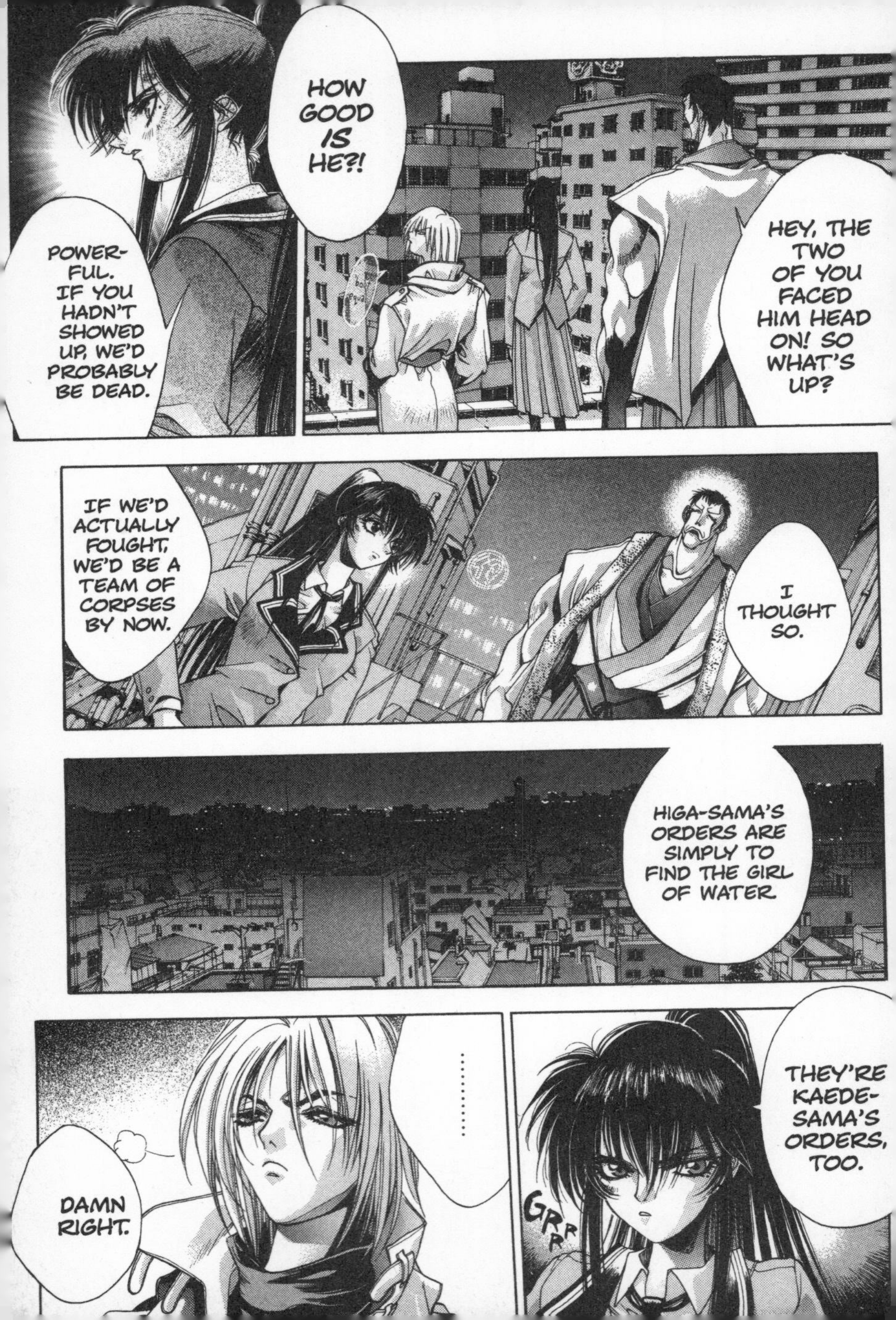
HEY, THE TWO OF YOU FACED HIM HEAD ON! SO WHAT'S UP?
HOW GOOD IS HE?!
POWER-FUL. IF YOU HADN'T SHOWED UP, WE'D PROBABLY BE DEAD.
I THOUGHT SO.
IF WE'D ACTUALLY FOUGHT, WE'D BE A TEAM OF CORPSES BY NOW.
HIGA-SAMA'S ORDERS ARE SIMPLY TO FIND THE GIRL OF WATER
THEY'RE KAEDE-SAMA'S ORDERS, TOO.
GRRR
....
DAMN RIGHT.

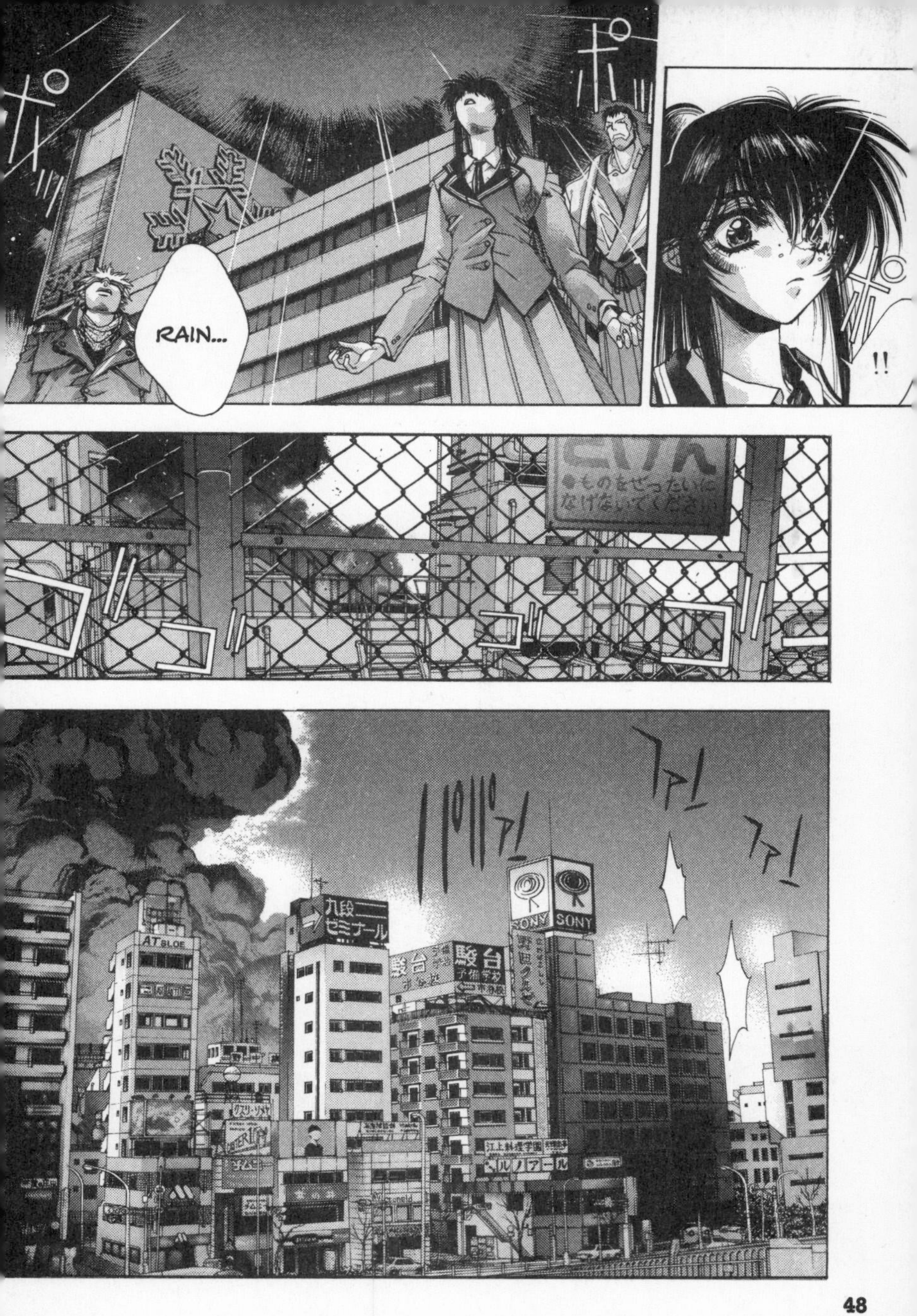
!!
RAIN...
九段ゼミナール
駿台
SONY
SONY

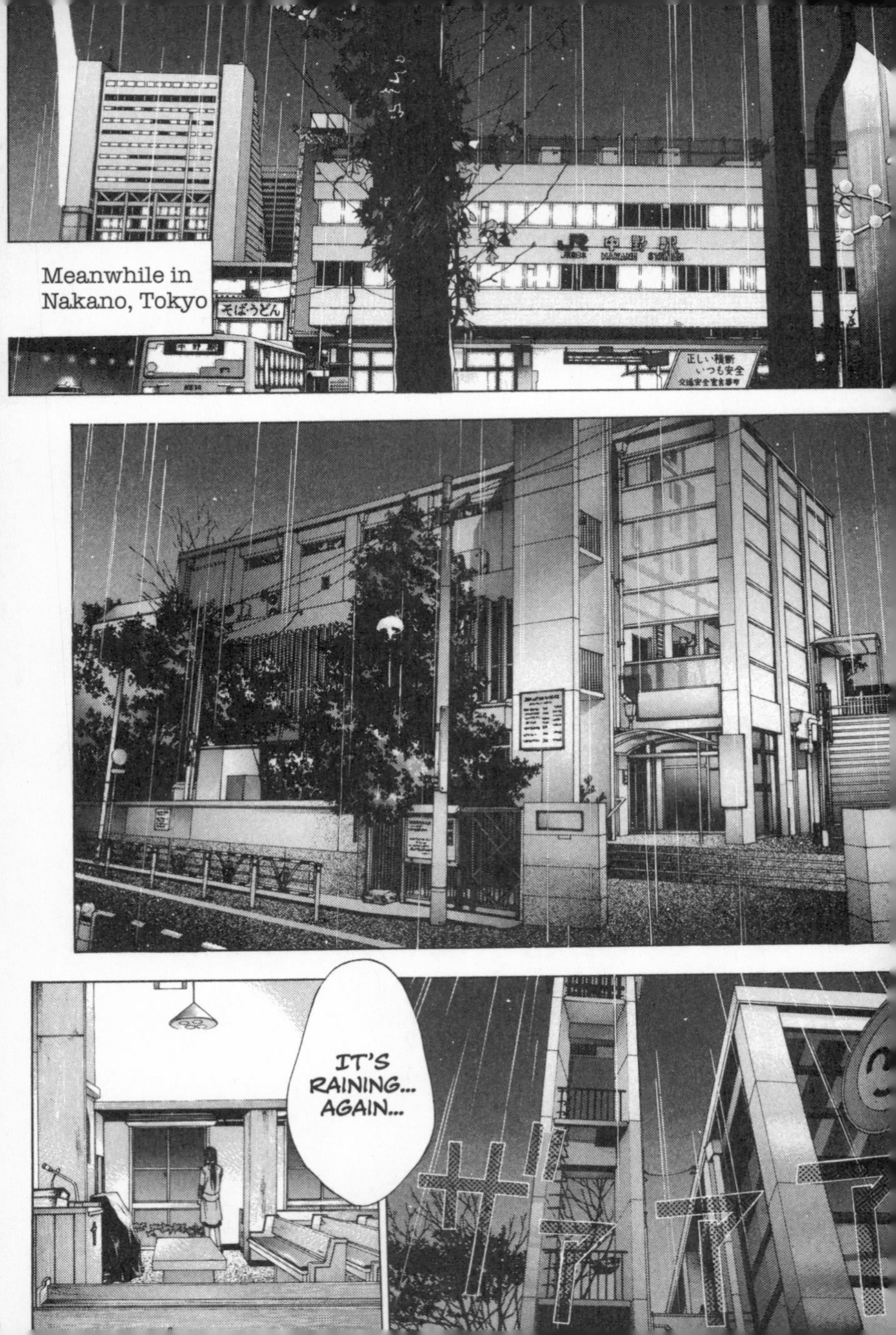
Meanwhile in Nakano, Tokyo
中野駅
そばうどん
中野駅
正しい横断
いつも安全
IT'S RAINING... AGAIN...

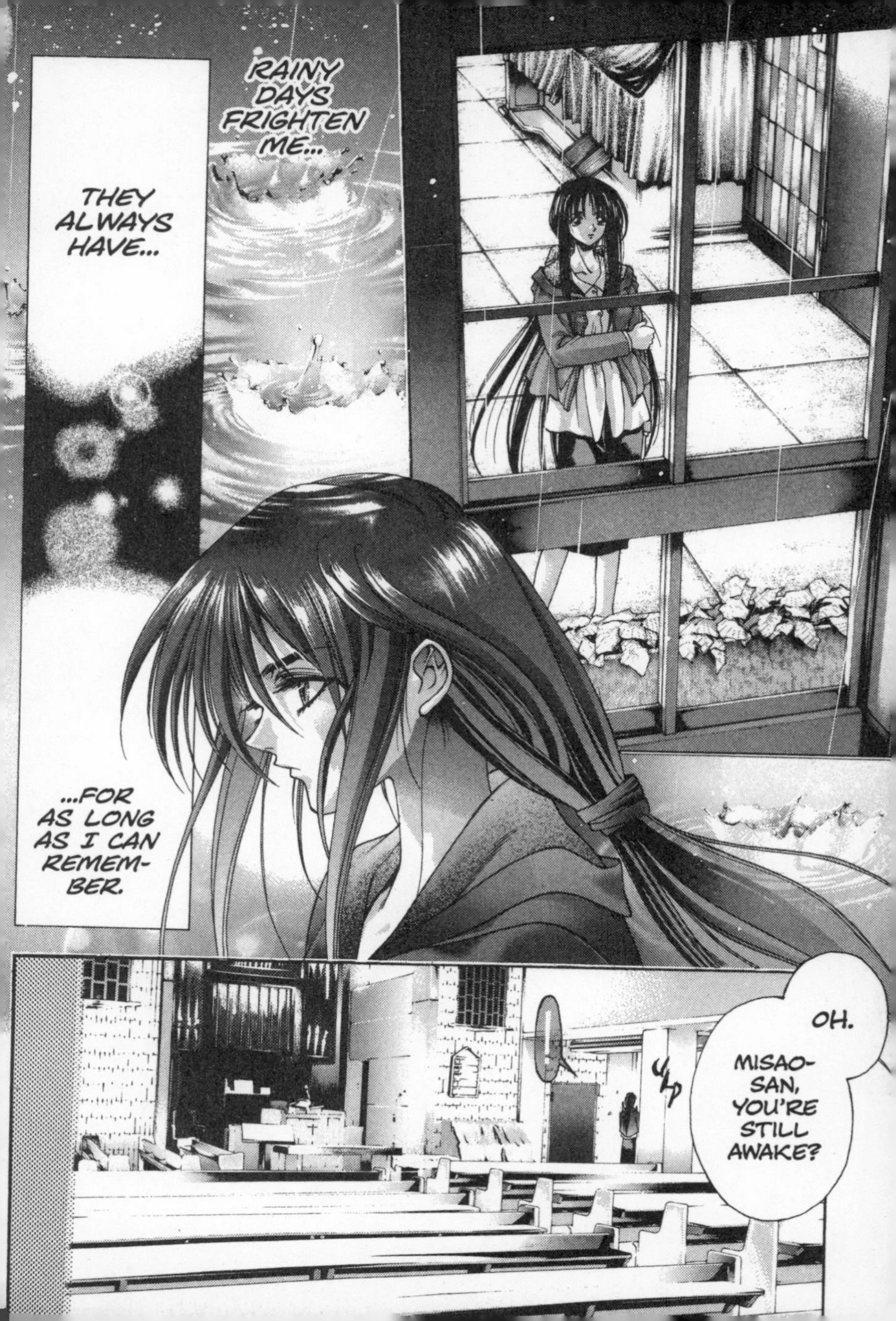
RAINY DAYS FRIGHTEN ME...
THEY ALWAYS HAVE...
...FOR AS LONG AS I CAN REMEMBER.
OH.
MISAO-SAN, YOU'RE STILL AWAKE?
ULP
!

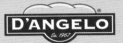

D'ANGELO
Est. 1967

$2.00 OFF

any medium or large sandwich

Not valid with any other coupons, discounts or offers. Valid at participating locations only. Please mention coupon when ordering.

Valid through 9/30/09 CPN 0085

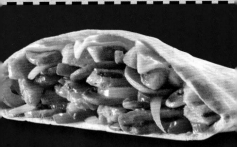

Chicken Stir Fry Pokket®

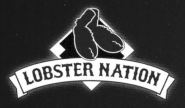

LOBSTER NATION

Try Our 100% Real Lobster Lineup

- **Traditional Lobster Sandwich**
- **Baked Stuffed Lobster Sandwich**
- **Lobster Roll**

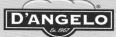

D'ANGELO *Est. 1967*

$3⁰⁰ OFF

any lobster sandwich

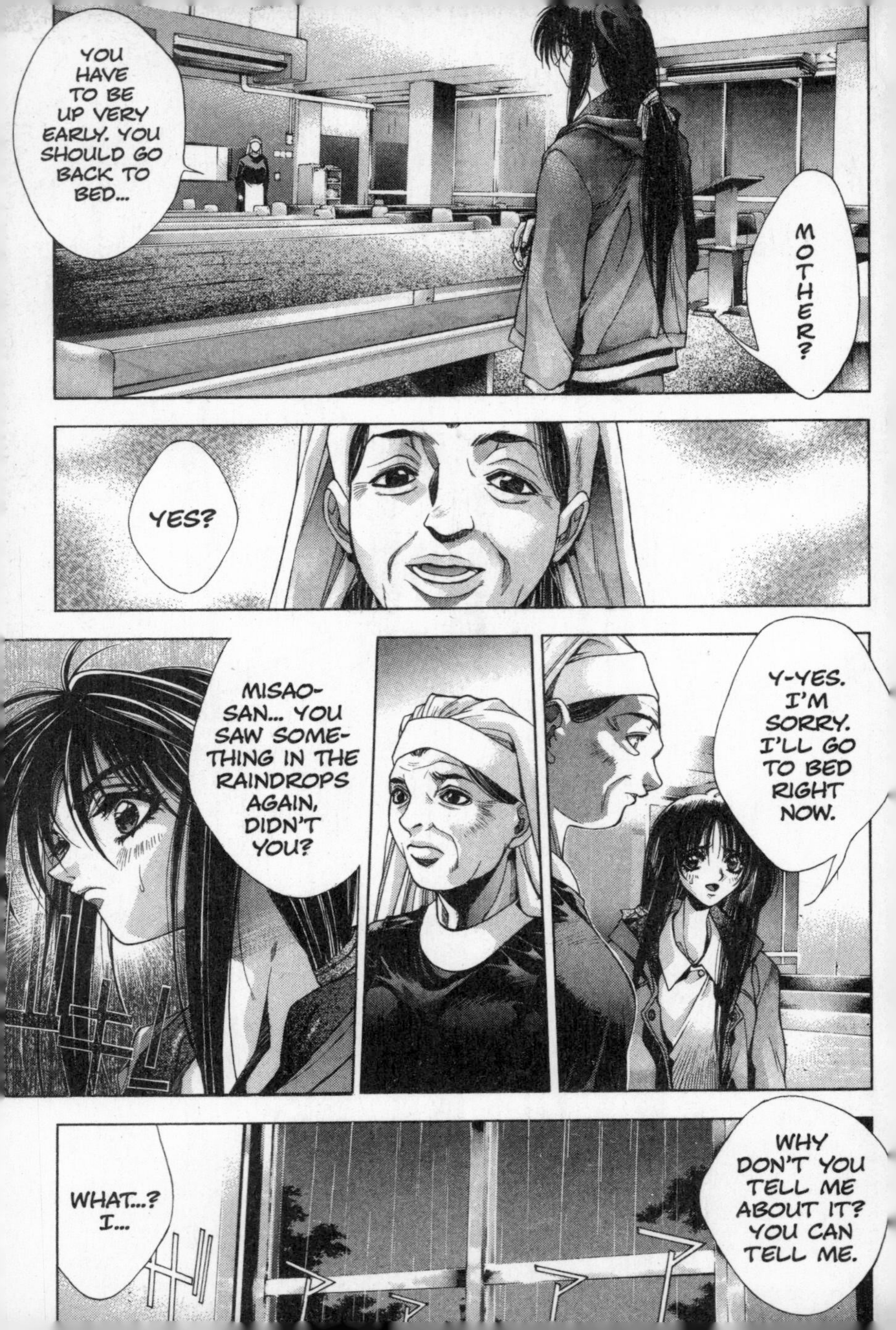
MOTHER?
YOU HAVE TO BE UP VERY EARLY. YOU SHOULD GO BACK TO BED...
YES?
Y-YES. I'M SORRY. I'LL GO TO BED RIGHT NOW.
MISAO-SAN... YOU SAW SOME-THING IN THE RAINDROPS AGAIN, DIDN'T YOU?
WHY DON'T YOU TELL ME ABOUT IT? YOU CAN TELL ME.
WHAT...? I...

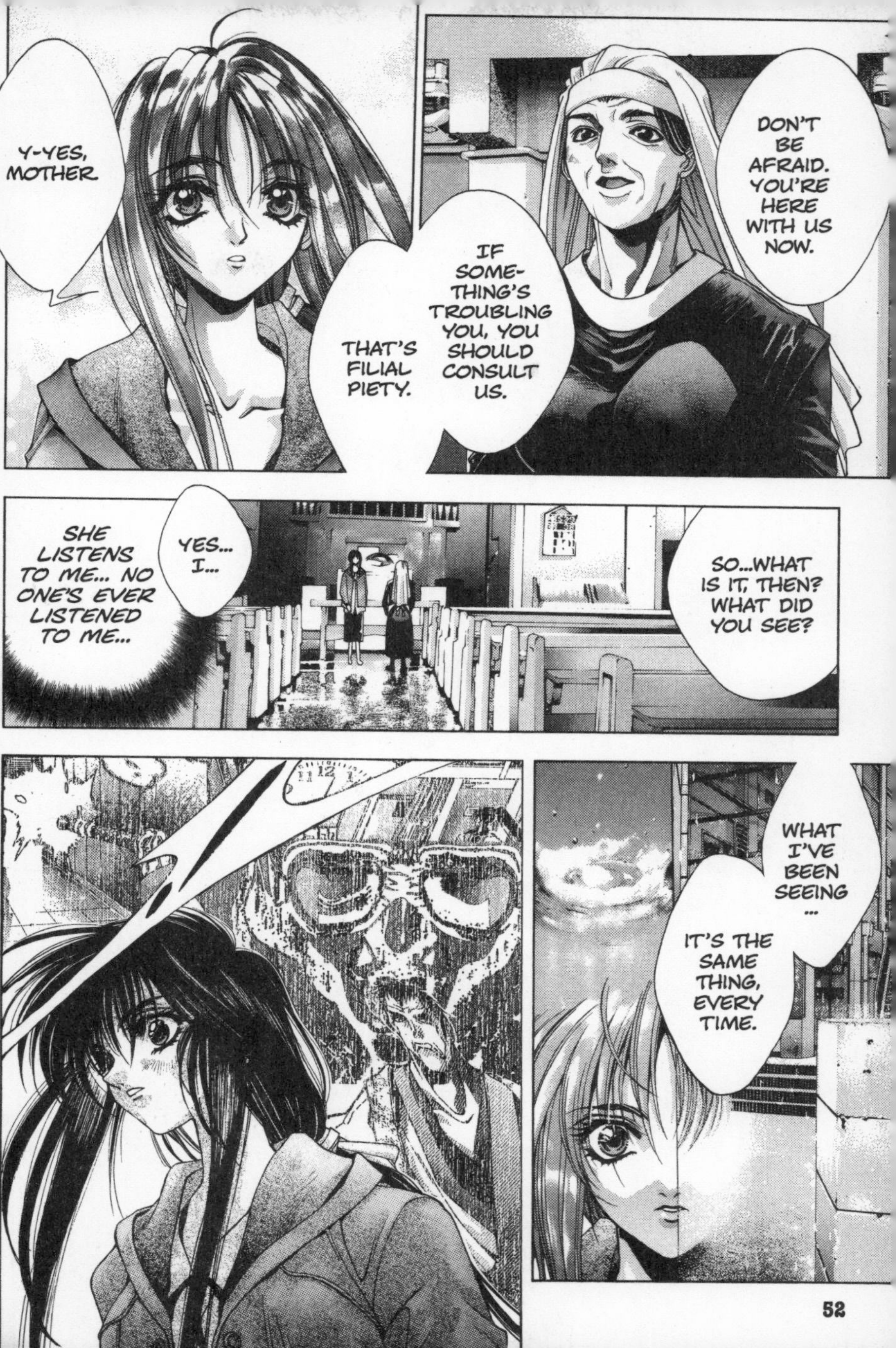
DON'T BE AFRAID. YOU'RE HERE WITH US NOW.
IF SOME-THING'S TROUBLING YOU, YOU SHOULD CONSULT US.
THAT'S FILIAL PIETY.
Y-YES, MOTHER
SO...WHAT IS IT, THEN? WHAT DID YOU SEE?
YES... I...
SHE LISTENS TO ME... NO ONE'S EVER LISTENED TO ME...
WHAT I'VE BEEN SEEING ...
IT'S THE SAME THING, EVERY TIME.

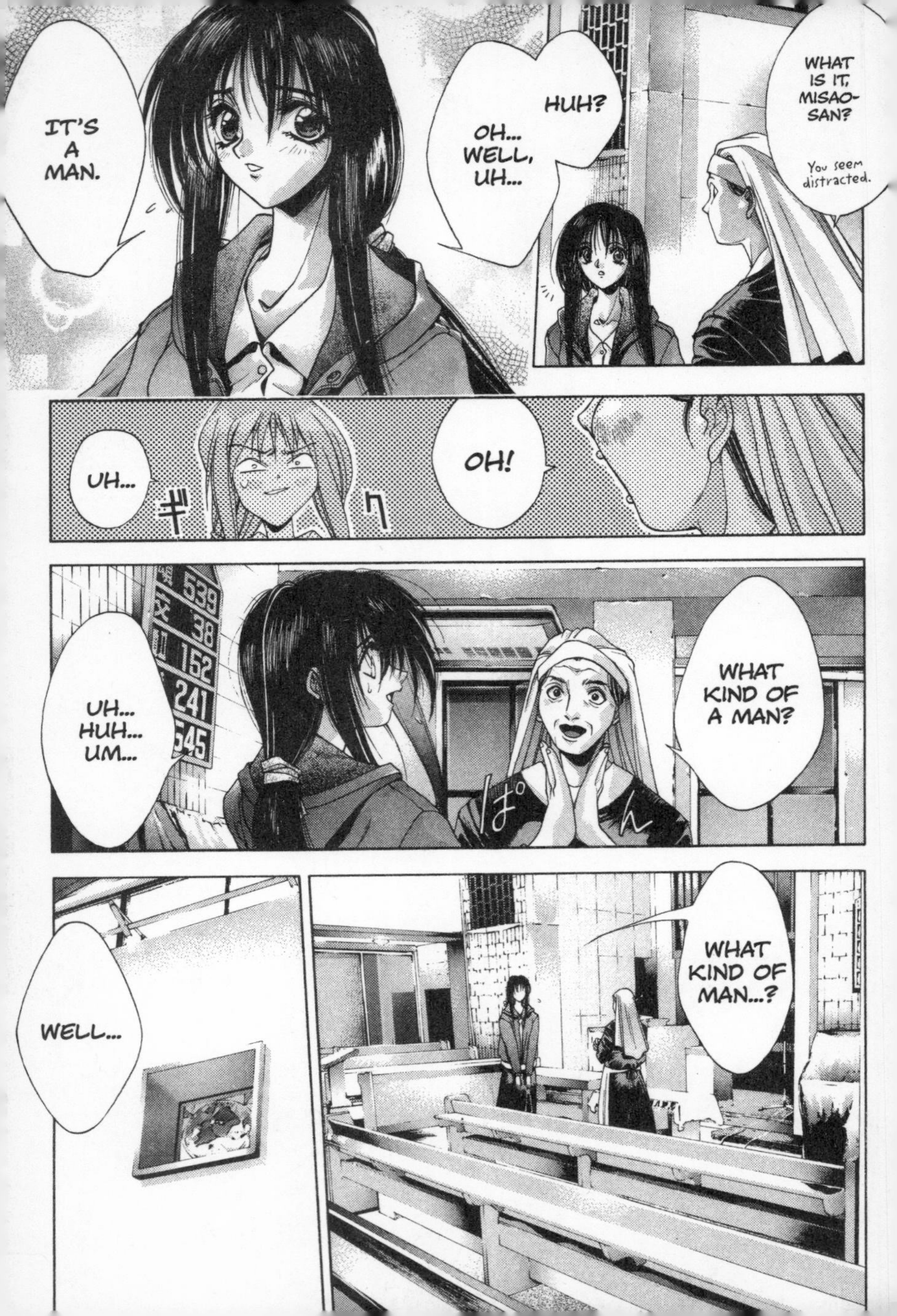
WHAT IS IT, MISAO-SAN?
You seem distracted.
HUH?
OH... WELL, UH...
IT'S A MAN.
OH!
UH...
ギ
ク
WHAT KIND OF A MAN?
ぱん
539
38
152
241
545
UH... HUH... UM...
WHAT KIND OF MAN...?
WELL...

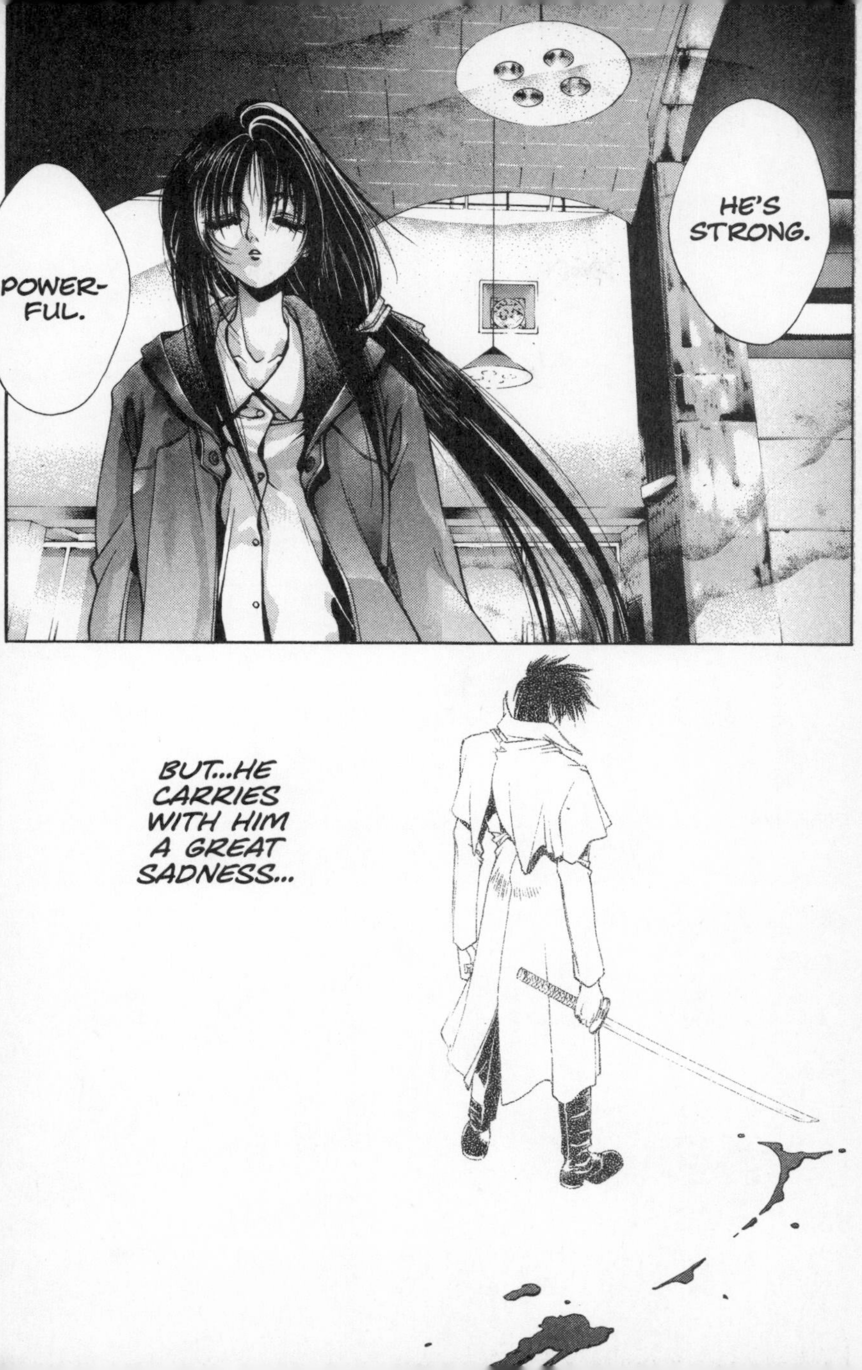
HE'S STRONG.
POWER-FUL.
BUT...HE CARRIES WITH HIM A GREAT SADNESS...

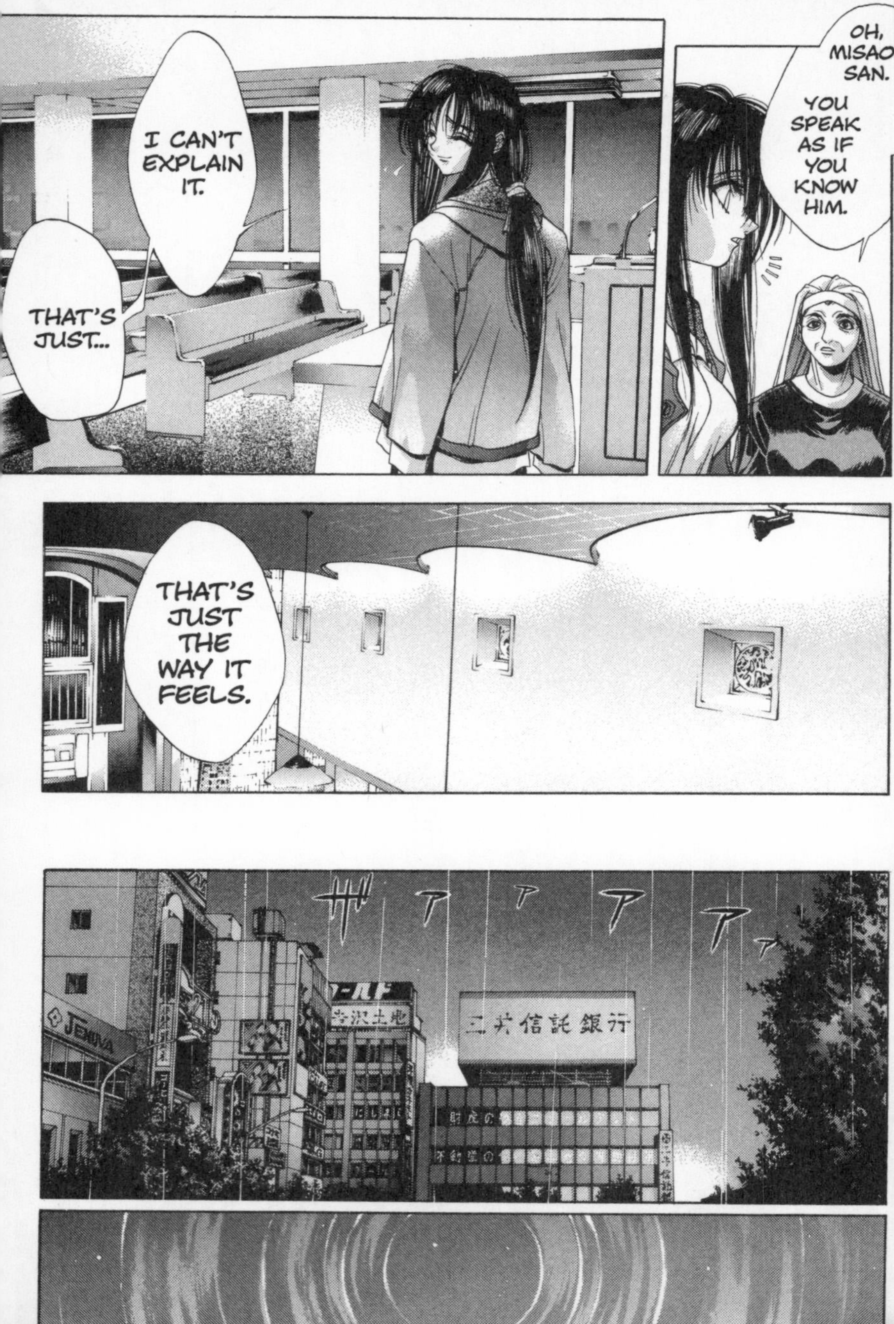
OH, MISAO-SAN.
YOU SPEAK AS IF YOU KNOW HIM.
I CAN'T EXPLAIN IT.
THAT'S JUST...
THAT'S JUST THE WAY IT FEELS.
ザァァァァァ

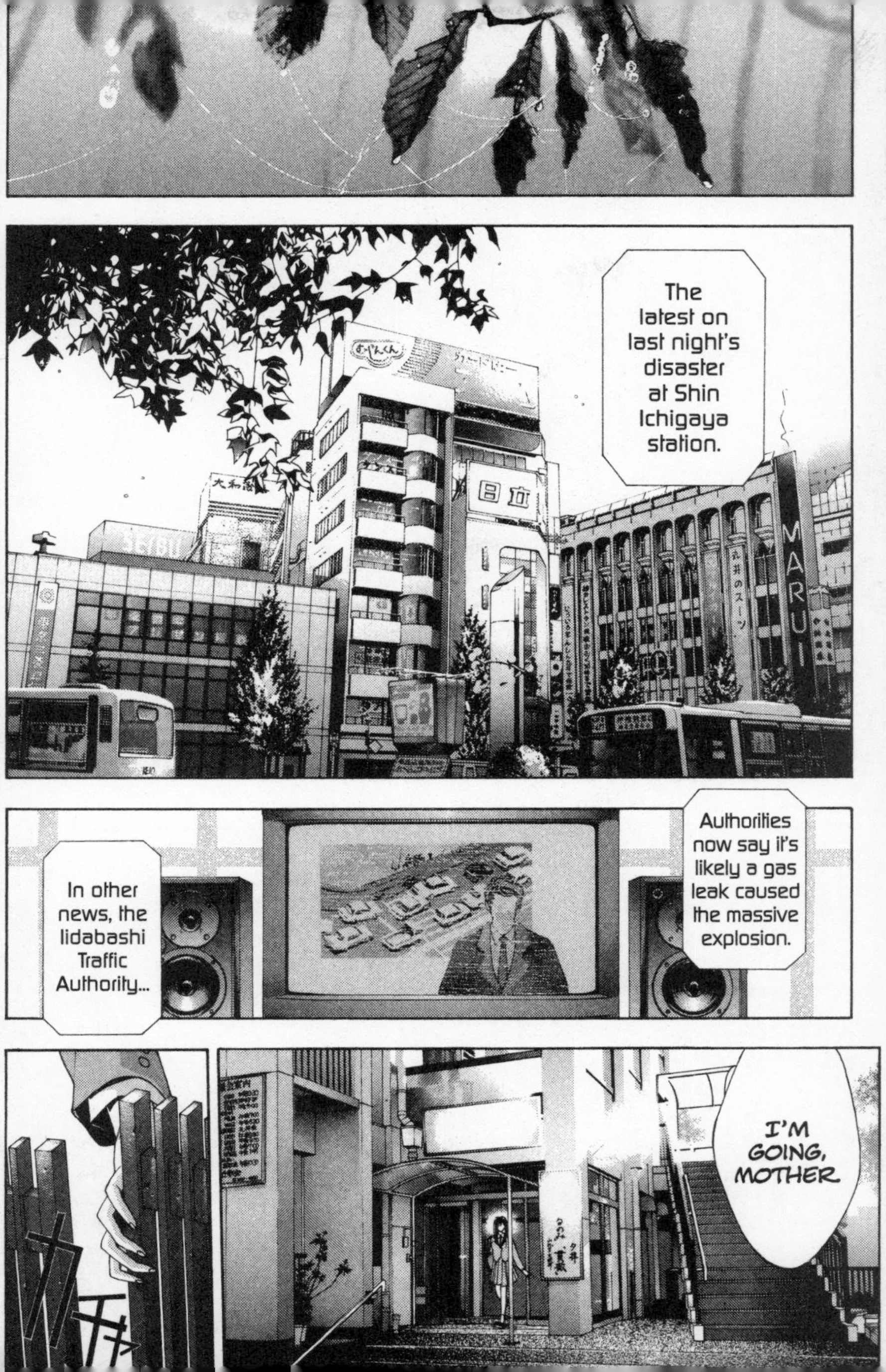
The latest on last night's disaster at Shin Ichigaya station.
Authorities now say it's likely a gas leak caused the massive explosion.
In other news, the Iidabashi Traffic Authority...
I'M GOING, MOTHER

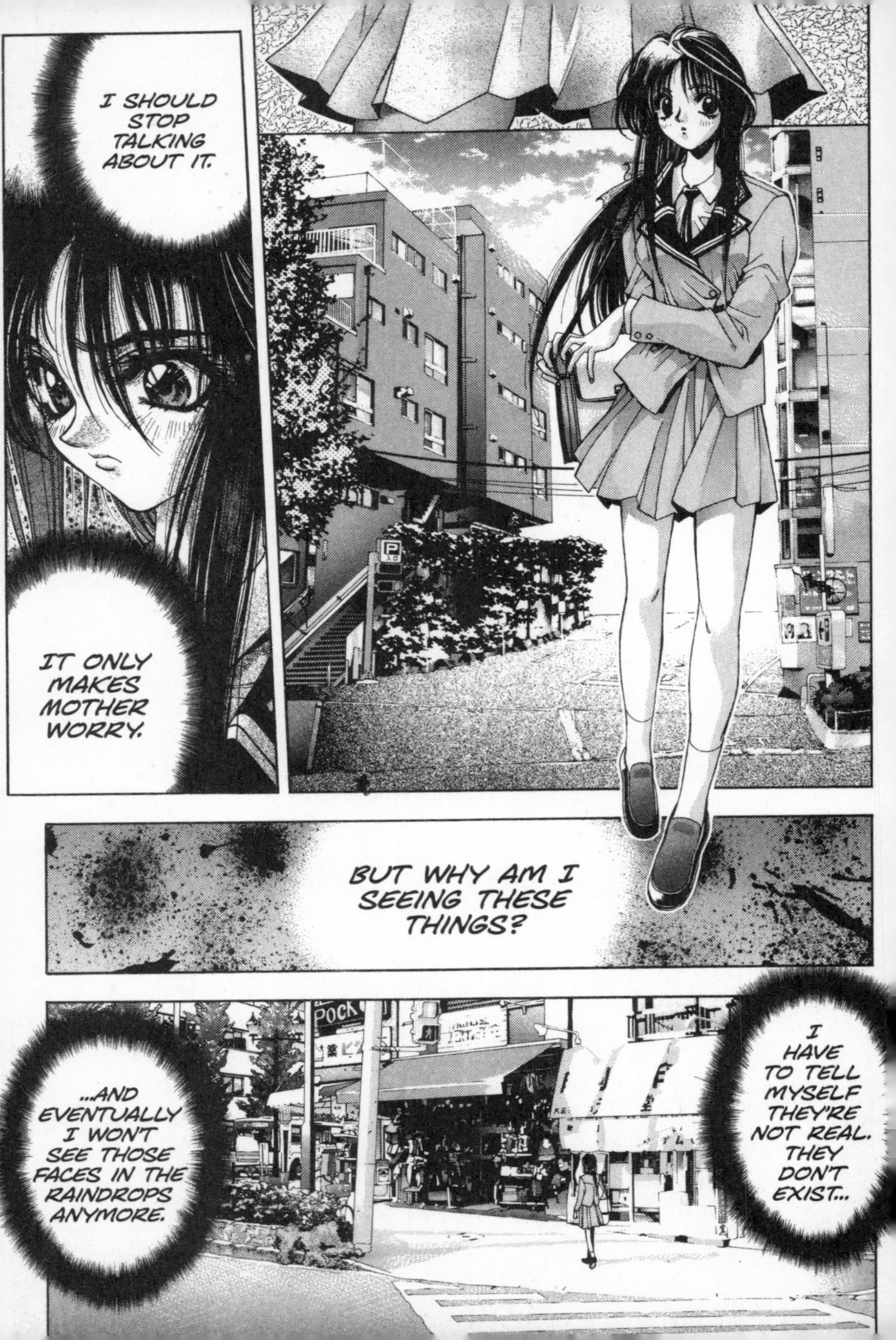
I SHOULD STOP TALKING ABOUT IT.
IT ONLY MAKES MOTHER WORRY.
BUT WHY AM I SEEING THESE THINGS?
I HAVE TO TELL MYSELF THEY'RE NOT REAL. THEY DON'T EXIST...
...AND EVENTUALLY I WON'T SEE THOSE FACES IN THE RAINDROPS ANYMORE.

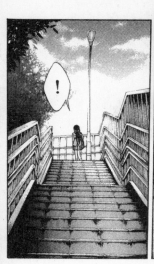

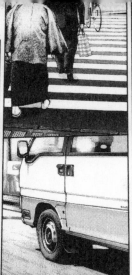

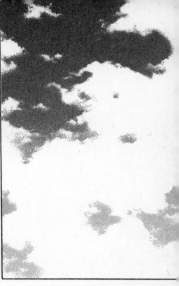

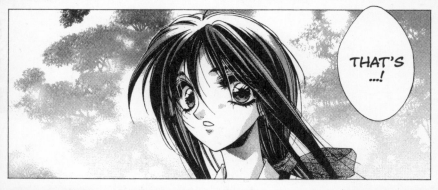

THAT'S
...!

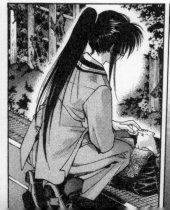

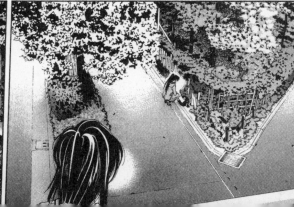

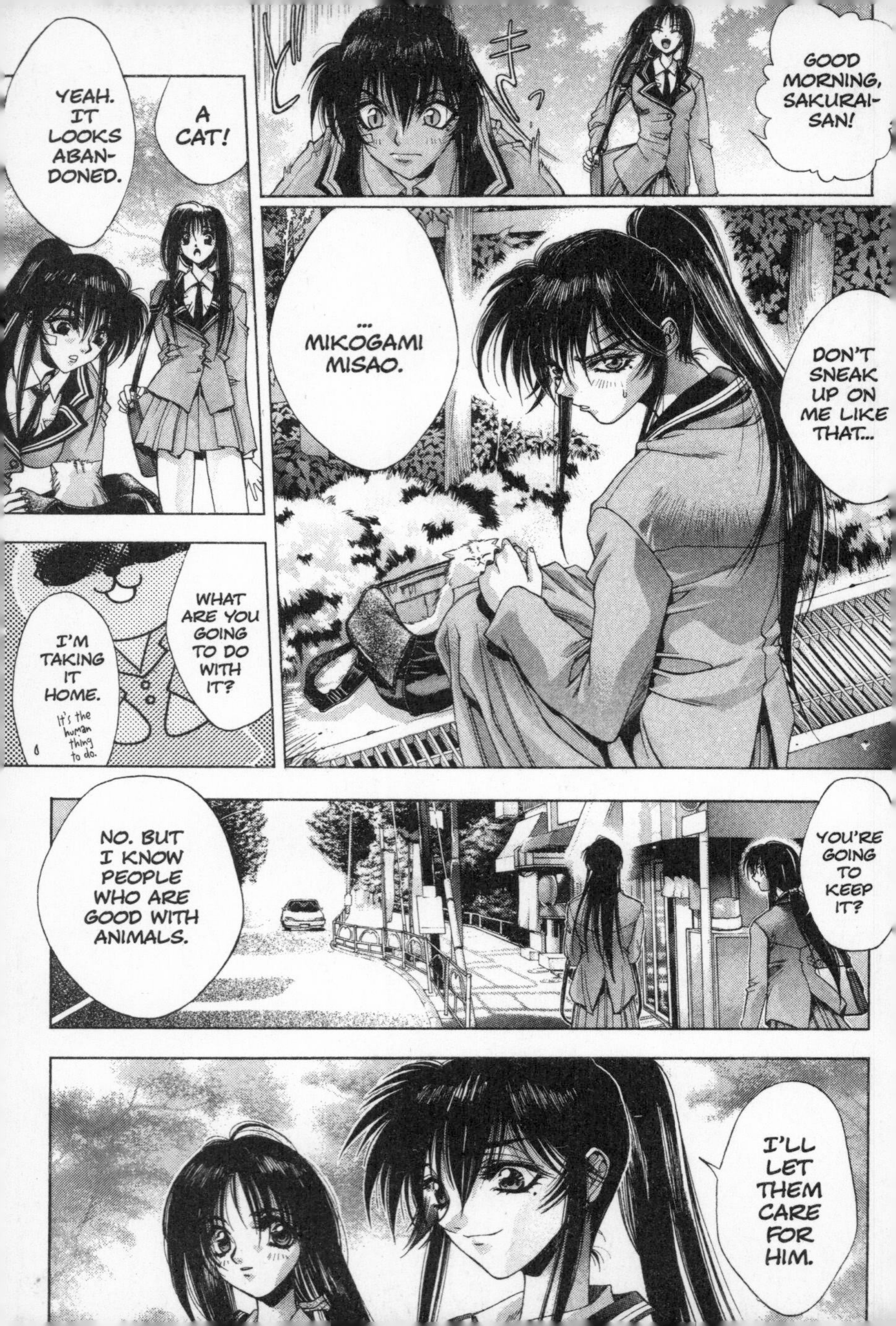
GOOD MORNING, SAKURAI-SAN!
... MIKOGAMI MISAO.
DON'T SNEAK UP ON ME LIKE THAT...
A CAT!
YEAH. IT LOOKS ABANDONED.
WHAT ARE YOU GOING TO DO WITH IT?
I'M TAKING IT HOME.
It's the human thing to do.
YOU'RE GOING TO KEEP IT?
NO. BUT I KNOW PEOPLE WHO ARE GOOD WITH ANIMALS.
I'LL LET THEM CARE FOR HIM.

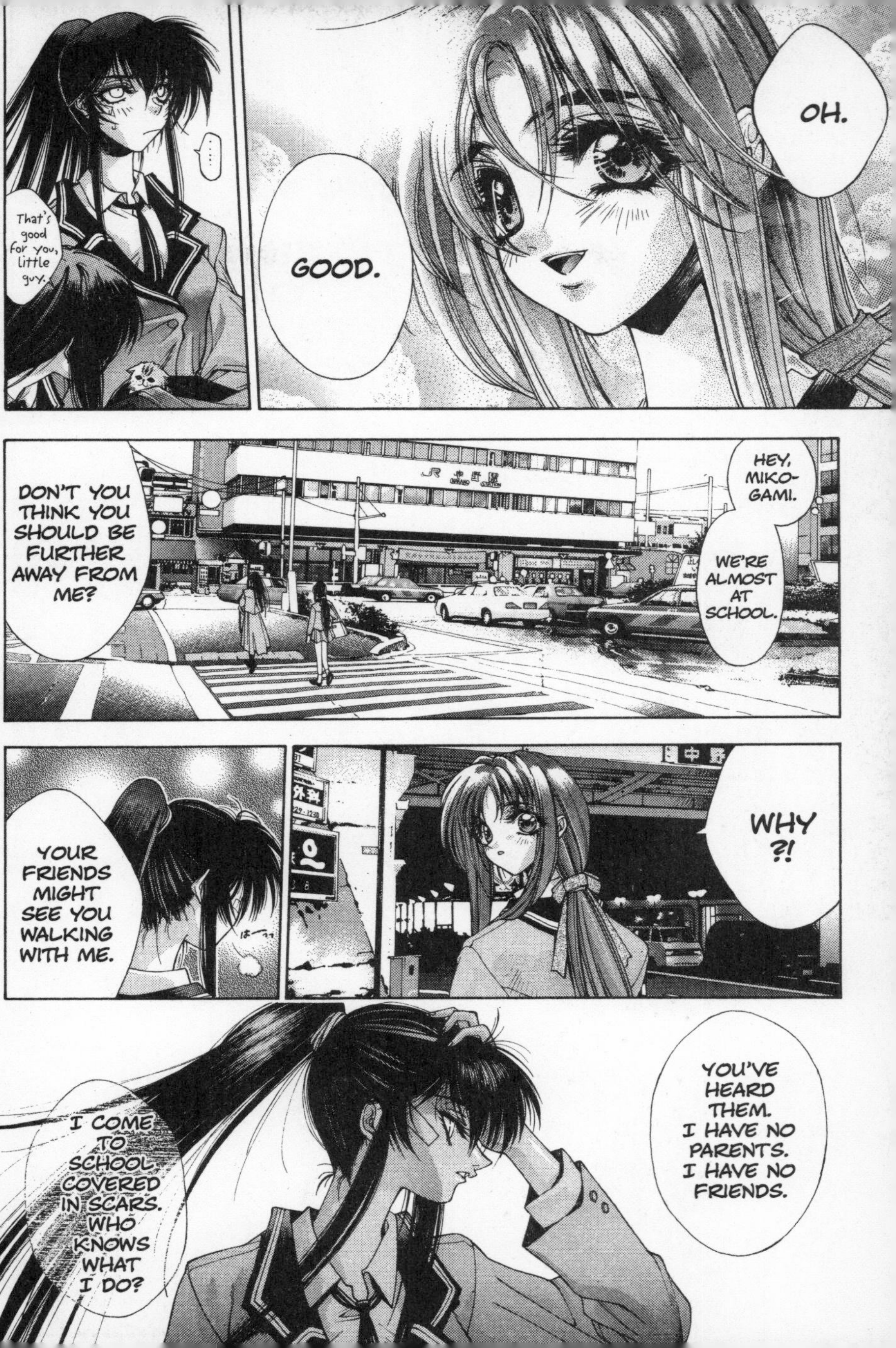
OH.
GOOD.
...
That's good for you, little guy.
HEY, MIKO-GAMI.
WE'RE ALMOST AT SCHOOL.
DON'T YOU THINK YOU SHOULD BE FURTHER AWAY FROM ME?
中野
WHY?!
YOUR FRIENDS MIGHT SEE YOU WALKING WITH ME.
はーっ
YOU'VE HEARD THEM. I HAVE NO PARENTS. I HAVE NO FRIENDS.
I COME TO SCHOOL COVERED IN SCARS. WHO KNOWS WHAT I DO?

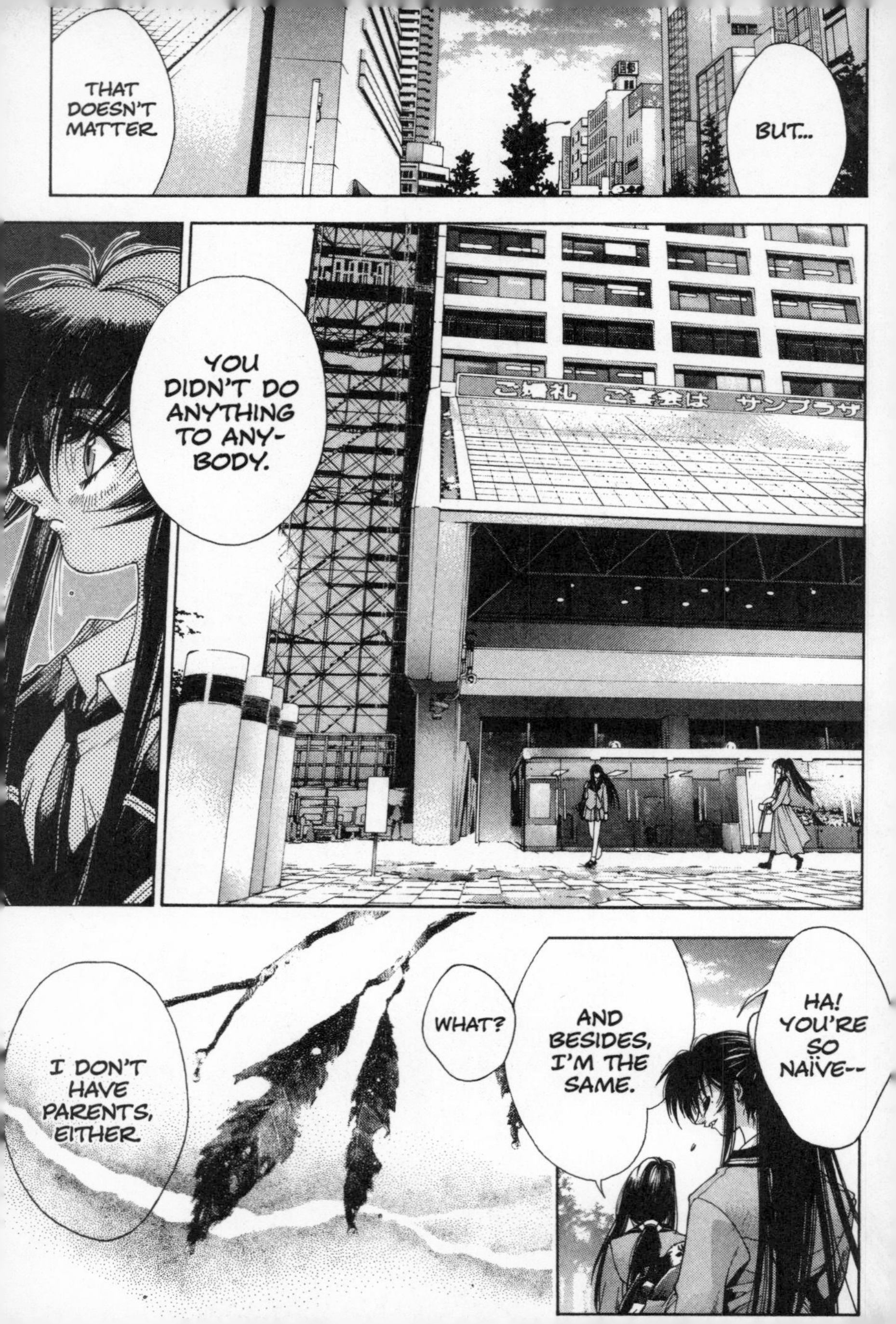
BUT...
THAT DOESN'T MATTER
ご婚礼 ご宴会は サンプラザ
YOU DIDN'T DO ANYTHING TO ANY-BODY.
HA! YOU'RE SO NAÏVE--
AND BESIDES, I'M THE SAME.
WHAT?
I DON'T HAVE PARENTS, EITHER.

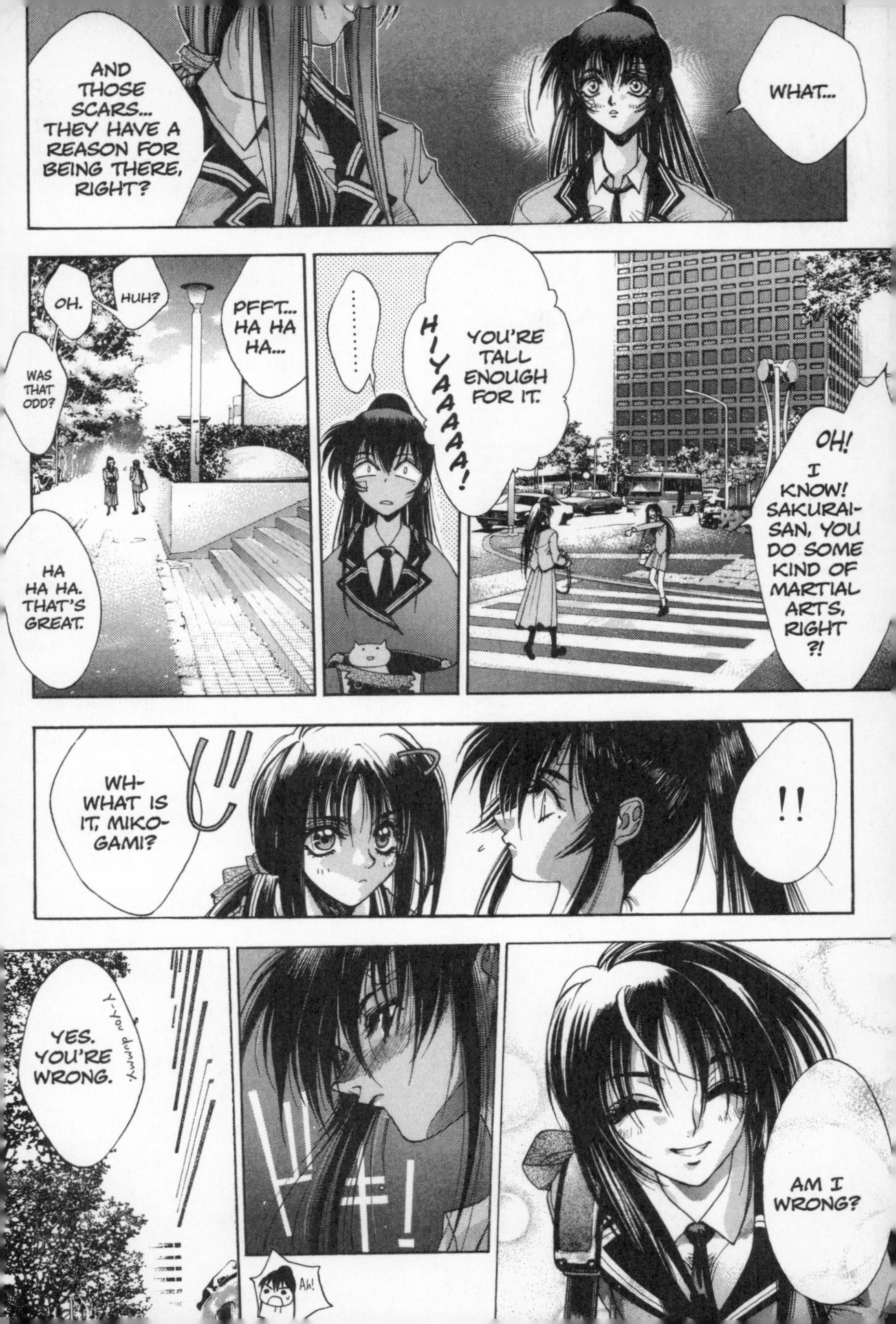
WHAT...
AND THOSE SCARS... THEY HAVE A REASON FOR BEING THERE, RIGHT?
OH! I KNOW! SAKURAI-SAN, YOU DO SOME KIND OF MARTIAL ARTS, RIGHT?!
YOU'RE TALL ENOUGH FOR IT.
HIYAAAAAA!
......
PFFT... HA HA HA...
HUH?
OH.
WAS THAT ODD?
HA HA HA. THAT'S GREAT.
!!
WH-WHAT IS IT, MIKO-GAMI?
AM I WRONG?
Ah!
Y-Y-you dummy
YES. YOU'RE WRONG.

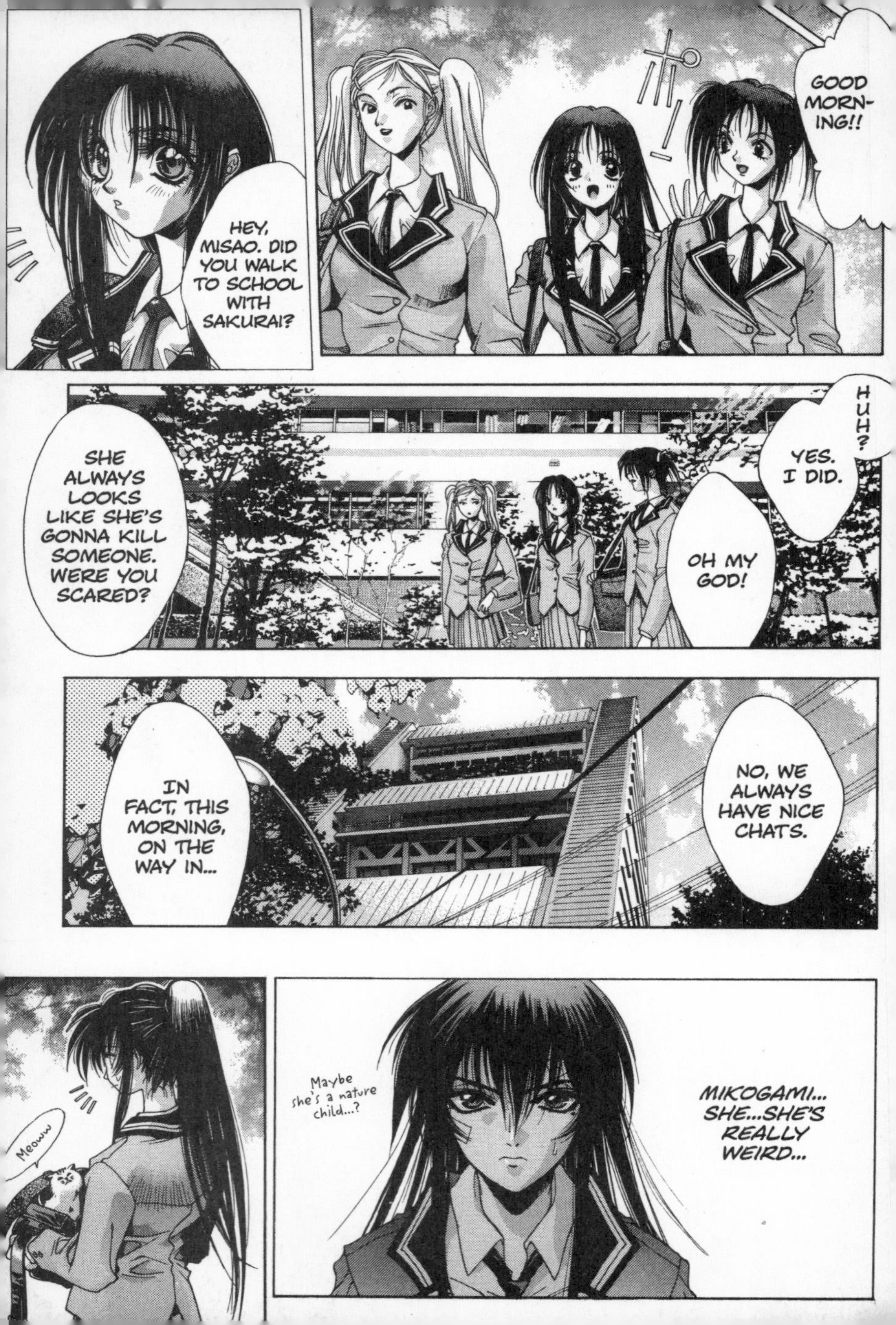
GOOD MORNING!!
HEY, MISAO. DID YOU WALK TO SCHOOL WITH SAKURAI?
HUH?
YES. I DID.
OH MY GOD!
SHE ALWAYS LOOKS LIKE SHE'S GONNA KILL SOMEONE. WERE YOU SCARED?
NO, WE ALWAYS HAVE NICE CHATS.
IN FACT, THIS MORNING, ON THE WAY IN...
MIKOGAMI... SHE...SHE'S REALLY WEIRD...
Maybe she's a nature child...?
Meowww

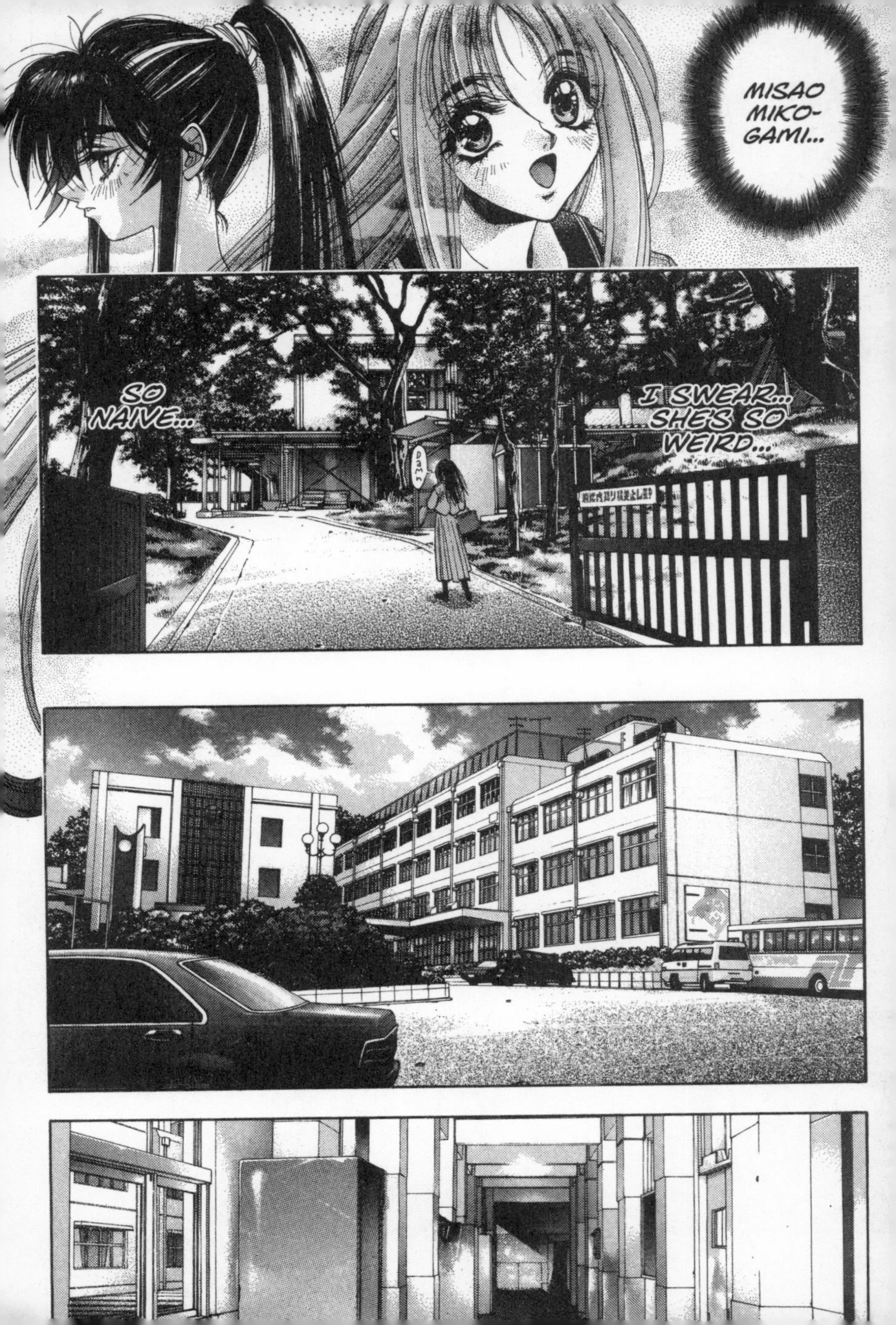
MISAO MIKO-GAMI...
I SWEAR... SHE'S SO WEIRD...
SO NAIVE...
Damn

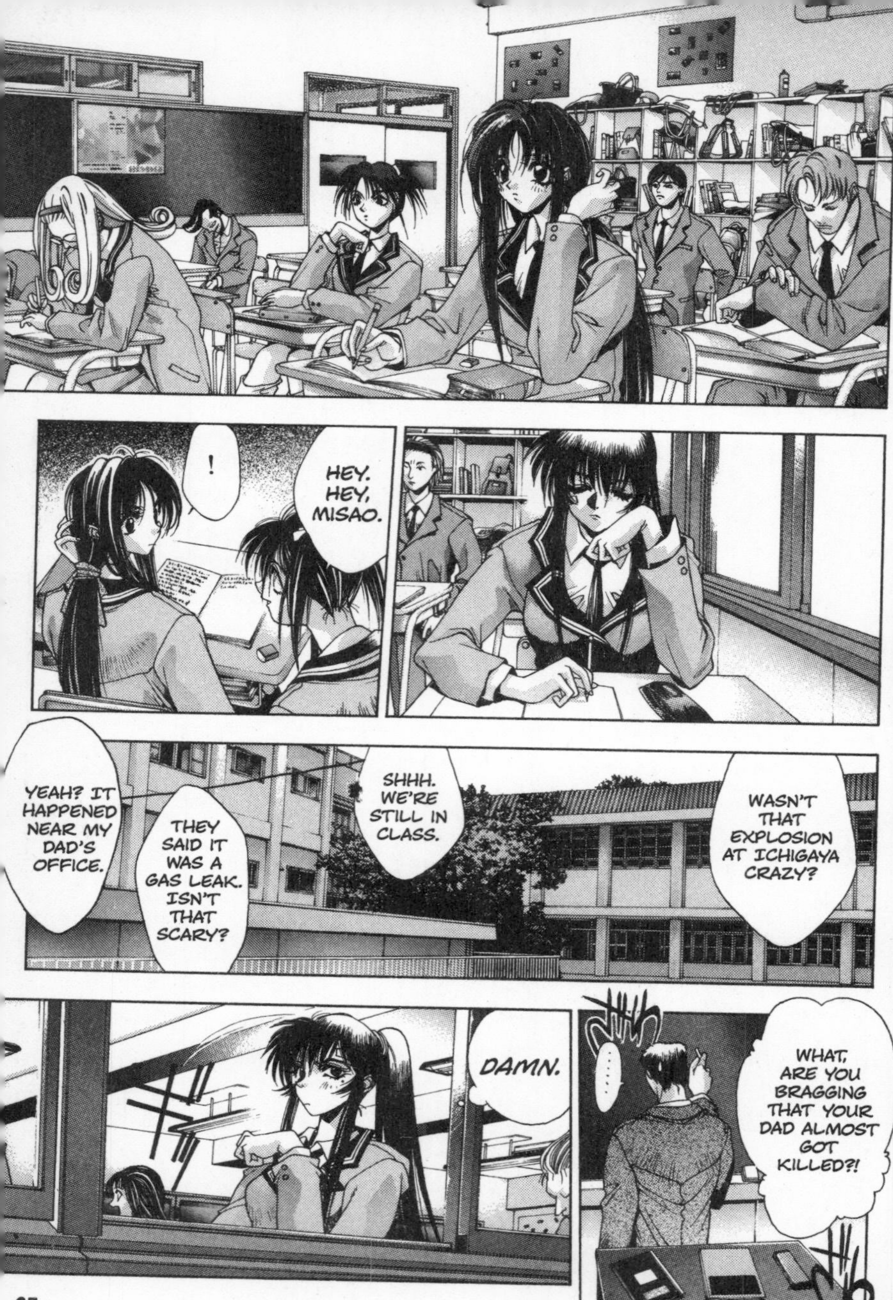
HEY. HEY, MISAO.
!
WASN'T THAT EXPLOSION AT ICHIGAYA CRAZY?
SHHH. WE'RE STILL IN CLASS.
THEY SAID IT WAS A GAS LEAK. ISN'T THAT SCARY?
YEAH? IT HAPPENED NEAR MY DAD'S OFFICE.
WHAT, ARE YOU BRAGGING THAT YOUR DAD ALMOST GOT KILLED?!
......
DAMN.

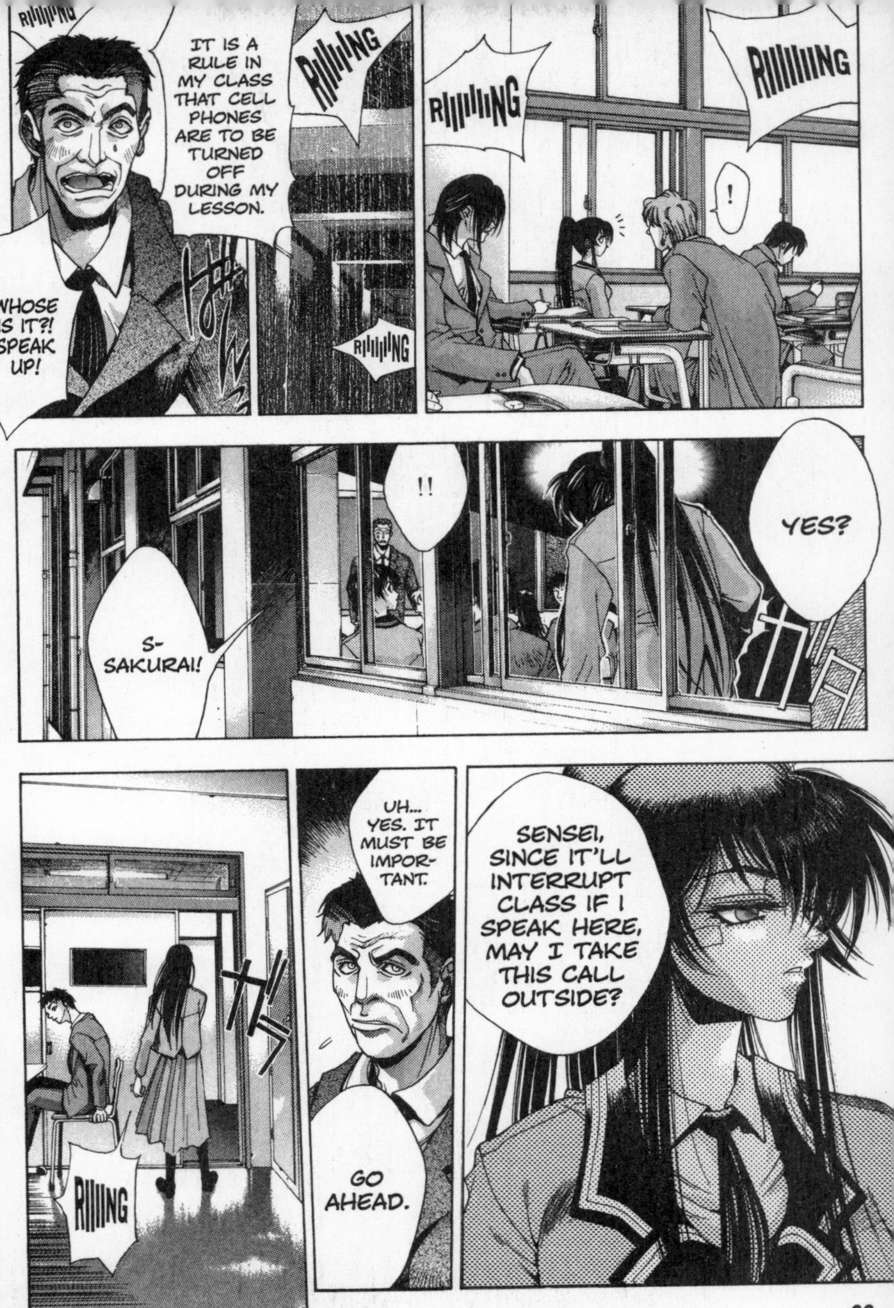
RIIIIING
RIIIIING
!
RIIIIING
RIIIING
RIIIING
IT IS A RULE IN MY CLASS THAT CELL PHONES ARE TO BE TURNED OFF DURING MY LESSON.
WHOSE IS IT?! SPEAK UP!
YES?
!!
S- SAKURAI!
SENSEI, SINCE IT'LL INTERRUPT CLASS IF I SPEAK HERE, MAY I TAKE THIS CALL OUTSIDE?
UH... YES. IT MUST BE IMPOR-TANT.
GO AHEAD.
RIIIING

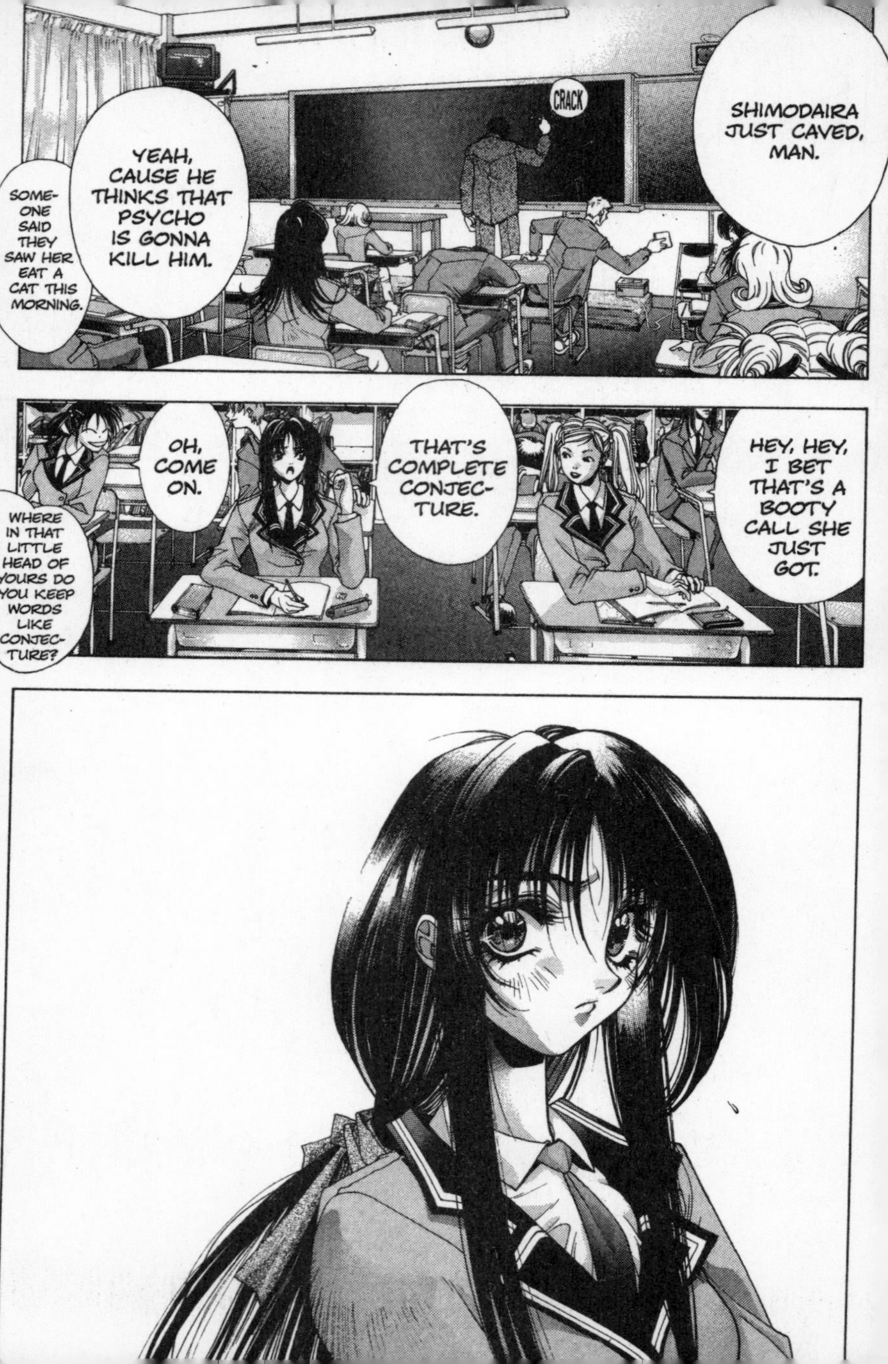
SHIMODAIRA JUST CAVED, MAN.
CRACK
YEAH, CAUSE HE THINKS THAT PSYCHO IS GONNA KILL HIM.
SOME-ONE SAID THEY SAW HER EAT A CAT THIS MORNING.
HEY, HEY, I BET THAT'S A BOOTY CALL SHE JUST GOT.
THAT'S COMPLETE CONJEC-TURE.
OH, COME ON.
WHERE IN THAT LITTLE HEAD OF YOURS DO YOU KEEP WORDS LIKE CONJEC-TURE?

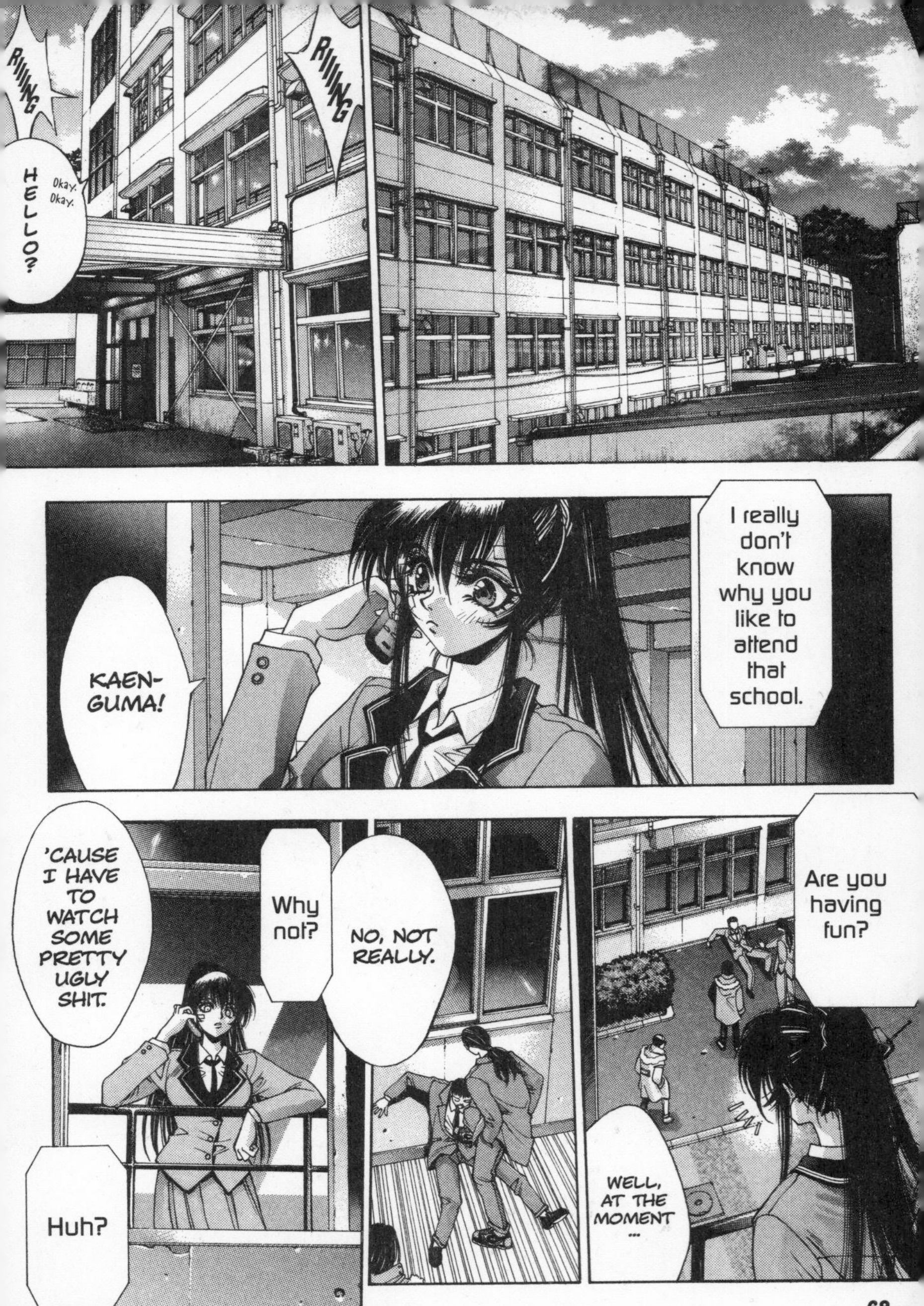
RIIING
RIIING
HELLO?
Okay. Okay.
I really don't know why you like to attend that school.
KAEN-GUMA!
Are you having fun?
WELL, AT THE MOMENT ...
NO, NOT REALLY.
Why not?
'CAUSE I HAVE TO WATCH SOME PRETTY UGLY SHIT.
Huh?

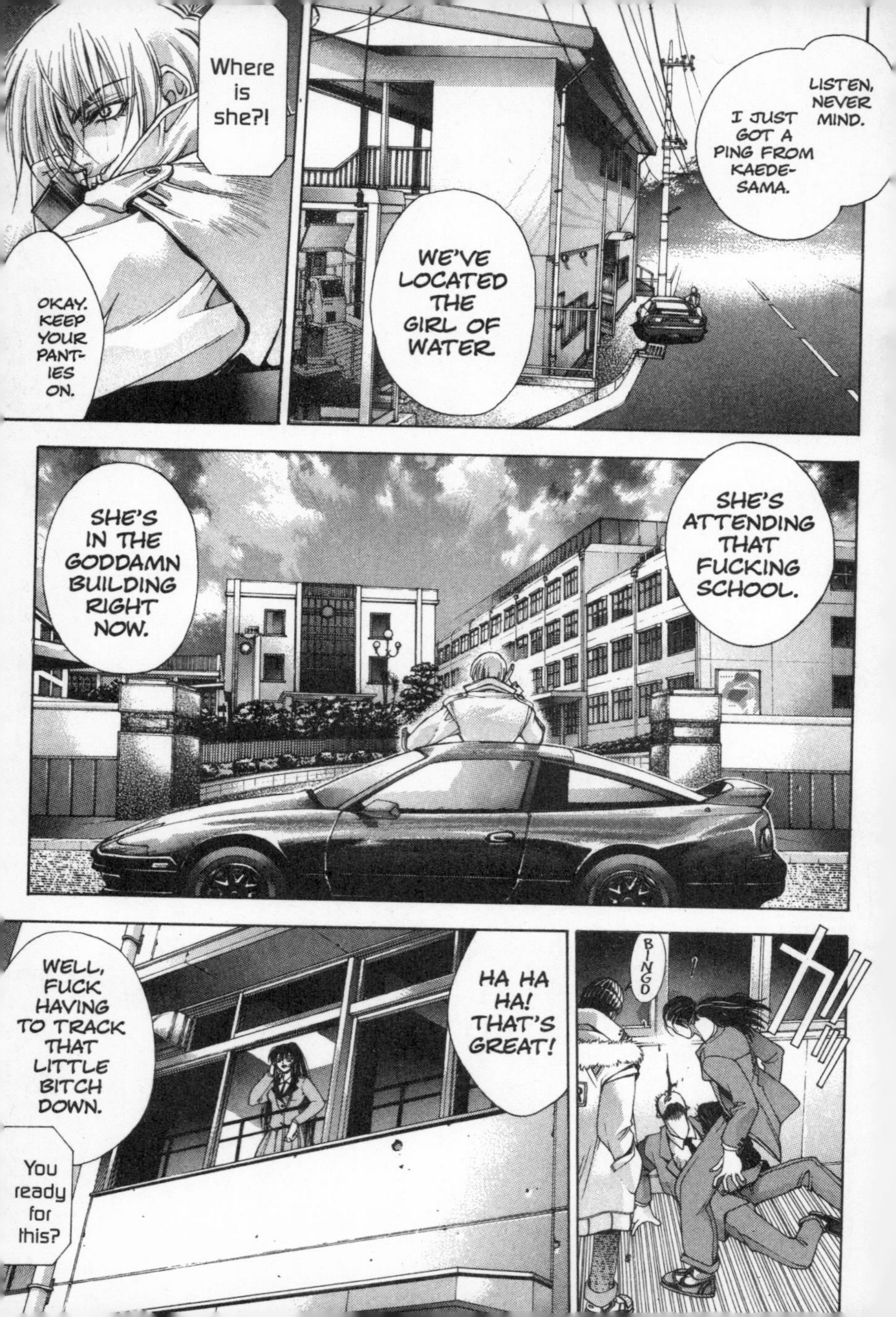
LISTEN, NEVER MIND.
I JUST GOT A PING FROM KAEDE-SAMA.
WE'VE LOCATED THE GIRL OF WATER
Where is she?!
OKAY. KEEP YOUR PANTIES ON.
SHE'S ATTENDING THAT FUCKING SCHOOL.
SHE'S IN THE GODDAMN BUILDING RIGHT NOW.
BINGO
!
HA HA HA! THAT'S GREAT!
WELL, FUCK HAVING TO TRACK THAT LITTLE BITCH DOWN.
You ready for this?

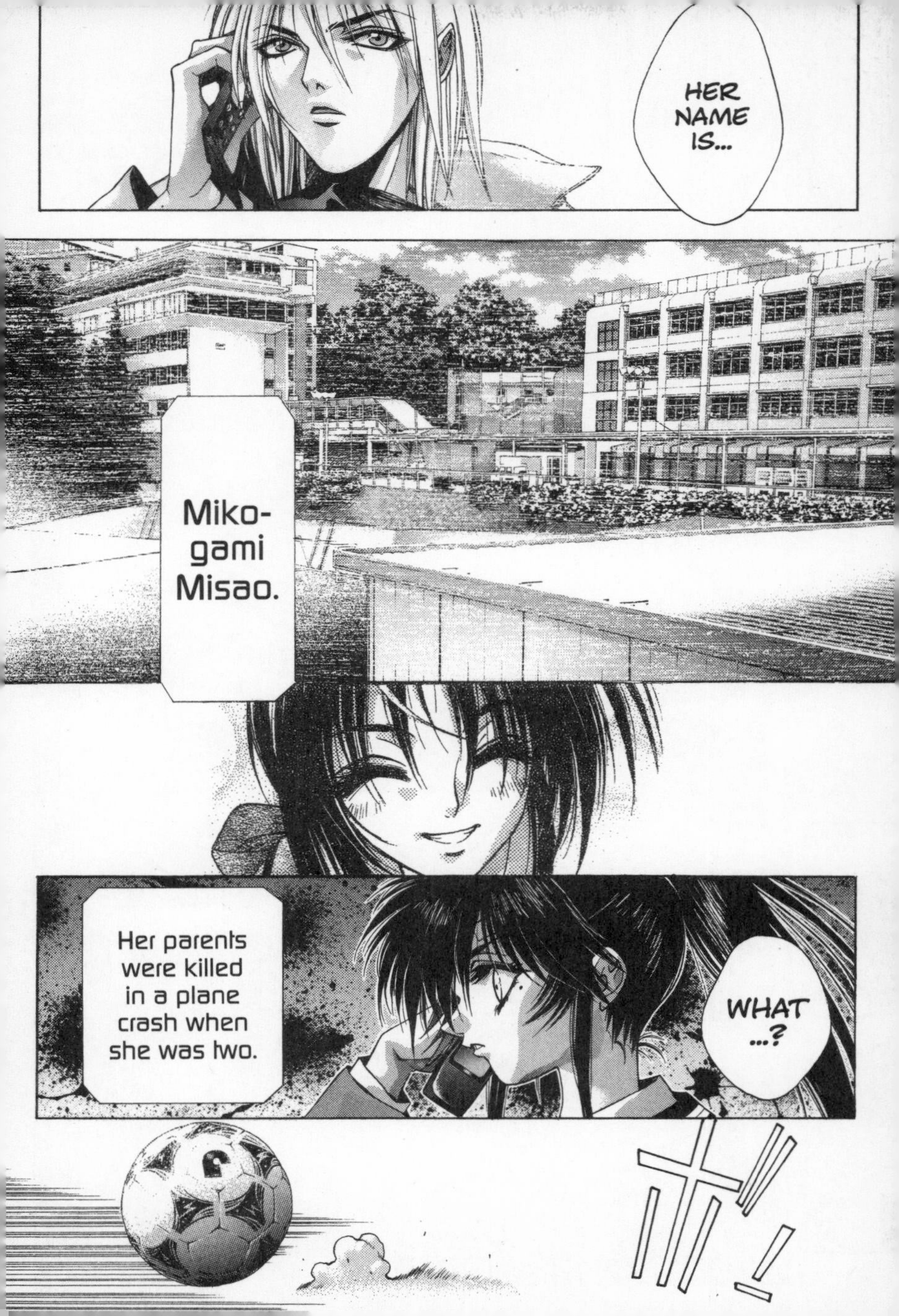
HER NAME IS...
Miko-gami Misao.
WHAT ...?
Her parents were killed in a plane crash when she was two.

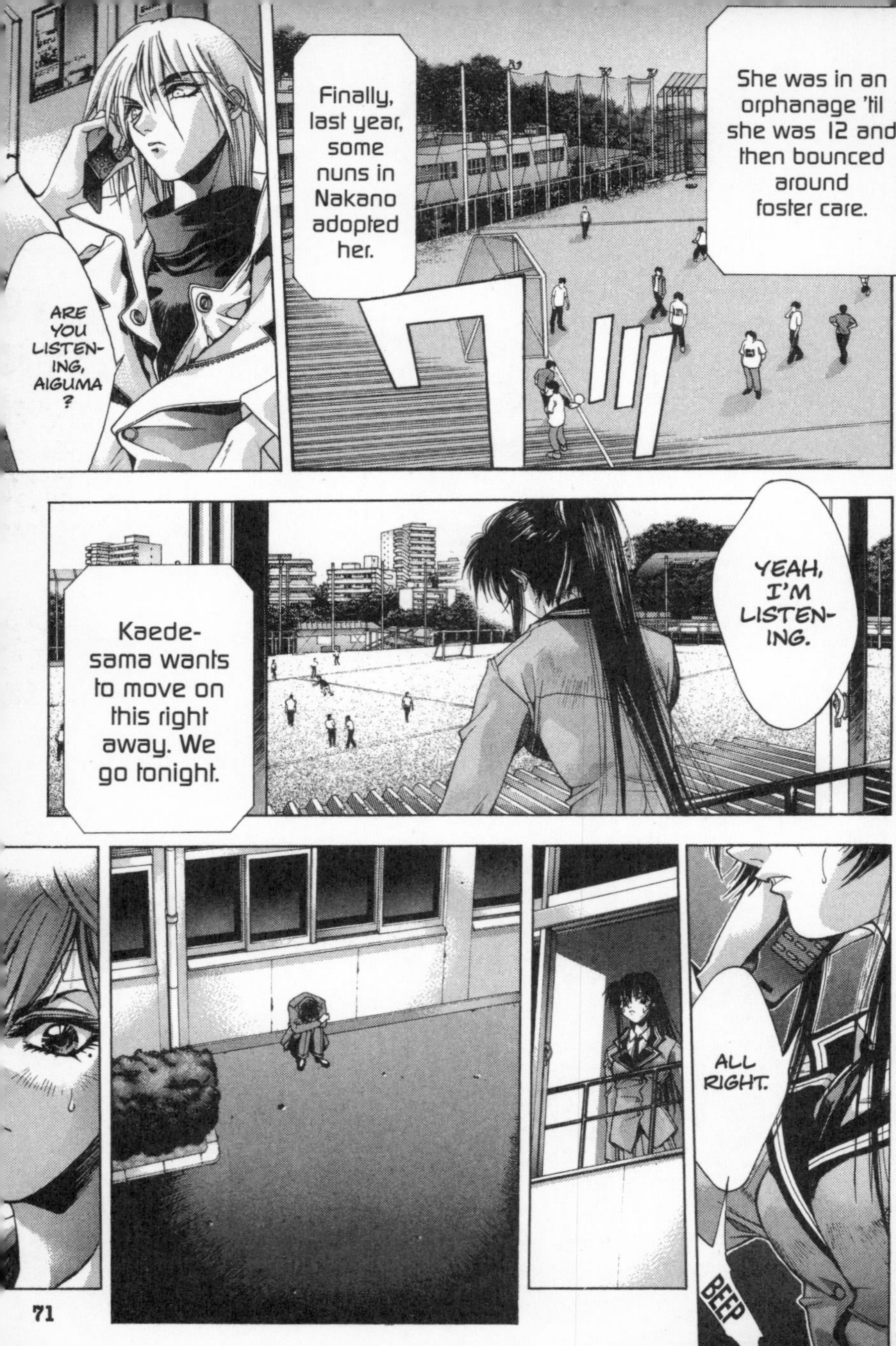
She was in an orphanage 'til she was 12 and then bounced around foster care.
Finally, last year, some nuns in Nakano adopted her.
ARE YOU LISTENING, AIGUMA?
YEAH, I'M LISTENING.
Kaede-sama wants to move on this right away. We go tonight.
ALL RIGHT.
BEEP

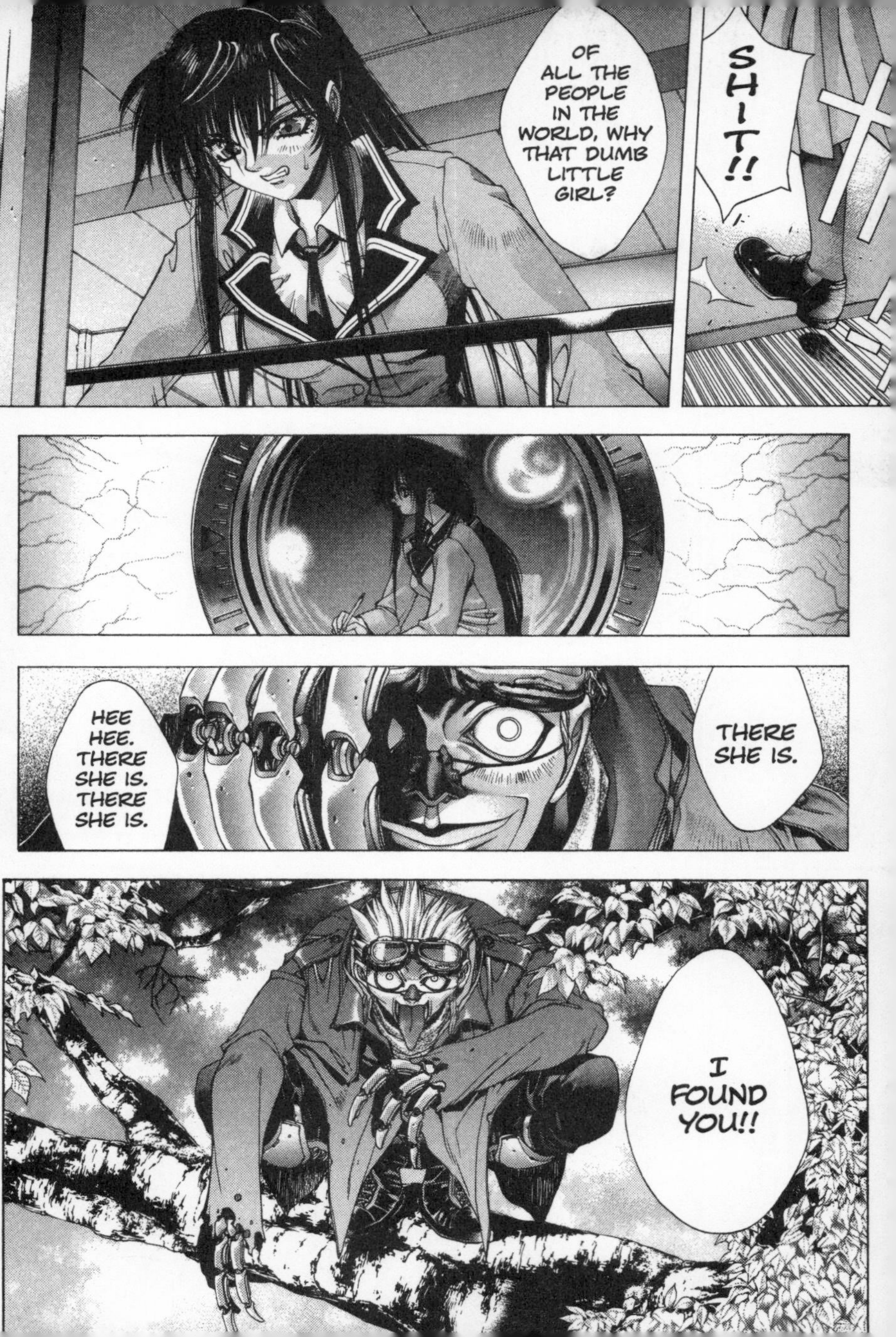
SHIT!!
OF ALL THE PEOPLE IN THE WORLD, WHY THAT DUMB LITTLE GIRL?
THERE SHE IS.
HEE HEE. THERE SHE IS. THERE SHE IS.
I FOUND YOU!!

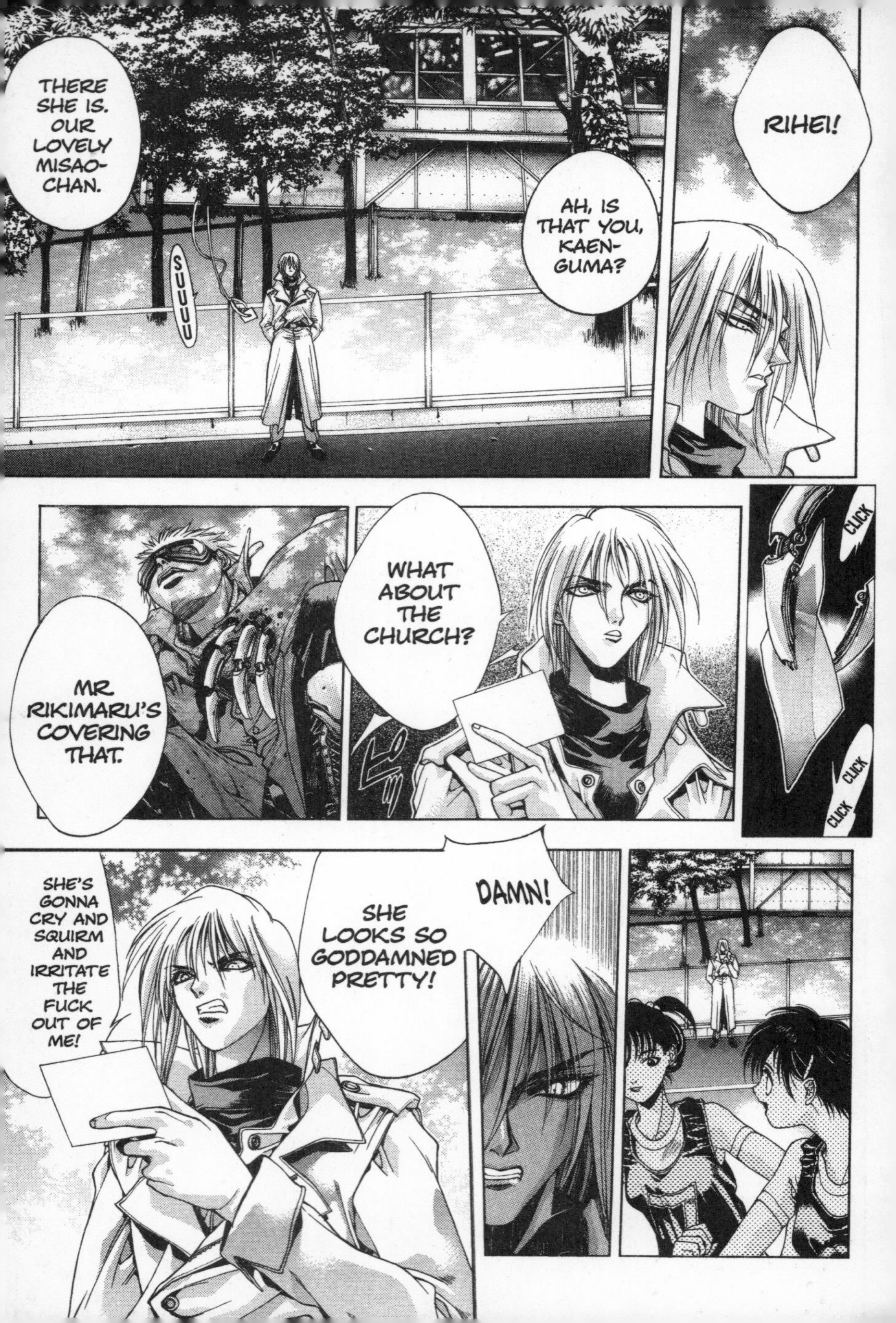
RIHEI!
AH, IS THAT YOU, KAEN-GUMA?
THERE SHE IS. OUR LOVELY MISAO-CHAN.
SUUUU
CLICK
CLICK
CLICK
WHAT ABOUT THE CHURCH?
MR RIKIMARU'S COVERING THAT.
DAMN!
SHE LOOKS SO GODDAMNED PRETTY!
SHE'S GONNA CRY AND SQUIRM AND IRRITATE THE FUCK OUT OF ME!

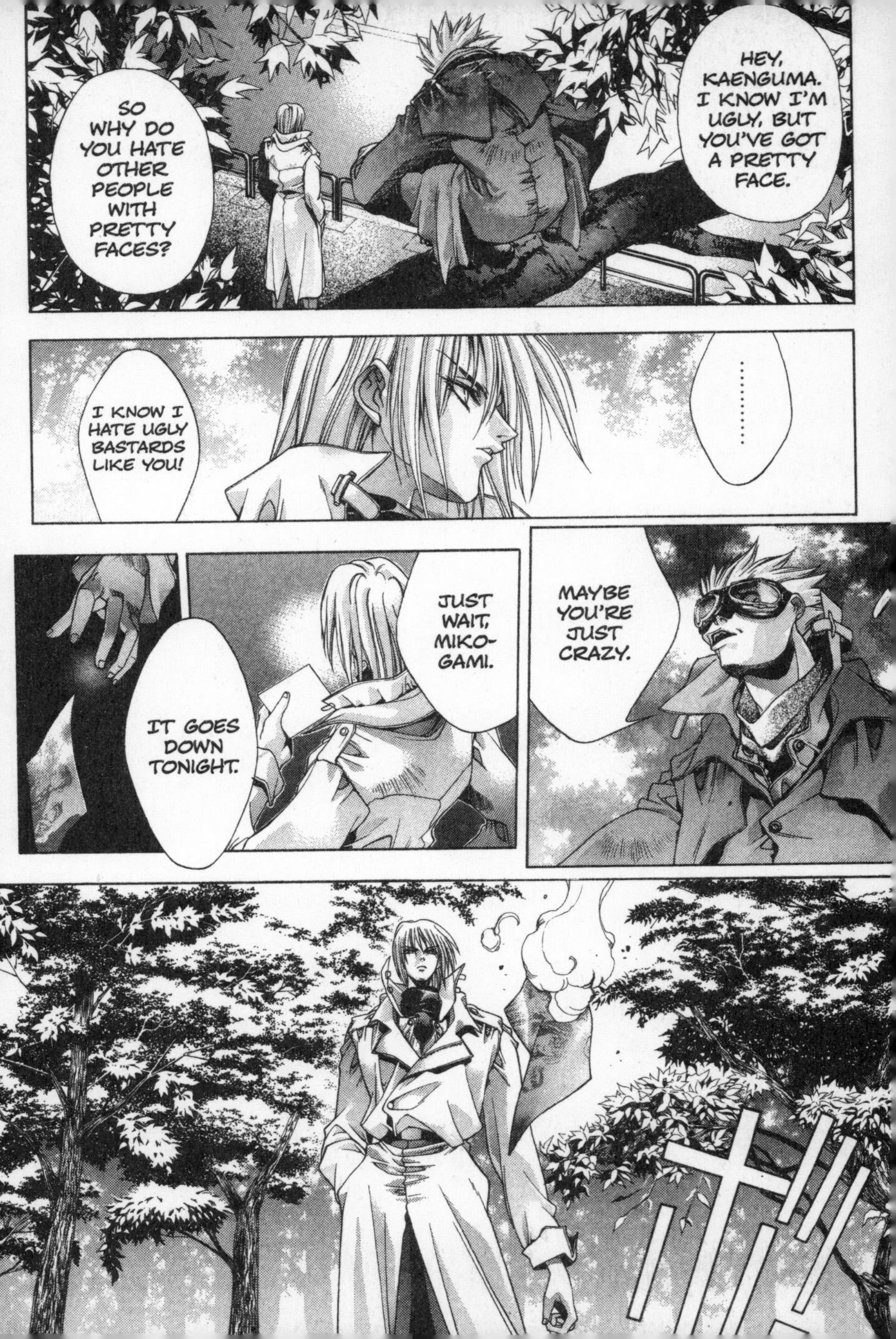
HEY, KAENGUMA. I KNOW I'M UGLY, BUT YOU'VE GOT A PRETTY FACE.
SO WHY DO YOU HATE OTHER PEOPLE WITH PRETTY FACES?
......
I KNOW I HATE UGLY BASTARDS LIKE YOU!
MAYBE YOU'RE JUST CRAZY.
JUST WAIT, MIKO-GAMI.
IT GOES DOWN TONIGHT.

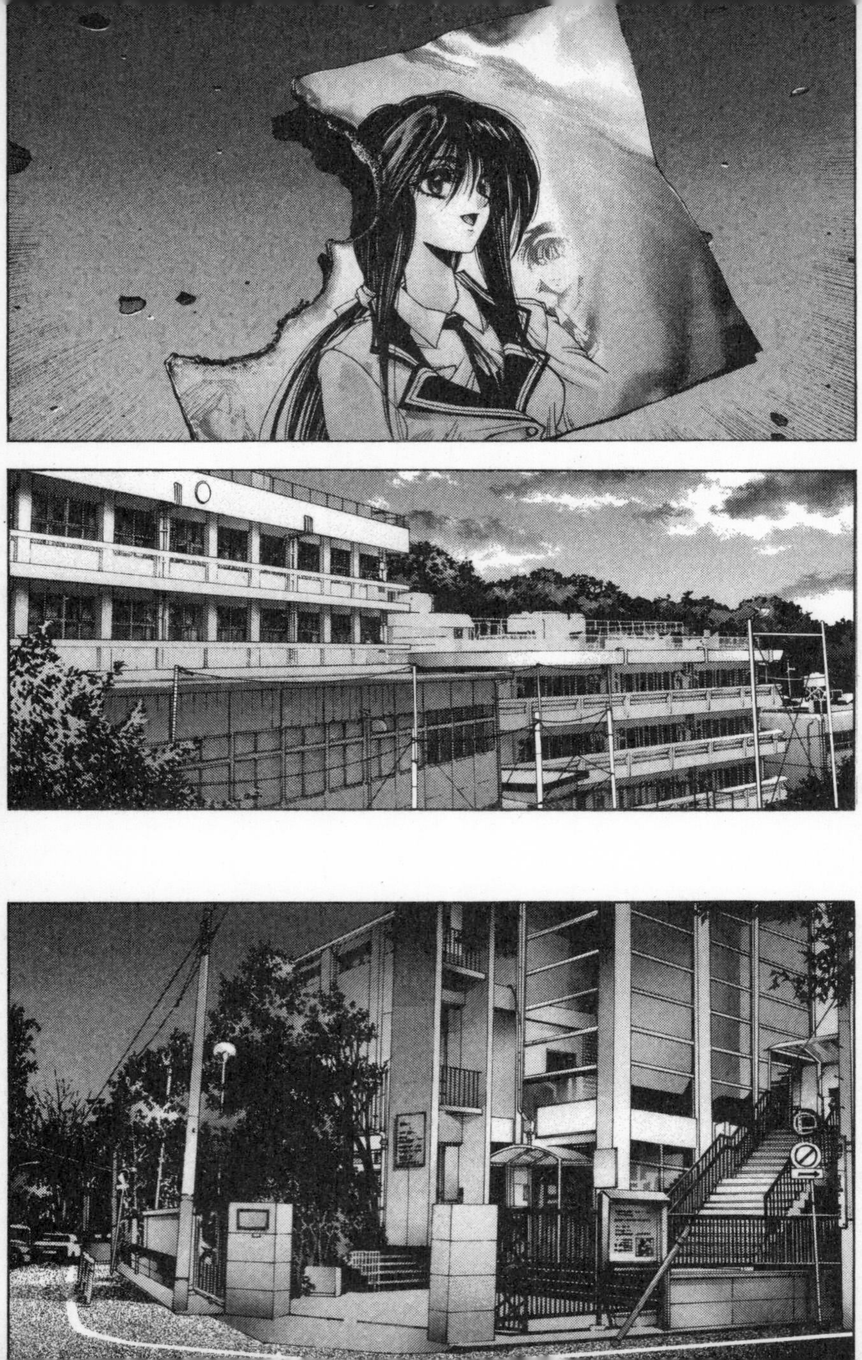

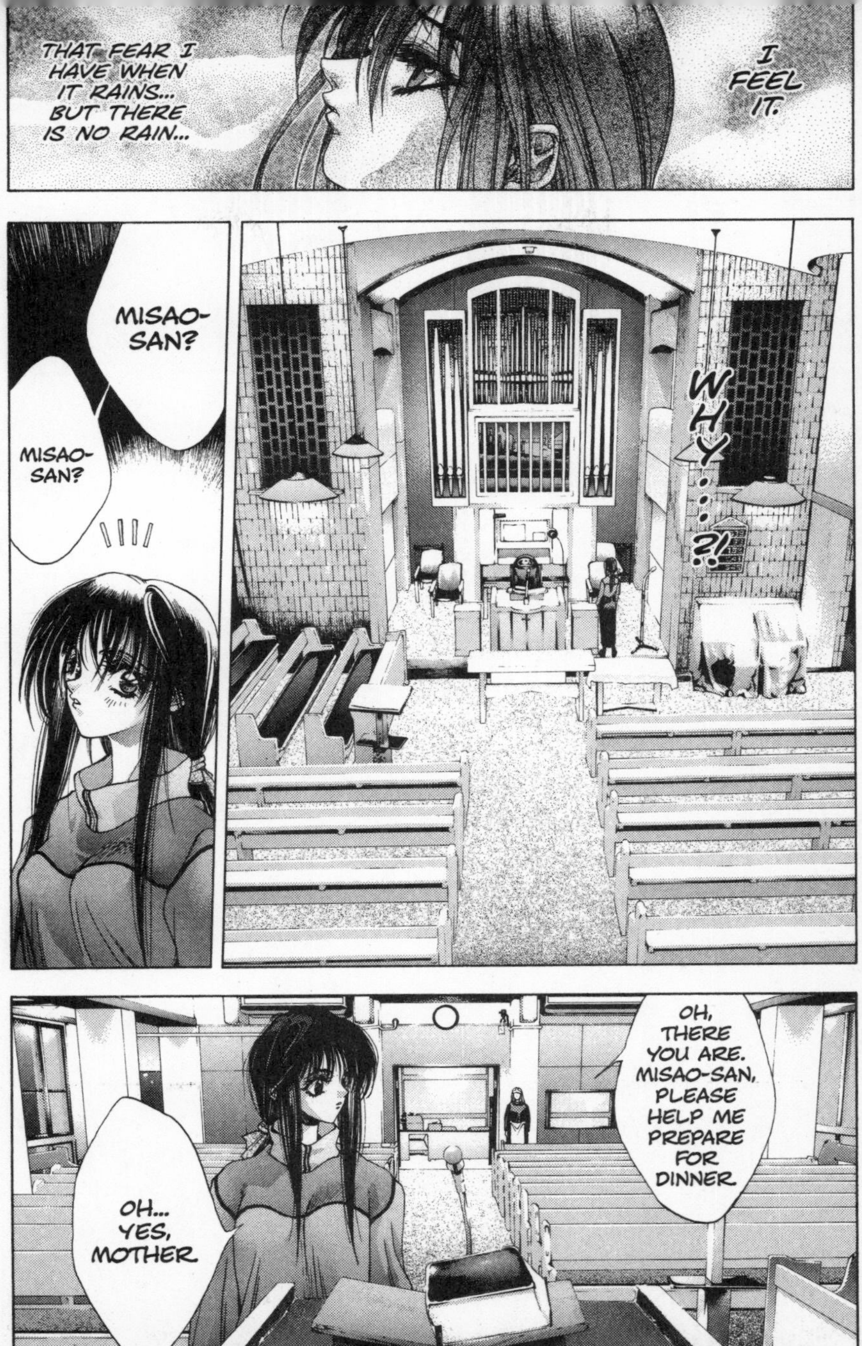
I FEEL IT.
THAT FEAR I HAVE WHEN IT RAINS... BUT THERE IS NO RAIN...
WHY...?!
MISAO-SAN?
MISAO-SAN?
OH, THERE YOU ARE. MISAO-SAN, PLEASE HELP ME PREPARE FOR DINNER
OH... YES, MOTHER

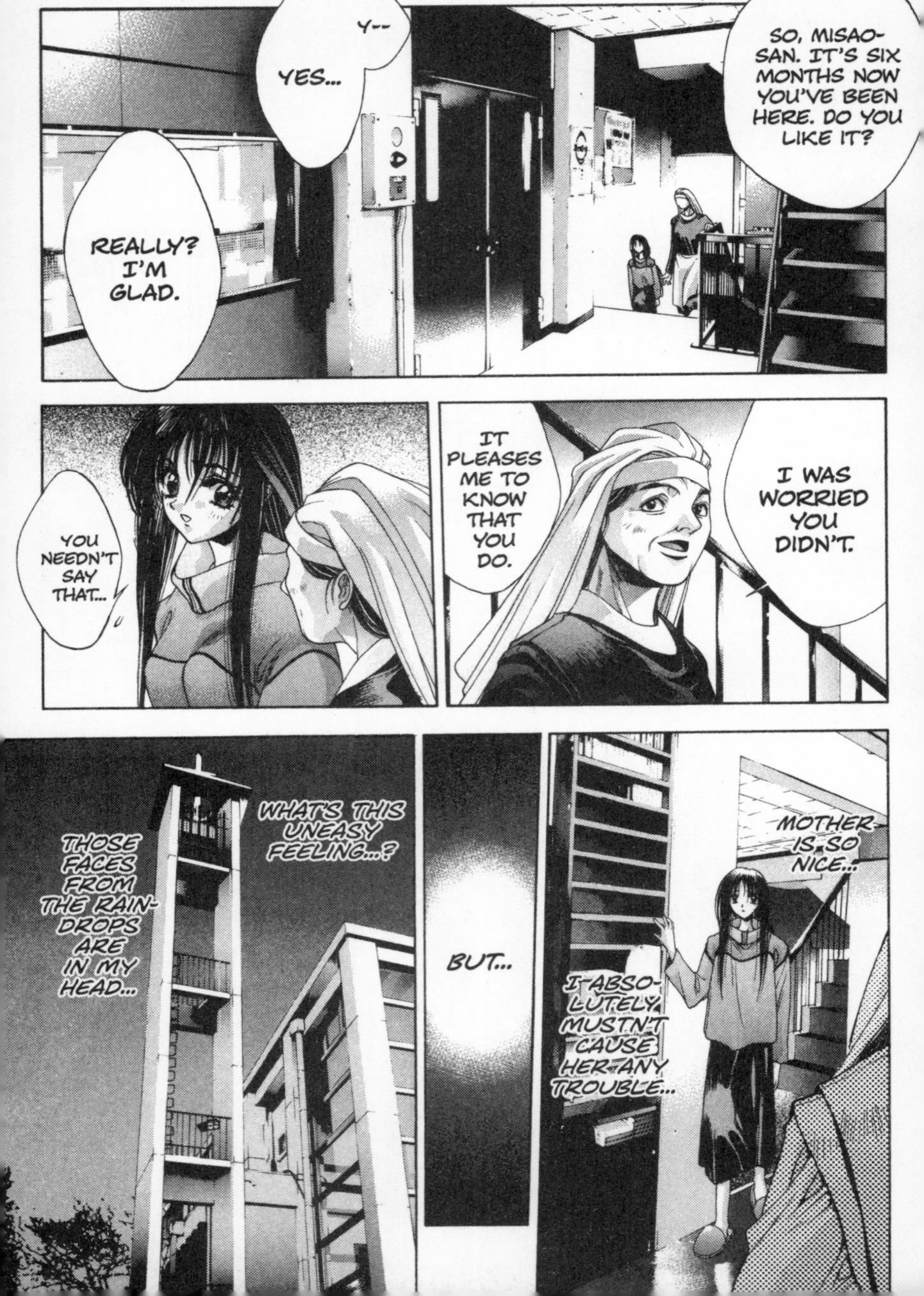
SO, MISAO-SAN. IT'S SIX MONTHS NOW YOU'VE BEEN HERE. DO YOU LIKE IT?
Y-- YES...
REALLY? I'M GLAD.
I WAS WORRIED YOU DIDN'T.
IT PLEASES ME TO KNOW THAT YOU DO.
YOU NEEDN'T SAY THAT...
MOTHER IS SO NICE...
I ABSOLUTELY MUSTN'T CAUSE HER ANY TROUBLE...
BUT...
WHAT'S THIS UNEASY FEELING...?
THOSE FACES FROM THE RAINDROPS ARE IN MY HEAD...

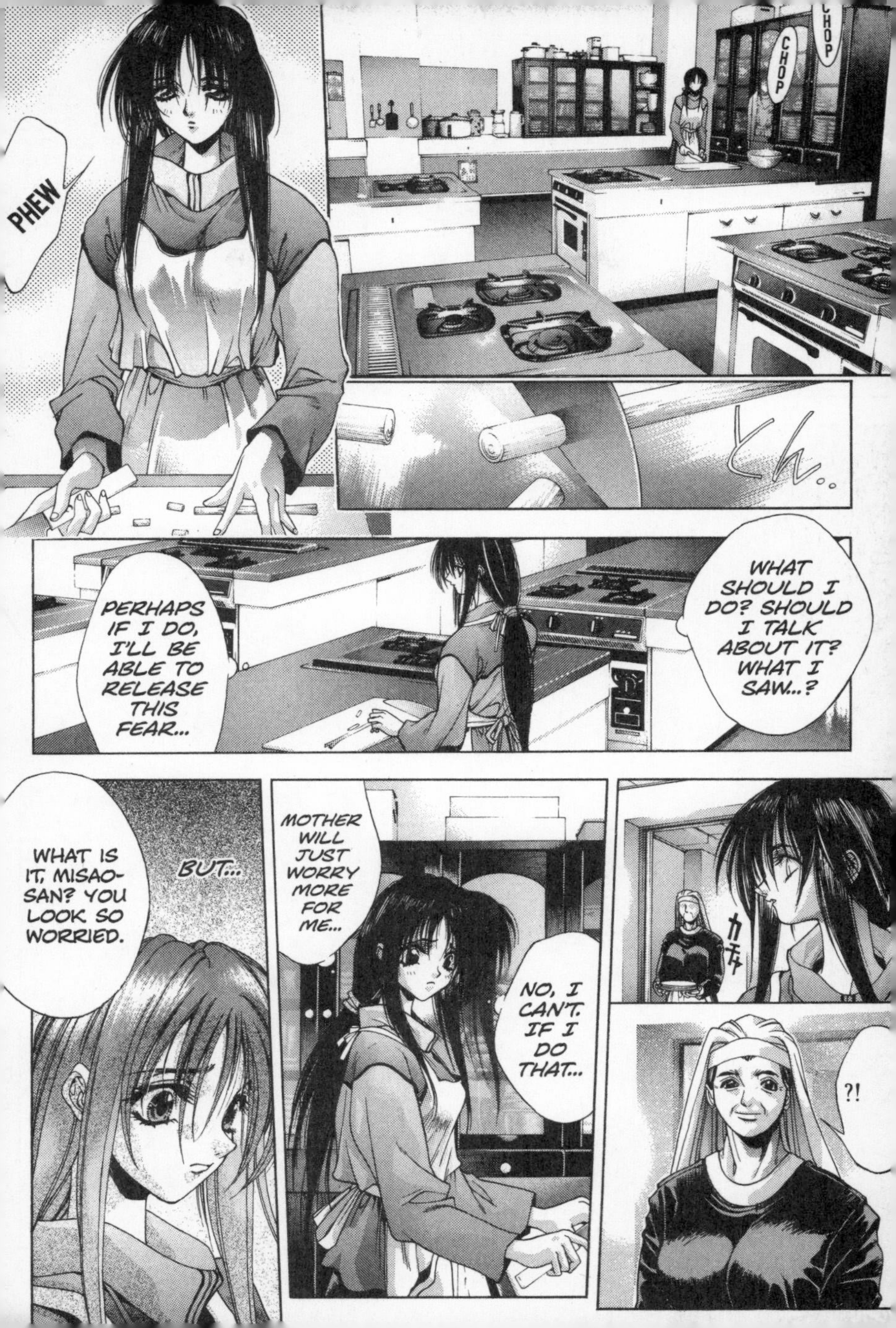
CHOP
CHOP
とん..
PHEW
WHAT SHOULD I DO? SHOULD I TALK ABOUT IT? WHAT I SAW...?
PERHAPS IF I DO, I'LL BE ABLE TO RELEASE THIS FEAR...
カチャ
?!
MOTHER WILL JUST WORRY MORE FOR ME...
NO, I CAN'T. IF I DO THAT...
BUT...
WHAT IS IT, MISAO-SAN? YOU LOOK SO WORRIED.

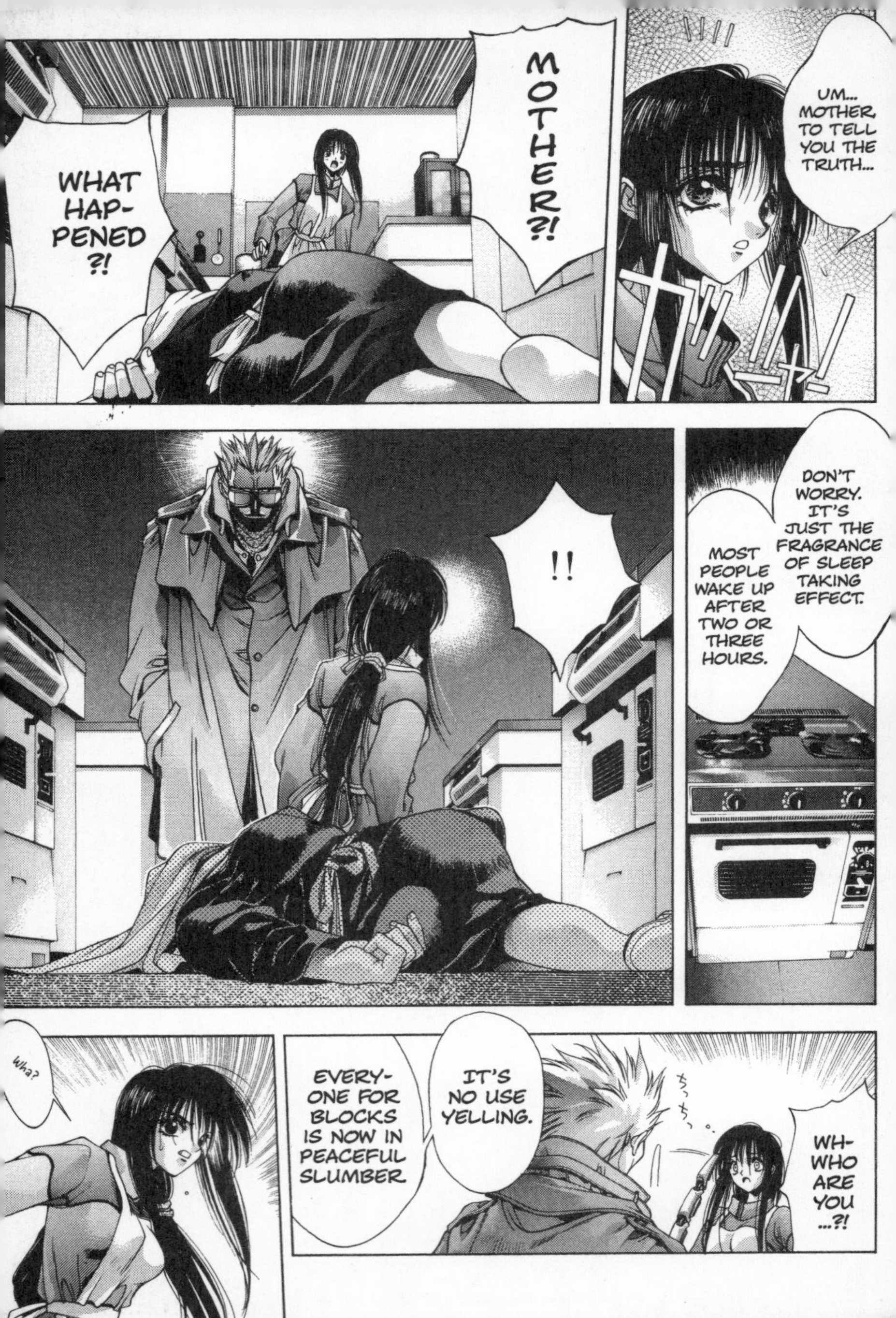
UM... MOTHER TO TELL YOU THE TRUTH...
MOTHER?!
WHAT HAP-PENED ?!
DON'T WORRY. IT'S JUST THE FRAGRANCE OF SLEEP TAKING EFFECT.
MOST PEOPLE WAKE UP AFTER TWO OR THREE HOURS.
!!
WH-WHO ARE YOU ...?!
IT'S NO USE YELLING.
EVERY-ONE FOR BLOCKS IS NOW IN PEACEFUL SLUMBER
Wha?

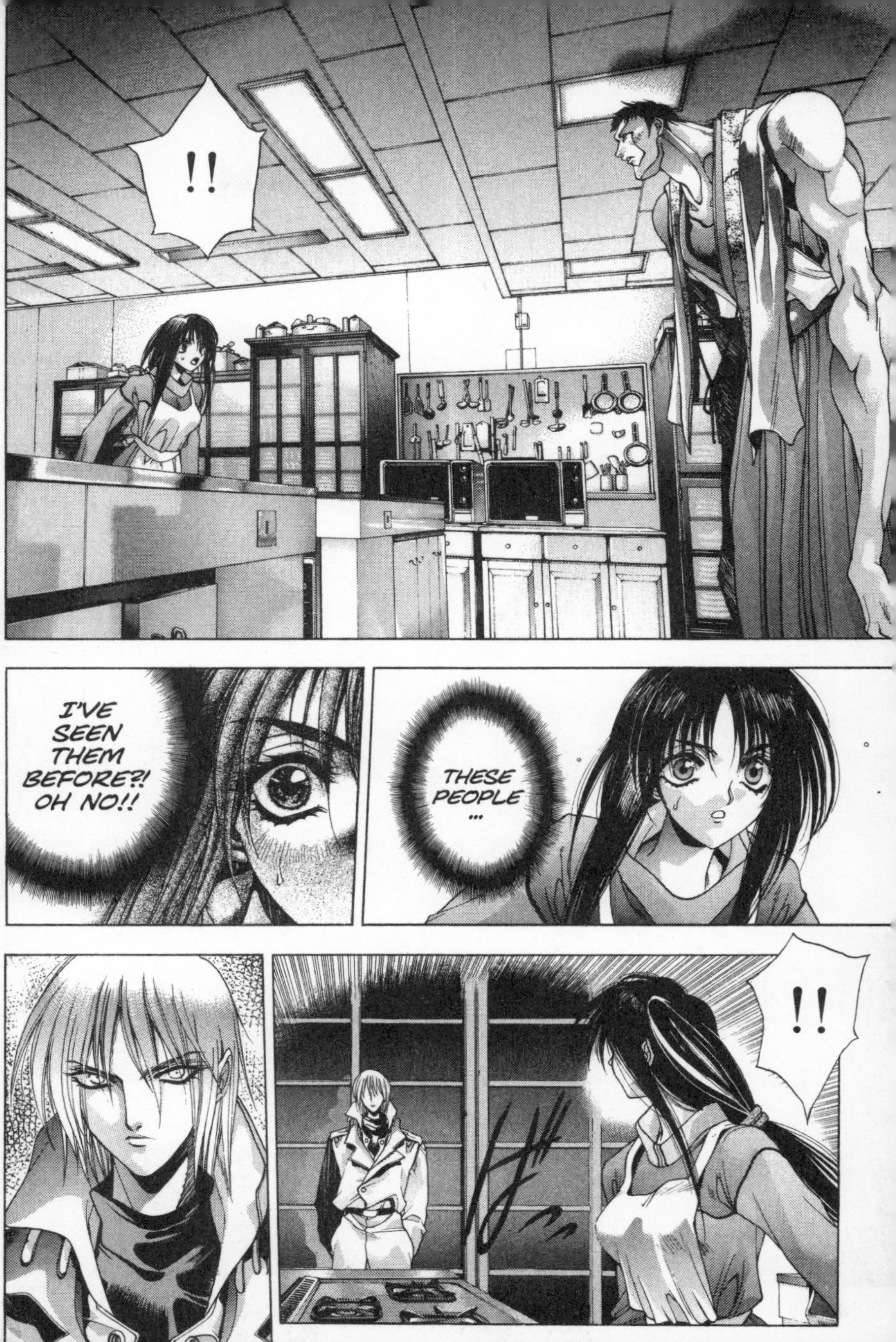
!!
THESE PEOPLE ...
I'VE SEEN THEM BEFORE?! OH NO!!
!!

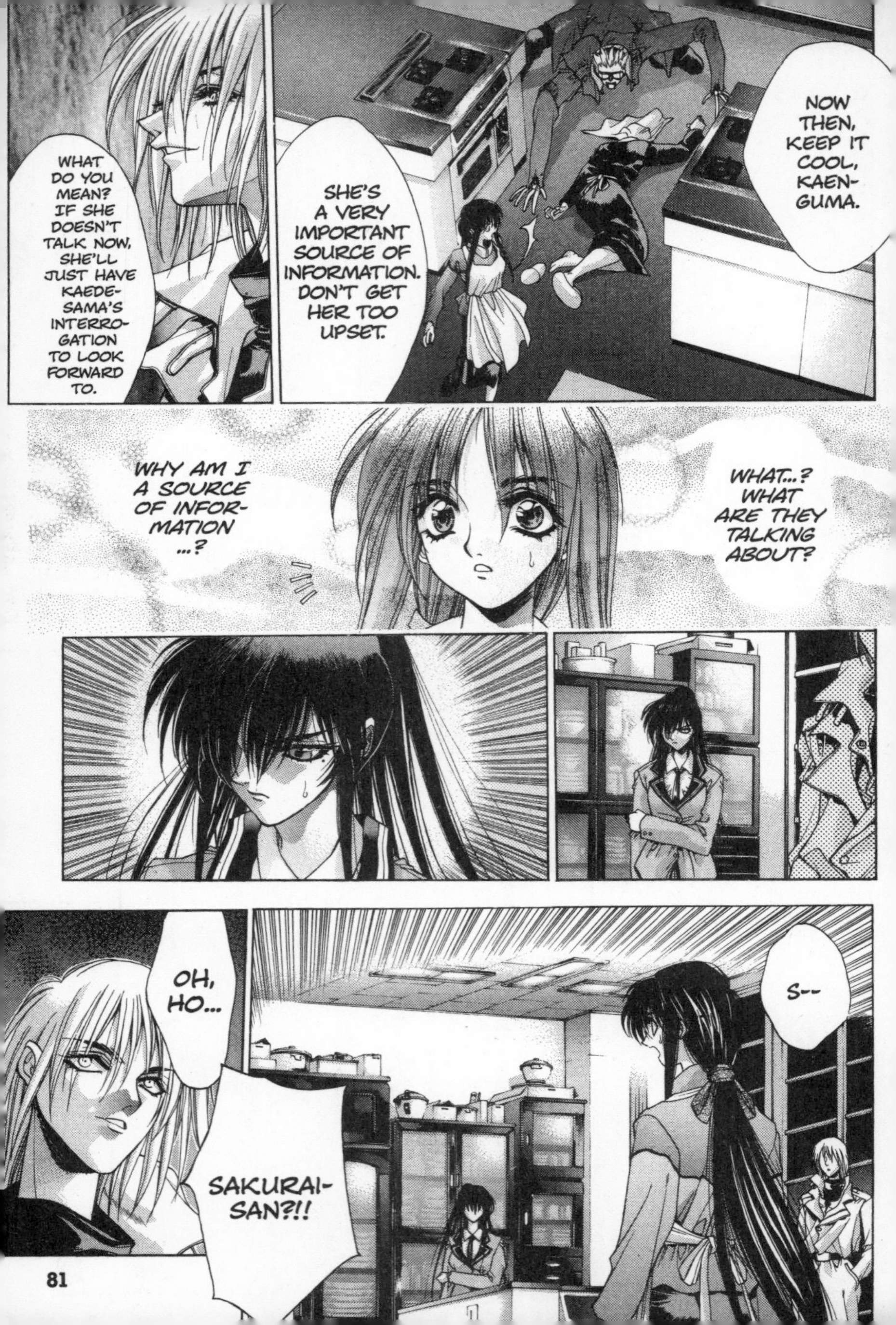
NOW THEN, KEEP IT COOL, KAEN-GUMA.
SHE'S A VERY IMPORTANT SOURCE OF INFORMATION. DON'T GET HER TOO UPSET.
WHAT DO YOU MEAN? IF SHE DOESN'T TALK NOW, SHE'LL JUST HAVE KAEDE-SAMA'S INTERRO-GATION TO LOOK FORWARD TO.
WHAT...? WHAT ARE THEY TALKING ABOUT?
WHY AM I A SOURCE OF INFOR-MATION ...?
S--
OH, HO...
SAKURAI-SAN?!!

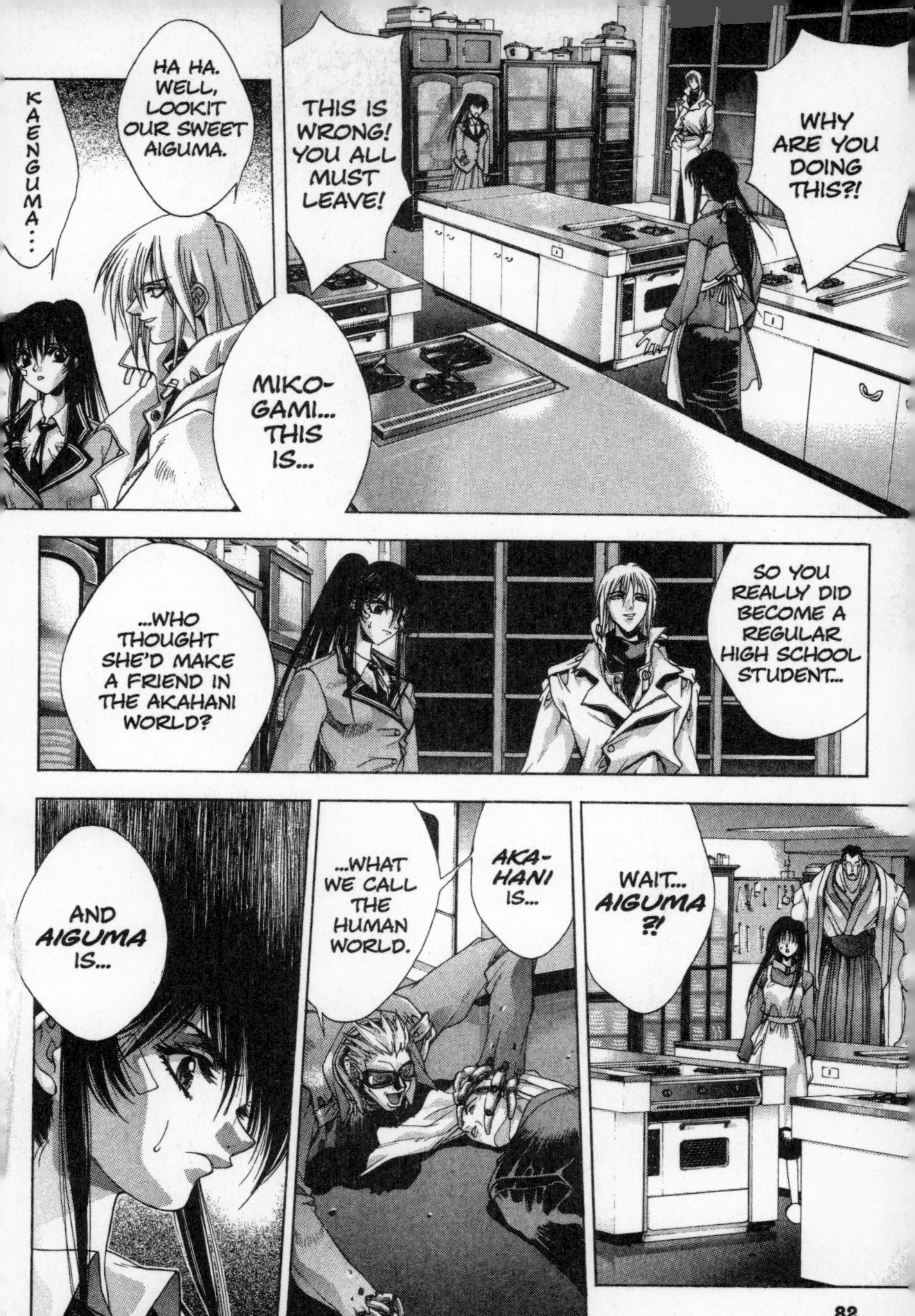
WHY ARE YOU DOING THIS?!
THIS IS WRONG! YOU ALL MUST LEAVE!
MIKO-GAMI... THIS IS...
HA HA. WELL, LOOKIT OUR SWEET AIGUMA.
KAENGUMA...
SO YOU REALLY DID BECOME A REGULAR HIGH SCHOOL STUDENT...
...WHO THOUGHT SHE'D MAKE A FRIEND IN THE AKAHANI WORLD?
WAIT... AIGUMA?!
AKA-HANI IS...
...WHAT WE CALL THE HUMAN WORLD.
AND AIGUMA IS...

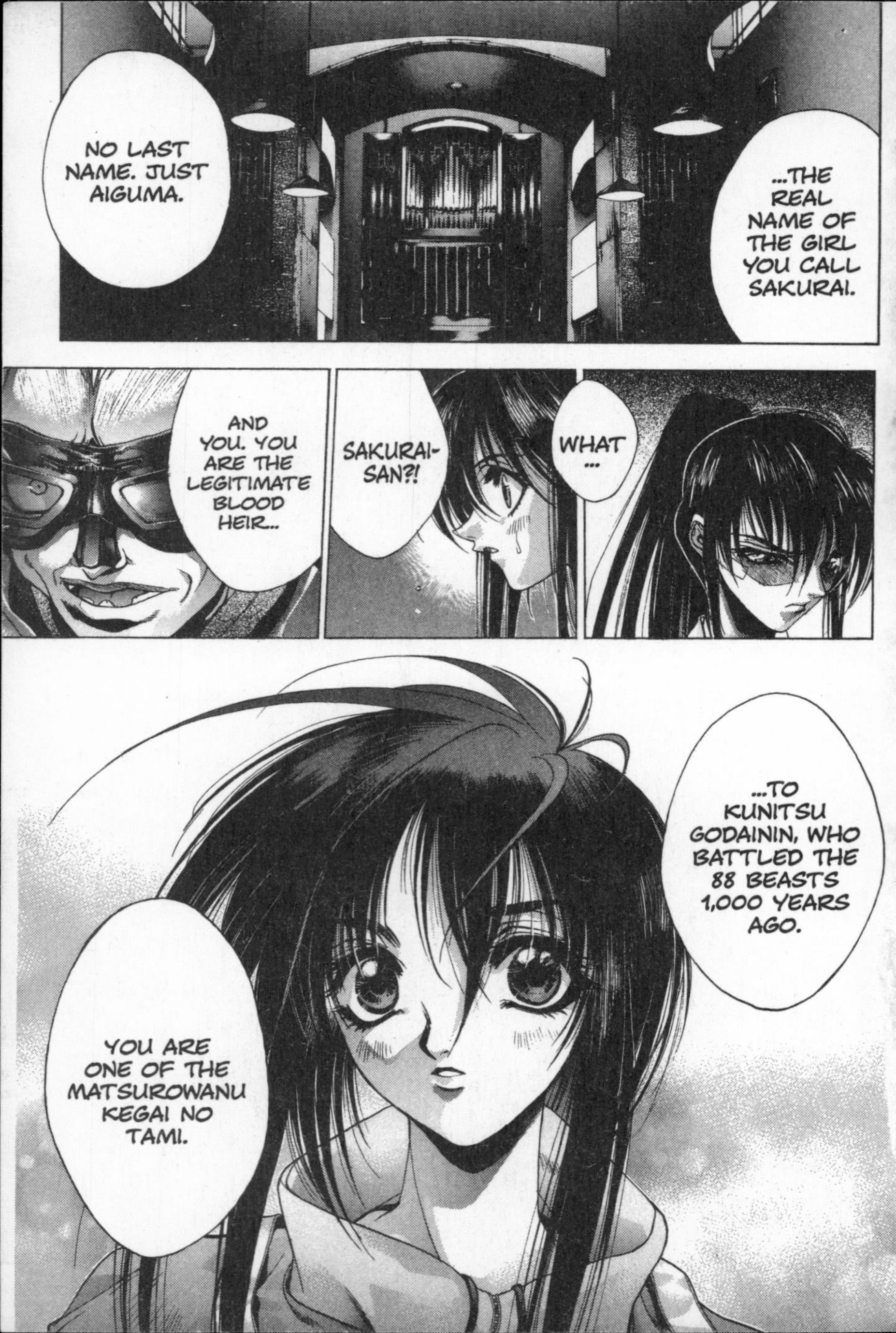
...THE REAL NAME OF THE GIRL YOU CALL SAKURAI.
NO LAST NAME. JUST AIGUMA.
WHAT ...
SAKURAI-SAN?!
AND YOU. YOU ARE THE LEGITIMATE BLOOD HEIR...
...TO KUNITSU GODAININ, WHO BATTLED THE 88 BEASTS 1,000 YEARS AGO.
YOU ARE ONE OF THE MATSUROWANU KEGAI NO TAMI.

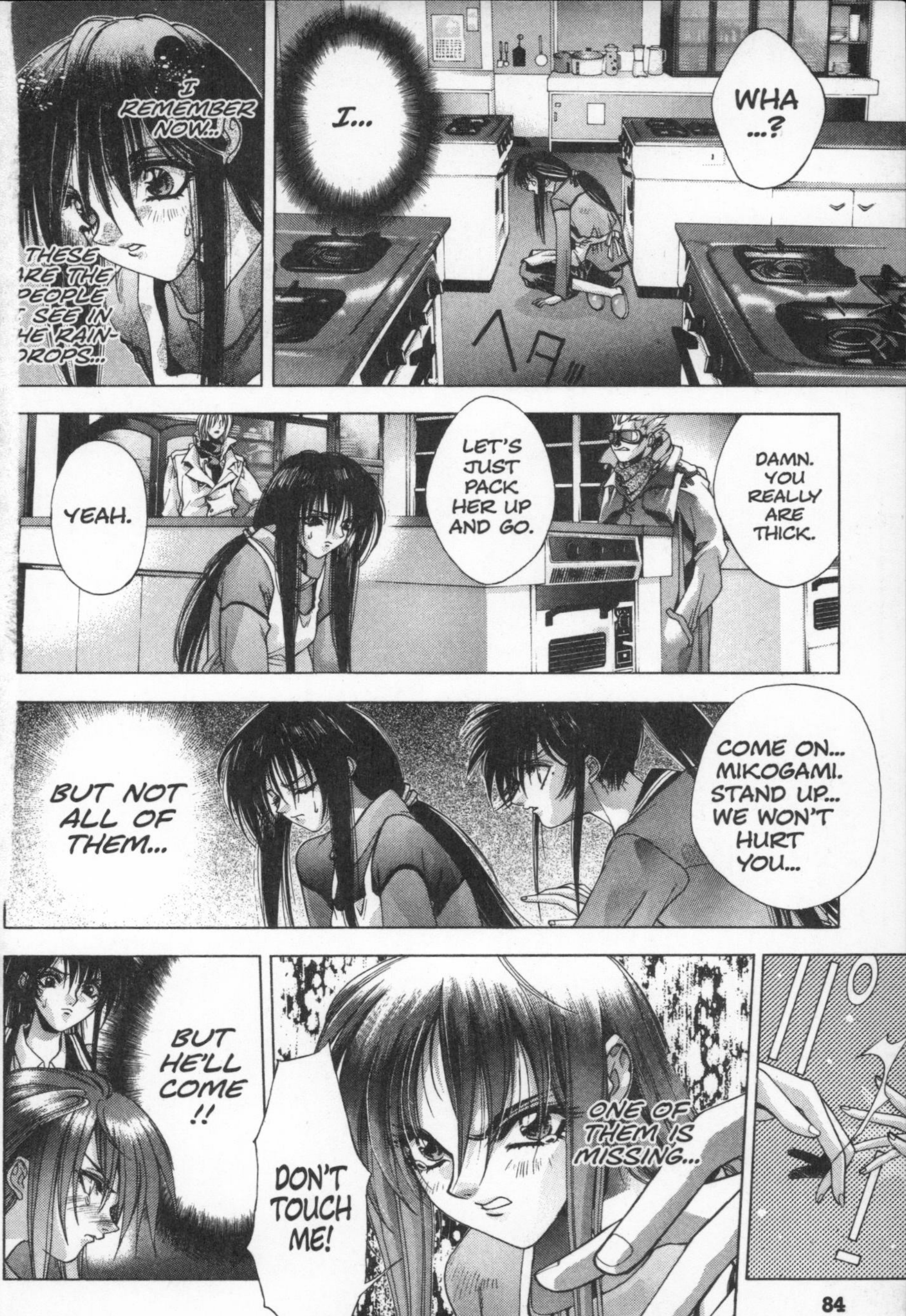
WHA ...?
I...
I REMEMBER NOW...
THESE ARE THE PEOPLE I SEE IN THE RAIN-DROPS...
DAMN. YOU REALLY ARE THICK.
LET'S JUST PACK HER UP AND GO.
YEAH.
COME ON... MIKOGAMI. STAND UP... WE WON'T HURT YOU...
BUT NOT ALL OF THEM...
ONE OF THEM IS MISSING...
DON'T TOUCH ME!
BUT HE'LL COME!!

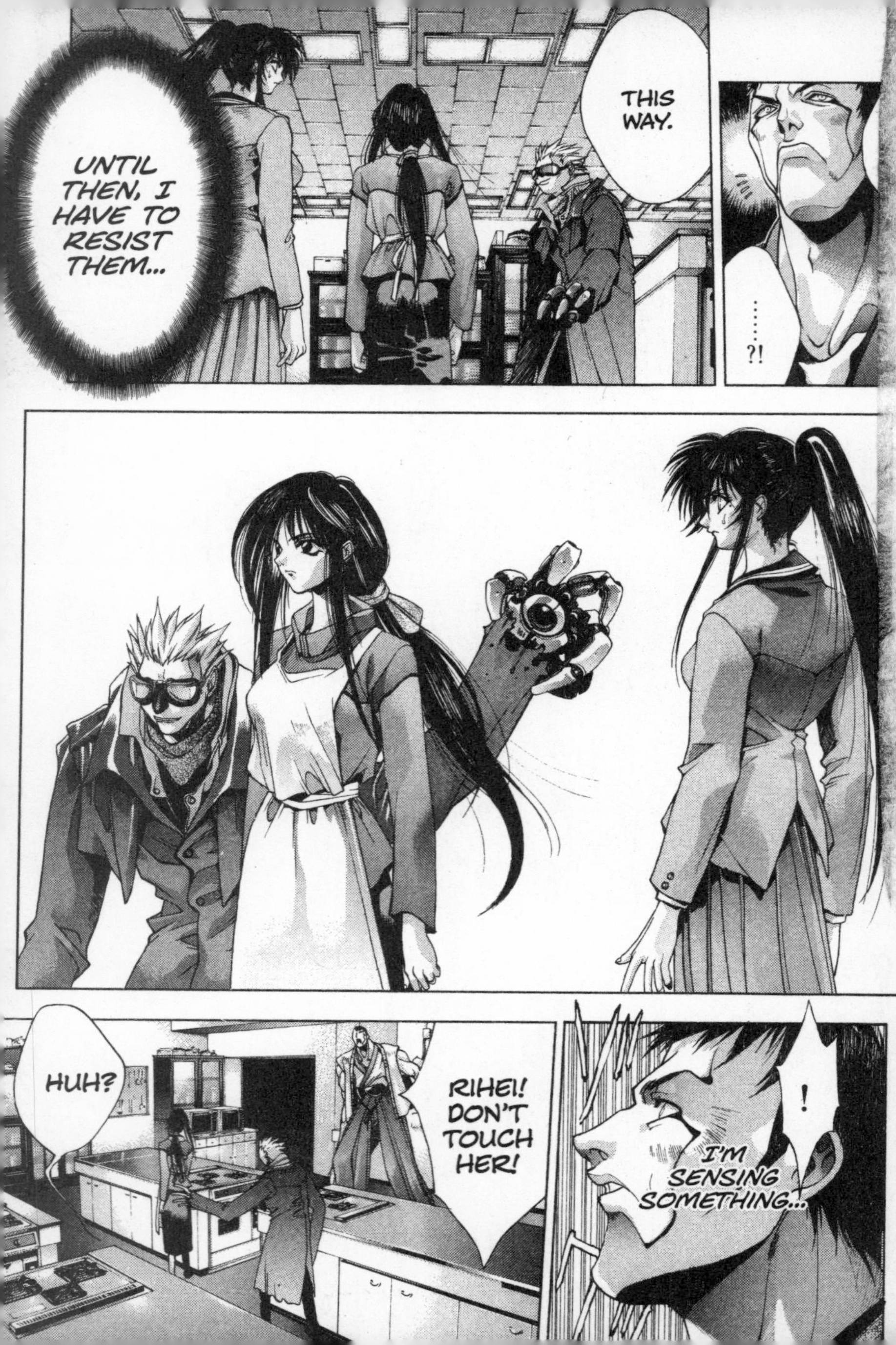
......
?!
THIS WAY.
UNTIL THEN, I HAVE TO RESIST THEM...
!
I'M SENSING SOMETHING...
RIHEI! DON'T TOUCH HER!
HUH?

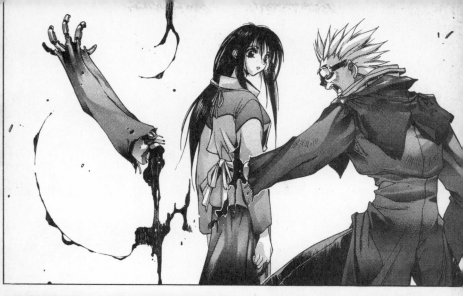

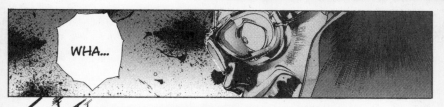

WHA...

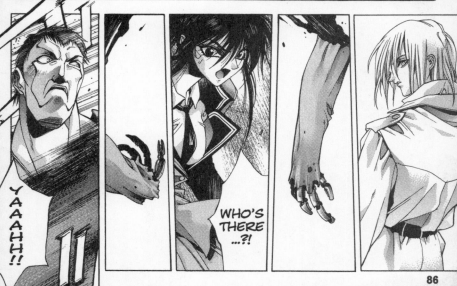

YAAAHH!!

WHO'S
THERE
...?!

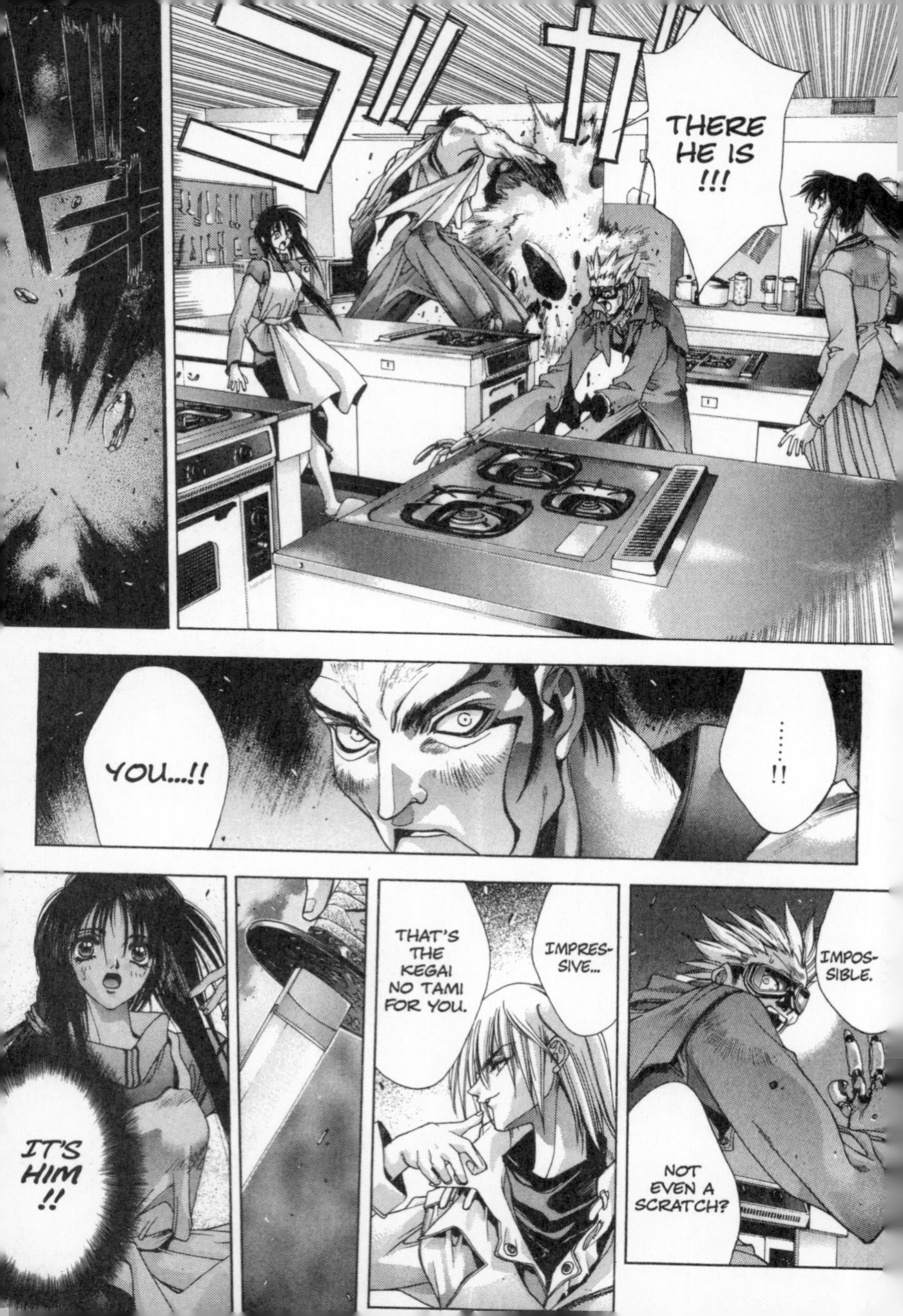
THERE HE IS !!!
......!!
YOU...!!
IMPOS-SIBLE.
NOT EVEN A SCRATCH?
IMPRES-SIVE...
THAT'S THE KEGAI NO TAMI FOR YOU.
IT'S HIM !!

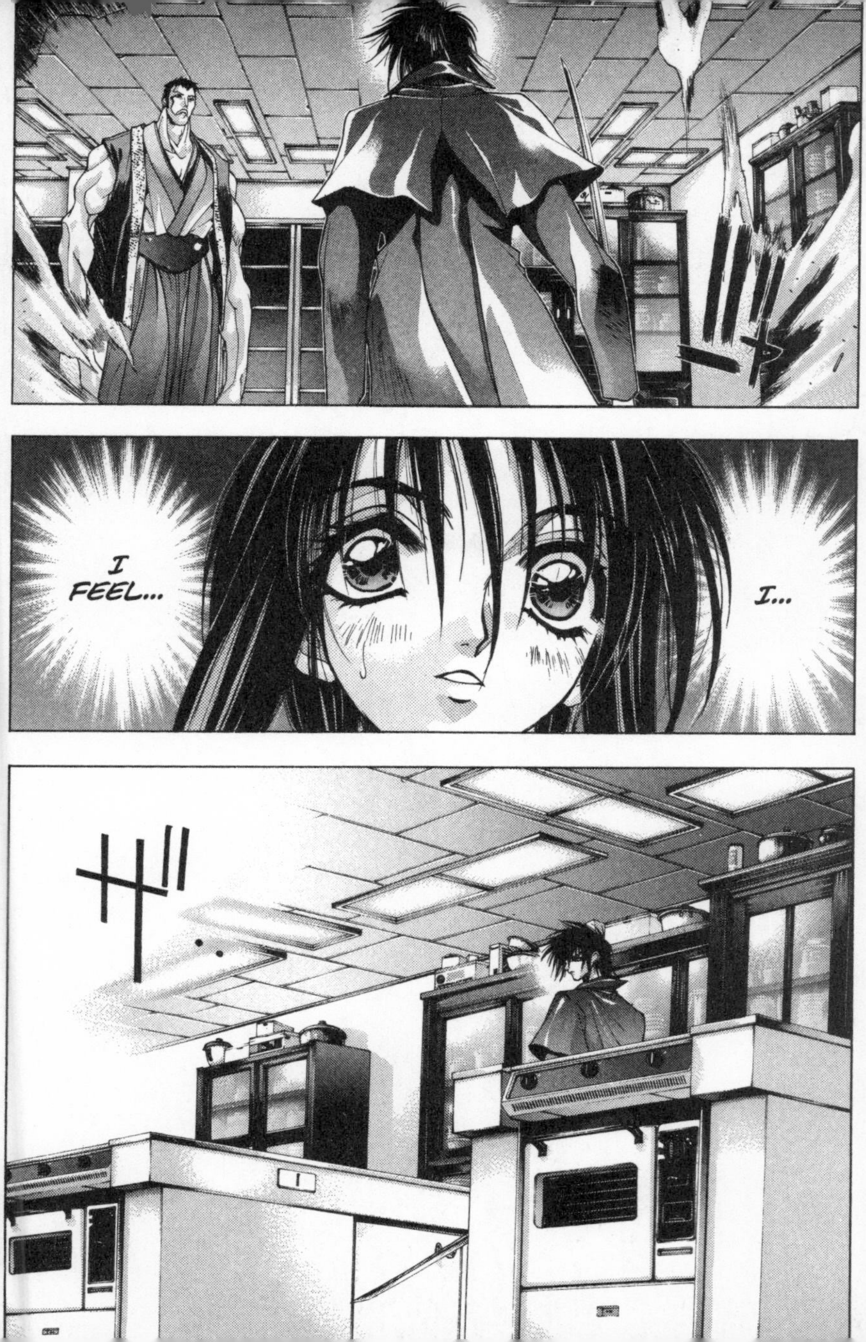
I...
I FEEL...

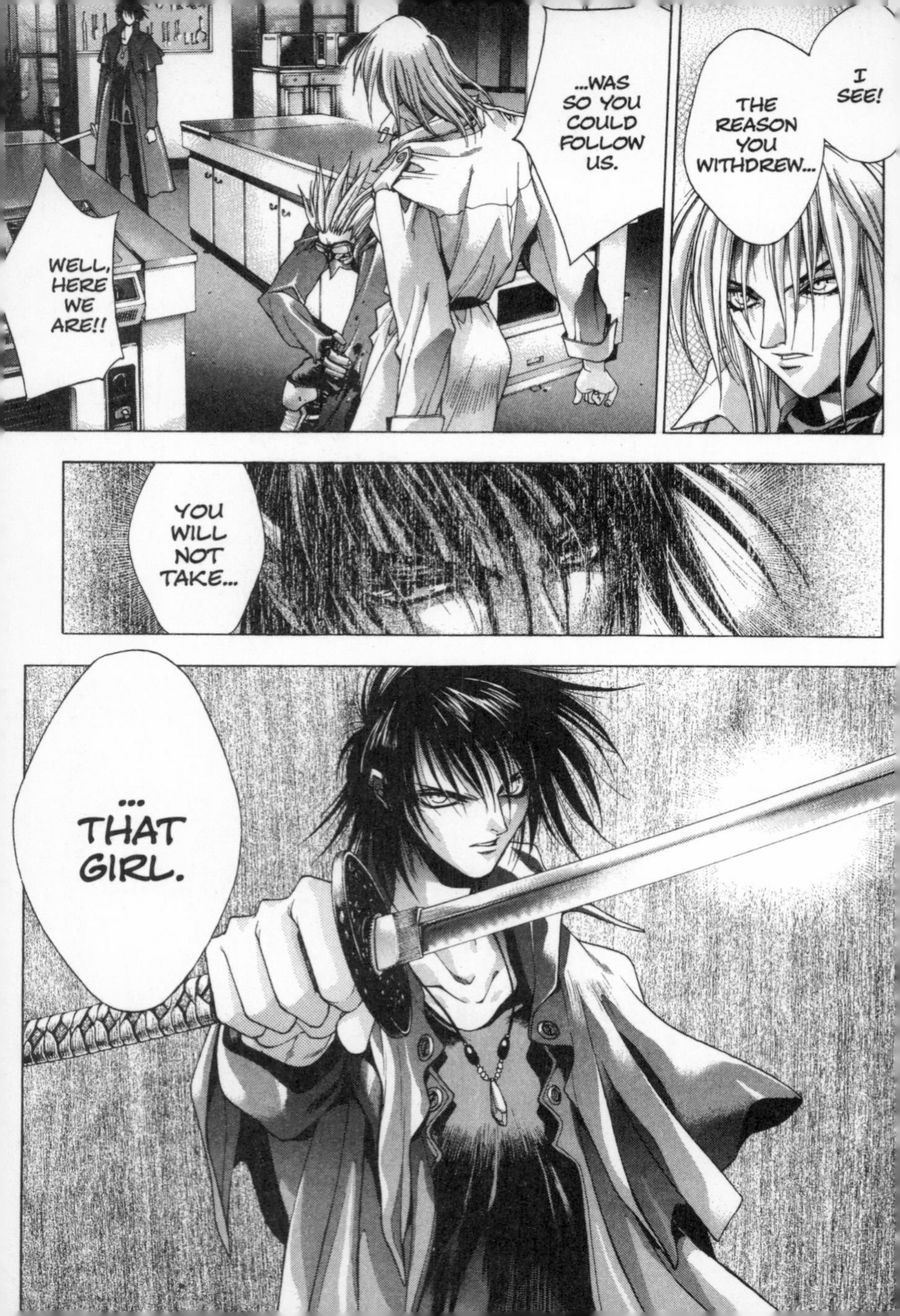
I SEE!
THE REASON YOU WITHDREW...
...WAS SO YOU COULD FOLLOW US.
WELL, HERE WE ARE!!
YOU WILL NOT TAKE...
...THAT GIRL.

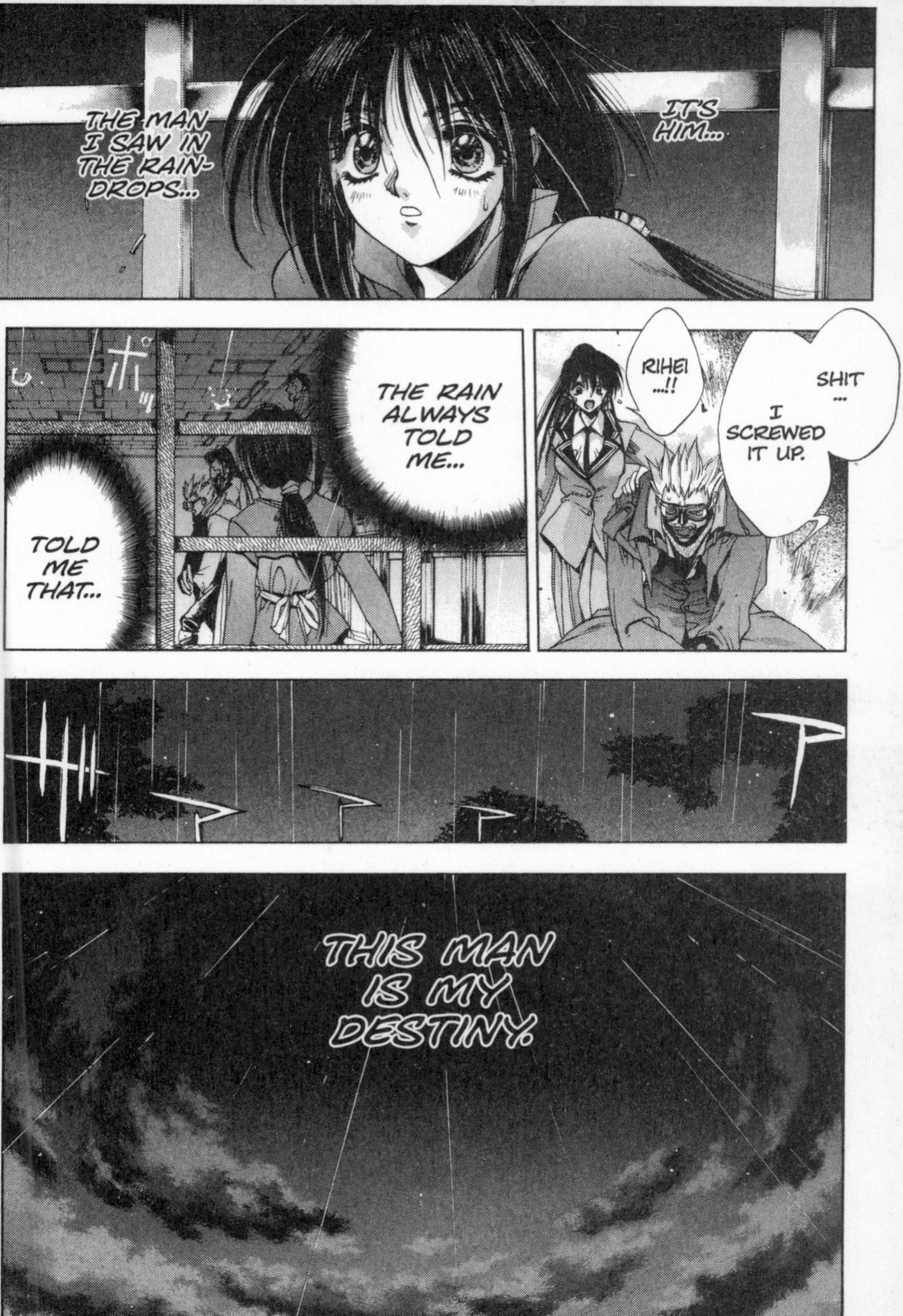
IT'S HIM...
THE MAN I SAW IN THE RAIN-DROPS...
RIHEI ...!!
SHIT ... I SCREWED IT UP.
THE RAIN ALWAYS TOLD ME...
TOLD ME THAT...
THIS MAN IS MY DESTINY.

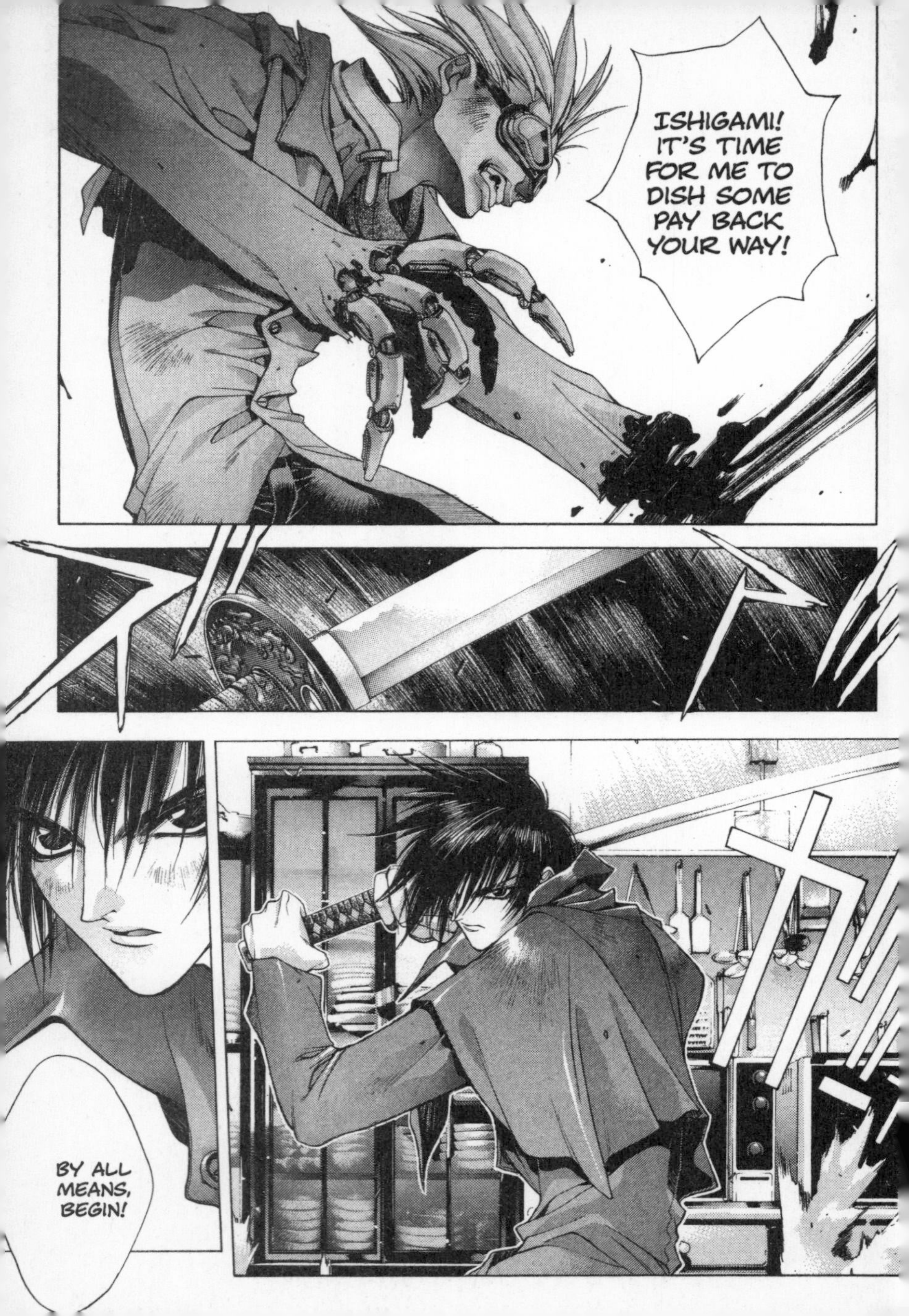
ISHIGAMI! IT'S TIME FOR ME TO DISH SOME PAY BACK YOUR WAY!
BY ALL MEANS, BEGIN!

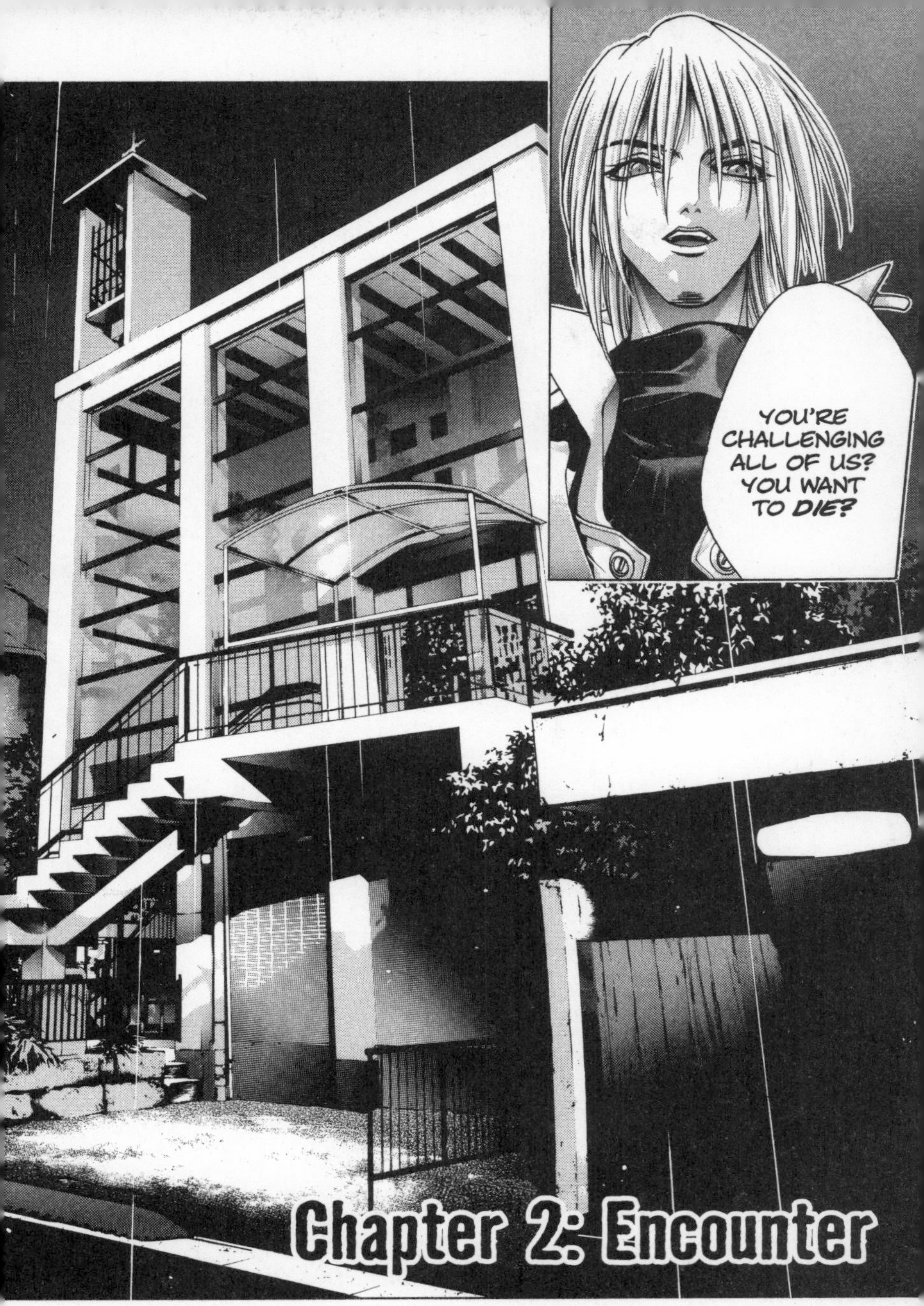
YOU'RE CHALLENGING ALL OF US? YOU WANT TO *DIE*?
Chapter 2: Encounter

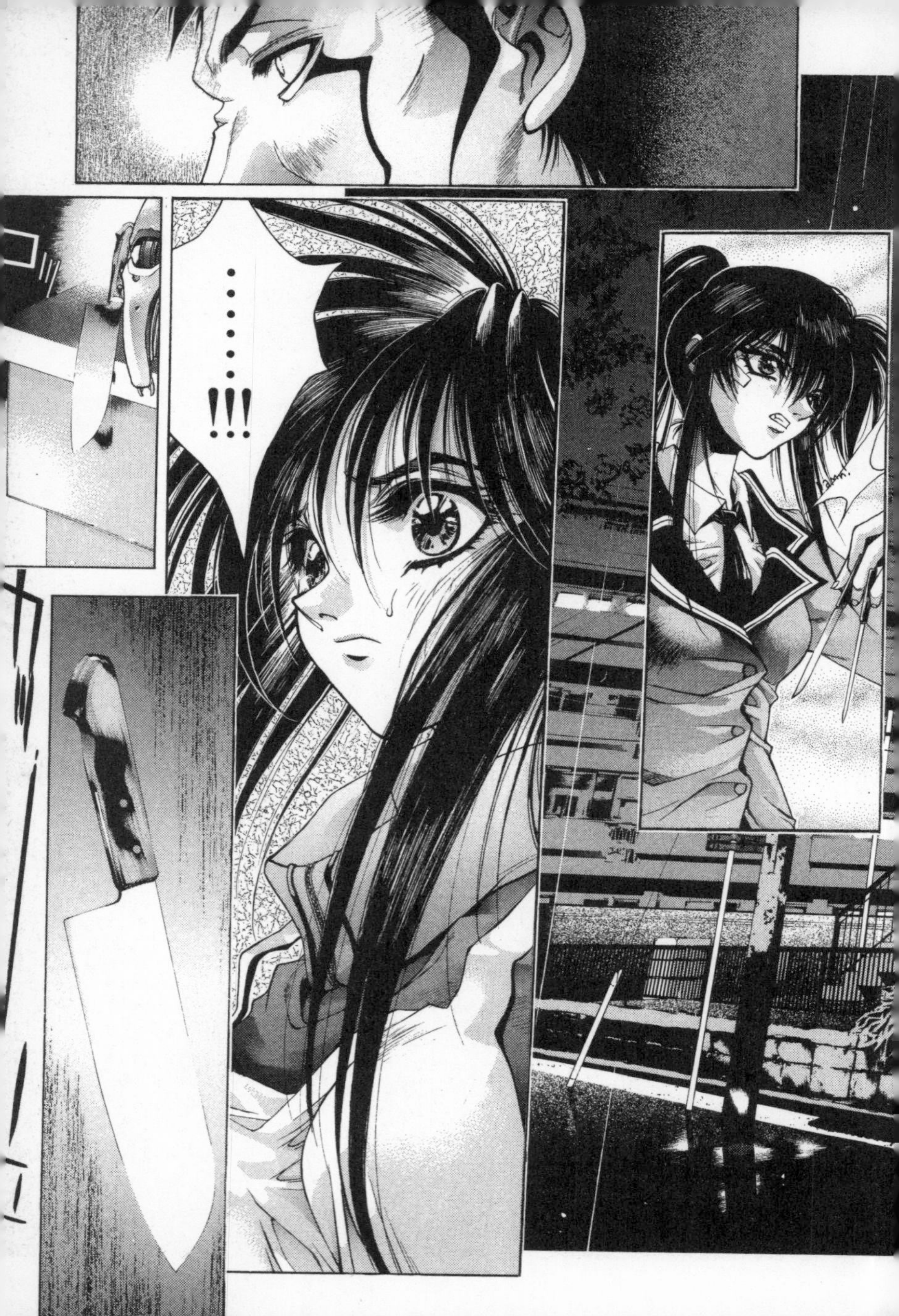
......!!!

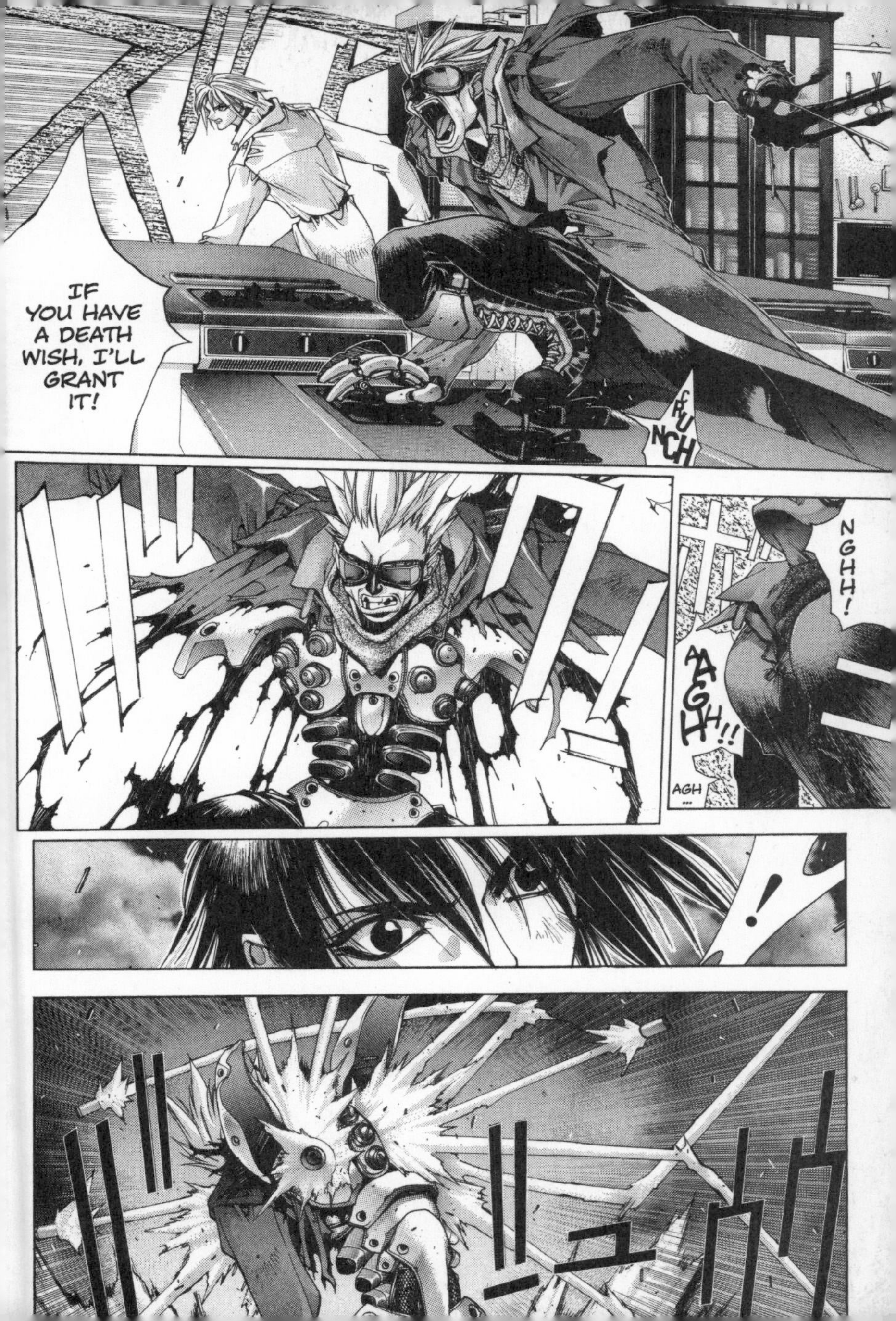
IF YOU HAVE A DEATH WISH, I'LL GRANT IT!
CRUNCH
NGHH!
AAGH!!
AGH ...

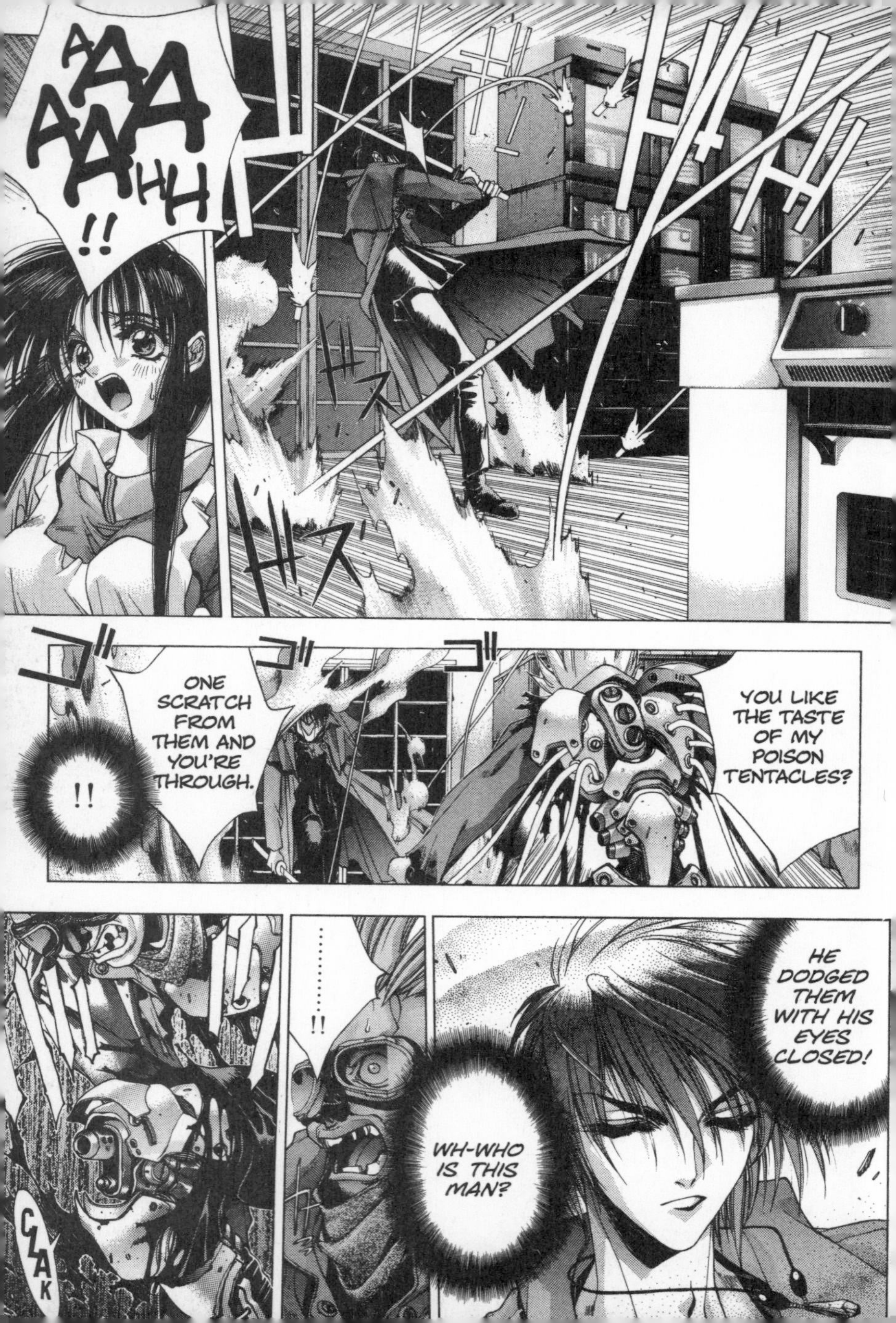
AAAAAAHH!!
YOU LIKE THE TASTE OF MY POISON TENTACLES?
ONE SCRATCH FROM THEM AND YOU'RE THROUGH.
!!
HE DODGED THEM WITH HIS EYES CLOSED!
WH-WHO IS THIS MAN?
......!!
CLAK

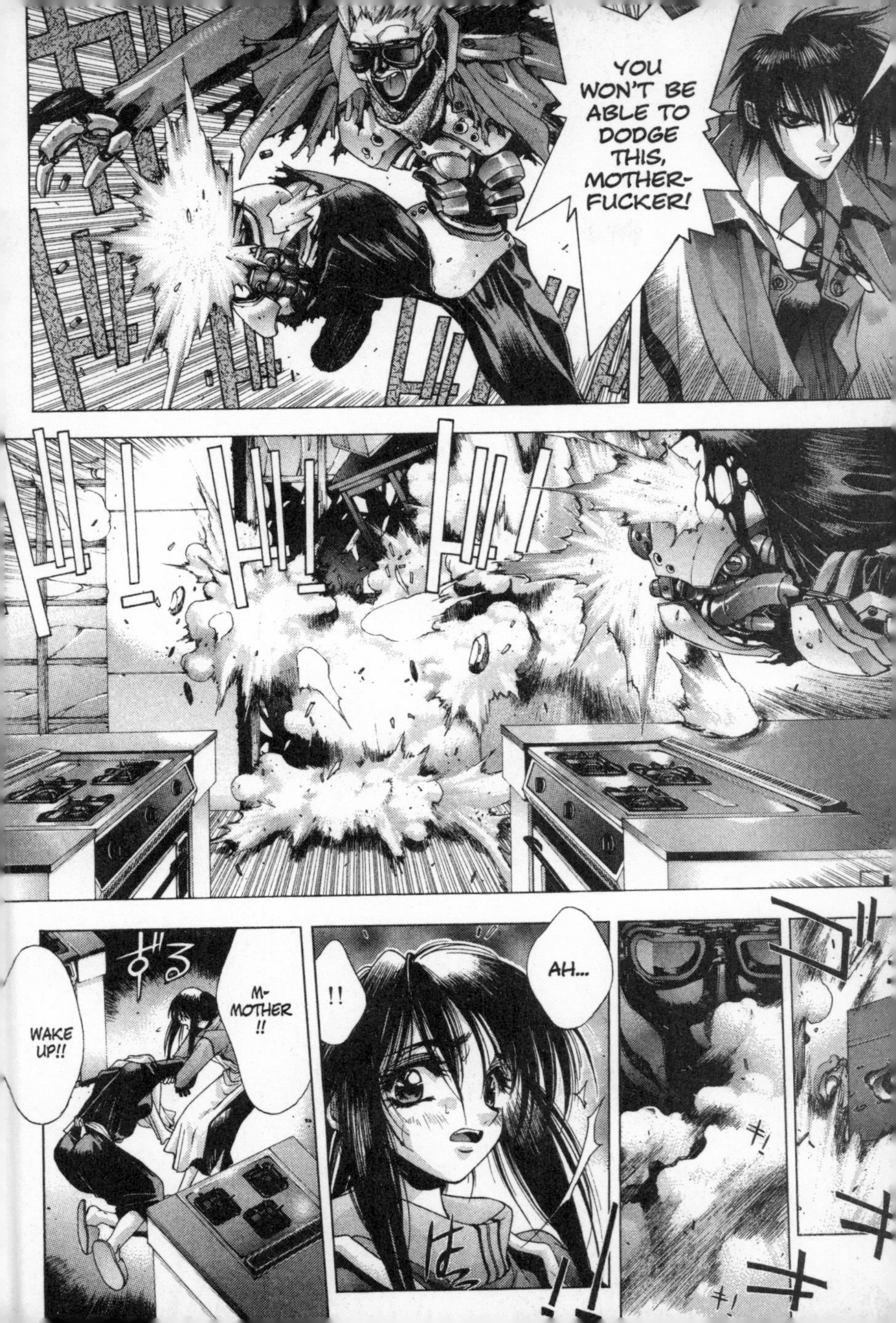
YOU WON'T BE ABLE TO DODGE THIS, MOTHER-FUCKER!
AH...
!!
M-MOTHER !!
ずる
WAKE UP!!

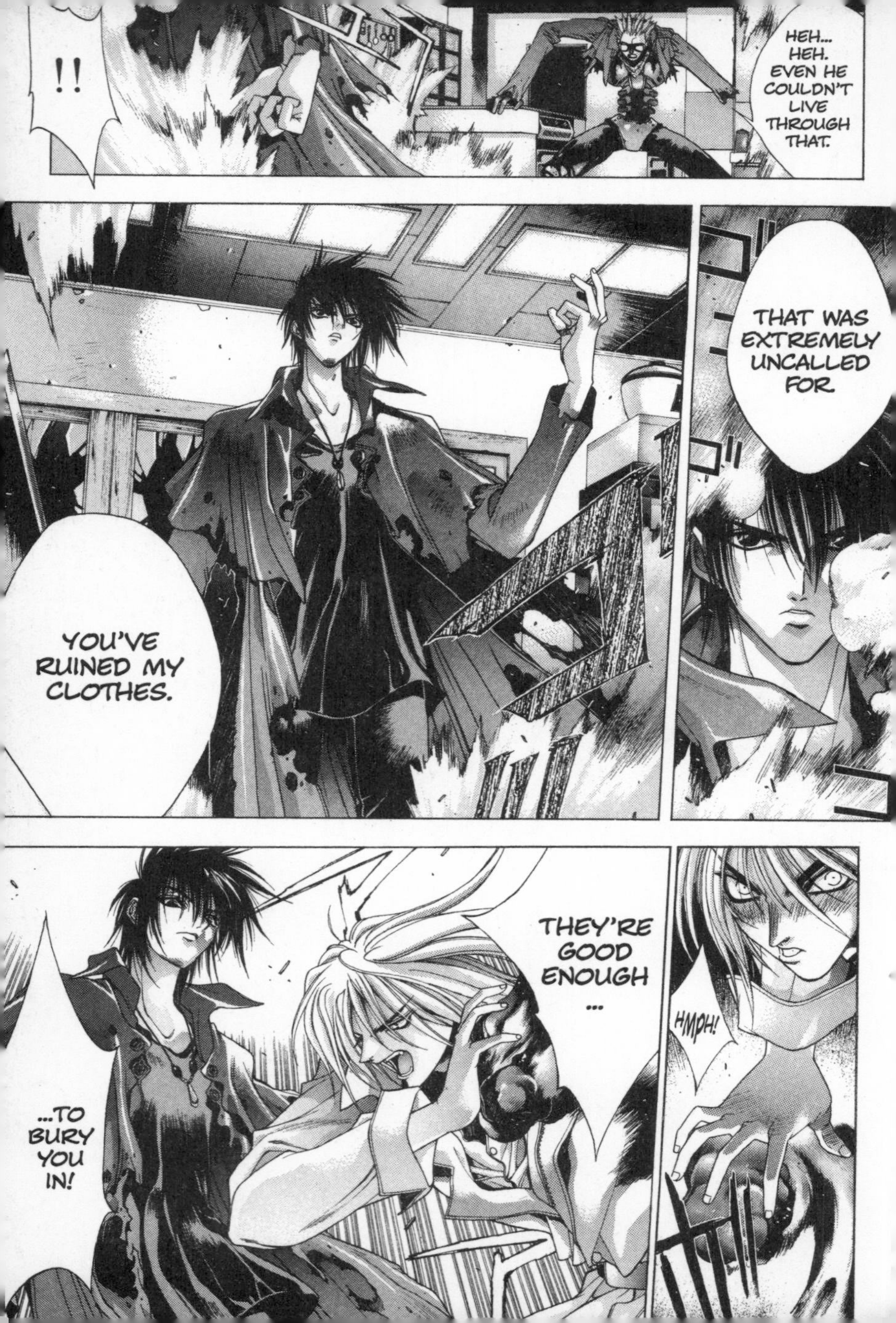
HEH... HEH. EVEN HE COULDN'T LIVE THROUGH THAT.
!!
THAT WAS EXTREMELY UNCALLED FOR.
YOU'VE RUINED MY CLOTHES.
HMPH!
THEY'RE GOOD ENOUGH ...
...TO BURY YOU IN!

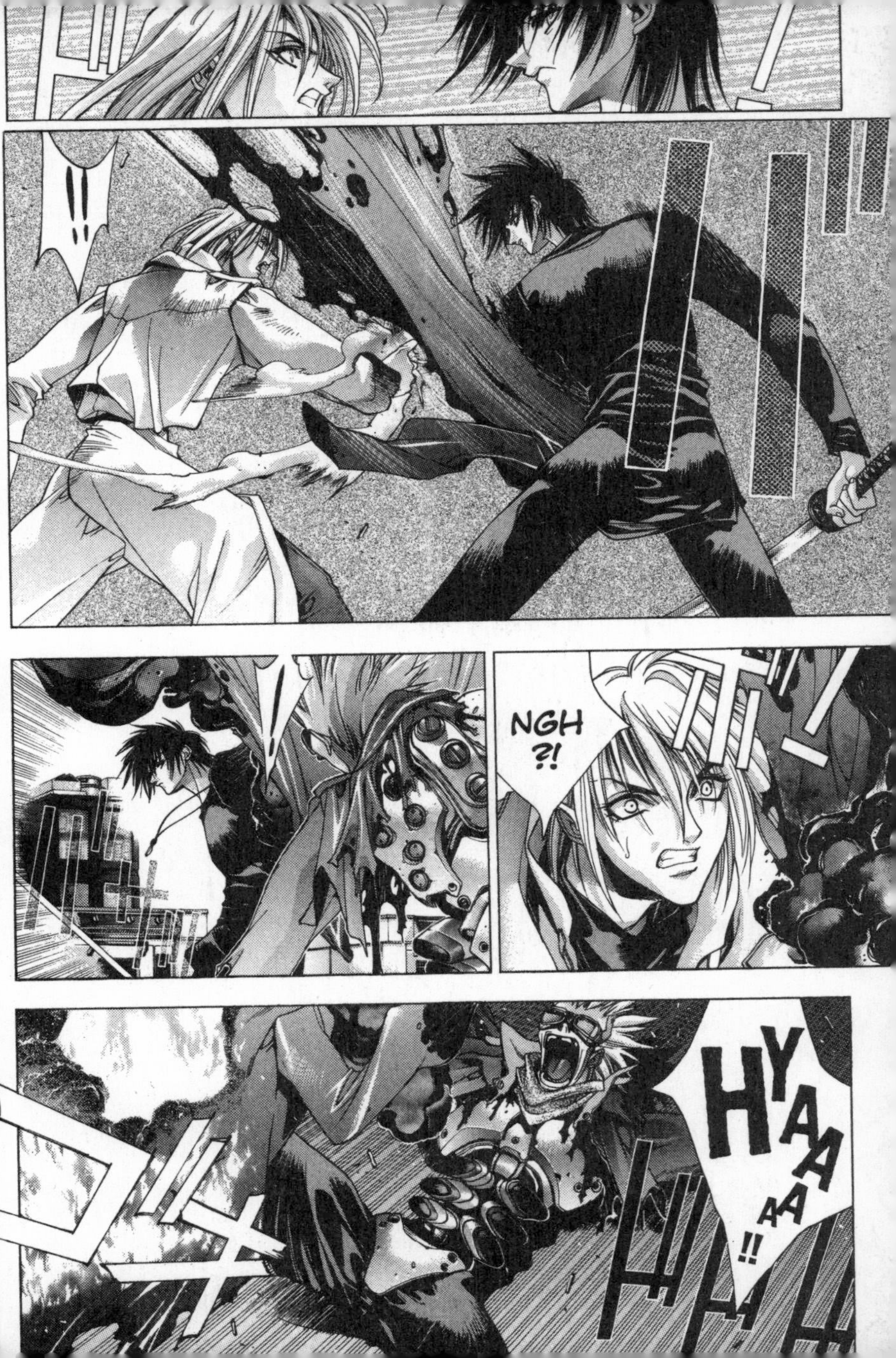
!!
NGH ?!
HYAAAAA!!

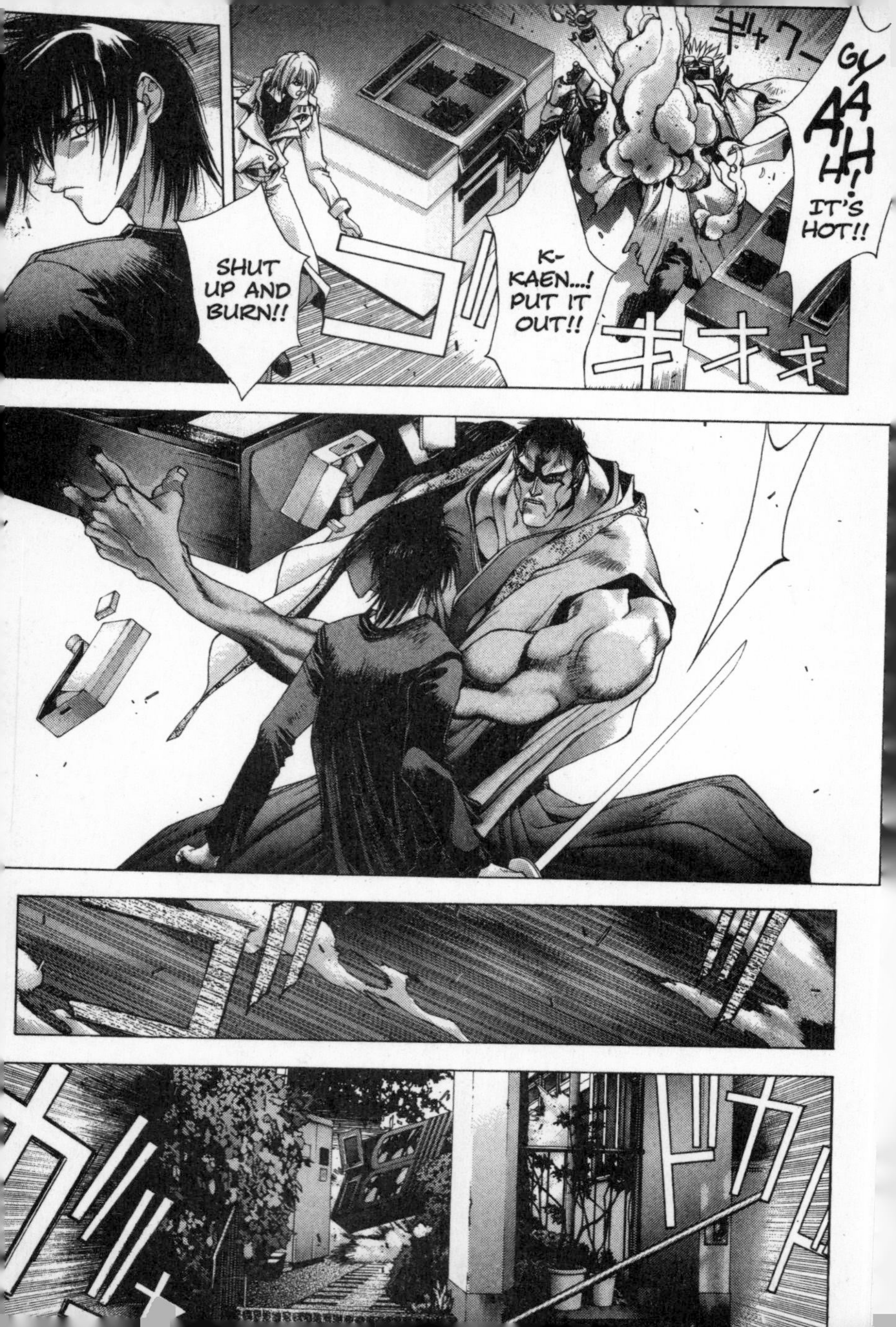
GYAAHH!
IT'S HOT!!
K-KAEN...! PUT IT OUT!!
SHUT UP AND BURN!!

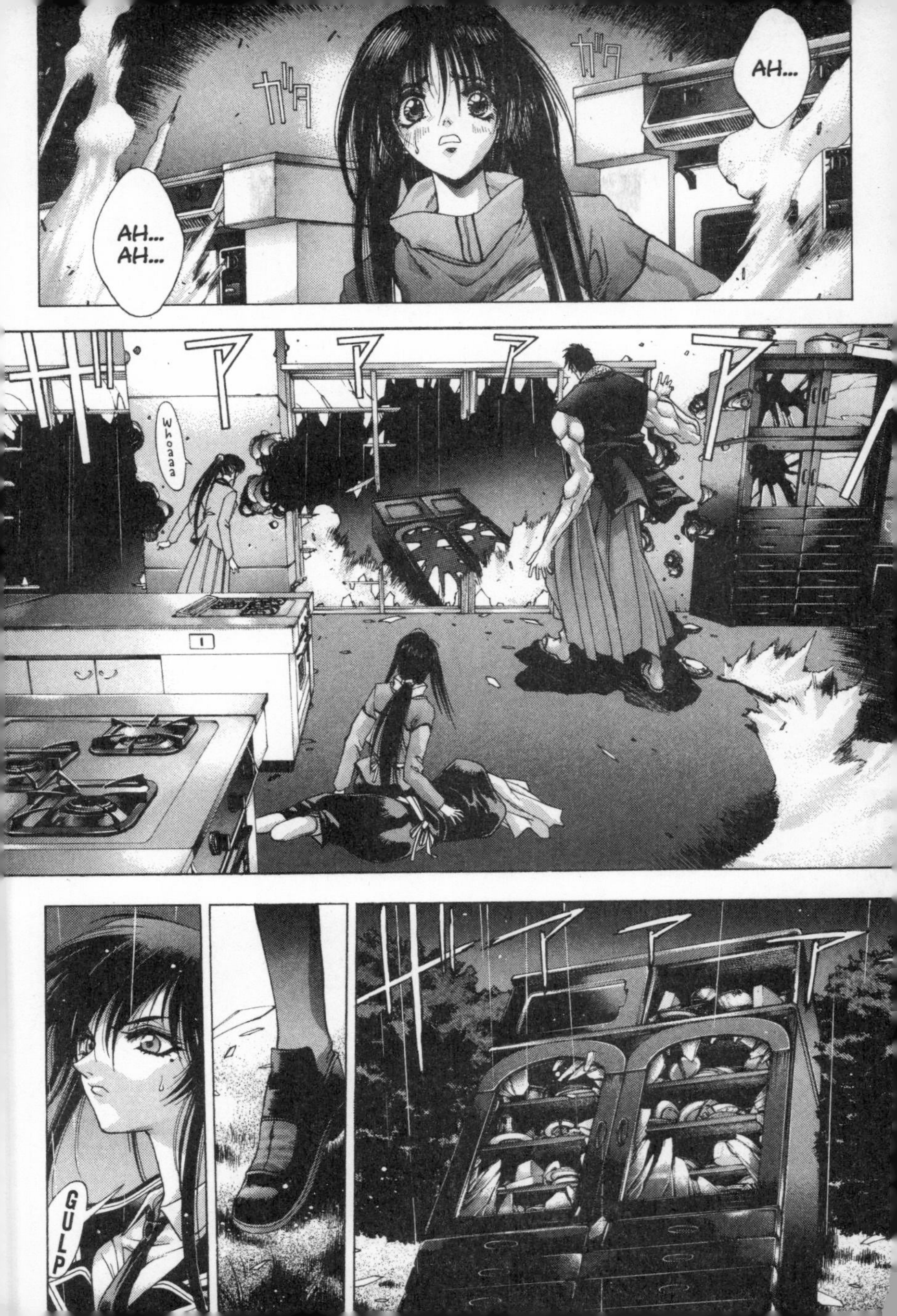
AH...
AH...
AH...
Whoaaa
GULP

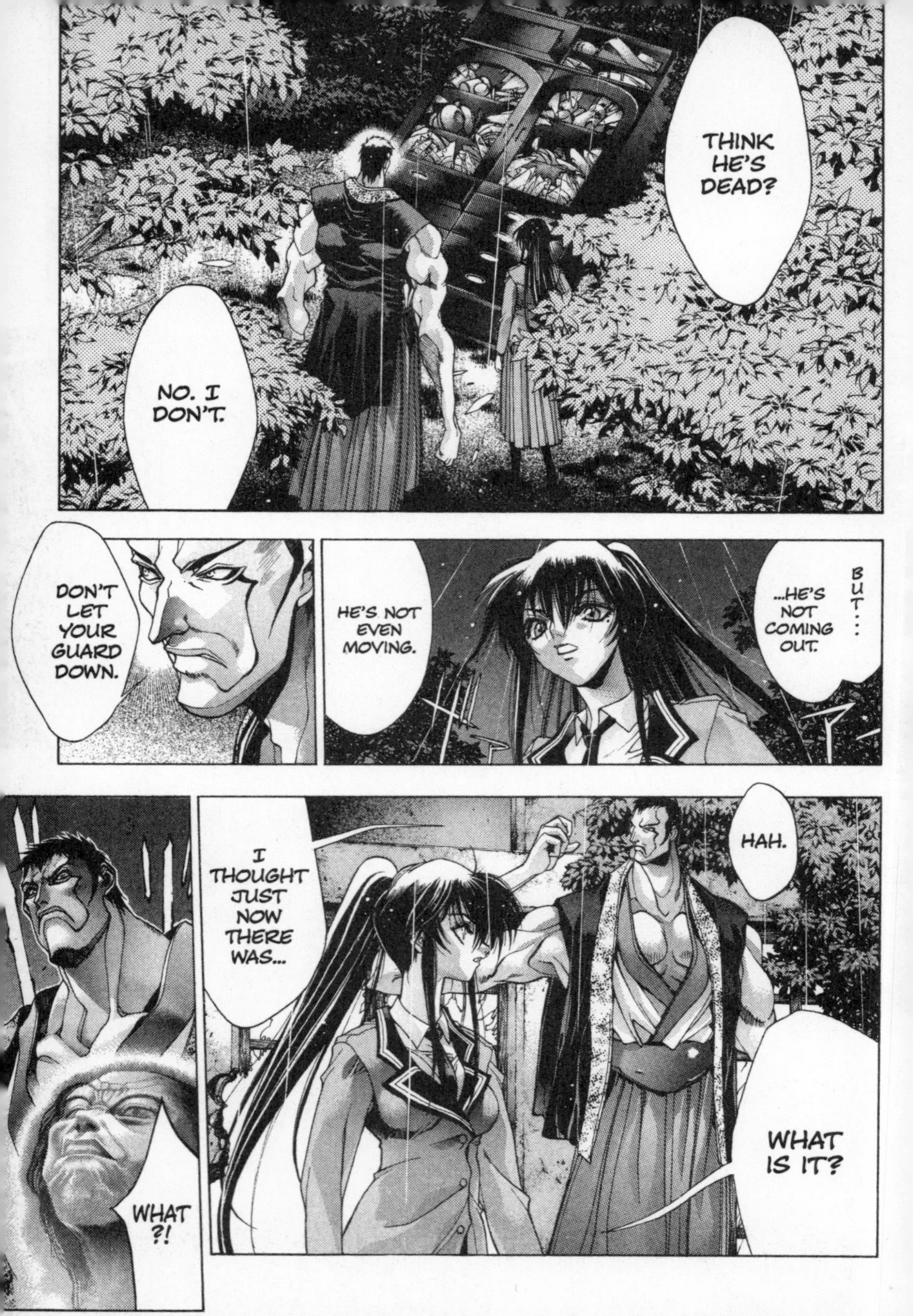
THINK HE'S DEAD?
NO. I DON'T.
BUT...
...HE'S NOT COMING OUT.
HE'S NOT EVEN MOVING.
DON'T LET YOUR GUARD DOWN.
HAH.
I THOUGHT JUST NOW THERE WAS...
WHAT IS IT?
WHAT?!

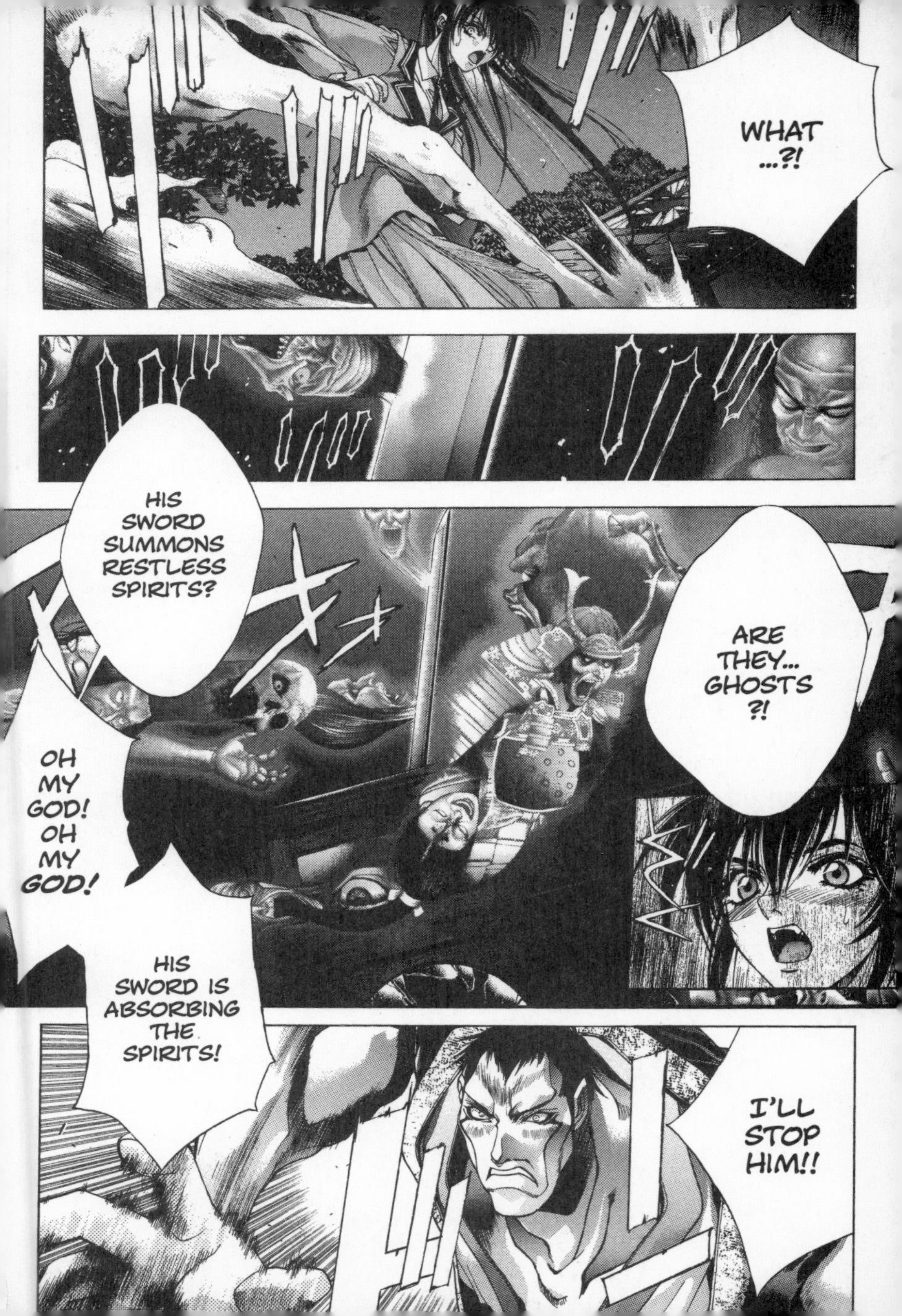
WHAT ...?!
ARE THEY... GHOSTS ?!
HIS SWORD SUMMONS RESTLESS SPIRITS?
OH MY GOD! OH MY GOD!
HIS SWORD IS ABSORBING THE SPIRITS!
I'LL STOP HIM!!

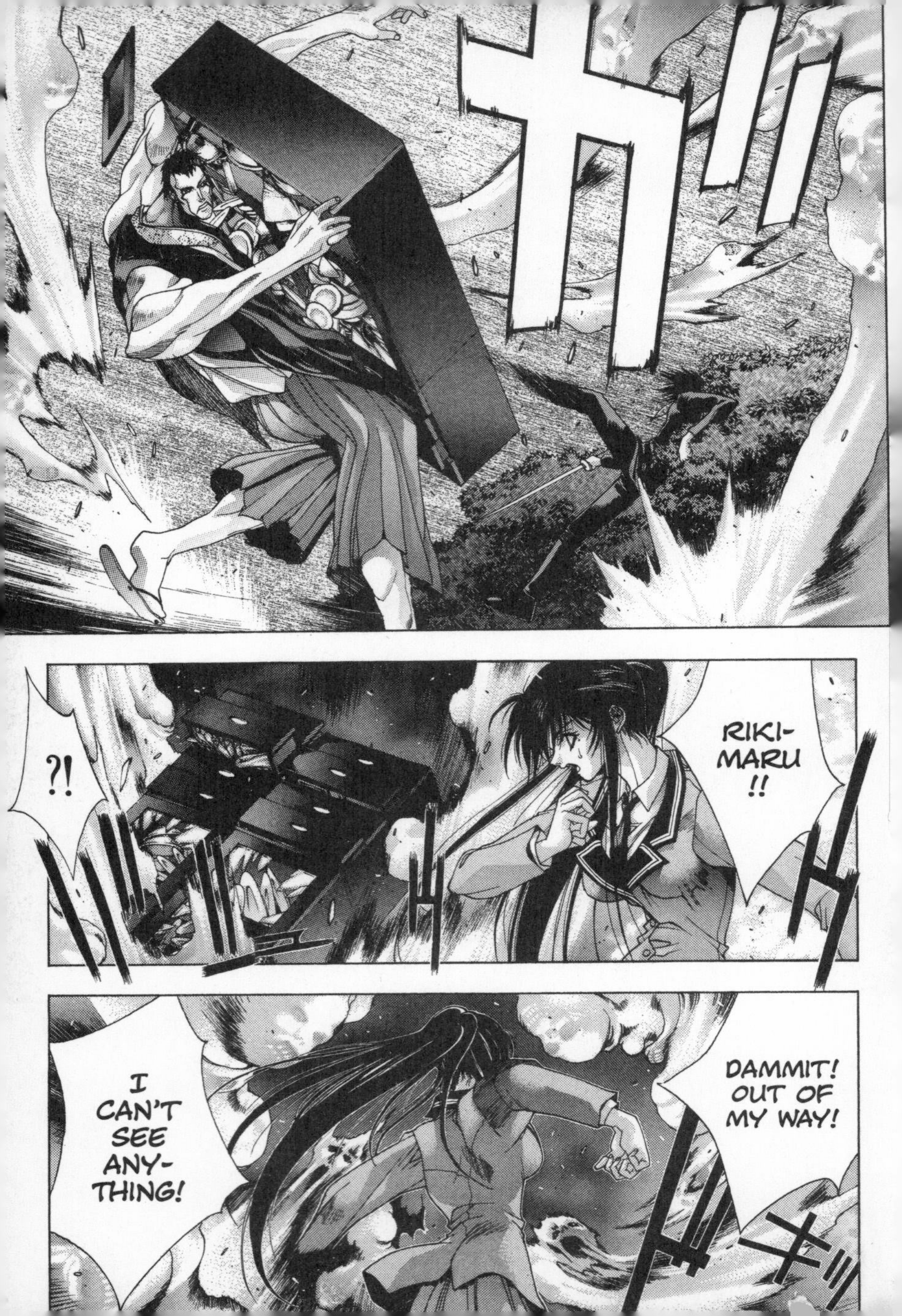
RIKI-MARU !!
?!
DAMMIT! OUT OF MY WAY!
I CAN'T SEE ANY-THING!

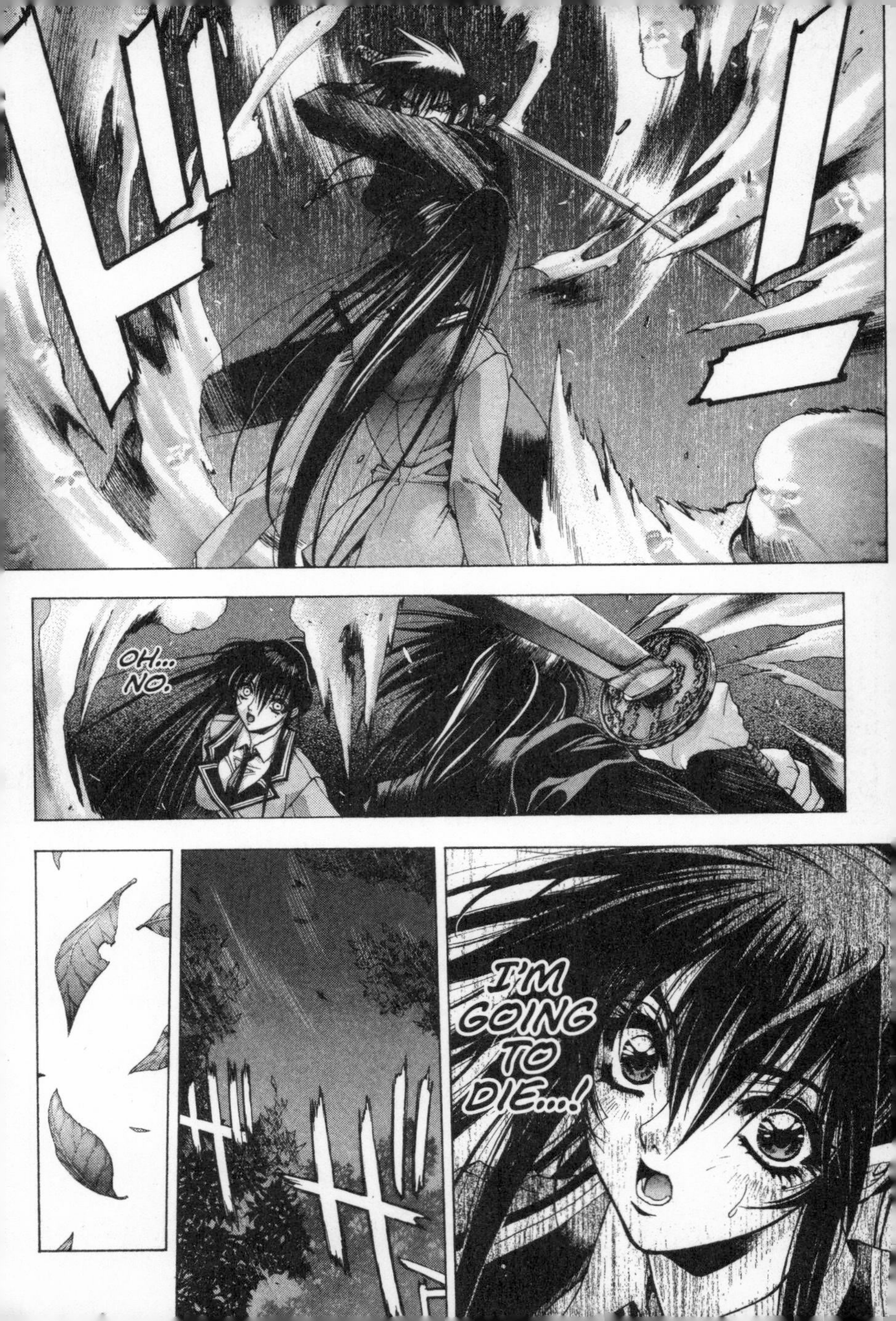
OH... NO.
I'M GOING TO DIE...!

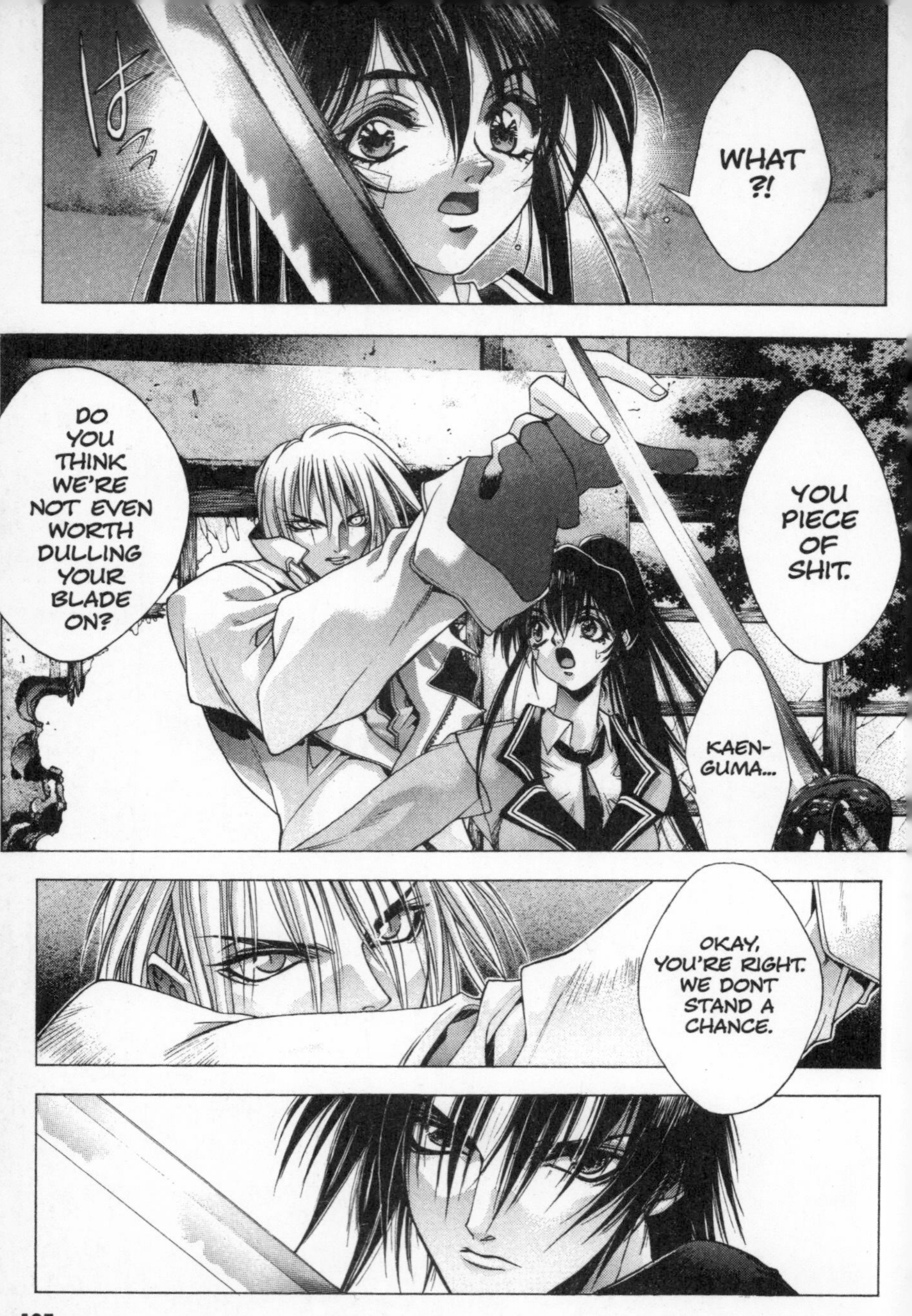
はっ
WHAT ?!
YOU PIECE OF SHIT.
DO YOU THINK WE'RE NOT EVEN WORTH DULLING YOUR BLADE ON?
KAEN-GUMA...
OKAY, YOU'RE RIGHT. WE DONT STAND A CHANCE.

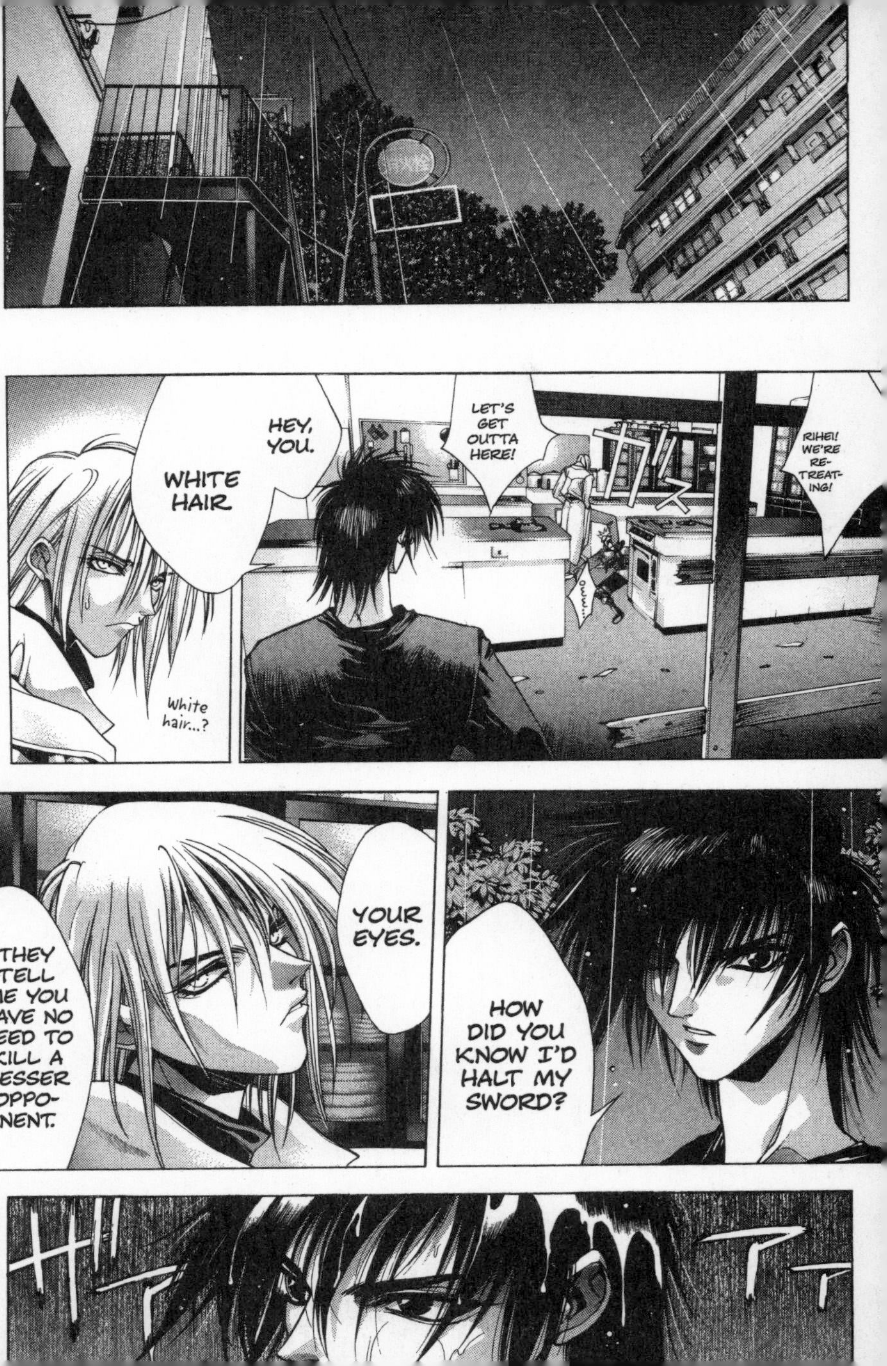
RIHEI! WE'RE RE-TREATING!
LET'S GET OUTTA HERE!
Oww...
HEY, YOU.
WHITE HAIR
White hair...?
HOW DID YOU KNOW I'D HALT MY SWORD?
YOUR EYES.
THEY TELL ME YOU HAVE NO NEED TO KILL A LESSER OPPO-NENT.

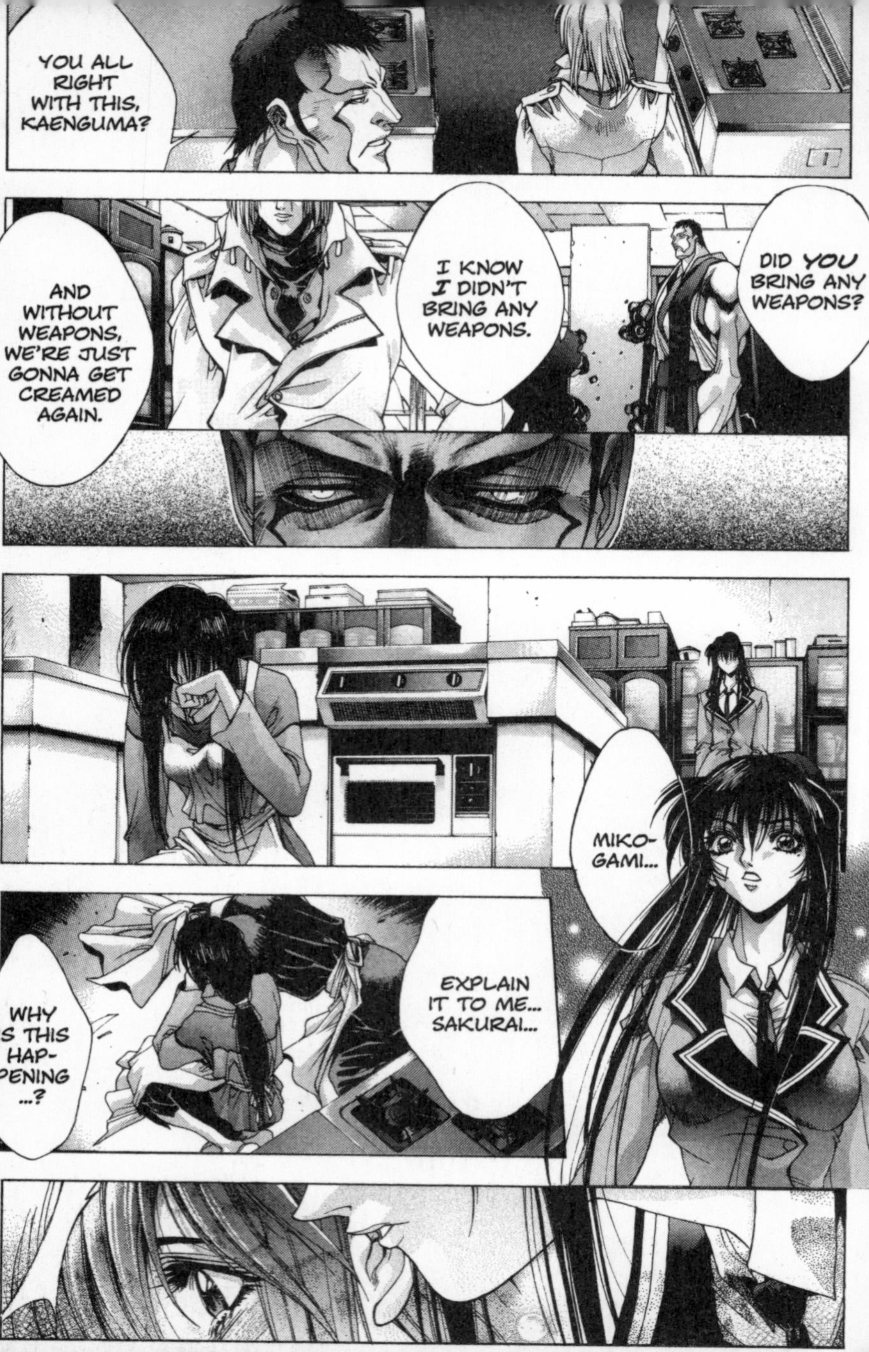
YOU ALL RIGHT WITH THIS, KAENGUMA?
DID YOU BRING ANY WEAPONS?
I KNOW I DIDN'T BRING ANY WEAPONS.
AND WITHOUT WEAPONS, WE'RE JUST GONNA GET CREAMED AGAIN.
MIKO-GAMI...
EXPLAIN IT TO ME... SAKURAI...
WHY IS THIS HAP-PENING ...?

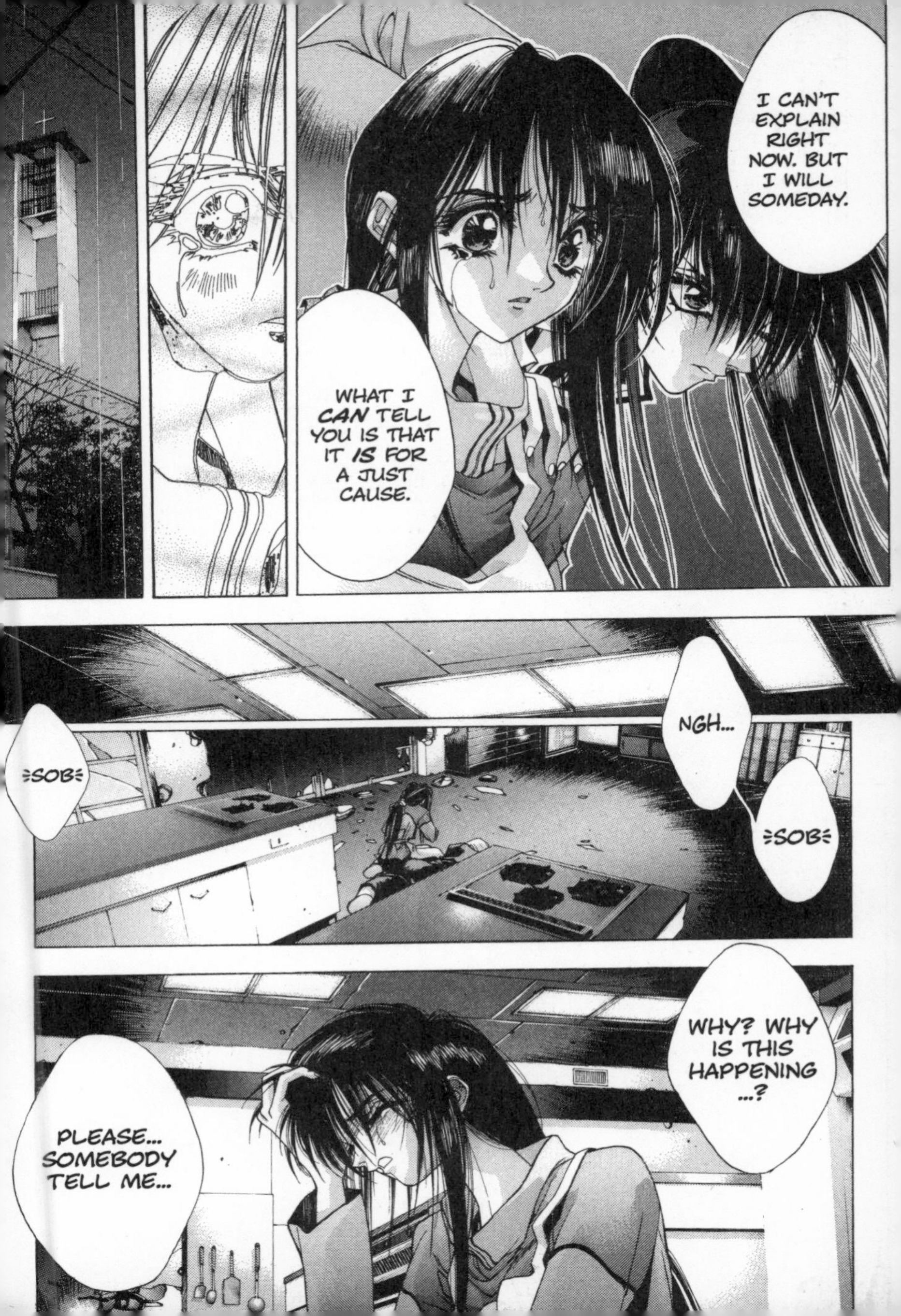
I CAN'T EXPLAIN RIGHT NOW. BUT I WILL SOMEDAY.
WHAT I *CAN* TELL YOU IS THAT IT *IS* FOR A JUST CAUSE.
NGH...
≈SOB≈
≈SOB≈
WHY? WHY IS THIS HAPPENING ...?
PLEASE... SOMEBODY TELL ME...

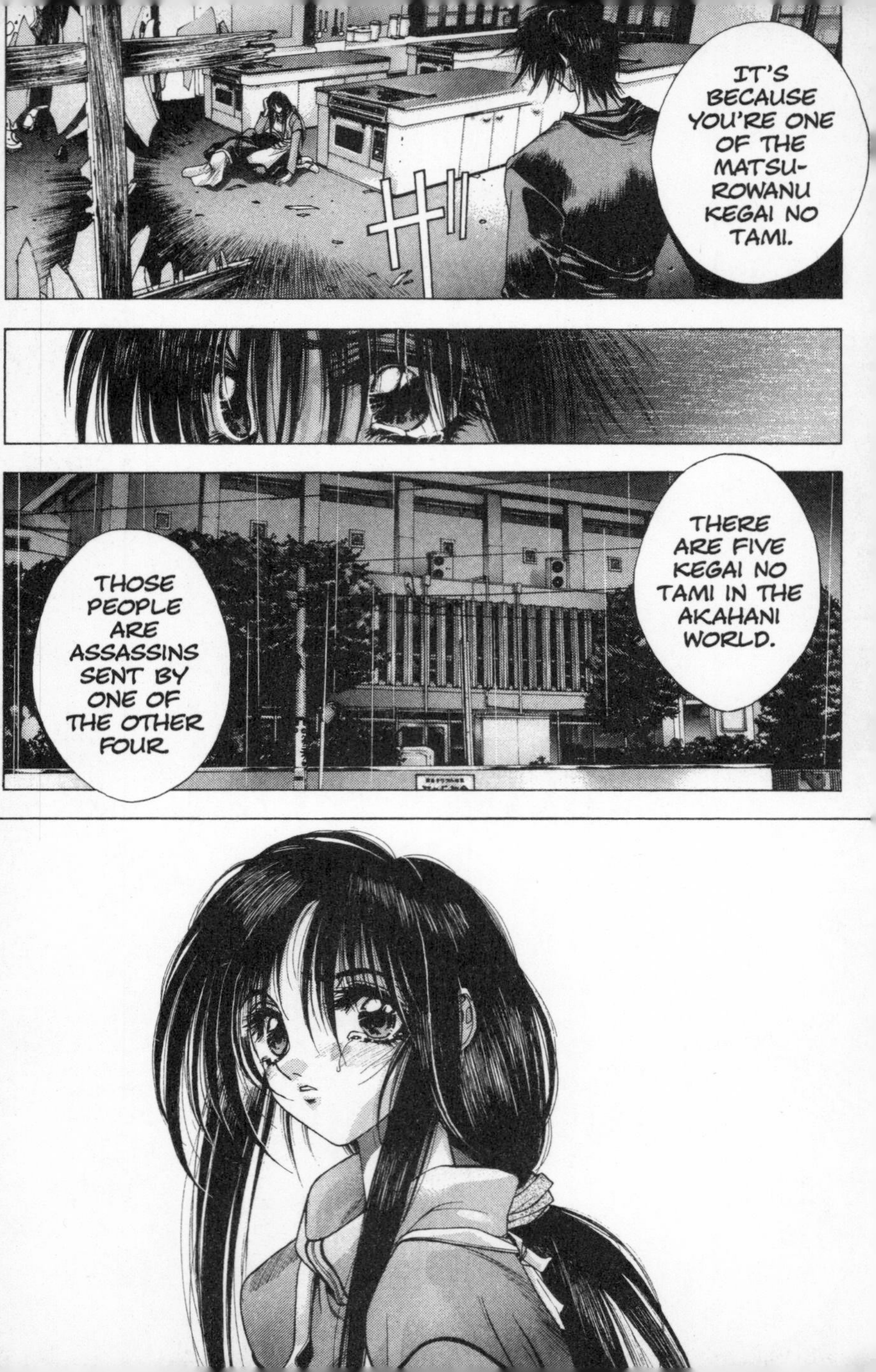
IT'S BECAUSE YOU'RE ONE OF THE MATSU-ROWANU KEGAI NO TAMI.
THERE ARE FIVE KEGAI NO TAMI IN THE AKAHANI WORLD.
THOSE PEOPLE ARE ASSASSINS SENT BY ONE OF THE OTHER FOUR

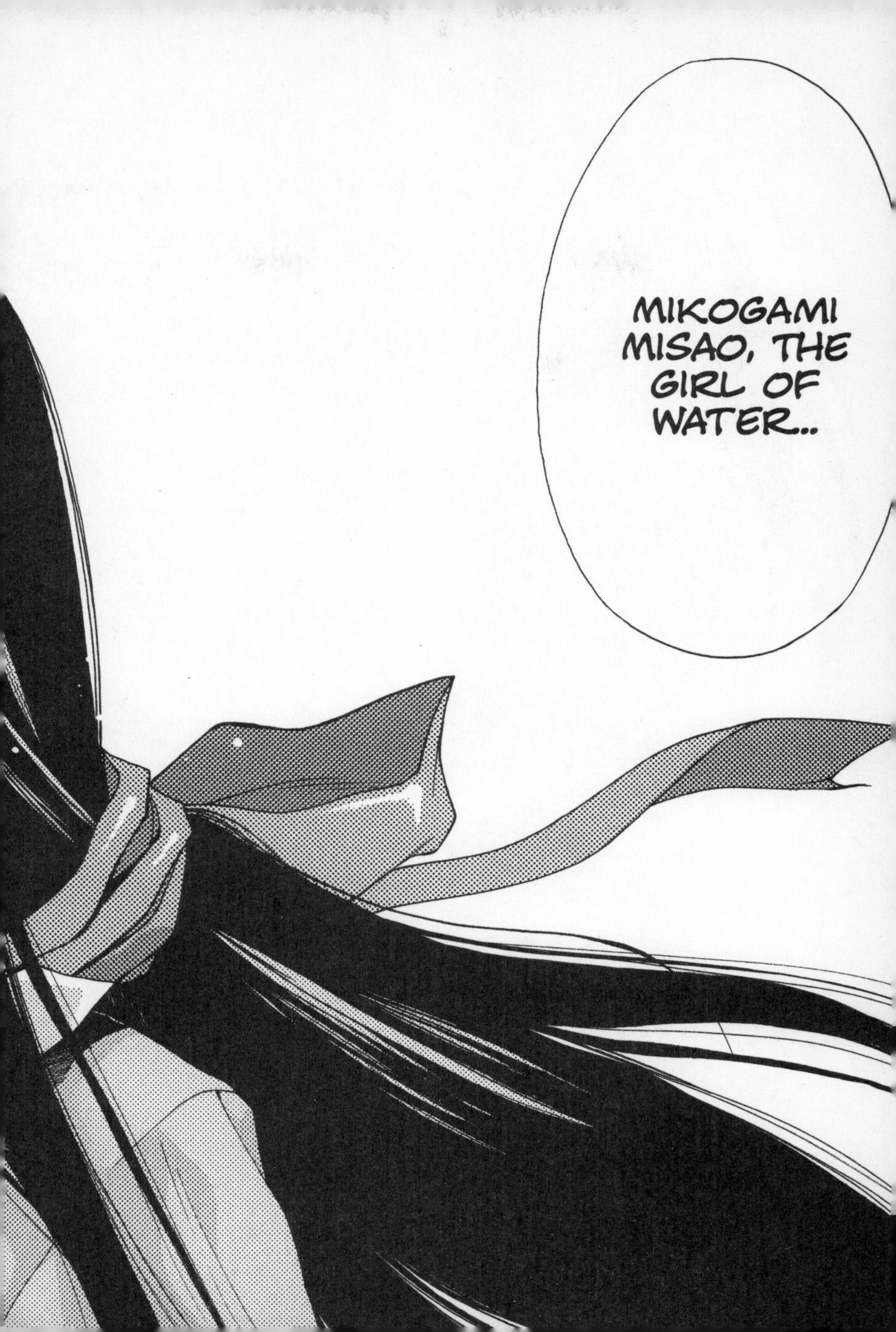
MIKOGAMI MISAO, THE GIRL OF WATER...

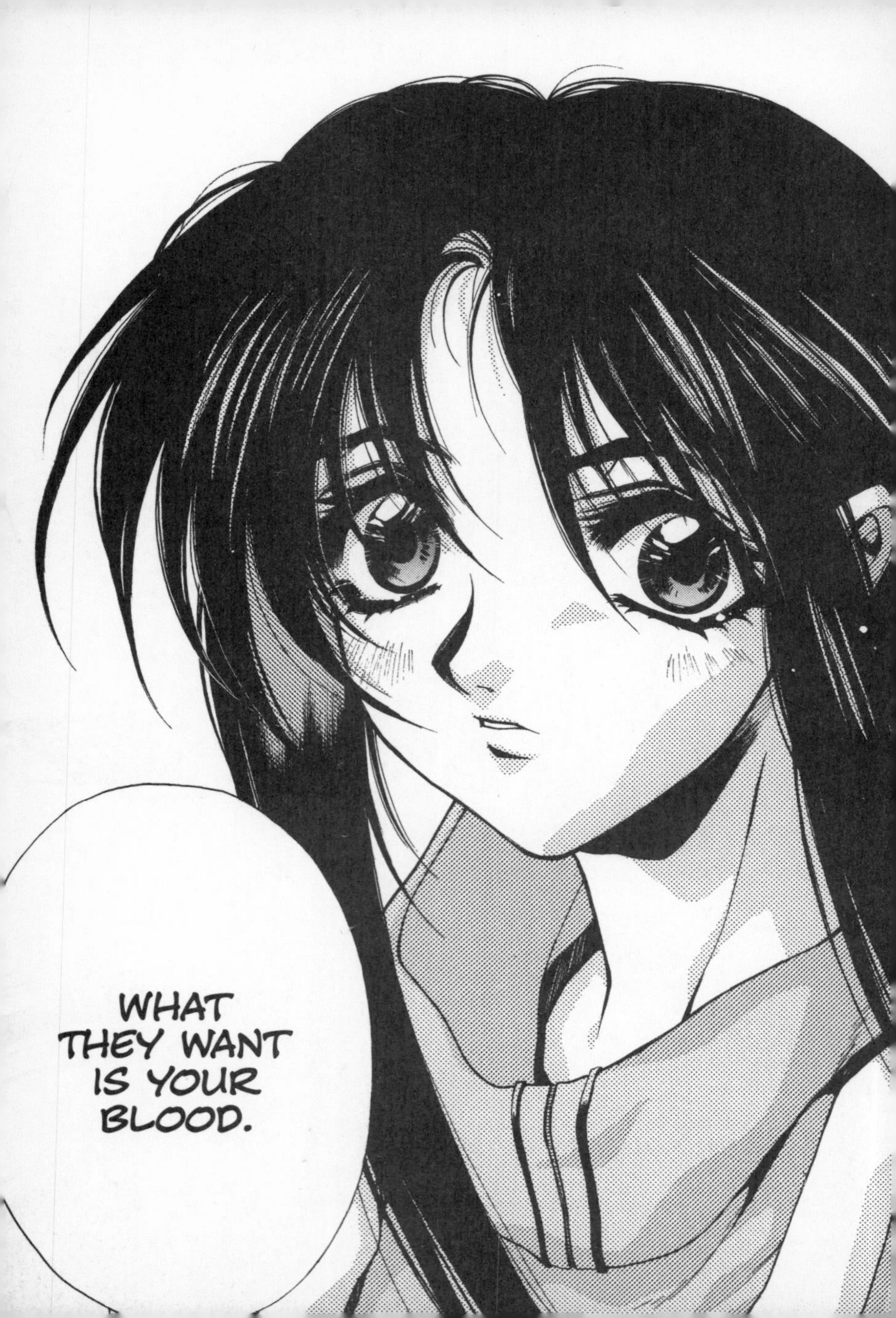
WHAT THEY WANT IS YOUR BLOOD.

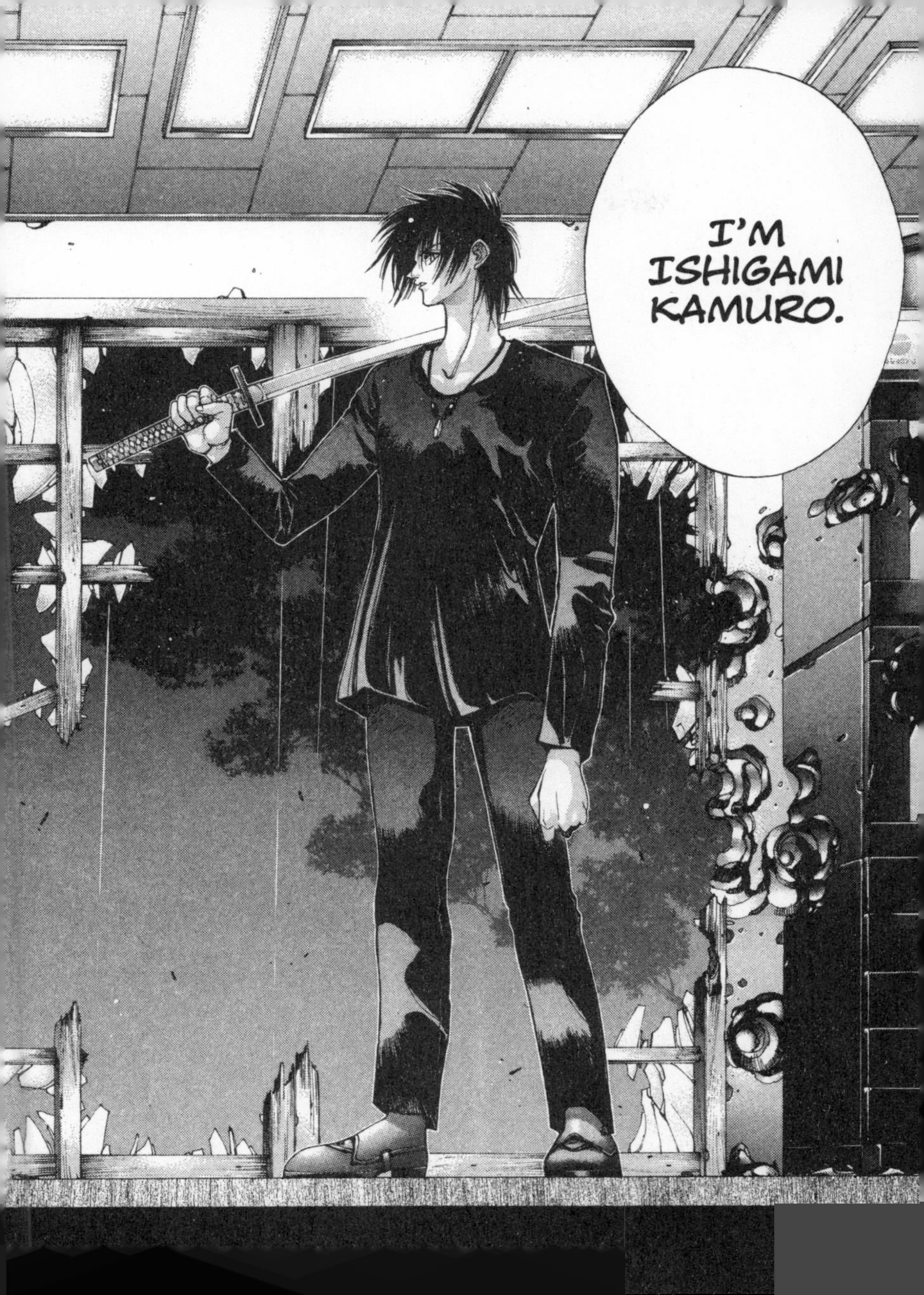
I'M ISHIGAMI KAMURO.

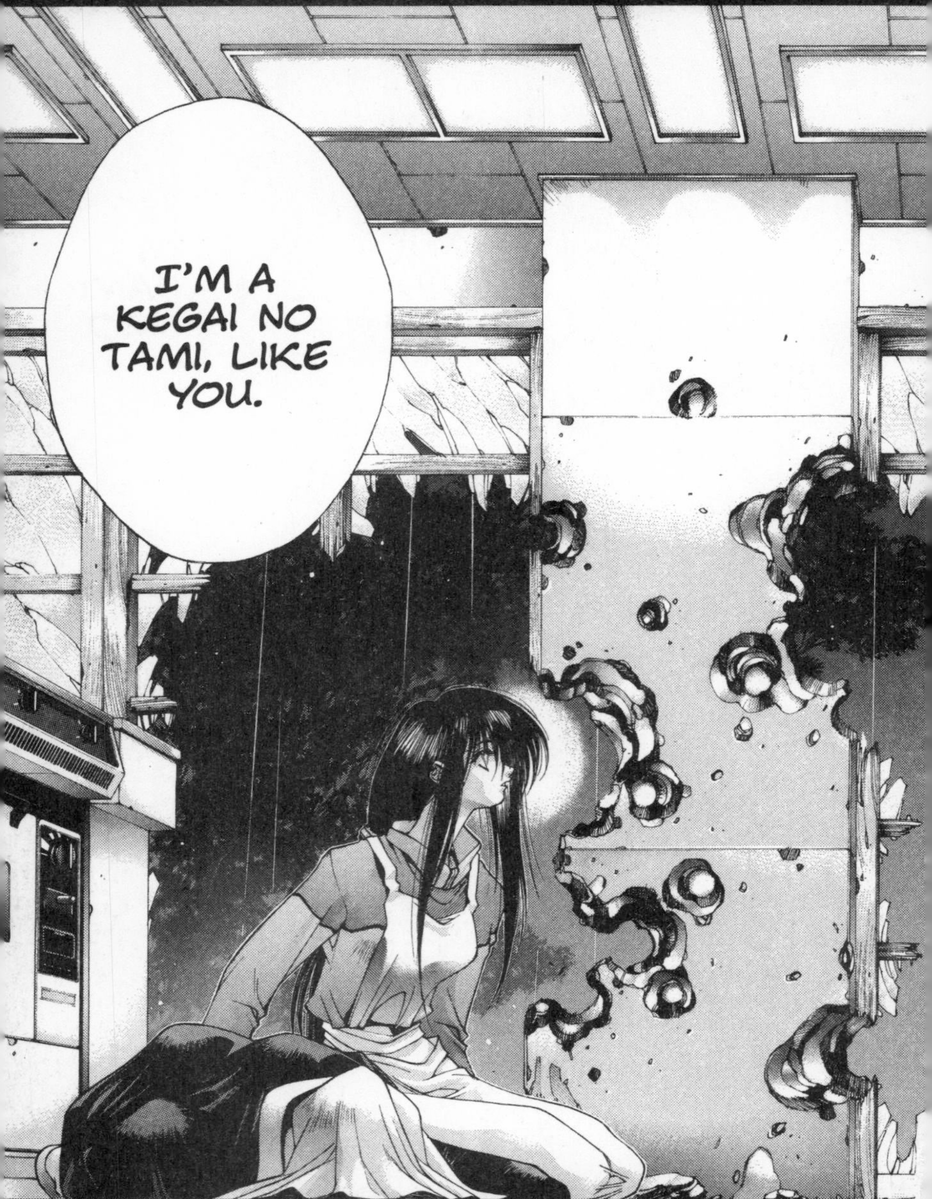
I'M A KEGAI NO TAMI, LIKE YOU.

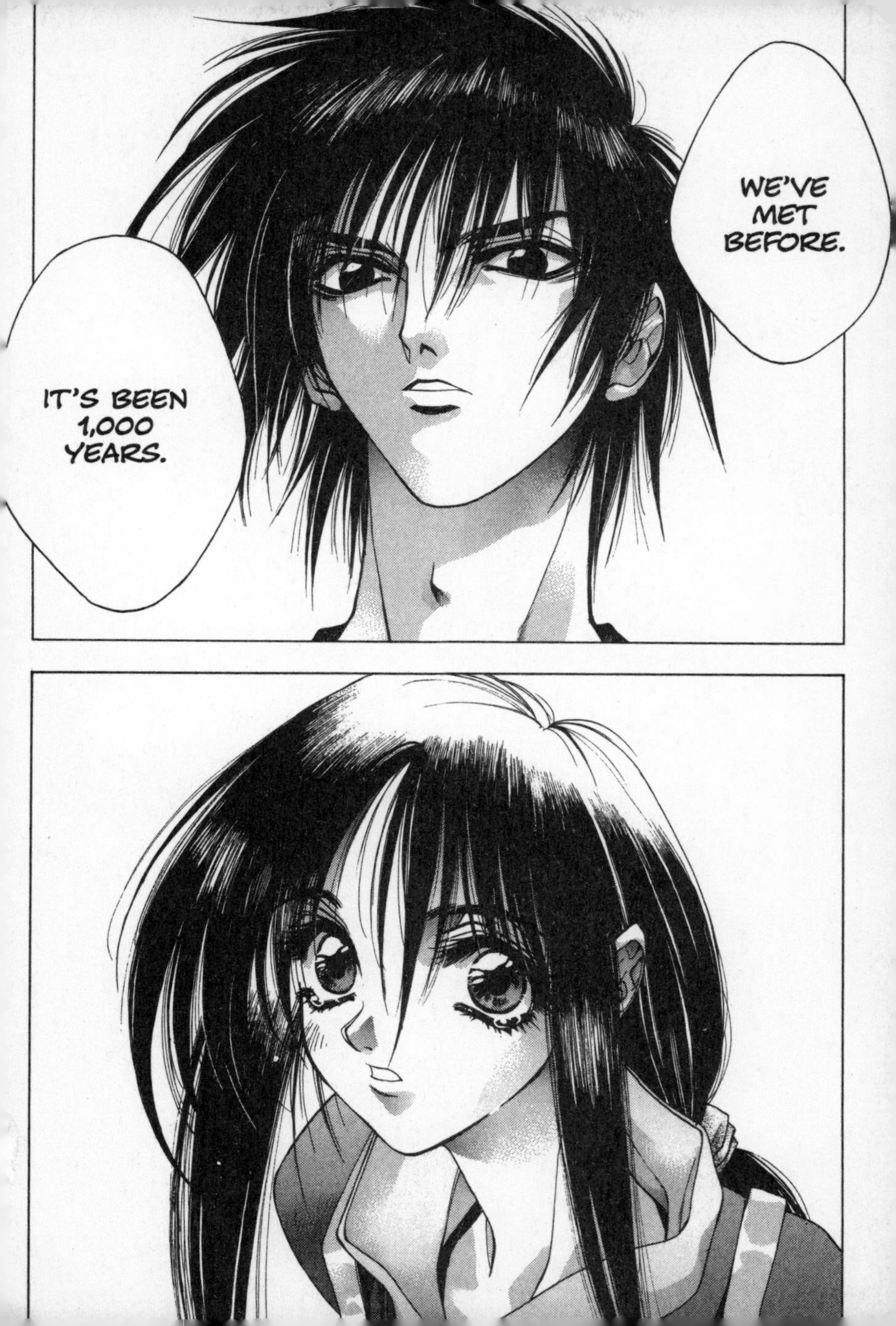
WE'VE MET BEFORE.
IT'S BEEN 1,000 YEARS.

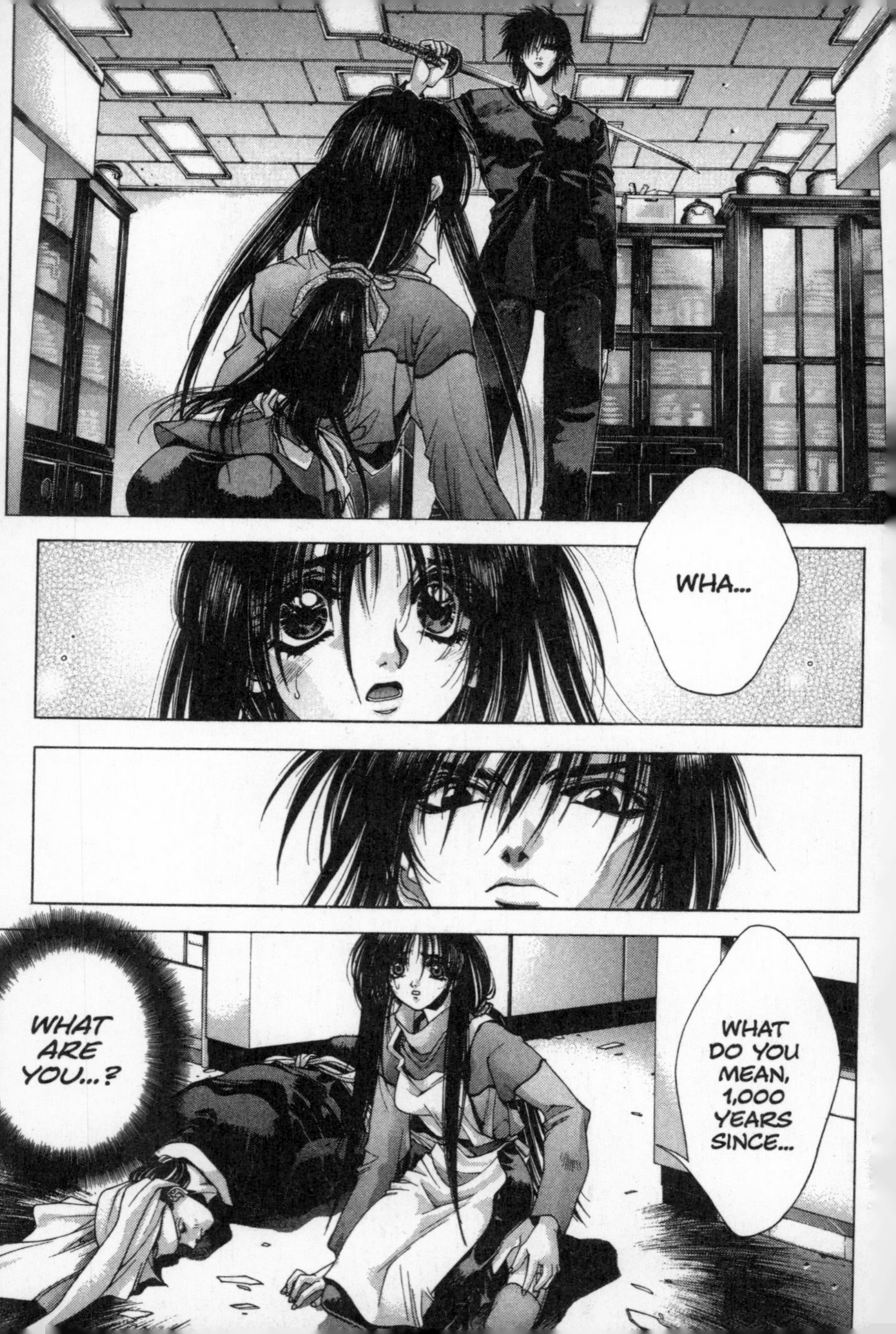
WHA...
WHAT DO YOU MEAN, 1,000 YEARS SINCE...
WHAT ARE YOU...?

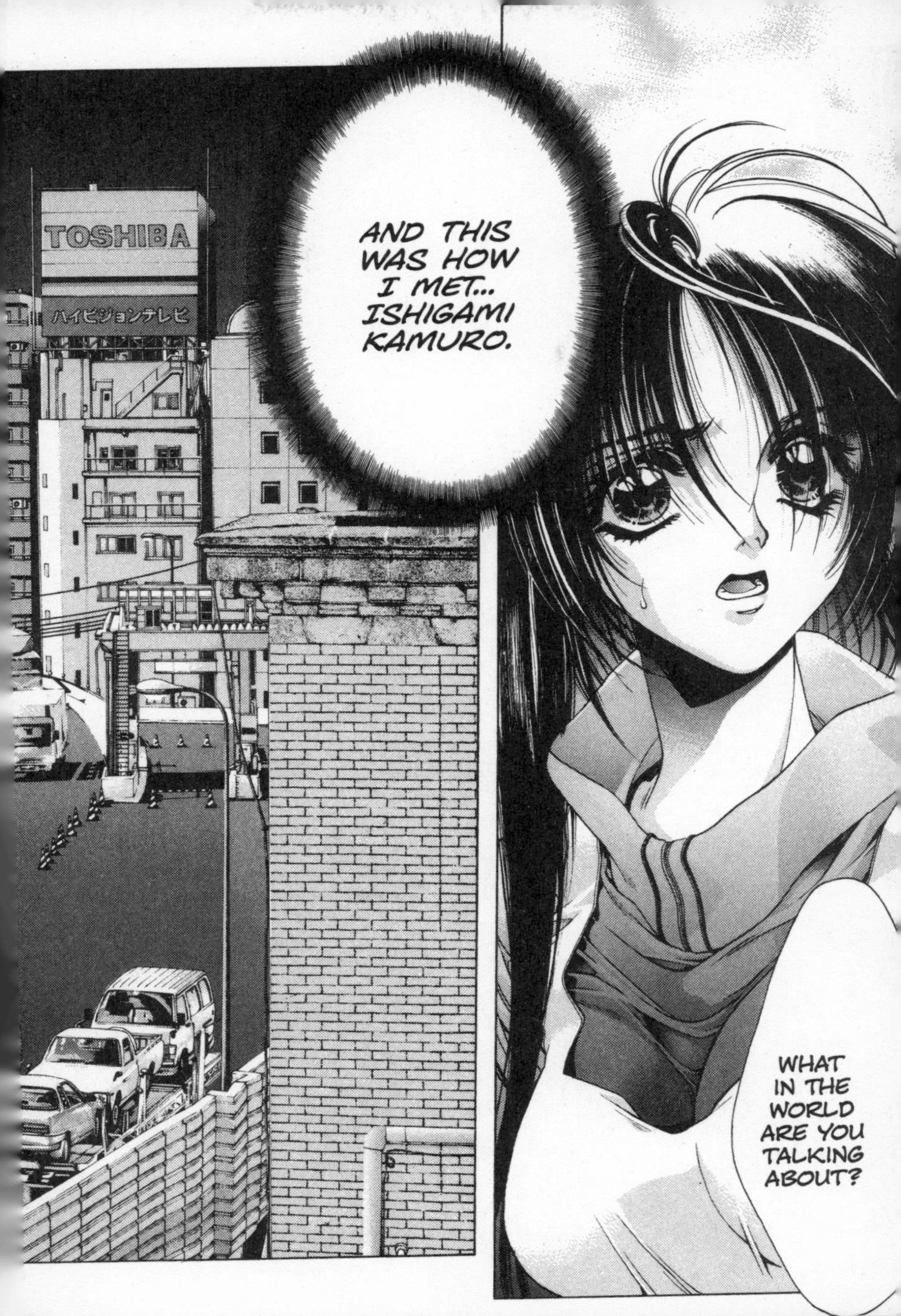
WHAT IN THE WORLD ARE YOU TALKING ABOUT?
AND THIS WAS HOW I MET... ISHIGAMI KAMURO.
TOSHIBA
ハイビジョンテレビ

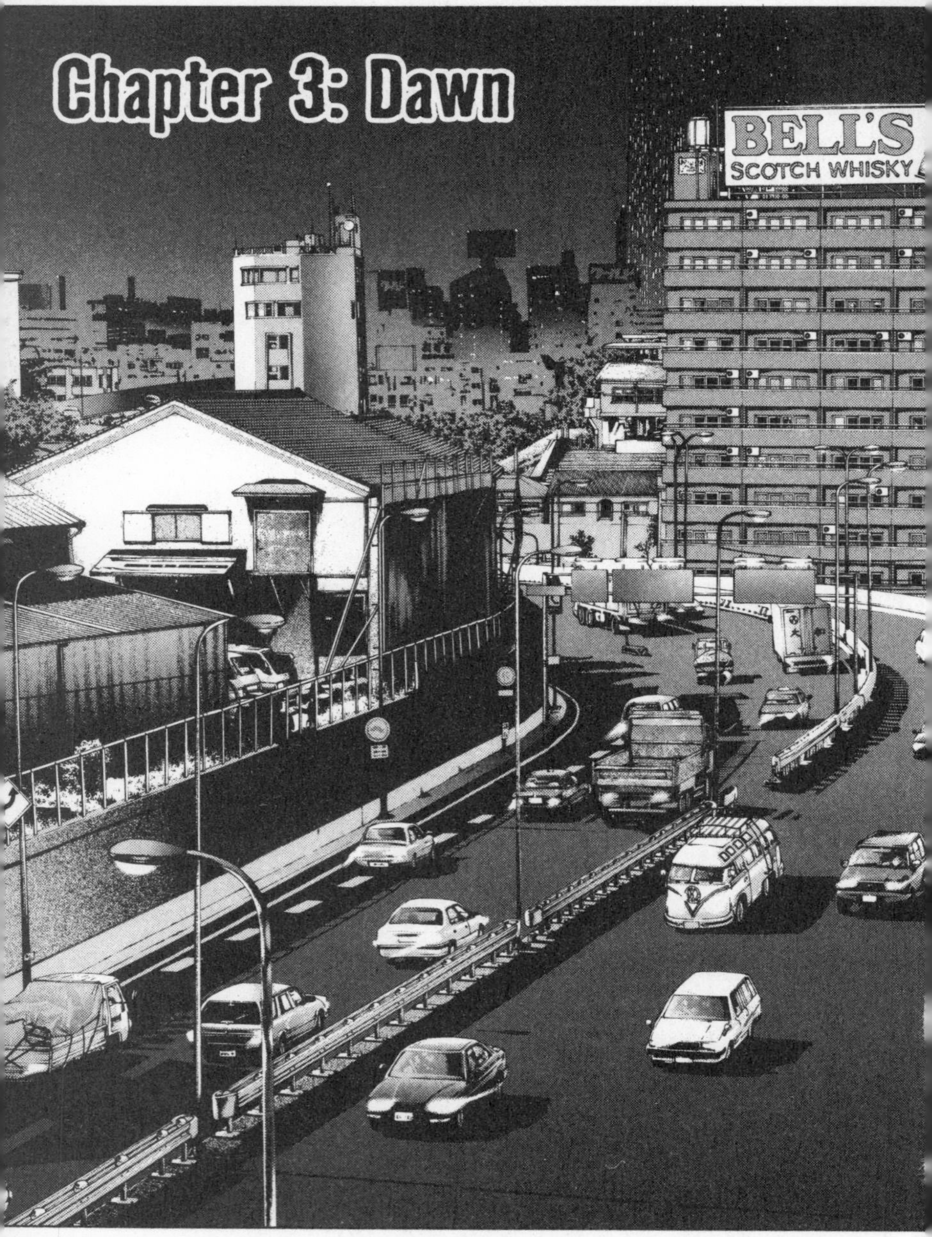
Chapter 3: Dawn
BELL'S
SCOTCH WHISKY

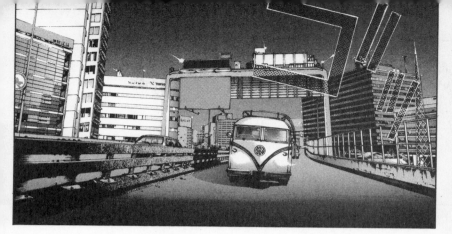

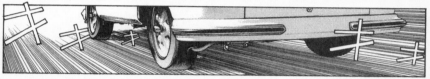

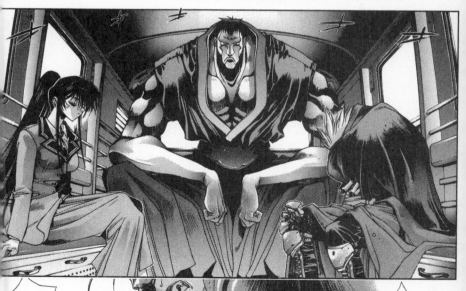

IT
HURTS...

SHIT.

SHIT.

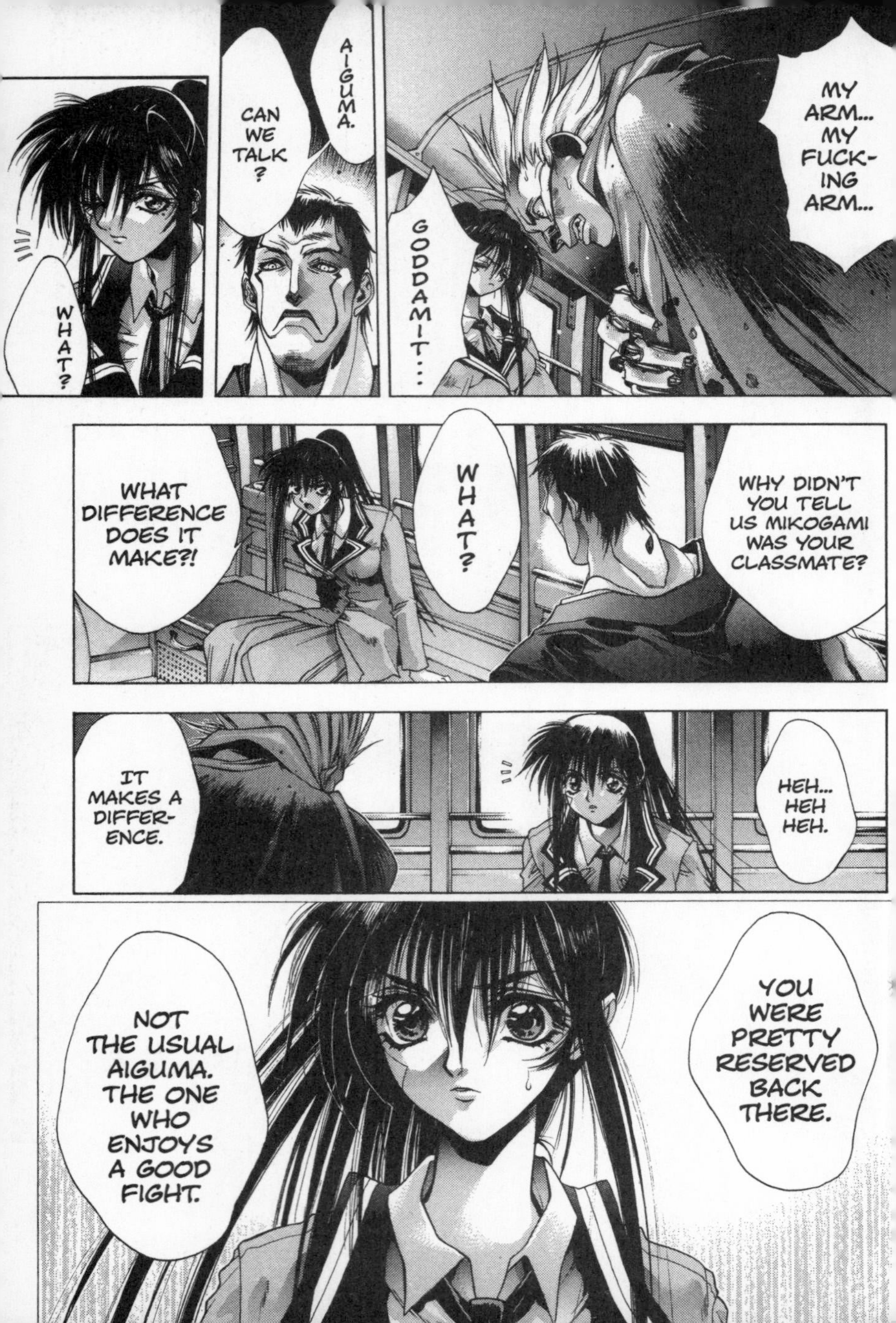
MY ARM... MY FUCKING ARM...
GODDAMIT...
AIGUMA.
CAN WE TALK?
WHAT?
WHY DIDN'T YOU TELL US MIKOGAMI WAS YOUR CLASSMATE?
WHAT?
WHAT DIFFERENCE DOES IT MAKE?!
HEH... HEH HEH.
IT MAKES A DIFFERENCE.
YOU WERE PRETTY RESERVED BACK THERE.
NOT THE USUAL AIGUMA. THE ONE WHO ENJOYS A GOOD FIGHT.

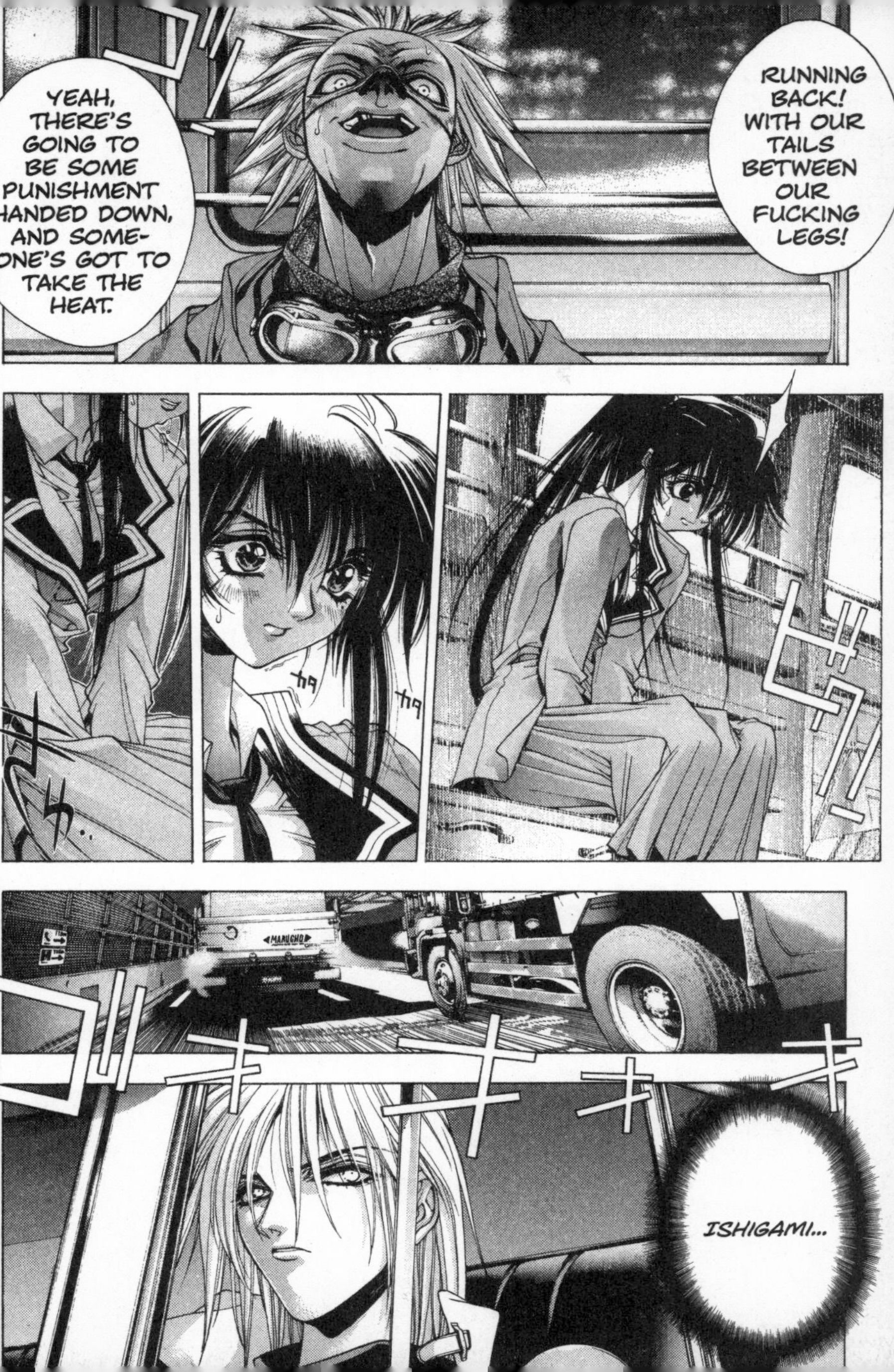
RUNNING BACK! WITH OUR TAILS BETWEEN OUR FUCKING LEGS!
YEAH, THERE'S GOING TO BE SOME PUNISHMENT HANDED DOWN, AND SOME-ONE'S GOT TO TAKE THE HEAT.
ISHIGAMI...

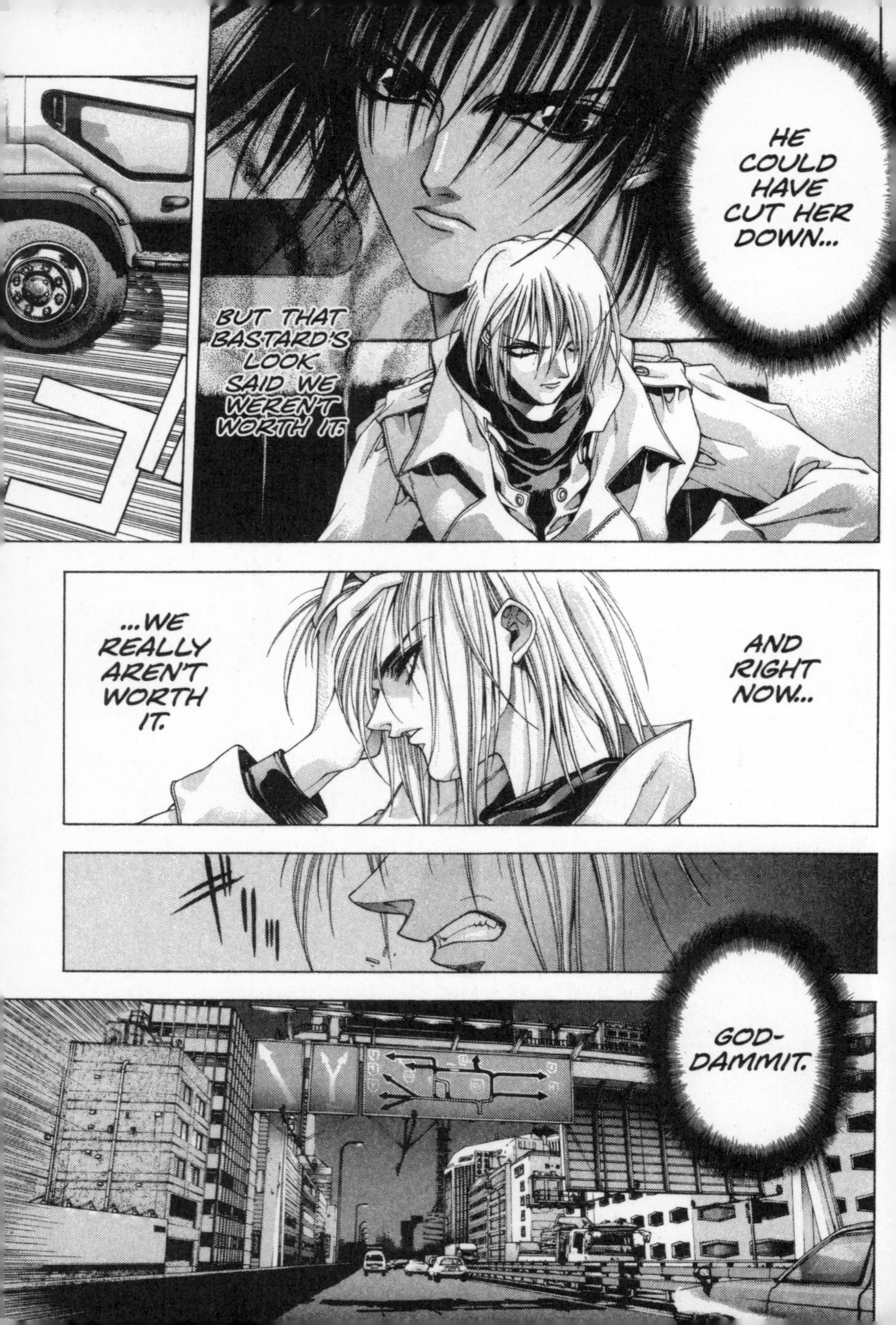
HE COULD HAVE CUT HER DOWN...
BUT THAT BASTARD'S LOOK SAID WE WEREN'T WORTH IT.
AND RIGHT NOW...
...WE REALLY AREN'T WORTH IT.
GOD-DAMMIT.

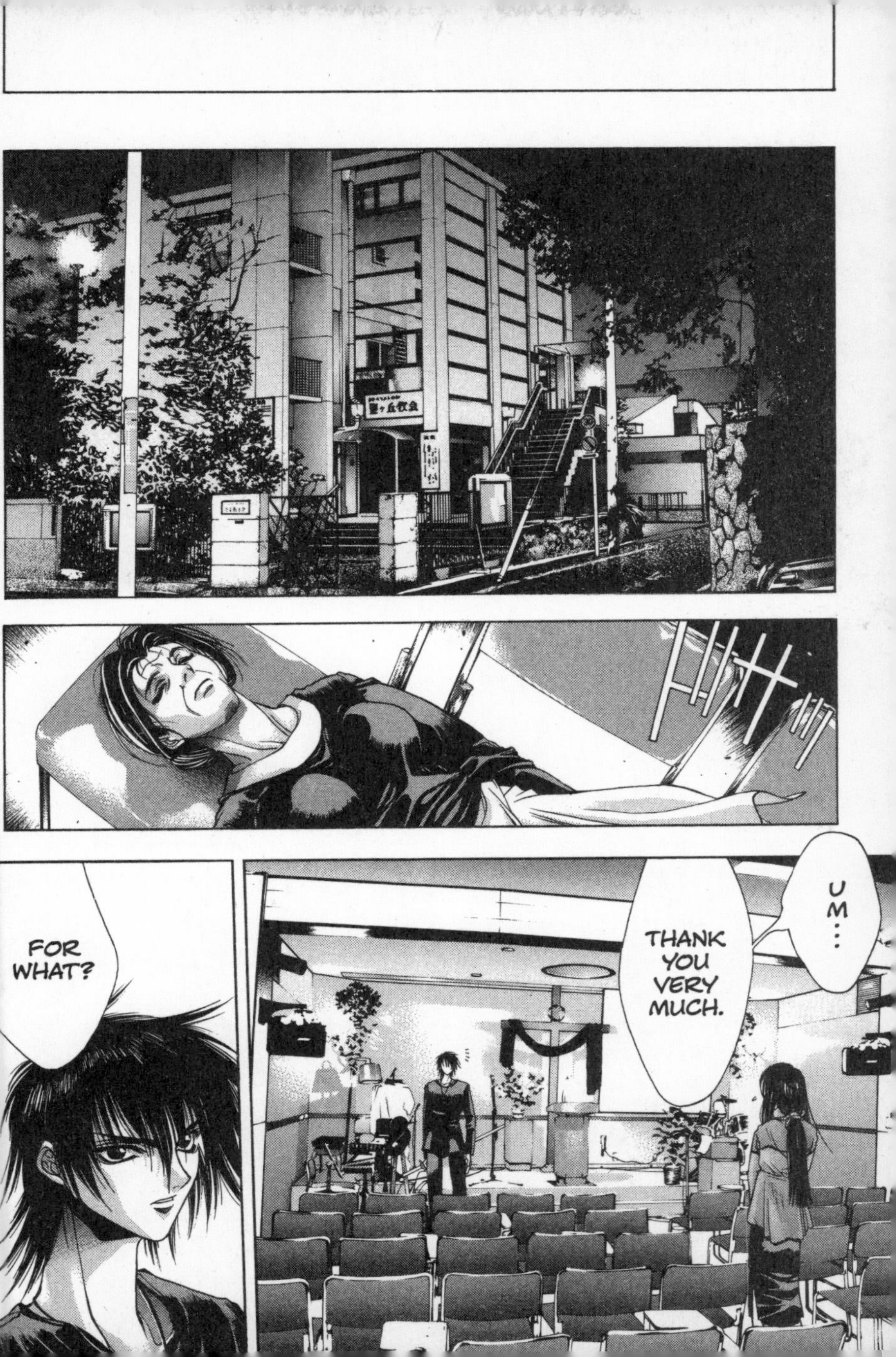
UM...
THANK YOU VERY MUCH.
FOR WHAT?

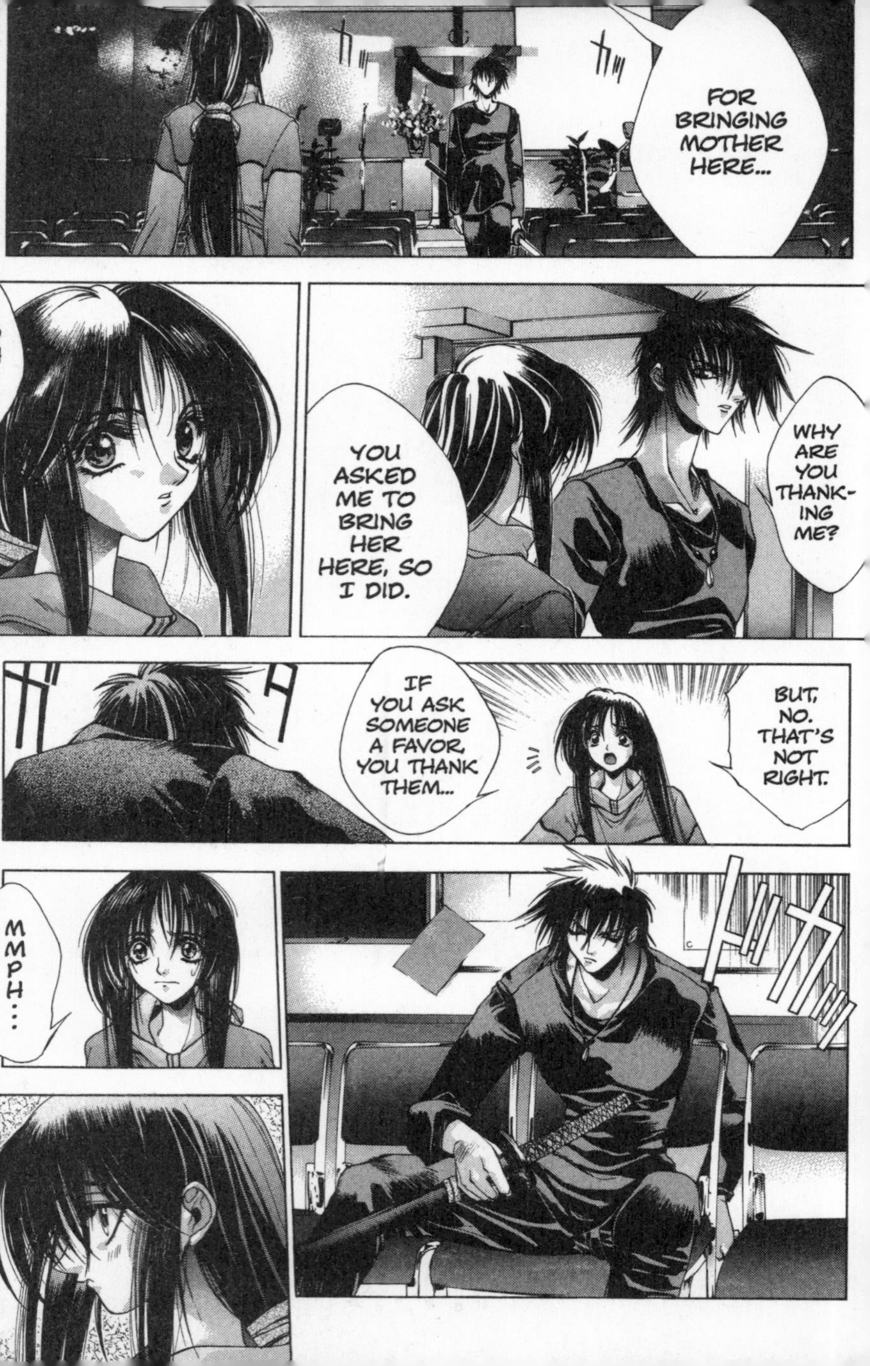
FOR BRINGING MOTHER HERE...
WHY ARE YOU THANKING ME?
YOU ASKED ME TO BRING HER HERE, SO I DID.
OH...
BUT, NO. THAT'S NOT RIGHT.
IF YOU ASK SOMEONE A FAVOR YOU THANK THEM...
MMPH...

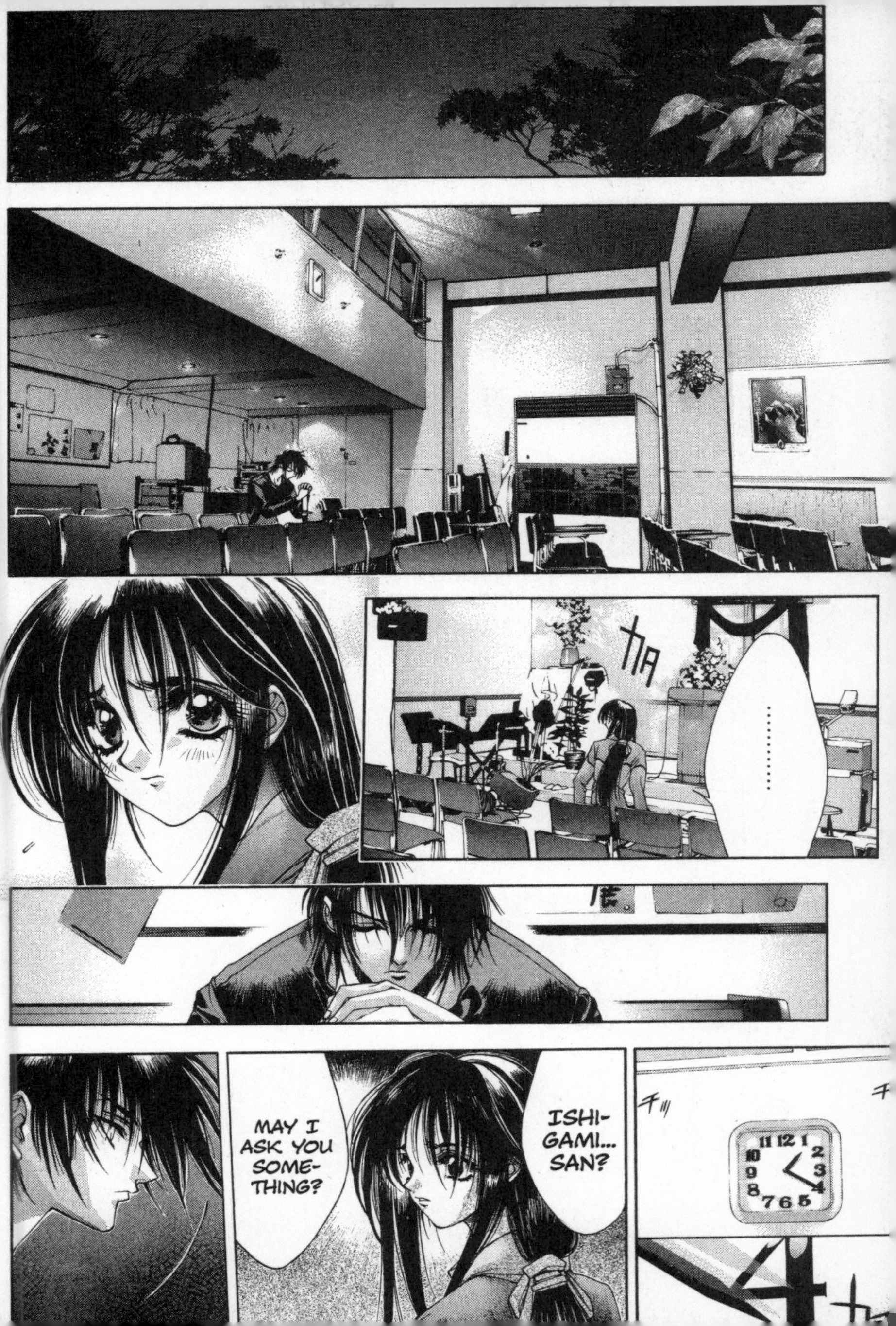
……
ISHI-GAMI... SAN?
MAY I ASK YOU SOMETHING?

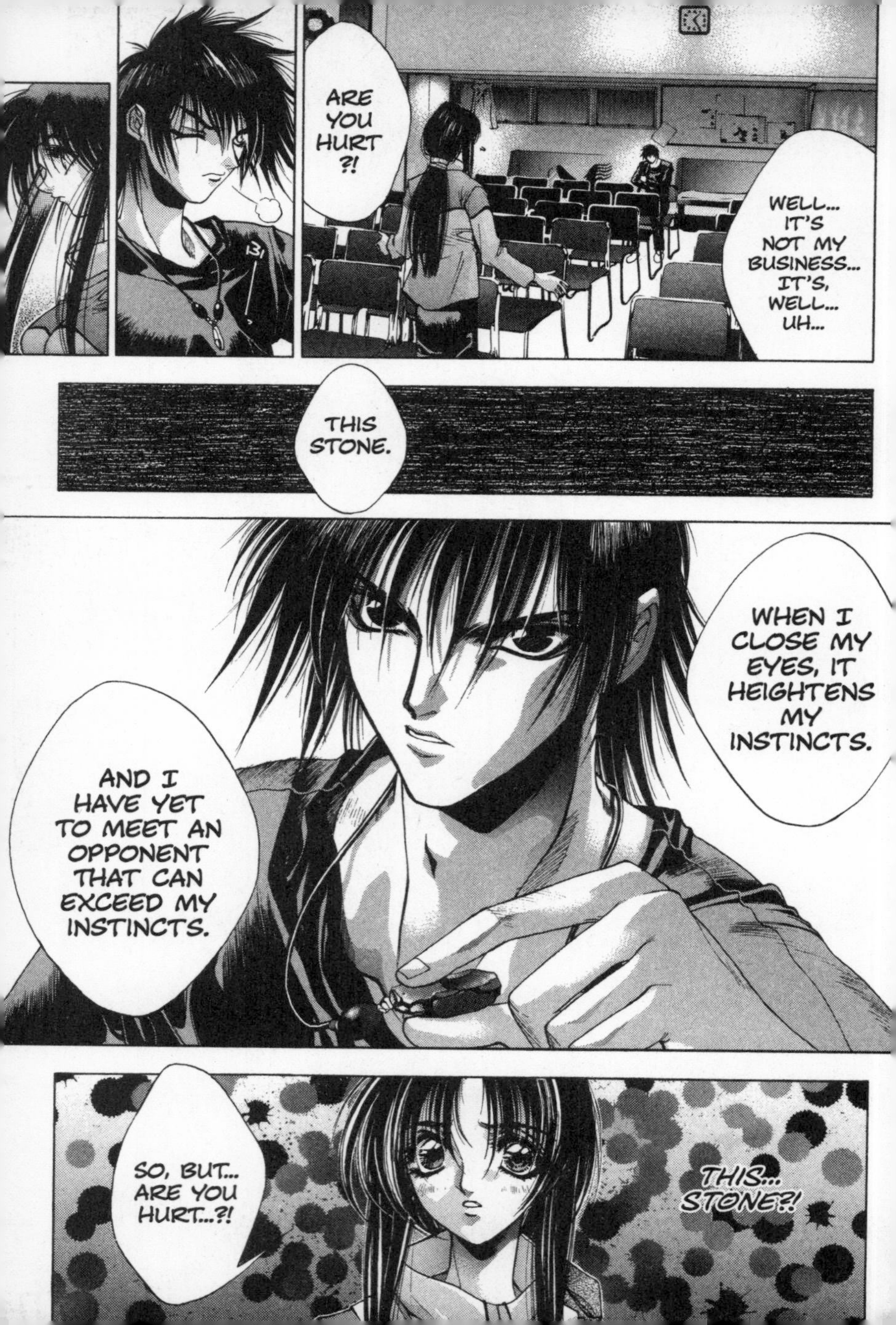
ARE YOU HURT ?!
WELL... IT'S NOT MY BUSINESS... IT'S, WELL... UH...
THIS STONE.
WHEN I CLOSE MY EYES, IT HEIGHTENS MY INSTINCTS.
AND I HAVE YET TO MEET AN OPPONENT THAT CAN EXCEED MY INSTINCTS.
THIS... STONE?!
SO, BUT... ARE YOU HURT...?!

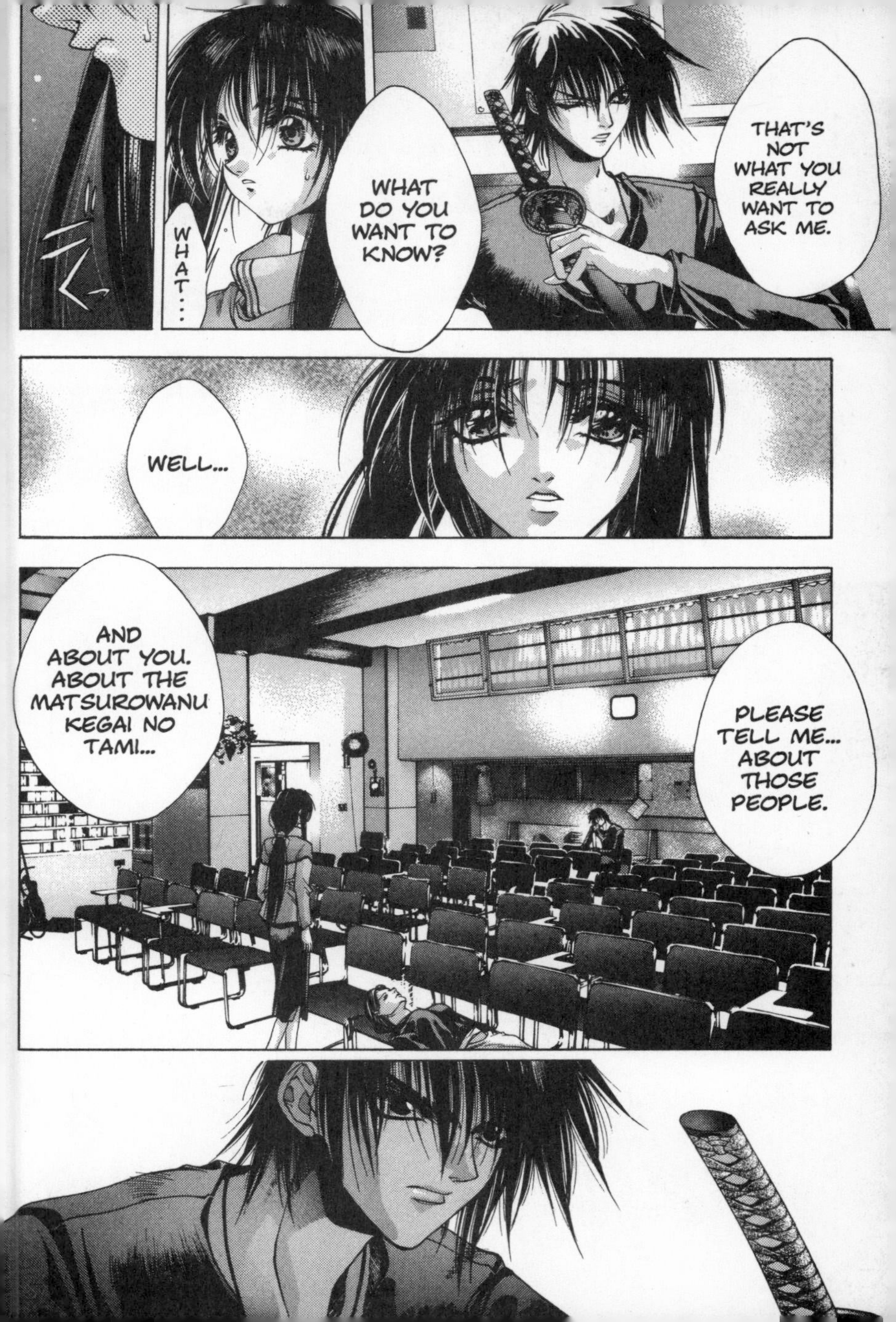
THAT'S NOT WHAT YOU REALLY WANT TO ASK ME.
WHAT DO YOU WANT TO KNOW?
WHAT...
WELL...
PLEASE TELL ME... ABOUT THOSE PEOPLE.
AND ABOUT YOU. ABOUT THE MATSUROWANU KEGAI NO TAMI...

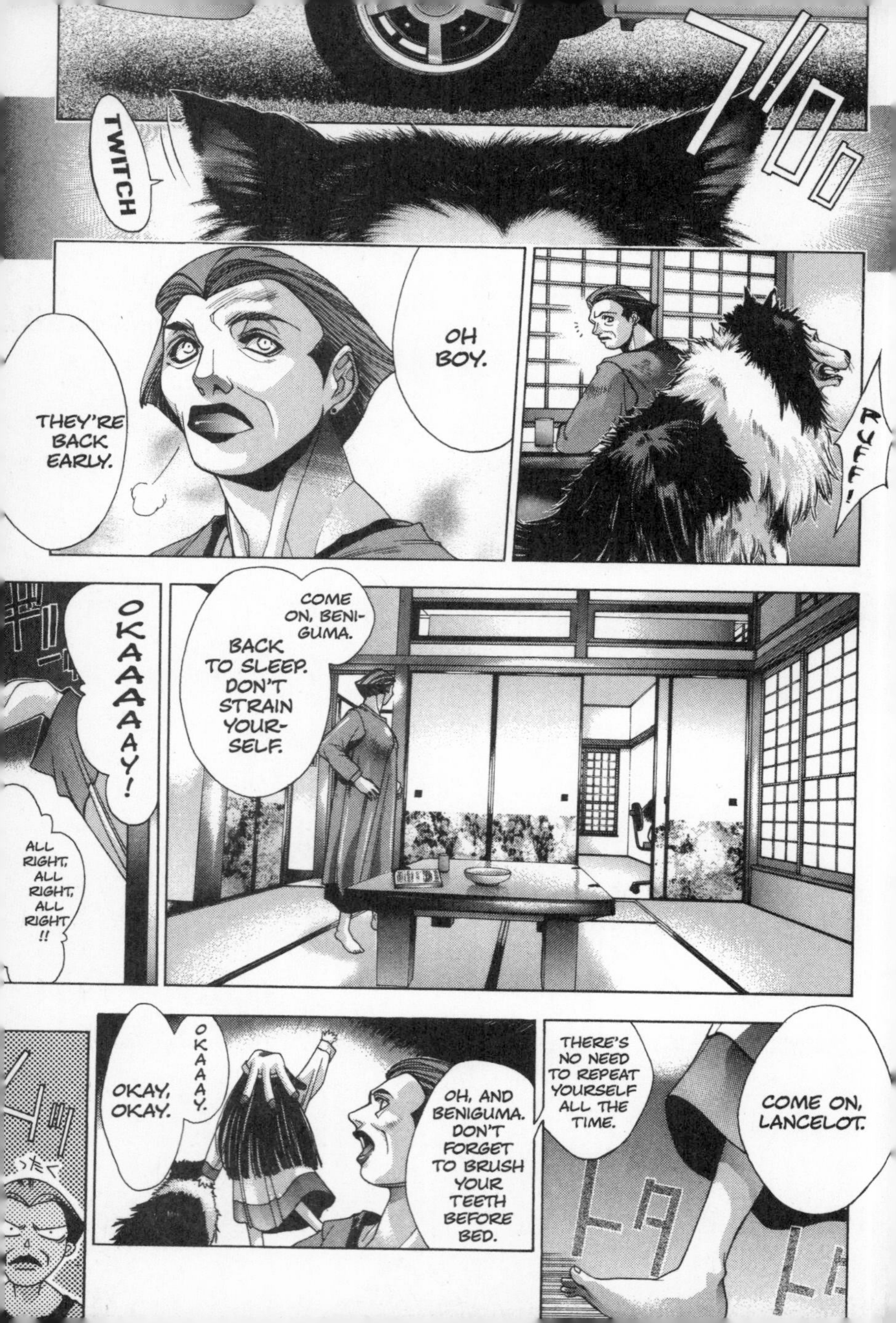
TWITCH
RUFF!
OH BOY.
THEY'RE BACK EARLY.
COME ON, BENIGUMA.
BACK TO SLEEP. DON'T STRAIN YOURSELF.
OKAAAAAAY!
ALL RIGHT, ALL RIGHT, ALL RIGHT!!
COME ON, LANCELOT.
THERE'S NO NEED TO REPEAT YOURSELF ALL THE TIME.
OH, AND BENIGUMA. DON'T FORGET TO BRUSH YOUR TEETH BEFORE BED.
OKAAAAY.
OKAY, OKAY.

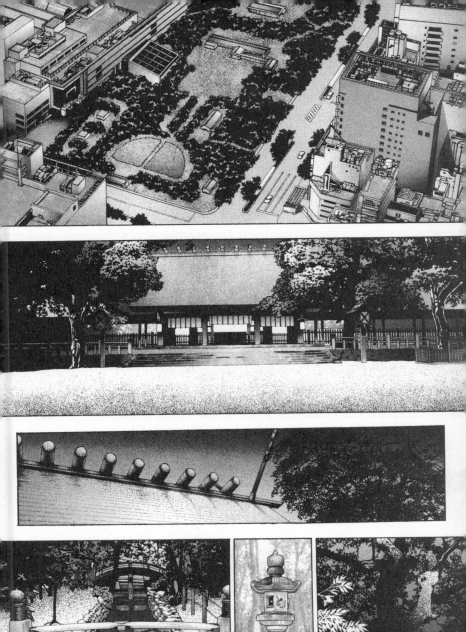

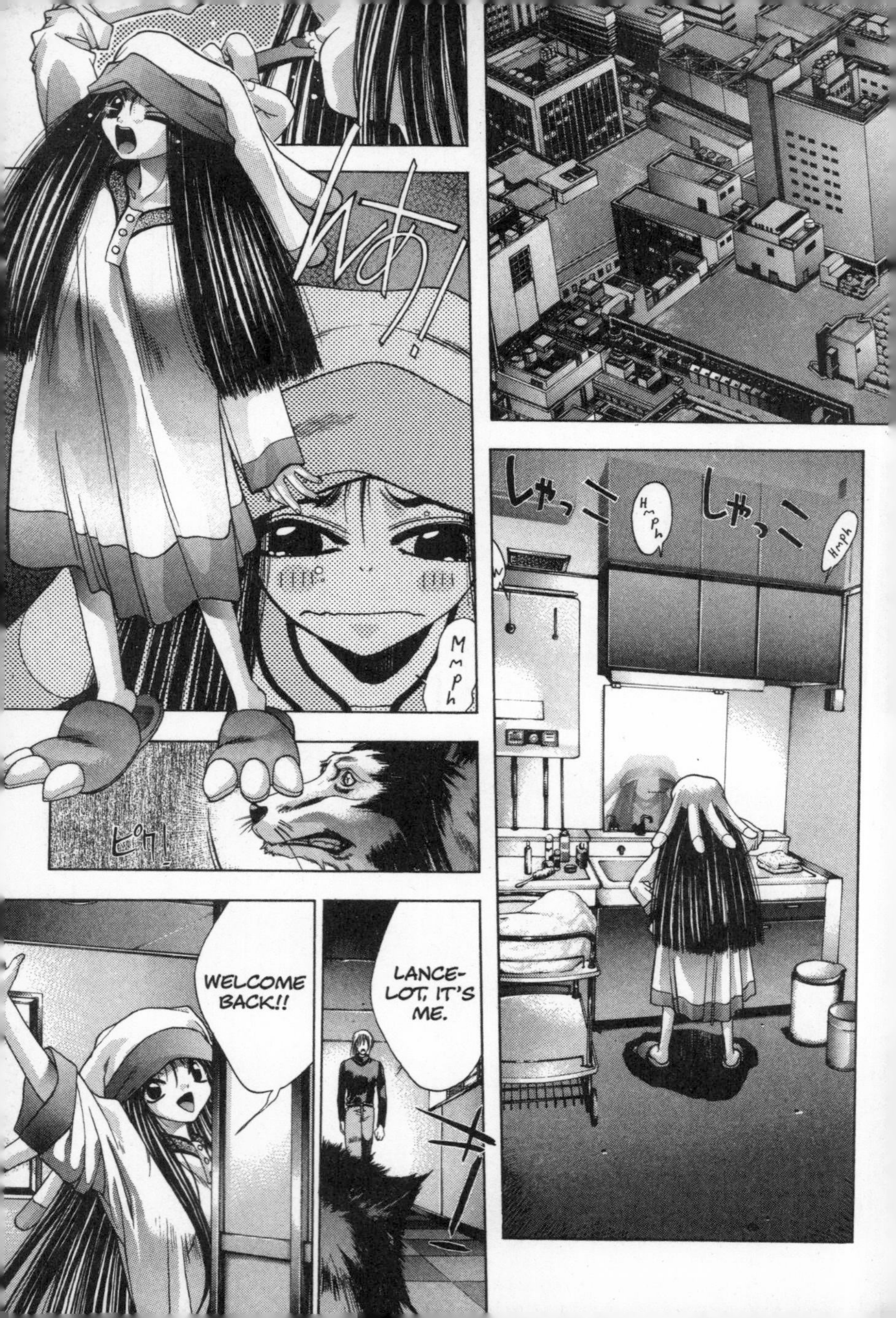
Hmph
しゃっこ
Hmph
しゃっこ
わあ!!
Mmph
ピク!
LANCE-LOT, IT'S ME.
WELCOME BACK!!

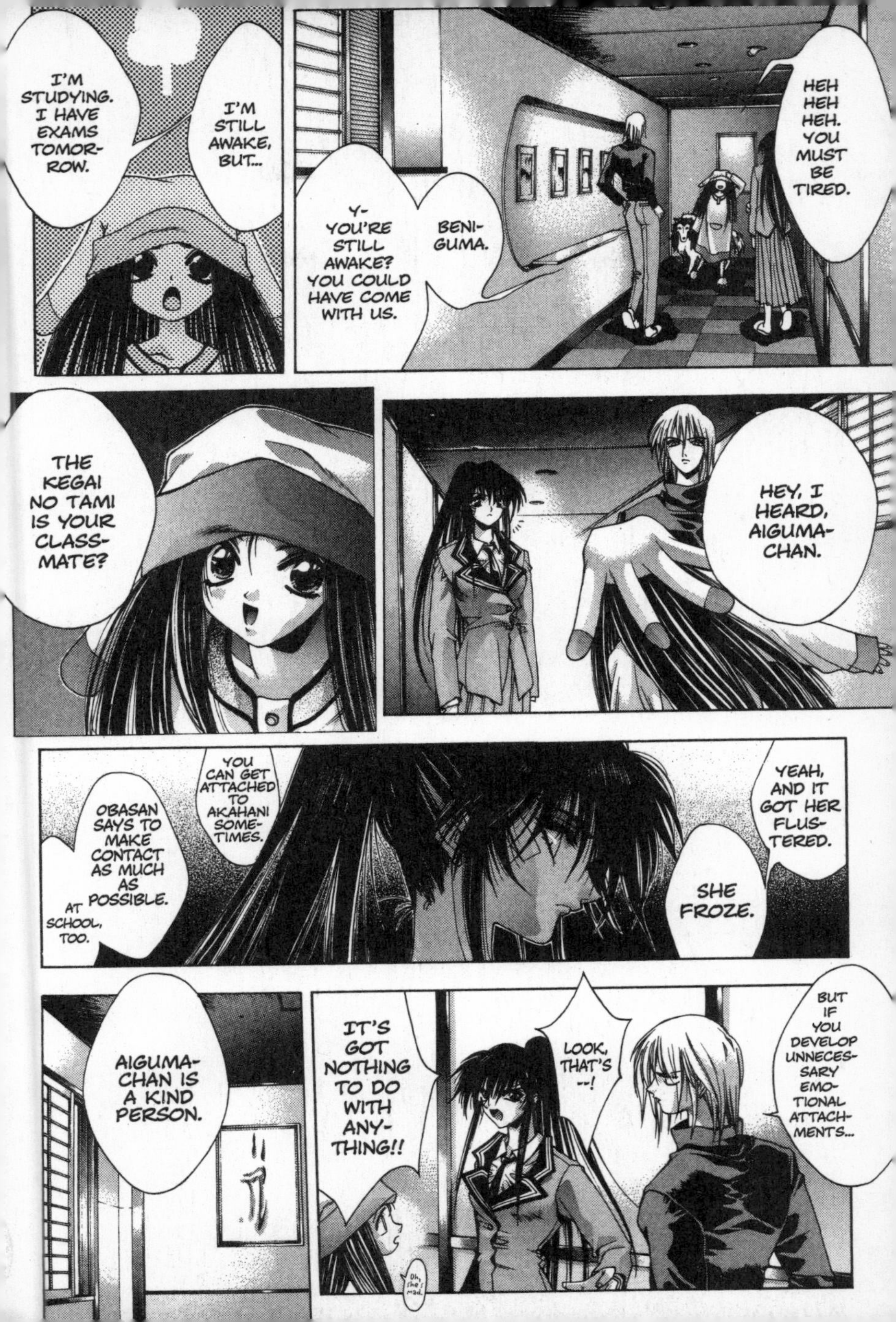
HEH HEH HEH. YOU MUST BE TIRED.
BENI-GUMA.
Y-YOU'RE STILL AWAKE? YOU COULD HAVE COME WITH US.
I'M STILL AWAKE, BUT...
I'M STUDYING. I HAVE EXAMS TOMORROW.
HEY, I HEARD, AIGUMA-CHAN.
THE KEGAI NO TAMI IS YOUR CLASSMATE?
YEAH, AND IT GOT HER FLUSTERED.
SHE FROZE.
YOU CAN GET ATTACHED TO AKAHANI SOMETIMES.
OBASAN SAYS TO MAKE CONTACT AS MUCH AS POSSIBLE.
AT SCHOOL, TOO.
BUT IF YOU DEVELOP UNNECESSARY EMOTIONAL ATTACHMENTS...
LOOK, THAT'S--!
IT'S GOT NOTHING TO DO WITH ANYTHING!!
Oh, she's mad.
AIGUMA-CHAN IS A KIND PERSON.

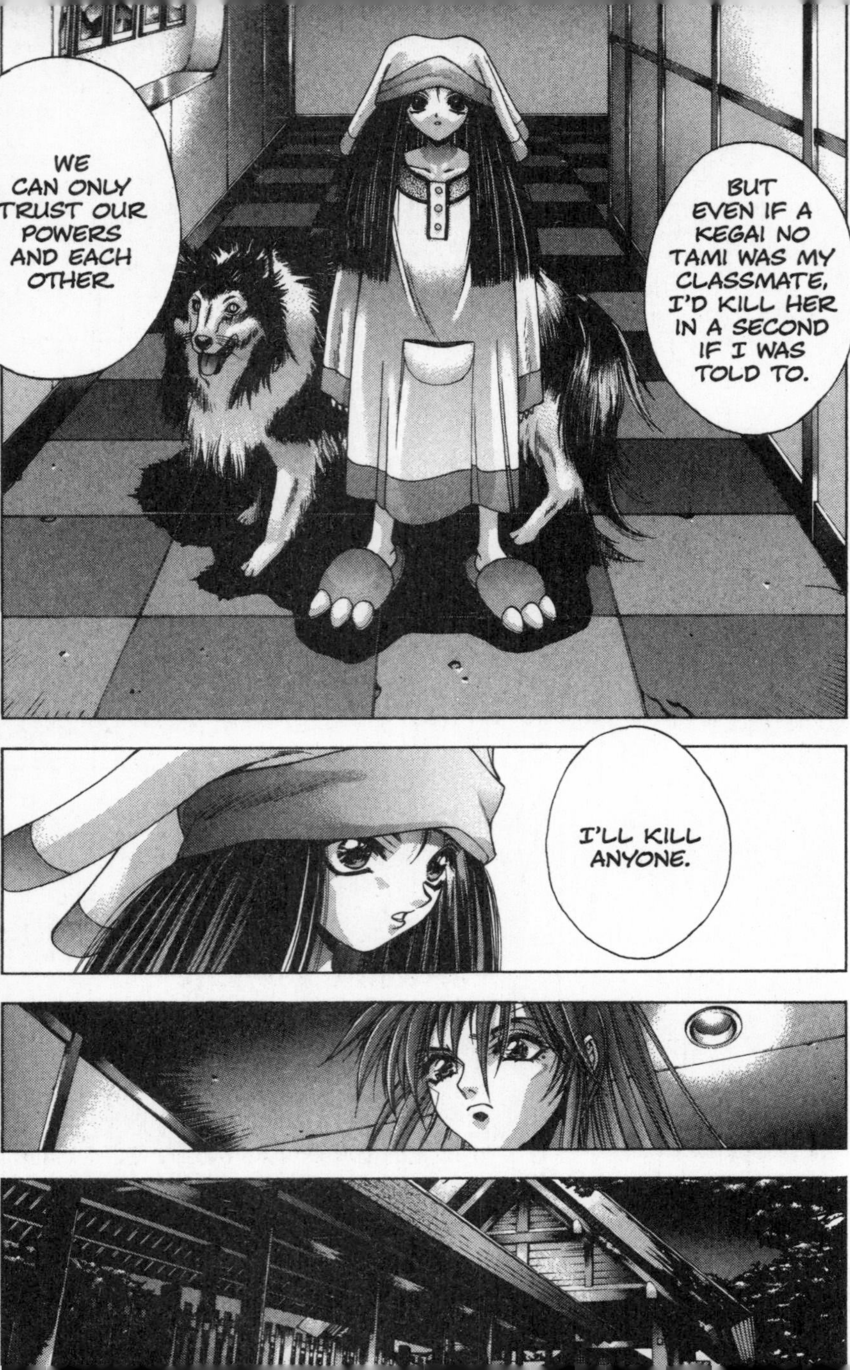
BUT EVEN IF A KEGAI NO TAMI WAS MY CLASSMATE, I'D KILL HER IN A SECOND IF I WAS TOLD TO.
WE CAN ONLY TRUST OUR POWERS AND EACH OTHER
I'LL KILL ANYONE.

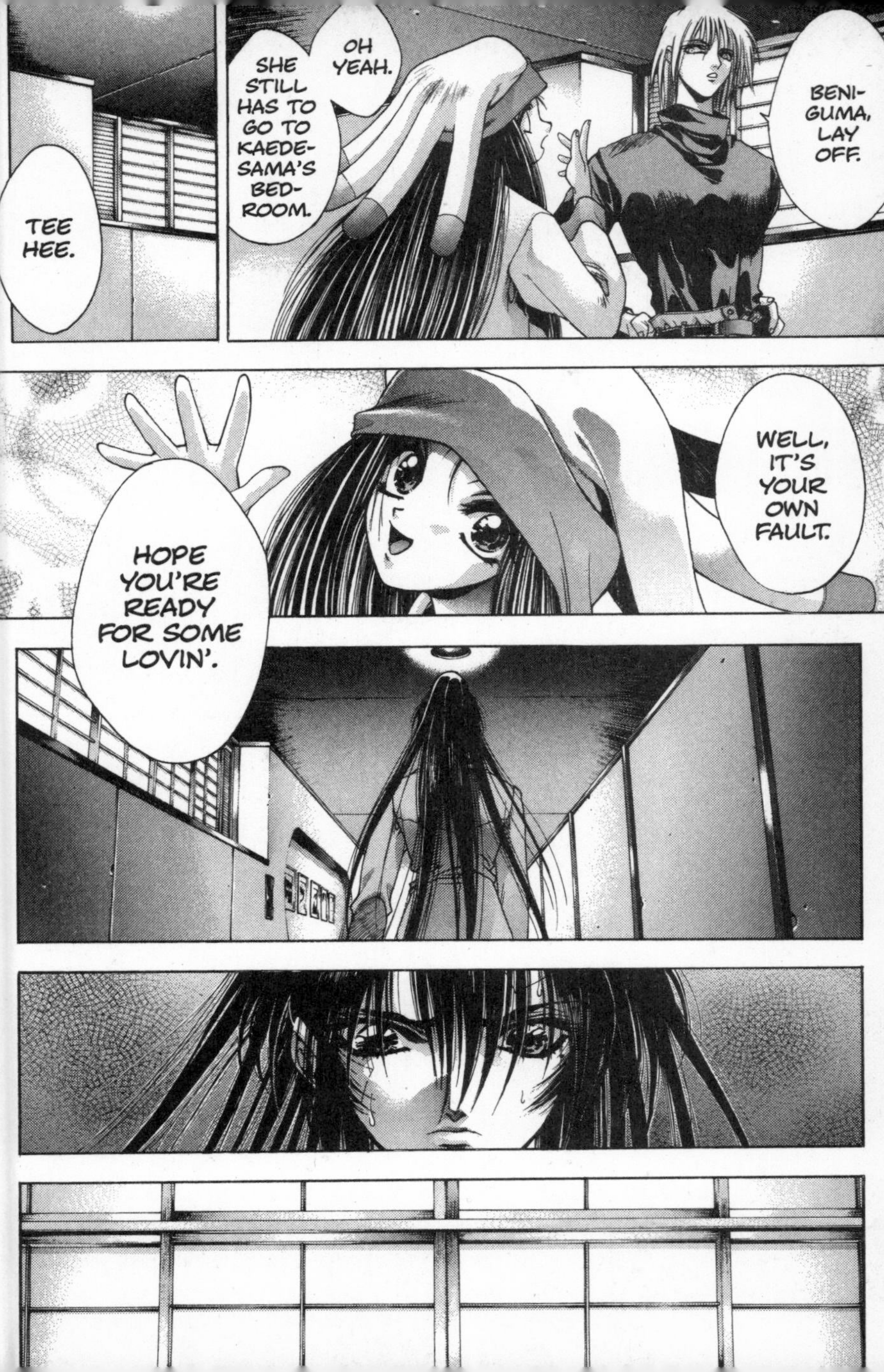
BENI-GUMA, LAY OFF.
OH YEAH.
SHE STILL HAS TO GO TO KAEDE-SAMA'S BEDROOM.
TEE HEE.
WELL, IT'S YOUR OWN FAULT.
HOPE YOU'RE READY FOR SOME LOVIN'.

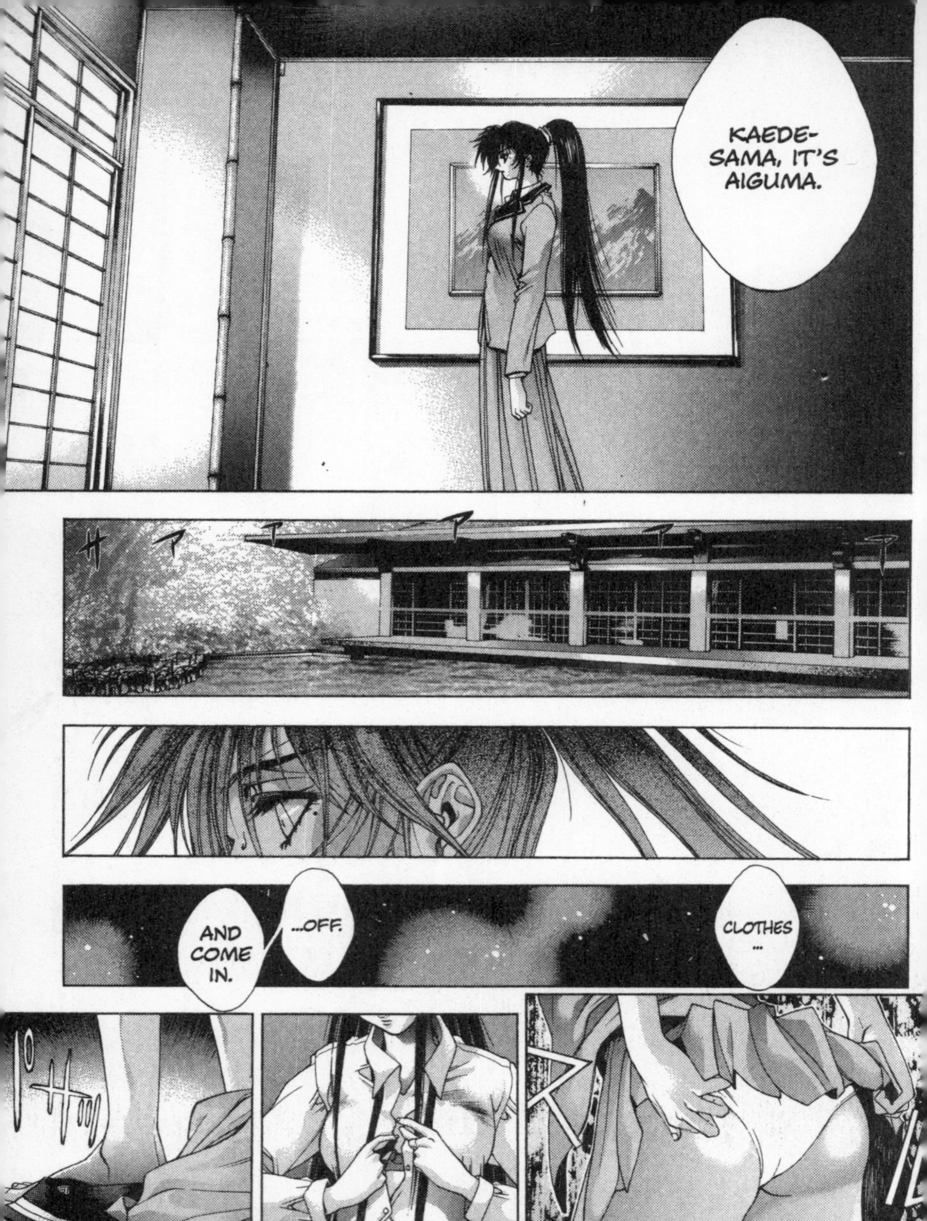
KAEDE-SAMA, IT'S AIGUMA.
CLOTHES ...
...OFF.
AND COME IN.

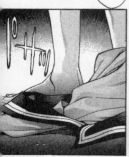

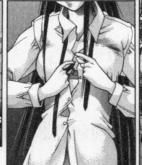

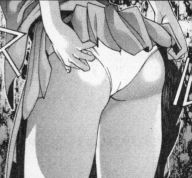

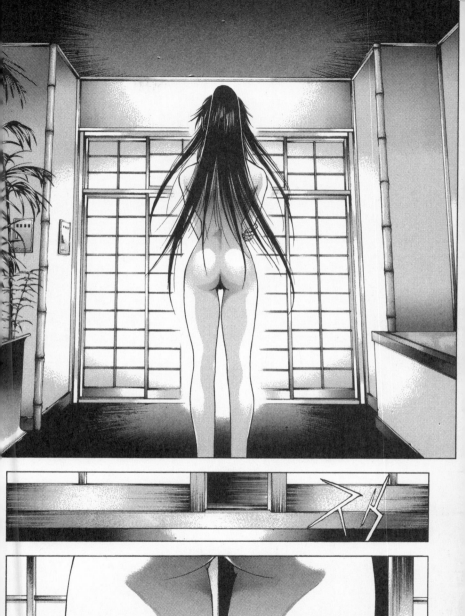
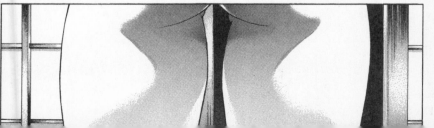

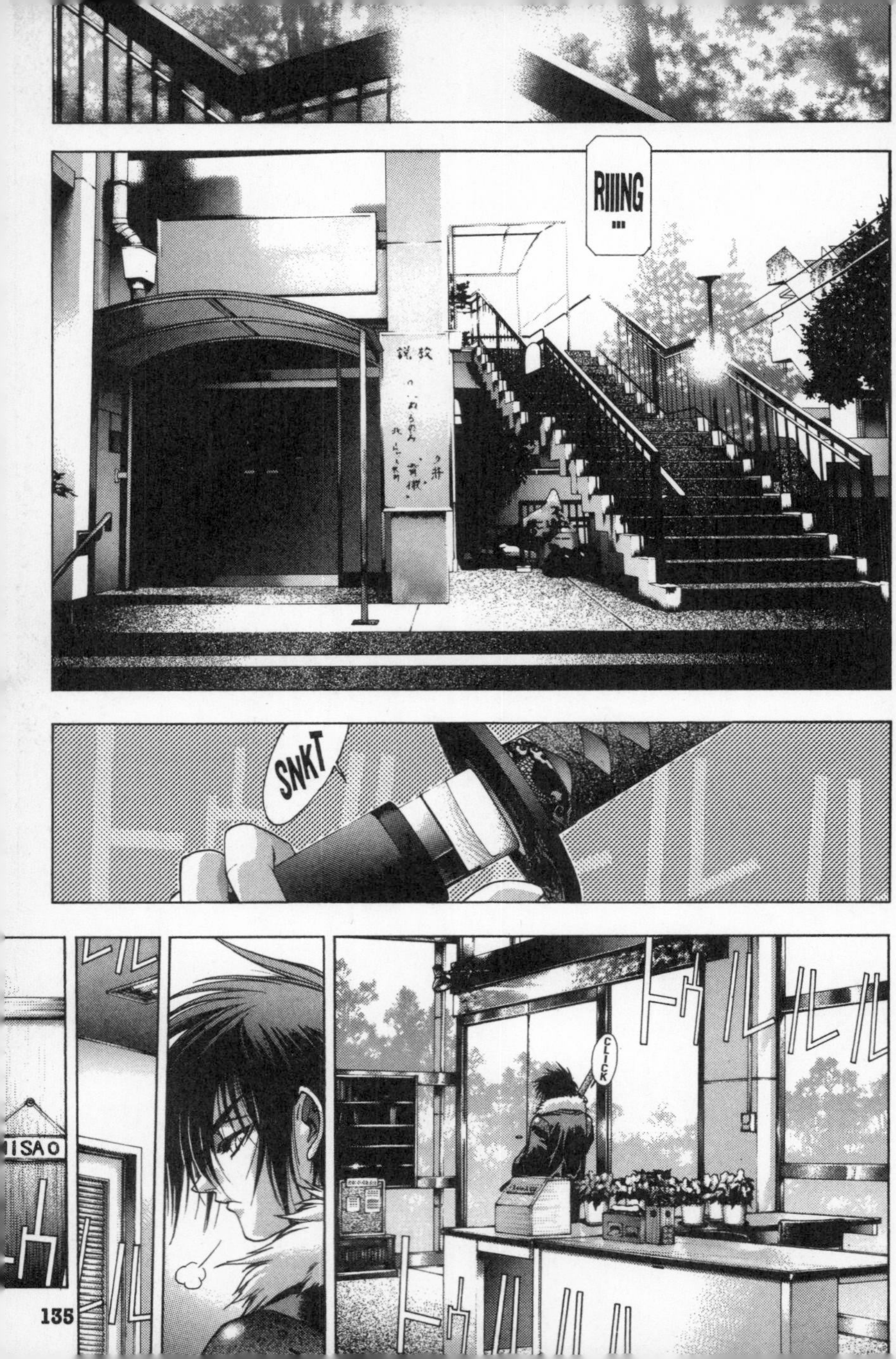
RIIING
...
SNKT
CLICK

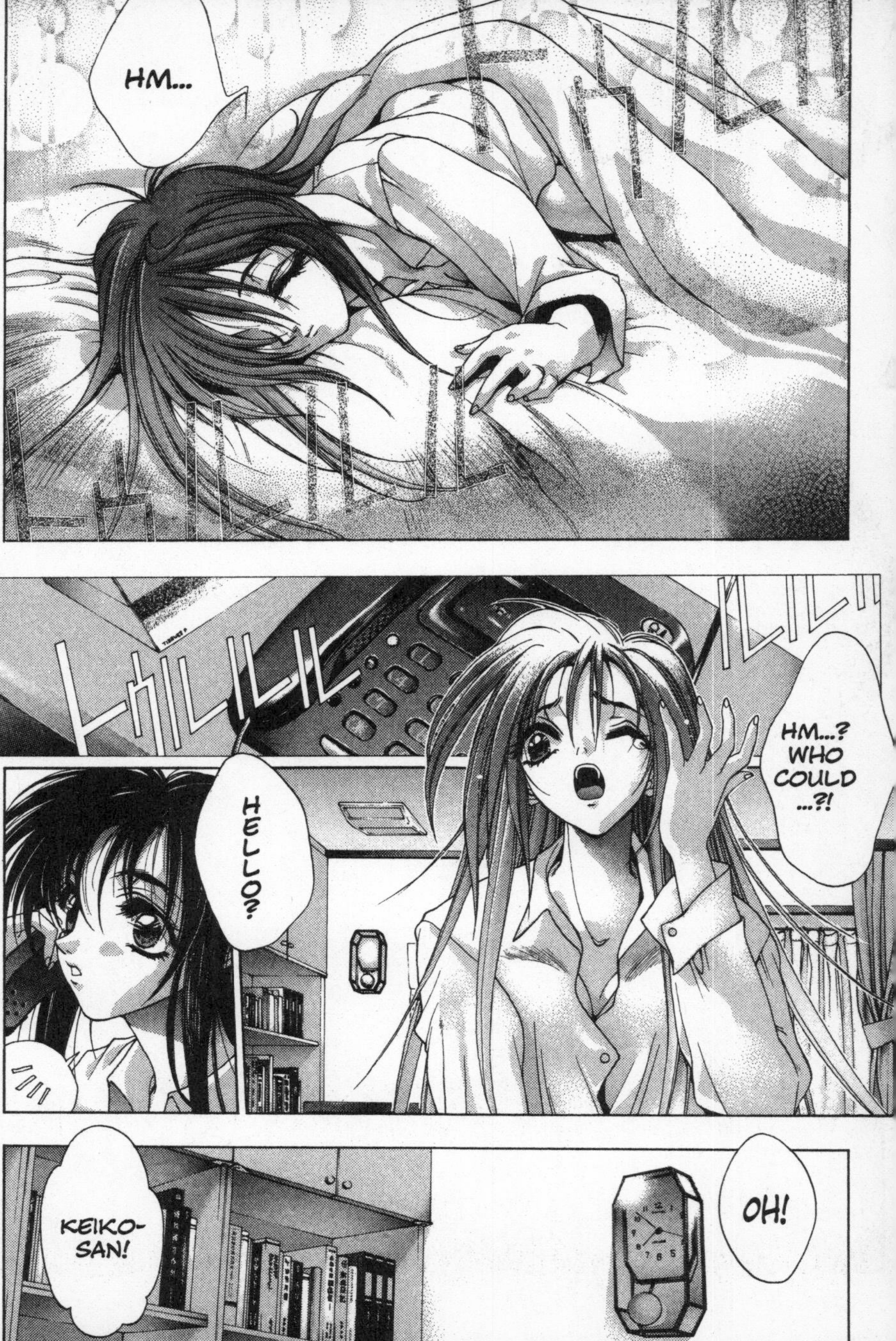
HM...
HM...? WHO COULD ...?!
HELLO?
OH!
KEIKO-SAN!

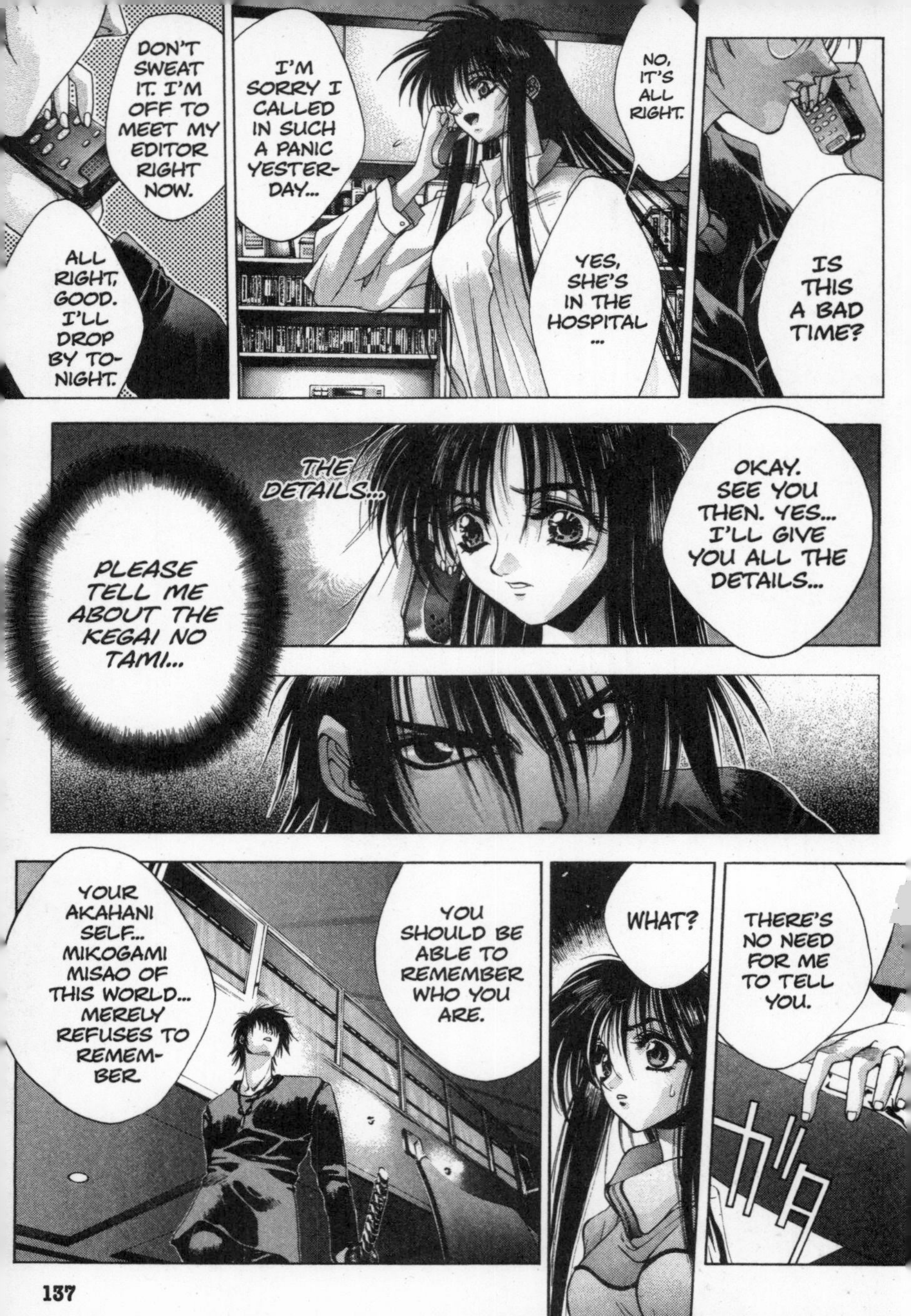
IS THIS A BAD TIME?
NO, IT'S ALL RIGHT.
I'M SORRY I CALLED IN SUCH A PANIC YESTER-DAY...
YES, SHE'S IN THE HOSPITAL...
DON'T SWEAT IT. I'M OFF TO MEET MY EDITOR RIGHT NOW.
ALL RIGHT, GOOD. I'LL DROP BY TO-NIGHT.
OKAY. SEE YOU THEN. YES... I'LL GIVE YOU ALL THE DETAILS...
THE DETAILS...
PLEASE TELL ME ABOUT THE KEGAI NO TAMI...
THERE'S NO NEED FOR ME TO TELL YOU.
WHAT?
YOU SHOULD BE ABLE TO REMEMBER WHO YOU ARE.
YOUR AKAHANI SELF... MIKOGAMI MISAO OF THIS WORLD... MERELY REFUSES TO REMEM-BER

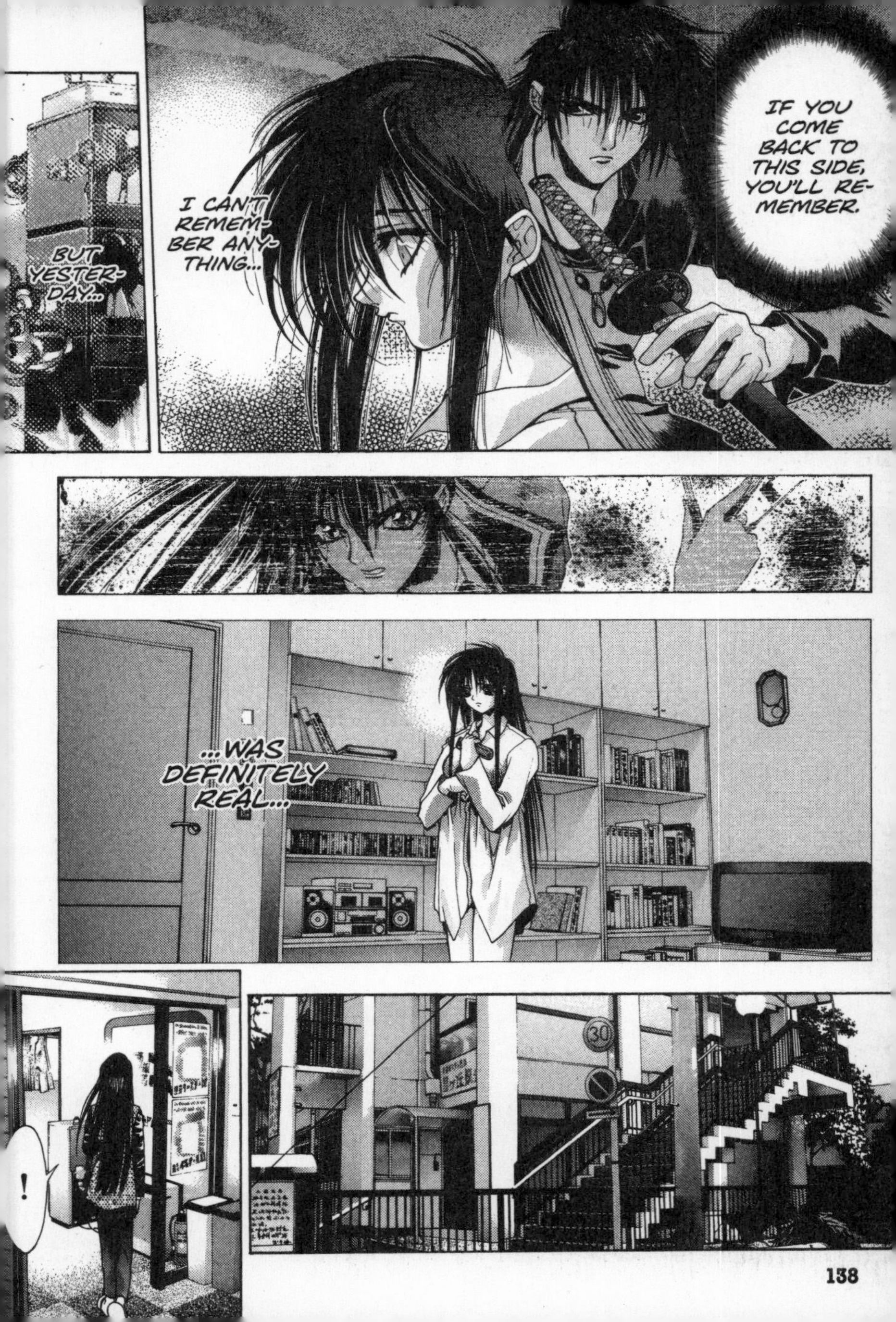
IF YOU COME BACK TO THIS SIDE, YOU'LL RE-MEMBER.
I CAN'T REMEM-BER ANY-THING...
BUT YESTER-DAY...
...WAS DEFINITELY REAL...
!

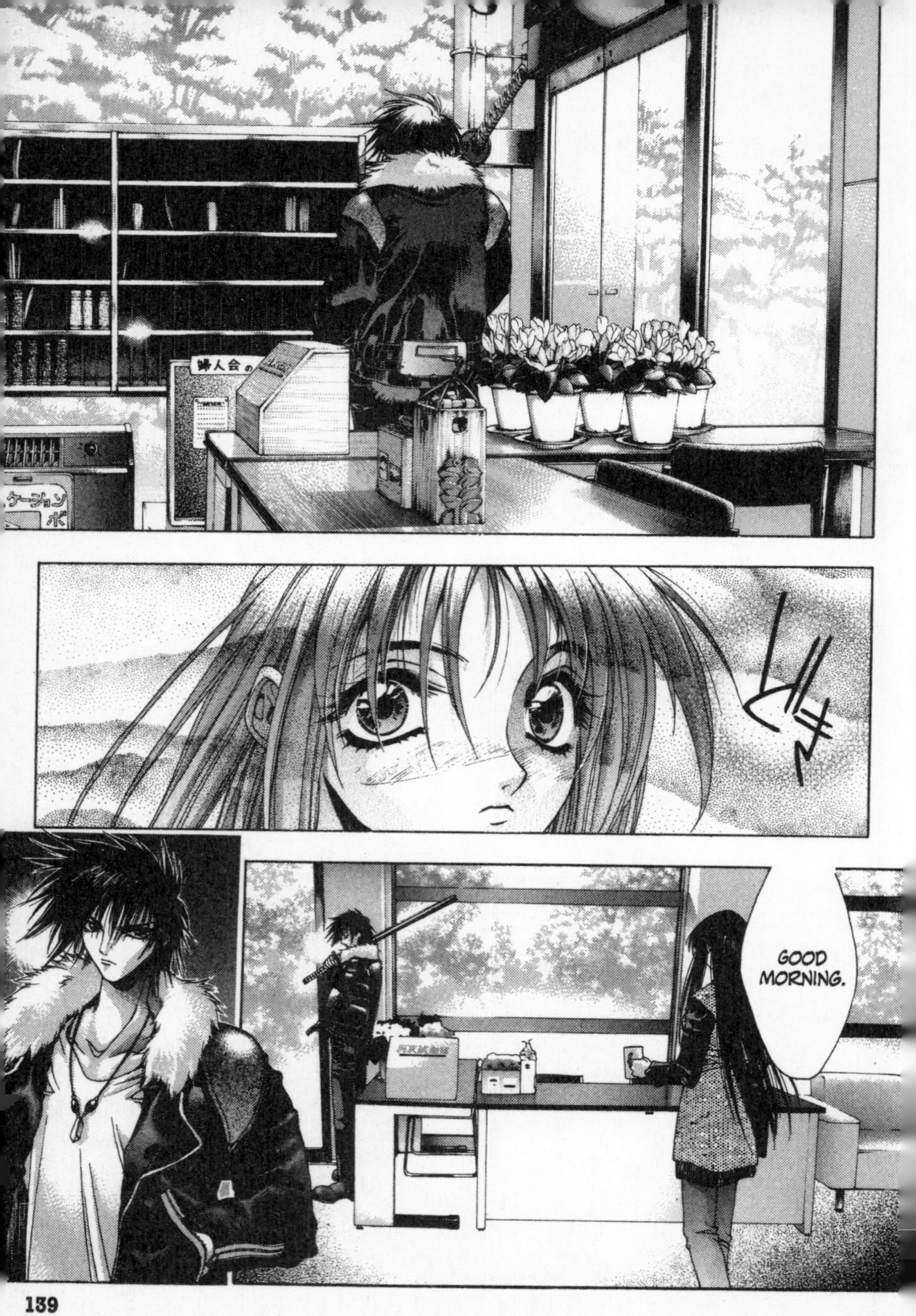
GOOD MORNING.

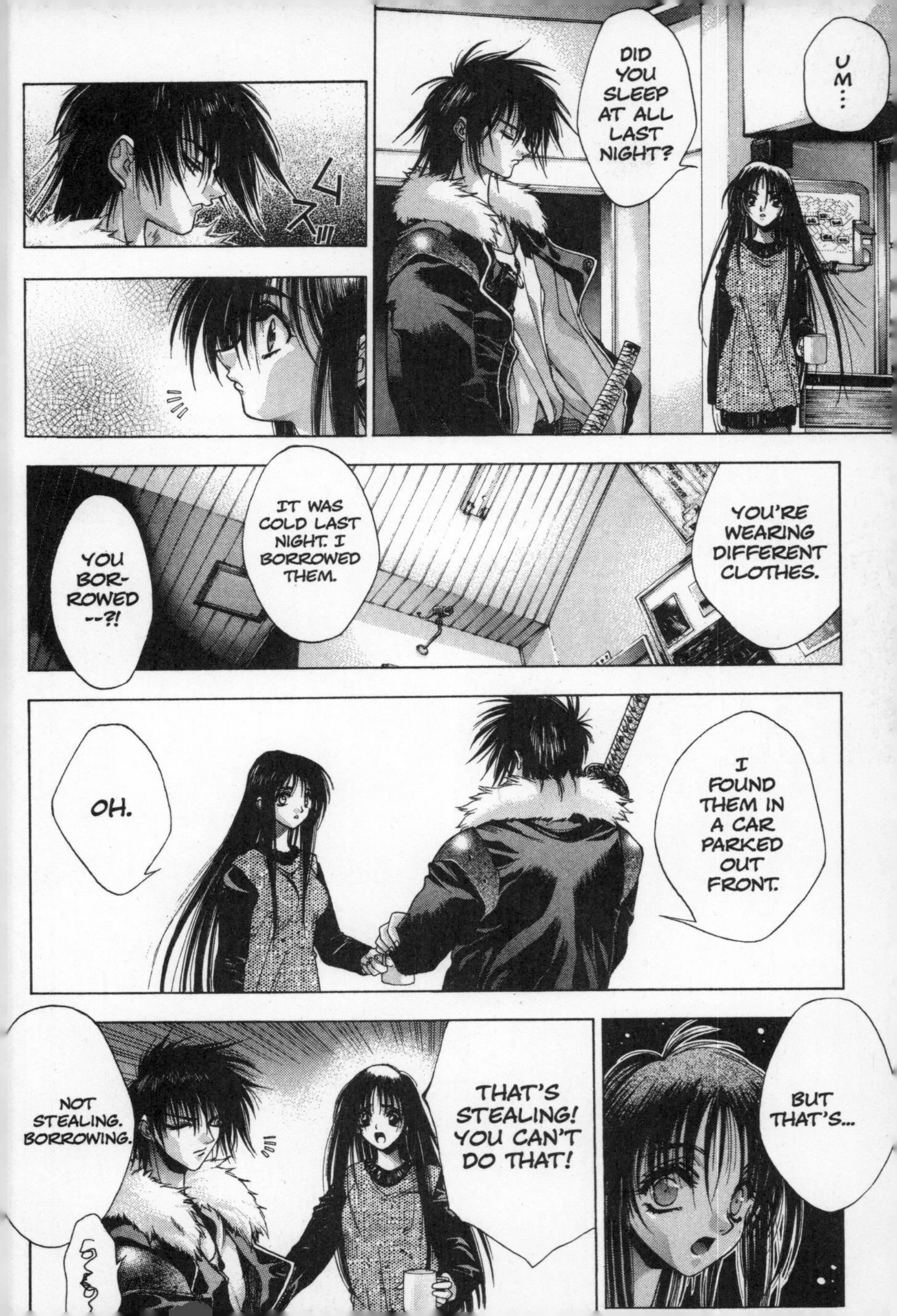
UM...
DID YOU SLEEP AT ALL LAST NIGHT?
ムスッ
YOU'RE WEARING DIFFERENT CLOTHES.
IT WAS COLD LAST NIGHT. I BORROWED THEM.
YOU BOR-ROWED--?!
I FOUND THEM IN A CAR PARKED OUT FRONT.
OH.
BUT THAT'S...
THAT'S STEALING! YOU CAN'T DO THAT!
NOT STEALING. BORROWING.

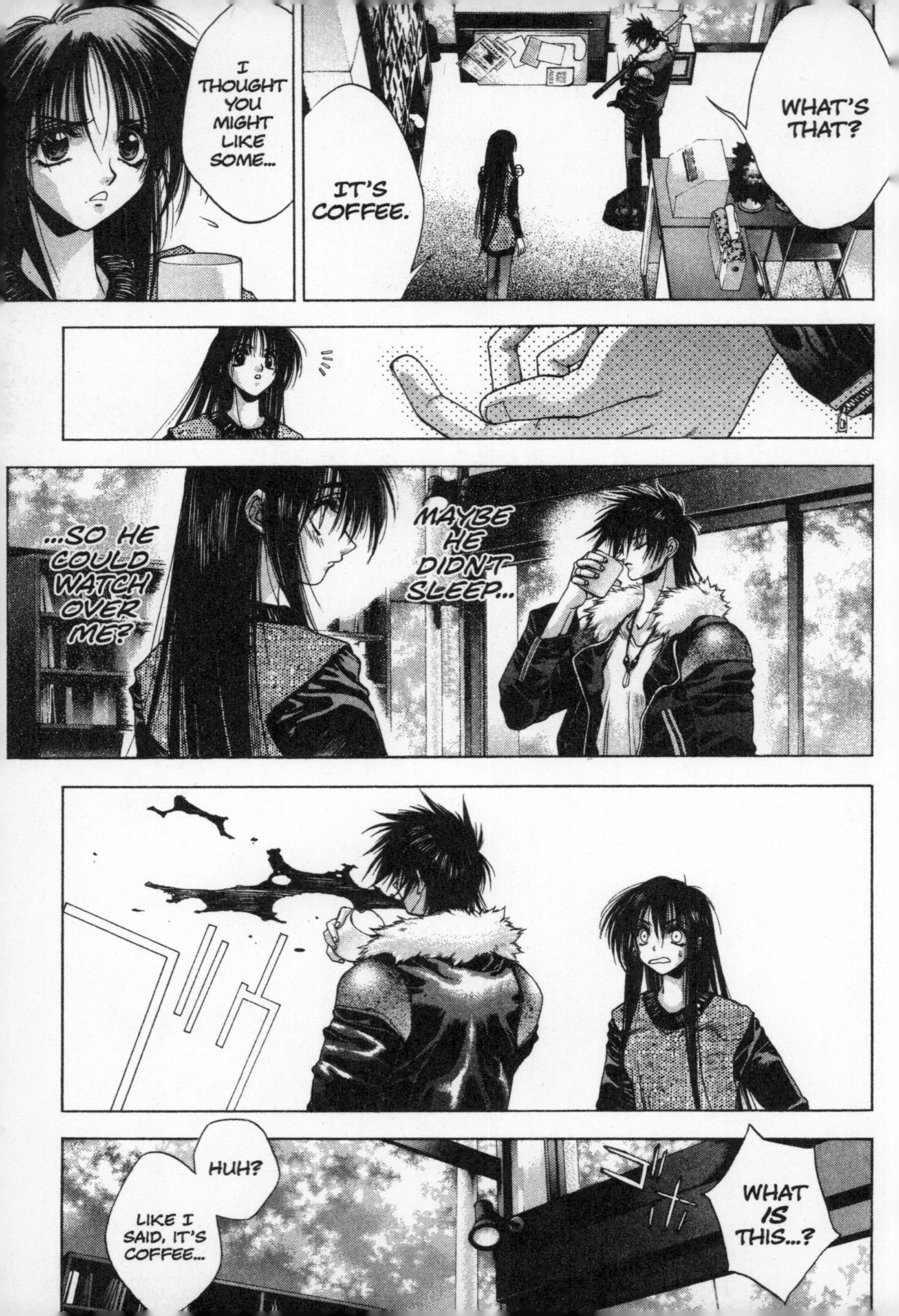
WHAT'S THAT?
IT'S COFFEE.
I THOUGHT YOU MIGHT LIKE SOME...
MAYBE HE DIDN'T SLEEP...
...SO HE COULD WATCH OVER ME?
WHAT *IS* THIS...?
HUH?
LIKE I SAID, IT'S COFFEE...

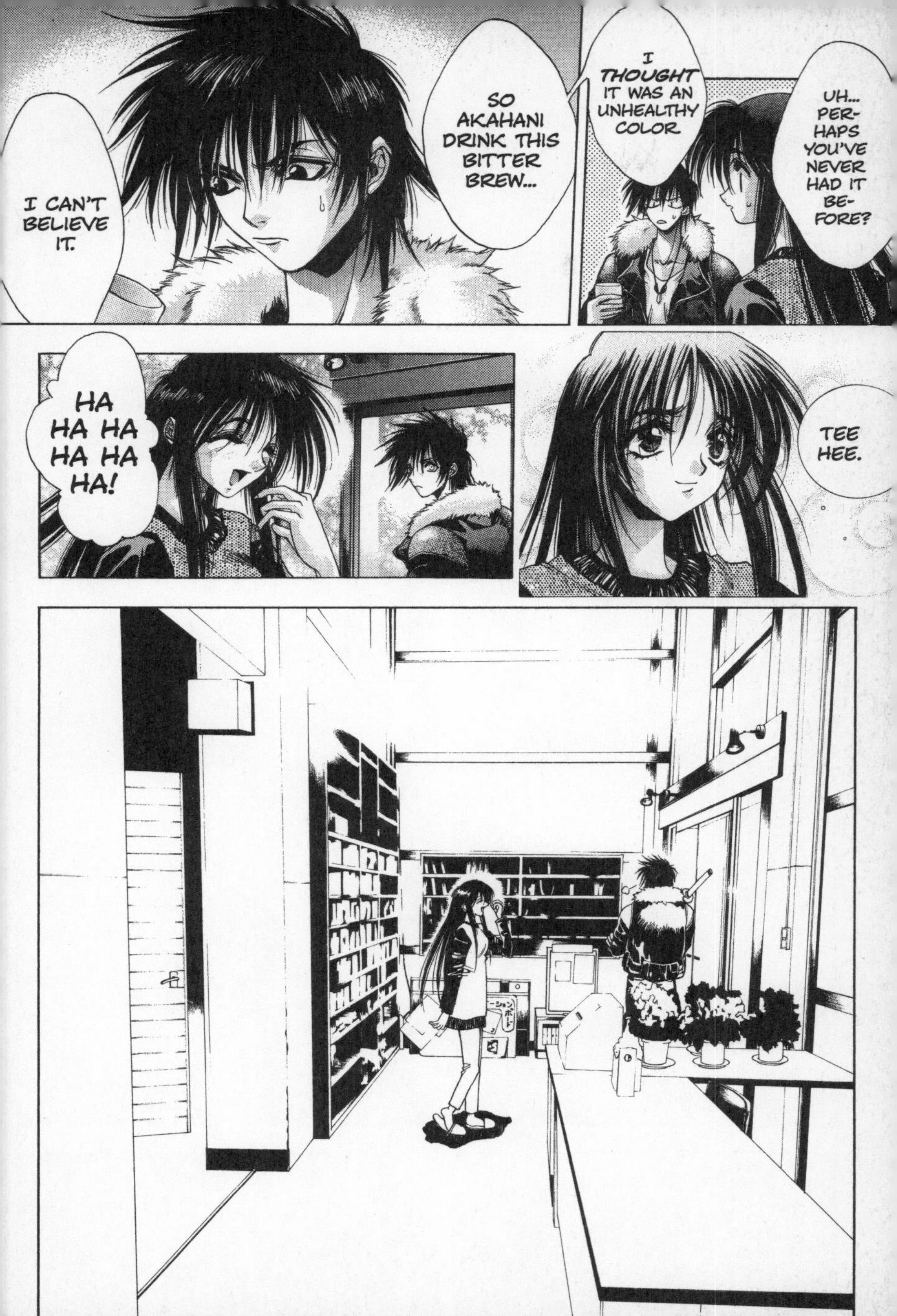
UH... PER-HAPS YOU'VE NEVER HAD IT BE-FORE?
I *THOUGHT* IT WAS AN UNHEALTHY COLOR
SO AKAHANI DRINK THIS BITTER BREW...
I CAN'T BELIEVE IT.
TEE HEE.
HA HA HA HA HA HA!

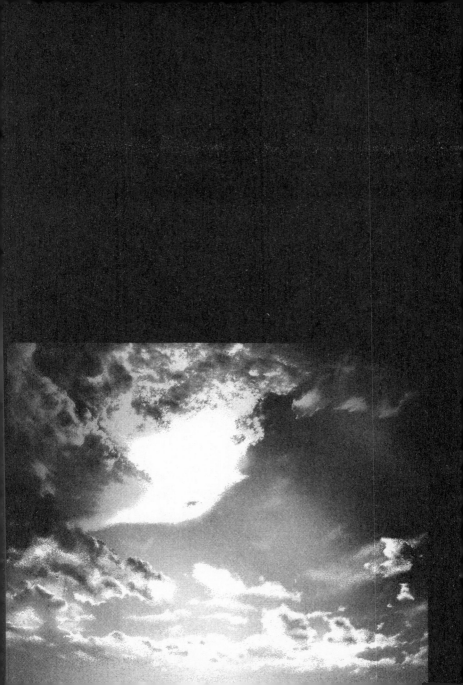

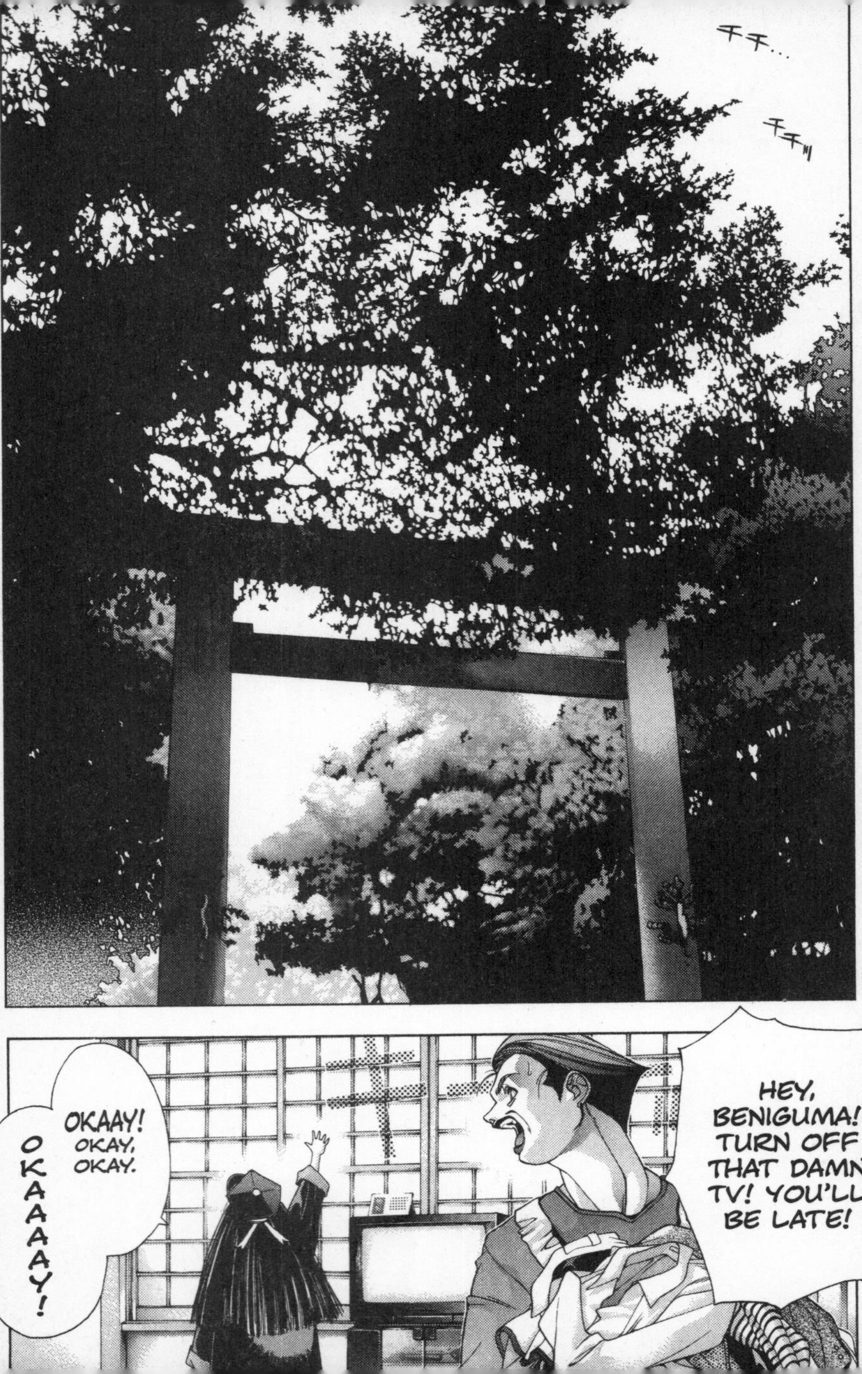
チチ...
チチッ
HEY, BENIGUMA! TURN OFF THAT DAMN TV! YOU'LL BE LATE!
OKAAY! OKAY, OKAY.
OKAAAAAY!

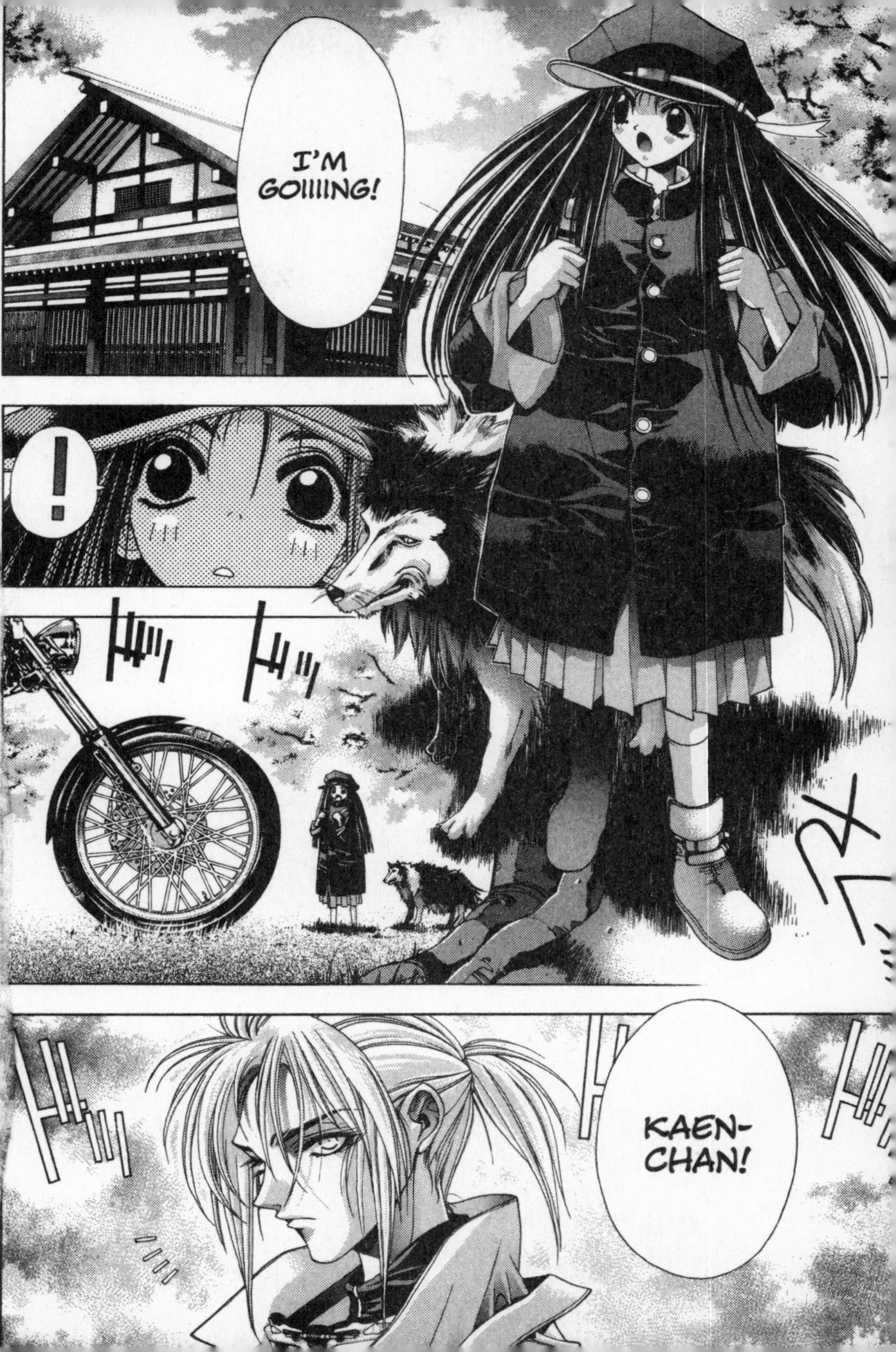
I'M GOIIIING!
!
KAEN-CHAN!

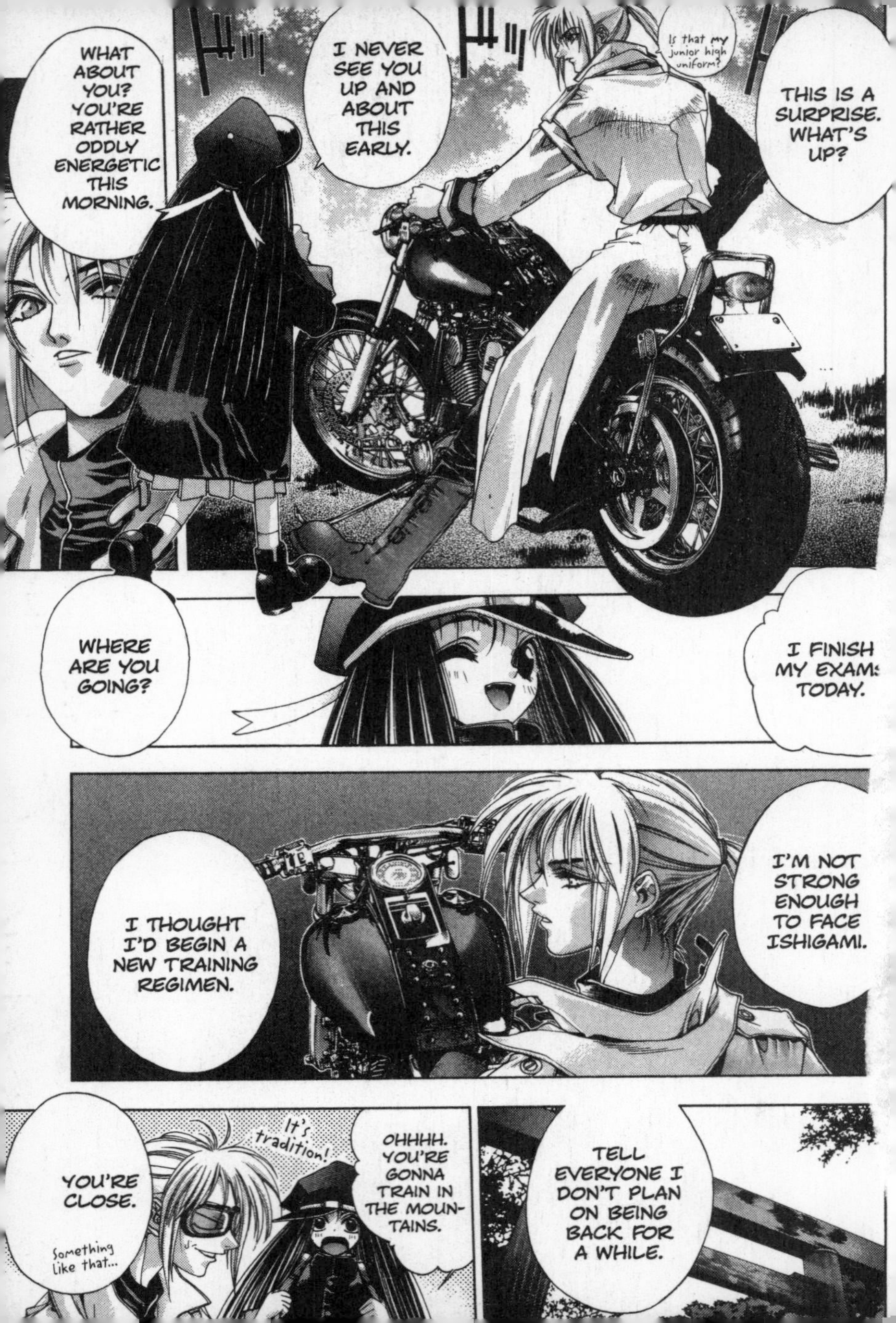
THIS IS A SURPRISE. WHAT'S UP?
Is that my junior high uniform?
I NEVER SEE YOU UP AND ABOUT THIS EARLY.
WHAT ABOUT YOU? YOU'RE RATHER ODDLY ENERGETIC THIS MORNING.
...
I FINISH MY EXAMS TODAY.
WHERE ARE YOU GOING?
I'M NOT STRONG ENOUGH TO FACE ISHIGAMI.
I THOUGHT I'D BEGIN A NEW TRAINING REGIMEN.
TELL EVERYONE I DON'T PLAN ON BEING BACK FOR A WHILE.
OHHHH. YOU'RE GONNA TRAIN IN THE MOUN-TAINS.
It's tradition!
YOU'RE CLOSE.
Something like that...

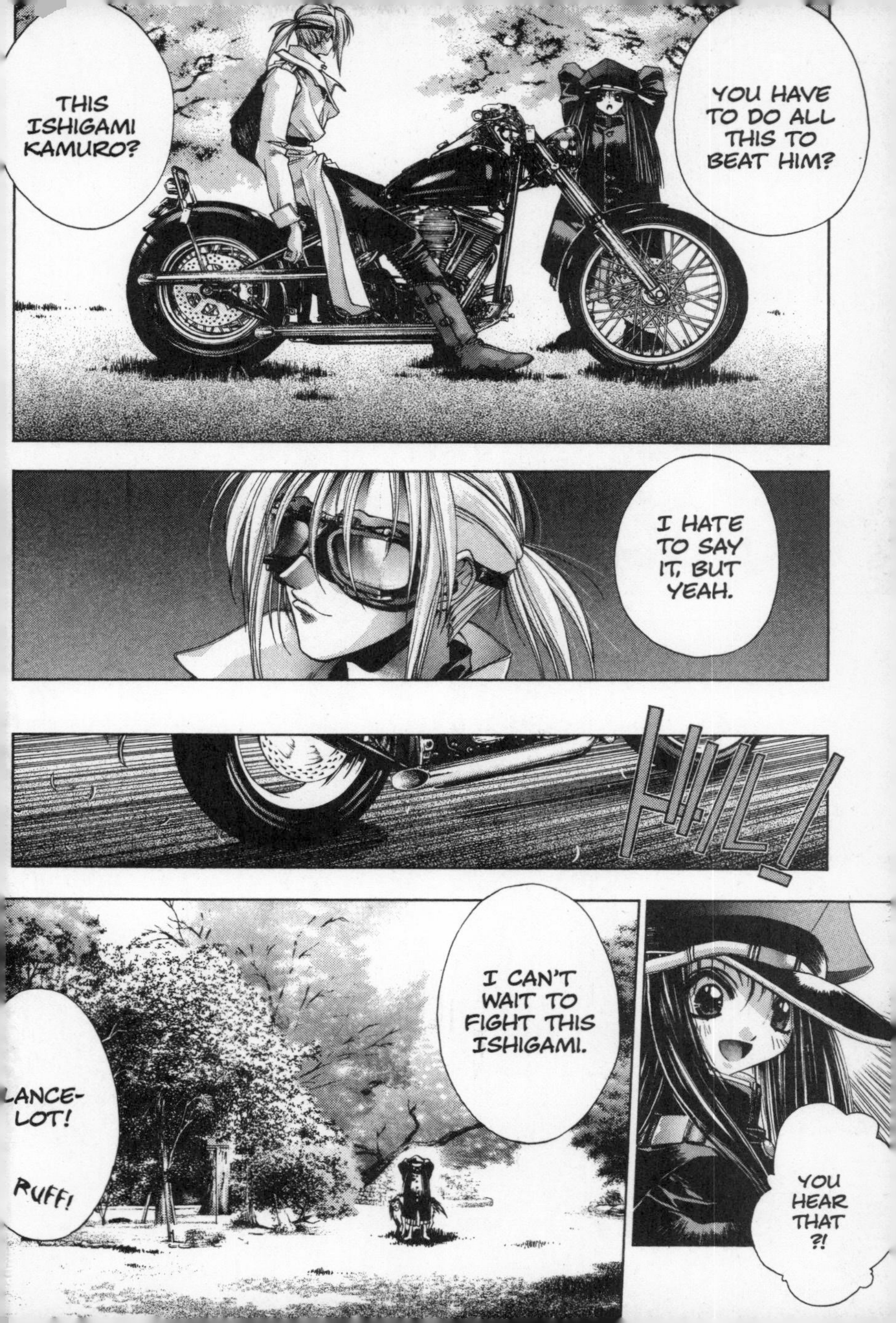
YOU HAVE TO DO ALL THIS TO BEAT HIM?
THIS ISHIGAMI KAMURO?
I HATE TO SAY IT, BUT YEAH.
YOU HEAR THAT ?!
I CAN'T WAIT TO FIGHT THIS ISHIGAMI.
LANCE-LOT!
RUFF!

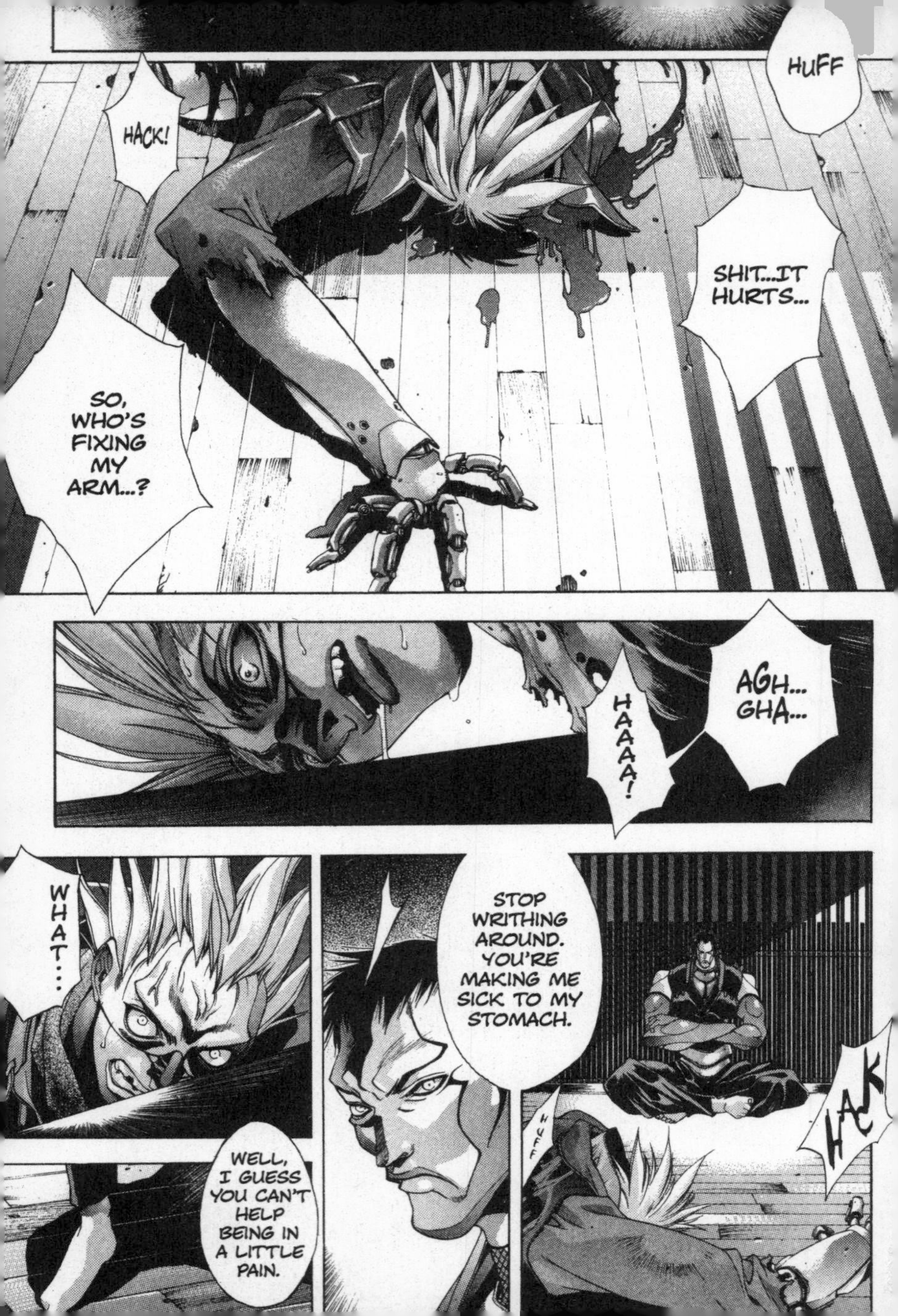
HUFF
HACK!
SHIT...IT HURTS...
SO, WHO'S FIXING MY ARM...?
AGH... GHA...
HAAAAA!
STOP WRITHING AROUND. YOU'RE MAKING ME SICK TO MY STOMACH.
HACK
HUFF
WELL, I GUESS YOU CAN'T HELP BEING IN A LITTLE PAIN.
WHAT...

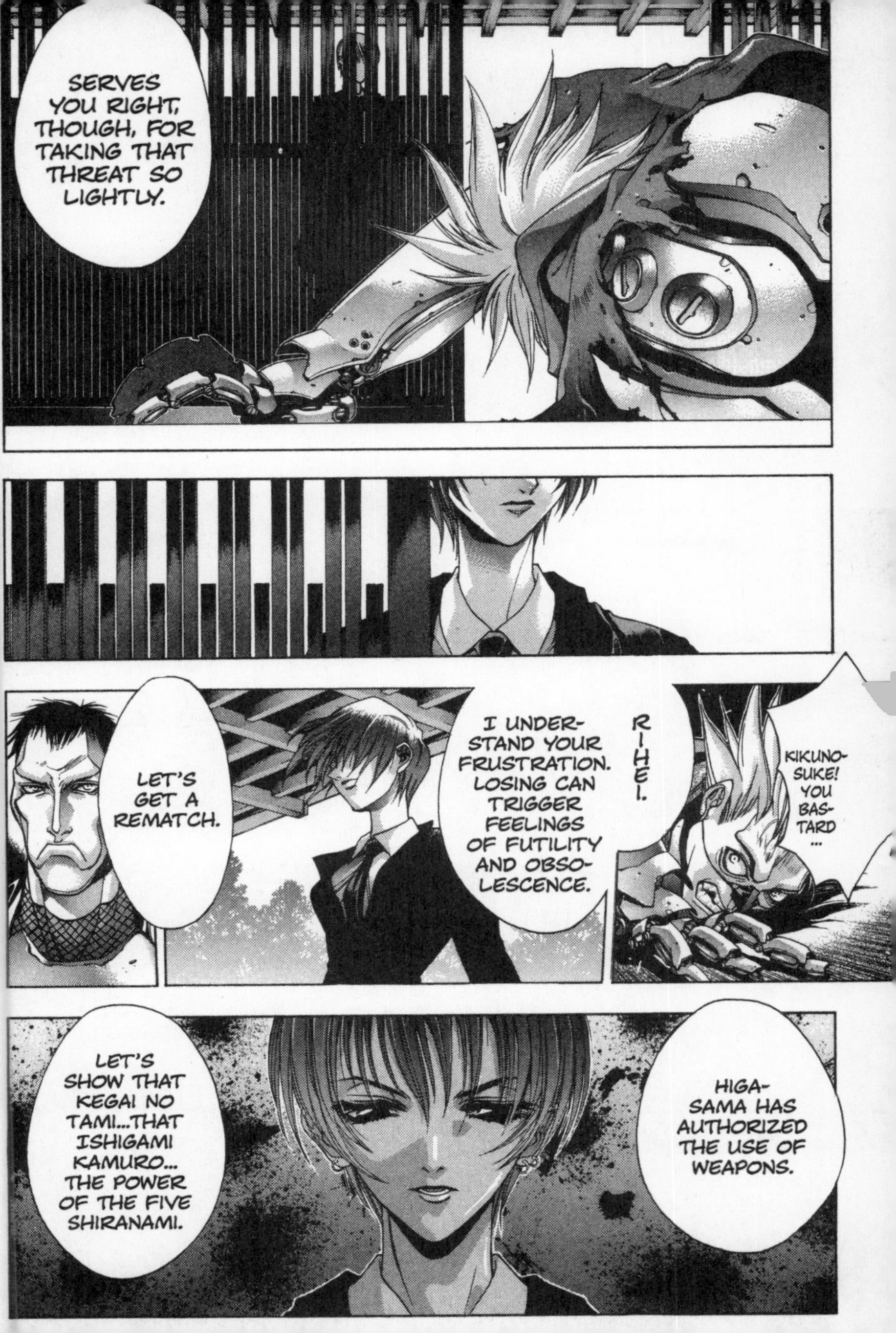

SERVES YOU RIGHT, THOUGH, FOR TAKING THAT THREAT SO LIGHTLY.
KIKUNO-SUKE! YOU BAS-TARD...
RIHEI.
I UNDER-STAND YOUR FRUSTRATION. LOSING CAN TRIGGER FEELINGS OF FUTILITY AND OBSO-LESCENCE.
LET'S GET A REMATCH.
HIGA-SAMA HAS AUTHORIZED THE USE OF WEAPONS.
LET'S SHOW THAT KEGAI NO TAMI...THAT ISHIGAMI KAMURO... THE POWER OF THE FIVE SHIRANAMI.

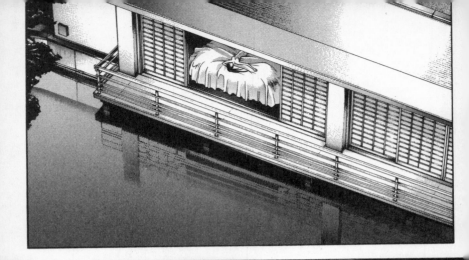

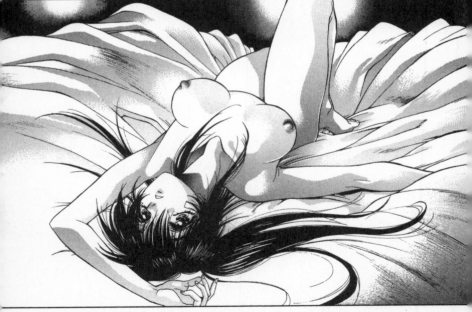

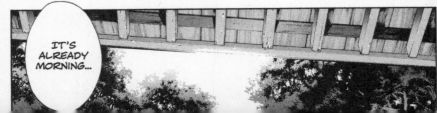

IT'S
ALREADY
MORNING...

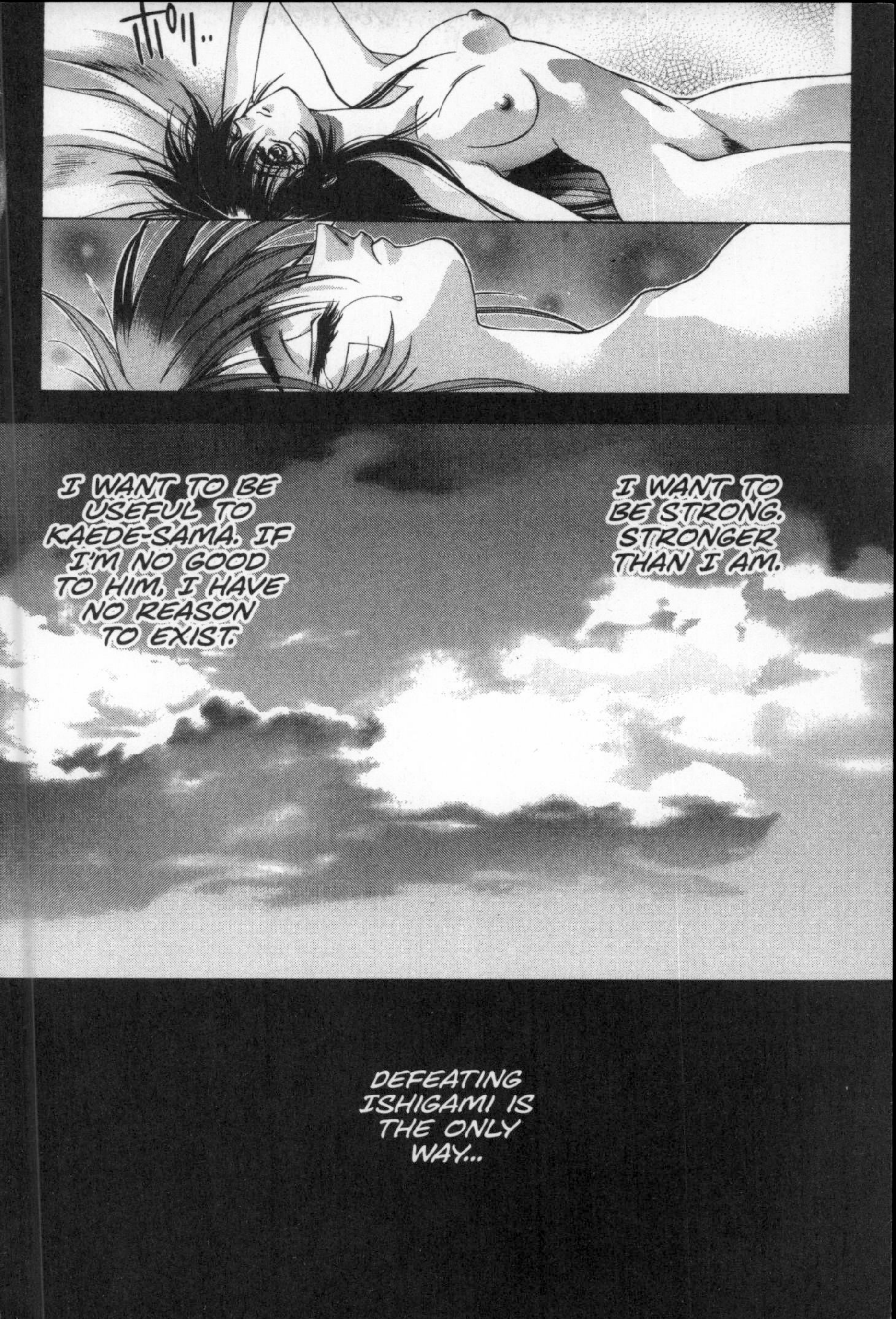
I WANT TO BE STRONG. STRONGER THAN I AM.
I WANT TO BE USEFUL TO KAEDE-SAMA. IF I'M NO GOOD TO HIM, I HAVE NO REASON TO EXIST.
DEFEATING ISHIGAMI IS THE ONLY WAY...

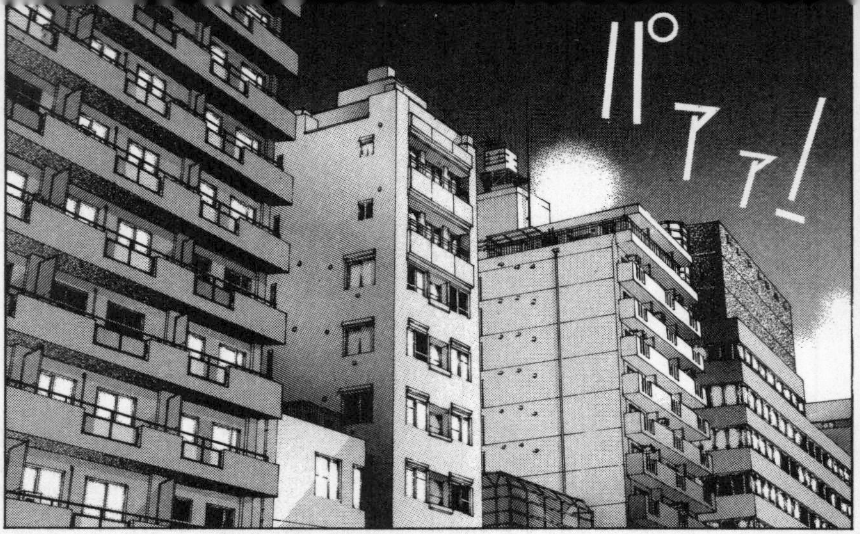
パァァ！
5: Weekly Tansei Editorial Division

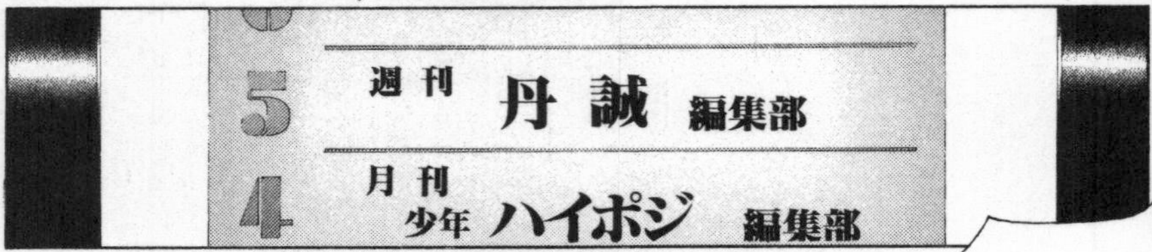
5
週刊 丹誠 編集部
4
月刊 少年 ハイポジ 編集部
4: Monthly Shonen Hi-Posi Editorial Division

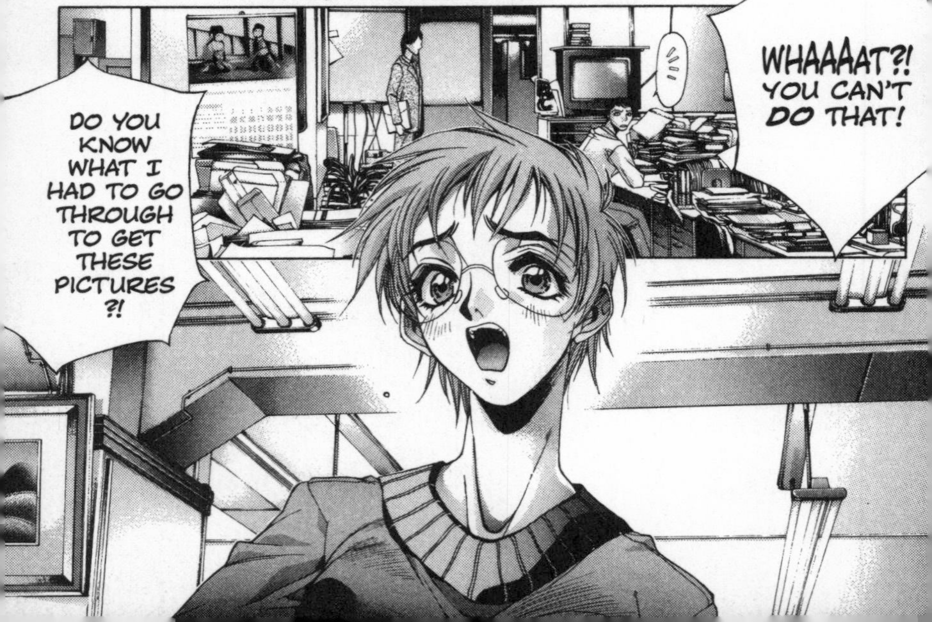
WHAAAAT?! YOU CAN'T DO THAT!
DO YOU KNOW WHAT I HAD TO GO THROUGH TO GET THESE PICTURES?!

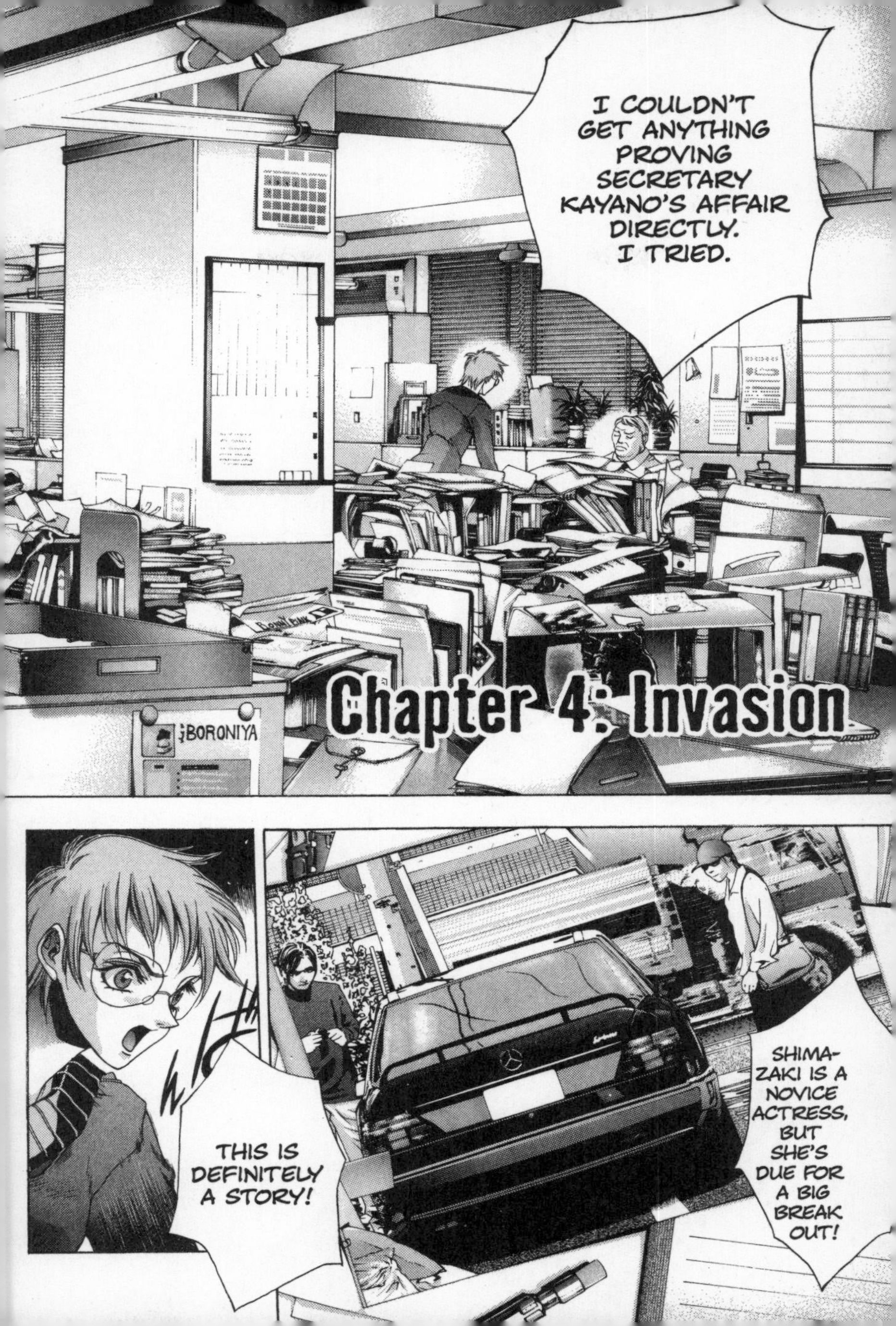
I COULDN'T GET ANYTHING PROVING SECRETARY KAYANO'S AFFAIR DIRECTLY. I TRIED.
Chapter 4: Invasion
BORONIYA
SHIMAZAKI IS A NOVICE ACTRESS, BUT SHE'S DUE FOR A BIG BREAK OUT!
THIS IS DEFINITELY A STORY!

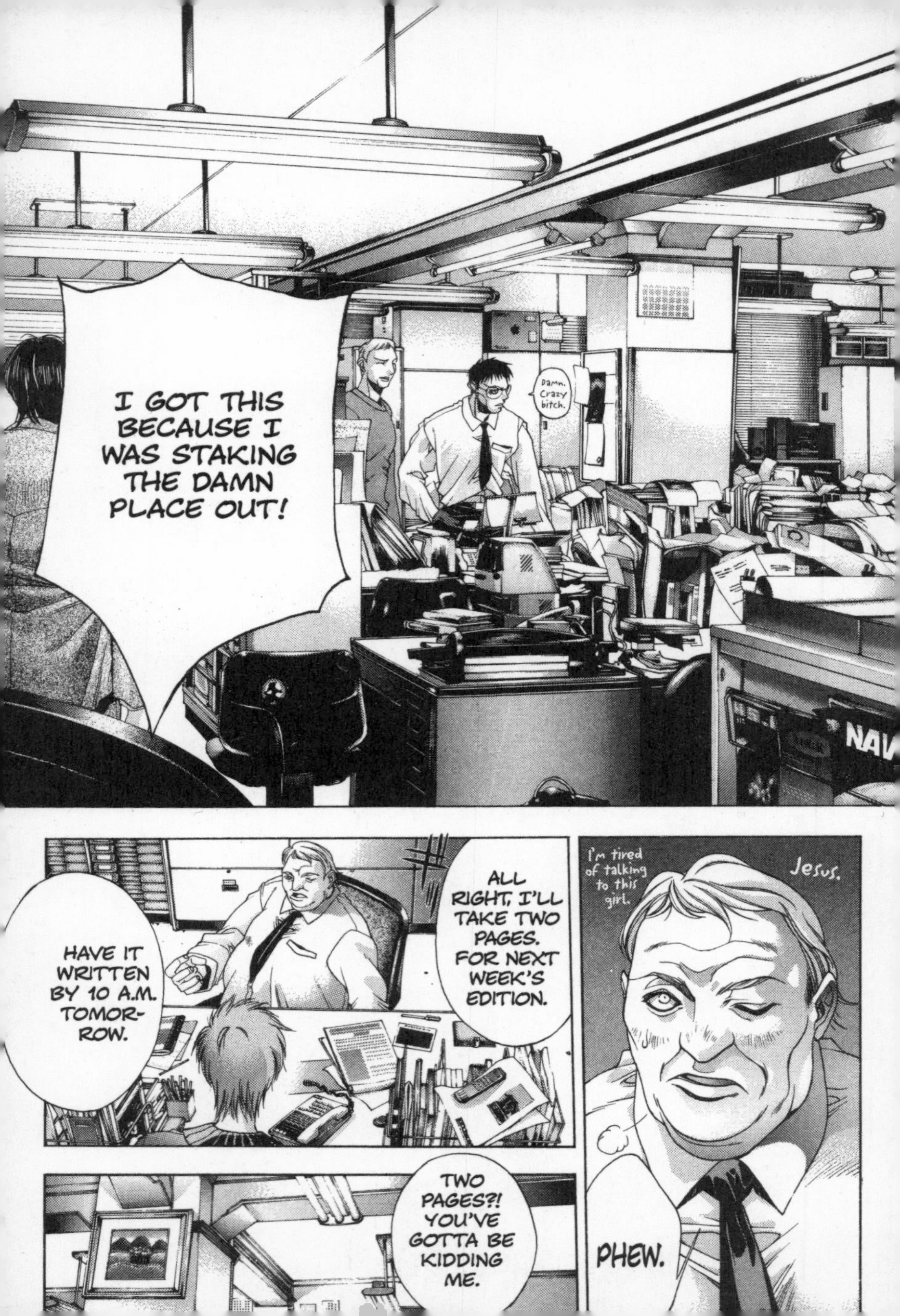
Damn. Crazy bitch.
I GOT THIS BECAUSE I WAS STAKING THE DAMN PLACE OUT!
Jesus.
I'm tired of talking to this girl.
PHEW.
ALL RIGHT, I'LL TAKE TWO PAGES. FOR NEXT WEEK'S EDITION.
HAVE IT WRITTEN BY 10 A.M. TOMOR-ROW.
TWO PAGES?! YOU'VE GOTTA BE KIDDING ME.

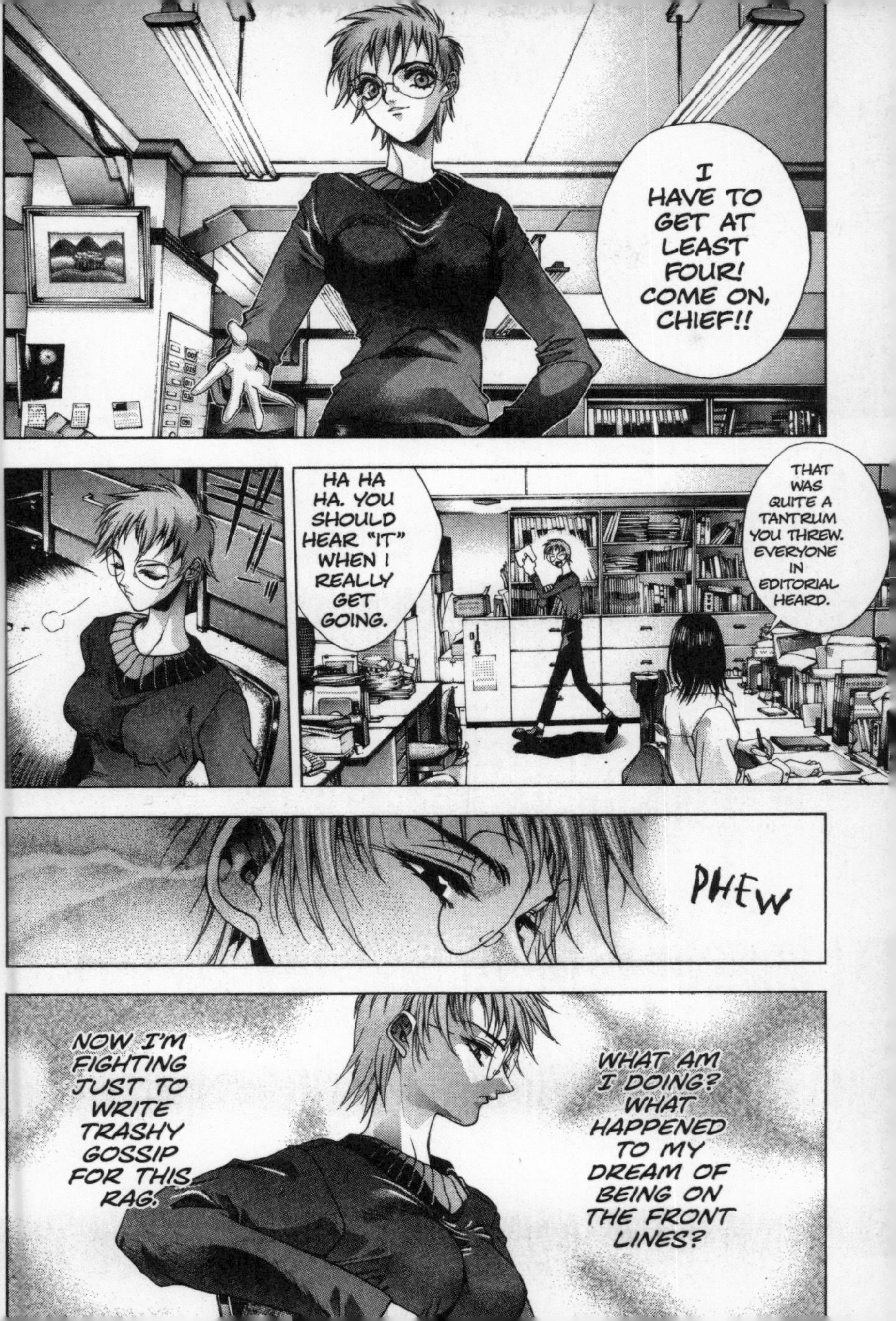
I HAVE TO GET AT LEAST FOUR! COME ON, CHIEF!!
THAT WAS QUITE A TANTRUM YOU THREW. EVERYONE IN EDITORIAL HEARD.
HA HA HA. YOU SHOULD HEAR "IT" WHEN I REALLY GET GOING.
PHEW
WHAT AM I DOING? WHAT HAPPENED TO MY DREAM OF BEING ON THE FRONT LINES?
NOW I'M FIGHTING JUST TO WRITE TRASHY GOSSIP FOR THIS RAG.

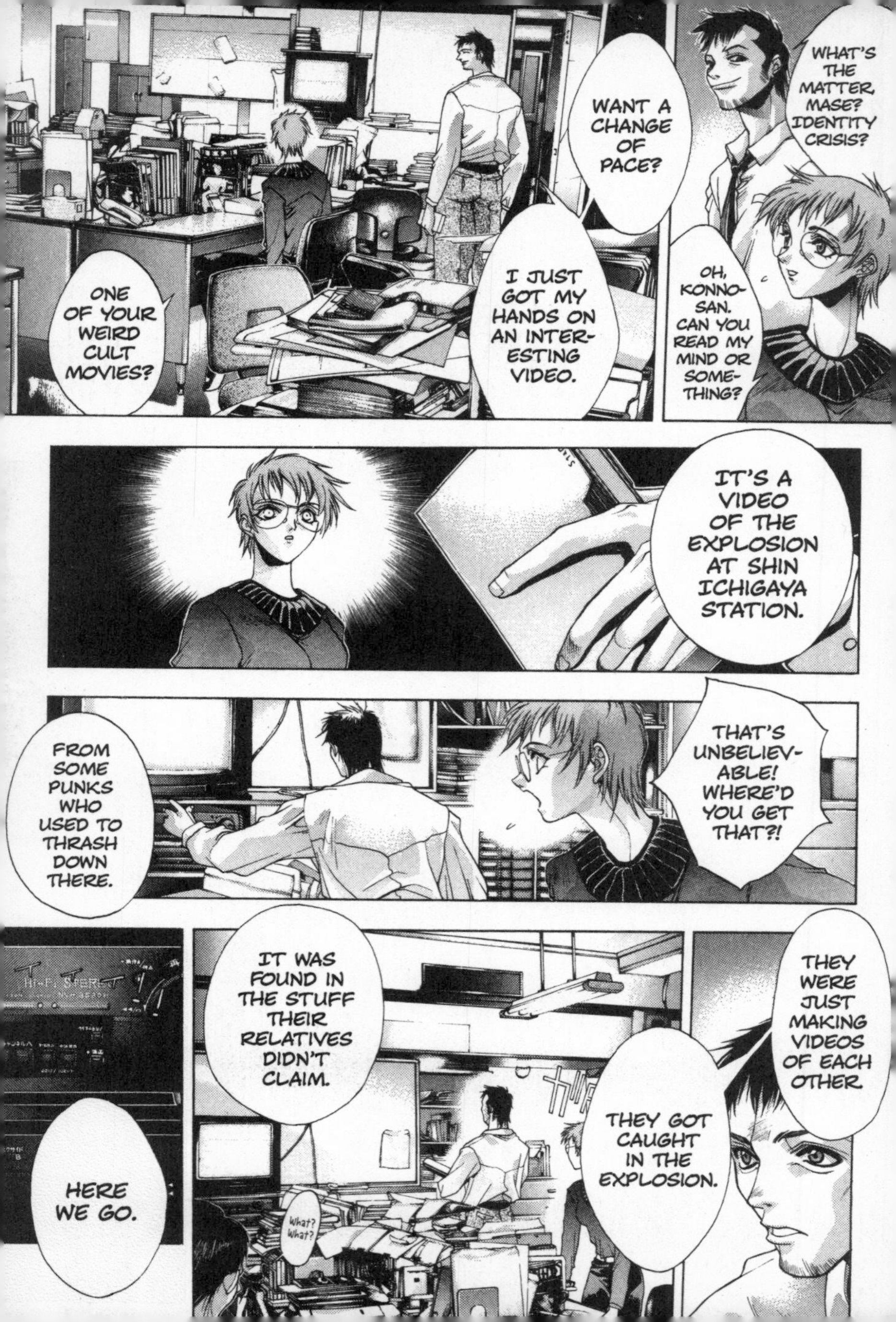
WHAT'S THE MATTER, MASE? IDENTITY CRISIS?
OH, KONNO-SAN. CAN YOU READ MY MIND OR SOMETHING?
WANT A CHANGE OF PACE?
I JUST GOT MY HANDS ON AN INTERESTING VIDEO.
ONE OF YOUR WEIRD CULT MOVIES?
IT'S A VIDEO OF THE EXPLOSION AT SHIN ICHIGAYA STATION.
THAT'S UNBELIEVABLE! WHERE'D YOU GET THAT?!
FROM SOME PUNKS WHO USED TO THRASH DOWN THERE.
THEY WERE JUST MAKING VIDEOS OF EACH OTHER.
THEY GOT CAUGHT IN THE EXPLOSION.
IT WAS FOUND IN THE STUFF THEIR RELATIVES DIDN'T CLAIM.
What? What?
HERE WE GO.

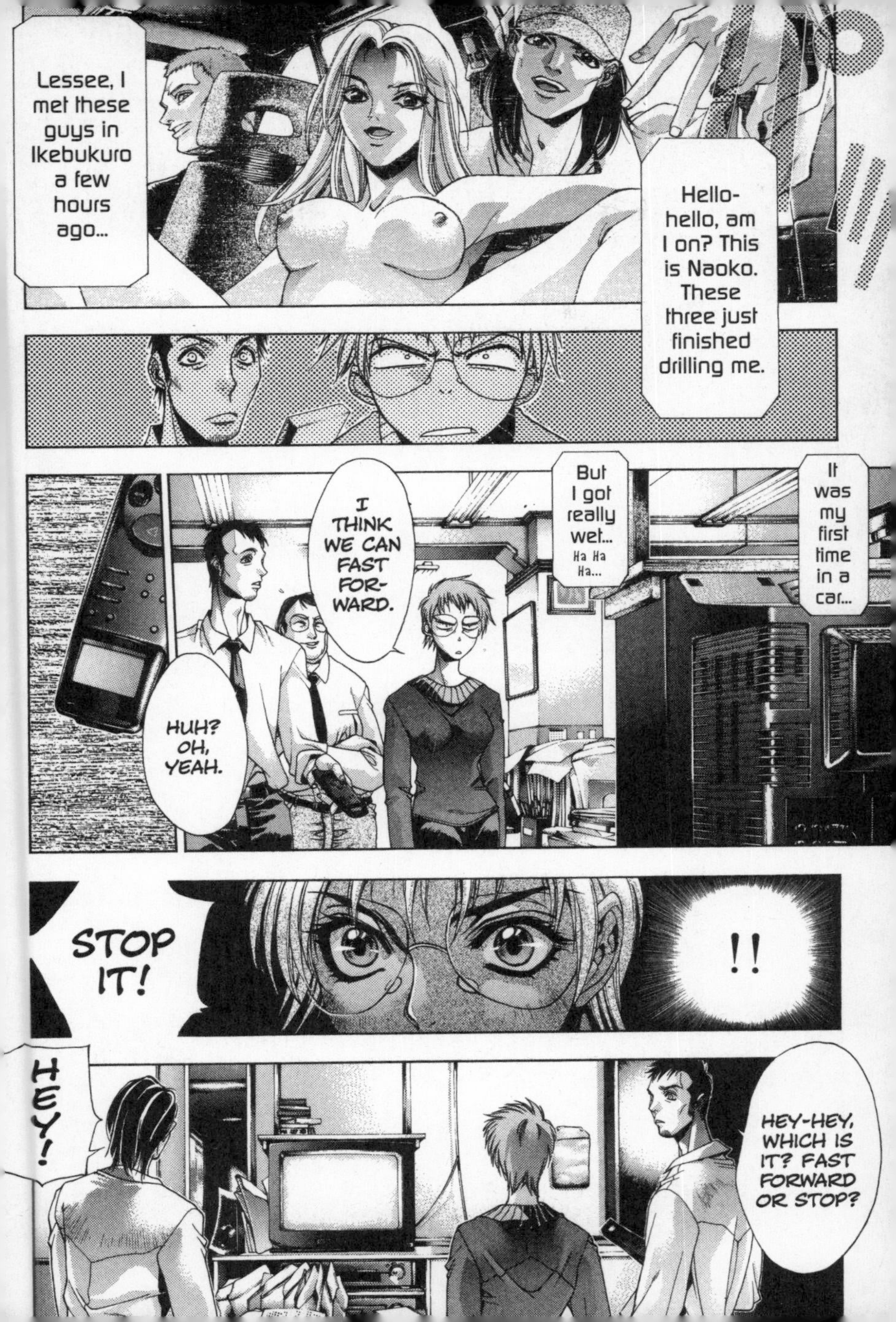
Hello-hello, am I on? This is Naoko. These three just finished drilling me.
Lessee, I met these guys in Ikebukuro a few hours ago...
It was my first time in a car...
But I got really wet... Ha Ha Ha...
I THINK WE CAN FAST FORWARD.
HUH? OH, YEAH.
!!
STOP IT!
HEY-HEY, WHICH IS IT? FAST FORWARD OR STOP?
HEY!

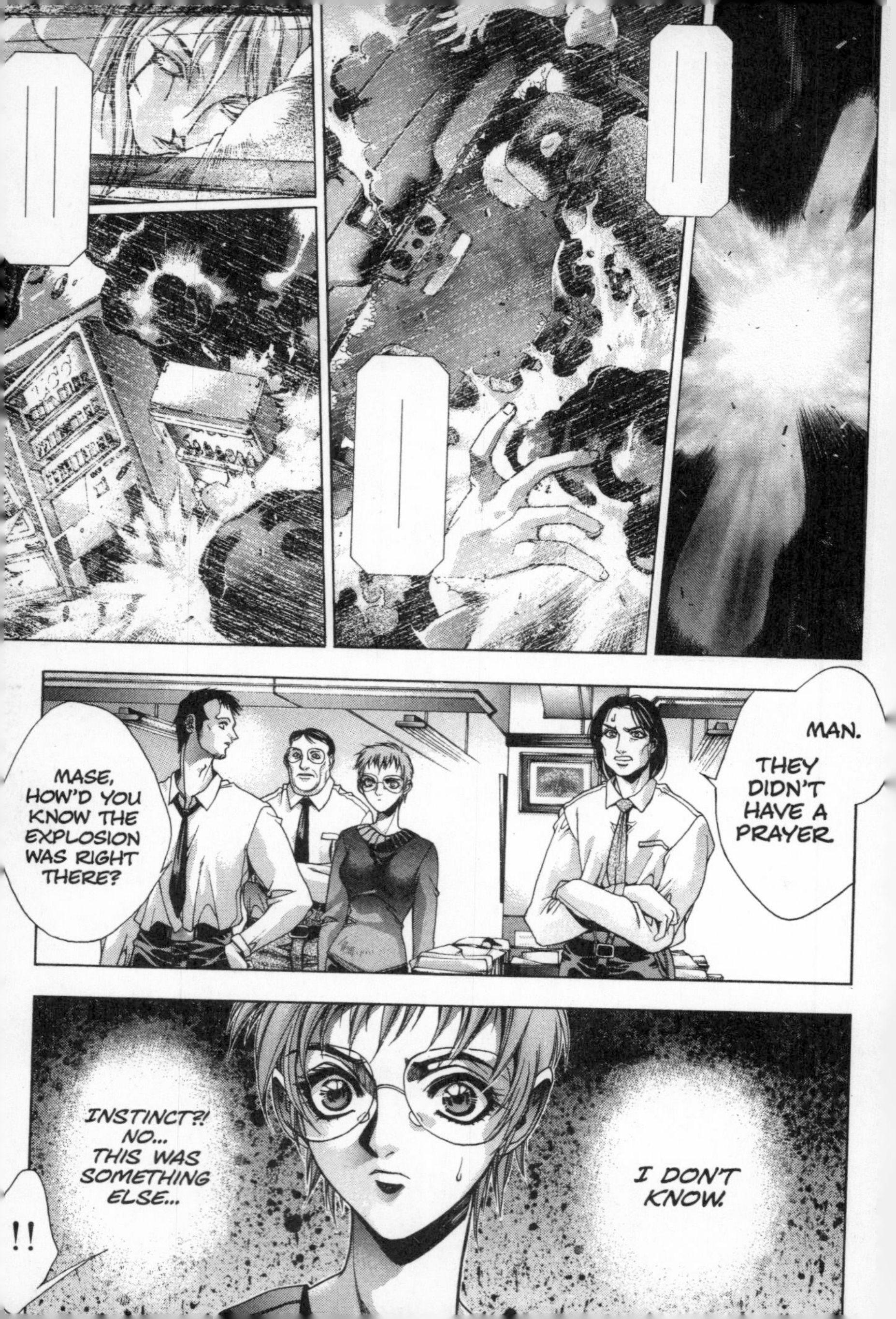
MAN.
THEY DIDN'T HAVE A PRAYER.
MASE, HOW'D YOU KNOW THE EXPLOSION WAS RIGHT THERE?
I DON'T KNOW.
INSTINCT?! NO... THIS WAS SOMETHING ELSE...
!!

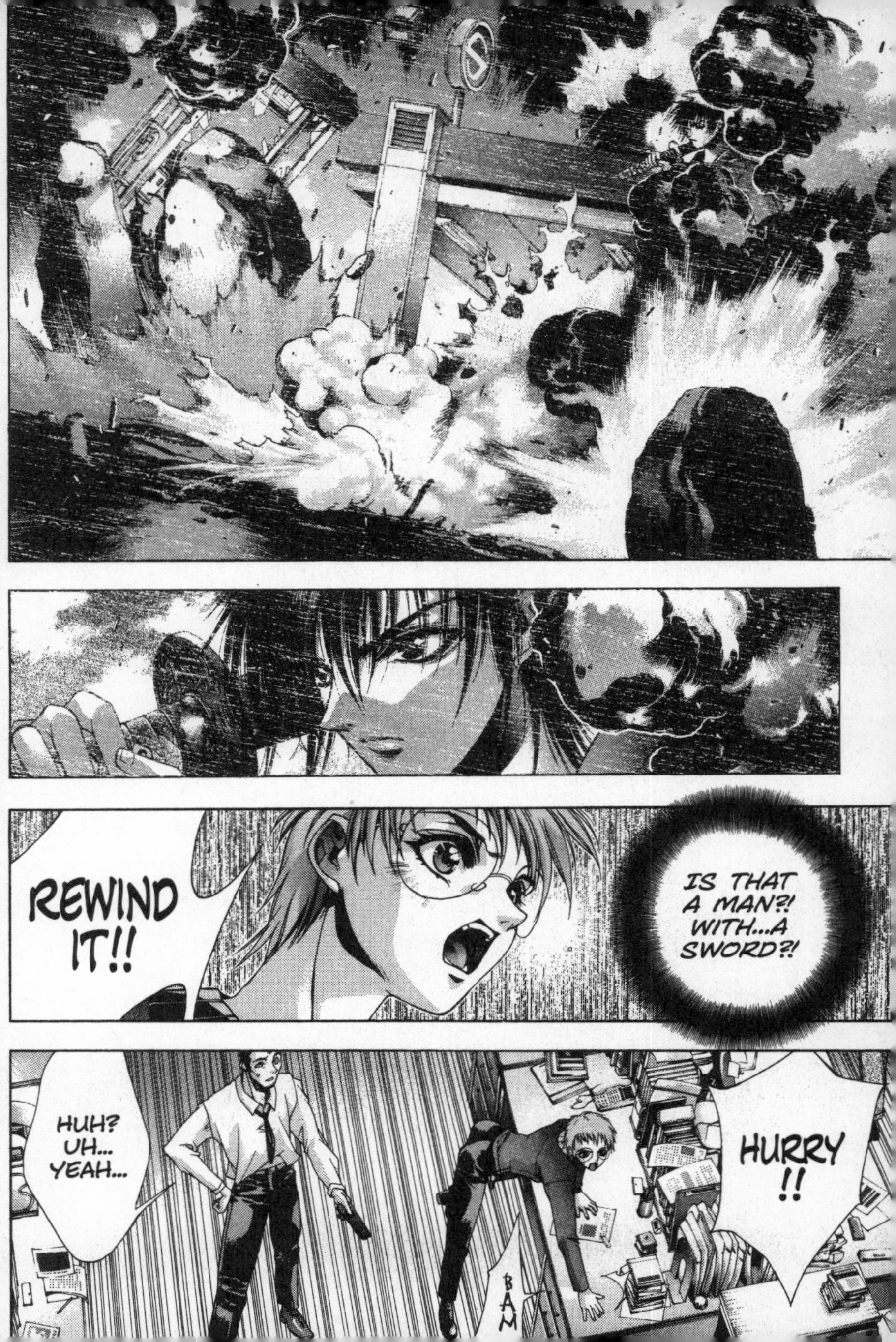
IS THAT A MAN?! WITH...A SWORD?!
REWIND IT!!
HURRY !!
BAM
HUH? UH... YEAH...

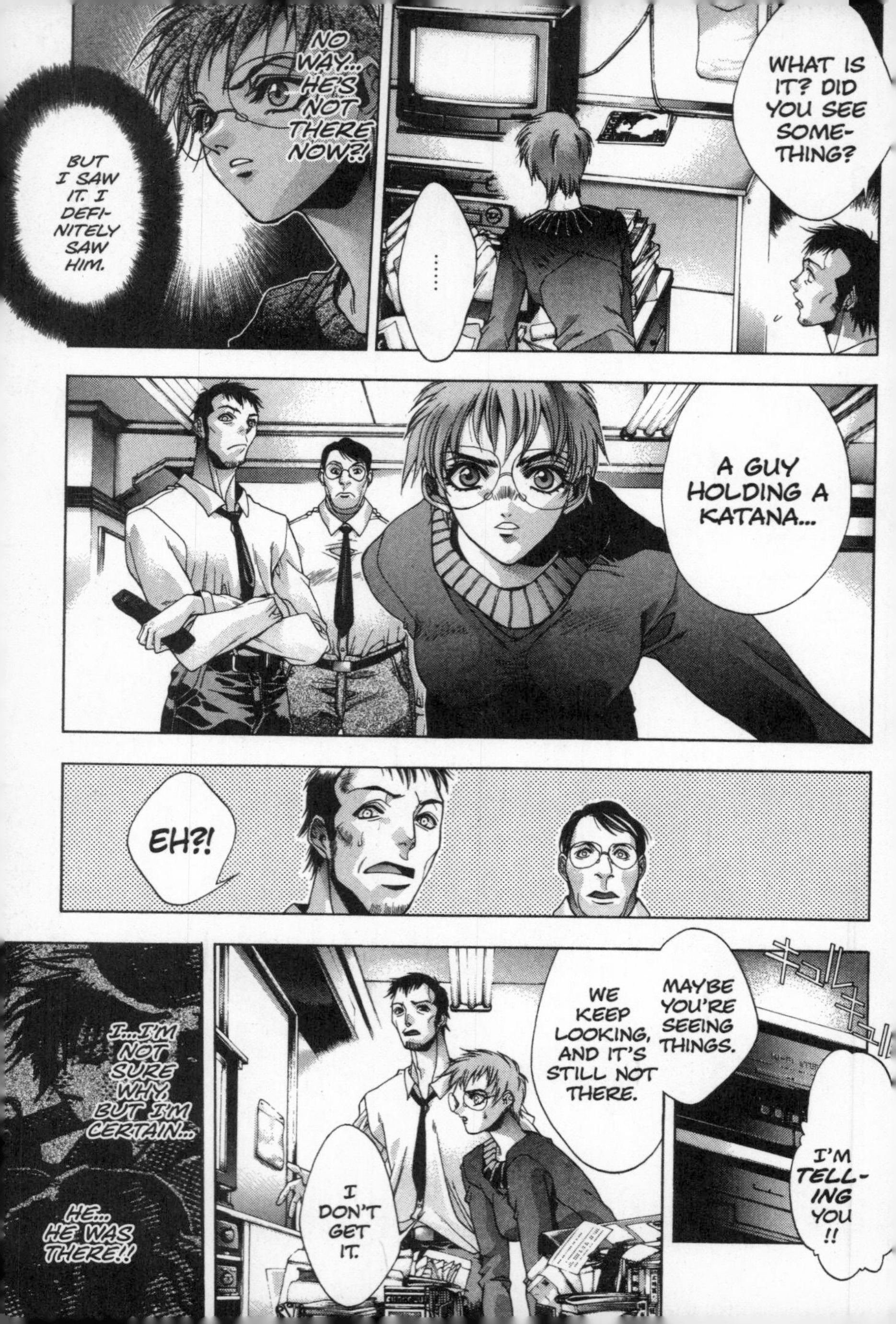
WHAT IS IT? DID YOU SEE SOME-THING?
......
NO WAY... HE'S NOT THERE NOW?!
BUT I SAW IT. I DEFI-NITELY SAW HIM.
A GUY HOLDING A KATANA...
EH?!
キュルキュル
MAYBE YOU'RE SEEING THINGS.
WE KEEP LOOKING, AND IT'S STILL NOT THERE.
I'M TELL-ING YOU!!
I DON'T GET IT.
I...I'M NOT SURE WHY, BUT I'M CERTAIN...
HE... HE WAS THERE!!

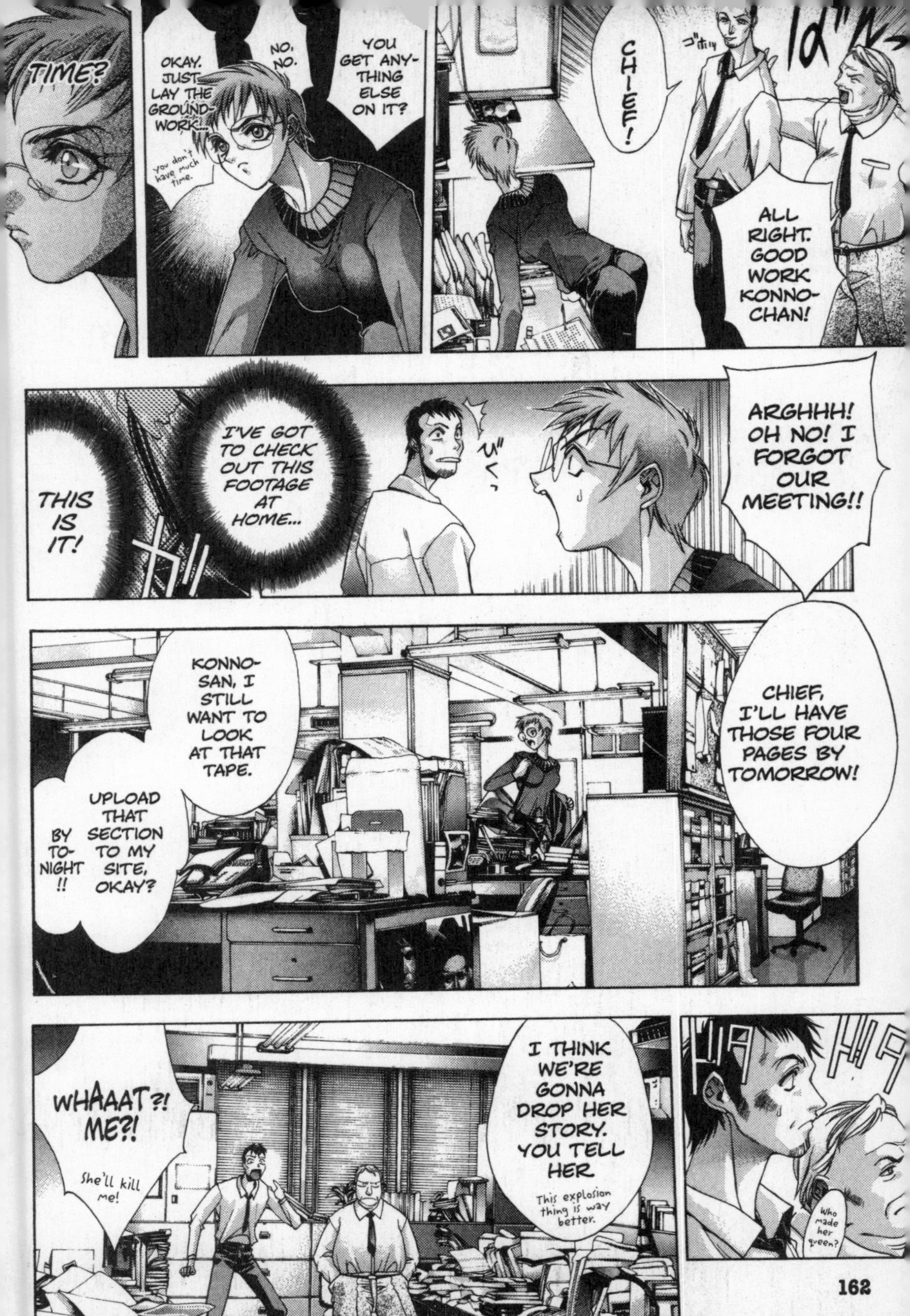
ALL RIGHT. GOOD WORK KONNO-CHAN!
CHIEF!
YOU GET ANYTHING ELSE ON IT?
NO, NO.
OKAY. JUST LAY THE GROUNDWORK...
you don't have much time.
TIME?
ARGHHH! OH NO! I FORGOT OUR MEETING!!
I'VE GOT TO CHECK OUT THIS FOOTAGE AT HOME...
THIS IS IT!
CHIEF, I'LL HAVE THOSE FOUR PAGES BY TOMORROW!
KONNO-SAN, I STILL WANT TO LOOK AT THAT TAPE.
UPLOAD THAT SECTION TO MY SITE, OKAY?
BY TONIGHT!!
Who made her queen?
I THINK WE'RE GONNA DROP HER STORY. YOU TELL HER
This explosion thing is way better.
WHAAAT?! ME?!
She'll kill me!

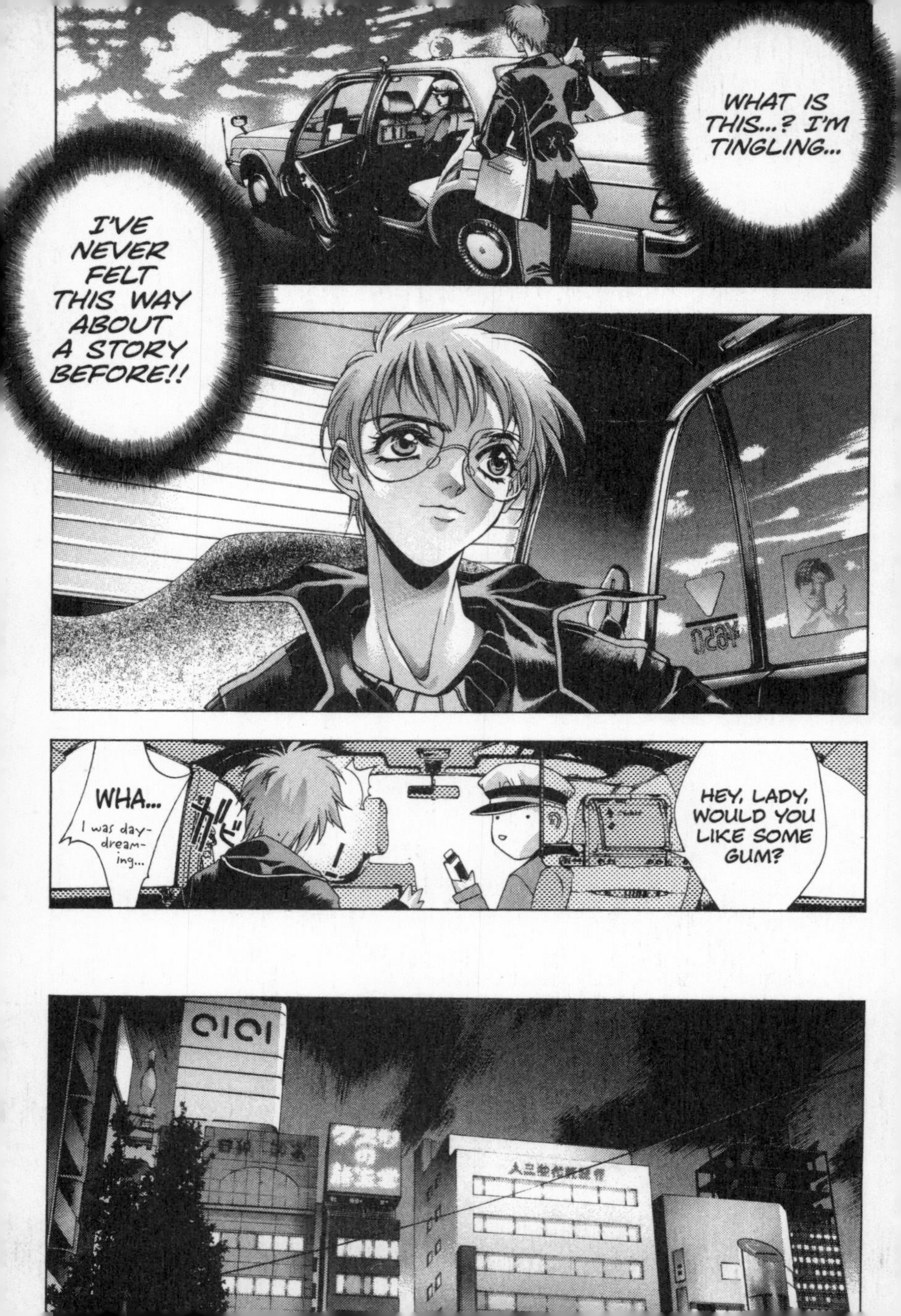
WHAT IS THIS...? I'M TINGLING...
I'VE NEVER FELT THIS WAY ABOUT A STORY BEFORE!!
HEY, LADY, WOULD YOU LIKE SOME GUM?
WHA...
I was day-dreaming...

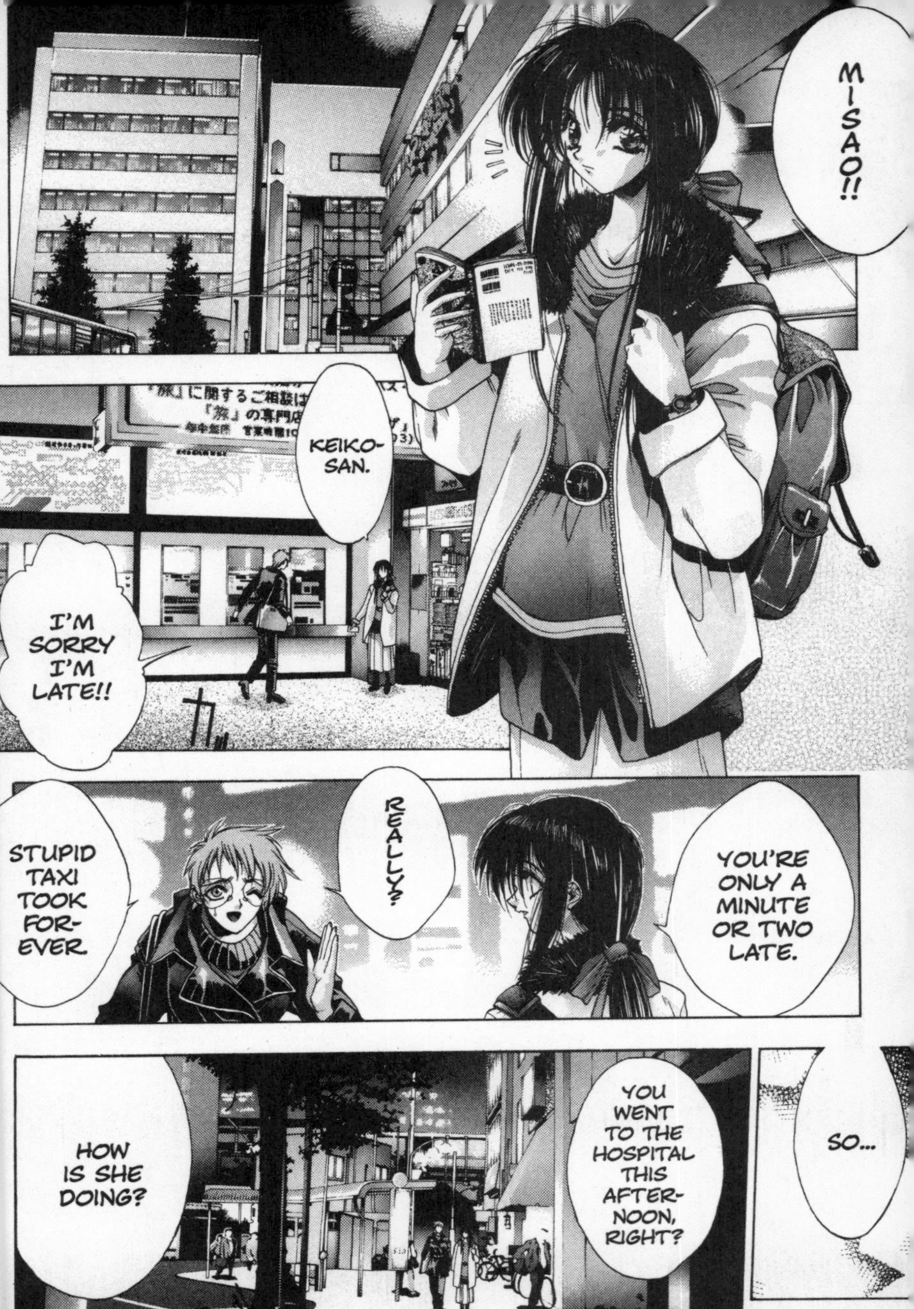
MISAO!!
KEIKO-SAN.
I'M SORRY I'M LATE!!
YOU'RE ONLY A MINUTE OR TWO LATE.
REALLY?
STUPID TAXI TOOK FOR-EVER.
SO...
YOU WENT TO THE HOSPITAL THIS AFTER-NOON, RIGHT?
HOW IS SHE DOING?

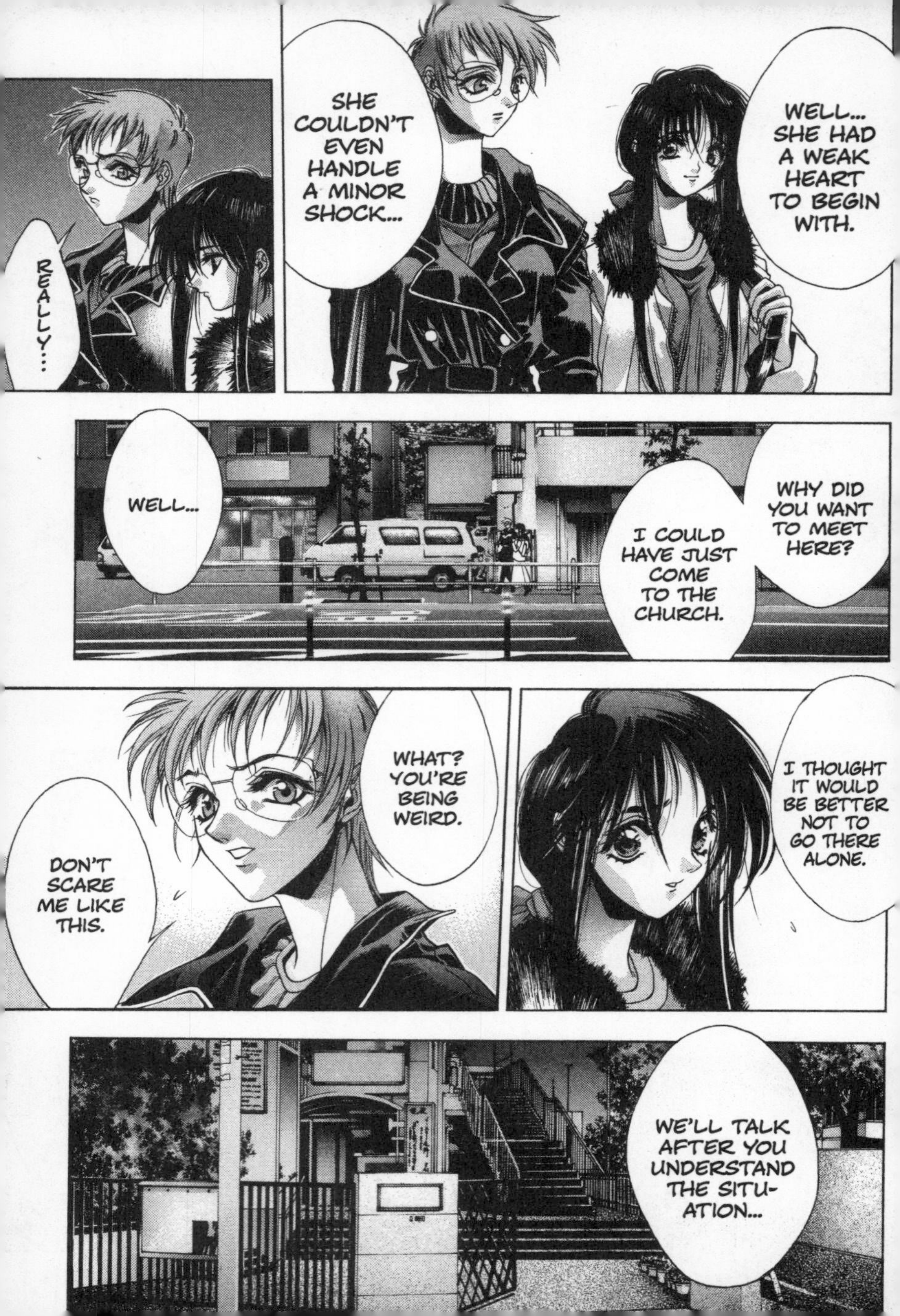
WELL... SHE HAD A WEAK HEART TO BEGIN WITH.
SHE COULDN'T EVEN HANDLE A MINOR SHOCK...
REALLY...
WHY DID YOU WANT TO MEET HERE?
I COULD HAVE JUST COME TO THE CHURCH.
WELL...
I THOUGHT IT WOULD BE BETTER NOT TO GO THERE ALONE.
WHAT? YOU'RE BEING WEIRD.
DON'T SCARE ME LIKE THIS.
WE'LL TALK AFTER YOU UNDERSTAND THE SITU-ATION...

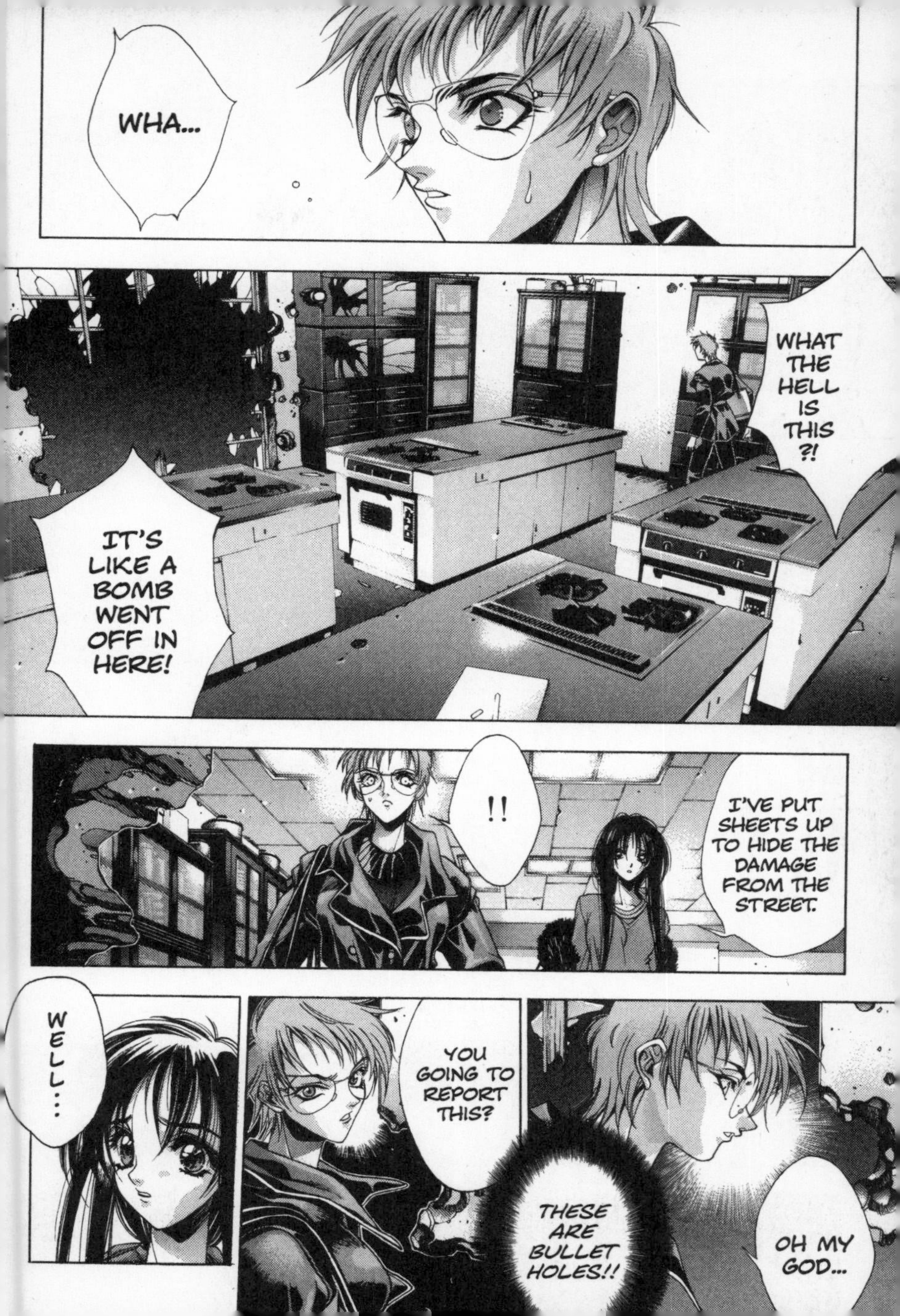
WHA...
WHAT THE HELL IS THIS ?!
IT'S LIKE A BOMB WENT OFF IN HERE!
I'VE PUT SHEETS UP TO HIDE THE DAMAGE FROM THE STREET.
!!
OH MY GOD...
THESE ARE BULLET HOLES!!
YOU GOING TO REPORT THIS?
WELL...

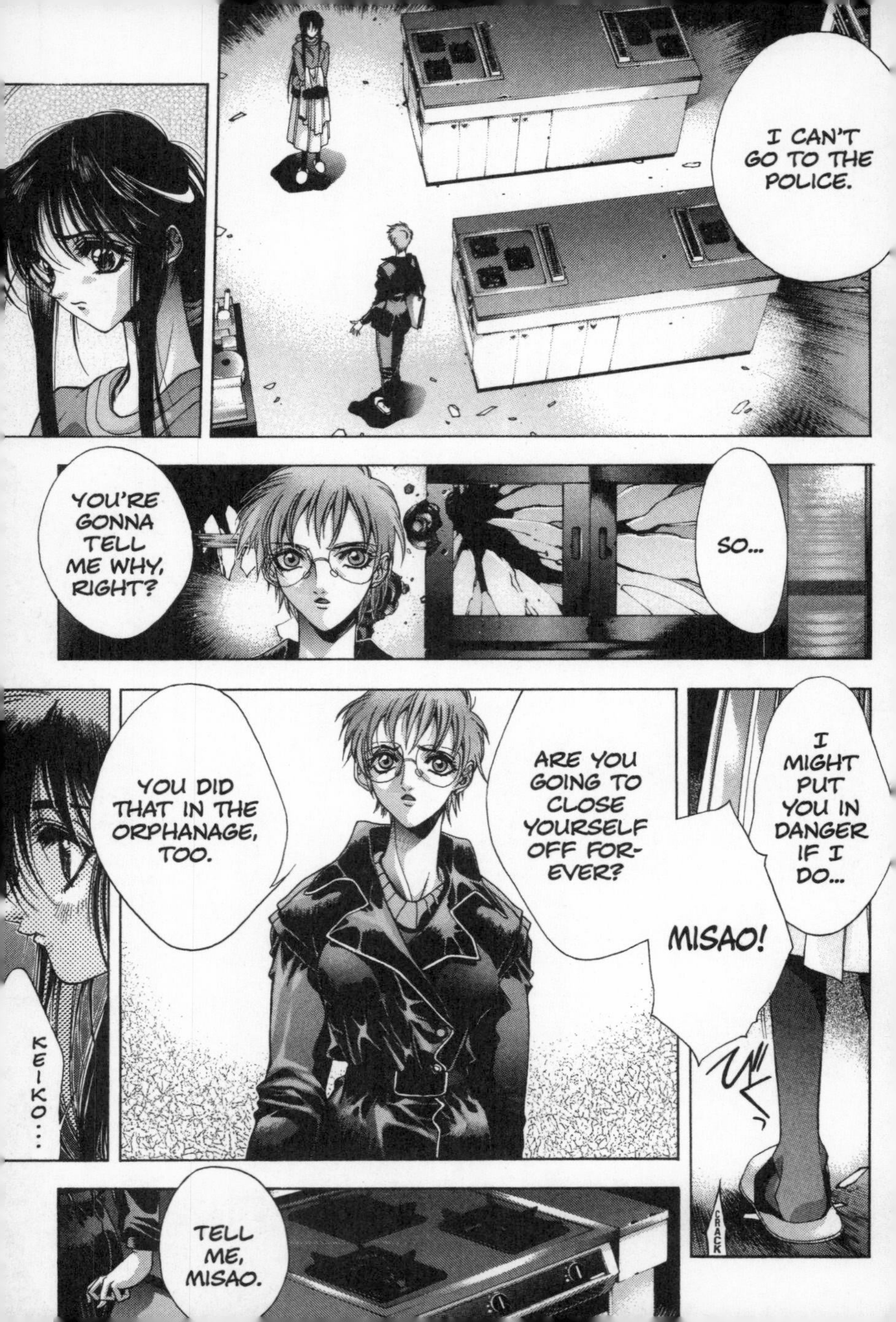
I CAN'T GO TO THE POLICE.
SO...
YOU'RE GONNA TELL ME WHY, RIGHT?
I MIGHT PUT YOU IN DANGER IF I DO...
CRACK
ARE YOU GOING TO CLOSE YOURSELF OFF FOR-EVER?
YOU DID THAT IN THE ORPHANAGE, TOO.
MISAO!
KEIKO...
TELL ME, MISAO.

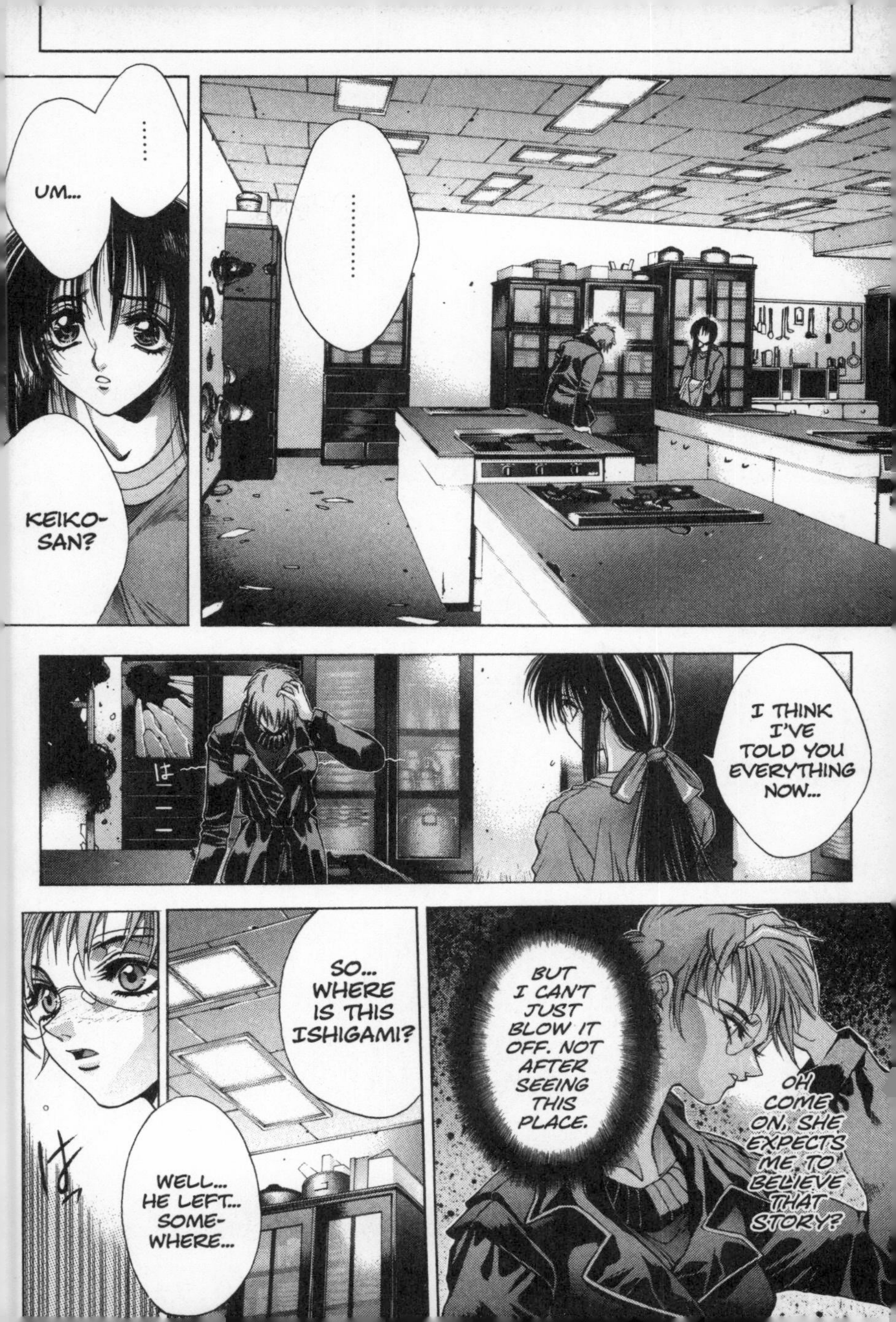
....
......
UM...
KEIKO-SAN?
I THINK I'VE TOLD YOU EVERYTHING NOW...
OH COME ON, SHE EXPECTS ME TO BELIEVE THAT STORY?
BUT I CAN'T JUST BLOW IT OFF. NOT AFTER SEEING THIS PLACE.
SO... WHERE IS THIS ISHIGAMI?
WELL... HE LEFT... SOME-WHERE...

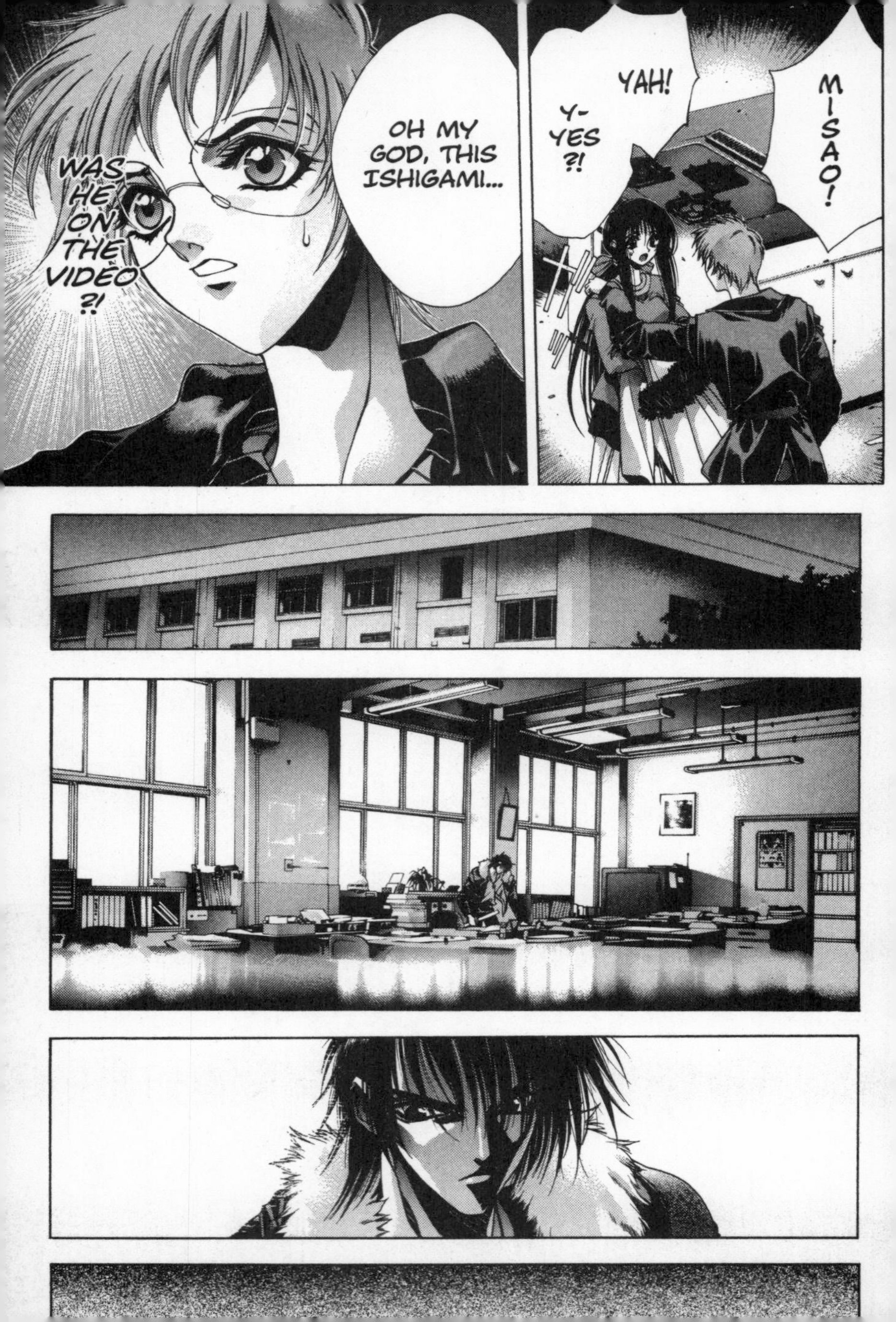
MISAO!
YAH!
Y-YES?!
OH MY GOD, THIS ISHIGAMI...
WAS HE ON THE VIDEO?!

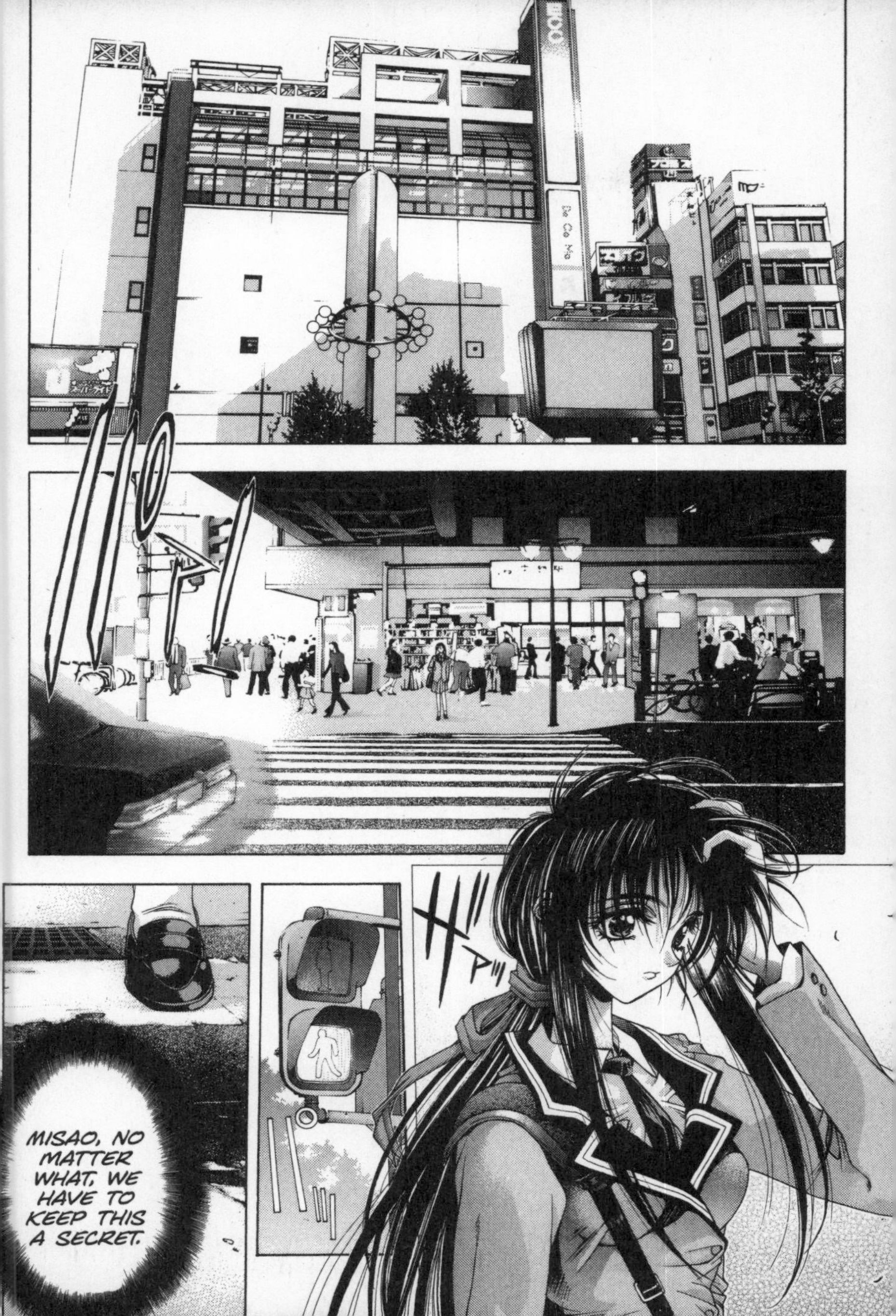
MISAO, NO MATTER WHAT, WE HAVE TO KEEP THIS A SECRET.

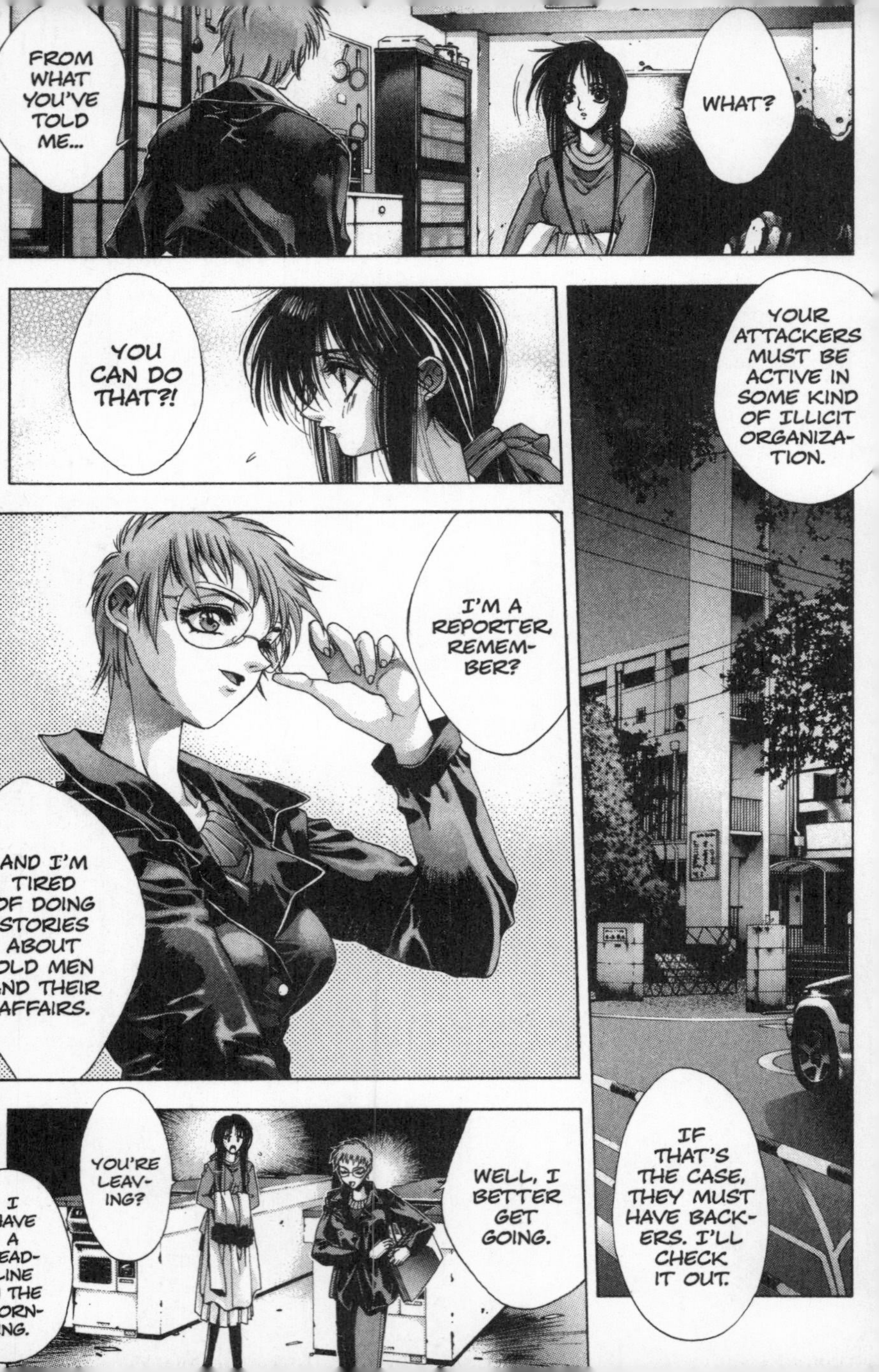
WHAT?
FROM WHAT YOU'VE TOLD ME...
YOUR ATTACKERS MUST BE ACTIVE IN SOME KIND OF ILLICIT ORGANIZA-TION.
IF THAT'S THE CASE, THEY MUST HAVE BACK-ERS. I'LL CHECK IT OUT.
YOU CAN DO THAT?!
I'M A REPORTER, REMEM-BER?
AND I'M TIRED OF DOING STORIES ABOUT OLD MEN AND THEIR AFFAIRS.
WELL, I BETTER GET GOING.
YOU'RE LEAV-ING?
I HAVE A DEAD-LINE IN THE MORN-ING.

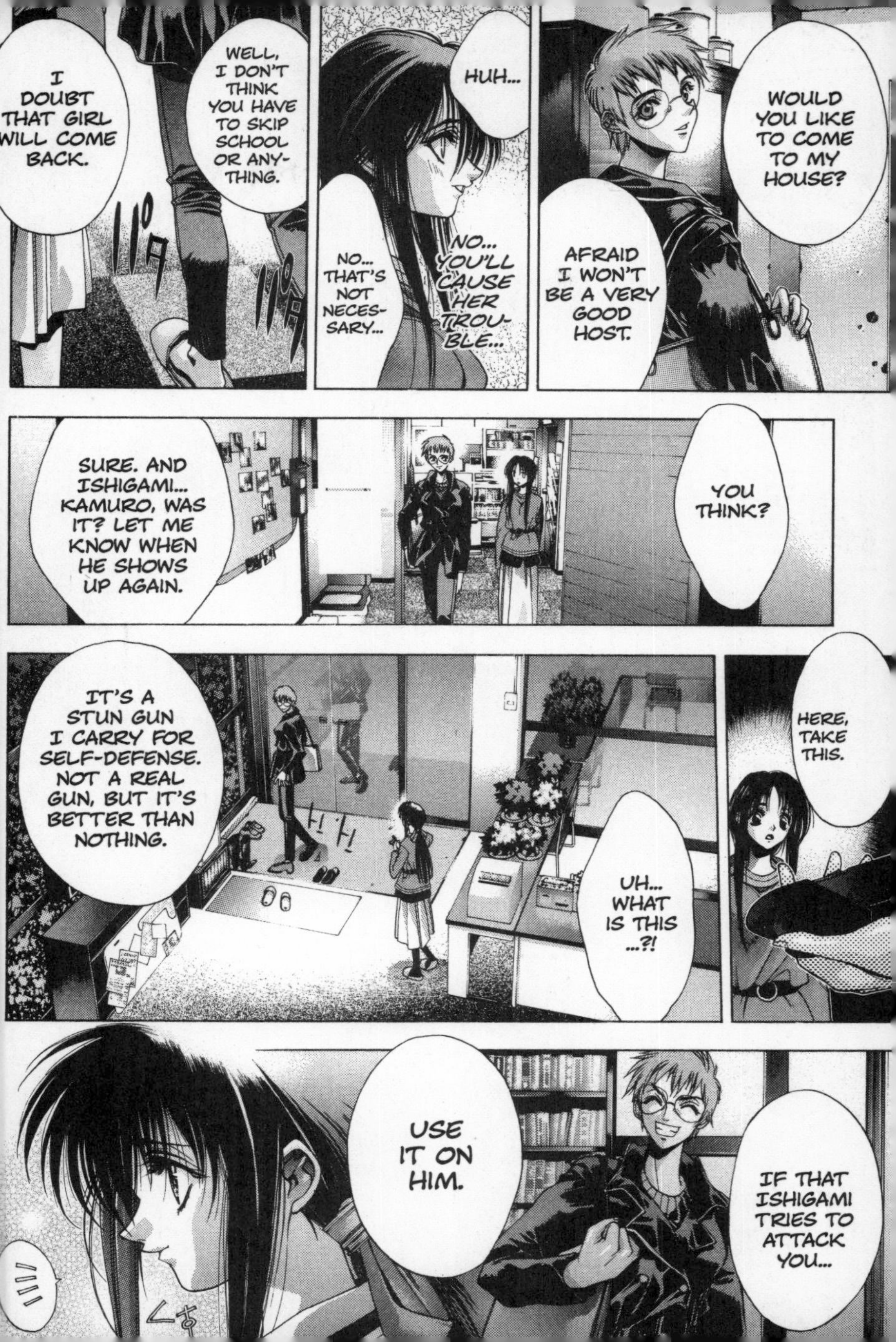
WOULD YOU LIKE TO COME TO MY HOUSE?
AFRAID I WON'T BE A VERY GOOD HOST.
HUH...
NO... YOU'LL CAUSE HER TROUBLE...
NO... THAT'S NOT NECES-SARY...
WELL, I DON'T THINK YOU HAVE TO SKIP SCHOOL OR ANY-THING.
I DOUBT THAT GIRL WILL COME BACK.
パタ
パタ
YOU THINK?
SURE. AND ISHIGAMI... KAMURO, WAS IT? LET ME KNOW WHEN HE SHOWS UP AGAIN.
HERE, TAKE THIS.
UH... WHAT IS THIS ...?!
IT'S A STUN GUN I CARRY FOR SELF-DEFENSE. NOT A REAL GUN, BUT IT'S BETTER THAN NOTHING.
IF THAT ISHIGAMI TRIES TO ATTACK YOU...
USE IT ON HIM.

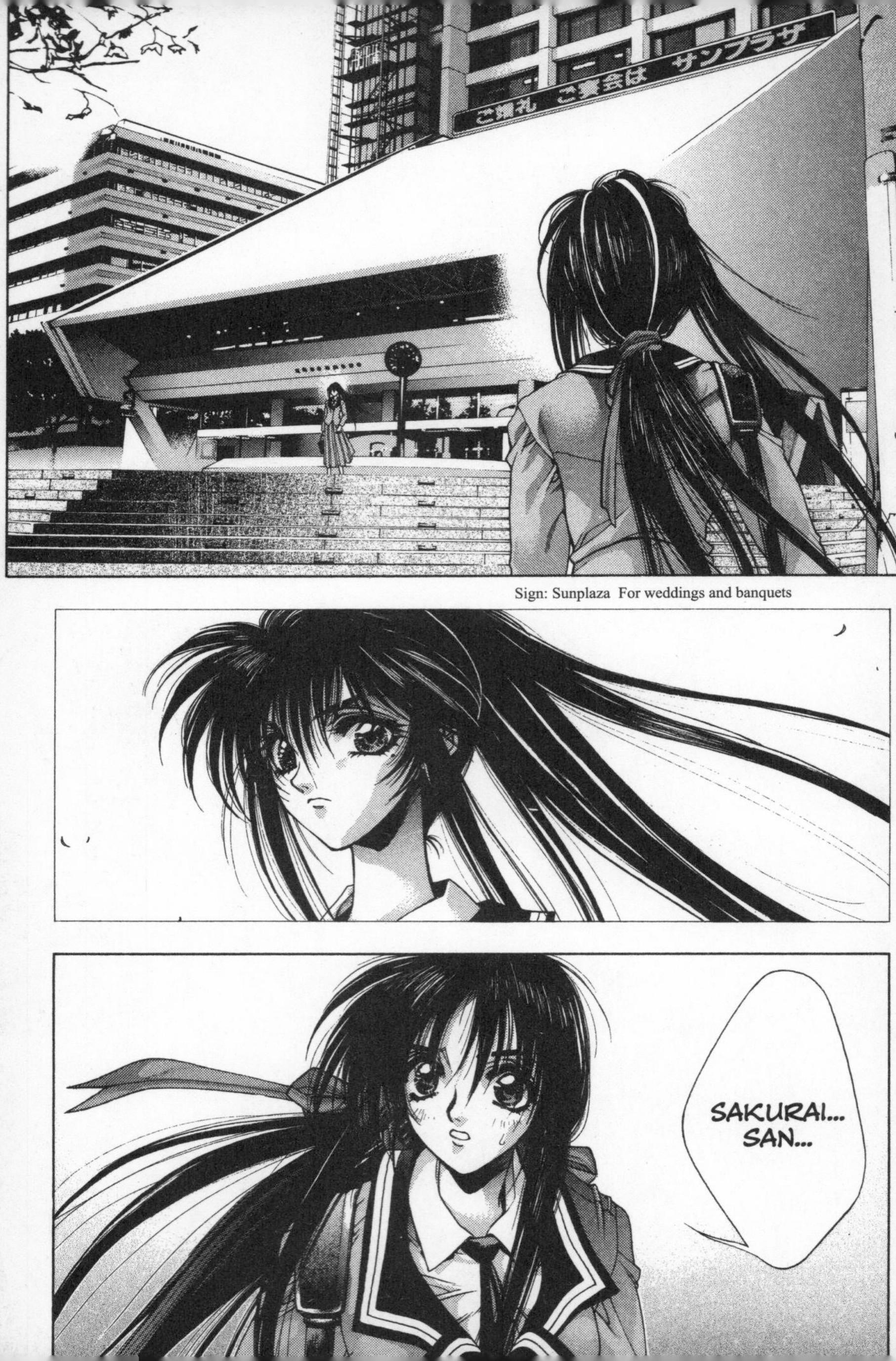
ご婚礼　ご宴会は　サンプラザ
Sign: Sunplaza For weddings and banquets
SAKURAI... SAN...

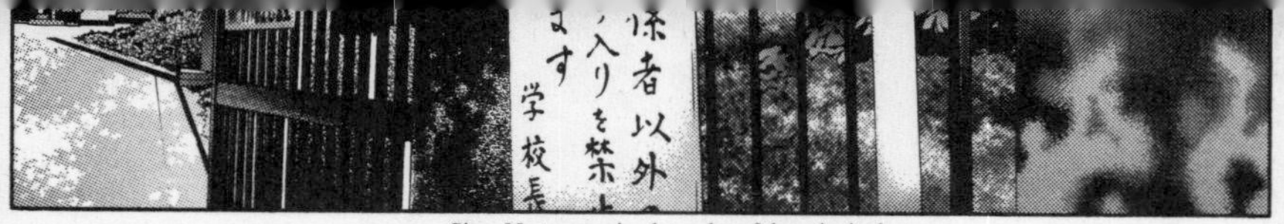
係者以外
入りを禁
ます
学校長
Sign: No trespassing by order of the principal

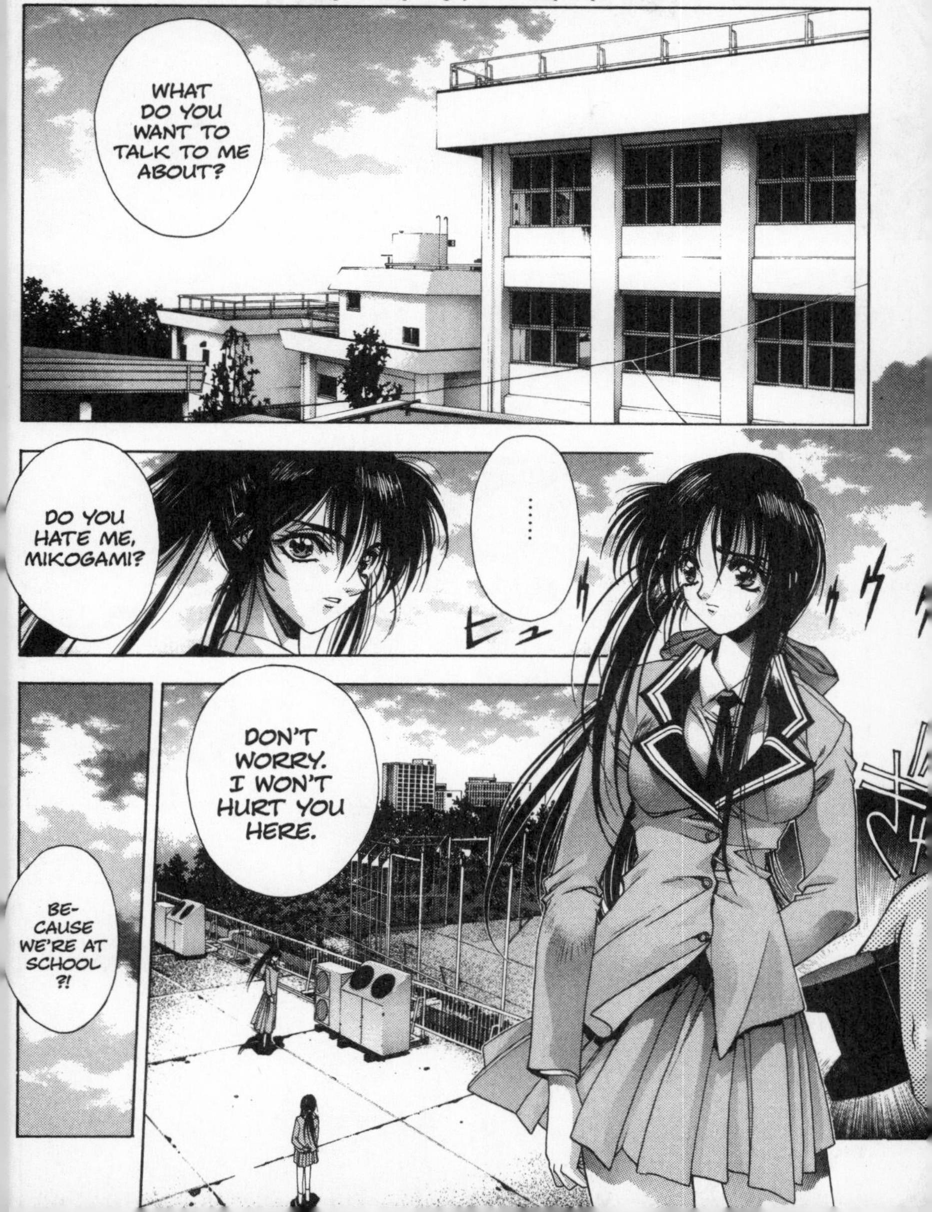
WHAT DO YOU WANT TO TALK TO ME ABOUT?
......
DO YOU HATE ME, MIKOGAMI?
ヒュ
DON'T WORRY. I WON'T HURT YOU HERE.
BE-CAUSE WE'RE AT SCHOOL ?!

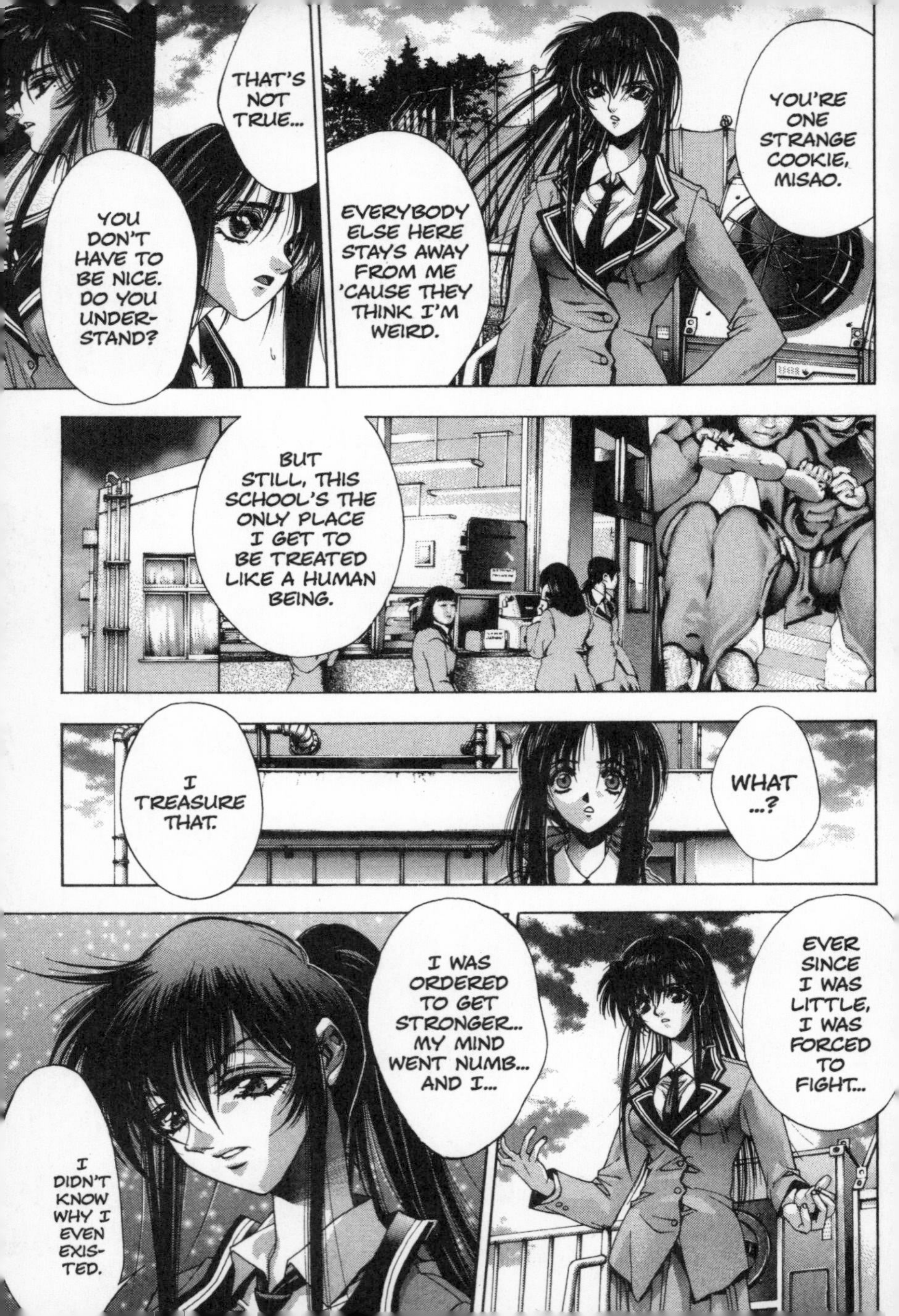
YOU'RE ONE STRANGE COOKIE, MISAO.
EVERYBODY ELSE HERE STAYS AWAY FROM ME 'CAUSE THEY THINK I'M WEIRD.
THAT'S NOT TRUE...
YOU DON'T HAVE TO BE NICE. DO YOU UNDER-STAND?
BUT STILL, THIS SCHOOL'S THE ONLY PLACE I GET TO BE TREATED LIKE A HUMAN BEING.
WHAT ...?
I TREASURE THAT.
EVER SINCE I WAS LITTLE, I WAS FORCED TO FIGHT...
I WAS ORDERED TO GET STRONGER... MY MIND WENT NUMB... AND I...
I DIDN'T KNOW WHY I EVEN EXIS-TED.

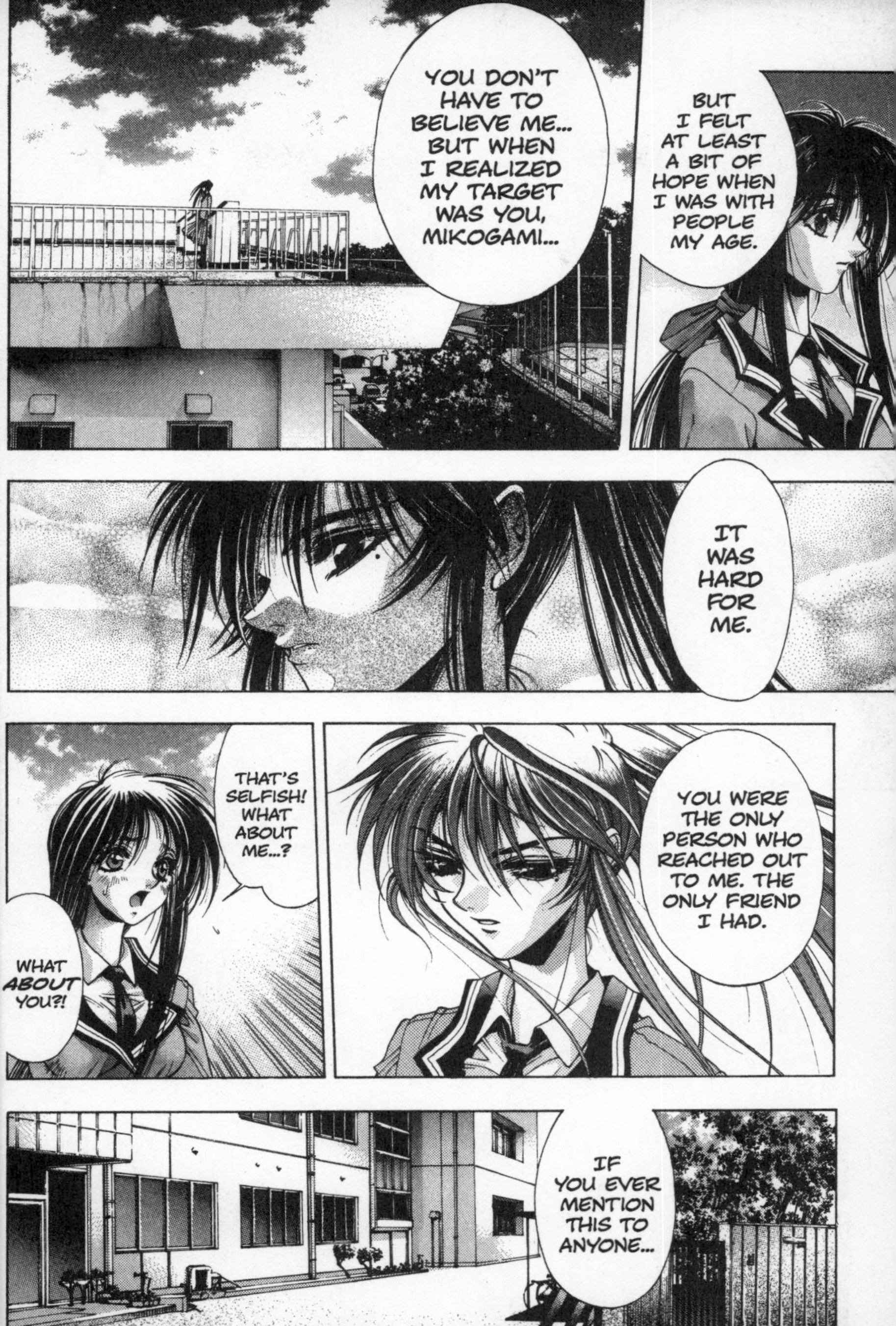
BUT I FELT AT LEAST A BIT OF HOPE WHEN I WAS WITH PEOPLE MY AGE.
YOU DON'T HAVE TO BELIEVE ME... BUT WHEN I REALIZED MY TARGET WAS YOU, MIKOGAMI...
IT WAS HARD FOR ME.
YOU WERE THE ONLY PERSON WHO REACHED OUT TO ME. THE ONLY FRIEND I HAD.
THAT'S SELFISH! WHAT ABOUT ME...?
WHAT ABOUT YOU?!
IF YOU EVER MENTION THIS TO ANYONE...

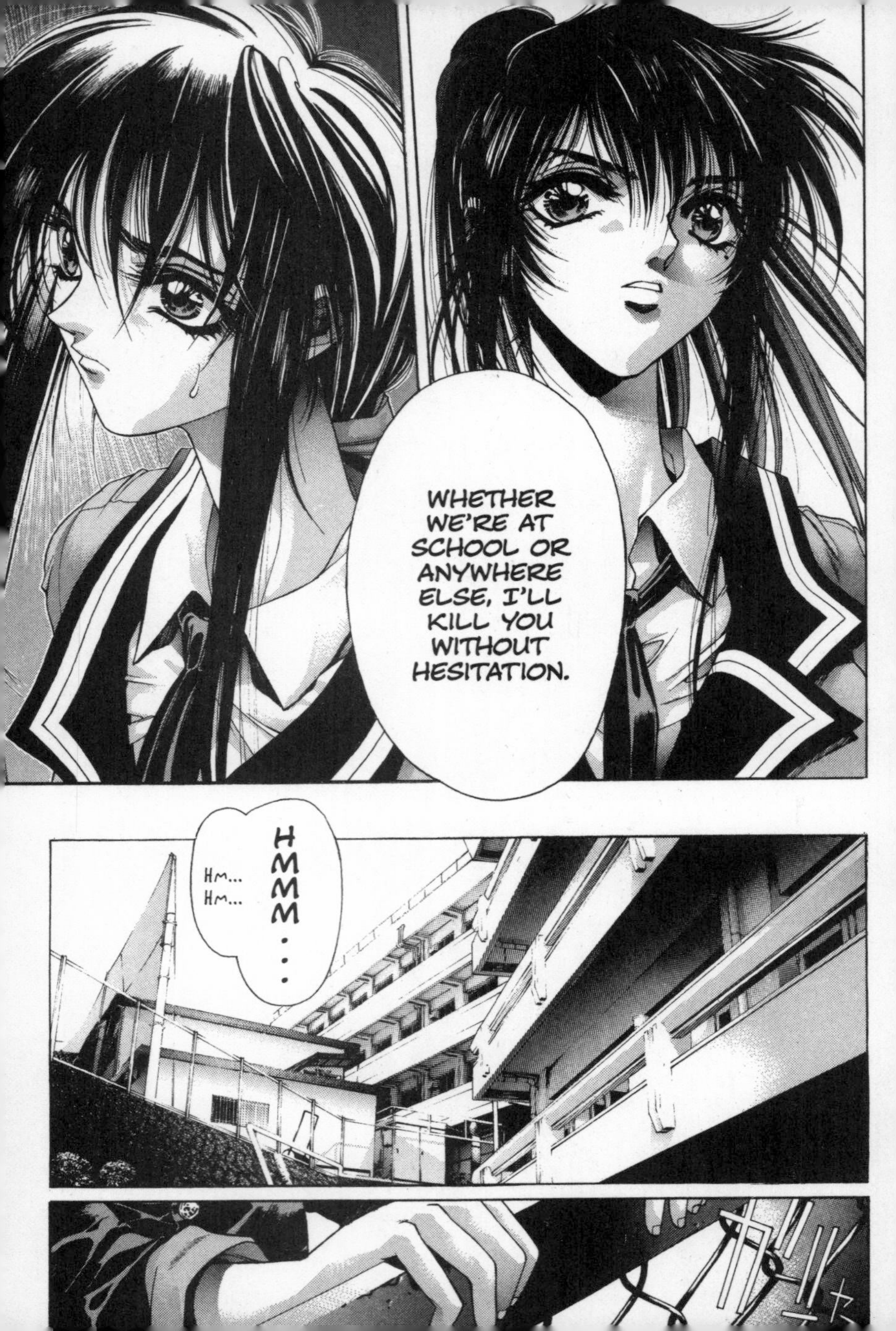
WHETHER WE'RE AT SCHOOL OR ANYWHERE ELSE, I'LL KILL YOU WITHOUT HESITATION.
HMMM...
Hm... Hm...

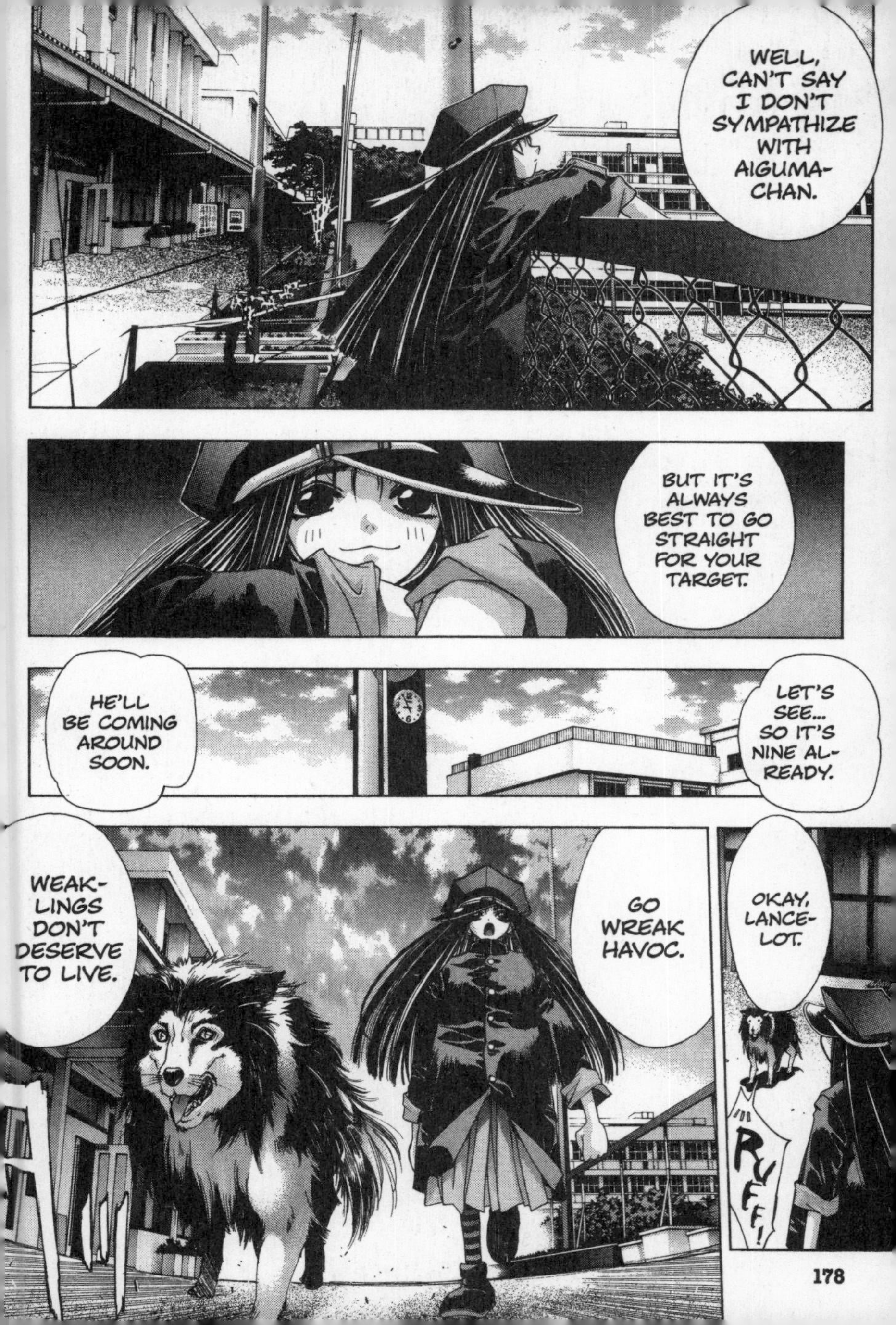
WELL, CAN'T SAY I DON'T SYMPATHIZE WITH AIGUMA-CHAN.
BUT IT'S ALWAYS BEST TO GO STRAIGHT FOR YOUR TARGET.
LET'S SEE... SO IT'S NINE AL-READY.
HE'LL BE COMING AROUND SOON.
OKAY, LANCE-LOT.
RUFF!
GO WREAK HAVOC.
WEAK-LINGS DON'T DESERVE TO LIVE.

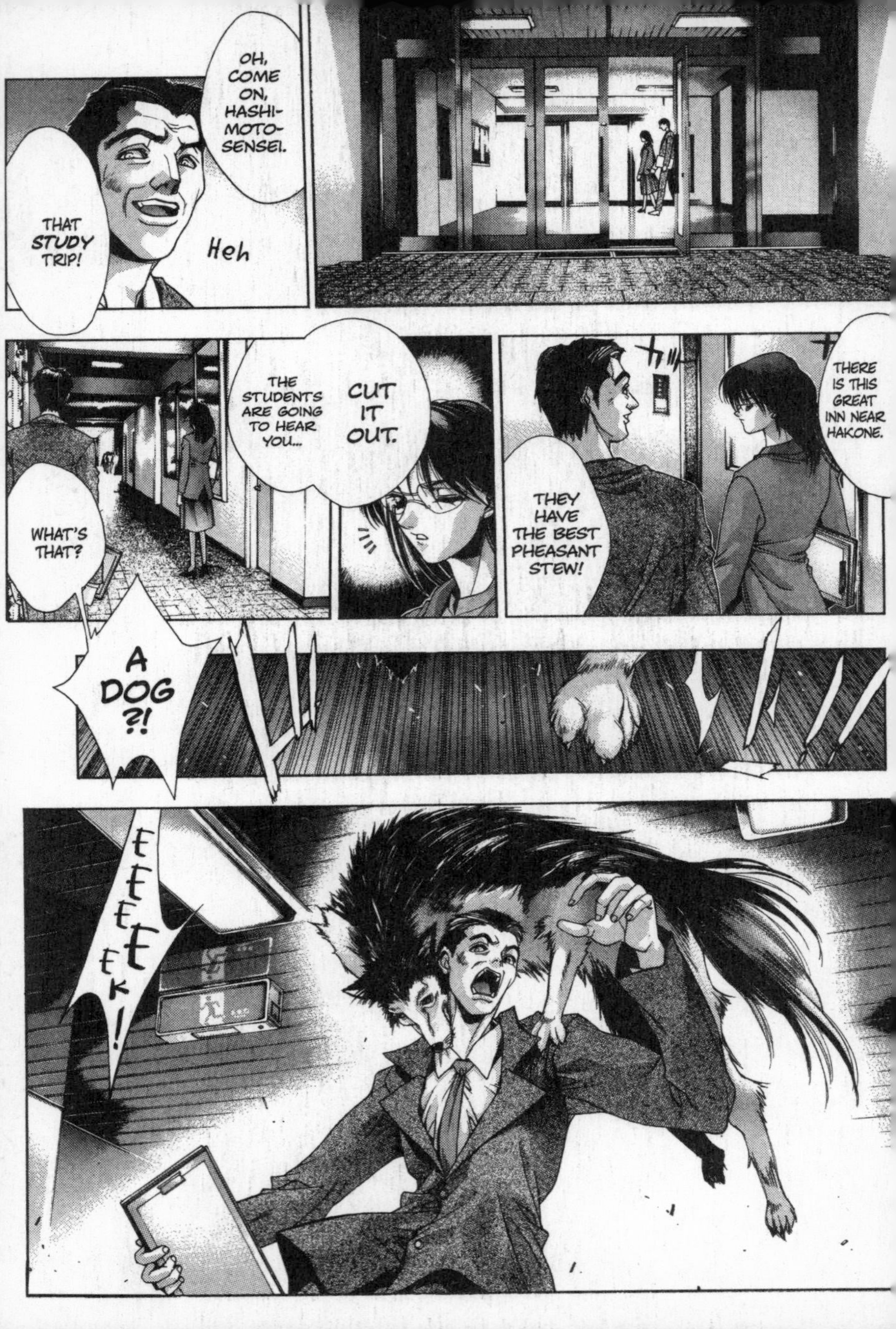
OH, COME ON, HASHI-MOTO-SENSEI.
THAT STUDY TRIP!
Heh
THERE IS THIS GREAT INN NEAR HAKONE.
THEY HAVE THE BEST PHEASANT STEW!
THE STUDENTS ARE GOING TO HEAR YOU...
CUT IT OUT.
WHAT'S THAT?
A DOG ?!
EEEEEEK!

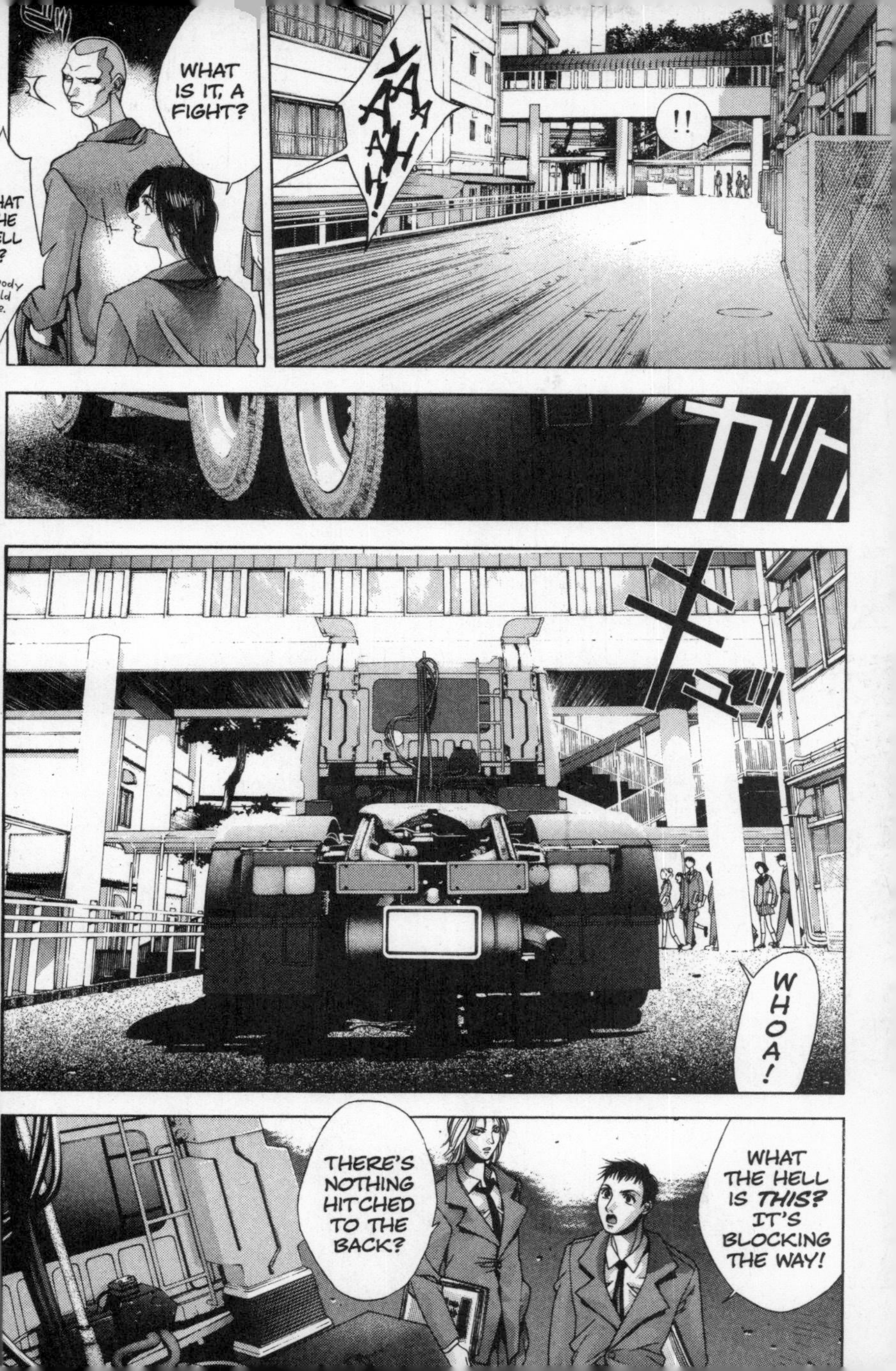
YAAAAH!
!!
WHAT IS IT, A FIGHT?
WHAT THE HELL?
Nobody told me.
WHOA!
WHAT THE HELL IS *THIS?* IT'S BLOCKING THE WAY!
THERE'S NOTHING HITCHED TO THE BACK?

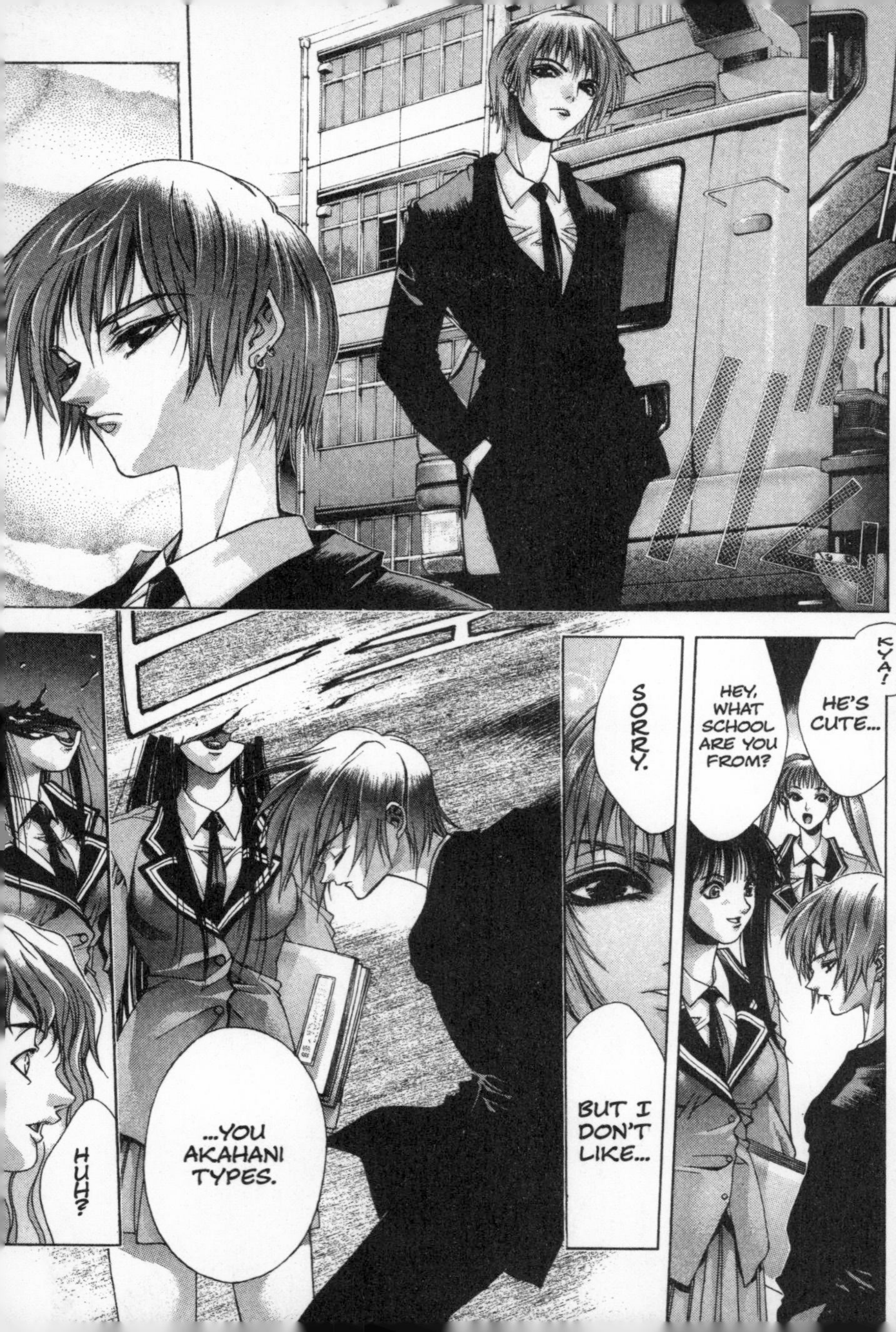
KYA!
HE'S CUTE...
HEY, WHAT SCHOOL ARE YOU FROM?
SORRY.
BUT I DON'T LIKE...
...YOU AKAHANI TYPES.
HUH?

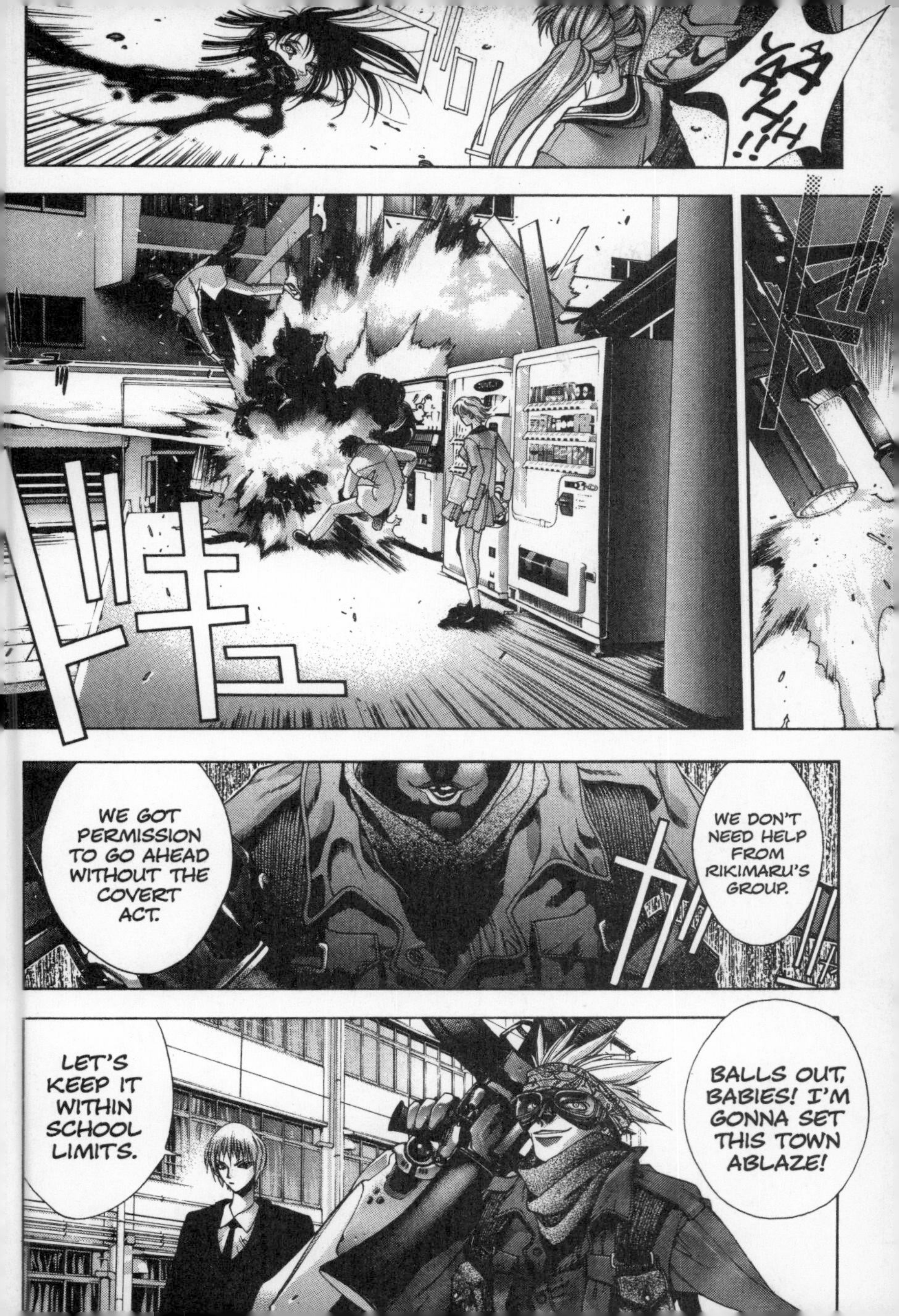
AAAHH!!
WE DON'T NEED HELP FROM RIKIMARU'S GROUP.
WE GOT PERMISSION TO GO AHEAD WITHOUT THE COVERT ACT.
BALLS OUT, BABIES! I'M GONNA SET THIS TOWN ABLAZE!
LET'S KEEP IT WITHIN SCHOOL LIMITS.

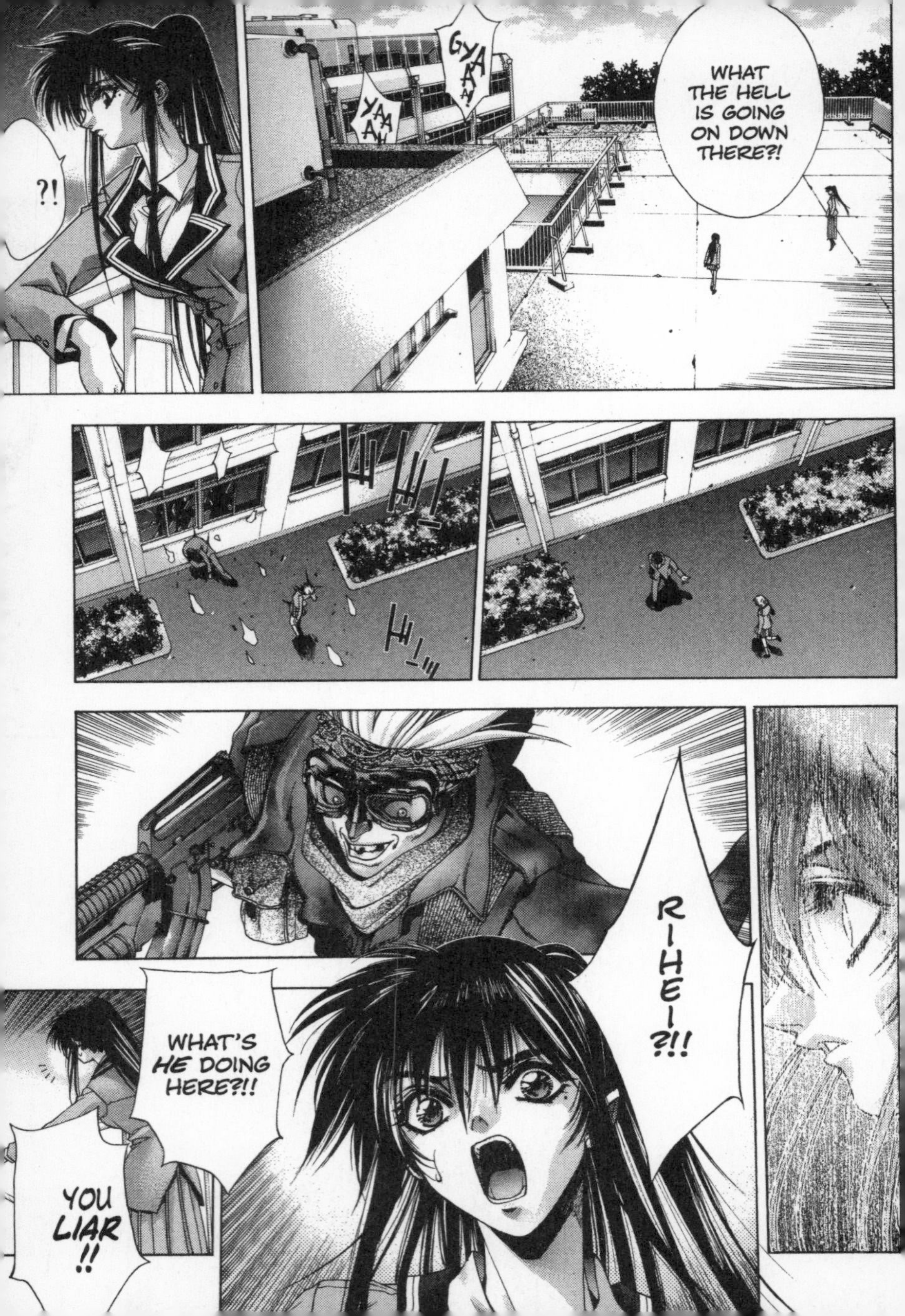
WHAT THE HELL IS GOING ON DOWN THERE?!
GYAAAA!
YAAAAH
?!
RIHEI ?!!
WHAT'S HE DOING HERE?!!
YOU LIAR !!

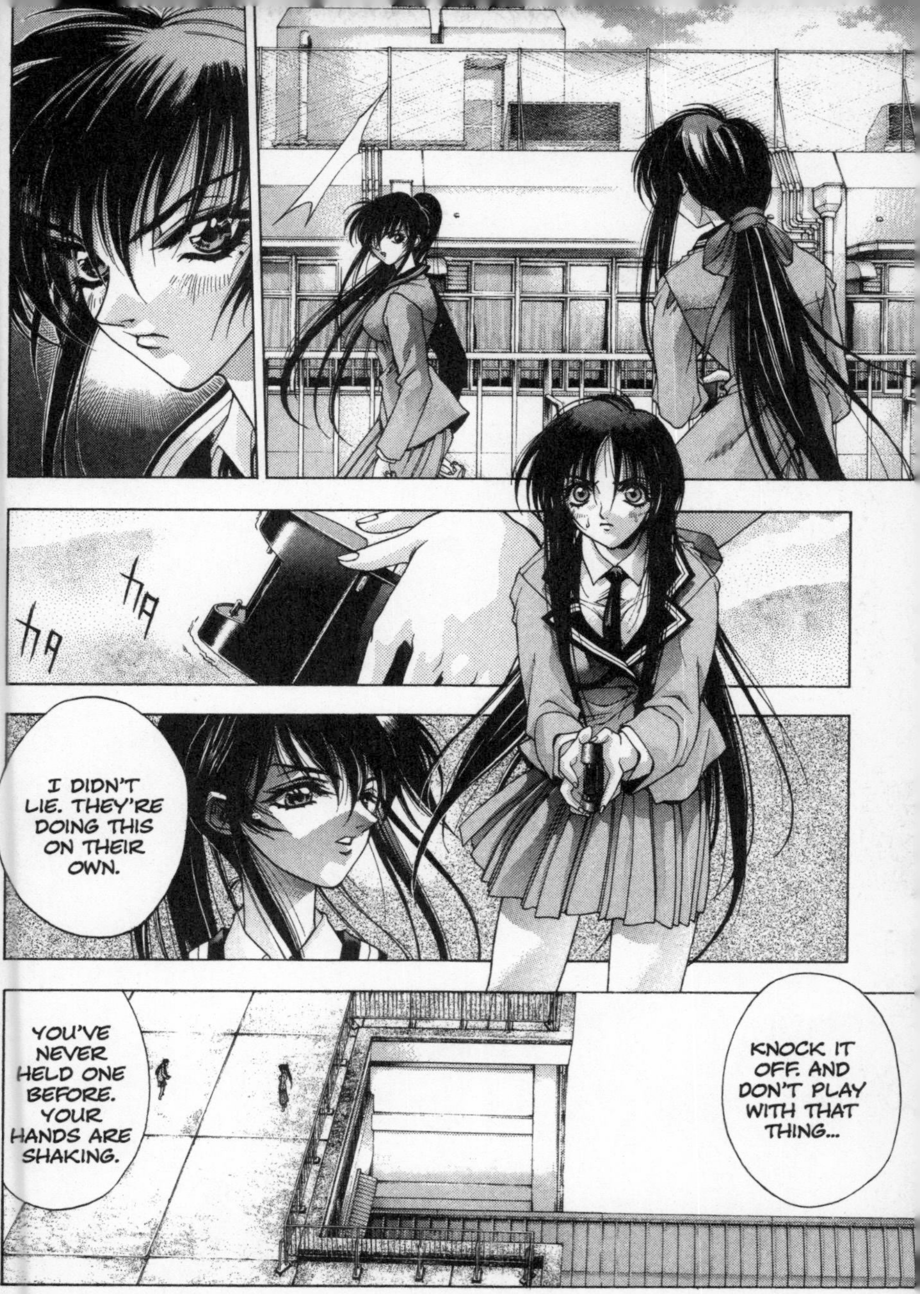
HA
HA
I DIDN'T LIE. THEY'RE DOING THIS ON THEIR OWN.
KNOCK IT OFF. AND DON'T PLAY WITH THAT THING...
YOU'VE NEVER HELD ONE BEFORE. YOUR HANDS ARE SHAKING.

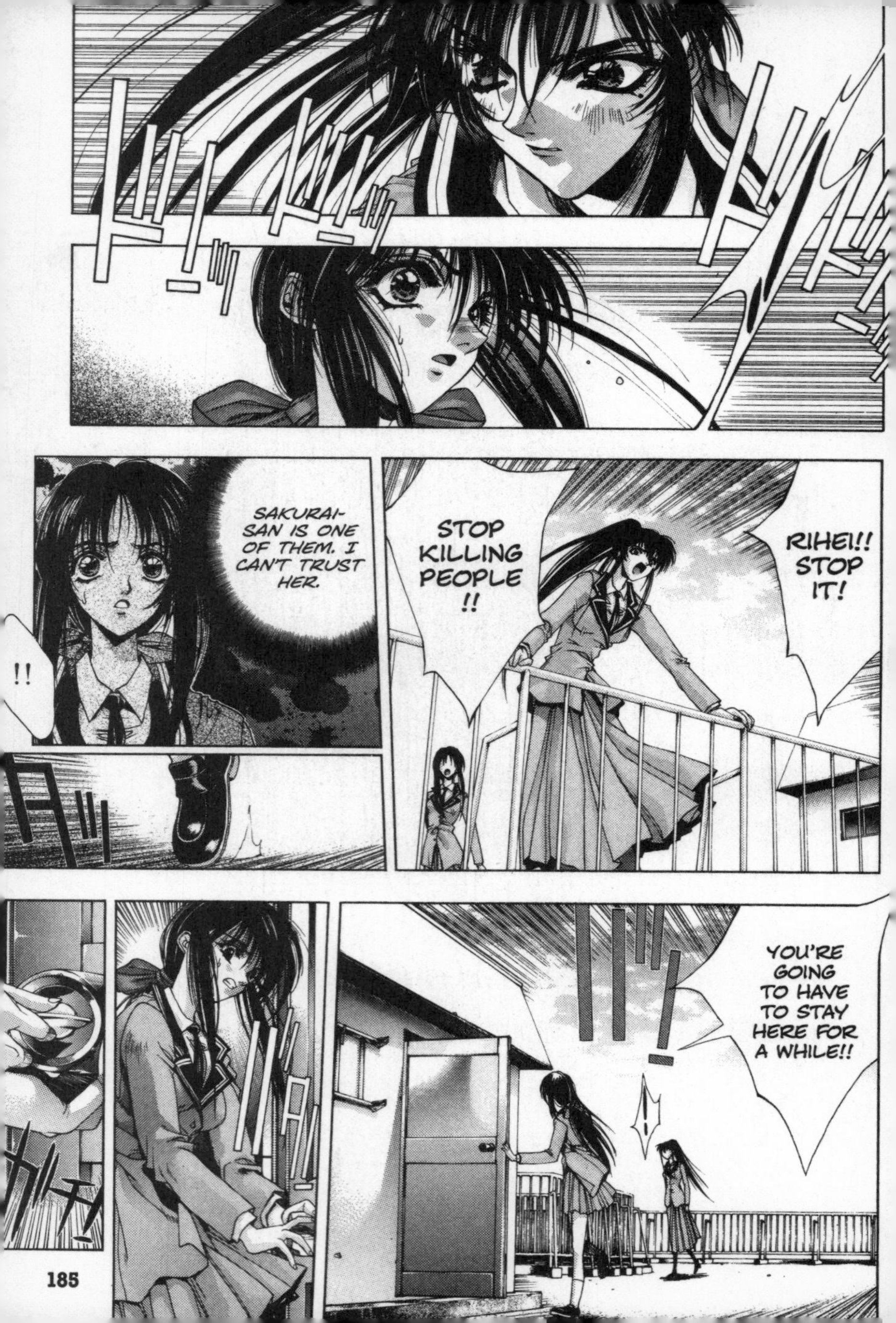
RIHEI!! STOP IT!
STOP KILLING PEOPLE !!
SAKURAI-SAN IS ONE OF THEM. I CAN'T TRUST HER.
!!
YOU'RE GOING TO HAVE TO STAY HERE FOR A WHILE!!

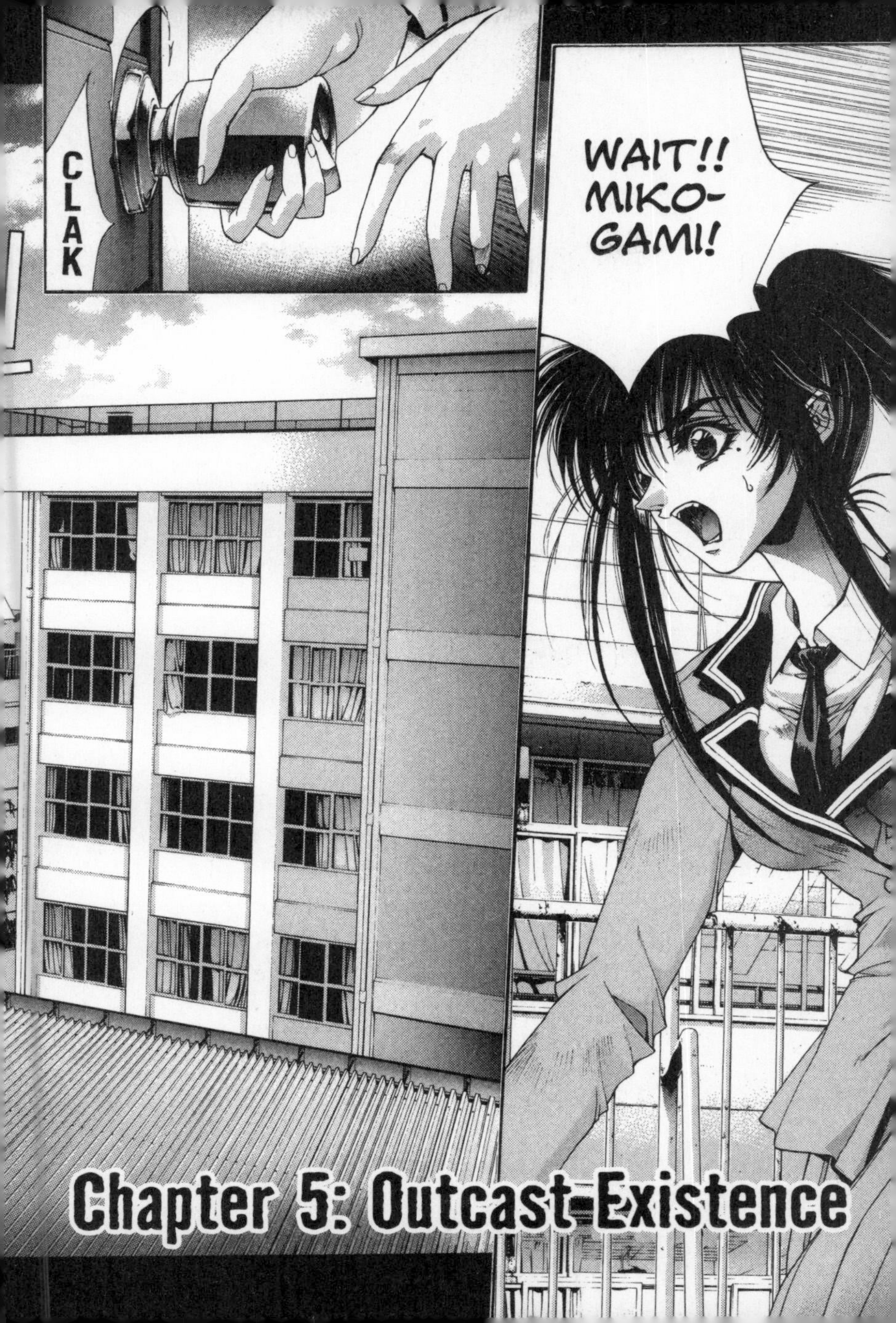
WAIT!! MIKO-GAMI!
CLAK
Chapter 5: Outcast-Existence

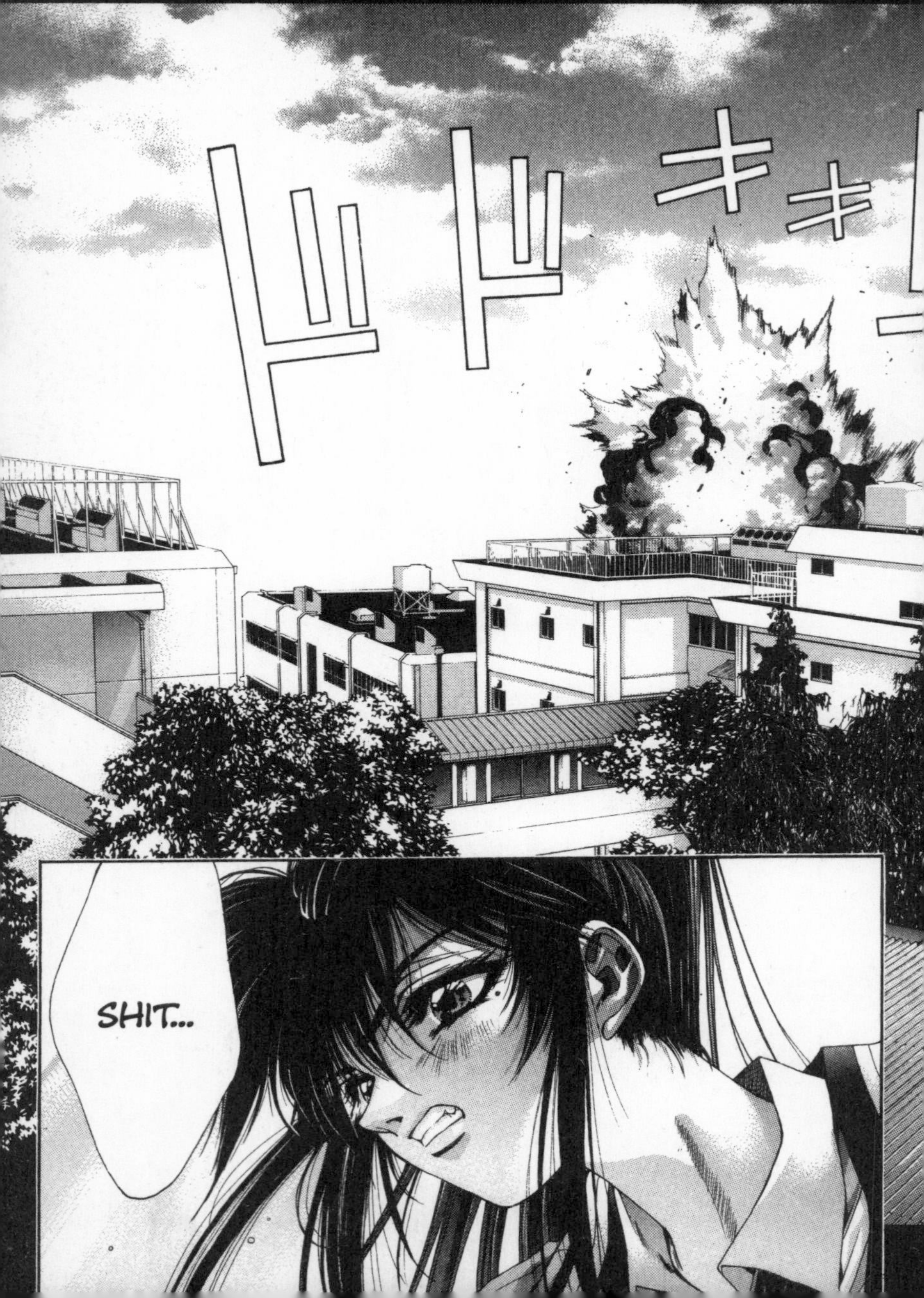
SHIT...

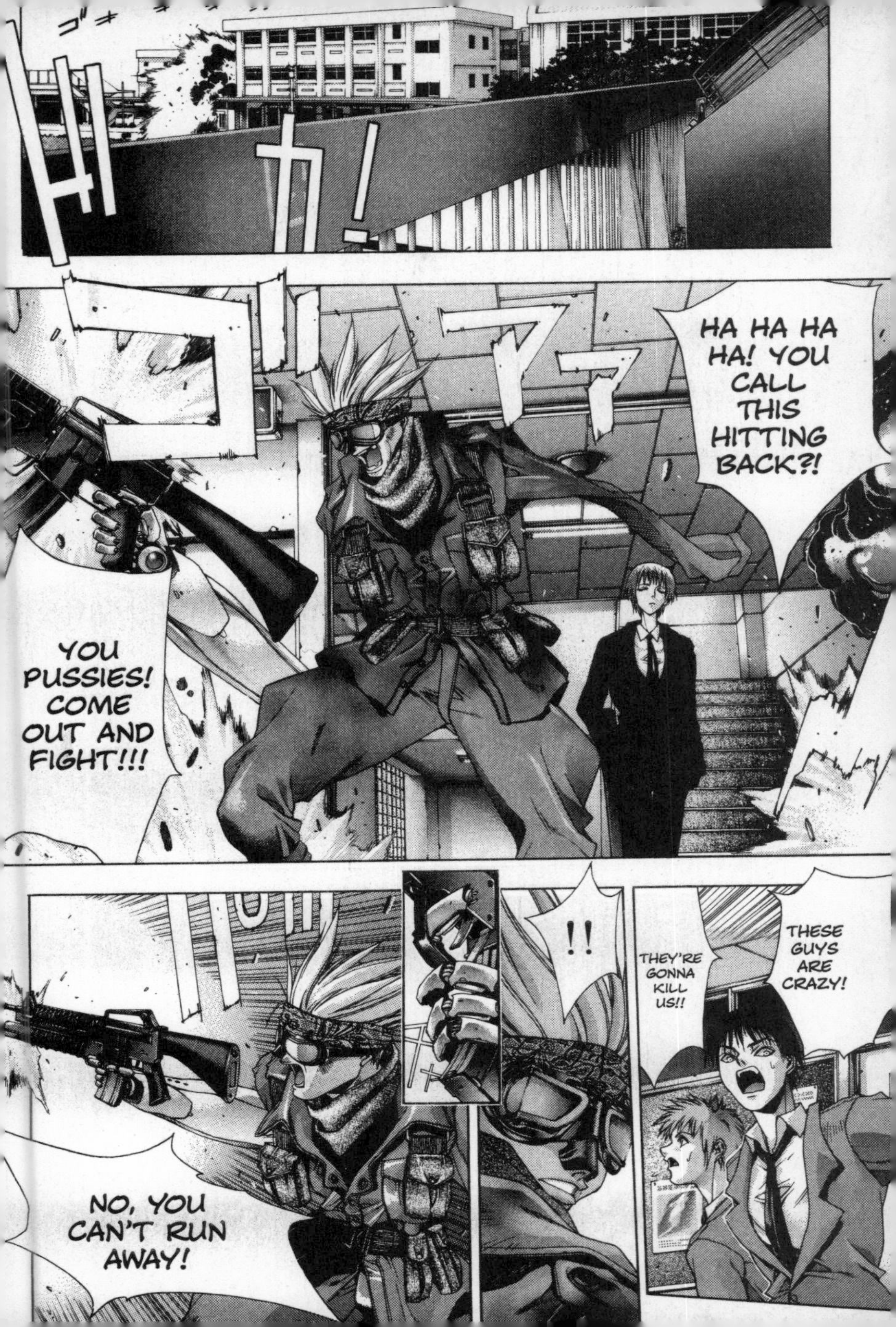
HA HA HA HA! YOU CALL THIS HITTING BACK?!
YOU PUSSIES! COME OUT AND FIGHT!!!
THESE GUYS ARE CRAZY!
THEY'RE GONNA KILL US!!
!!
NO, YOU CAN'T RUN AWAY!

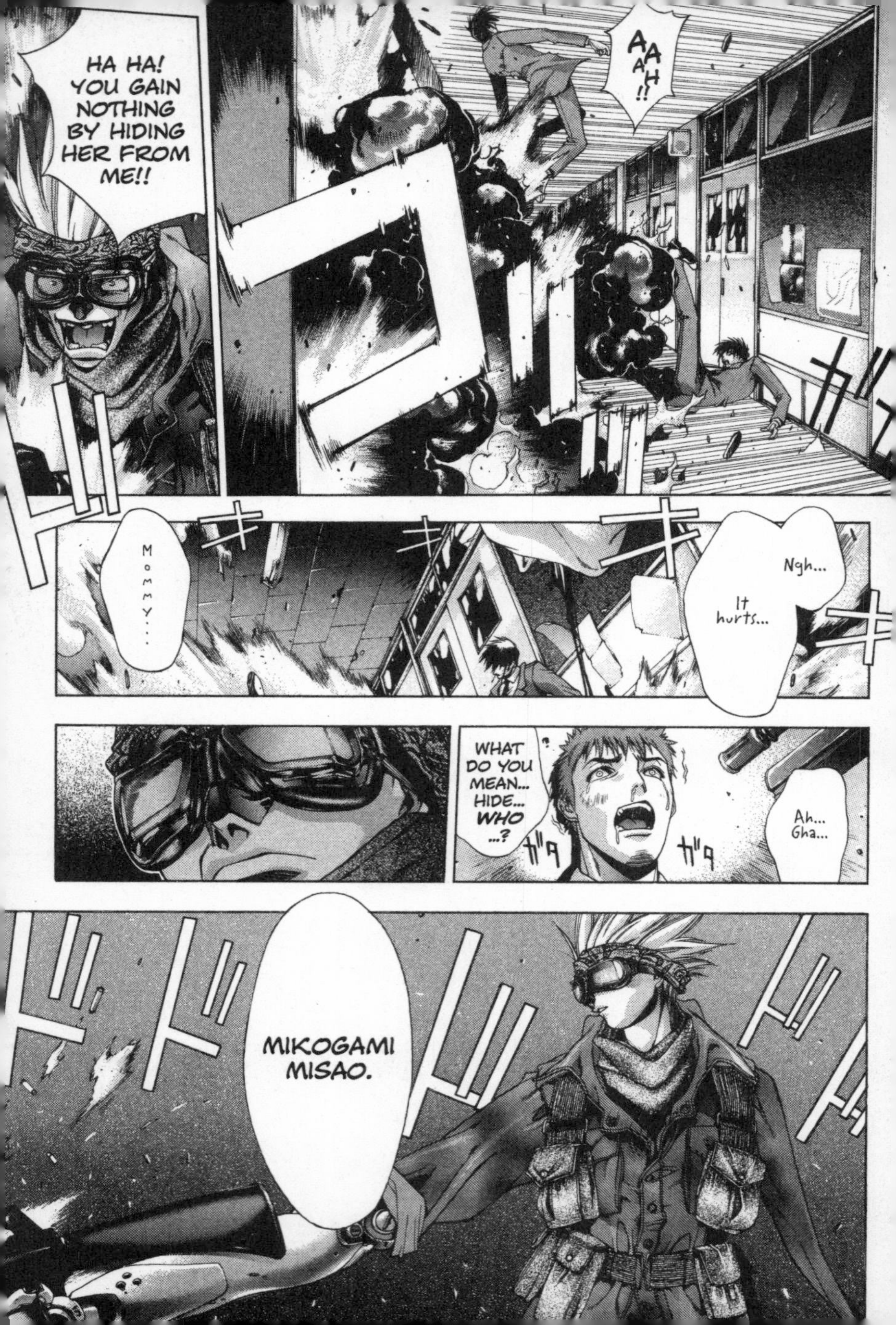
AAAH!!
HA HA! YOU GAIN NOTHING BY HIDING HER FROM ME!!
Ngh... It hurts...
Mommy...
Ah... Gha...
WHAT DO YOU MEAN... HIDE... WHO ...?
MIKOGAMI MISAO.

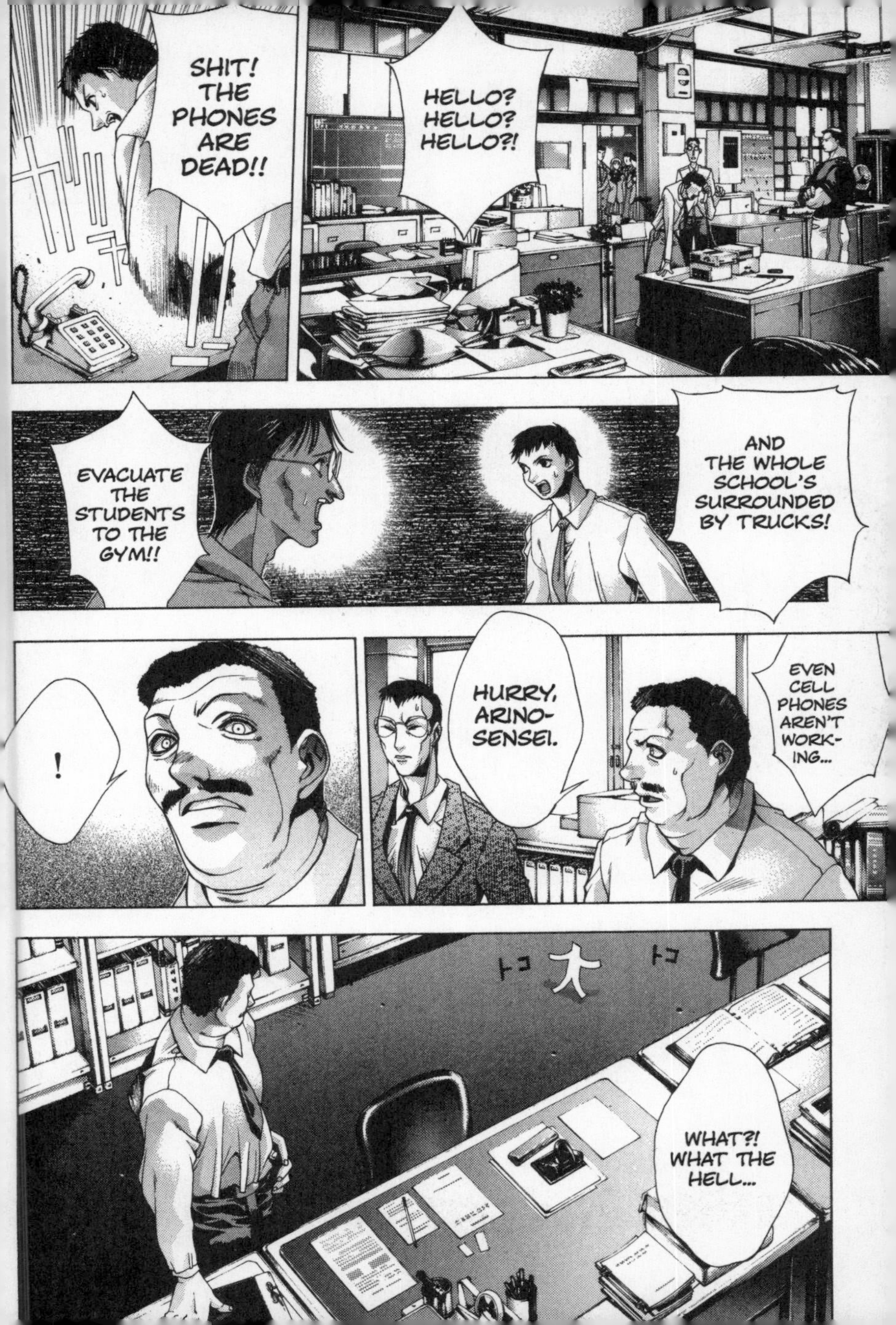
HELLO? HELLO? HELLO?!
SHIT! THE PHONES ARE DEAD!!
AND THE WHOLE SCHOOL'S SURROUNDED BY TRUCKS!
EVACUATE THE STUDENTS TO THE GYM!!
EVEN CELL PHONES AREN'T WORK-ING...
HURRY, ARINO-SENSEI.
!
トコ
トコ
WHAT?! WHAT THE HELL...

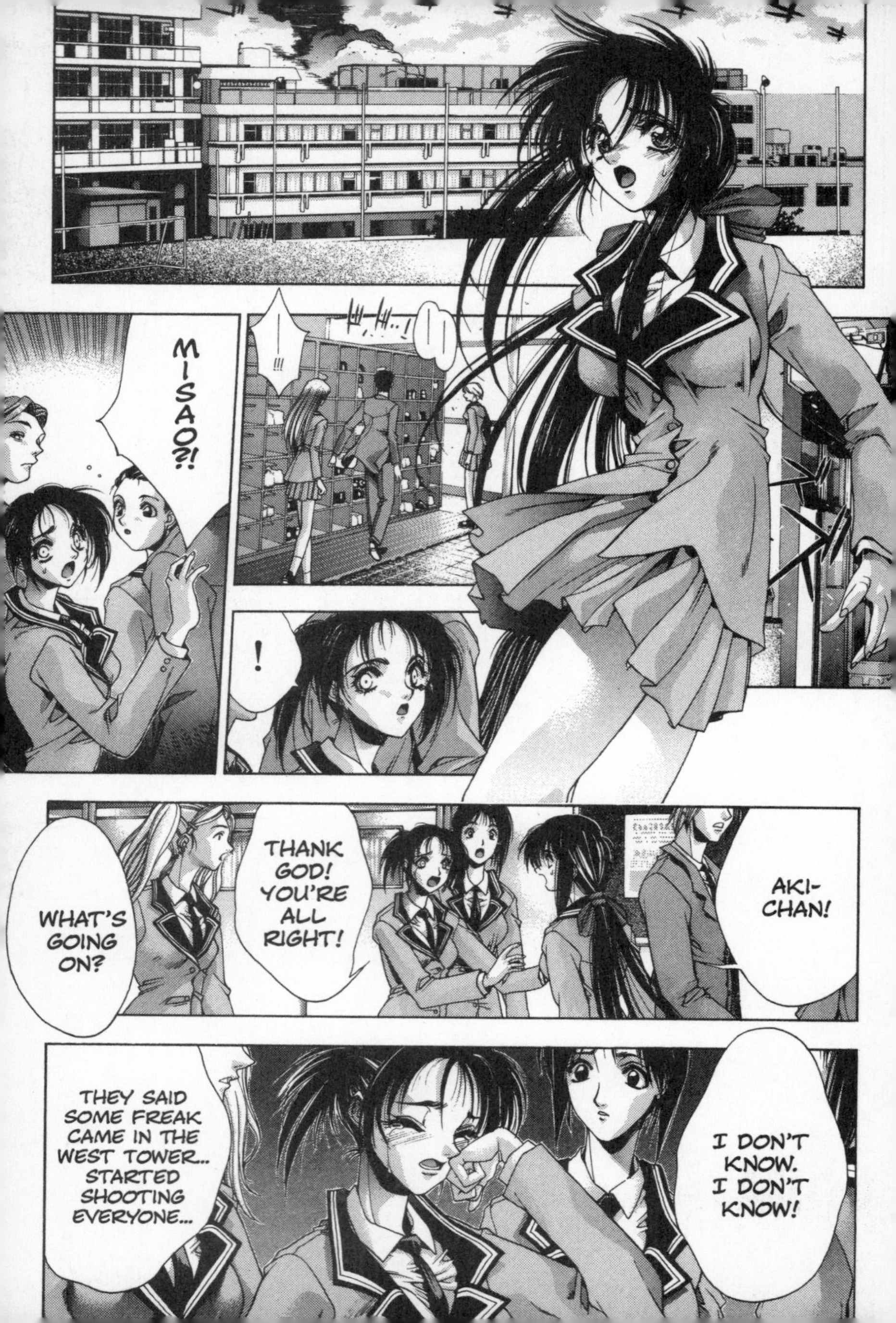

!
!!!
!
MISAO?!
AKI-CHAN!
THANK GOD! YOU'RE ALL RIGHT!
WHAT'S GOING ON?
I DON'T KNOW. I DON'T KNOW!
THEY SAID SOME FREAK CAME IN THE WEST TOWER.. STARTED SHOOTING EVERYONE...

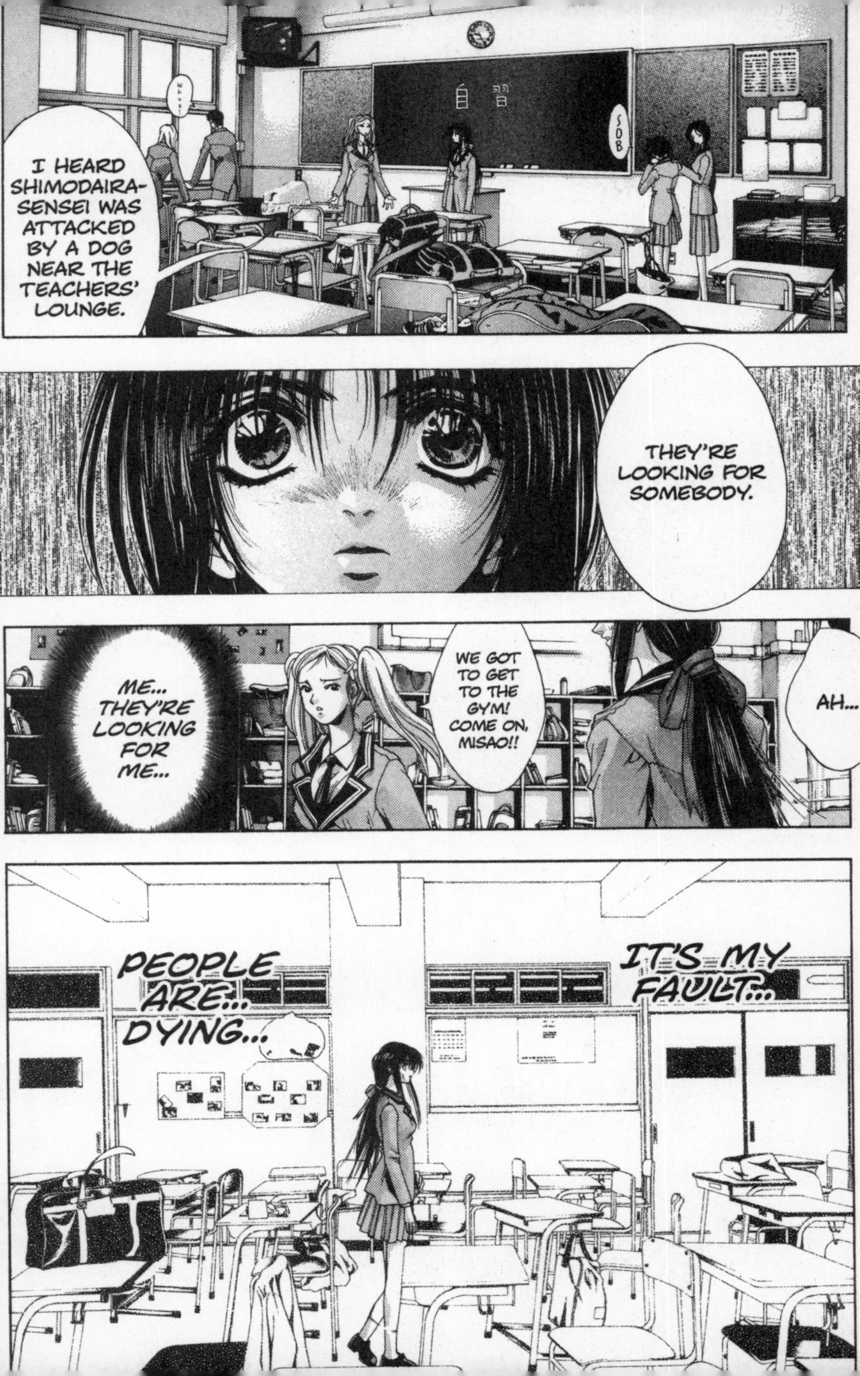
SOB
Whoa!
I HEARD SHIMODAIRA-SENSEI WAS ATTACKED BY A DOG NEAR THE TEACHERS' LOUNGE.
THEY'RE LOOKING FOR SOMEBODY.
AH...
WE GOT TO GET TO THE GYM! COME ON, MISAO!!
ME... THEY'RE LOOKING FOR ME...
IT'S MY FAULT...
PEOPLE ARE... DYING...

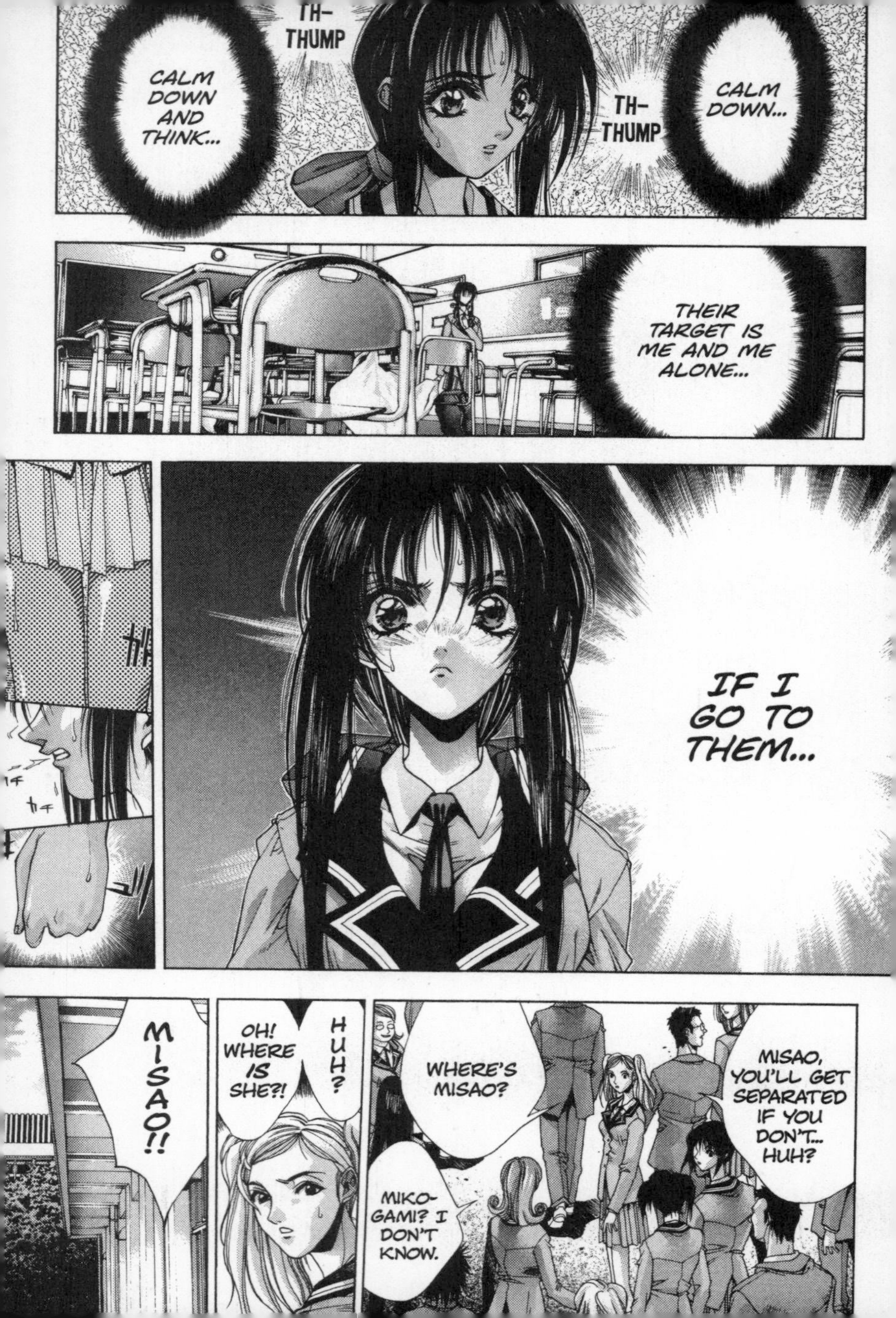
CALM DOWN...
TH-THUMP
TH-THUMP
CALM DOWN AND THINK...
THEIR TARGET IS ME AND ME ALONE...
IF I GO TO THEM...
MISAO, YOU'LL GET SEPARATED IF YOU DON'T... HUH?
WHERE'S MISAO?
MIKO-GAMI? I DON'T KNOW.
HUH?
OH! WHERE IS SHE?!
MISAO!!

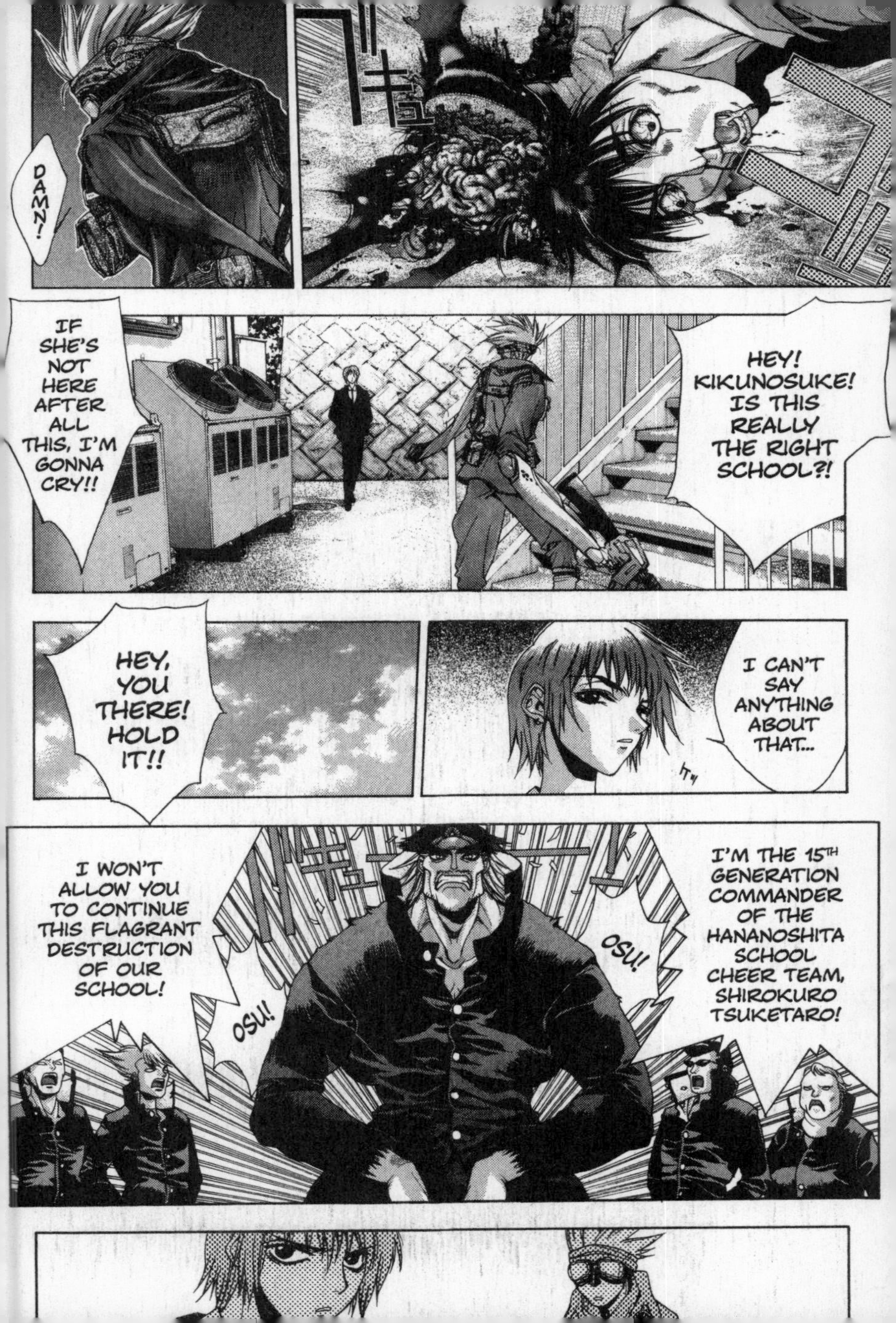
DAMN!
HEY! KIKUNOSUKE! IS THIS REALLY THE RIGHT SCHOOL?!
IF SHE'S NOT HERE AFTER ALL THIS, I'M GONNA CRY!!
I CAN'T SAY ANYTHING ABOUT THAT...
HEY, YOU THERE! HOLD IT!!
I'M THE 15TH GENERATION COMMANDER OF THE HANANOSHITA SCHOOL CHEER TEAM, SHIROKURO TSUKETARO!
OSU!
OSU!
I WON'T ALLOW YOU TO CONTINUE THIS FLAGRANT DESTRUCTION OF OUR SCHOOL!

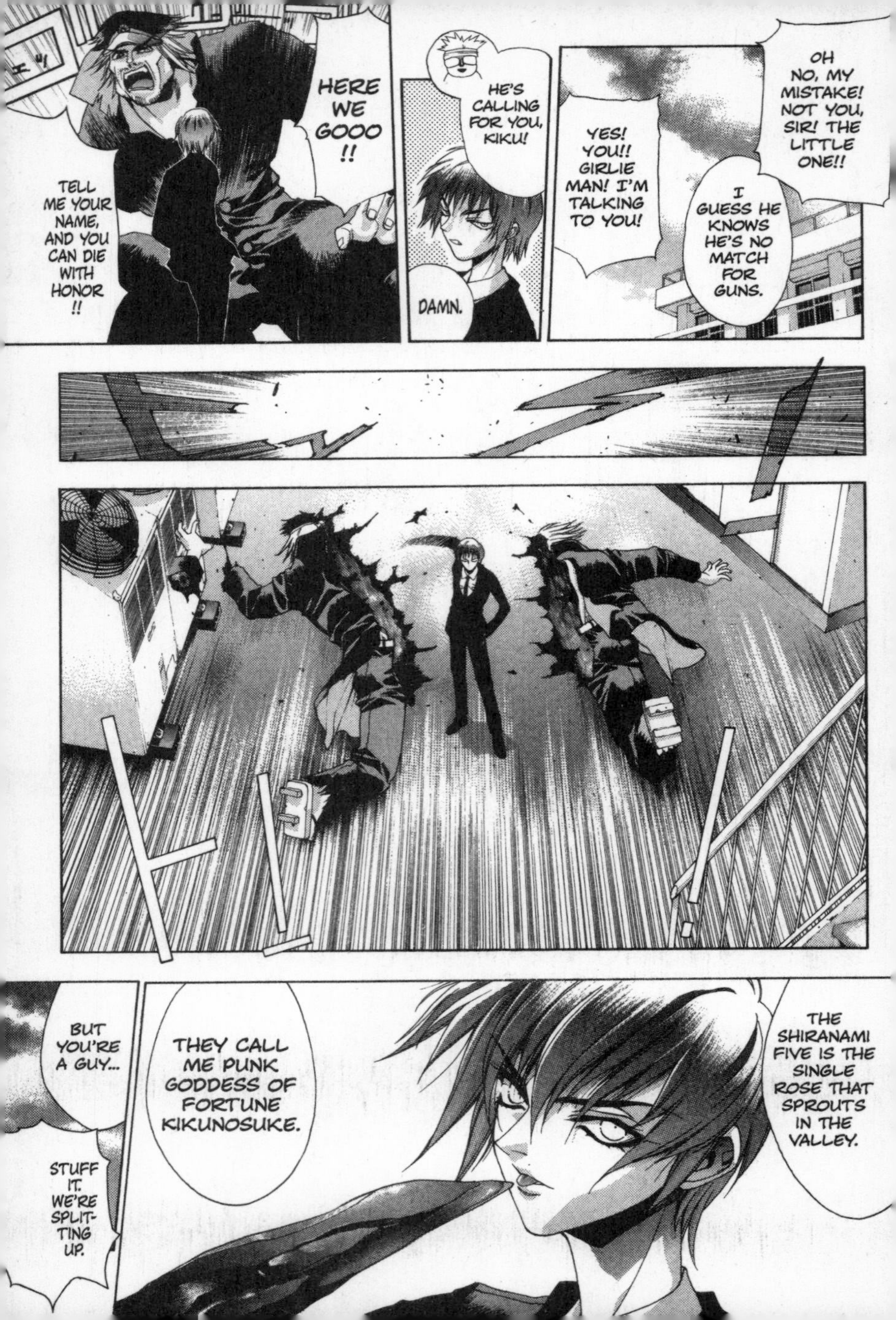
OH NO, MY MISTAKE! NOT YOU, SIR! THE LITTLE ONE!!
I GUESS HE KNOWS HE'S NO MATCH FOR GUNS.
HE'S CALLING FOR YOU, KIKU!
YES! YOU!! GIRLIE MAN! I'M TALKING TO YOU!
DAMN.
HERE WE GOOO !!
TELL ME YOUR NAME, AND YOU CAN DIE WITH HONOR !!
THE SHIRANAMI FIVE IS THE SINGLE ROSE THAT SPROUTS IN THE VALLEY.
THEY CALL ME PUNK GODDESS OF FORTUNE KIKUNOSUKE.
BUT YOU'RE A GUY...
STUFF IT. WE'RE SPLIT-TING UP.

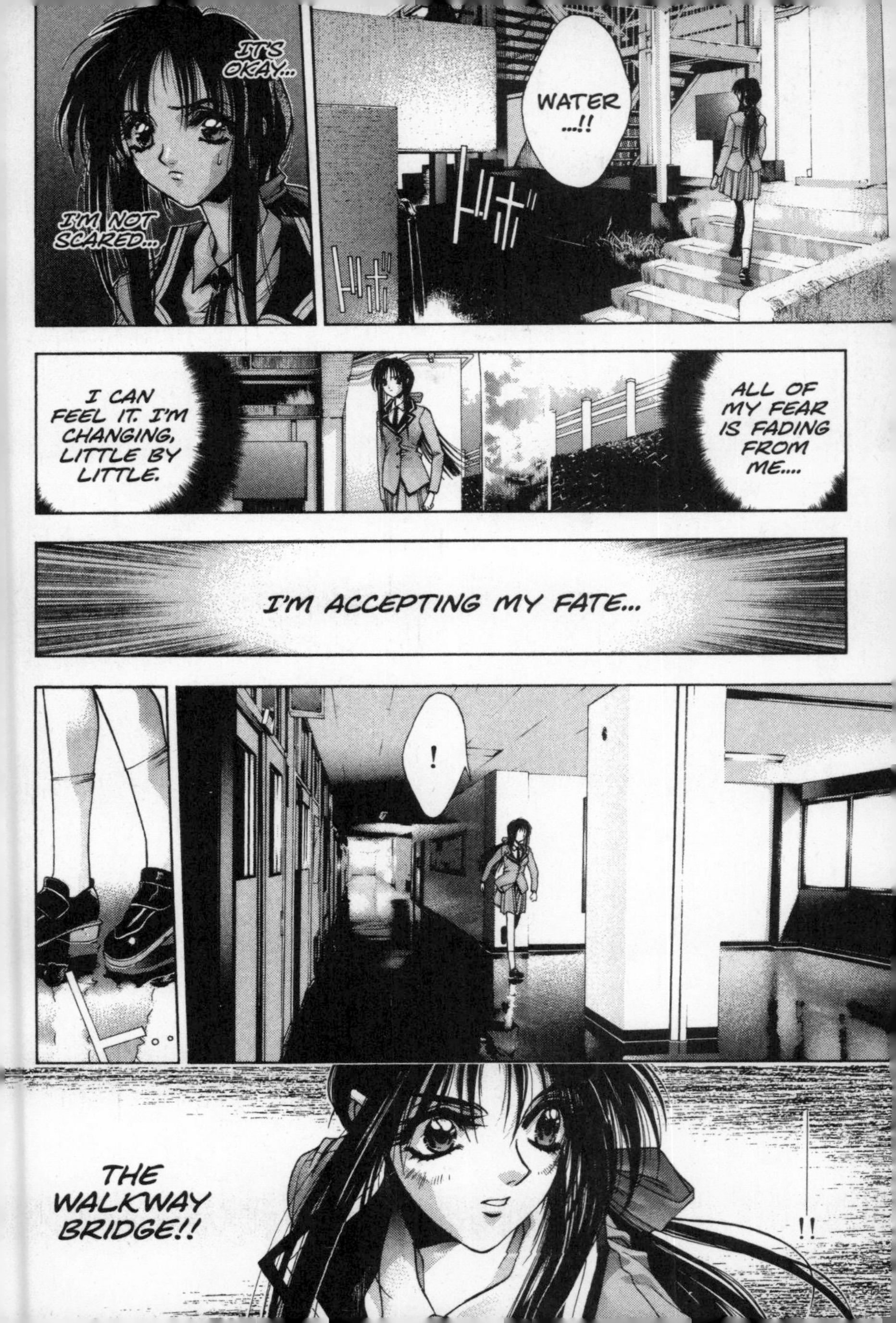
WATER ...!!
IT'S OKAY...
I'M NOT SCARED...
ALL OF MY FEAR IS FADING FROM ME....
I CAN FEEL IT. I'M CHANGING, LITTLE BY LITTLE.
I'M ACCEPTING MY FATE...
!
!!
THE WALKWAY BRIDGE!!

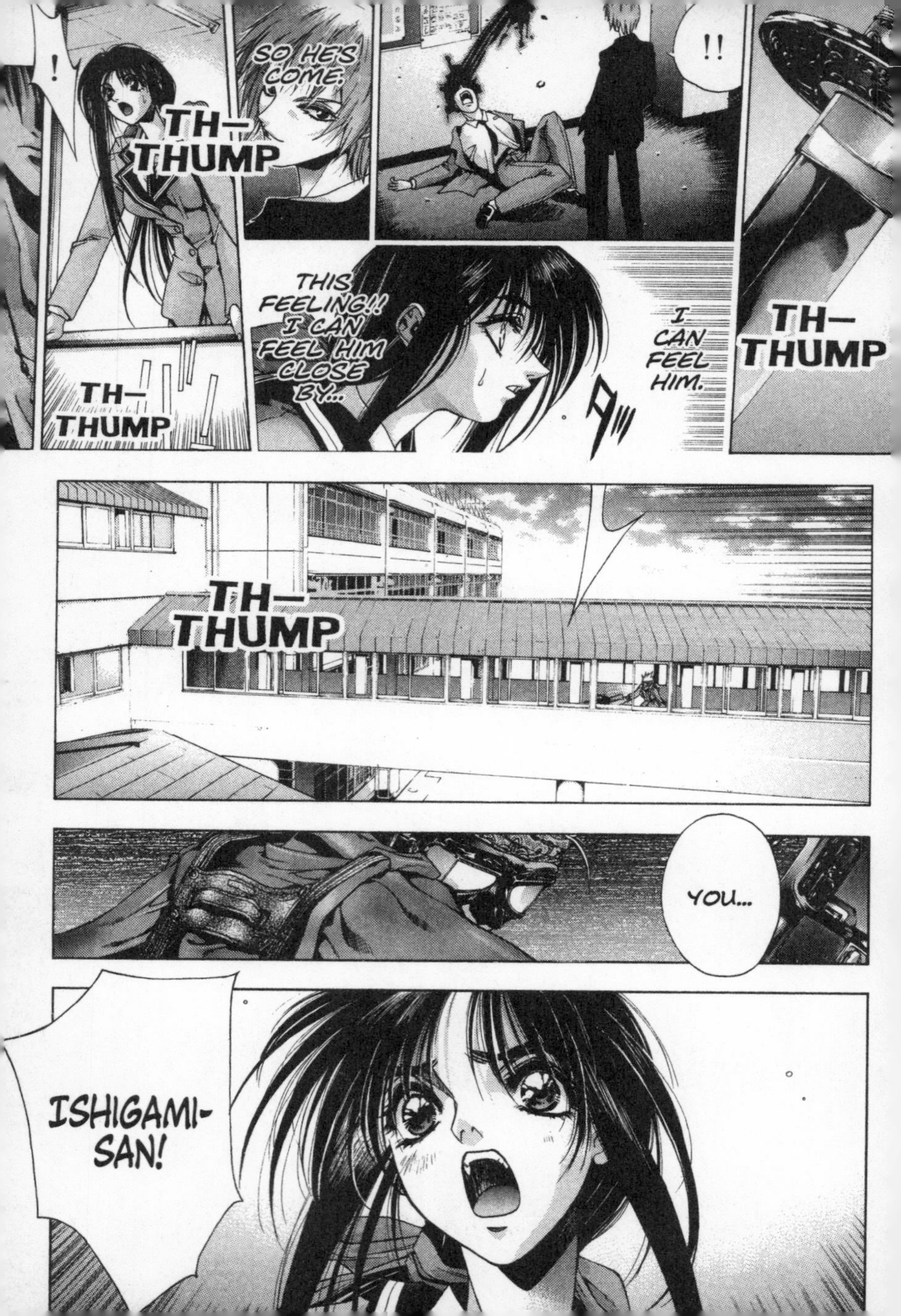
TH—THUMP
!!
SO HE'S COME.
TH—THUMP
I CAN FEEL HIM.
THIS FEELING!! I CAN FEEL HIM CLOSE BY...
!
TH—THUMP
TH—THUMP
YOU...
ISHIGAMI-SAN!

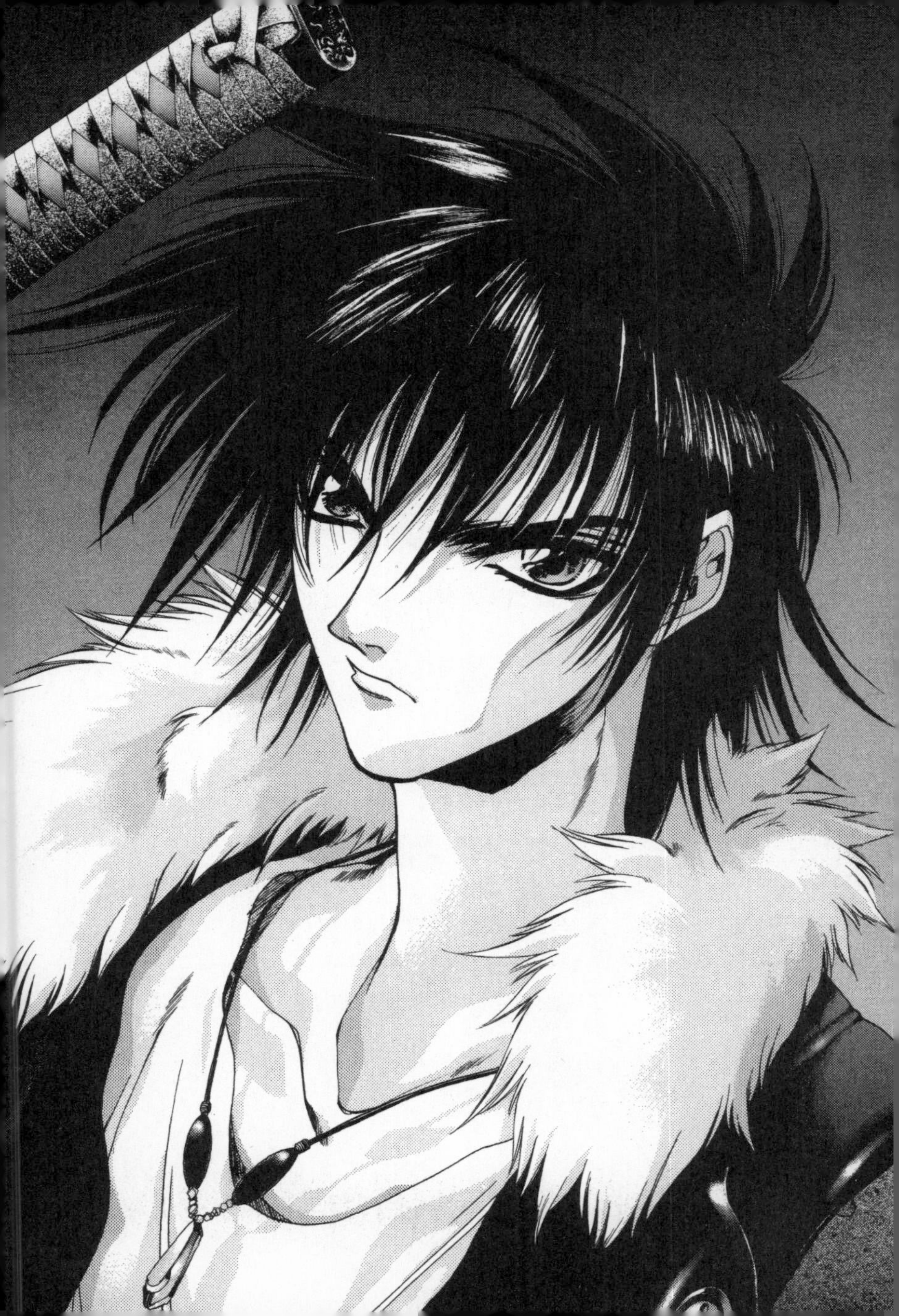

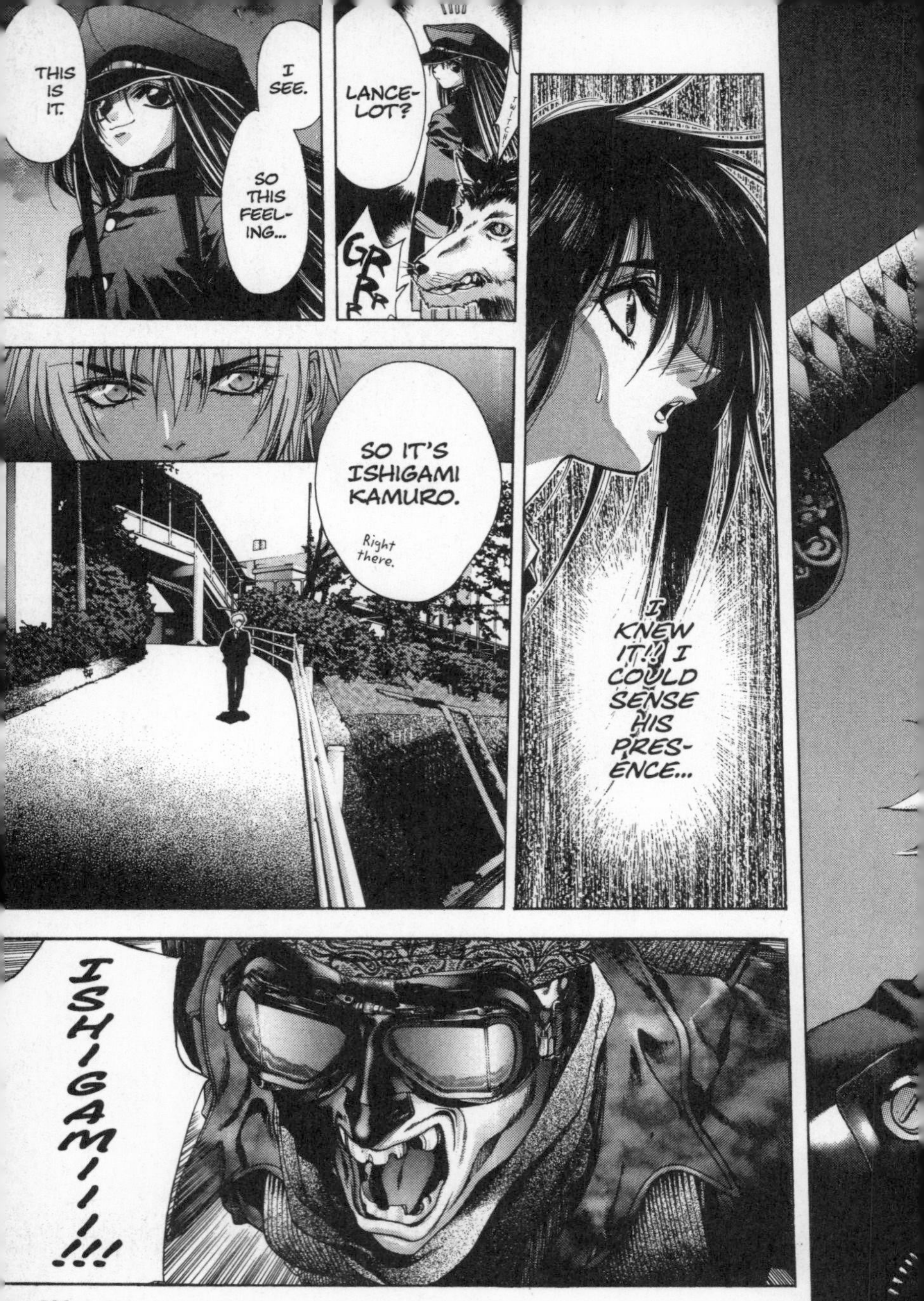
I KNEW IT!! I COULD SENSE HIS PRESENCE...
LANCE-LOT?
TWITCH
GRRRR
I SEE.
SO THIS FEEL-ING...
THIS IS IT.
SO IT'S ISHIGAMI KAMURO.
Right there.
ISHIGAMI!!!!

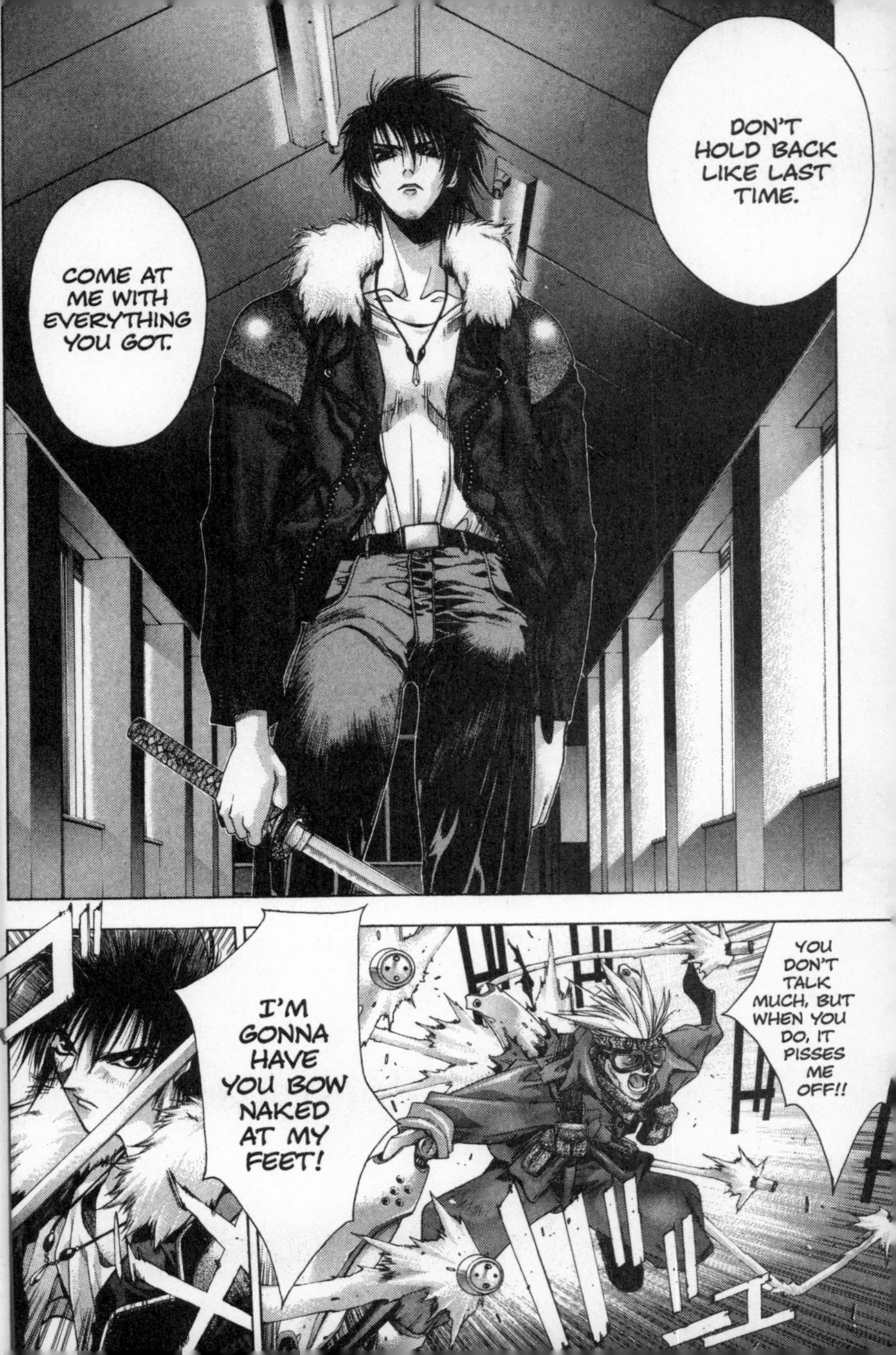
DON'T HOLD BACK LIKE LAST TIME.
COME AT ME WITH EVERYTHING YOU GOT.
YOU DON'T TALK MUCH, BUT WHEN YOU DO, IT PISSES ME OFF!!
I'M GONNA HAVE YOU BOW NAKED AT MY FEET!

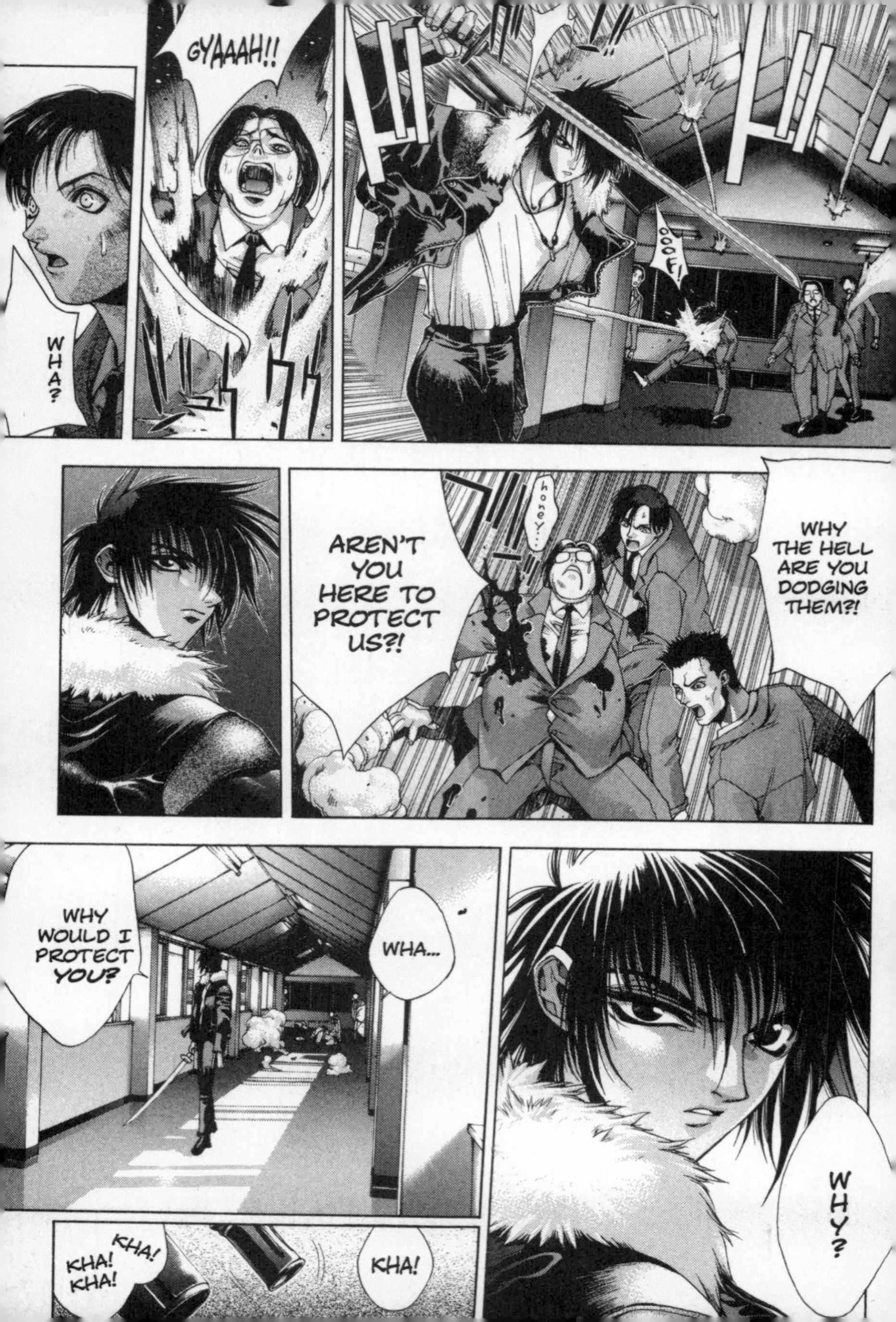
OOOF!
GYAAAH!!
WHA?
WHY THE HELL ARE YOU DODGING THEM?!
honey...
AREN'T YOU HERE TO PROTECT US?!
WHY?
WHA...
WHY WOULD I PROTECT YOU?
KHA!
KHA! KHA! KHA!

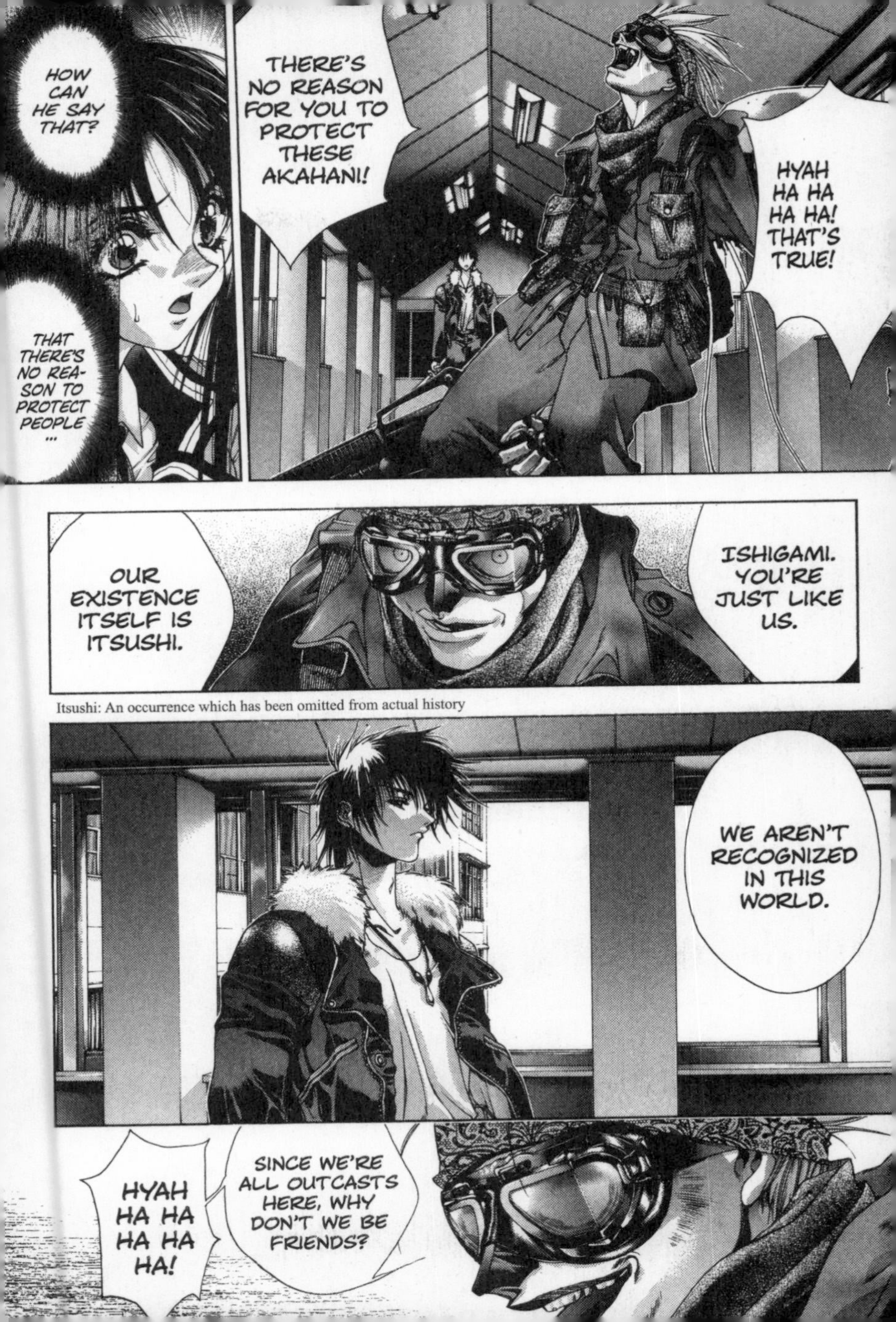
THERE'S NO REASON FOR YOU TO PROTECT THESE AKAHANI!
HYAH HA HA HA HA! THAT'S TRUE!
HOW CAN HE SAY THAT?
THAT THERE'S NO REA-SON TO PROTECT PEOPLE ...
ISHIGAMI. YOU'RE JUST LIKE US.
OUR EXISTENCE ITSELF IS ITSUSHI.
WE AREN'T RECOGNIZED IN THIS WORLD.
SINCE WE'RE ALL OUTCASTS HERE, WHY DON'T WE BE FRIENDS?
HYAH HA HA HA HA HA!
Itsushi: An occurrence which has been omitted from actual history

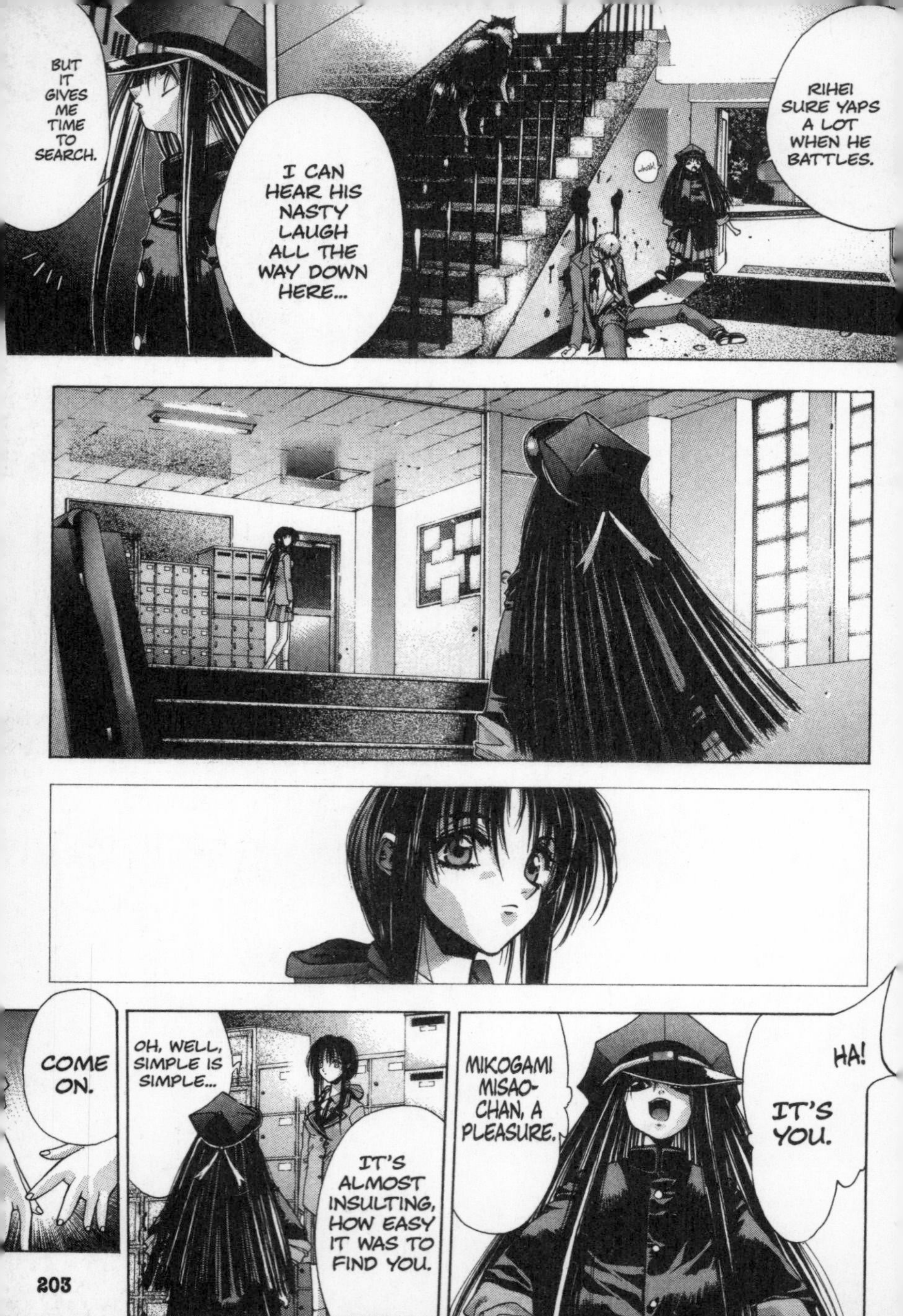
RIHEI SURE YAPS A LOT WHEN HE BATTLES.
I CAN HEAR HIS NASTY LAUGH ALL THE WAY DOWN HERE...
BUT IT GIVES ME TIME TO SEARCH.
HA!
IT'S YOU.
MIKOGAMI MISAO-CHAN, A PLEASURE.
OH, WELL, SIMPLE IS SIMPLE...
IT'S ALMOST INSULTING, HOW EASY IT WAS TO FIND YOU.
COME ON.

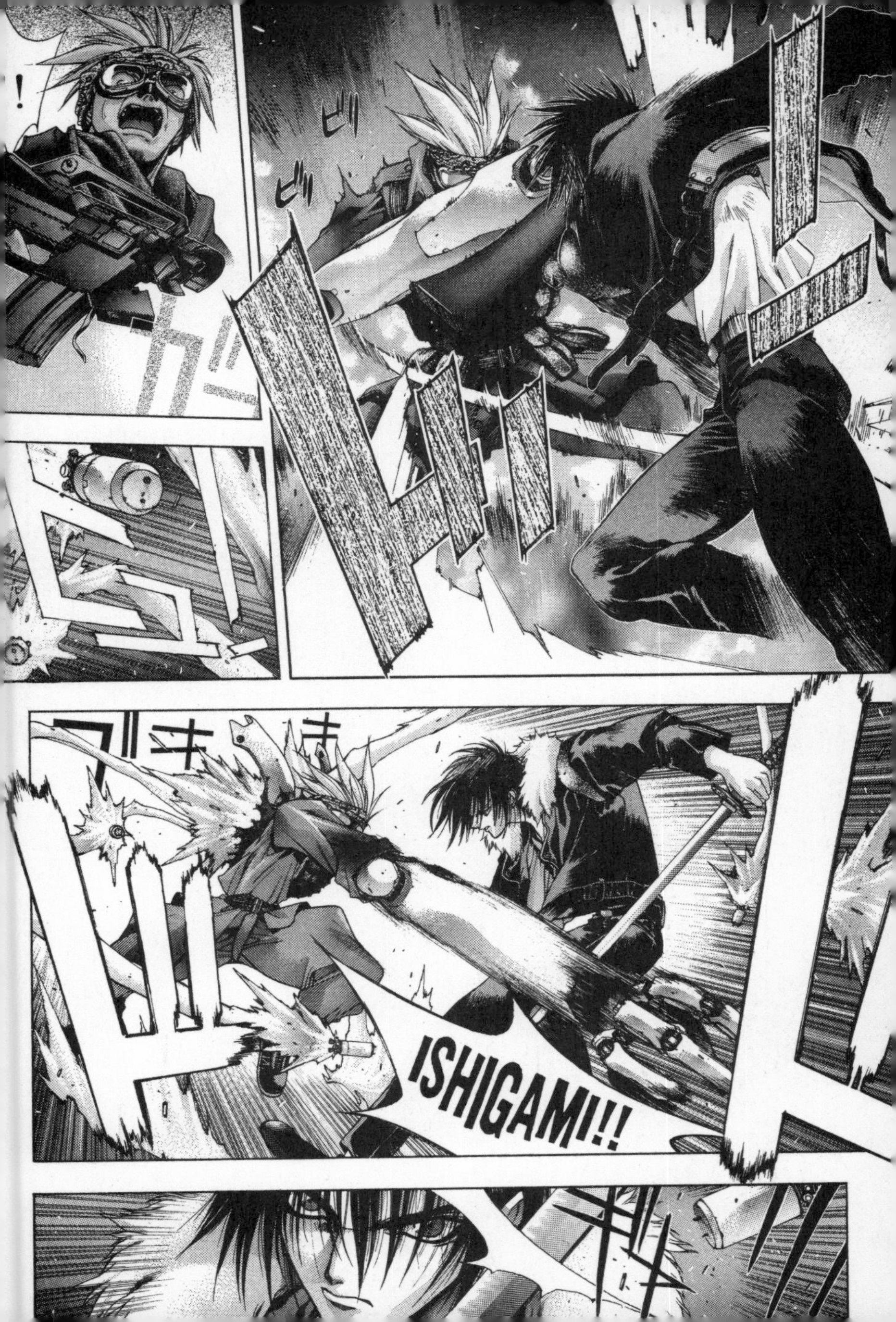
!
ISHIGAMI!!

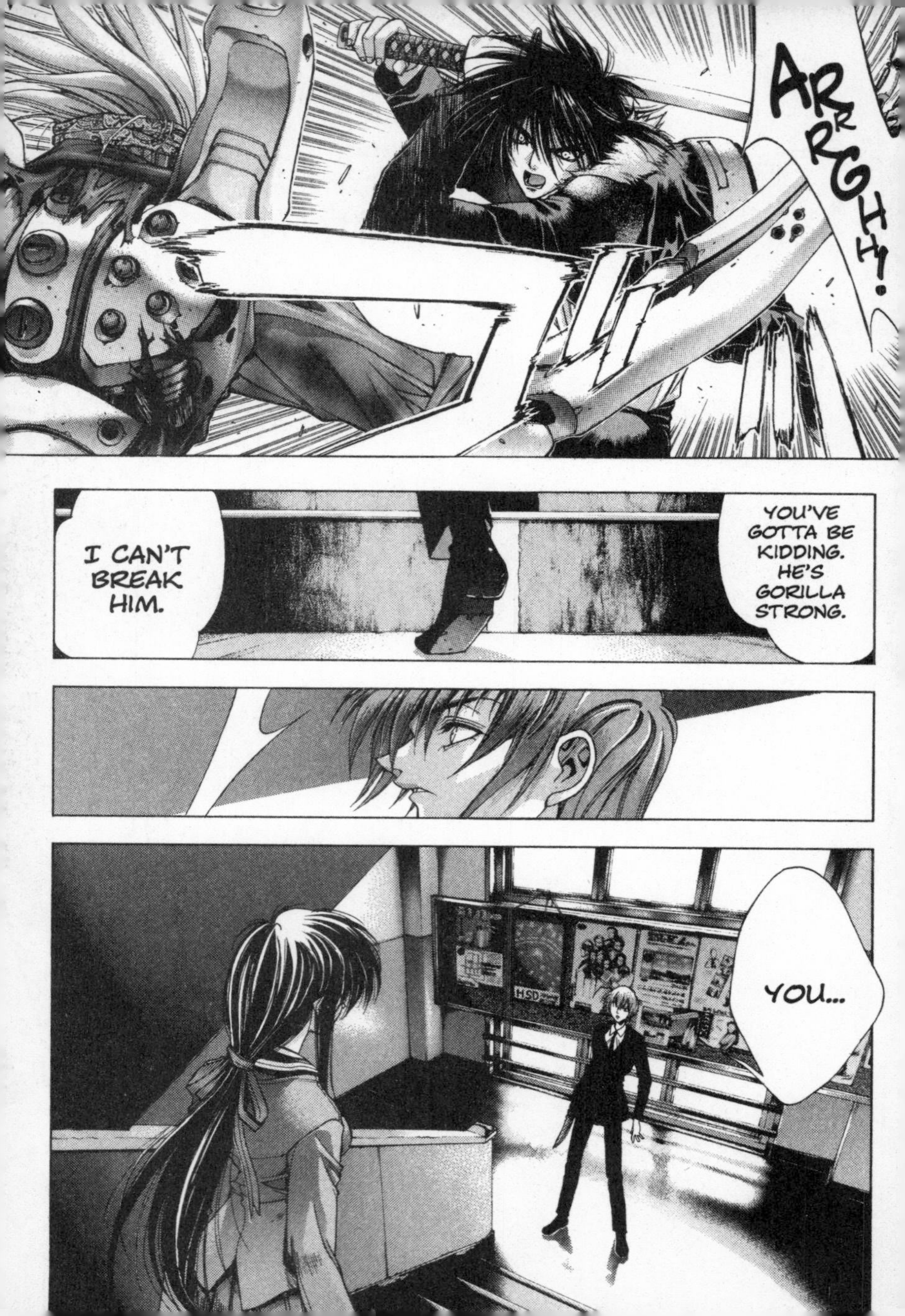
ARRRGHH!
YOU'VE GOTTA BE KIDDING. HE'S GORILLA STRONG.
I CAN'T BREAK HIM.
YOU...

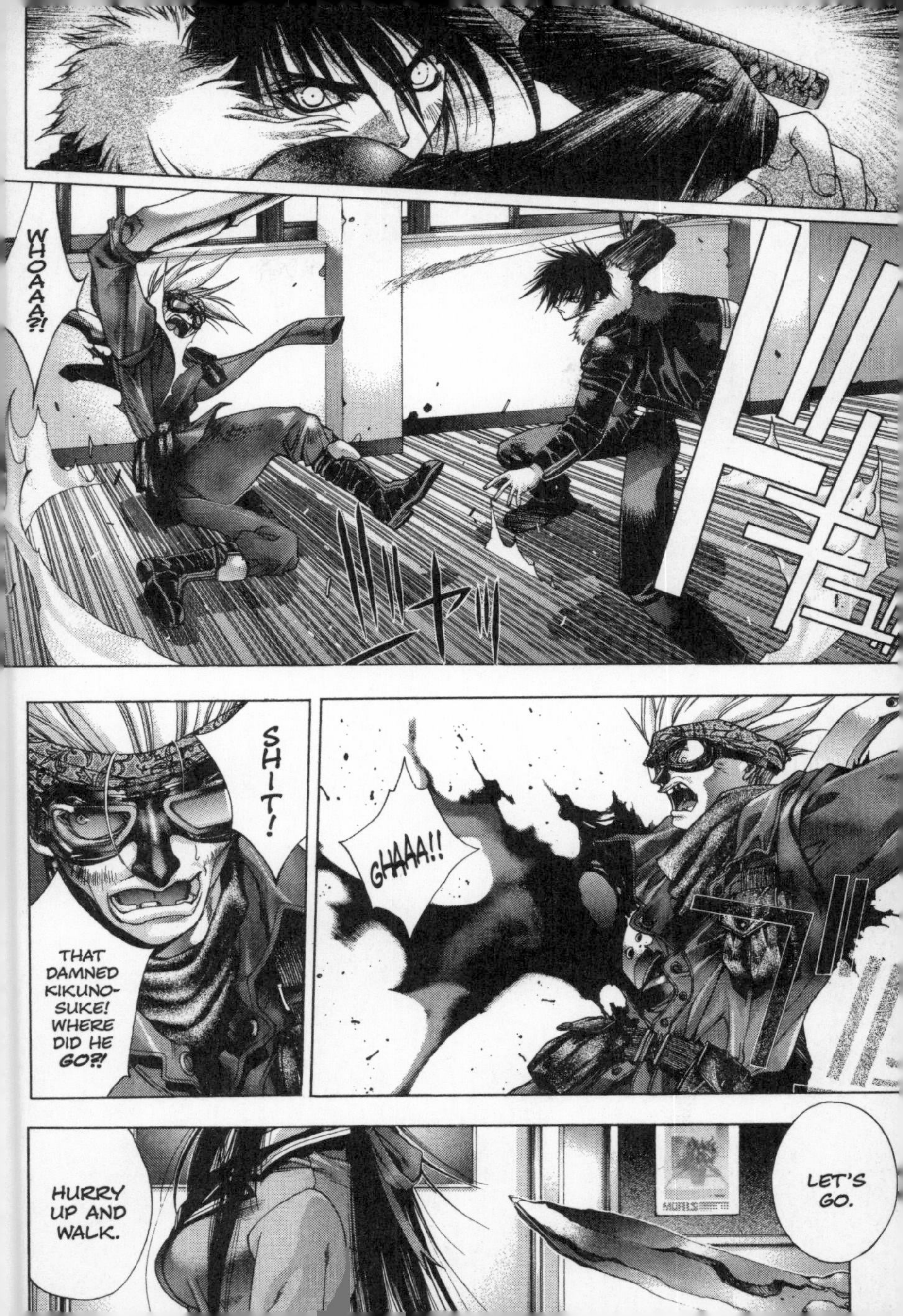
WHOAAA?!
GHAAA!!
SHIT!
THAT DAMNED KIKUNO-SUKE! WHERE DID HE GO?!
LET'S GO.
HURRY UP AND WALK.

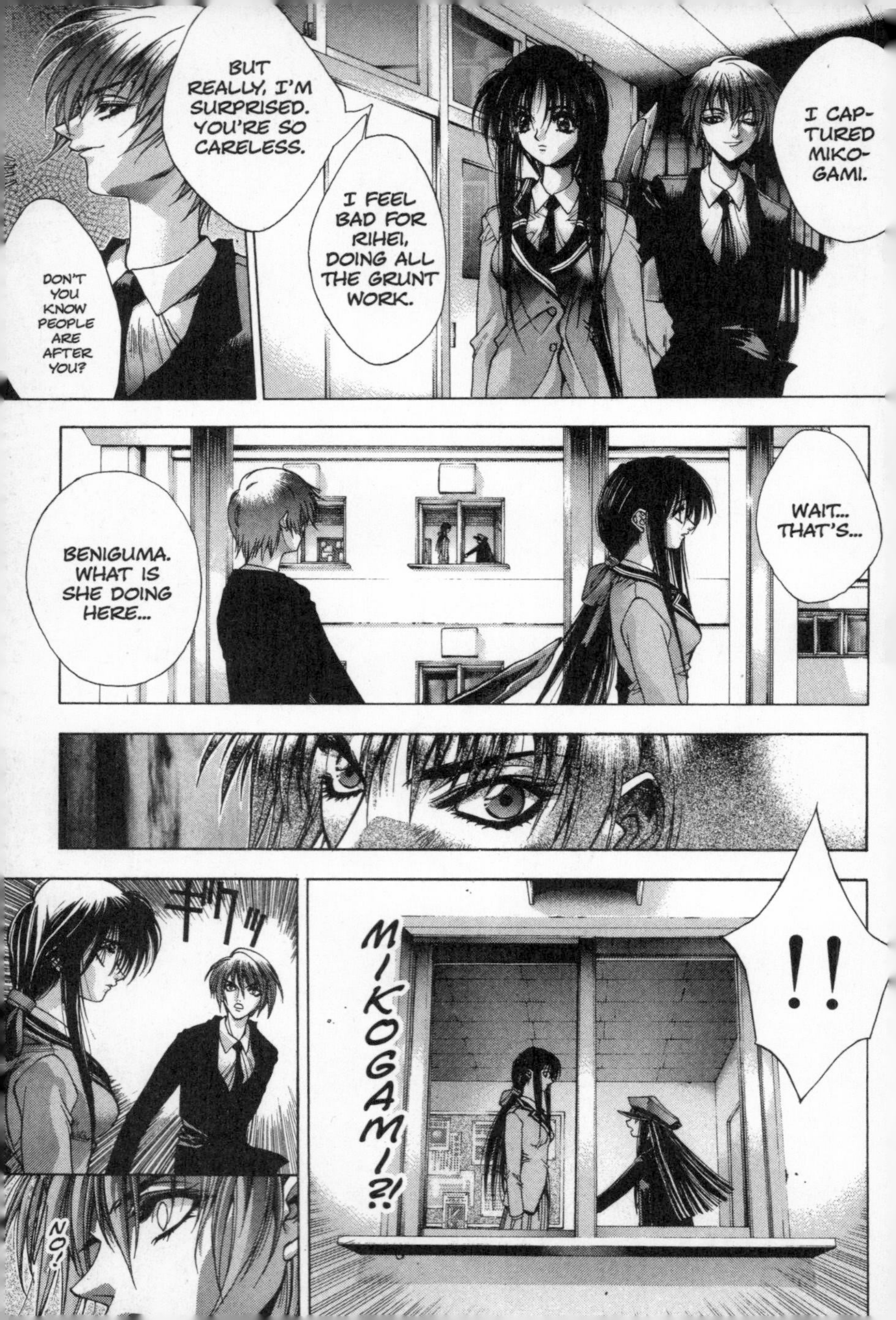
I CAP-
TURED
MIKO-
GAMI.
BUT REALLY, I'M SURPRISED. YOU'RE SO CARELESS.
I FEEL BAD FOR RIHEI, DOING ALL THE GRUNT WORK.
DON'T YOU KNOW PEOPLE ARE AFTER YOU?
WAIT... THAT'S...
BENIGUMA. WHAT IS SHE DOING HERE...
!!
MIKOGAMI?!
NO!

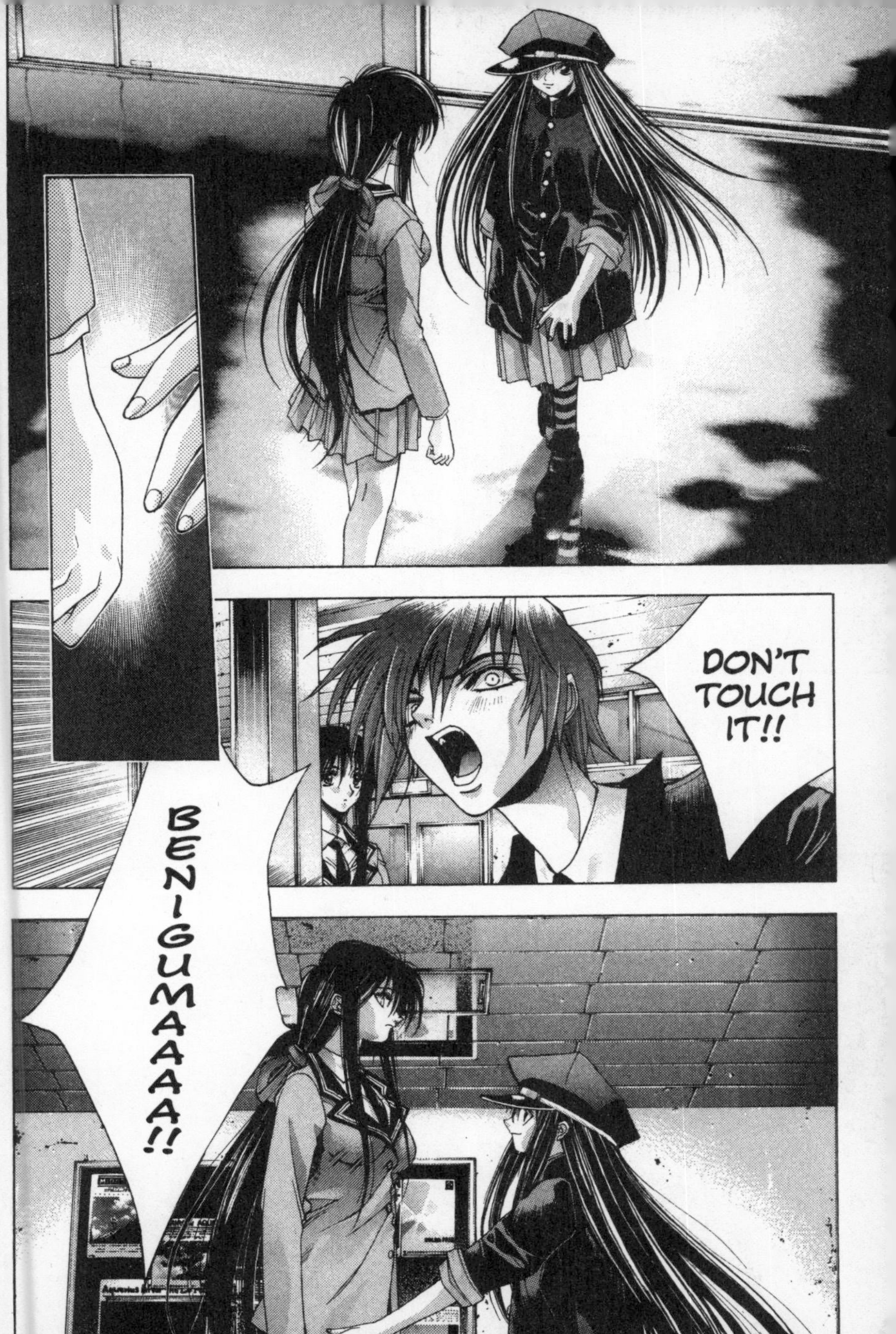
DON'T TOUCH IT!!
BENIGUMAAAAA!!

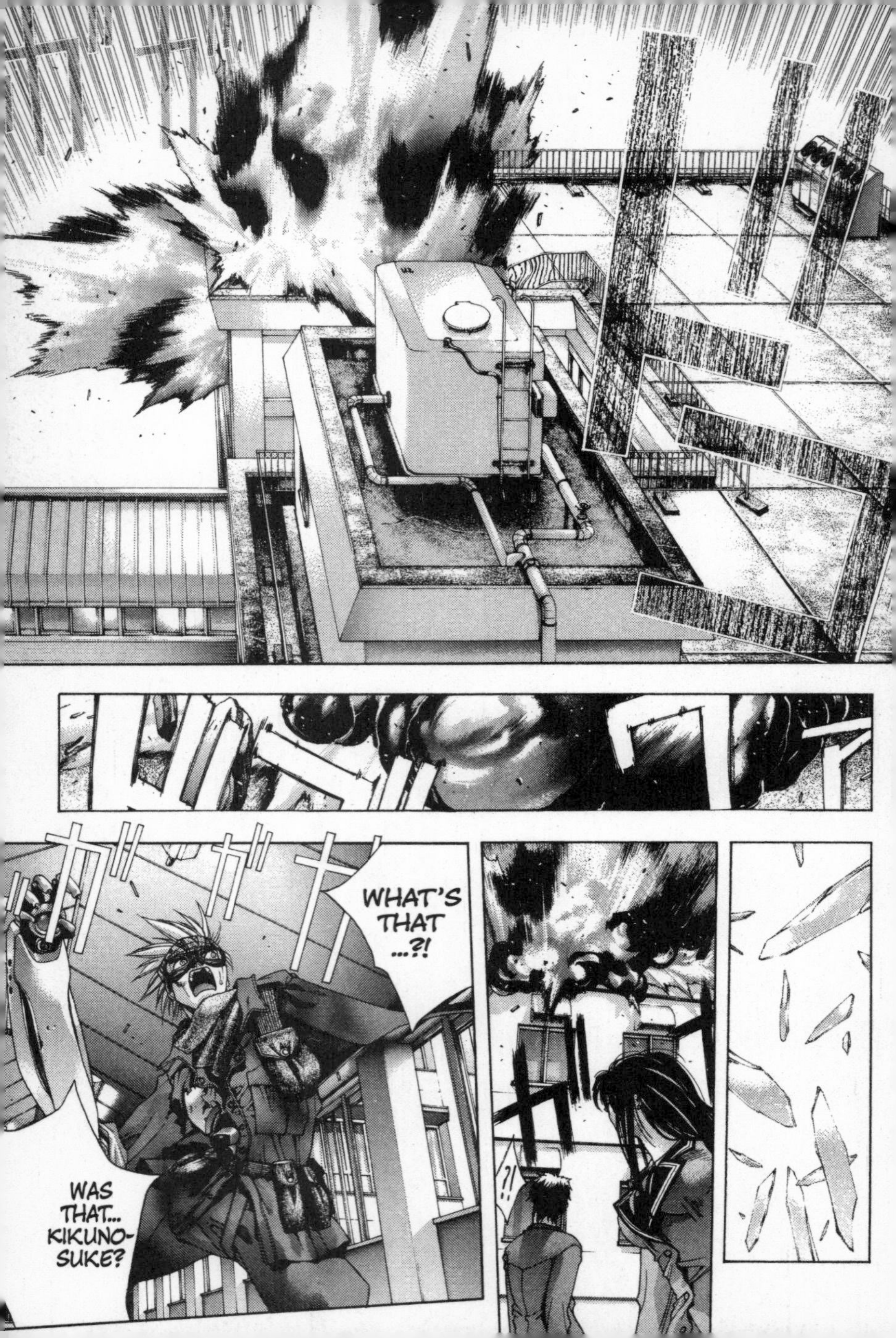
?!
WHAT'S THAT ...?!
WAS THAT... KIKUNO-SUKE?

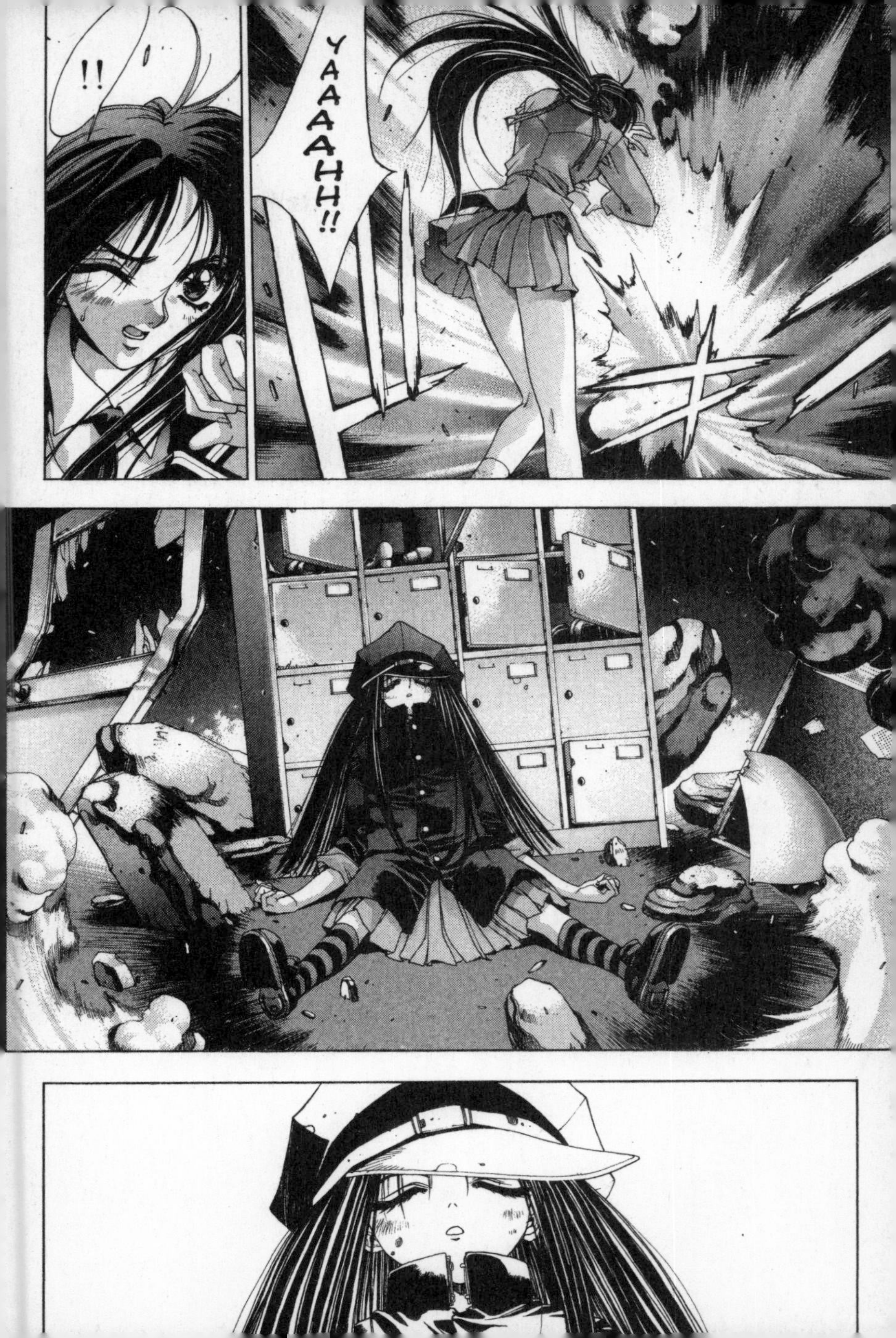
YAAAAAHH!!
!!

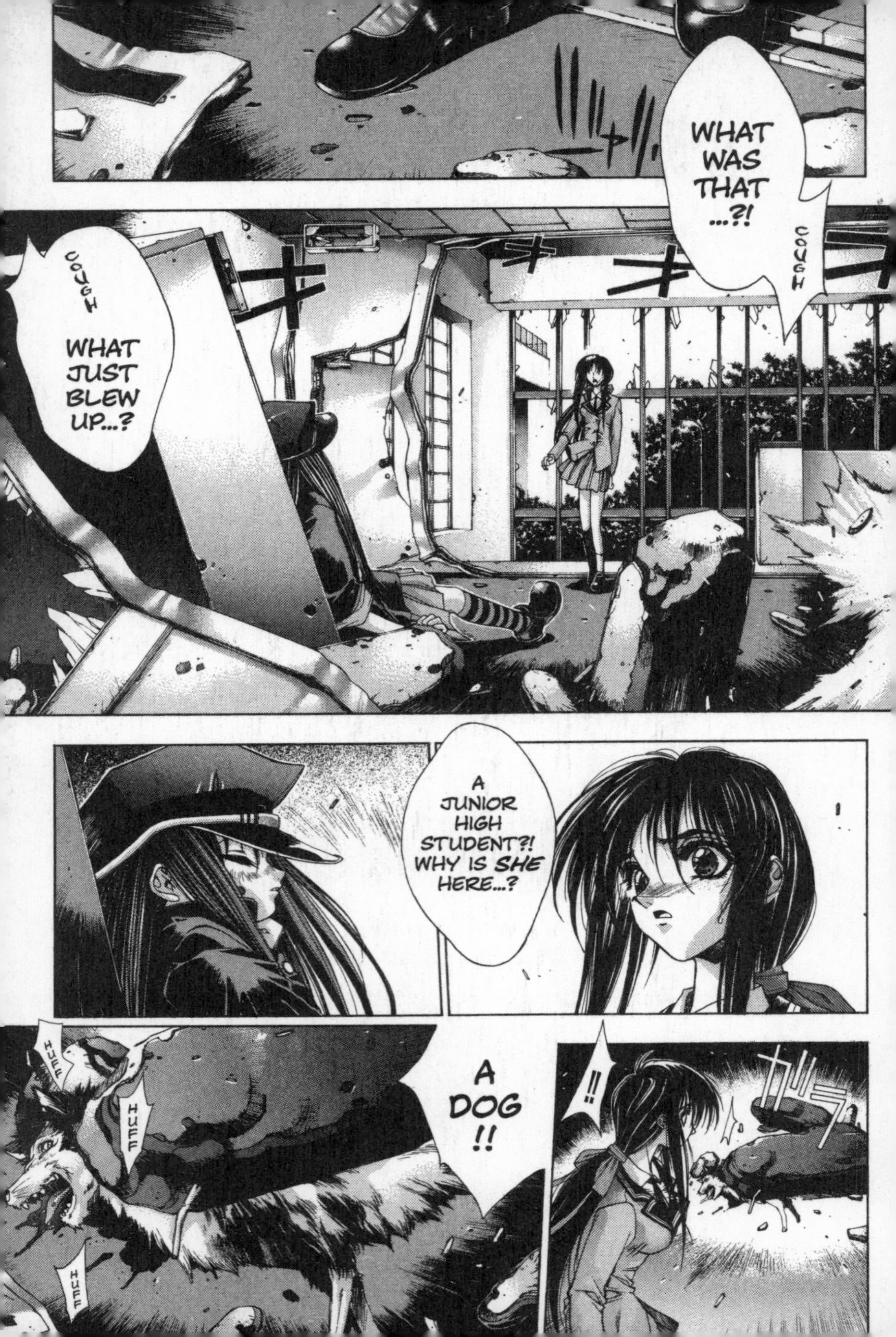
WHAT WAS THAT ...?!
COUGH
COUGH
WHAT JUST BLEW UP...?
A JUNIOR HIGH STUDENT?! WHY IS SHE HERE...?
!!
A DOG !!
HUFF
HUFF
HUFF

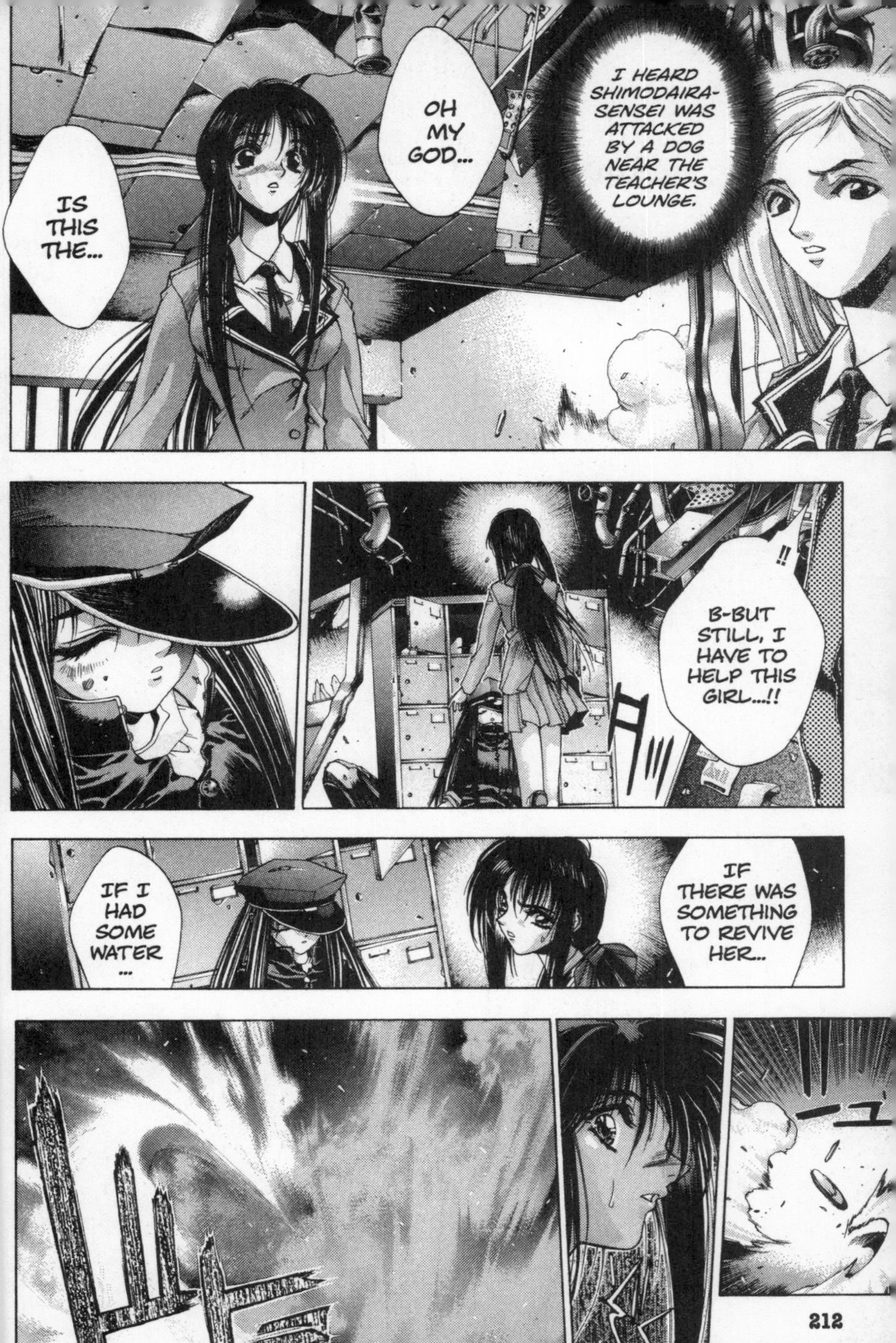
I HEARD SHIMODAIRA-SENSEI WAS ATTACKED BY A DOG NEAR THE TEACHER'S LOUNGE.
OH MY GOD...
IS THIS THE...
!!
B-BUT STILL, I HAVE TO HELP THIS GIRL...!!
IF THERE WAS SOMETHING TO REVIVE HER...
IF I HAD SOME WATER ...

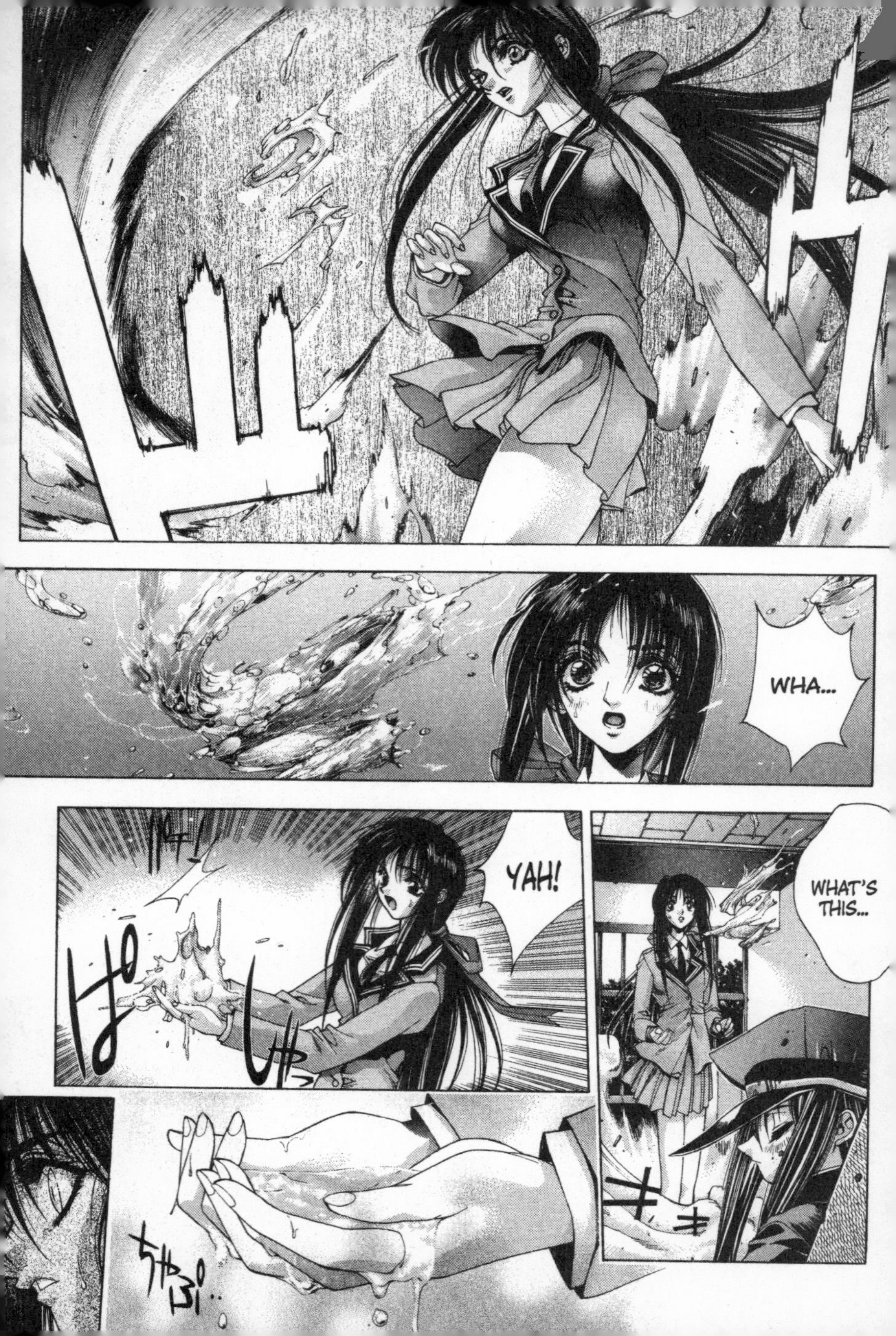
WHA...
WHAT'S THIS...
YAH!
ちゃぷ..

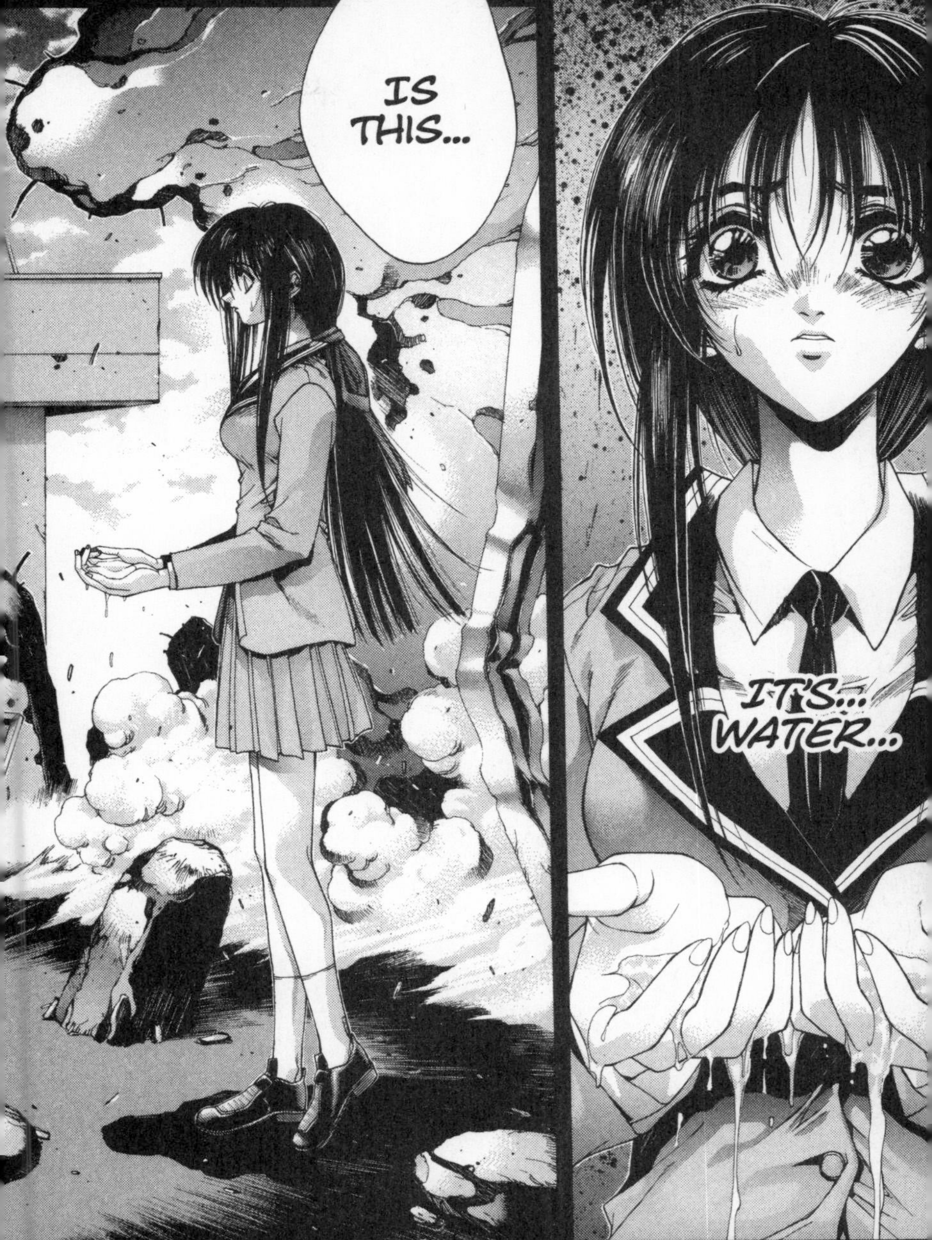
IT'S... WATER...
IS THIS...

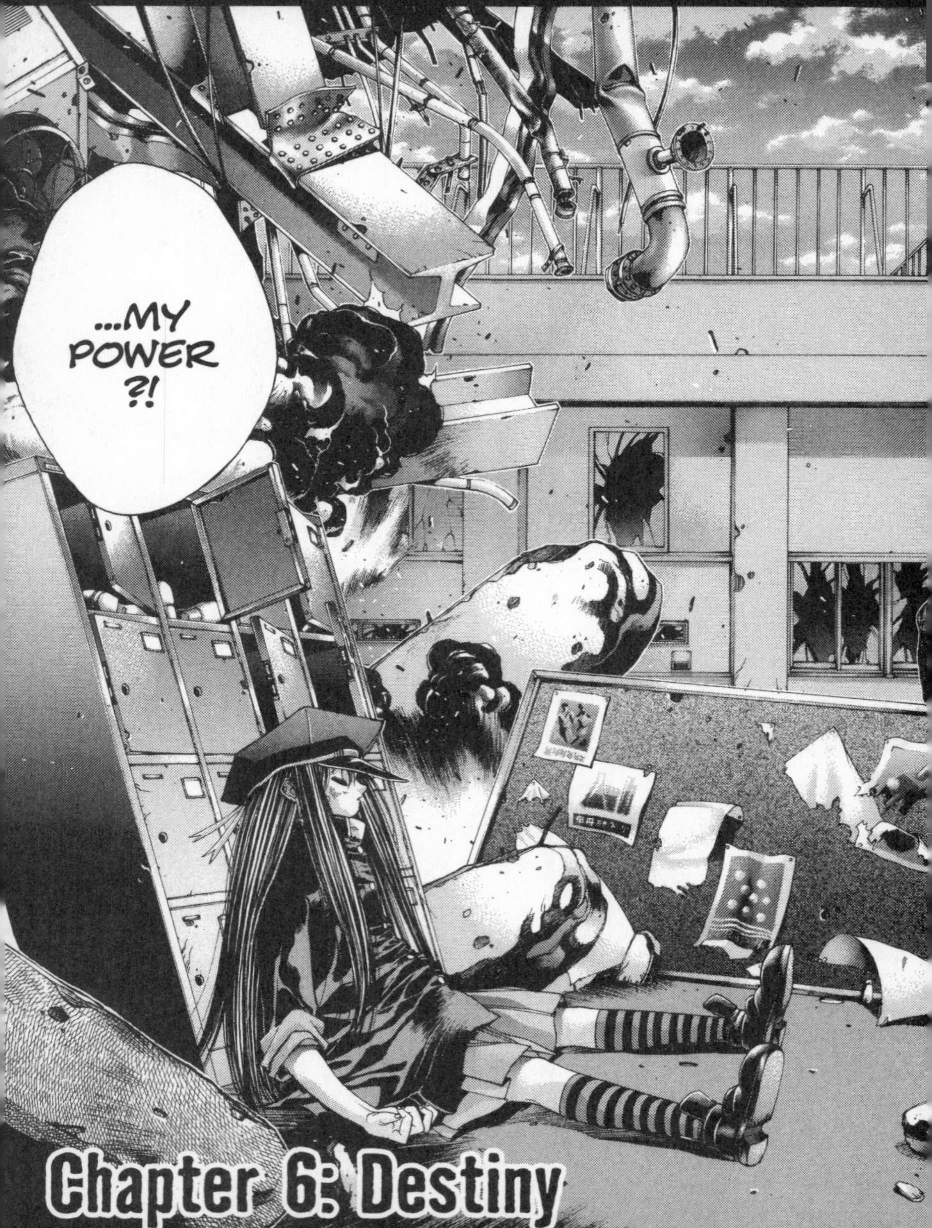
...MY POWER ?!

Chapter 6: Destiny

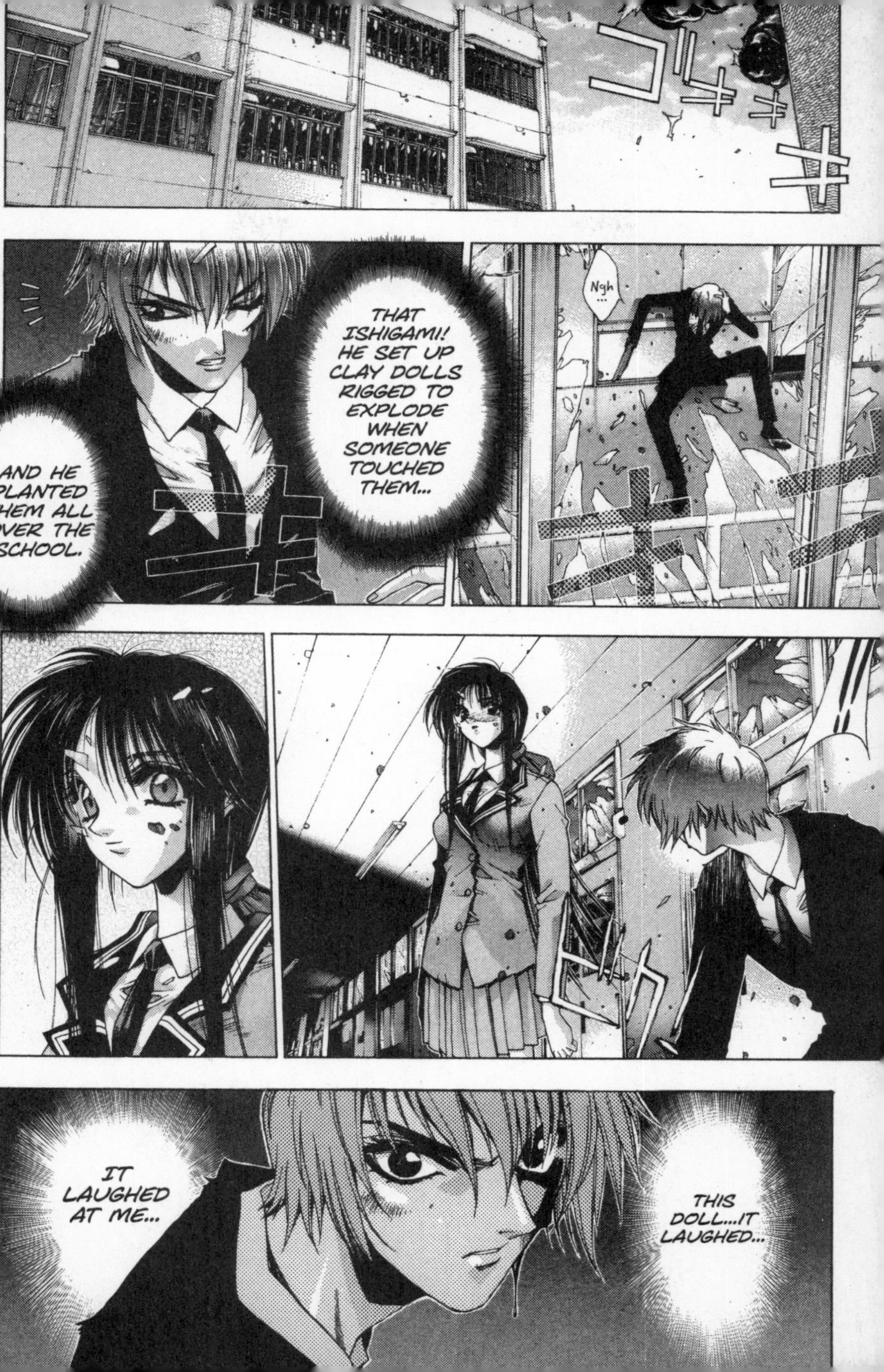
Ngh...
THAT ISHIGAMI! HE SET UP CLAY DOLLS RIGGED TO EXPLODE WHEN SOMEONE TOUCHED THEM...
AND HE PLANTED THEM ALL OVER THE SCHOOL.
THIS DOLL...IT LAUGHED...
IT LAUGHED AT ME...

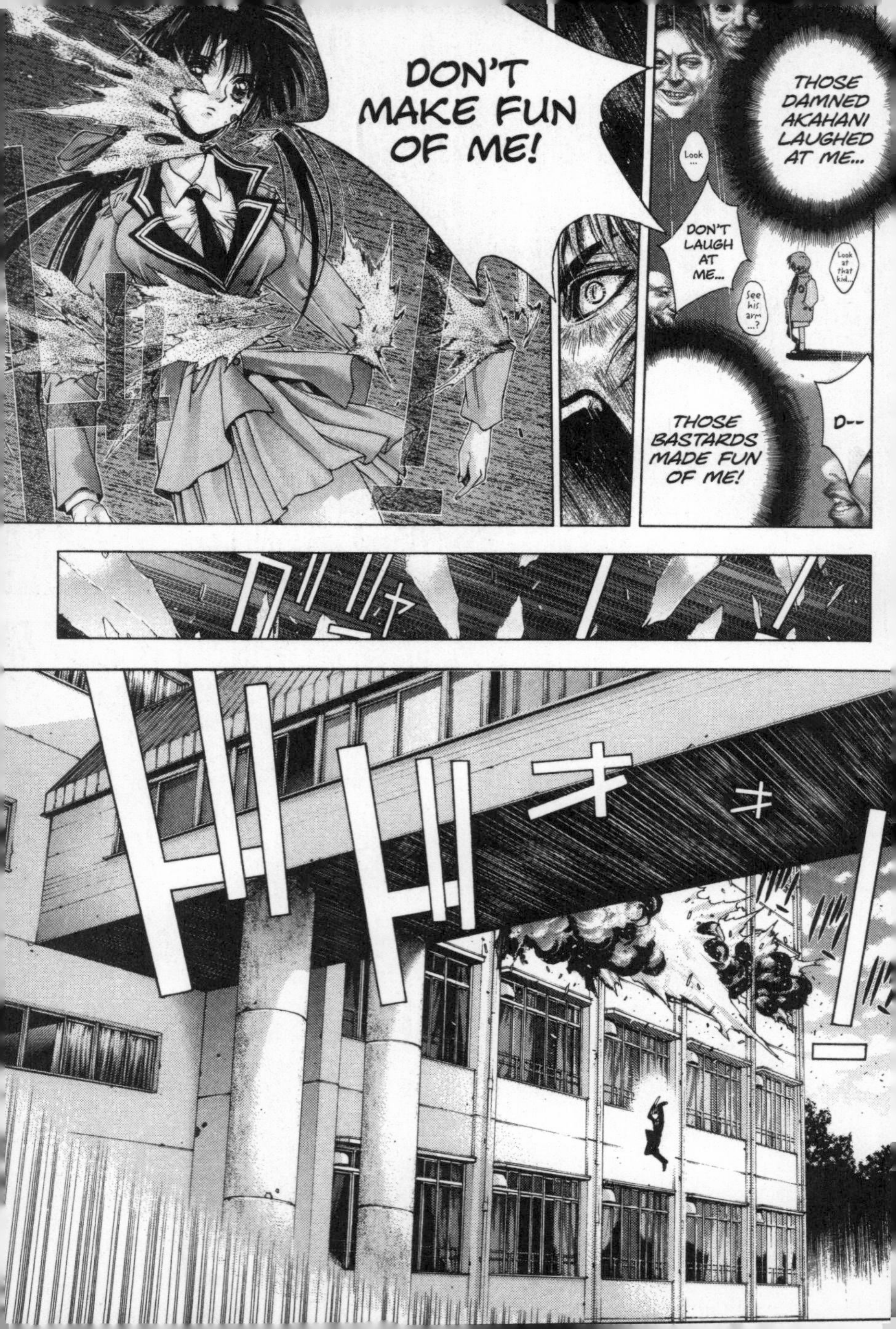
THOSE DAMNED AKAHANI LAUGHED AT ME...
Look at that kid...
Look ...
See his arm ...?
DON'T LAUGH AT ME...
D--
THOSE BASTARDS MADE FUN OF ME!
DON'T MAKE FUN OF ME!

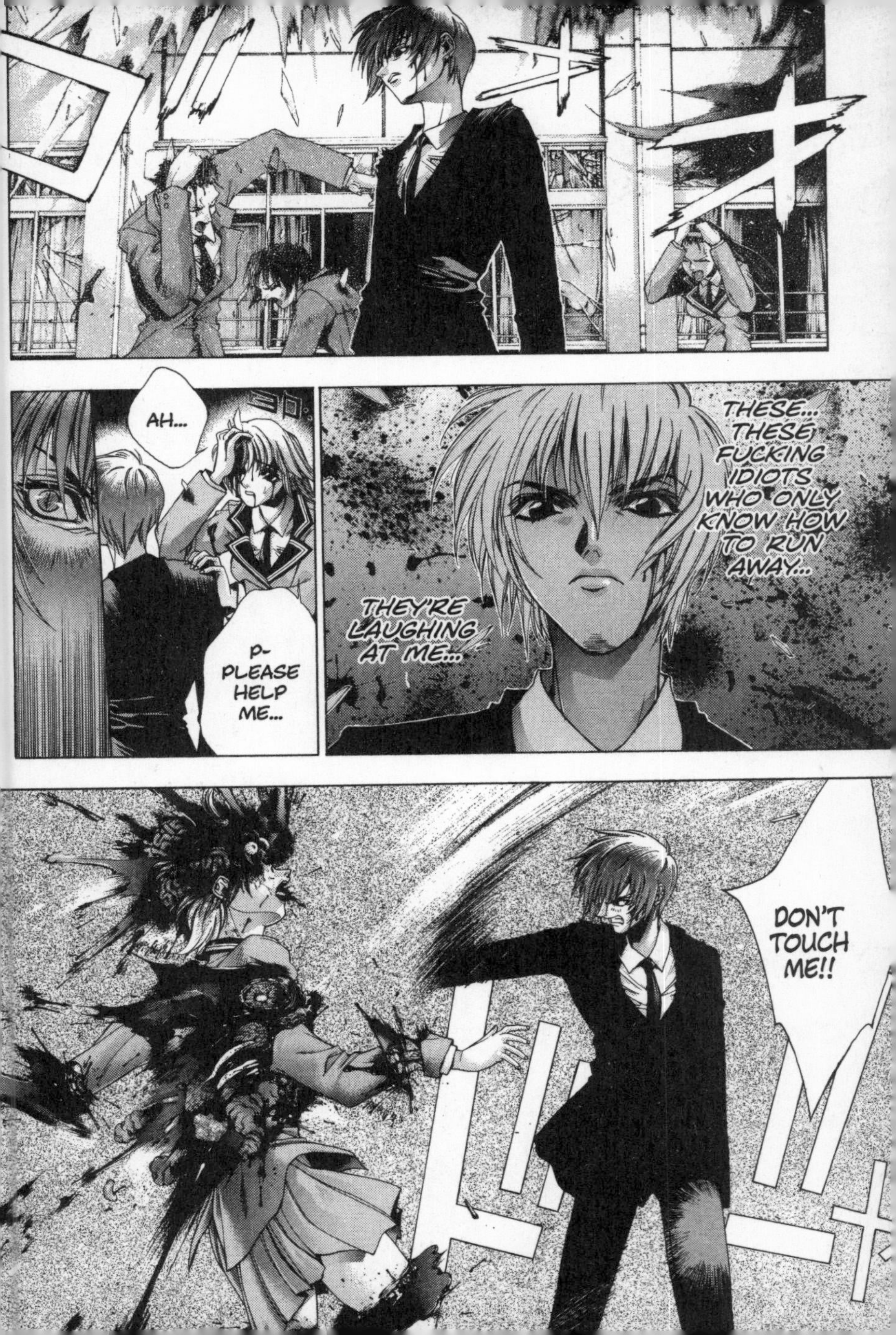
THESE... THESE FUCKING IDIOTS WHO ONLY KNOW HOW TO RUN AWAY...
THEY'RE LAUGHING AT ME...
AH...
P-PLEASE HELP ME...
DON'T TOUCH ME!!

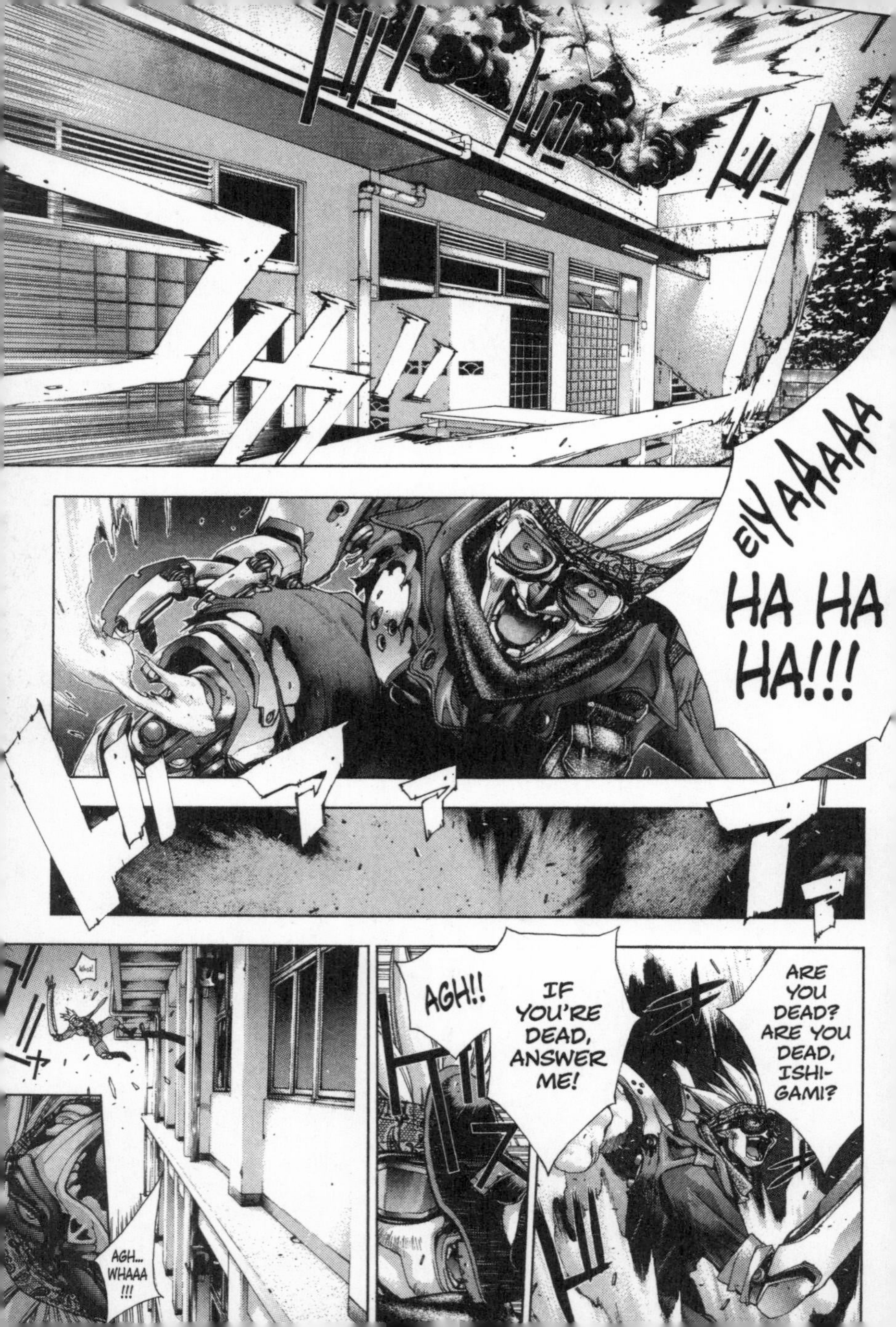
EIYAAAAA
HA HA HA!!!
ARE YOU DEAD? ARE YOU DEAD, ISHIGAMI?
IF YOU'RE DEAD, ANSWER ME!
AGH!!
Whoa!
AGH... WHAAA !!!

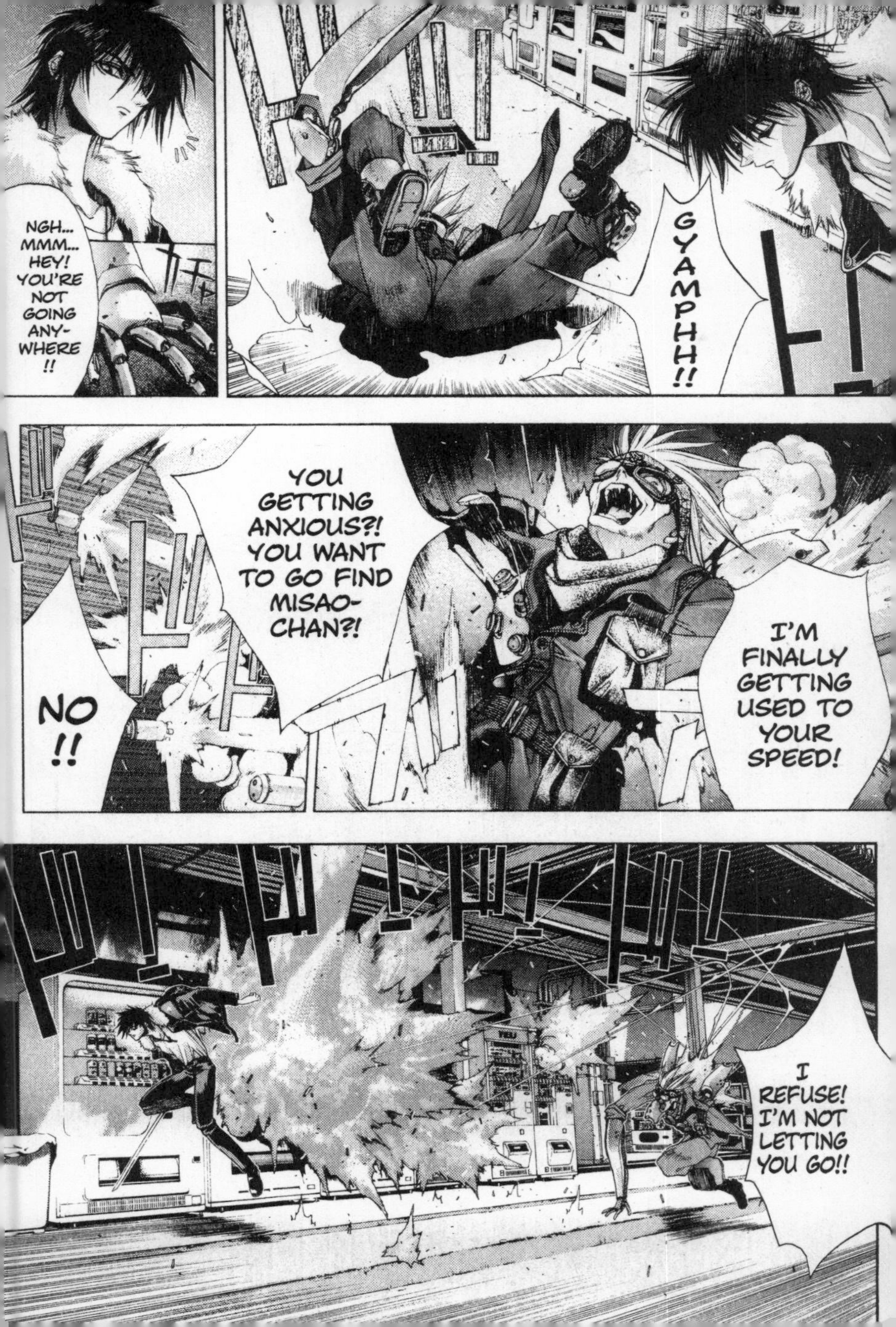
GYAMPHH!!
NGH... MMM... HEY! YOU'RE NOT GOING ANY-WHERE!!
I'M FINALLY GETTING USED TO YOUR SPEED!
YOU GETTING ANXIOUS?! YOU WANT TO GO FIND MISAO-CHAN?!
NO!!
I REFUSE! I'M NOT LETTING YOU GO!!

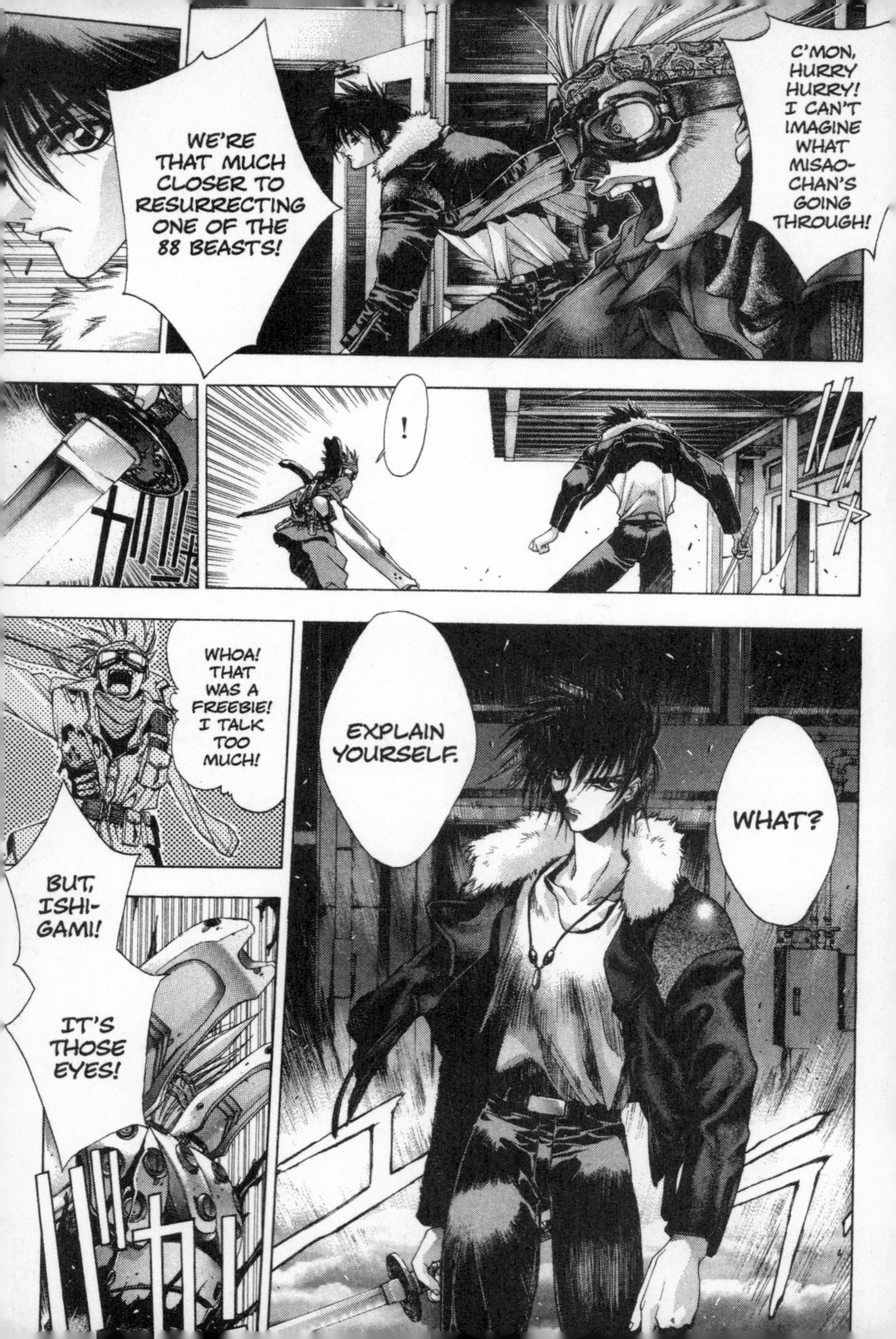
C'MON, HURRY HURRY! I CAN'T IMAGINE WHAT MISAO-CHAN'S GOING THROUGH!
WE'RE THAT MUCH CLOSER TO RESURRECTING ONE OF THE 88 BEASTS!
!
WHAT?
EXPLAIN YOURSELF.
WHOA! THAT WAS A FREEBIE! I TALK TOO MUCH!
BUT, ISHI-GAMI!
IT'S THOSE EYES!

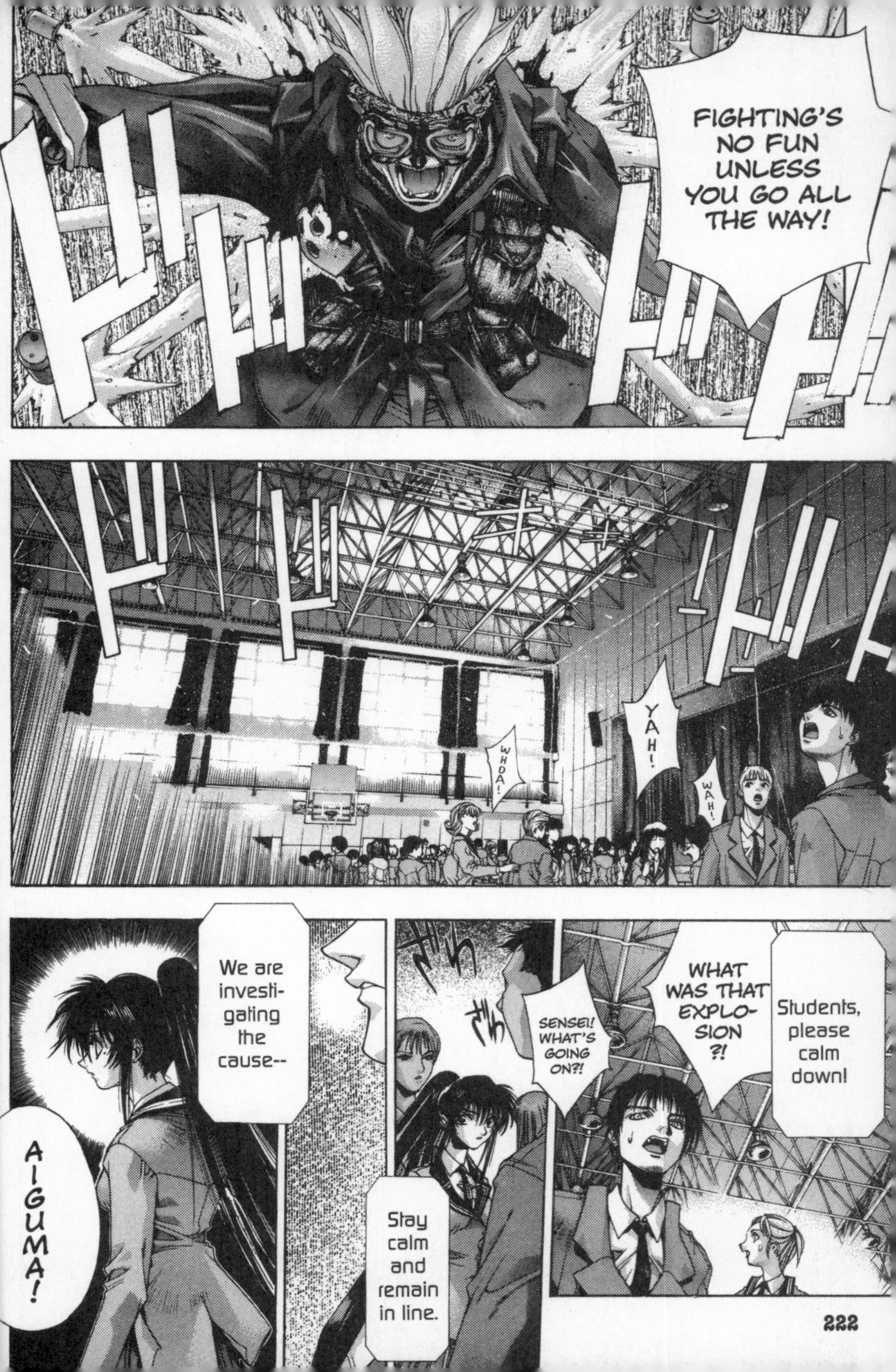
FIGHTING'S NO FUN UNLESS YOU GO ALL THE WAY!
YAH!
WAH!
WHOA!
Students, please calm down!
WHAT WAS THAT EXPLOSION?!
SENSEI! WHAT'S GOING ON?!
Stay calm and remain in line.
We are investigating the cause--
AIGUMA!

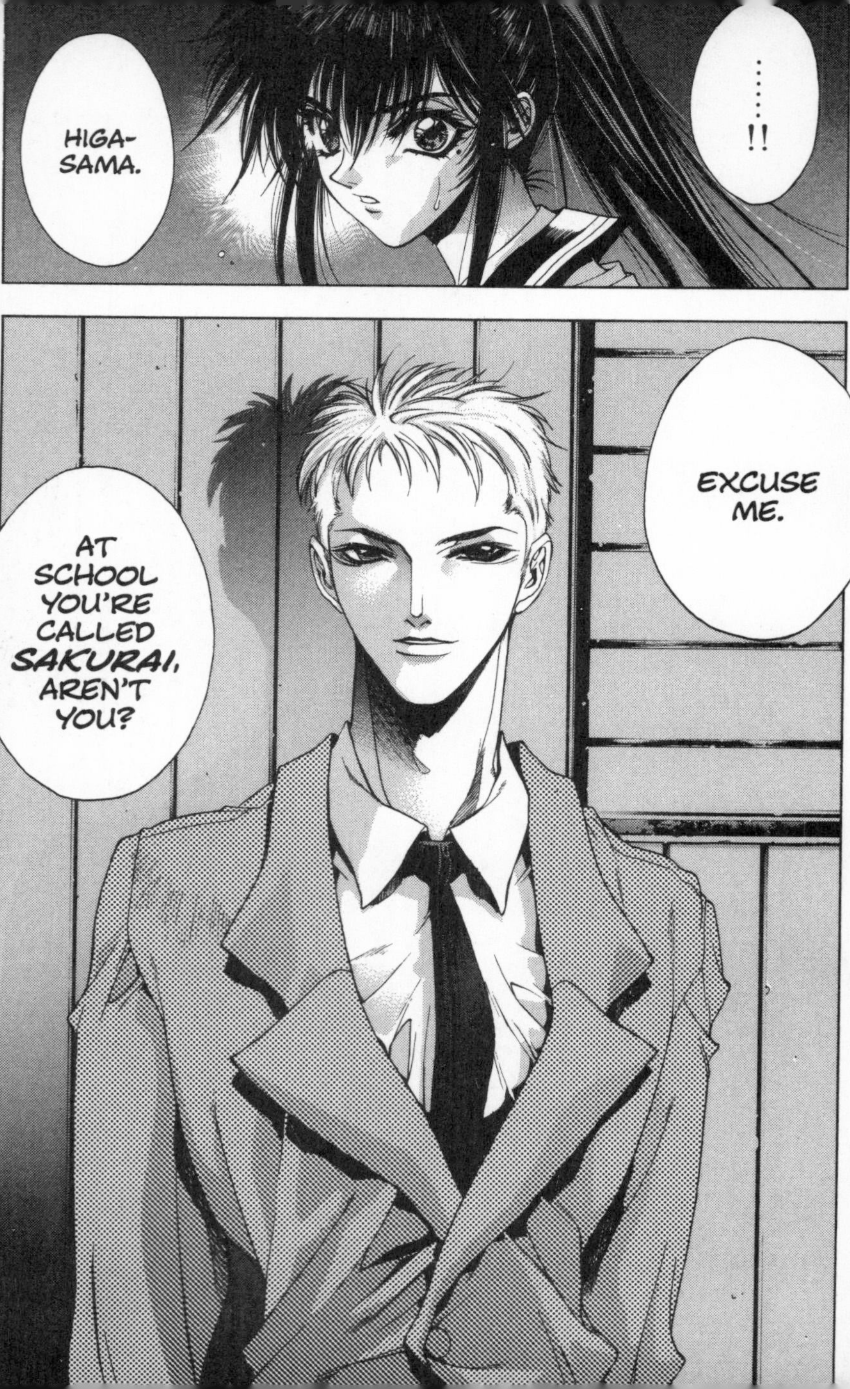
……!!
HIGA-SAMA.
EXCUSE ME.
AT SCHOOL YOU'RE CALLED **SAKURAI**, AREN'T YOU?

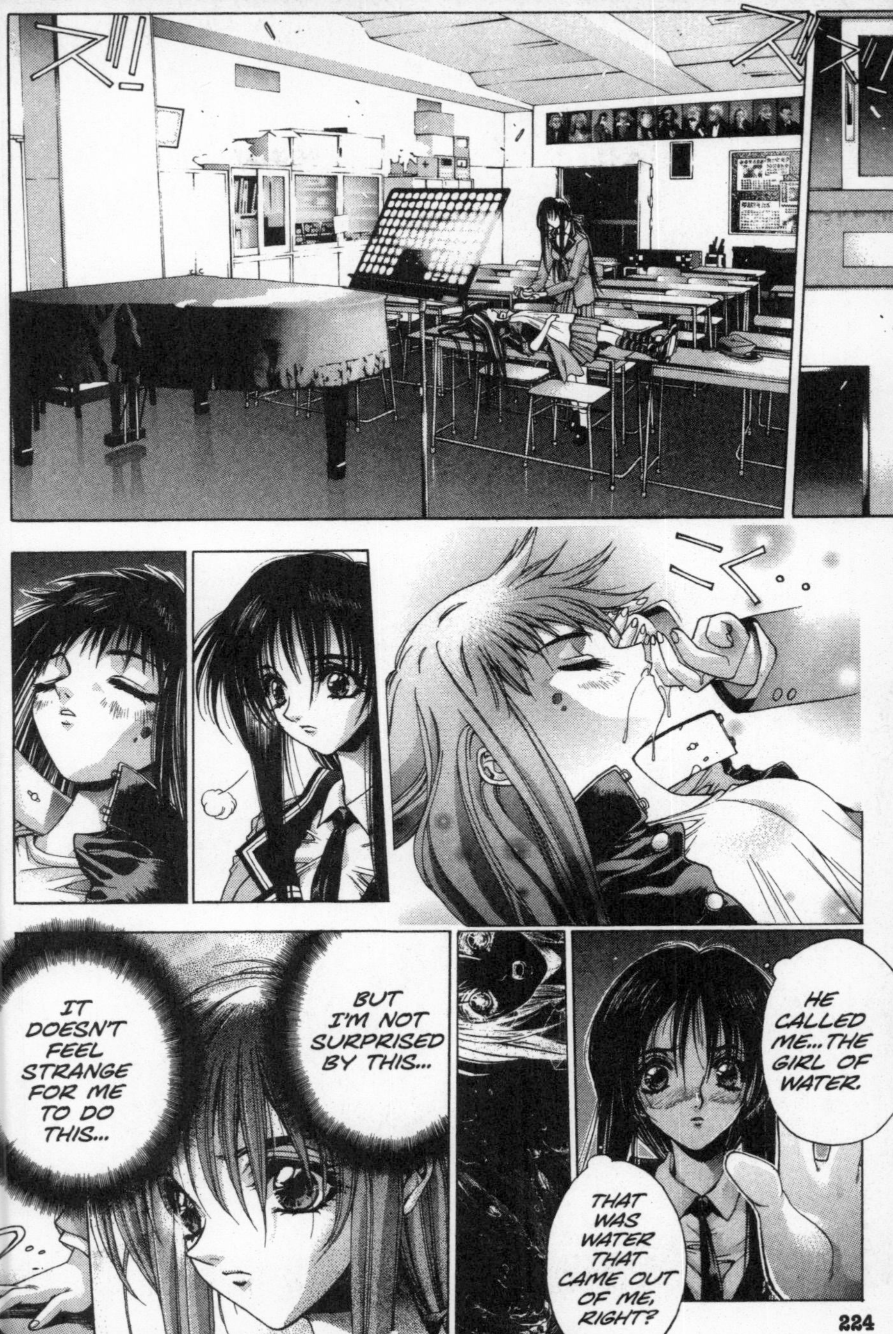
HE CALLED ME...THE GIRL OF WATER.
THAT WAS WATER THAT CAME OUT OF ME, RIGHT?
BUT I'M NOT SURPRISED BY THIS...
IT DOESN'T FEEL STRANGE FOR ME TO DO THIS...

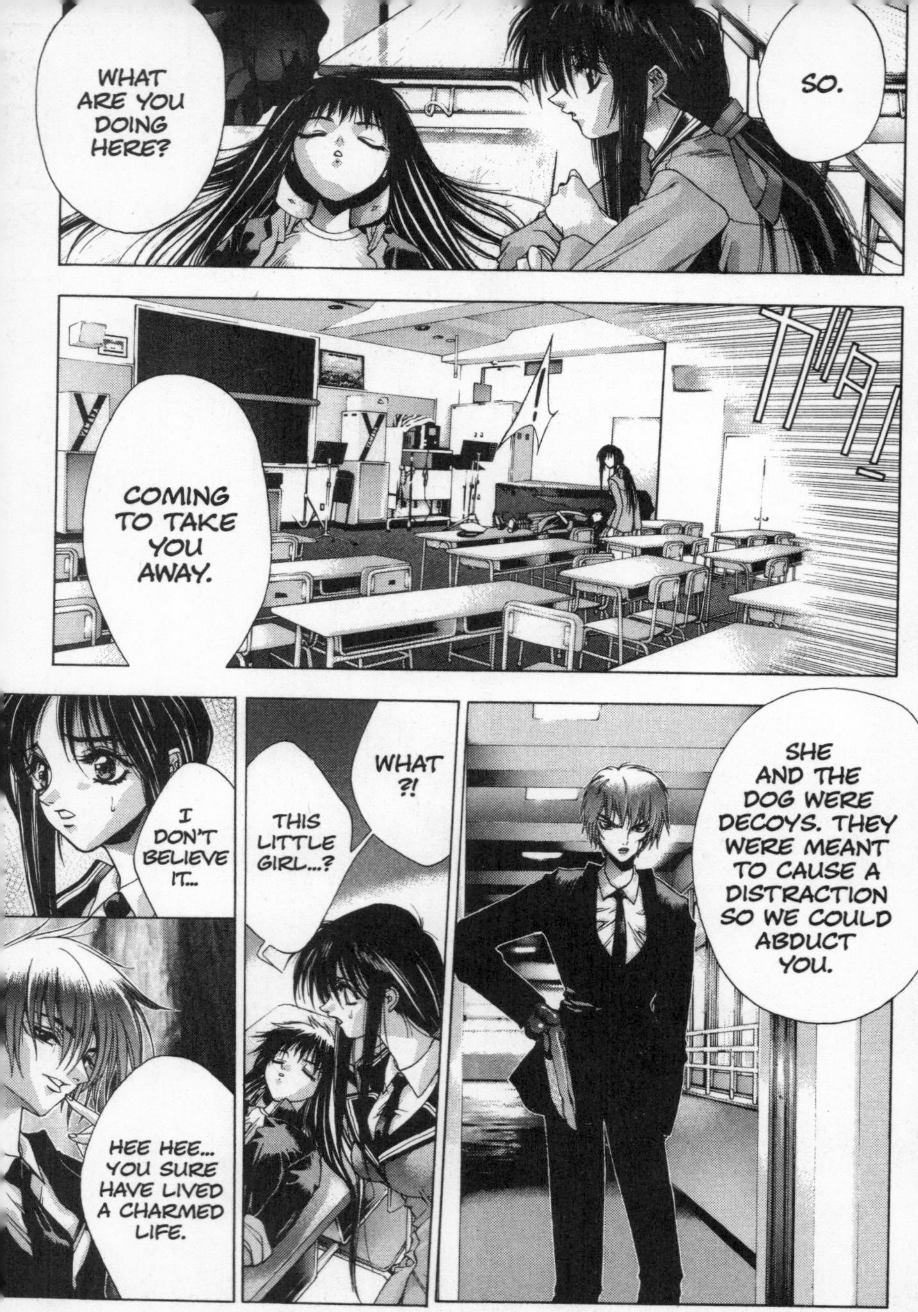
SO.
WHAT ARE YOU DOING HERE?
COMING TO TAKE YOU AWAY.
SHE AND THE DOG WERE DECOYS. THEY WERE MEANT TO CAUSE A DISTRACTION SO WE COULD ABDUCT YOU.
WHAT ?!
THIS LITTLE GIRL...?
I DON'T BELIEVE IT...
HEE HEE... YOU SURE HAVE LIVED A CHARMED LIFE.

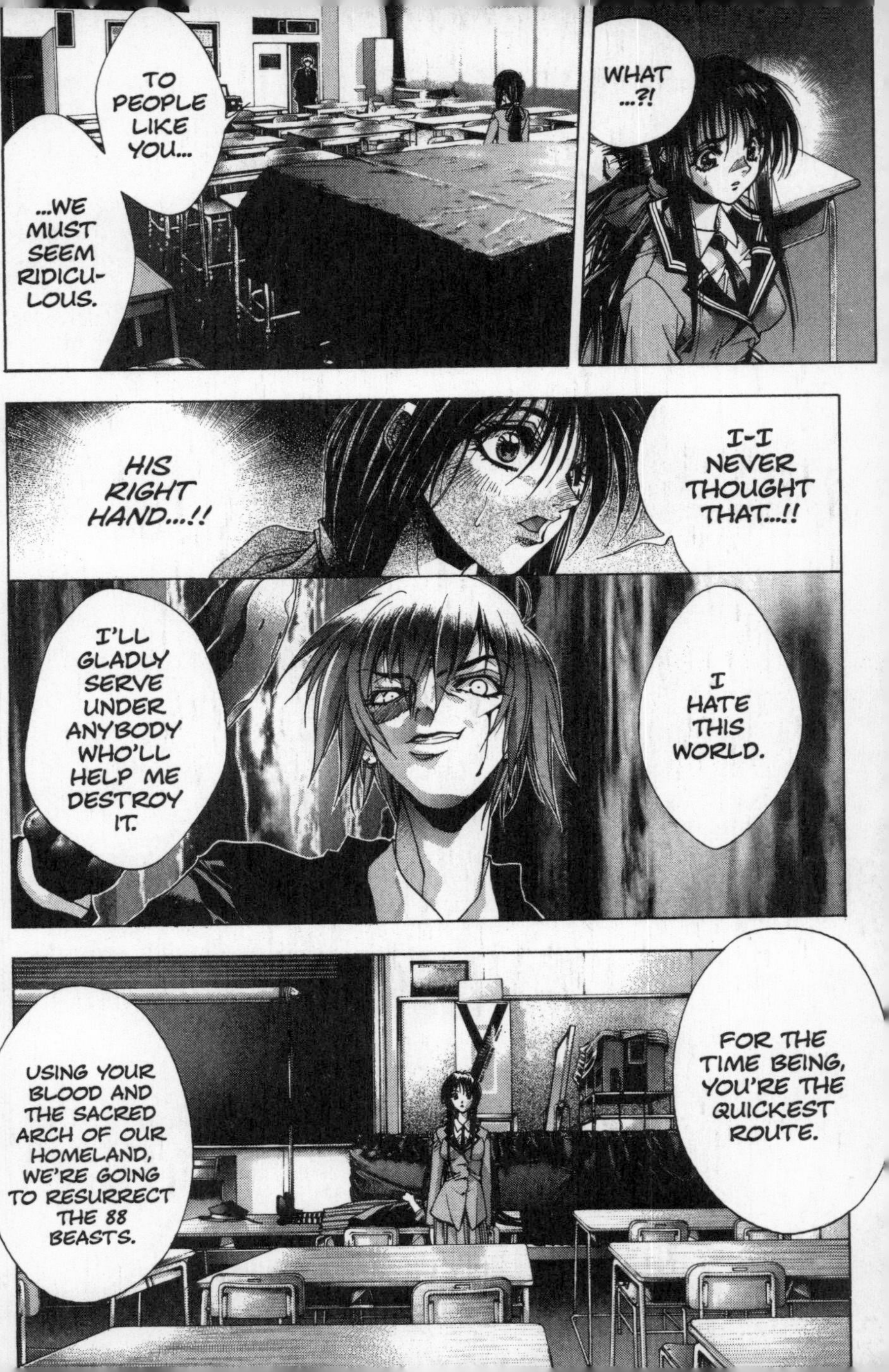
WHAT ...?!
TO PEOPLE LIKE YOU...
...WE MUST SEEM RIDICU-LOUS.
I-I NEVER THOUGHT THAT...!!
HIS RIGHT HAND...!!
I HATE THIS WORLD.
I'LL GLADLY SERVE UNDER ANYBODY WHO'LL HELP ME DESTROY IT.
FOR THE TIME BEING, YOU'RE THE QUICKEST ROUTE.
USING YOUR BLOOD AND THE SACRED ARCH OF OUR HOMELAND, WE'RE GOING TO RESURRECT THE 88 BEASTS.

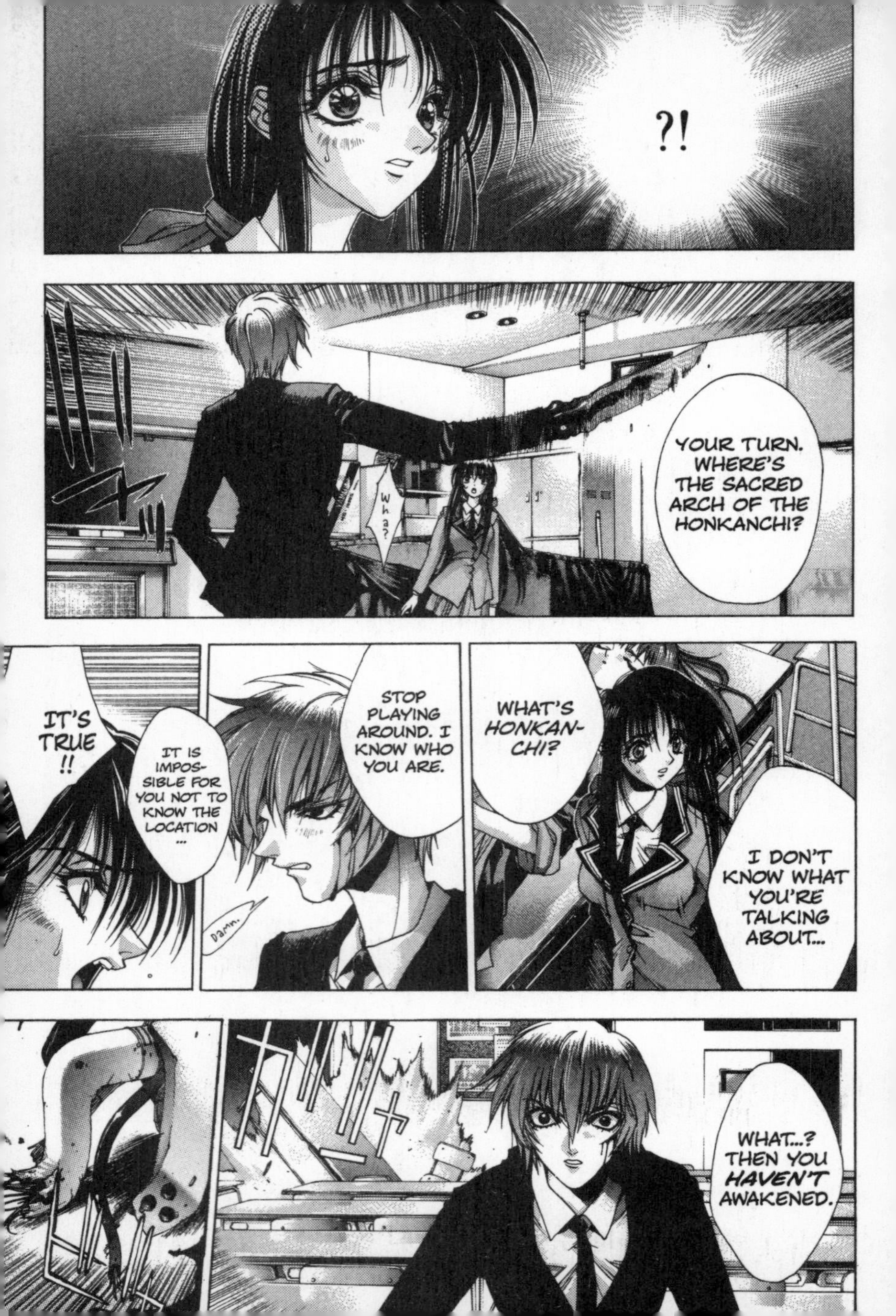
?!
YOUR TURN. WHERE'S THE SACRED ARCH OF THE HONKANCHI?
Wha?
WHAT'S HONKAN-CHI?
I DON'T KNOW WHAT YOU'RE TALKING ABOUT...
STOP PLAYING AROUND. I KNOW WHO YOU ARE.
Damn.
IT IS IMPOS-SIBLE FOR YOU NOT TO KNOW THE LOCATION...
IT'S TRUE!!
WHAT...? THEN YOU HAVEN'T AWAKENED.

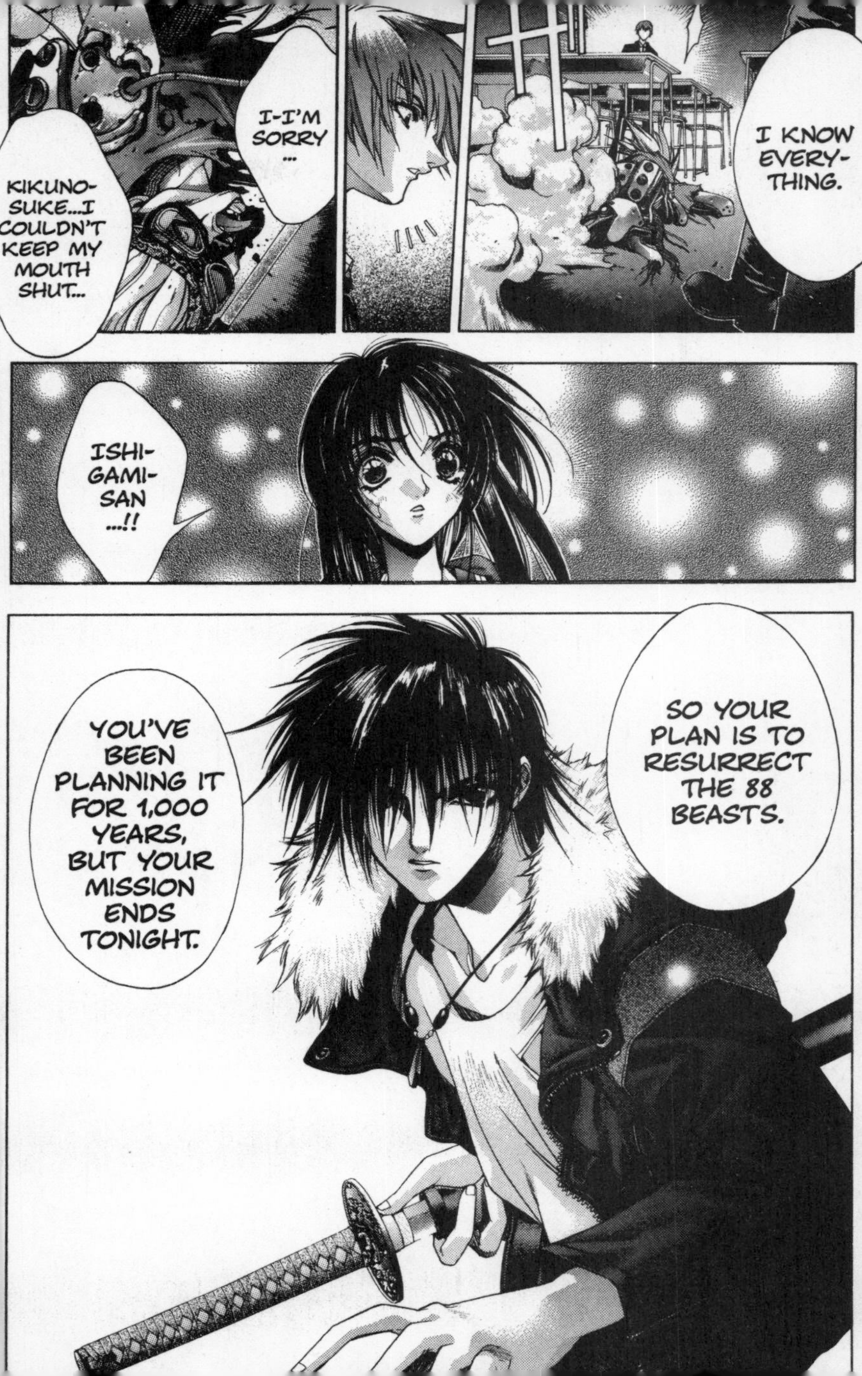
I KNOW EVERYTHING.
I-I'M SORRY ...
KIKUNOSUKE...I COULDN'T KEEP MY MOUTH SHUT...
ISHIGAMI-SAN ...!!
SO YOUR PLAN IS TO RESURRECT THE 88 BEASTS.
YOU'VE BEEN PLANNING IT FOR 1,000 YEARS, BUT YOUR MISSION ENDS TONIGHT.

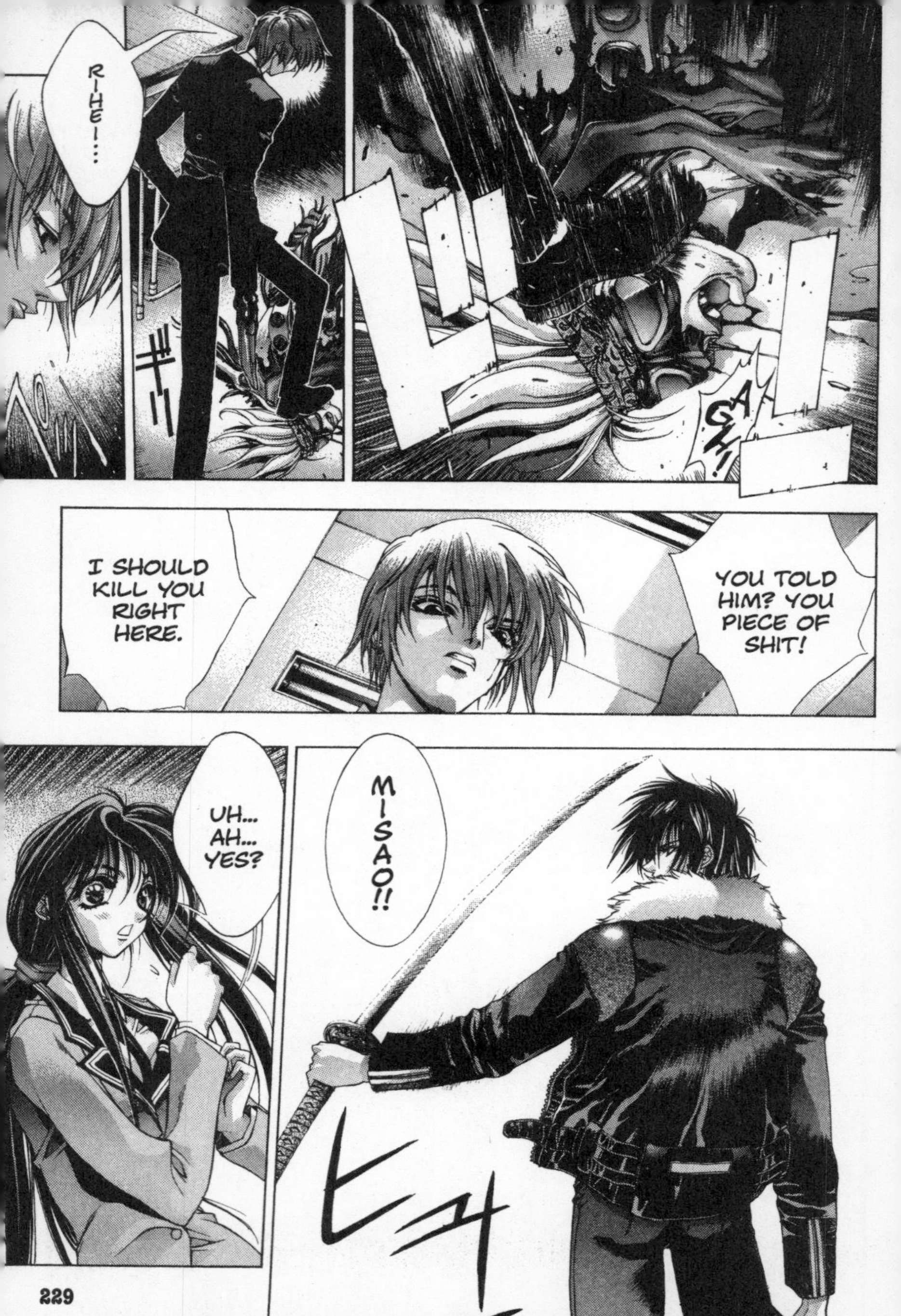
AGH!
RIHEI...
YOU TOLD HIM? YOU PIECE OF SHIT!
I SHOULD KILL YOU RIGHT HERE.
MISAO!!
UH... AH... YES?

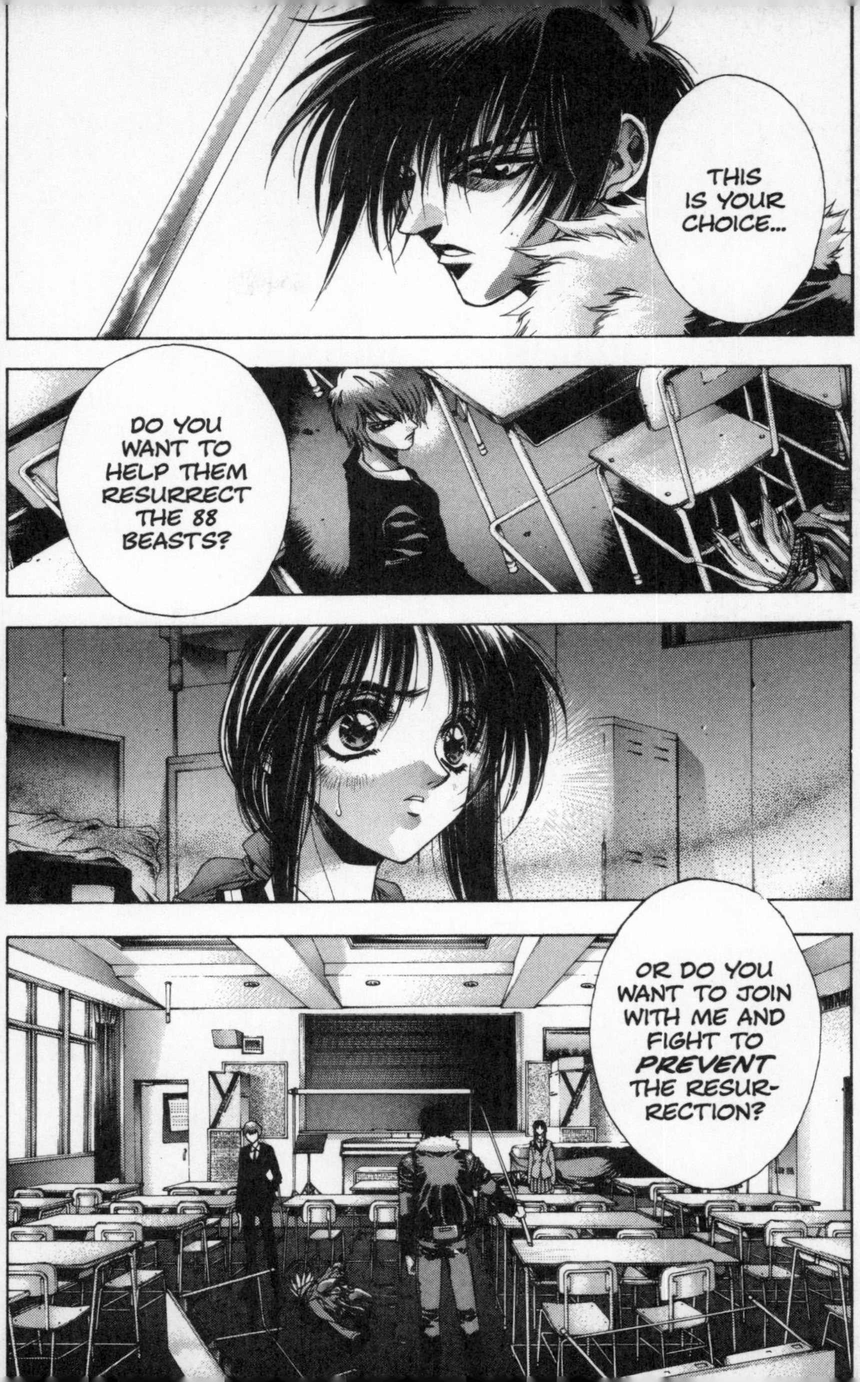
THIS IS YOUR CHOICE...
DO YOU WANT TO HELP THEM RESURRECT THE 88 BEASTS?
OR DO YOU WANT TO JOIN WITH ME AND FIGHT TO *PREVENT* THE RESURRECTION?

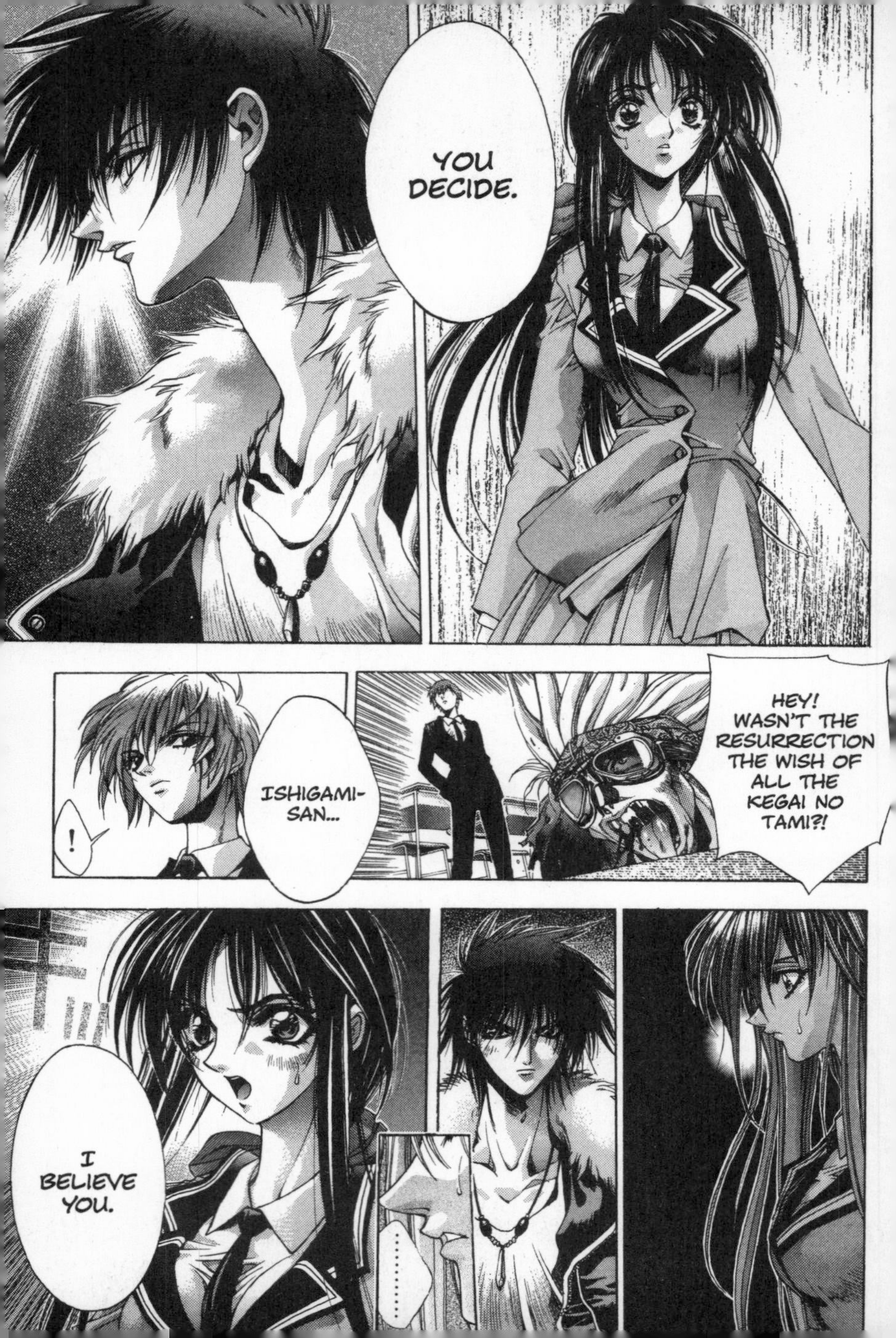
YOU DECIDE.
HEY! WASN'T THE RESURRECTION THE WISH OF ALL THE KEGAI NO TAMI?!
ISHIGAMI-SAN...
!
......
I BELIEVE YOU.

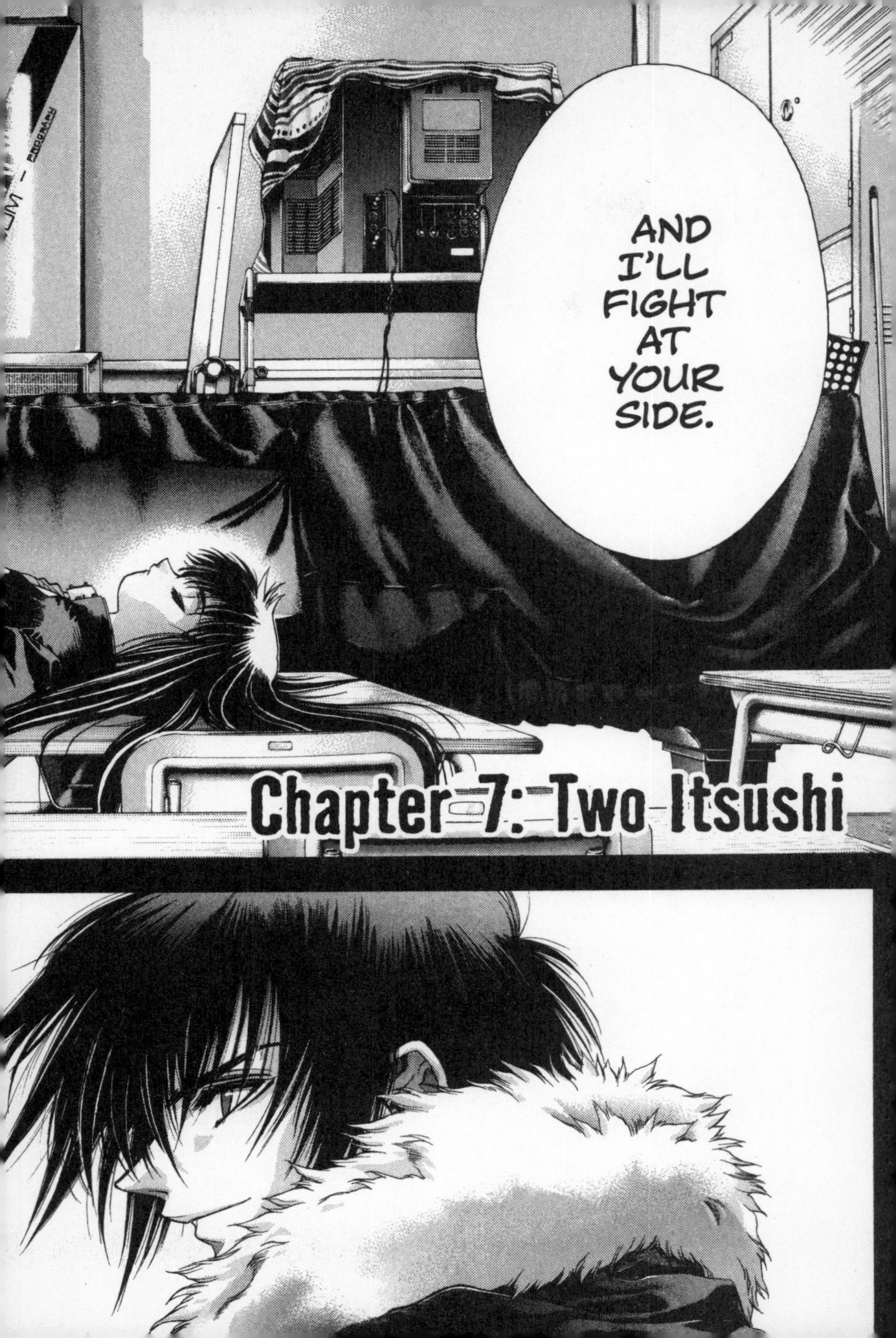
AND I'LL FIGHT AT YOUR SIDE.
Chapter 7: Two Itsushi

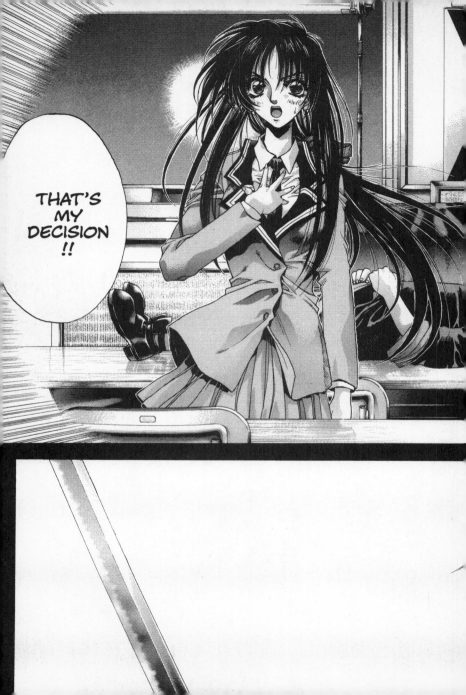

THAT'S
MY
DECISION
!!

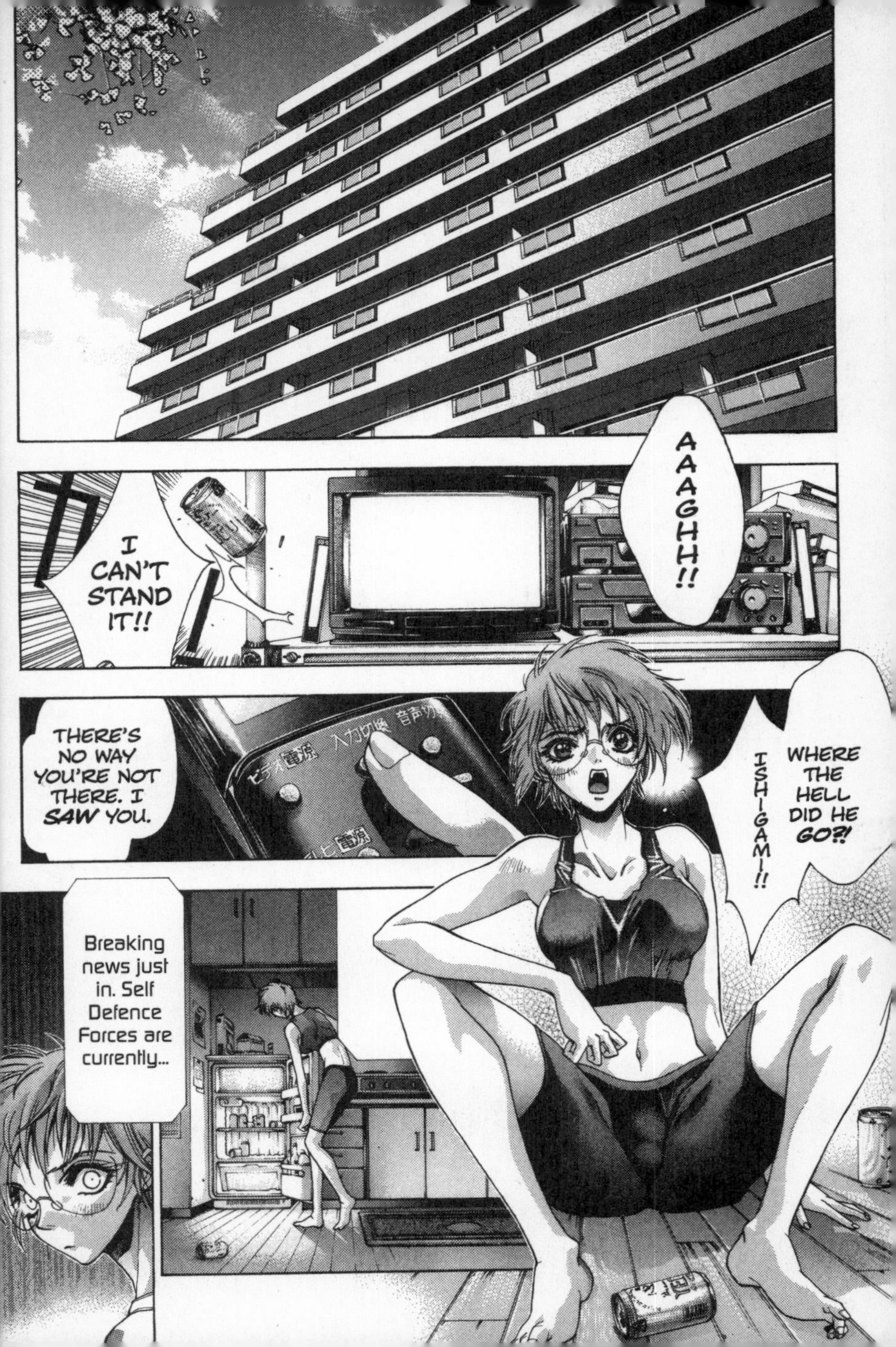
AAAGHH!!
I CAN'T STAND IT!!
WHERE THE HELL DID HE GO?!
ISHIGAMI!!
THERE'S NO WAY YOU'RE NOT THERE. I SAW YOU.
Breaking news just in. Self Defence Forces are currently...

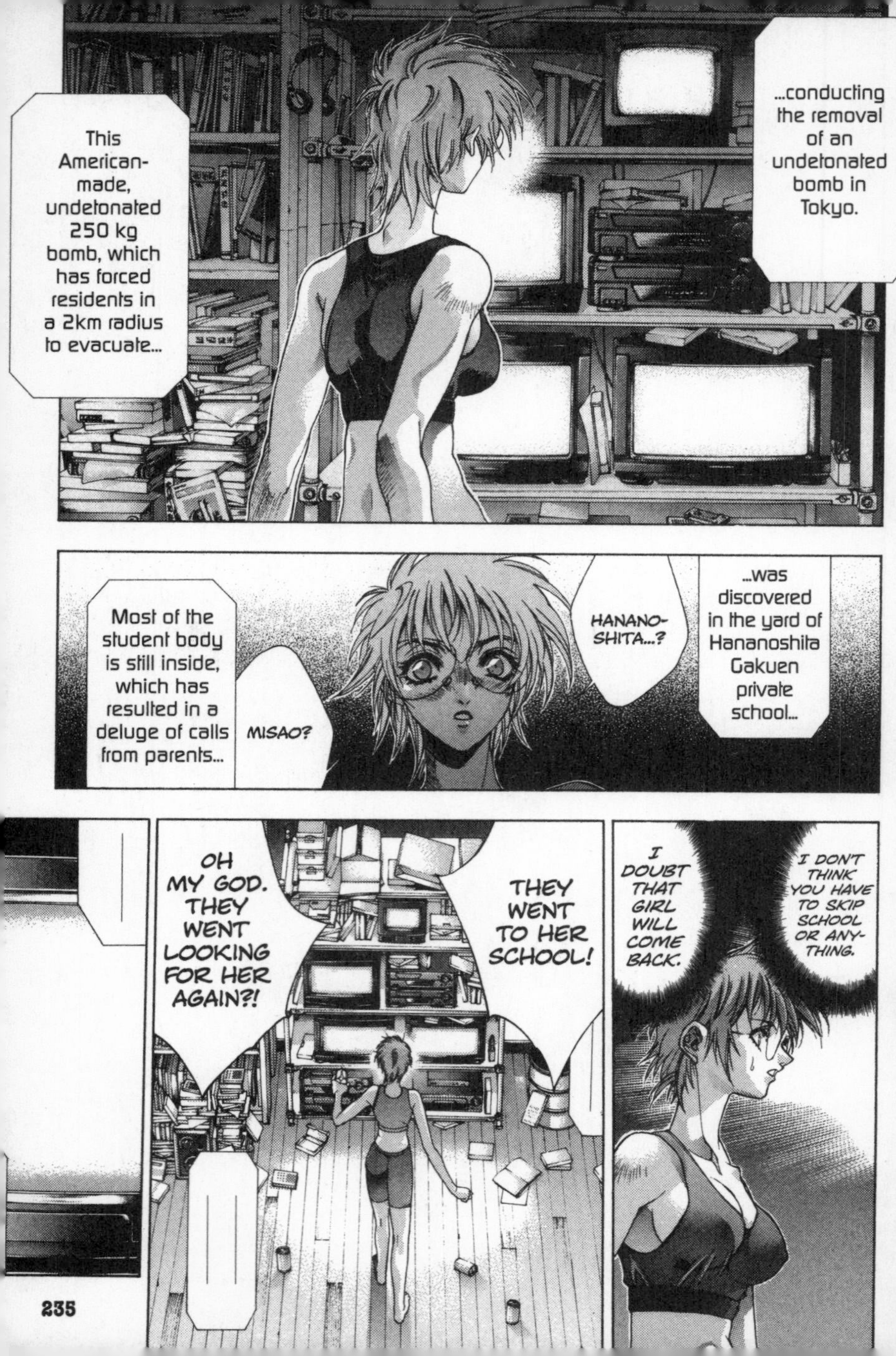
...conducting the removal of an undetonated bomb in Tokyo.
This American-made, undetonated 250 kg bomb, which has forced residents in a 2km radius to evacuate...
...was discovered in the yard of Hananoshita Gakuen private school...
HANANO-SHITA...?
MISAO?
Most of the student body is still inside, which has resulted in a deluge of calls from parents...
I DON'T THINK YOU HAVE TO SKIP SCHOOL OR ANY-THING.
I DOUBT THAT GIRL WILL COME BACK.
THEY WENT TO HER SCHOOL!
OH MY GOD. THEY WENT LOOKING FOR HER AGAIN?!

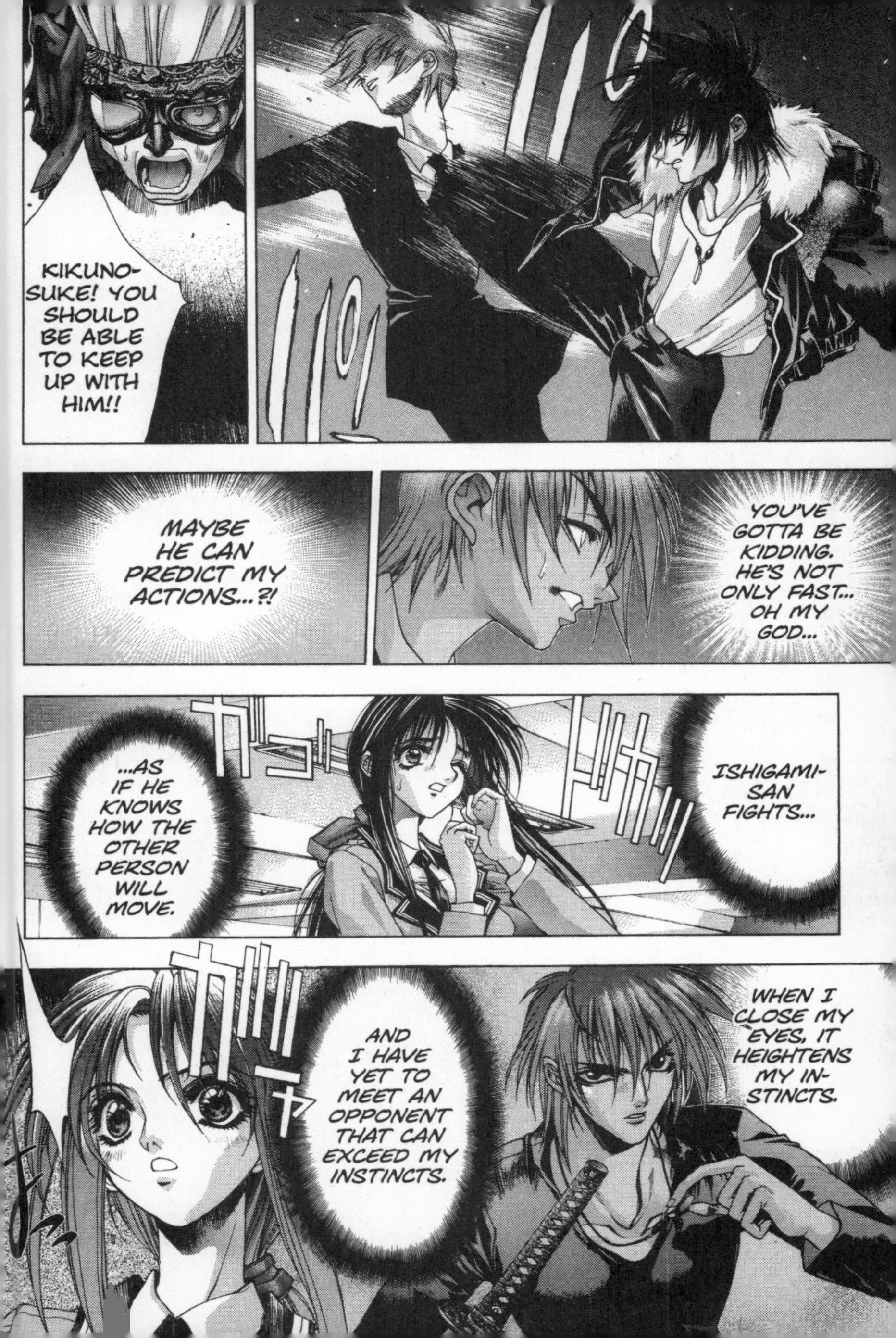
KIKUNO-SUKE! YOU SHOULD BE ABLE TO KEEP UP WITH HIM!!
YOU'VE GOTTA BE KIDDING. HE'S NOT ONLY FAST... OH MY GOD...
MAYBE HE CAN PREDICT MY ACTIONS...?!
ISHIGAMI-SAN FIGHTS...
...AS IF HE KNOWS HOW THE OTHER PERSON WILL MOVE.
WHEN I CLOSE MY EYES, IT HEIGHTENS MY IN-STINCTS.
AND I HAVE YET TO MEET AN OPPONENT THAT CAN EXCEED MY INSTINCTS.

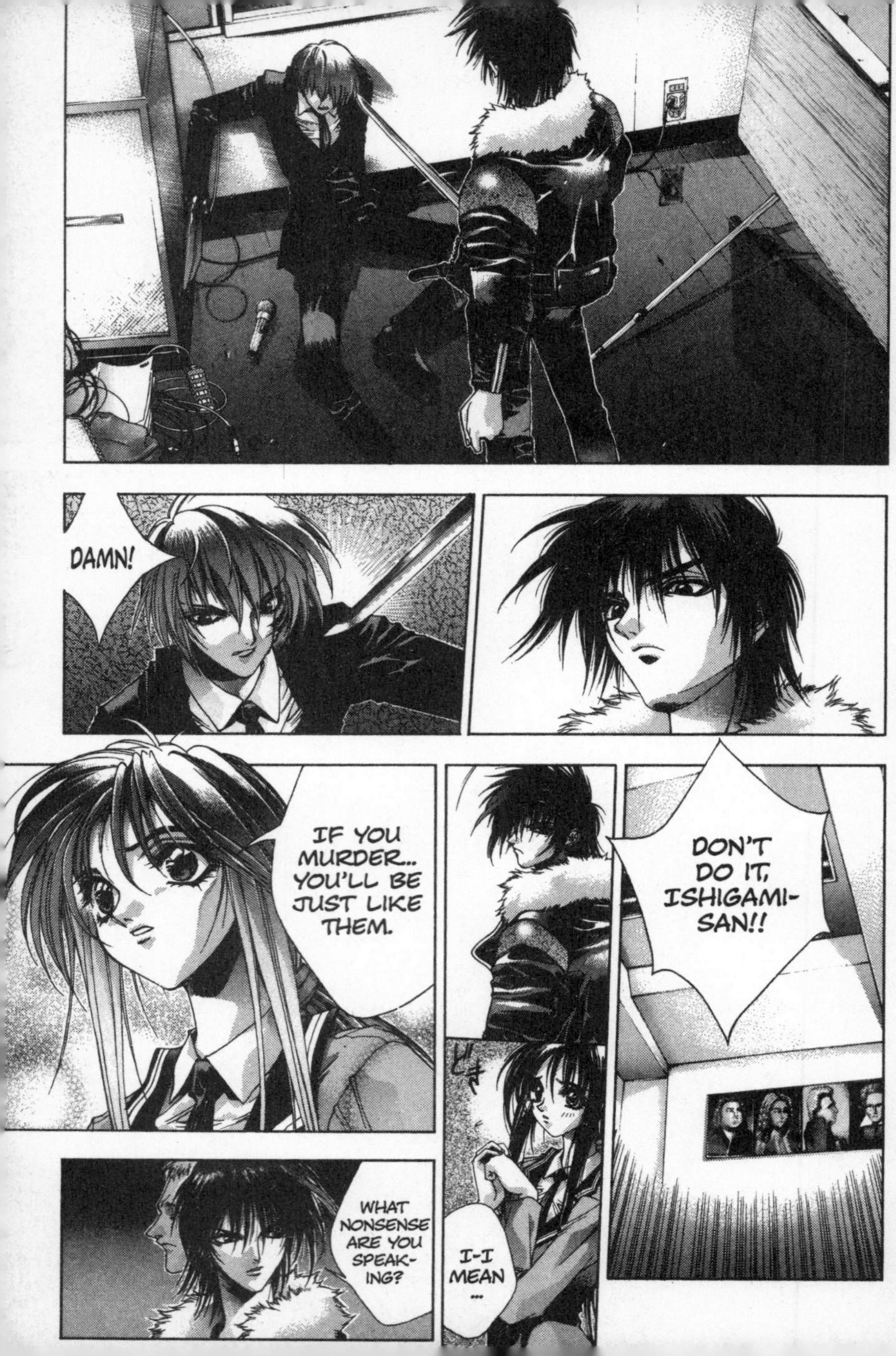
DAMN!
DON'T DO IT, ISHIGAMI-SAN!!
IF YOU MURDER... YOU'LL BE JUST LIKE THEM.
WHAT NONSENSE ARE YOU SPEAKING?
I-I MEAN ...

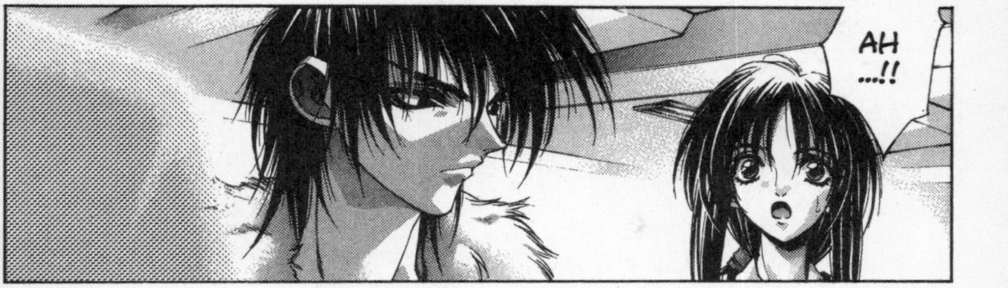
AH
...!!
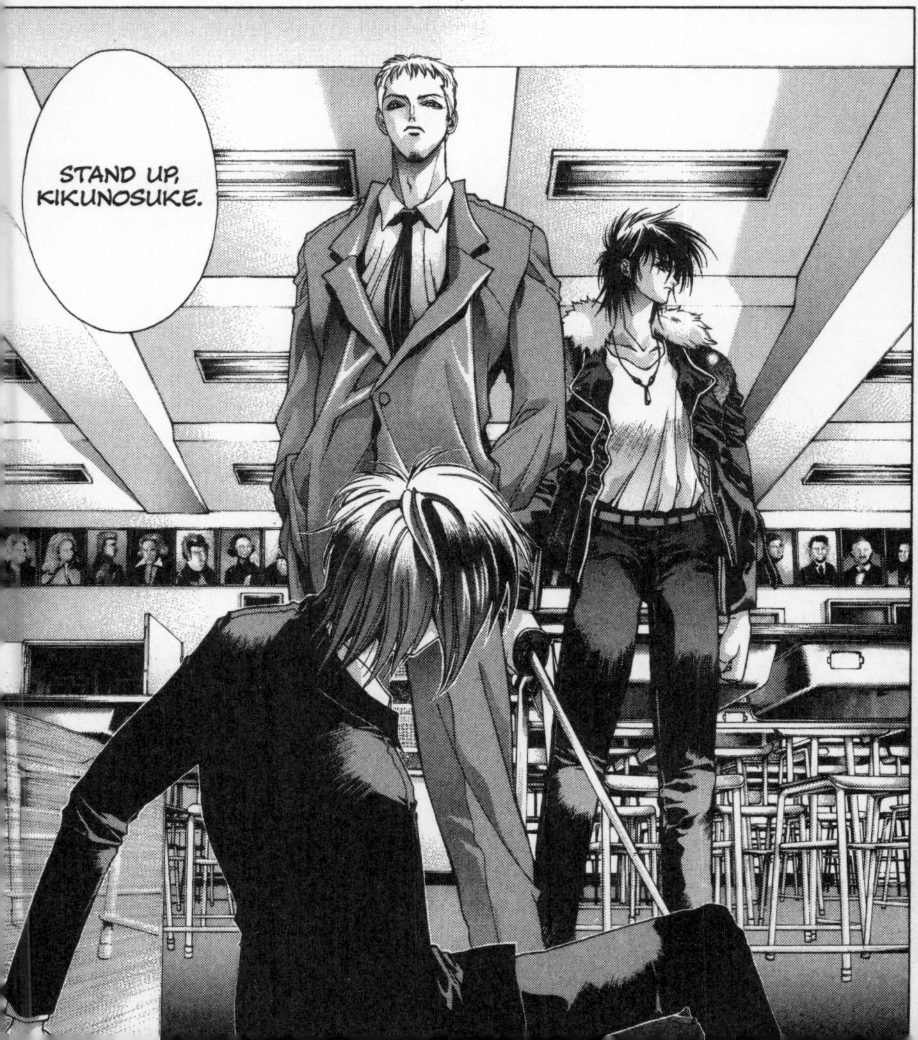
STAND UP, KIKUNOSUKE.

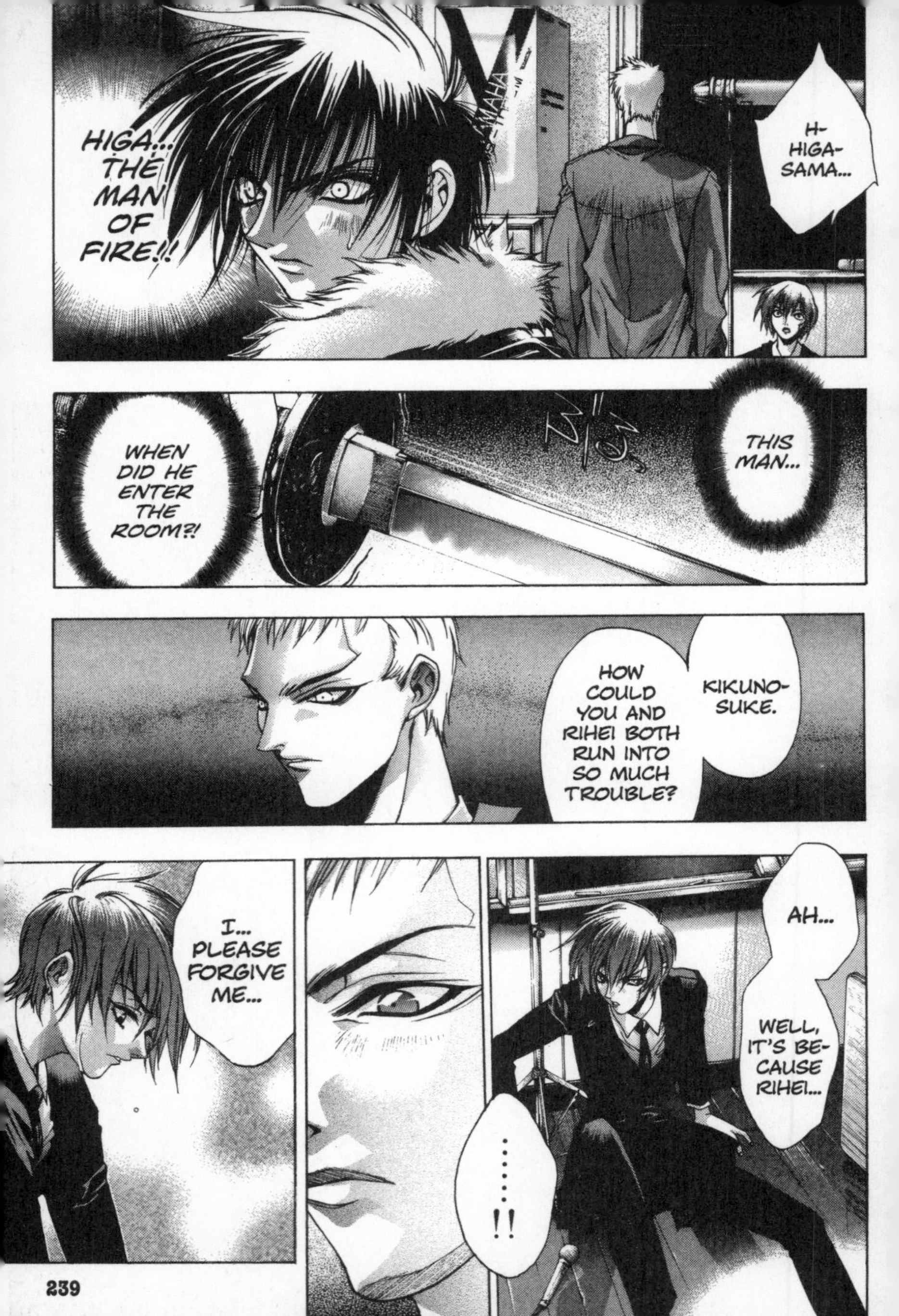
H-HIGA-SAMA...
HIGA... THE MAN OF FIRE!!
THIS MAN...
WHEN DID HE ENTER THE ROOM?!
KIKUNOSUKE.
HOW COULD YOU AND RIHEI BOTH RUN INTO SO MUCH TROUBLE?
AH...
WELL, IT'S BECAUSE RIHEI...
......!!
I... PLEASE FORGIVE ME...

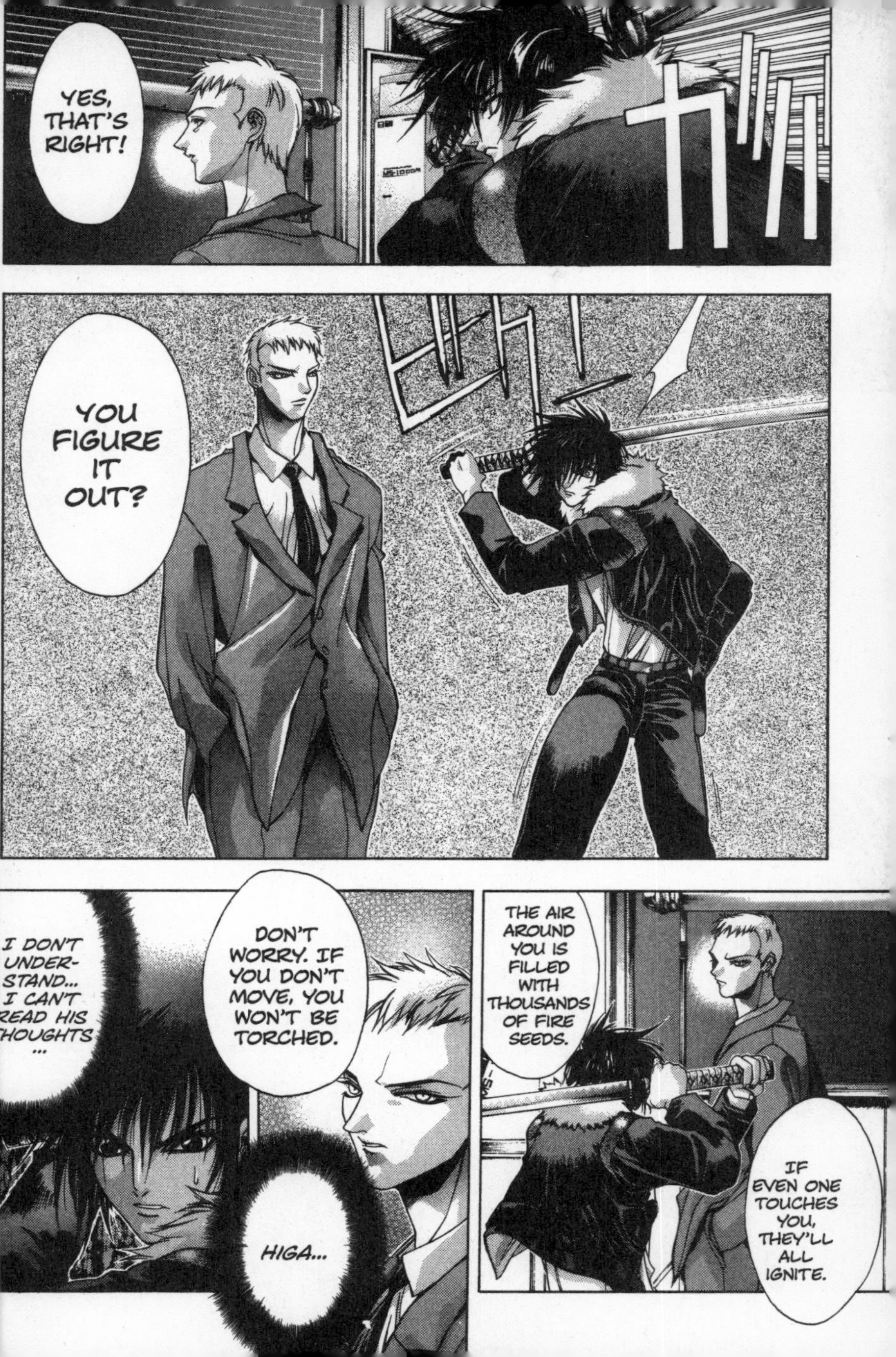
YES, THAT'S RIGHT!
YOU FIGURE IT OUT?
THE AIR AROUND YOU IS FILLED WITH THOUSANDS OF FIRE SEEDS.
IF EVEN ONE TOUCHES YOU, THEY'LL ALL IGNITE.
DON'T WORRY. IF YOU DON'T MOVE, YOU WON'T BE TORCHED.
I DON'T UNDERSTAND... I CAN'T READ HIS THOUGHTS...
HIGA...

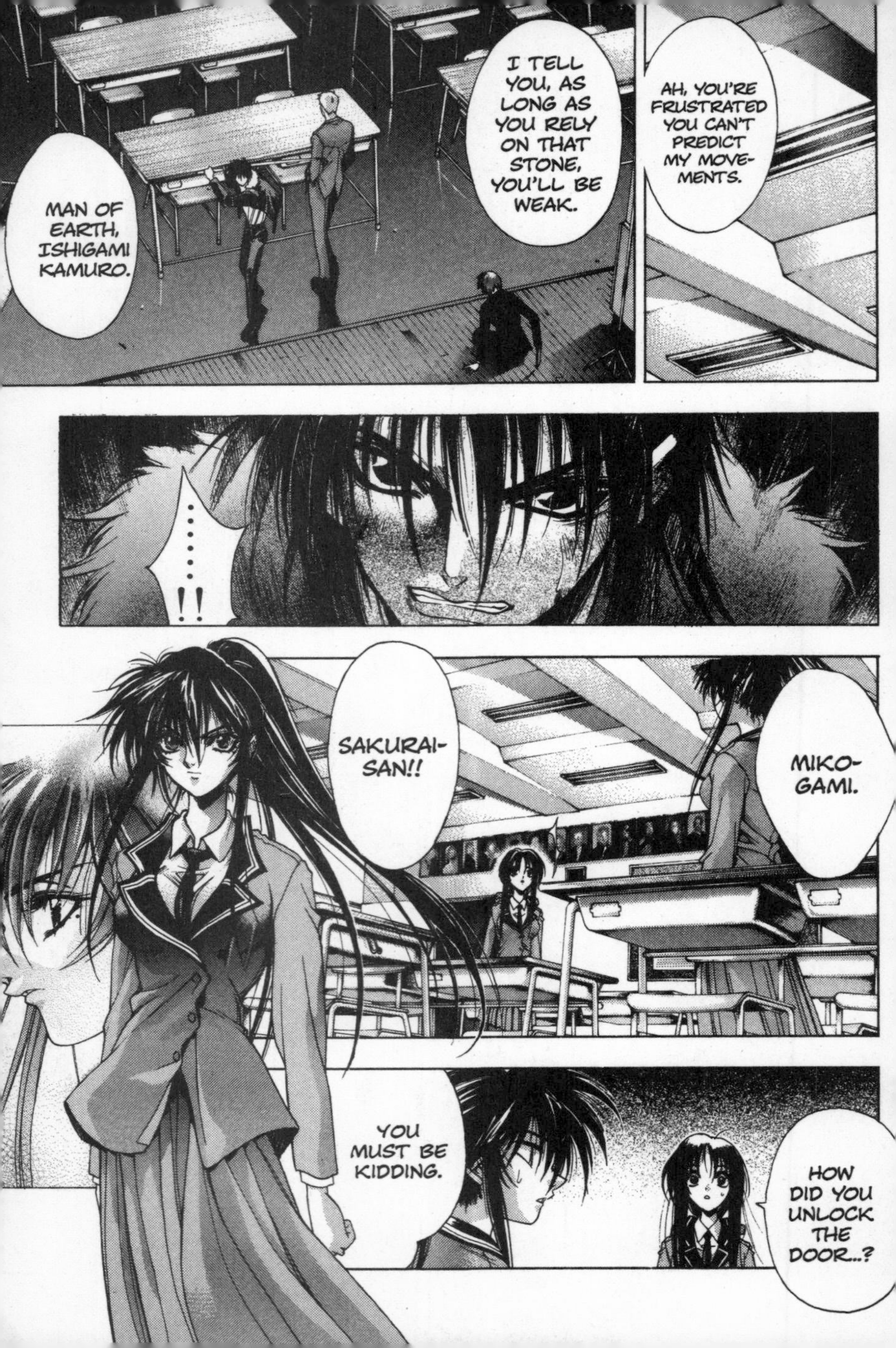
AH, YOU'RE FRUSTRATED YOU CAN'T PREDICT MY MOVE-MENTS.
I TELL YOU, AS LONG AS YOU RELY ON THAT STONE, YOU'LL BE WEAK.
MAN OF EARTH, ISHIGAMI KAMURO.
......
!!
MIKO-GAMI.
SAKURAI-SAN!!
HOW DID YOU UNLOCK THE DOOR...?
YOU MUST BE KIDDING.

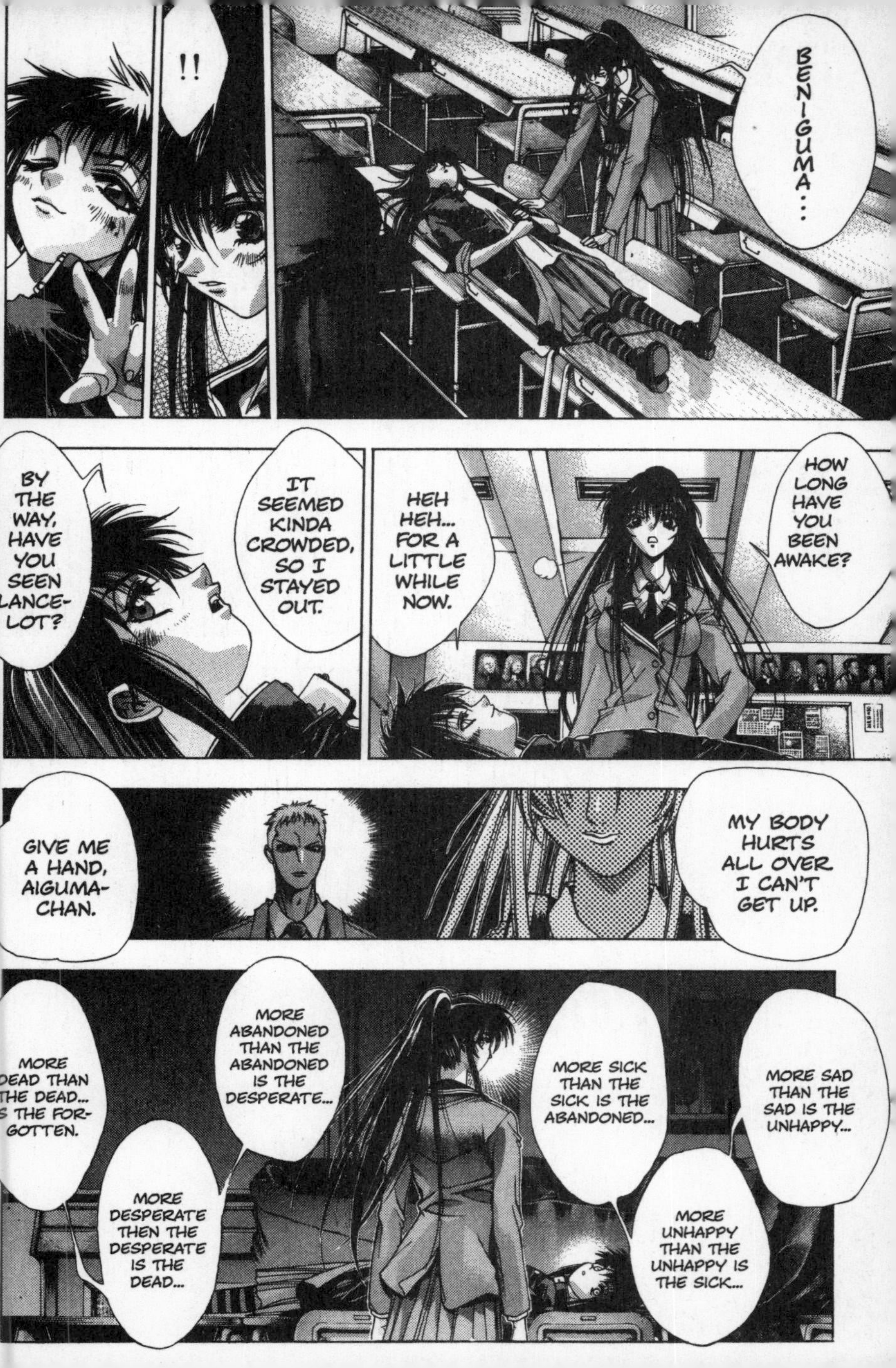
BENIGUMA...
!!
HOW LONG HAVE YOU BEEN AWAKE?
HEH HEH... FOR A LITTLE WHILE NOW.
IT SEEMED KINDA CROWDED, SO I STAYED OUT.
BY THE WAY, HAVE YOU SEEN LANCE-LOT?
MY BODY HURTS ALL OVER I CAN'T GET UP.
GIVE ME A HAND, AIGUMA-CHAN.
MORE SAD THAN THE SAD IS THE UNHAPPY...
MORE UNHAPPY THAN THE UNHAPPY IS THE SICK...
MORE SICK THAN THE SICK IS THE ABANDONED...
MORE ABANDONED THAN THE ABANDONED IS THE DESPERATE...
MORE DESPERATE THEN THE DESPERATE IS THE DEAD...
MORE DEAD THAN THE DEAD... IS THE FOR-GOTTEN.

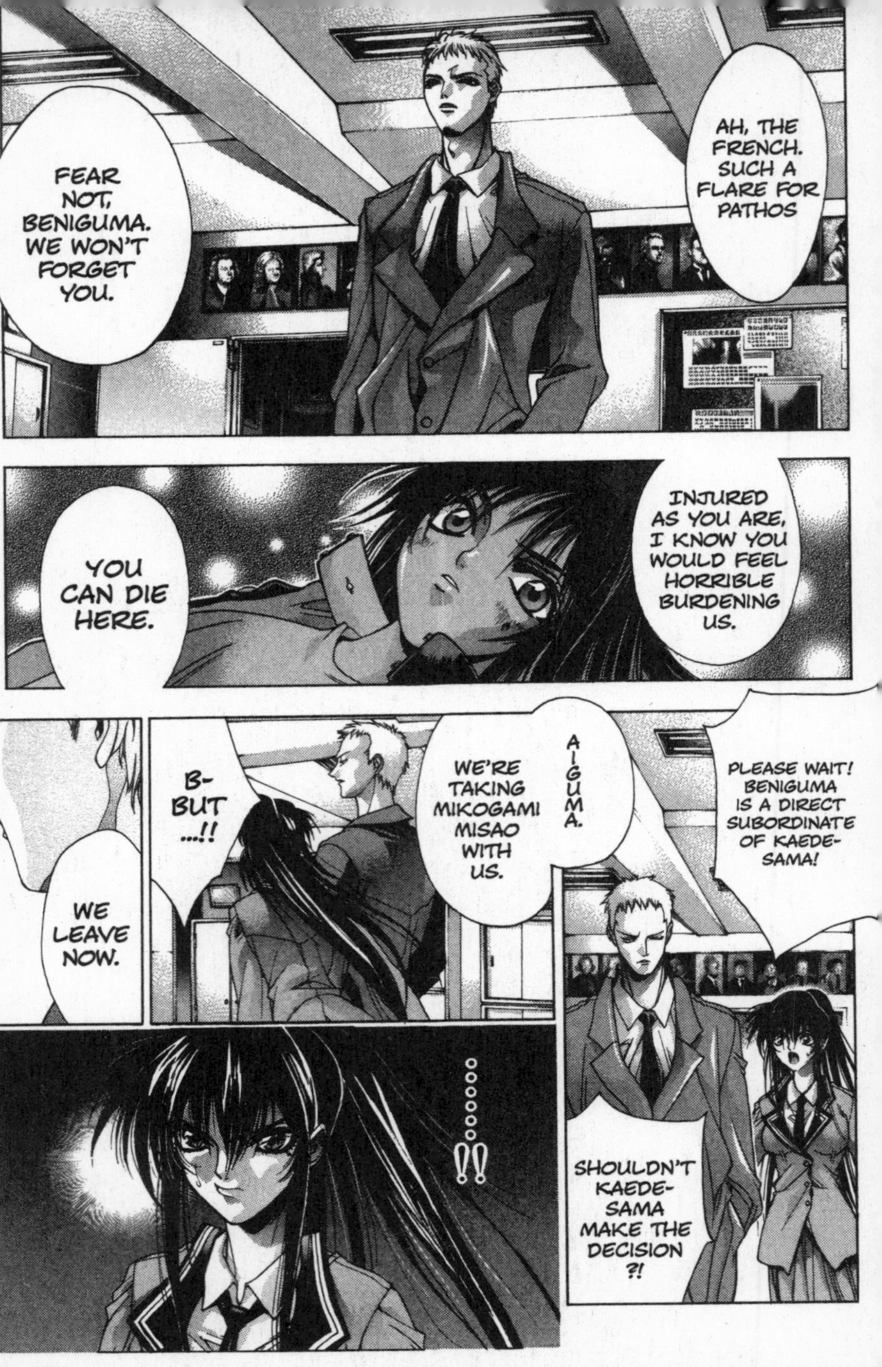
AH, THE FRENCH. SUCH A FLARE FOR PATHOS
FEAR NOT, BENIGUMA. WE WON'T FORGET YOU.
INJURED AS YOU ARE, I KNOW YOU WOULD FEEL HORRIBLE BURDENING US.
YOU CAN DIE HERE.
PLEASE WAIT! BENIGUMA IS A DIRECT SUBORDINATE OF KAEDE-SAMA!
SHOULDN'T KAEDE-SAMA MAKE THE DECISION ?!
AIGUMA.
WE'RE TAKING MIKOGAMI MISAO WITH US.
B-BUT ...!!
WE LEAVE NOW.
OOOOOOO!!

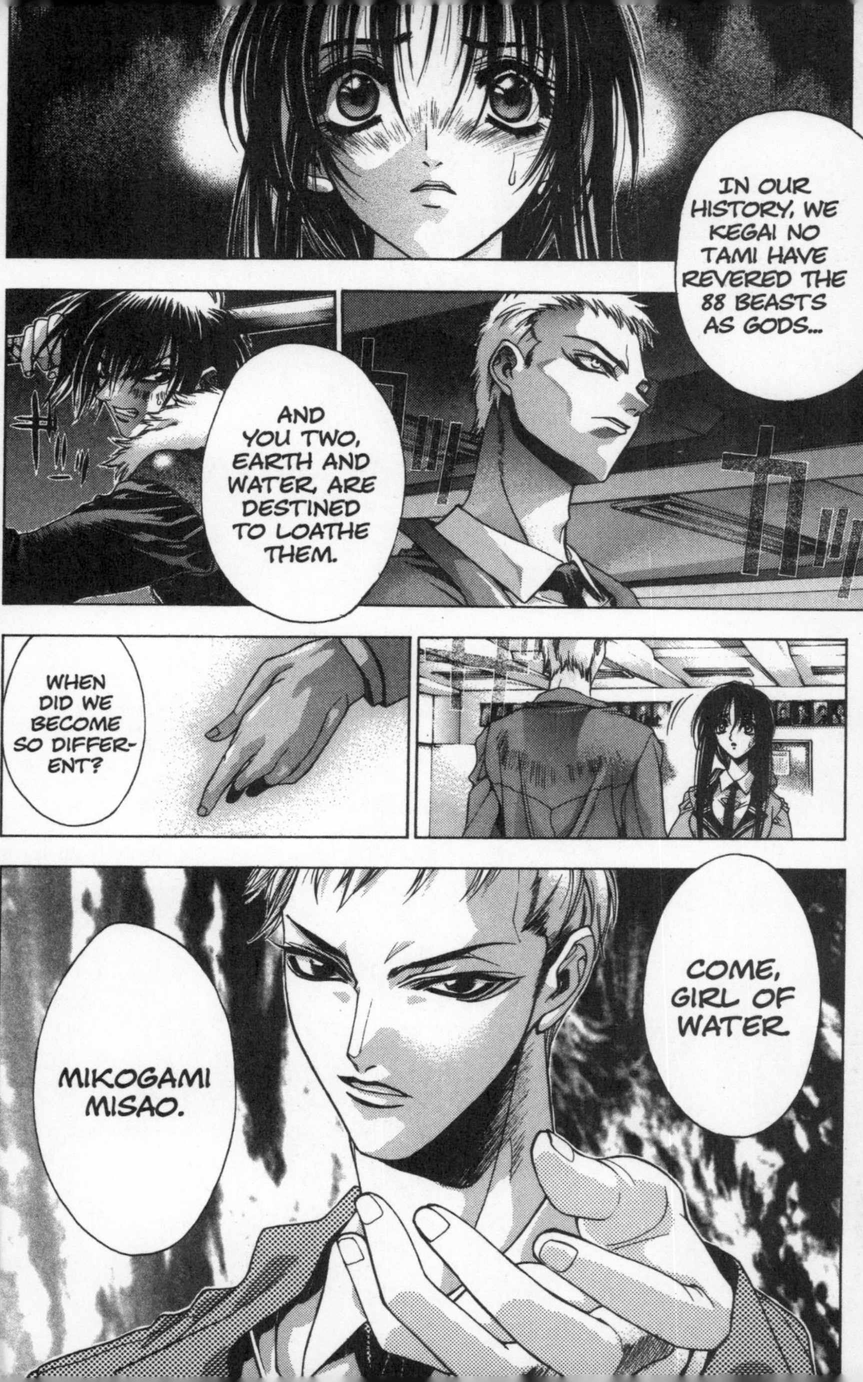
IN OUR HISTORY, WE KEGAI NO TAMI HAVE REVERED THE 88 BEASTS AS GODS...
AND YOU TWO, EARTH AND WATER, ARE DESTINED TO LOATHE THEM.
WHEN DID WE BECOME SO DIFFER-ENT?
COME, GIRL OF WATER
MIKOGAMI MISAO.

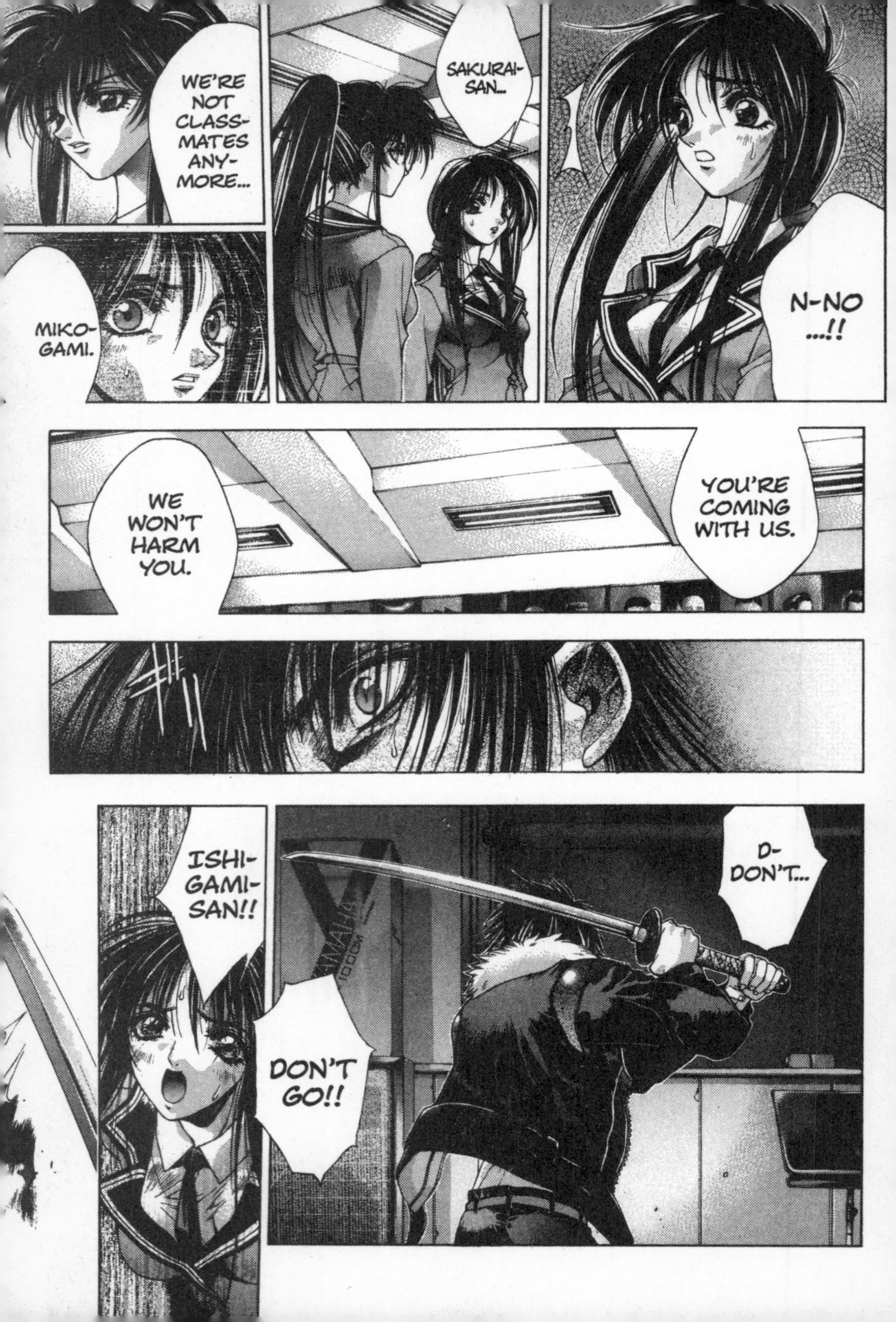
N-NO ...!!
SAKURAI-SAN...
WE'RE NOT CLASSMATES ANYMORE...
MIKO-GAMI.
YOU'RE COMING WITH US.
WE WON'T HARM YOU.
D-DON'T...
ISHI-GAMI-SAN!!
DON'T GO!!

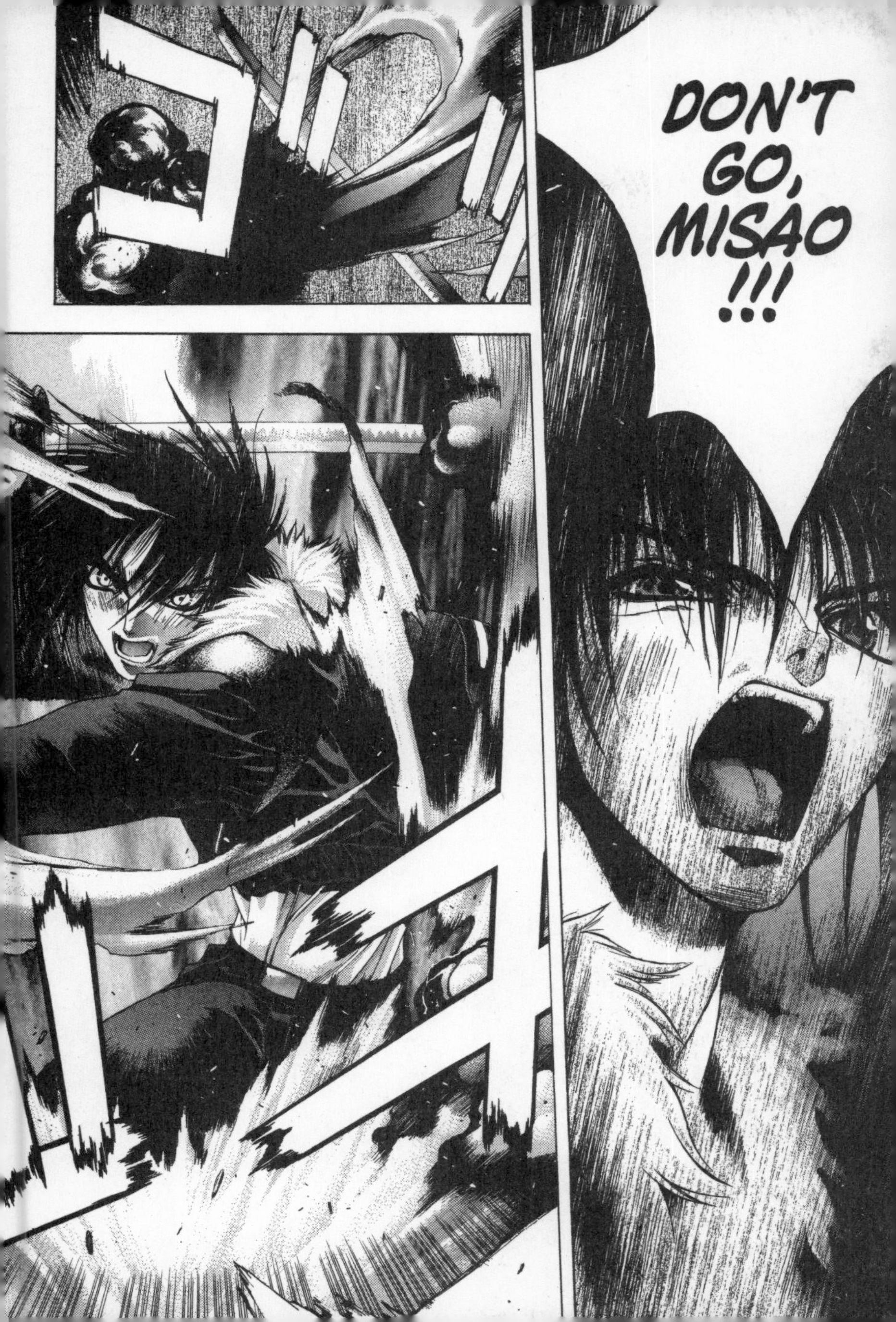
DON'T GO, MISAO !!!

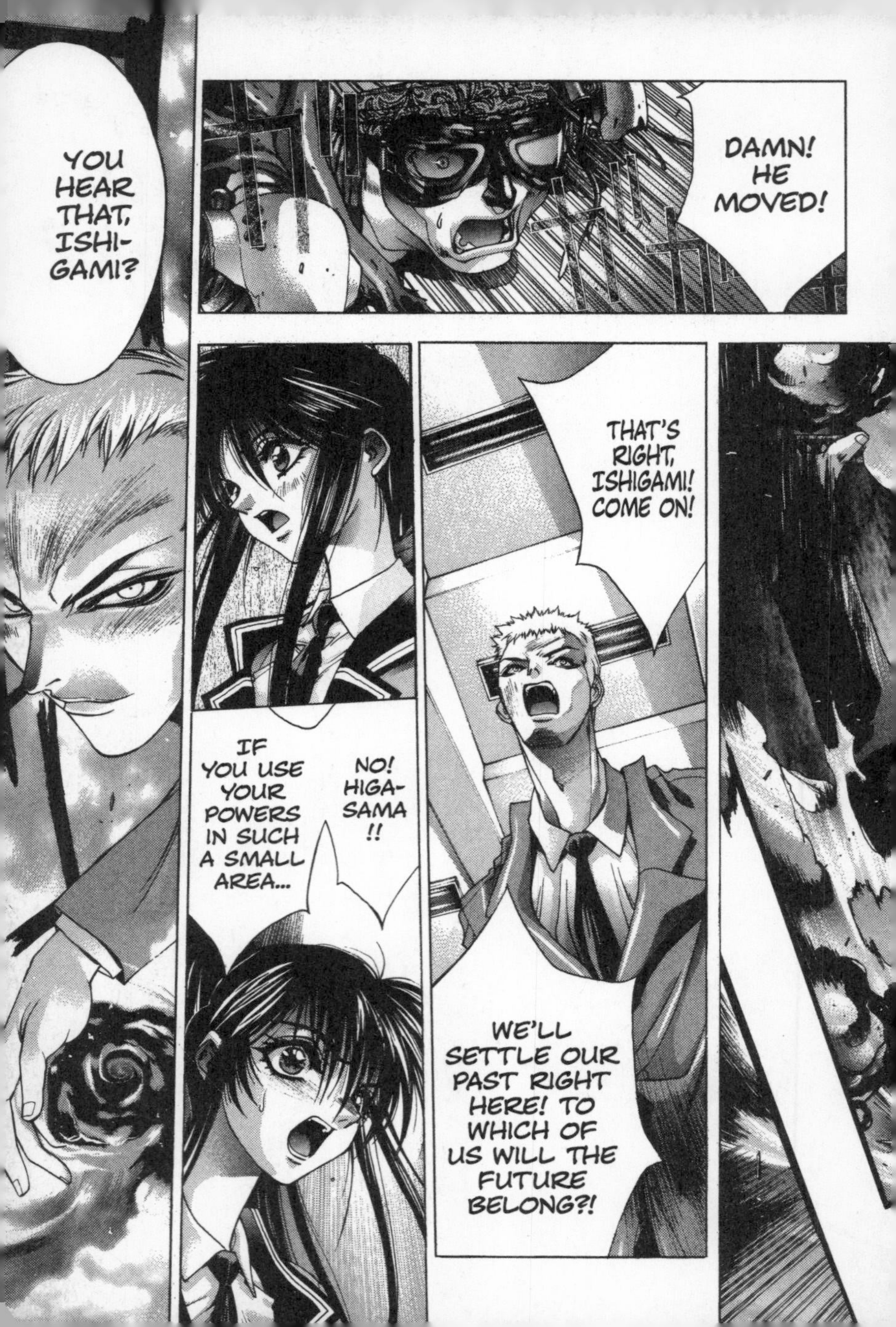
DAMN! HE MOVED!
THAT'S RIGHT, ISHIGAMI! COME ON!
WE'LL SETTLE OUR PAST RIGHT HERE! TO WHICH OF US WILL THE FUTURE BELONG?!
NO! HIGA-SAMA!!
IF YOU USE YOUR POWERS IN SUCH A SMALL AREA...
YOU HEAR THAT, ISHI-GAMI?

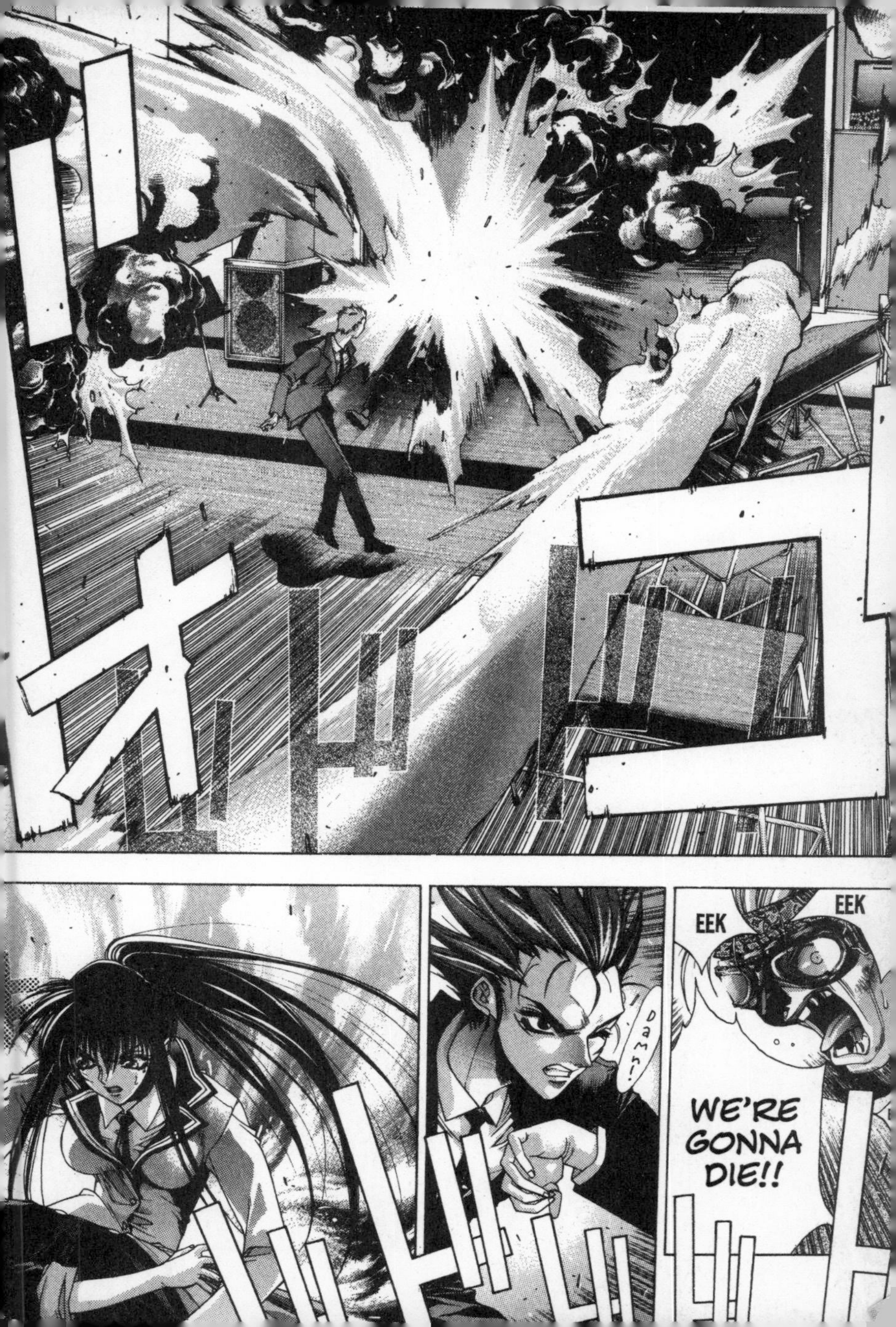
EEK
EEK
WE'RE GONNA DIE!!
Damn!

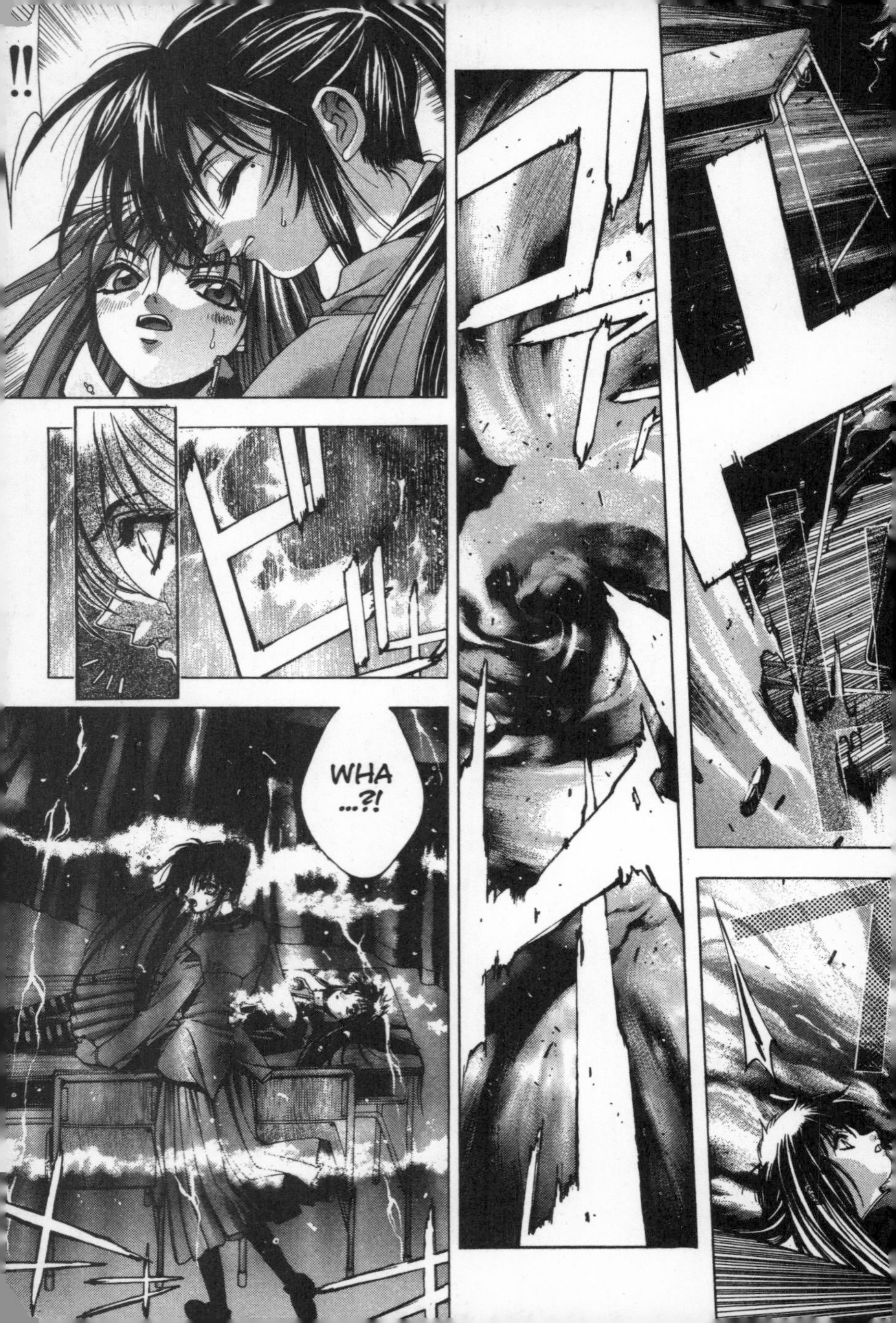
!!
WHA ...?!

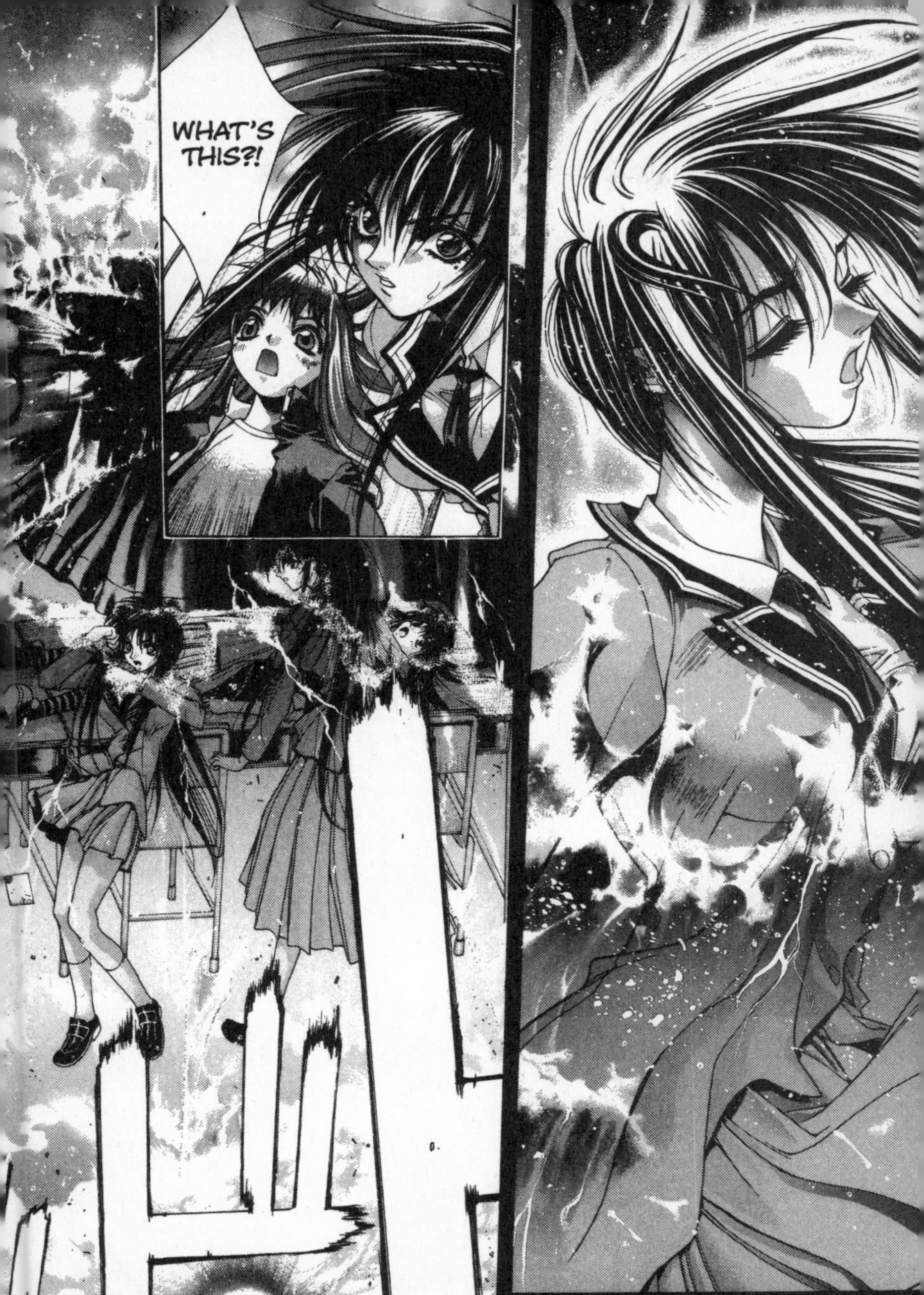
WHAT'S THIS?!

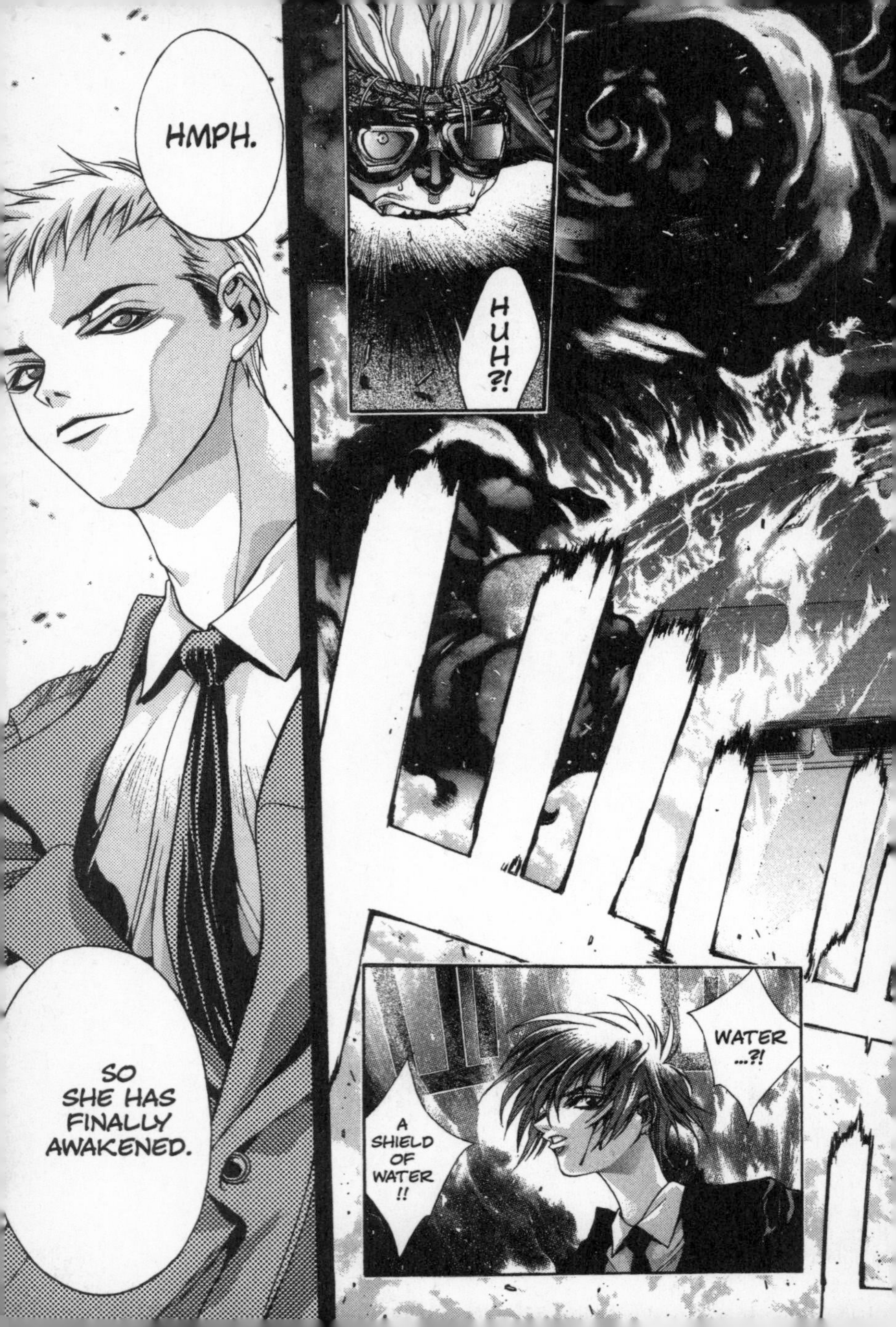
HUH?!
WATER ...?!
A SHIELD OF WATER !!
HMPH.
SO SHE HAS FINALLY AWAKENED.

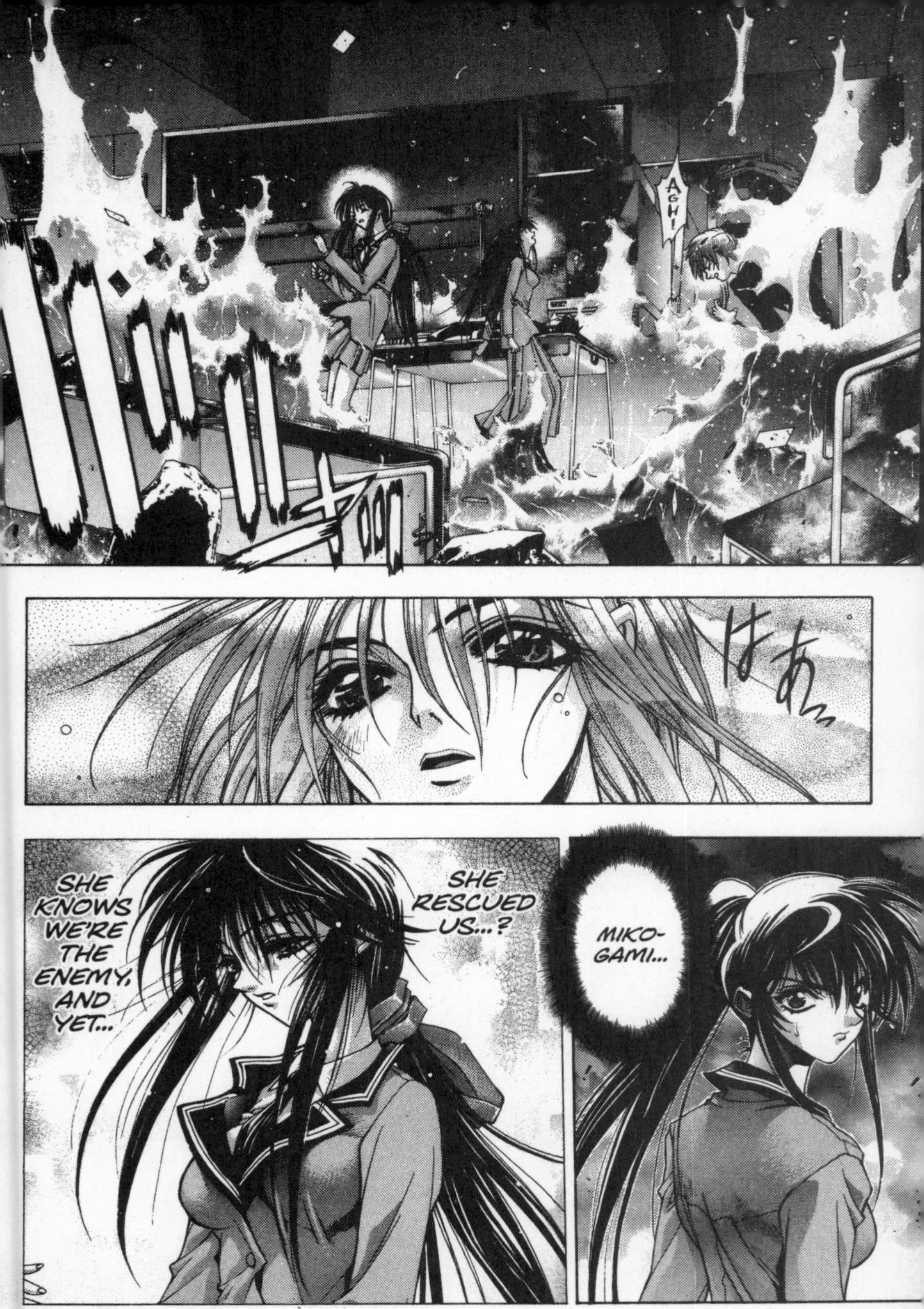
AGH!
はあ
MIKO-GAMI...
SHE RESCUED US...?
SHE KNOWS WE'RE THE ENEMY, AND YET...

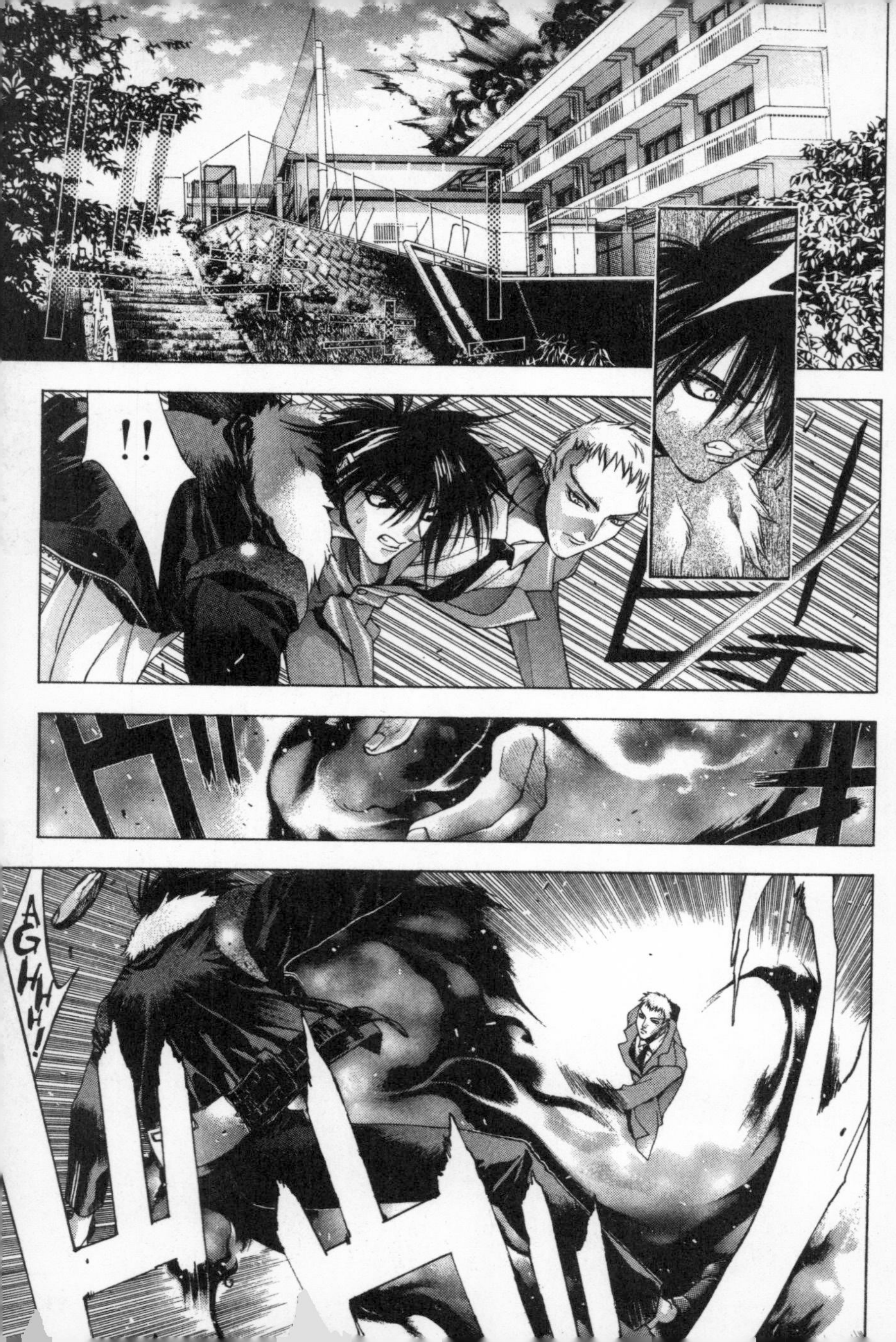
!!
AGHHH!

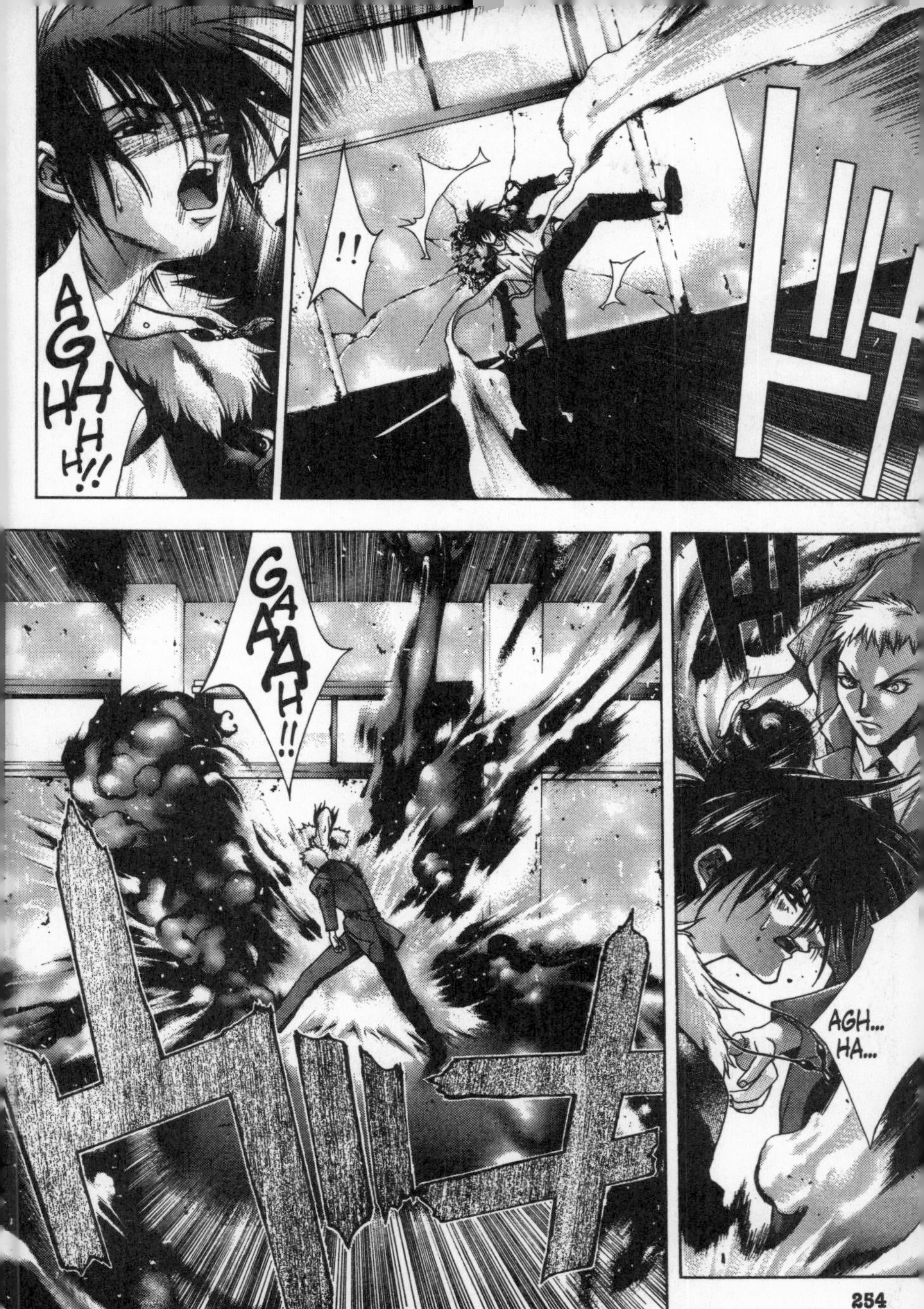
!!
!
AGHHHH!!
AGH... HA...
GAAAH!!

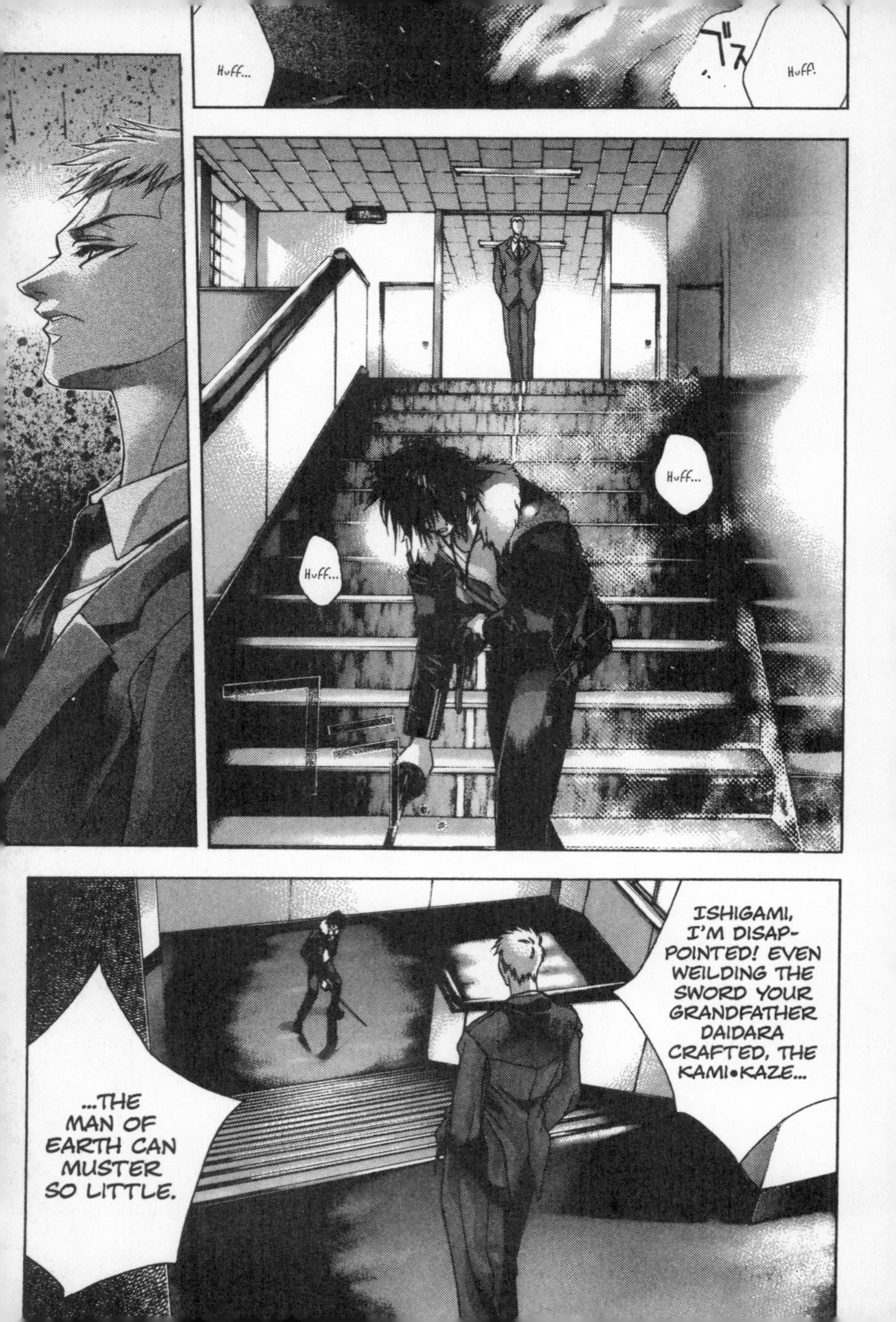
Huff!
Huff...
Huff...
Huff...
ISHIGAMI, I'M DISAP-POINTED! EVEN WEILDING THE SWORD YOUR GRANDFATHER DAIDARA CRAFTED, THE KAMI•KAZE...
...THE MAN OF EARTH CAN MUSTER SO LITTLE.

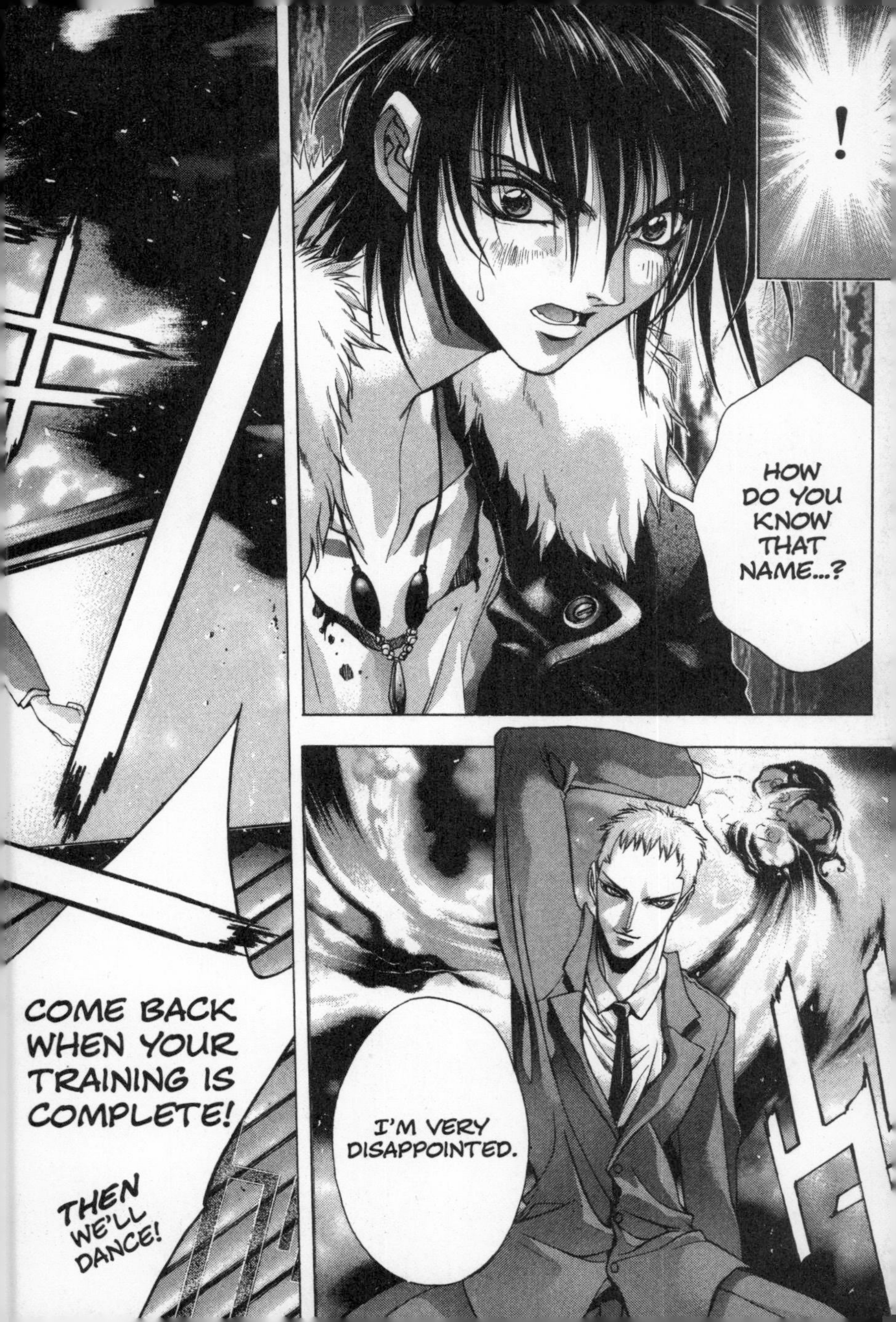
!
HOW DO YOU KNOW THAT NAME...?
I'M VERY DISAPPOINTED.
COME BACK WHEN YOUR TRAINING IS COMPLETE!
THEN WE'LL DANCE!

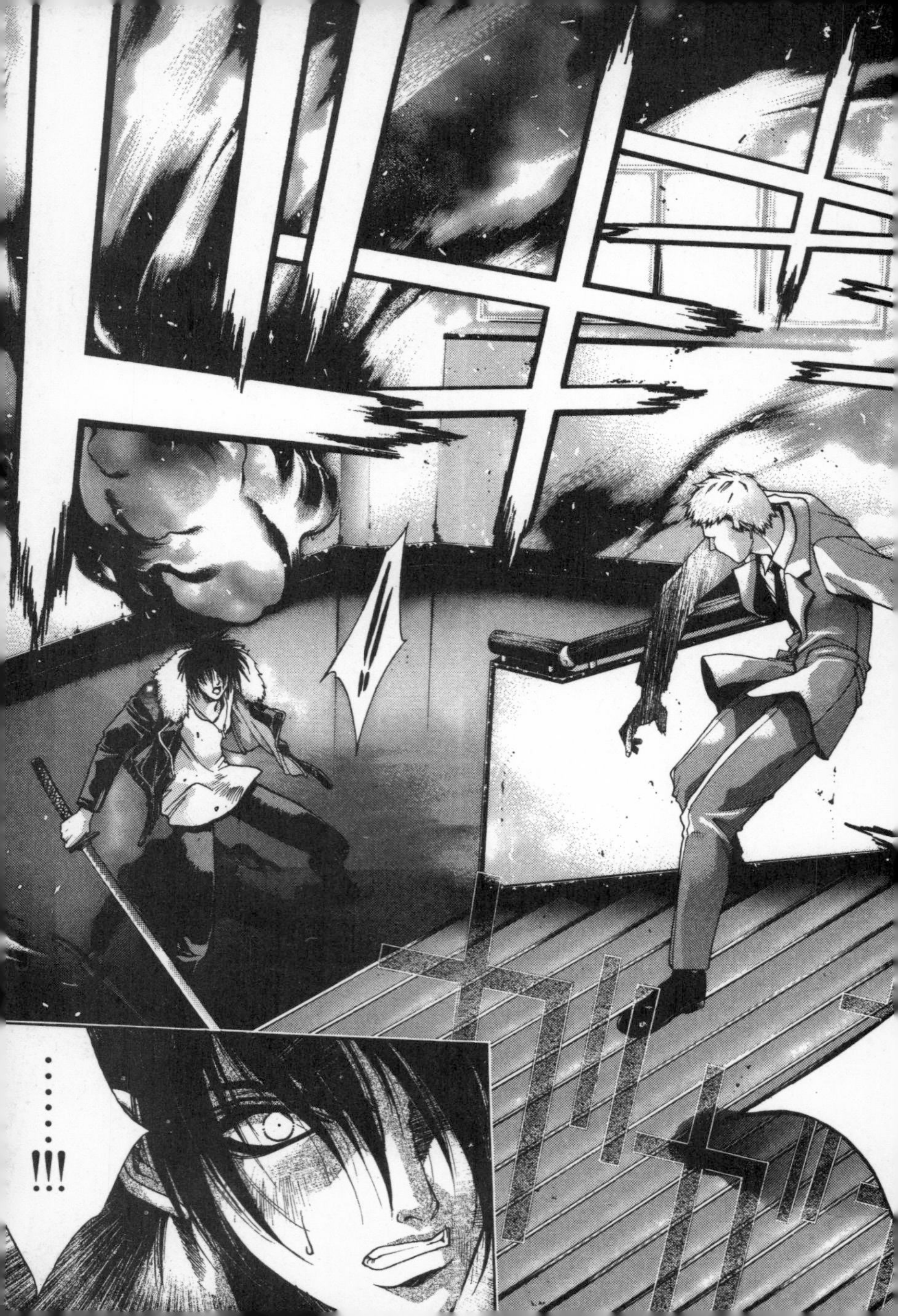
......!!!

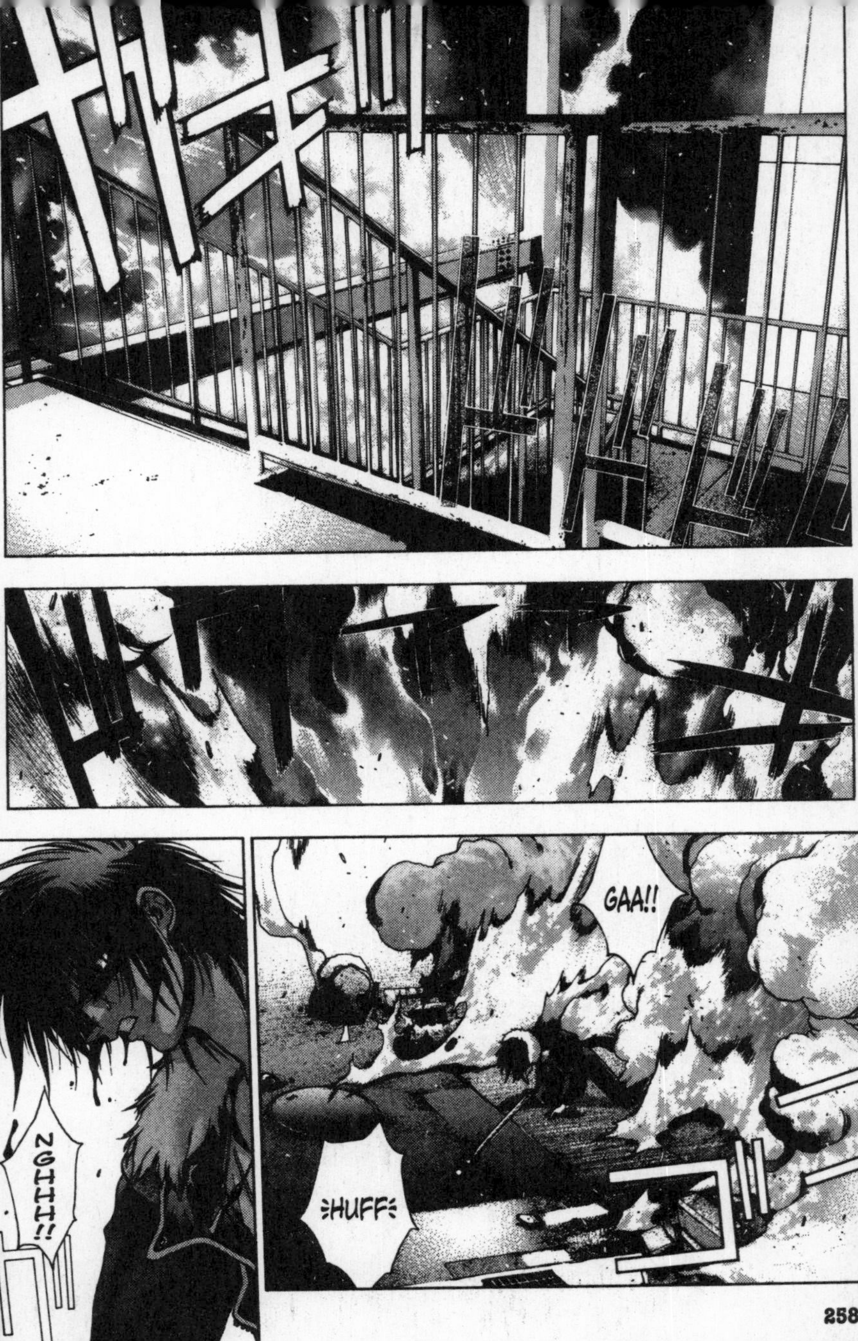
GAA!!
HUFF
NGHHHH!!

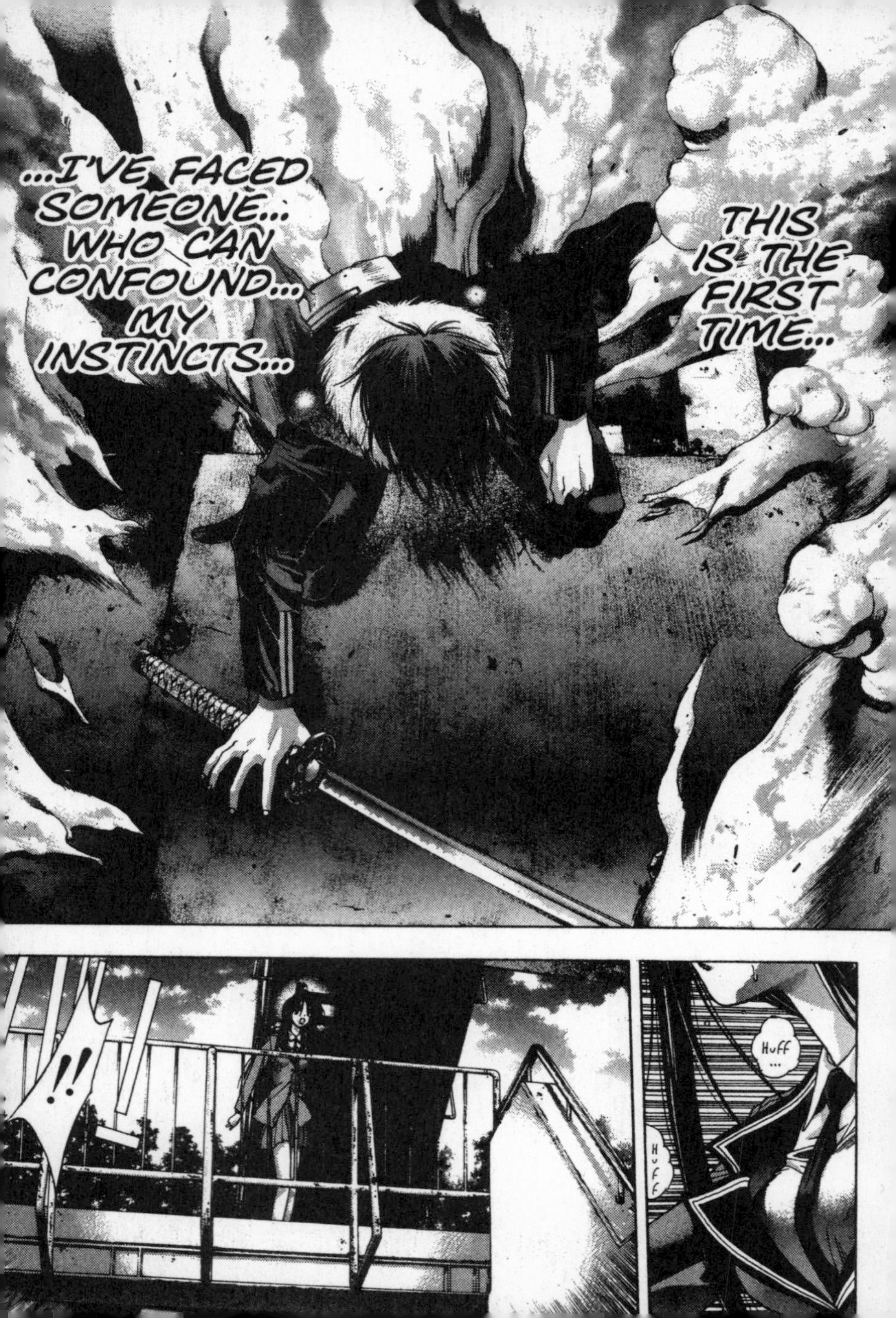
THIS IS THE FIRST TIME...
...I'VE FACED SOMEONE... WHO CAN CONFOUND... MY INSTINCTS...
HUFF ...
HUFF
!!

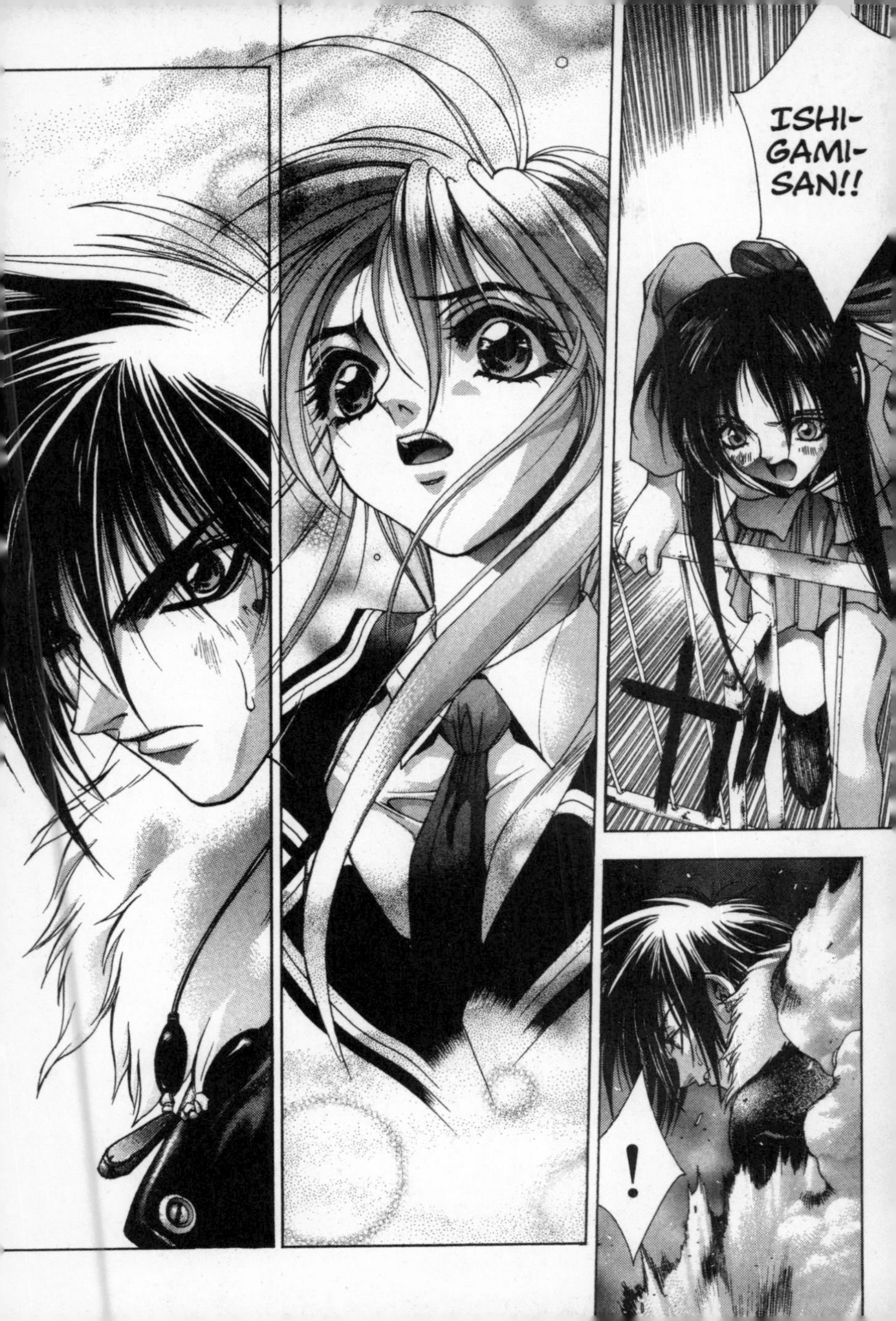
ISHI-GAMI-SAN!!
!

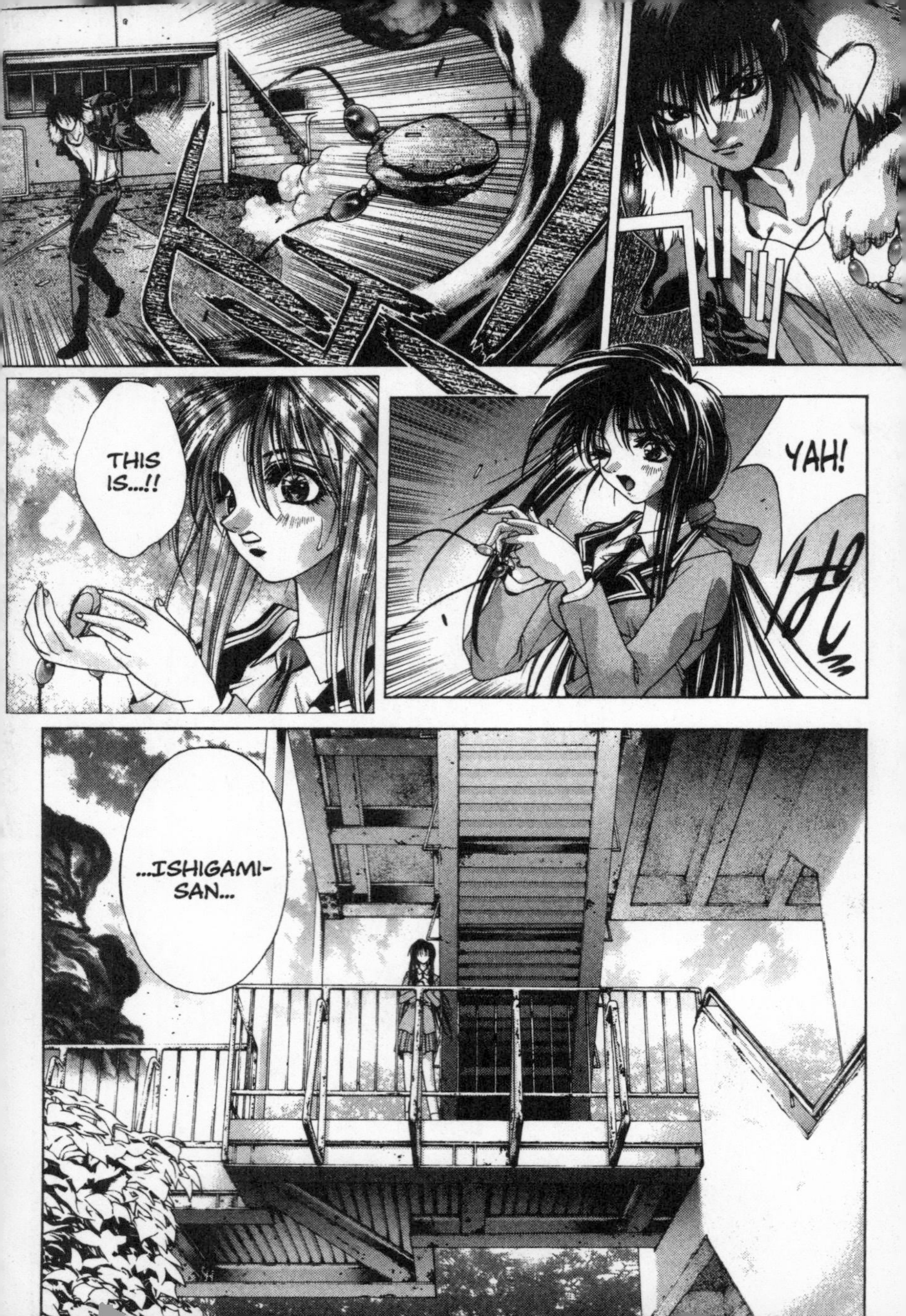
YAH!
THIS IS...!!
...ISHIGAMI-SAN...

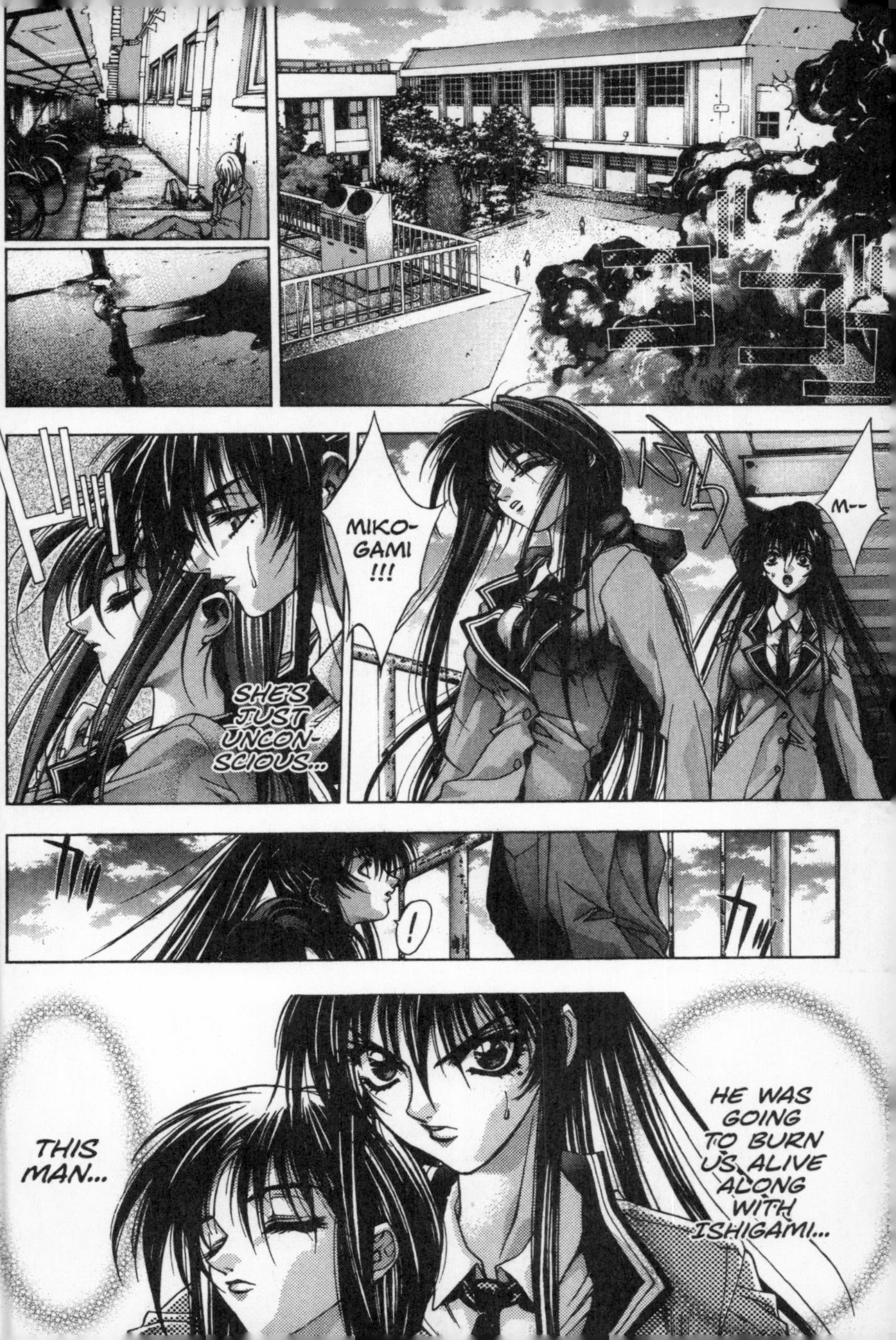
M--
MIKO-GAMI !!!
SHE'S JUST UNCON-SCIOUS...
!
HE WAS GOING TO BURN US ALIVE ALONG WITH ISHIGAMI...
THIS MAN...

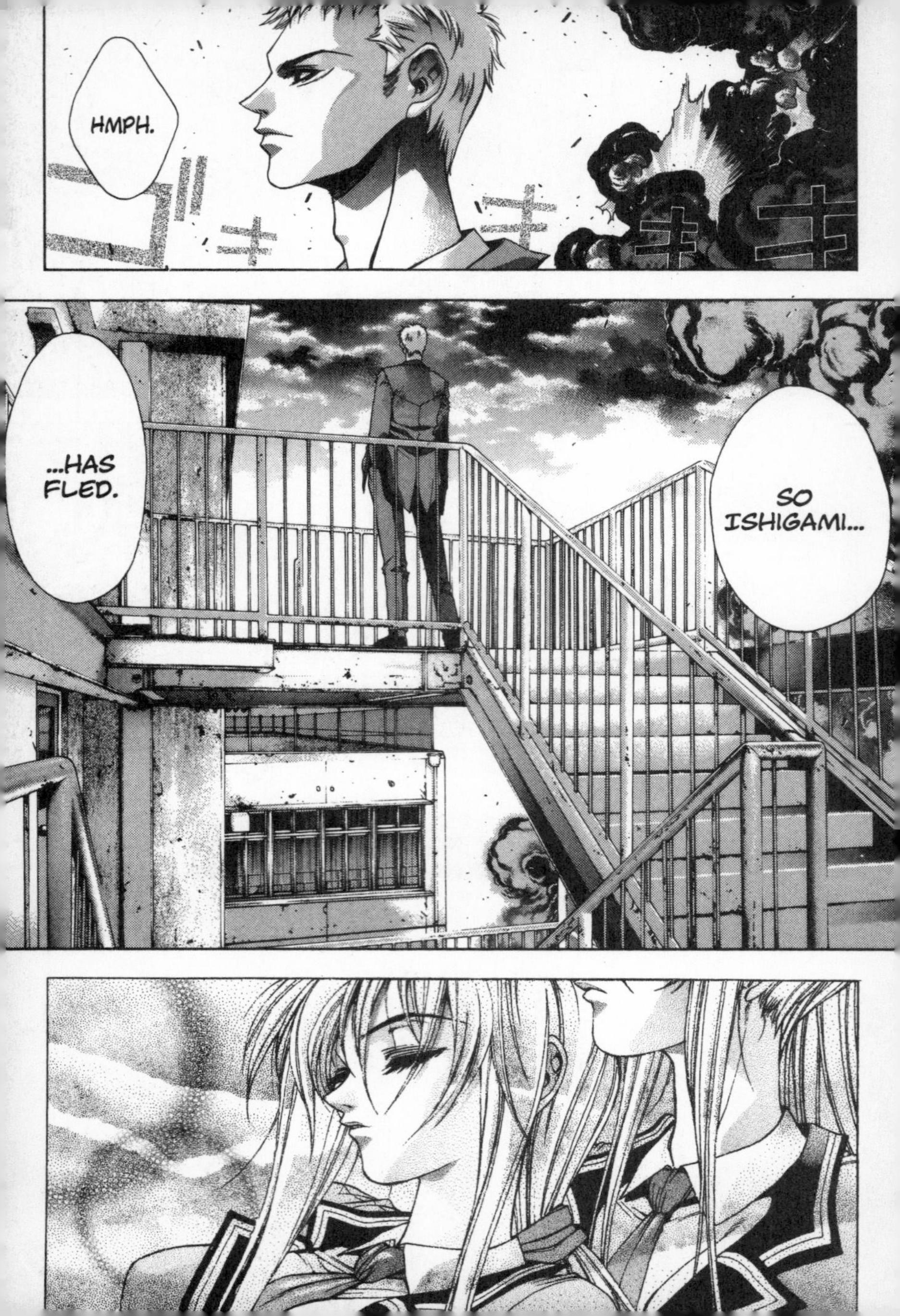
HMPH.
SO ISHIGAMI...
...HAS FLED.

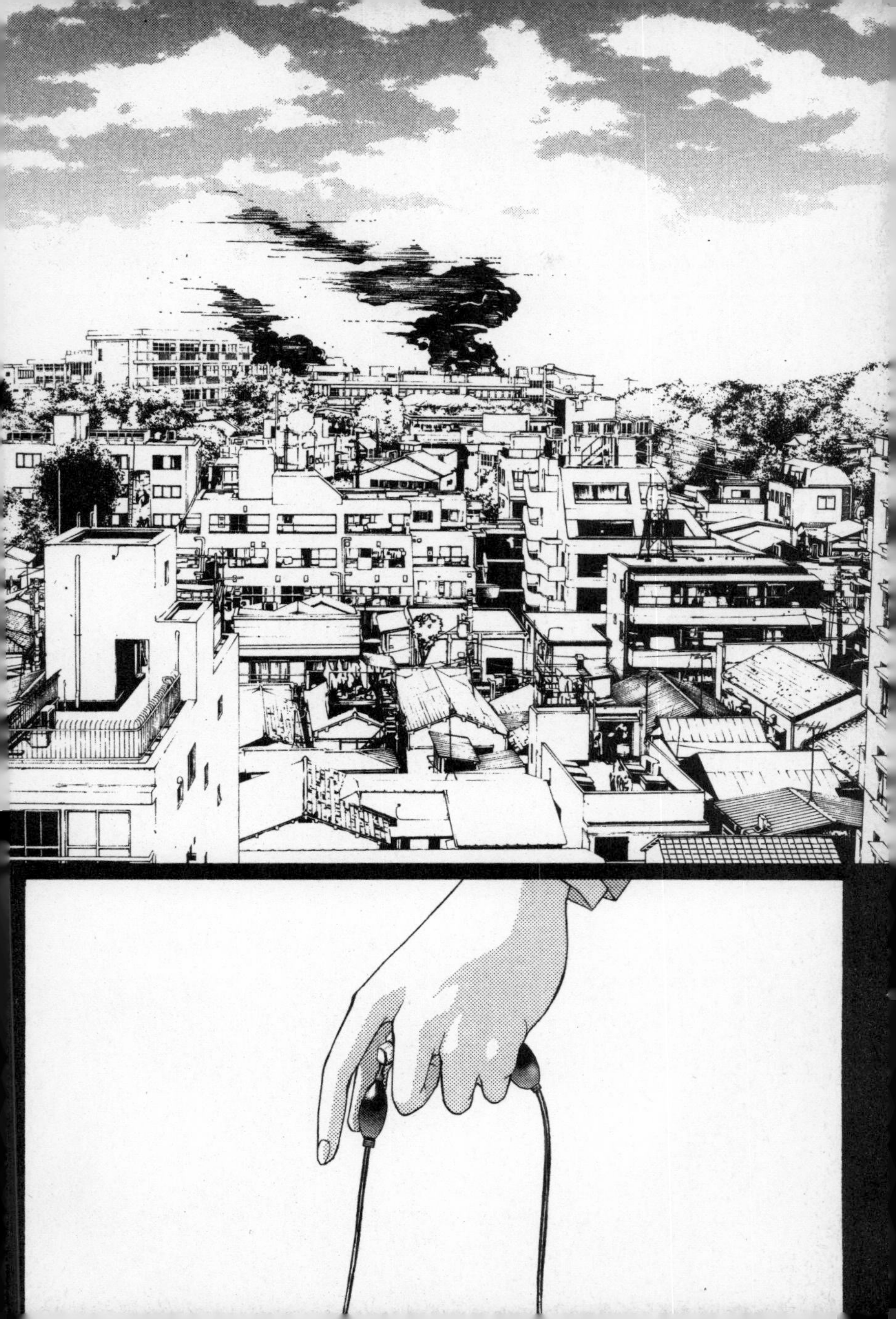

To be continued in VOLUME 2

STAFF

Hirofumi Sugimoto
Masahiro Uchida
Ryo Sugino
Naoki Hirose

●

Suguru Shibuya
Hiroki Sasaki
Masanobu Takahashi
Hitoshi Houjo
Odate Yokoo

●

Shiki Satoshi

In the next VOLUME of

KAMI◊KAZE™

Injured in the supernatural clash at the high school, Ishigami and Beniguma recover in the care of Keiko, distraught at the kidnapping of her dear friend Misao and determined to get some answers fast. The resurrection of the 88 beasts imminent and close, the now three unlikely allies travel to an old Hani village, where Ishigami is faced with a horrible choice.

TOKYOPOP SHOP

WWW.TOKYOPOP.COM/SHOP

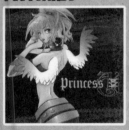
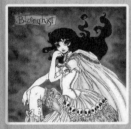

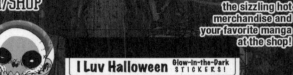
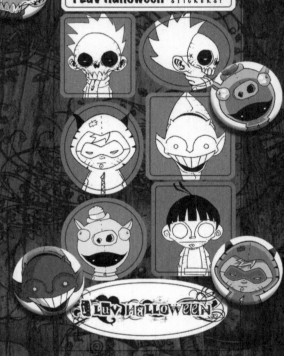

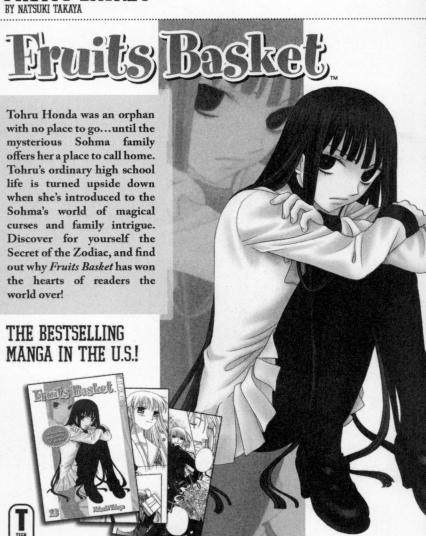

LIFE
BY KEIKO SUENOBU

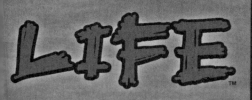

Ordinary high school teenagers...
Except that they're not.

L✝FE™

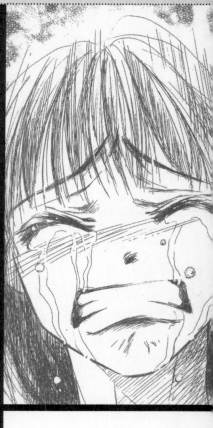

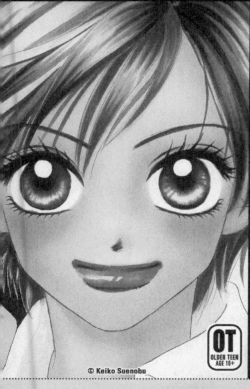

© Keiko Suenobu

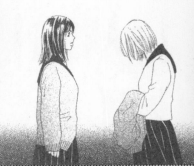

READ THE ENTIRE FIRST CHAPTER ONLINE FOR FREE:

Ayumu struggles with her studies, and the all-important high school entrance exams are approaching. Fortunately, she has help from her best bud Shii-chan, who is at the top of the class. But when the test results come back, the friends are surprised: Ayumu surpasses Shii-chan's scores and gets into the school of her choice—without Shii-chan! Losing her friend is so painful for Ayumu that she starts cutting herself to ease her sorrow. Finally, Ayumu seeks comfort in a new friend, Manami. But will Manami prove to be the friend that Ayumu truly needs? Or will Ayumu continue down a dark path?

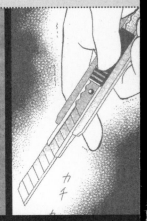

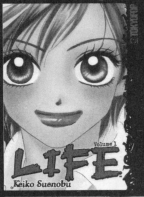

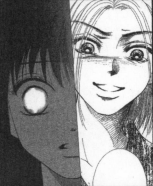

Volume 1

LIFE

Keiko Suenobu

It's about real teenagers...

It's about real high school...

It's about real life.

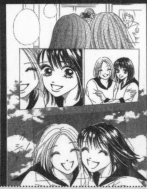

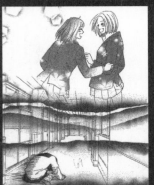

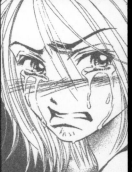

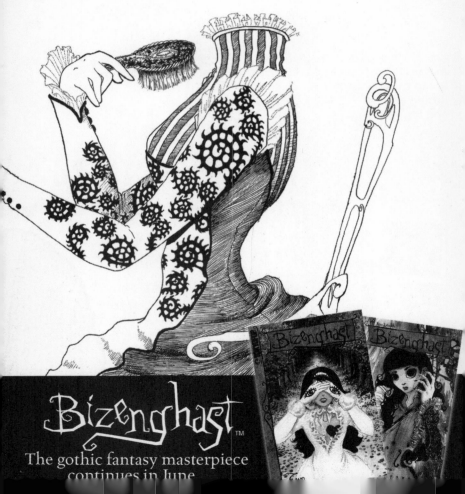

that I'm not like other people...

Bizenghast™

The gothic fantasy masterpiece
continues in June

STOP!

This is the back of the book.
You wouldn't want to spoil a great ending!

This book is printed "manga-style," in the authentic Japanese right-to-left format. Since none of the artwork has been flipped or altered, readers get to experience the story just as the creator intended. You've been asking for it, so TOKYOPOP® delivered: authentic, hot-off-the-press, and far more fun!

DIRECTIONS

1
2
3
4
5
6
7
8
9
10

If this is your first time reading manga-style, here's a quick guide to help you understand how it works.

It's easy... just start in the top right panel and follow the numbers. Have fun, and look for more 100% authentic manga from TOKYOPOP®!

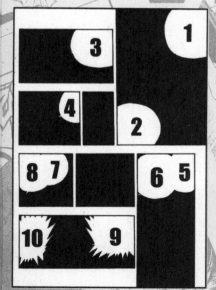

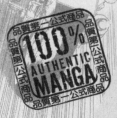